A–Z

OF

ℭLASSICAL MUSIC

A–Z

OF

CLASSICAL
MUSIC

EDITED BY CHARLES OSBORNE

Acknowledgements

London, Royal College of Music: pp. 10, 79, 94, 103, 191, 238, 335, 341, 355. – Mansell Collection: pp. 11, 13, 17, 20, 24, 33, 35, 39, 42, 49, 50, 56, 61, 68, 75, 85, 87, 88, 89, 106, 110, 116, 119, 155, 157, 169, 176, 205, 237, 239, 242, 246/47, 249, 266, 299, 305, 313, 327, 330, 333, 336, 337, 356, 358. – Snark International: Frontispiece, pp. 19, 21, 36, 43, 45, 69, 74, 81, 97, 100, 108, 123, 124, 166, 178, 195, 222, 228, 230/31, 240, 264, 275, 276, 279, 280, 287, 288, 300, 322, 329, 331, 365. – Paris, Bibliothèque Nationale: pp. 22, 32, 52, 96, 131, 142, 167, 168, 186, 189, 199, 201, 206, 233, 234, 243, 244, 245, 255, 272, 283, 306, 308. – Boudot-Lamotte: p. 23. – New York, Central Library: pp. 29, 30. – Paris, Archives Photographiques: pp. 34. – German National Archives: pp. 40. – Austrian Institute: pp. 44, 185, 295. – Prague, Theatremuseum: p. 47. – Paris, Bibliothèque du Conservatoire: pp. 57, 90, 173, 179, 216, 229, 292, 339, 340, 344, 362. – Collection Sirot: pp. 58, 77, 150, 154, 218, 316. – The Author: p. 60. – Roger-Viollet: p. 63. – Vienna, National Library: pp. 65, 76, 208, 296, 301, 325, 359, 373. – Hamburg, Staatsbibliothek: p. 67. – Reg Wilson: pp. 70, 282, 332, 350, 377. – Paris, Cultural American Centre: pp. 92, 137, 376. – Paris, Bibliothèque des Arts Décoratifs: p. 133. – Collection Speiser: pp. 134, 170, 281, 302, 348, 379. – London, British Library: pp. 135, 162, 164, 236, 366, 371. – Paris, Bibliothèque de l'Opéra: pp. 146, 152, 204, 261. – London, National Portrait Gallery: p. 159. – Collection Meyer: pp. 174, 224, 252, 259, 273, 309, 353. – Prague, National Library: p. 184. – Paris, Archives Heugel: pp. 193, 321, 323. – Eric Shanes: p. 210. – Berlin, National Bibliothek: p. 251. – Milan, National Library: p. 265. – Paris, Théâtre des Champs-Elysées: pp. 270, 286. – Bologna, Museo Civico: p. 290. – Paris, Librairie du Globe: p. 346. – Photo Schob: p. 361. – Turino, Library: p. 363. Jacket – Painting entitled *The Music Party* by Phillip Mercier by courtesy of The National Portrait Gallery London

Contributors

Ernest Chapman (E.C.)
Joan Chissell (J.C.)
Alan Blyth (A.B.)
Gerald Gifford (G.G.)
Professor Denis Arnold (D.A.)
Frank Granville Barker (F.G.B.)
Colin Wilson (C.W.)
Christopher Headington (C.H.)
Brendan G. Carroll (B.G.C.)
Robert Layton (R.L.)
Jerrold Northrop Moore (J.N.M.)
Edward Higginbottom (E.H.)
Jeremy Noble (J.N.)

Charles Osborne (C.O.)
Richard Osborne (R.O.)
Dr. Mosco Carner (Mos.C.)
Nicholas Chadwick (N.C.)
Noel Goodwin (N.G.)
Charles Cudworth (C.C.)
Peter Gammond (P.G.)
Christopher Grier (C.G.)
Christopher Palmer (C. P.)
Eric Walter White (E.W.W.)
Stephen Walsh (S.W.)
Martin Cooper (M.C.)
Humphrey Searle (H.S.)

Foreword

These biographies are addressed to the music enthusiast who does not already have full-length biographies of his favourite composers on his bookshelves, and the collection is based on the proposition that one can deepen one's understanding of a man's music by knowing something about his life. The entries, therefore, are not merely lists of works, but essays in each of which the major events of a composer's life are set forth and, where appropriate, related to his music. I have not confined the collection to the 'great' composers, but have cast my nets more widely. On the other hand, I do not seek to be comprehensive. The criterion for inclusion has been whether one was likely to encounter the music of the composer in question in the concert hall or the opera house, not just on an isolated and rare occasion but with reasonable frequency. Consequently, none of the four known Charpentiers, for example, will be found in these pages, although it is possible, if not very probable, that something or other by two of them – Marc-Antoine Charpentier (1634–1704) and Gustave Charpentier (1860–1956) – might turn up in a concert pro-gramme or at an opera house. But Villa-Lobos and Korngold, though not necessarily composers of the first rank, are included be-cause their music, though hardly 'in fashion' at present, is nevertheless heard from time to time.

No unanimity of approach has been forced upon the contributors, beyond a general in-junction to tell the story of the composer's life clearly and concisely, and to comment on the music in non-technical language. The great composers have, in general, more space devoted to them than the lesser figures, though again this is not consistently the case. The popular composer of the second rank who has led a long and interesting life may have a longer entry than the great genius who lived for nothing beyond his music and who died young. It is my hope that the reader may, by reading about composers in whom he has not hitherto taken an interest, be led to explore their work and thus to extend his own knowledge of and enjoyment in the art of music.

C.O.

ADAM, Adolphe
(b. Paris, 24 July 1803;
d. Paris, 3 May 1856)

Although his father, Louis Adam, was a pianist, teacher and composer of some importance in Paris, Adolphe Adam was discouraged from taking up music himself as a profession. His father sent him to an ordinary school and refused to allow him musical instruction, which the lad, however, acquired secretly. When he was fourteen, his father relented to the extent that the boy was allowed to enter the Paris Conservatoire, but only after Adolphe had solemnly sworn that he would never compose music for the theatre!

The first instrument which the young musician mastered was the organ, which was soon followed by the harmonium on which he used to improvise and compose tunes. One of his teachers was the composer Boïeldieu, master of the *opéra comique*, who took a particular interest in his young pupil. Adam was later to acknowledge that most of what he knew of composition came from Boïeldieu. It was certainly Boïeldieu who led him away from his solemn promise to his father, towards the attractions of the theatre and *opéra comique*. When Boïeldieu's *La Dame blanche* was being prepared for performance in 1825, he allowed his twenty-two-year-old pupil to compose the overture, or rather to construct it from Boïeldieu's themes.

Adam's first *opéra comique*, *Pierre et Catherine*, was produced in Paris, at the theatre called the Opéra-Comique, in 1829. It was only a one-act piece, but it was followed the next year by a three-act work, *Danilowa*, whose immediate success encouraged the young composer promptly to embark upon another. His talent, he discovered, was a facile one. Melodies came easily to him, and orchestration gave him no trouble. His prolific melodic gift was, in fact, his greatest asset; had he been a little more interested in the other aspects of composition, Adam's music might have risen to greater heights. But the comic operas that flowed from his pen were invariably successful with audiences, so he was hardly encouraged to experiment. One of the most charming of the operas is *Le Postilion de Longjumeau* with its fearsome entrance aria requiring the tenor to produce a high D in the chest register. *Le Postilion de Longjumeau* was staged in 1836 at the Opéra-Comique where the vast majority of Adam's operas were given their premières. His one or two grand operas, such as *Richard en Palestine* (produced at the

Opéra in 1844) were failures, but his reputation in comic opera is secure, though apart from *Le Postilion de Longjumeau* few of them are encountered on the stage today. Adam also composed a number of ballet scores, not only for Paris but also for Berlin, St Petersburg and London. One of these, *Giselle*, produced at the Paris Opéra in 1841, is still immensely popular with ballet audiences today.

Adam was generous in his encouragement of younger composers. In 1847 he founded the Théâtre National, to produce new works by young composers. The 1848 revolution put an end to this enterprise, in which Adam lost all his savings, and incurred debts which were to cripple him for the remainder of his life. In 1849 he became a professor of composition at the Paris Conservatoire. His death in 1856 was sudden.

C.O.

ALBÉNIZ, Isaac
(b. Camprodón, 29 May 1860;
d. Cambó-les-Bains, 18 May 1909)

A caricature of Albéniz published in *La ilustración musical* of Barcelona in 1883 carried the caption: '*Como hombre, un nino – Como pianista, un gigante*' ('As a man, a midget – As a pianist, a giant'). Albéniz was then twenty-three, and about to settle down to marriage and study after a picaresque childhood and adolescence which had already taken him half-way round the world. He was born in Gerona, the son of a tax collector. Exceptionally precocious, he learned the piano almost instinctively, and improvised at a public concert in Barcelona when he was four. At seven he was taken to Paris, where he sailed through the entry examinations for the Conservatoire, tossed a ball through one of its hallowed windows and was refused admission, officially on account of his extreme youth.

Nothing daunted, he became a vagabond, running away from home and the Madrid Conservatory a year later, and supporting himself by his piano playing – chiefly in a vaudeville stunt with his back to the keyboard using the backs of his fingers, palms upwards. By the time he was fifteen, having stowed away on a westbound ship, he had explored Buenos Aires and Cuba, toured the USA from New York to San Francisco, and given concerts in Liverpool, London and Leipzig on the way back. His handicap was a fundamental lack of self-discipline. Felipe Pedrell found him unteachable so far as theoretical principles were concerned. Albéniz did try. He studied at different times with Pedrell in Barcelona; with Liszt in Weimar and Rome; at Madrid, Leipzig and Brussels; with d'Indy and Dukas in Paris, but the exuberance of an instinctive improviser would not be tamed.

Most of his music is for the piano, from the light salon pieces of his adolescence, through the colourful nationalistic works like the *Cantos de España* and *Suite española*, to the ultimate stylisation of this in his last piano suite, *Iberia*. At the same time, Albéniz was convinced he had a neglected gift for the stage, which is no doubt why he accepted a handsome stipend from an English banker, Francis Money-Coutts, to turn the latter's verse-dramas into operas. This 'pact of Faust', as Albéniz later called it, first involved a trilogy on the Arthurian legends. The composer plodded doggedly through *Merlin* and half of *Lancelot*, in a weak imitation of Wagner, before giving up. He then set *Henry Clifford*, a Wars of the Roses romance premièred at Barcelona in 1895 (and sung in Italian), and persuaded his patron to use a Spanish novel for *Pepita Jiménez*, which travelled from Barcelona in 1896 to Prague, Paris and Brussels, and has recently been revived. He also wrote three unsuccessful *zarzuelas,* or Spanish operettas.

Albéniz, however, was not really an orchestral composer. He lacked the technique and the feeling for it. 'I am a Moor', he would proclaim, and the Moorish rhythms, harmonic traits and ornate decoration of Andalucian music was what he most loved to reflect in his own. It mainly took the guitar for its instrumental model and the piano for its means of expression. An association with Fauré and his circle in Paris, where Albéniz went to live in 1893, gave him loftier aspirations, and the piano hardly seems adequate to realise the full beauty of the 12 pieces that make up *Iberia*. They tax keyboard technique to the limit: Albéniz wrote that he came near to burning the music when he found much of it almost unplayable. They nevertheless remain unsurpassed as an idealisation of southern Spanish music and dance forms, and represent the last extravagance of the composer before his death on the 18th May 1909, after a short illness.

N.G.

ARNE, Thomas
(b. London, 12 March 1710;
d. London, 5 March 1778)

Thomas Augustine Arne was born at the Crown and Cushion, King Street, Covent Garden, where the Indian Kings had lodged during their visit to London in the reign of Queen Anne. His father (also Thomas) was by trade an upholsterer and coffin-maker. The young Thomas was sent to Eton College where he is said to have spent part of his spare time practising on a 'miserable, cracked, common-flute'. Burney described his passion for music as a young man.

> He used to avail himself of the privilege of a servant, by borrowing livery and going into the upper gallery of the opera, which was ther appropriated to domestics. At home he had contrived to secrete a spinet in his room, upon which, after muffling the strings with a handkerchief, he used to practise in the night while the rest of the family were asleep.

In addition, he took lessons in violin-playing and taught himself composition.

Thomas was not the only musician in the family. His sister, Susannah Maria, and younger brother, Michael, were both singers of distinction. Thanks to her elder brother's training, Susannah made a successful début at the Little Theatre in the Haymarket in 1733 in Lampe's 'English opera' *Amelia*; and a few months later their father unexpectedly produced Handel's *Acis and Galatea* as an 'English pastoral opera', also at the Little Theatre, with Susannah in the role of Galatea. Meanwhile, Thomas was engaged on a new setting of Addison's libretto for *Rosamund*, and this was most successful when brought out at Lincoln's Inn Fields Theatre (1733) with Susannah in the title role and Michael as the page.

In 1734 Susannah contracted what was to prove a disastrous marriage with Theophilus Cibber, the son of Colley Cibber, the actor, playwright and manager, and thereafter she was launched on a new career as an actress. In 1737 Thomas married Cecilia, one of three musical daughters of Anthony Young, the organist of All Hallows, Barking. A natural son, christened Michael like his uncle, was born in 1740 and in course of time became a composer too. Thomas had a strong streak of profligacy in his nature; and about 1755 his marriage seemed on the verge of collapse. Nevertheless, he and Cecilia came together again; and in his Will (dated 6th December

1777) he left all his estate to be divided equally between 'my beloved wife Cecilia and my only son Michael'.

Arne's reputation as a lyric composer was established in 1738 with his setting of Milton's *Comus*. Burney's opinion was that in this masque 'he introduced a light airy, original, and pleasing melody, wholly different from that of Purcell or Handel'. Arne himself is reported to have said that the test of a good melody was such a one as 'would grind about the streets on the organ'.

Arne was attracted by the masque as a theatrical form; and in the summer of 1740 he produced two further masques for a gala performance at Cliefden, Buckinghamshire – *The Judgment of Paris*, a setting of Congreve's original libretto, and *Alfred*, which contained a patriotic 'Ode in Honour of Great Britain'. The latter rapidly achieved independent popularity under the title 'Rule, Britannia!'

Arne.

In the course of his life, he paid three separate visits to Dublin, where his music became very popular. Returning to London after his first visit (1742/4) he was appointed resident composer at Drury Lane; but the three comic operas he produced there in 1745 – *The Temple of Dullness*, *The Picture*, and *King Pepin's Campaign* – did not prove successful. Garrick now had the idea of commissioning an afterpiece each from Arne and Boyce (*q.v.*). *The Chaplet* (1749) by Boyce was much liked; but not so Arne's *Don Saverio* (1750). At this period he seems to have had more success with the numerous ballads, dialogues, duets and trios he wrote for the public gardens, particularly Vauxhall where his wife frequently performed, than with his music for the theatre.

Shortly after Handel's death in 1759, the University of Oxford conferred the degree of Doctor of Music on Arne, and in 1760 he had the good fortune to meet a first-class librettist, the young Isaac Bickerstaff, recently arrived in London from Ireland. Their first work of collaboration was the delightful little 'dramatic pastoral', *Thomas and Sally*, which was brought out at Covent Garden. Bickerstaff then provided Arne with the text of an oratorio, *Judith*, which was produced at Drury Lane in 1761, and the libretto of a comic opera, which was an altered version of the old ballad opera, *The Village Opera*. Arne selected, arranged, and scored music by seventeen different composers, including himself, to produce *Love in a Village*, as it was now called, one of the best pasticcio operas of the century (Covent Garden, 1762).

Shortly before *Love in a Village*, he decided to compose an English version of an Italian *opera seria* for Covent Garden, and his choice of libretto fell on Metastasio's *Artaserse*. In its English form *Artaxerxes* (1762) caught the public's taste and kept its position in the repertory until well into the 19th century. An attempt to repeat this success with *Olimpiade*, where Arne set Metastasio's original Italian libretto for the King's Theatre in the Haymarket (1765), was a failure.

In 1770 he set out to persuade Garrick to revive Purcell's *King Arthur* at Drury Lane in a new version where he himself would be responsible for the alterations and additions to the score. Some of the arguments in his correspondence with Garrick sound very arrogant.

The air 'Let not a moon-born elf' is after the two first bars of Purcell very bad. Hear mine. . . . I wish you would only give me

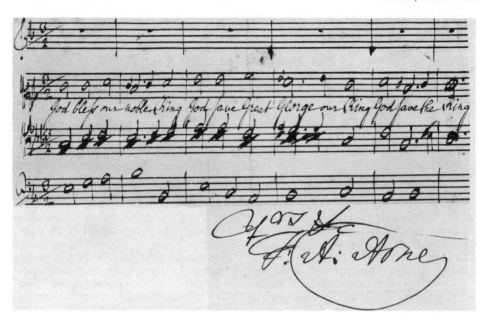

Early version of 'God Save the King' by Dr Arne.

AUBER, Daniel
(b. Caen, 29 Jan 1782; d. Paris, 12 May 1871)

leave to doctor this performance. I would certainly make it pleasing to the public.

But when it came to the point, Arne seems to have behaved with considerable discretion and, according to Charles Dibdin, 'so far from mutilating Purcell . . . his whole study was to place his idolised predecessor in that conspicuous situation the brilliancy of his reputation demanded.'

Towards the end of his life Arne wrote a number of minor comic operas, including *The Guardian Outwitted* (1764), *The Cooper* (1772), *The Rose* (1772), *Achilles in Petticoats* (1773), and *May-Day* (1775). In *The Fairy Prince* (1771) he reverted to his earlier style of masque, choosing the text of Ben Jonson's *Oberon* for his setting. And in *The Golden Pippin* (1773) he imitated the example of the 'English burletta' *Midas*, which had been launched in Dublin in 1762 on an amazingly successful career. He died in Bow Street, Covent Garden.

E.W.W.

Auber was one of the leading figures in that sophisticated world of French opera that lies between the grand and the light known as *opéra comique*. He was born in Normandy and came from an artistic and vaguely aristocratic family. His grandfather had gone to seek his fortune in Paris and became official artist and sculptor at the court of Louis XVI. His father was also a court official and passed on to his son a great love of music, horses and painting. Later making a modest fortune as a shopkeeper, he hoped that his son Daniel would be able to combine business and art and sent him to London in 1802 to learn the trade of selling paintings. In London he wrote several songs which had public performances and was gradually drawn more and more toward a career in music. He returned to France in 1804, settled in Paris, studied for a time with Cherubini, then gave himself wholly to composition.

He became friendly with a distinguished French cellist, Jacques La Marre (later spelt Lamare) who was much admired by Clementi. Auber wrote four 'cello concertos which were published under Lamare's name in 1804 and well received on the strength of his popularity. When it eventually became known that Auber was the composer it gave him a ready-made reputation and led to him writing a violin concerto for Jacques Mazas which was played with great success at the Conservatoire and afterwards in London by Sainton.

Auber was by nature a peculiarly timid person, modest and shy – so much so that he was said never to have attended the performance of any of his own works. His first attempt at opera was predictably modest, a setting of a libretto by Jacques Marie Boutet de Monville, *L'Erreur d'un moment,* which had previously been set by Dezède. It was given an amateur performance at the Salle Doyen in 1805 and another opera, *Couvin,* was privately performed in 1812. He also wrote a mass in that year from which he later extracted material for use in the opera *Masaniello.* His first public stage performance came with *Le Séjour militaire* at the Paris Opéra-Comique on the 27th February 1813. It was a failure and for the next six years Auber made no further assaults on the operatic stage but lived an obscure and perilous existence performing various menial musical tasks. In 1819 *Le Testament et les billets-doux* was equally unsuccessful but, by now, he was certain of his vocation and was rewarded by the general acclaim of his *La Bergère châtelaine* which opened at the Opéra-Comique on the 27th January 1820. This was two days before his thirty-eighth birthday – so it had been a long, hard road.

From now on he was to write a regular series of operatic successes, most of his best works being the result of his regular collaboration with Eugène Scribe, one of the finest librettists of the day. He was to write almost fifty operas, the last *Rêve d'amour* premièred at the Opéra-Comique in 1869. Auber, in spite of his fame, remained the quiet, gentle, epicurean Parisian gentleman who shunned publicity to such an extent that he never appeared in public as a conductor. With characteristic modesty he said that if he ever listened to one of his own works he would probably never write another note.

He became a member of the Académie in 1829 and received many awards both in France and abroad. He was appointed Director of the Conservatoire in 1842 and remained in this post until he died in 1871. In 1857 he was graced by Napoleon III with the title of 'maître de chapelle'. He wrote a modest number of songs, a few orchestral and chamber compositions, five piano works and a very successful ballet *Marco Spada,* based on the libretto of his opera of the same name which was written in 1852. The music for the 1857 ballet was not taken from the opera but adapted from many of his most popular works.

Auber's reputation might be said to rest firmly on his operatic writings though today very few of them are performed, and even the names that are known to all, *Le Cheval de bronze, Le Domino noir, Les Diamants de la couronne,* are remembered for their light, vivacious and tuneful overtures – as with so many of Rossini's works. At the time these works had tremendous esteem. *Les Diamants de la couronne* was a major success in Paris in 1841 and an even greater one in London three years later. In these *opéra comique* scores Auber epitomised the grace and elegance of the genre, combining vitality and the simple amorous grace of the popular French chanson, with a very careful and lucid setting of words. In this he followed in the steps of Boïeldieu and proved himself a strong rival of such contemporaries as Adam and Hérold. His orchestration was particularly apt and brilliant. The works of these composers were the intermediate step between the comic operas of Mozart, Rossini and Donizetti and the frivolous operettas of Offenbach, Lecocq and Messager. The *opéra comique* regularly introduced dialogue and was thus able to add extra strength to dramatic characters in the plot.

Auber had the depth of musical imagination to be able to step aside from his lighter works and write in more serious vein. The work that established his European reputation was the five-act opera *La Muette de Portici,* more commonly known abroad as *Masaniello* – the name of its leading character. The overture and much that follows owes a strong debt to Rossini, but it was rich enough in dramatic effects, subtle instrumentation and original harmonies to win high praise from no less a high-priest of opera than Wagner. Within twelve years of its première it had been performed a hundred times at the Paris Opéra and by 1880 had received 500 French performances. It was performed many times in New York and London in the 1800s and there was a successful Berlin revival in 1953. Another work to gain international favour was the three-act *opéra comique, Fra Diavolo* first produced in 1830, with a strong musical score and a well constructed plot. This also travelled the world in the 1800s and was revived in New York in 1910, Berlin in 1934, at La Scala, Milan in the same year, by the Sadler's Wells company in London in

Caricature of Auber by Gill.

1935, in Berlin in 1936 and in Stockholm in 1948. It remains popular in Germany and has provided a good tenor role for many singers including Bonci and Schipa.

There is a slight prejudice against French opera abroad, in favour of the German and Italian schools, but there is always a probability that the delights of *opéra comique* will get a deserved and rewarding reassessment. The works of Auber will certainly stand revival when the climate is right, and then the merits of both his operatic and orchestral works will get their due appreciation.

P.G.

AURIC, Georges
(b. Lodève, 15 Feb 1899)

Composer, critic, administrator and elder statesman of French music, Georges Auric is the most prominent surviving member of *Les Six*, the group of lively young Paris-based musicians, who, animated by Jean Cocteau, caused such a stir in the 1920s. Born in Lodève in Hérault in 1899, he attended Montpellier Conservatoire and later, when his family moved to Montmartre, became a pupil of Vincent d'Indy at the Schola Cantorum and of Gédalge at the Conservatoire – like Durey, Tailleferre, Milhaud, Honegger and Auric's exact contemporary Poulenc. 1913 saw the introduction of this gifted, self-assured youth to Satie, who was to prove a major influence on his early development. That Cocteau should have dedicated his manifesto, *Coq et Arlequin* (1918) to him was significant. Auric became the standard bearer of *Les Six* in their spirited reaction against romantic rhetoric, portentousness and also Impressionism.

An urbane, witty and fashionable iconoclast, he was taken up by Diaghilev for whom he wrote *Les Fâcheux* (1923) and *Les Matelots* (1924). Those scores, together with his *Sonatine*, *Pastorales* and *Impromptus* for piano and his song settings of Chalupt, Cocteau, de Nerval and Louise de Vilmorin gave the impression of a pragmatic musical personality, rather facile, and given to conciseness, irony and an appearance of artistic flippancy.

Beneath the elegant, impersonal mask however another Auric was emerging, as demonstrated in his lyrically powerful Piano Sonata in F (1932). This was a breakaway from the simplistic austerity advocated by the orthodox aesthetic of *Les Six* and even won the approval of Cortot, normally no friend to their activities. Unfortunately, the sonata's hostile critical reception discouraged Auric from pursuing 'pure' music systematically, and in general his orchestral and chamber music (including his trio for oboe, clarinet and bassoon and his violin sonata) is incidental to his major creative pre-occupation. This was to be music for the stage and especially for the screen. Between the early 1930s and the 1950s, his film scores, of which he claims to have lost count, set a new standard of professionalism, imagination and idiomatic agility. Once again however it was Cocteau who inspired the finest results, in *Le Sang d'un poète*, *l'Éternel Retour*, *la Belle et la Bête* and *Orphée*. Other outstanding scores included *A nous la liberté*, *Symphonie Pastorale* and *l'Aigle a deux têtes*.

(In *Moulin Rouge* he even managed to write a theme song which swept the world.)

Meanwhile Auric's ballet scores for *Le Peintre et son modèle* and *Phèdre* in 1949 and 1950 indicated the new dimensions of dramatic expression and even violence towards which he was gravitating. His perspectives had broadened to embrace serialism as well as other contemporary trends, proof of which came in his high-tension tripartite Partita for two pianos. The mock-dissonant grimaces and relaxed tunefulness of the 20s had been left far behind.

It remains to cite Auric's critical work for *Marianne, Paris-Soir, Les Nouvelles littéraires* and, during the war, the *Nouvelle Revue française*, his presidency of the Lamoureux concerts, his six years as General Administrator of the Paris Opéra and his election to the Académie des Beaux-Arts.

C.G.

BACH, Carl Philipp Emanuel
(b. Weimar, 8 March 1714;
d. Hamburg, 15 Dec 1788)

Carl Philipp Emanuel Bach was the second surviving son of the great Johann Sebastian by his first wife Maria Barbara. Georg Philipp Telemann was one of his godparents. Carl Philipp was educated at St Thomas's School, Leipzig, and subsequently at the University of Frankfurt-on-the-Oder. Here he was an active member of the Collegium Musicum, and on one occasion in 1737, performed some of his compositions before the Margrave and Friedrich Wilhelm of Prussia, the tyrannical father of Frederick the Great, his future patron.

Carl Philipp was appointed cembalist in the *Kapelle* of Frederick the Great in 1740, claiming proudly in his autobiography that he 'had the honour of accompanying on the clavier, quite alone, at Charlottenburg, the first flute solo that Frederick played after becoming King'. Frederick's taste in music was conservative – although his repertoire included some three hundred concertos these were all either by himself or his flute-teacher Quantz. Quantz was held in high royal favour, as was the *Kapellmeister* Carl Heinrich Graun, a prolific composer of opera. Despite his close association with the royal flute playing Carl Philipp failed to achieve the importance at Court of either Quantz or Graun, whose names, according to Dr Burney, were more sacred in Berlin than those of Luther and Clavin. The King's flute playing suffered from a certain instability of tempo with which the cembalist was obliged to comply; one imagines that a certain amount of Bach's unwillingness would have been apparent to the King. Bach, however, demonstrated his formal devotion in the dedication of his six *Prussian Sonatas* to Frederick. One of the most important products of Carl Philipp's service in the Prussian Court was his didactic work *Versuch über die Wahre Art das Klavier zu Spielen* published in two parts in 1753 and 1762 – the first methodical treatment of the subject. Both by this treatise on technique and through his keyboard compositions, Carl Philipp may be regarded as the founder of modern piano playing.

As early as 1750, Carl Philipp had applied for appointments elsewhere, signifying discontent with his conditions at the Prussian Court. He confided a wish to Dr Burney for a life of 'more tranquility and independence', and in 1767 this was fulfilled. Carl Philipp succeeded his godfather Telemann as music director of the five principal churches in Hamburg. Burney, who visited Hamburg in 1777, described Carl Philipp as 'rather short in stature, with black hair and eyes, and brown complexion, a very animated countenance, and of cheerful and lively disposition'. The composer spent the remaining years of his life respected as the principal musician of Hamburg. He died on the 15th December 1788, and although plans were formulated to erect monuments in his honour at Hamburg and Weimar, they were never carried out. News of his death did not spread far, and as late as 1795, Haydn visited Hamburg in the hope of meeting him.

Historically, Carl Philipp Emanuel Bach is of the greatest importance standing in the transitionary period which separates the Baroque from the Classical, J. S. Bach from Haydn. In terms of musical style he rejected the contrapuntal manner of his father in favour of a more homophonic treatment of material, condemning canons, for instance, as 'dry and despicable pieces of pedantry that one might compose who would give his time to them'. Delicacy of workmanship and minute attention to musical expression are the hallmarks of Carl Philipp's style. A prolific composer whose output included oratorios, symphonies, songs and chamber music, his most important contribution was in the field of keyboard music. The *Prussian Sonatas* of 1742 were in many respects revolutionary, a collection of *Württemburg Sonatas* followed two years later, and subsequently there were important collections of sonatas '*für Kenner und Liebhaber*'. Although his later sonatas were intended for the forte-piano, Carl Philipp's favourite instrument was the clavichord whose capacity for delicate dynamic shading enchanted him. The clavichord was the perfect medium for one whose works were to represent the essence of the *empfindsamer Stil*.

G.G.

BACH, Johann Christian
(b. Leipzig, 5 Sept 1735;
d. London, 1 Jan 1782)

Johann Christian Bach was the youngest son of Johann Sebastian Bach by his second wife, Anna Magdalena. His first musical instruction was from his father, but as the latter died in 1750 when Johann Christian was only fifteen, the boy was taken into the household of his half-brother Carl Philipp Emanuel, in Berlin, who forwarded the lad's musical education, until such time as Johann Christian found himself in Italy, under the patronage of a certain Count Agostino Litta, in Milan. It is said that he went there in the company of a female Italian opera singer though of this nothing is known for sure, but in 1754, brother Carl noted that Johann Christian had 'gone to Italy'. In Italy he certainly was, by the late 1750s, and there became a pupil (by post, it would seem) of the celebrated Padre Martini of Milan, who came to regard him like a son. Perhaps it was through Martini's influence, or merely to qualify for a job as an Italian church organist, but it is certain that in that country Johann Christian abandoned the Protestantism of his forefathers and became a Roman Catholic convert, which faith he henceforward adhered to, even later on in Protestant England. As a Roman Catholic, he became organist of Milan Cathedral, and even composed some splendid pieces of Latin church music, which are well worthy of revival. But church music was not to absorb him for long; Italy was full of opera houses and invitations to compose operas for them too appealing; Johann Christian's first Italian opera (a setting of Metastasio's *Artaserse*) was produced at Turin in the Carnival Season of 1761, and later the same year his *Catone in Utica* was produced very successfully in Naples, to be followed the next year (1762) with a setting of Metastasio's very popular *Alessandro in Indie* libretto. Young Bach was obviously a rising star in the Italian operatic field. But then a strange thing happened, as it had happened to his great compatriot Handel, some fifty years before. Johann Christian found himself going to London, to compose an opera for the Italian opera house there. So he arrived in the English capital in the summer of 1762, as 'Mr John Bach, a Saxon Master of Musick . . .' At first he was disappointed with the voices placed at his disposal and so only attempted to direct comic operas and pasticcios – operas with music selected from the works of other composers – until he heard that singer Anna de' Amicis, whose voice charmed him, and he then composed for her the opera seria of *Orione ossia Diana Vendicata*, which took the town by storm, from the first notes of the splendid overture, in which Dr Burney stated that clarinets were used for the first time in the London opera. Actually, there is some doubt about his claim, since they are known to have been used by Handel, and Dr Arne certainly scored for them in some of his operas.

So young Bach was launched upon his English career. In a short time he passed from being a mere 'Saxon Master of Musick' to 'our trusty and well-beloved John Christian Bach, Gent'. He was appointed Music-Master to the young Queen Charlotte Sophia, wife of King George the Third. Both monarchs were fond of music; the King played the flute quite well and could strum a tune on the harpsichord, whilst his Queen was quite a competent keyboard player, who is said to have consoled her suffering fellow-travellers on the stormy sea-crossing from Germany to England 'with her executions on the harpsichord'; one can only hope that they were duly appreciative. Her first Music-Master in England had been the rather crotchety old Joseph Kelway, who was soon supplanted by the urbane and polished young Saxon, with whom the Queen could at least converse in her native tongue. John Bach, as he now was, became a great favourite in the Royal Household, dedicating to his royal patroness his own Op. 1, a set of very modern-sounding concertos. In a way, he stepped to some extent into the empty shoes of the dead Handel, who had died only a few years before, leaving a conspicuous void in English musical life, as there was no native composer of sufficient genius to occupy the great man's place. Not even Drs Boyce and Arne, gifted though they were, had sufficient

reputation to succeed the Beloved Saxon; it was left to another Saxon, who became 'the English Bach', to take over something of the great man's place, in due course. Young Bach was no great epic composer, like the departed Handel, but his music had something of the same consummate technical mastery as Handel's, albeit in an altogether different and more 'modern' style.

In London, Bach found some congenial spirits, some foreign, some British. Foremost among them was Carl Friedrich Abel, a celebrated viola da gamba virtuoso, who had once been a pupil of Bach's father Johann Sebastian. These two very kindred spirits now revived their old acquaintance and became close friends. They both played in the Queen's private chamber band, and actually set up house together and founded a long-popular series of concerts, known as the 'Bach-Abel Concerts' and later as the 'Hanover Square Concerts', devoted very largely to the performance of the 'modern' music of the day – among other things, Haydn's symphonies were played there, long before J. P. Salomon brought that great composer to London from Vienna. Another distinguished foreign musician resident in mid-18th-century London was Felice de' Giardini, brilliant violinist in the 'modern' style, who played for Bach, led the opera orchestra, and sometimes even tried his hand at the management, always a risky business. Then, later in the 1760s, they were joined by Johann Christian Fischer, the most distinguished oboist of the day, who also played Bach's music, and who later married one of Gainsborough's daughters. Gainsborough himself, of course, was a great music-lover and a close friend of both Bach and Abel, especially when he returned to London from Bath in the mid-1770s. He painted a remarkably fine portrait of John Christian, which still exists in two versions, one in Bologna, where Bach sent it at the request of his beloved old mentor Padre Martini, and one still in England.

London was a busy musical centre in the mid-18th century. Besides the Italian opera, there were two major English opera houses, and several smaller ones, as well as several series of indoor concerts, run by clubs and societies, and the open-air concerts at the various Pleasure Gardens, which provided music often of a very high standard in the summer months and were really the ancestors of the modern Promenade Concerts. Chief of these were Vauxhall and Ranelagh, at which

Portrait of J. C. Bach attributed to Gainsborough.

some of the finest musicians in London, both native and foreign, did not disdain to perform. Mr Bach's music, both vocal and instrumental, was in high demand there, and among other things he composed some of the very finest and most enchantingly melodious of all the innumerable sets of Vauxhall Songs, which serve to make one wish that he had had more opportunity to compose music to English words.

Although it had been his rising young reputation as a composer of Italian opera which had initially brought him to London, his actual connection with the London opera house became increasingly sporadic as the years went by. He found himself more in demand as a keyboard-player, concert-giver and composer of melodious chamber-music than as an opera-composer. Still, he did maintain a somewhat tenuous connection with the lyric stage. After *Orione*, came *Zanaida* (also in 1763 and described as a 'tragic' opera, although its sparkling little B flat symphony-overture is anything but tragic). But thereafter Bach's London operatic appearances became increasingly irregular, as new fashionable idols came and went. In 1765 he produced his *Adriano in Siria* (Metastasio again, as librettist); then two years later, in 1767, came the fine *Carattaco*, an Italian opera on a British subject, which was highly successful, as *Orione* had been some four years before. Its choral numbers were particularly admired and do indeed make one wish that the London Bach had tackled an English oratorio, after the Handelian fashion. But when, in 1770, he did compose an oratorio, it was to an Italian opera seria type text (*Gioas, Re di Giuda*) and failed miserably. At his royal patroness's suggestion, the composer played an organ concerto, Handel-fashion, 'between the acts' but it was a light-hearted, 'modern' work and failed to please the English 'organ-hunters', who actually hissed it. But although it failed to please at the oratorio, the John Christian kind of organ concerto was just the thing at Vauxhall and was to prove a lasting success to James Hook, for his own nightly organ concerts there, just as John Christian's other keyboard concertos, were to provide a model for the youthful Mozart, who had met the English Bach in London in 1764 and through him was introduced to English musical society. Mozart never forgot his beloved 'Herr Bach von London', his kindness, or his music. Anyone who knows the music of the two men is constantly being reminded of the younger man's artistic indebtedness to the older.

The early 1770s found the English Bach at the height of his career as performer and composer. He had by then established himself thoroughly as a composer of agreeable instrumental music in the modern idiom; his symphonies, concertos, sonatas and chamber pieces were in great demand with every publisher throughout Europe and especially in London. In the late 1760s he had had the acumen to see the future importance of the pianoforte, in place of the older harpsichord. Although he was not the first British performer to play the new instrument (John Burton, Charles Dibdin and even Thomas Gray and the Rev. William Mason had the precedence there) he was the first performer of any real consequence to feature it in a public concert. He bought one of Zumpe's little 'square' forte pianos in April 1768, and a 'Thatch'd House' concert in St James's Street, in June of that year, featured a 'Solo on the Piano Forte, by Mr Bach'. His very popular Op. 5 set of six keyboard sonatas, published that same year, were entitled 'pour le clavecin ou le piano forte', one of the first of many to be so described, right up until the time of early Beethoven.

Although his London operatic fame had

faded a little before the advent of newer idols, such as Sacchini, and perhaps because of a rather mangled version he himself had mounted of Gluck's *Orpheus*, flattering invitations came from abroad to compose operas for important foreign theatres, such as that at Mannheim, where his *Temistocle* was a triumphant success in November 1772; some years later came the rather less successful, although still very beautiful *Lucio Silla* of 1776, best known nowadays for its overture, the first of his orchestral works to be revived in modern times, as 'Sinfonia in B flat, Op. 18, No. 2'.

The 1772 Mannheim visit had been a fateful one for John Christian, by then in his late thirties and still unmarried. According to the Mozarts (who were great purveyors of musical gossip) Bach fell in love in Mannheim with the very beautiful teen-age daughter of his friend the flute-player J. B. Wendling. If so, nothing came of the affair and she later became the mistress of the Elector Carl Theodor. Bach, back home in London, married an old friend, Cecilia Grassi, the opera singer, who, although no great beauty, made him a very congenial wife, if contemporary accounts are to be believed.

Although his connection with the London Italian opera house had become very tenuous, by the late 1770s, nevertheless he did compose one more splendid opera seria for the London stage. This was *La Clemenza di Scipione*, described as a 'new Serious Opera with Grand Chorusses' when it was first performed at the Haymarket on the 4th April 1778. In this work there is no hint of failing powers on the part of the composer; rather it contains many signs that his style was broadening towards the coming Classical Viennese style. It had a fair success and was revived many years later, long after Bach's death, as a vehicle for the talents of the famous singer Mrs Billington.

One more flattering invitation for an operatic composition came from Paris, a most unexpected quarter, although Bach's instrumental music was well known and popular there. For the Paris opera, he composed his splendid *Amadis des Gaules*, to a modified version of an old text written nearly a century before by the famous poet Quinault, for Lully. Bach went over to Paris, to hear the singers, in the summer of 1778, and there met his young friend Mozart, who wrote back to his father in Salzburg, saying that 'Mr Bach von London' had been in Paris for a fortnight and how pleased they had been to see each other again, adding 'he is an honest man and

treats people fairly; I love him . . . with all my heart, and respect him . . .'

Unfortunately, *Amadis des Gaules*, for all its great melodic beauty, subtle orchestration and some of the most enchanting ballet music of the whole period, not even excepting that of Rameau and Gluck, was a comparative failure, pleasing neither the Gluckists nor the Piccinnists. Bach went home to London a worried man. Any hope that he was going to repair his foundering fortunes with a great French success had evaporated; his receipts were falling, and his own appearances drew less acclaim than they had even a few short years before. Newer piano-players such as Muzio Clementi and J. S. Schroeter were attracting the crowds (and the pupils!) and Bach's falling revenues were rendered even more serious by the depredations of a dishonest housekeeper who took Bach's money, but omitted to pay his bills. He still had his royal connections, of course, and moved to Richmond, partly to be near the court at Kew, partly for the sake of the more salubrious air. But it was in vain. His health gradually worsened, and although it is very difficult to discover from contemporary accounts exactly what was the cause of his ill-health, it seems that he may have died from worry, more than anything else, for he left debts amounting to £4,000, a very large sum in those days. A handful of friends followed his coffin to the grave, in St Pancras' Churchyard, and the event itself roused little comment at the time, except that when young Mozart heard the news, some time later, for news travelled slowly in those days, he wrote home to Papa Leopold 'You will no doubt have heard that the English Bach is dead – what a loss for the musical world!'

C.C.

BACH, Johann Sebastian
(b. Eisenach, 21 March 1685;
d. Leipzig, 28 July 1750)

The Bach family in Northern Germany contained musicians from the early 16th century, and no doubt earlier. They remained of purely local fame until Johann Sebastian was born as the youngest child of Johann Ambrosius Bach. His education was irregular, but like

Engraving of J. S. Bach at the organ in the church at Leipzig.

Passio secudũ Joañe. a 4 Voci. 2 Obo. 2 Violini Viola e Cont.
di J. S. Bach

virtually every male in his family he studied music and, as the possessor of what was said to be an 'uncommonly fine soprano voice', sang in the church and school choirs. A famous, perhaps apocryphal story, told of Bach as a child, describes how he ruined his eyesight for life by his practice of copying out secretly, and by moonlight, volumes of clavier compositions by older German masters. At the age of fifteen, through the influence of the local cantor, Herder, Johann Sebastian gained an appointment as boy soprano at Lüneberg. Here he met the distinguished organist, Georg Böhm, at whose instigation he walked thirty miles to Hamburg to hear Böhm's old master, Johann Adam Reinken, play at the Katharinenkirche.

It was while he was still in his teens, and at Lüneberg, that Bach's earliest known compositions, preludes and variations for the organ, were produced. He had also studied the violin, and at the age of eighteen became, briefly, a violinist in the orchestra of Duke Johann Ernst of Weimar. Weeks later, however, he was appointed organist in the Bonifacius-Kirche at Arnstadt. It was here that he began to write his great series of church cantatas for performance at the Sunday services. In October 1705, he obtained a month's leave from Arnstadt, and made a pilgrimage, again on foot, to Buxtehude in Lübeck. Buxtehude, the most famous composer of his time in North Germany, was then an old man, though he was still active in Lübeck as organist. It is not known whether Bach took lessons from him, or indeed whether the two men met at all. The twenty-year-old composer may simply have listened to his performances without making himself known. But there is no doubt that Buxtehude's influence upon Bach was enormous, especially upon his compositions for the organ. After spending four months away from Arnstadt, Bach returned to find himself in trouble because of his prolonged absence, and also because of the strange and unusual style of the compositions he produced for the church. He began to look for employment elsewhere and, in 1707, at the age of twenty-two, went to Mühlhausen as organist. Here he married his cousin, Maria Barbara, and attempted to concentrate upon his duties and upon the composition of music for the

Poster for a concert conducted by J. S. Bach in Leipzig, 1734.

church. As a pious Lutheran, Bach viewed music less as art than as an adjunct of his religion. In Mühlhausen, he found a great deal of dissension within the Lutheran church, and within a year he had decided to remove himself from it, and to accept an engagement at Weimar where he knew he could pursue his own ideas in composition without opposition or controversy. In 1708, he became court organist at Weimar, and chamber musician to the reigning Duke Wilhelm Ernst. Here he was to remain for the next nine years.

It was only in the last three years of his Weimar period that Bach became *Konzertmeister* or conductor of the court orchestra. At first, his most important duty was as organist, and thus it was that many of his great compositions for the organ were composed during this time: the C minor Passacaglia and Fugue, the arrangements of Vivaldi concertos, the *Orgelbüchlein*, and a great many of the preludes and fugues. Bach's fame began to spread, both as composer for the organ and as performer. When, in 1714, he played for the future King Frederick I of Sweden, it is recorded that his feet 'flew over the pedalboard as if they had wings'. After he became *Konzertmeister* at Weimar, Bach began to produce, in addition to the organ works, a number of cantatas for performance in the

A page from J. S. Bach's St John Passion.

St Thomas Church, Leipzig.

court chapel. In 1716, the coveted position of *Kapellmeister* became vacant on the death of Johann Samuel Drese, and it was not unreasonable for Bach to expect that the post would be offered to him. It was not, however, and he began immediately to look for an opportunity to move again. Within months, such an opportunity presented itself at Cöthen, at the court of Prince Leopold. Leopold, whose sister had married the nephew of Bach's Weimar employer, became acquainted with Bach at Weimar, and offered him the position of *Kapellmeister* at Cöthen in August, 1717. But Bach's Weimar employer refused to let him go, and, annoyed at the manner in which Bach had asked to be released from his employment, had the composer placed under arrest, and confined for some weeks. It was not until early December that Duke Wilhelm August of Weimar finally allowed Bach to travel to Cöthen and take up his duties there.

Bach's principal duty in Cöthen was to conduct the court orchestra, in which the Prince himself liked to play the viola da gamba, and to provide compositions for it. The Brandenburg Concertos, so-called because of their dedication to Duke Christian Ludwig of Brandenburg, the suites for orchestra, the violin concertos and much chamber music, all date from the Cöthen years. For the most part, they were tranquilly happy years for Bach. His relationship with his Prince was one of mutual respect, and he travelled with his master twice to the spa of Carlsbad. The Prince became godfather to the youngest child of Bach's first marriage, but the child did not survive infancy. The charming secular cantata for solo soprano, '*Weichet nur, betrübte Schatten*', known as the Wedding Cantata, was composed for an unrecorded Cöthen occasion.

After four or five years, Bach again became restless. In 1720 his wife had died while he was absent from Cöthen with his employer. He returned to find her dead and buried. Cöthen no longer seemed so happy a place to him. Eighteen months later, he married again. His new wife, Anna Magdalena, was the daughter of Johann Caspar Wilcken, a musician. At the age of twenty, she became step-mother to Bach's growing children, whose education was now a matter of some concern to their father. In the Calvinist town of Cöthen, the best school was a Calvinist one, which Bach would not permit his children to attend. Also, his master had just married a youthful princess who, according to Bach, was opposed to the arts and therefore likely to make life difficult for him. When Johann Kuhnau, cantor of the Thomasschule, or St Thomas School in Leipzig, died in June 1722, Bach applied for the position. The Leipzig council preferred two of the other candidates for the post, Telemann and Graupner, but Telemann withdrew and Graupner failed to obtain a release from his previous employer. So the Council settled for Bach.

Display of instruments in Bach's house, Leipzig.

Beginning of Prelude no. 7 from J. S. Bach's
Wohltemperites Klavier.

While he had been at Cöthen, Bach had continued to improve and extend his reputation as an organist and as an advisor on church organs. It was also during his Cöthen period that the famous non-meeting of Bach and Handel occurred. Bach travelled to Halle in the autumn of 1719 specifically to meet Handel, but discovered that he had already returned to England. The two greatest composers of the age were never to meet, though they made two or three attempts to do so.

As Cantor of the Leipzig Thomasschule, Bach was required to instruct the scholars, tc compose music which would not be operatic in style, and to seek the Mayor's permission whenever he wished to leave the town. The Cantor was also responsible for the music in two churches, the Thomaskirche and the Nicolaikirche, whose choirs were provided by the School. The Cantor personally conducted the choir and orchestra of the Thomaskirche, and it was for the Sunday services in these churches that Bach's great series of church cantatas was composed. He was also expected to provide music for certain University occasions, but Bach's relations with the University were, from the beginning, uncordial. More congenial to him was the conductorship of one of Leipzig's two musical societies, for which he was happy to compose as well.

Although he found himself involved in various disputes with the Leipzig Council and other bodies, mostly arising over lines of demarcation, or what he regarded as slights to his eminence, Bach remained at Leipzig for the remainder of his life. When his son Carl

Philipp Emanuel, now aged twenty-six, was appointed to the service of the Prussian Emperor Frederick the Great, in 1740, this gave Bach an opportunity to extend his own reputation as far as the Prussian court. In 1747, at the invitation of Frederick the Great, Bach travelled to Berlin. The story is told of how; scanning one evening the list of passengers brought by the coach, Frederick suddenly exclaimed in excitement, 'Gentlemen, old Bach has arrived.' 'Old Bach' was immediately called for, and came from his son's lodgings still in his travelling clothes. An enjoyable evening was spent in impromptu musical performance, and in due course, upon

Organ played on by J. S. Bach at Arnstadt.

a theme which Frederick gave him that evening, Bach composed for the Emperor his 'Musical Offering'.

Bach's domestic life in Leipzig appears to have been tranquil and well-ordered. The four children of his first marriage were, over the years, increased by seven more. In 1749, Bach's eyesight began to fail, and soon he became completely blind. He died in his sixty-sixth year of a stroke, his eyesight having returned ten days before his death. He was buried in the Johanniskirche, though with no tablet to mark the spot. His grave was rediscovered in 1894 during excavations to extend the foundations of the church.

Bach was no innovator in music. For him, his art existed only as part of his religion. The perfection to which he brought polyphony was not something to which the generation immediately following him could be expected to respond. His greatness reveals itself, however, in this and in the variety of the forms of music in which he excelled. Understandably, he eschewed opera as being too frivolous. But in the realm of sacred music he has left a number of masterpieces. High among these are the 295 church cantatas, the *St Matthew Passion* which is a more deeply devout oratorio than Handel's *Messiah*, and the B minor Mass. The organ compositions have already been mentioned: Bach's finest secular works include the set of six Brandenburg Concertos and the forty-eight preludes and fugues of *The Well-tempered Clavier*.

C.O.

BALAKIREV, Mily
(b. Nizhny-Novgorod, 2 Jan 1837;
d. St Petersburg, 29 May 1910)

Balakirev was largely self-taught in music and early conceived a fondness for Chopin and a passion for Glinka which remained with him throughout his life. He started composing at the age of fifteen but entered the University of Kazan as a mathematics student. In 1855 he went to St Petersburg where he met Glinka whose spiritual heir he became and the guidance of whose circle he undertook after his death in 1857 – by which time Balakirev was quite well known as a pianist and composer. His first important composition, the *Overture on Three Russian Themes*, was written in 1858, but his *King Lear* music, though begun the same year, was not completed until 1861.

Balakirev always found difficulty in working systematically and in producing satisfactory definitive versions of his works, and over the next ten years only three substantial pieces were completed – the symphonic poem *Russia*, the *Overture on Czech Themes (In Bohemia)* and the piano fantasy *Islamey*. Meanwhile in 1862 he instigated the founding of the Russian Free School of Music and distinguished himself as teacher, adviser and father figure above all to the young nationalist-oriented group of composers who gathered around him and were later nicknamed 'The Mighty Handful': Mussorgsky, Rimsky-Korsakov and Borodin were all set to composing professionally as a result of Balakirev's encouragement, although several later rebelled against his 'benevolent despotism' (even Tchaikovsky was kept for a time under surveillance). In 1866 Balakirev went to Prague to supervise productions of Glinka's operas, and the following year succeeded Anton Rubinstein as principal conductor of the Russian Music Society. He gained even more control in musical circles when he assumed the directorship of the Free School, but his outspokenness and refusal to compromise led to his dismissal in 1869. In 1881 he again took charge of it after a prolonged mental and psychological crisis which effectively removed him from the musical scene for several years. In 1883 he was appointed Director of Music at the Imperial Chapel, and started editing the complete works of Glinka for publication. He resigned from the Imperial post in 1894 and devoted the last fifteen years of his life increasingly to composition: he completed the C major symphony begun thirty years before, the Second Symphony and much piano music.

As heir to the Glinka tradition Balakirev made an incalculable contribution to the nationalist cause in Russian music. He inherited all Glinka's love of folksong (he published three sets of arrangements) of instrumental colour and the tendency to compose in short bursts. The influence of Liszt and the fusion of folkmusic traits with exotic arabesque nurtured a highly-wrought, richly ornamental style in which genuine development, dramatic argument and thematic proliferation is often eschewed in favour of a play of harmonic and instrumental colour – e.g., *Islamey* and Balakirev's masterpiece *Tamara* (1882) which in terms of opulence of sound stands unrivalled in the music of its time. This work had important repercussions:

Rimsky-Korsakov's *Scheherezade* was directly indebted and so also, far more significantly, was Debussy's *Prélude à l'Après-midi d'un Faune*. Otherwise Balakirev is best represented by his First Symphony, his fine *Russia* and early *Overture on Three Russian Themes*, and a number of sterling songs.

C.P.

BALFE, Michael William
(b. Dublin, 15 May 1808;
d. Rowney Abbey, Herts, 20 Oct 1870)

Balfe was descended from families on both his father's and mother's side who were connected with music and the stage. His father was a dancing master and violinist; his grandfather had been a member of the Crow Street Theatre band; and his great-grandfather was reputed to have played in the orchestra at the first performance of Handel's *Messiah* in Dublin (1742). His mother was related to Leonard Macnally, author of the libretto of the comic opera *Robin Hood* (1784). The young Balfe was taught piano and violin by his father and became the pupil of William O'Rourke (later known as Rooke) who brought him before the Dublin public as solo violinist in a concerto by Mayseder at the early age of eight. After his father's death in 1823, he decided to leave Dublin and seek his fortune in London, where he was apprenticed to Charles Horn, the singer and composer, and engaged as a violinist in the Drury Lane orchestra for the 1823/4 season.

At this juncture the boy of sixteen met an Italian nobleman called Count Mazzara, who was so moved by his chance resemblance to his only son who had recently died that he invited him to Rome where he would meet the Count's wife and family and pursue his musical studies. Balfe accepted. The journey to Italy was broken in Paris, where Balfe was introduced to Luigi Cherubini. In Italy he studied under Paer in Rome and Vincenzo Frederici in Milan; and his first stage work, a ballet entitled *Il Naufragio di La Perouse*, was mounted at the Teatro alla Canobbiana, Milan, in the autumn of 1825.

On his return to Paris, he was introduced by Cherubini to Rossini, who agreed to recommend him to the Théâtre Italien, provided he studied singing for a period under Bordogni. In due course he made his operatic début as Figaro in *Il Barbiere di Seviglia*. Other engagements followed, including an appearance with Maria Malibran in *La Cenerentola*. Returning to Italy, he pursued a successful career as an opera singer (1830–4), which took him to many towns, including Palermo, Piacenza, Varese, Bergamo (where he met a Hungarian singer, Lina Roser, who became his wife), Pavia, Milan, and Venice.

Early in 1830 he was in Palermo, when the chorus of the Teatro Carolino struck for higher pay. The irate management decided to finish the season by mounting operas that needed no chorus; and Balfe, invited to write something new to fit this bill, promptly produced a little farce called *I Rivali di se stessi*. He wrote two other operas during this period – *Un avvertimento ai gelosi* for the Teatro Fraschini, Pavia (1831), and *Enrico Quarto al passo della Marna* for the Teatro Carcano, Milan (1833). On his return to England, he found that the Lyceum Theatre (English Opera House), rebuilt after a recent fire, was presenting a number of new English romantic operas with spoken dialogue. He was invited to contribute to this season. Edward Fitzball provided a libretto based on Madame de Genlis's novel, *Le Siège de La Rochelle*, and Balfe composed the score with great rapidity; but *The Siege of Rochelle* was eventually mounted, not at the Lyceum, but at Drury Lane, where Alfred Bunn, the manager, remembered Balfe from 1824 when he had played in the Drury Lane orchestra. *The Siege of Rochelle* was a great success when produced on the 29th October 1835 and launched Balfe on a wave of popularity. The following year he enjoyed an equally sensational success when he wrote *The Maid of Artois* specially for Malibran, who unfortunately died later that summer in Manchester at the early age of twenty-eight. A decline set in with his next three operas – *Catherine Grey* (1837), *Joan of Arc* (1837), and *Diadesté* (1838) – and *Falstaff* (1838), which he wrote to an Italian libretto for the Italian Opera at Her Majesty's Theatre, though brilliantly cast, was only partly successful.

Early in 1839 he was under contract to provide a new opera to a libretto written by Bunn (presumably *The Bohemian Girl*). He wrote the greater part of the score; but then Bunn got into such deep financial difficulties that he was adjudged bankrupt in 1840, and the new opera had to be put into cold storage. This meant that for the time being Balfe reverted to his old career of opera singer. But in 1841 he was so ill-advised as to try his hand at opera management on his own. Taking a lease of the

Lyceum, he produced a new opera of his (*Kēolanthe*) with his wife in the title role and promised to follow it with other new English operas. Unfortunately the enterprise collapsed after less than three months.

At that moment he received an invitation to write an opera for Madame Grisi at the Théâtre Italien in Paris. He had made excellent progress with the score, when to his disappointment this project too collapsed. He was on the point of returning to London, when an invitation to give a recital of his own compositions at the Salle Erard led to a meeting with the French librettist, A. E. Scribe, who suggested they should collaborate on a new opera for the Opéra-Comique. Balfe accepted; and *Le Puits d'Amour* was produced there on the 20th April 1843. Its success led to a demand for another comic opera from Balfe; and *Les Quatre Fils Aymon* (1844) was the result. Both operas were produced in London (under the titles of *Geraldine* and *The Castle of Aymon*); but their main success was achieved in Europe, particularly Germany. Before leaving Paris, Balfe was commissioned to write a serious opera for the Paris Opera house. The result was *L'Etoile de Séville* (1845), which received fifteen performances, but was not revived.

Meanwhile, by an extraordinary reversal of fortune Bunn had reappeared on the London theatrical scene and been appointed manager once more of Drury Lane. He forthwith reminded Balfe of the opera he had commissioned from him a few years previously. Balfe, who had used some of the music for other purposes, now refurbished the score, rewriting several numbers; and *The Bohemian Girl*, when produced at Drury Lane on the 27th November 1843, brought him the greatest success of his whole career. In a few days' time the opera's popular tunes were being whistled everywhere and ground out by every London street barrel-organ. Balfe followed up with several other operas for Drury Lane – a through-composed opera, with recitative, entitled *The Daughter of St Mark* (1844), and then four operas written to the usual formula with spoken dialogue: *The Enchantress* (1845), *The Bondman* (1846), *The Maid of Honour* (1847), and *The Sicilian Bride* (1852).

In 1846 Balfe was appointed conductor of the Italian Opera at Her Majesty's in succession to Costa. At the opening of his first season he conducted the first performance in London of Verdi's *Nabucodonosor*, which had been retitled *Nino* in order to circumvent the

new censorship regulations; but he was not a good conductor, and the appointment lapsed in 1852.

For a few years in the 1850s he travelled extensively in Europe. In 1850 he visited Berlin, where *The Bondman* was produced in a German version under the title of *Der Mulatte*. This was followed a year later by visits to Berlin and Vienna to attend productions of *The Bohemian Girl*, which proved very popular in its German guise as *Die Zigeunerin*. A considerable part of 1852 and 1853 was spent in St Petersburg – a rewarding visit insofar as he took part in various Court concerts and gave music lessons to the nobility – but none of his operas seem to have been produced. He broke his return journey in Vienna in order to supervise the production of a German adaption of *Keolanthe* (December 1853). He then revisited Italy where *La Zingara* (*The Bohemian Girl*) was produced in Trieste, Bologna, Brescia, and Bergamo. Ricordi, the Italian music publisher, commissioned a new opera from him for Trieste; but *Pittore e Duca* (1854), to a libretto by F. M. Piave, seems to have been a flop. Some years later an English version was given by the Carl Rosa Company under the title of *Moro, the Painter of Antwerp* (1882).

Back in England he found a new management for English opera had been set up by two singers, Louisa Pyne and William Harrison. They commissioned half a dozen new operas from him, of which *The Rose of Castile* (1857), *Satanella* (1858) and *The Puritan's Daughter* (1861) proved especially popular with the public. In 1864 Balfe retired into Hertfordshire, where the last years of his life were devoted to revising the score of *The Bohemian Girl* for production in Paris as *La Bohémienne* (1869) and to writing his last opera *The Knight of the Leopard*. He died on the 20th October 1870.

Balfe had a knack for pleasing the public; but his facile fluency and lack of self-criticism were fatal flaws in his music. Even his closest friends agreed his talent desperately needed discipline. Yet in his defence it must be admitted that he knew how to write for the voice, had a gift for melody, and an instinct for the effectiveness of music in the theatre. He was one of the few British composers to win an international reputation as an opera composer.

E.W.W.

BARBER, Samuel
(b. Westchester, Pa., 9 March 1910)

Of the generation of Benjamin Britten, Samuel Barber is the American composer who, in his approach to composition and in his own style, most resembles Britten. As a child and a young man, he was taught to sing by his aunt, the famous contralto Louise Homer. He began composing while still a child, and then studied at the Curtis Institute in Philadelphia. He continued his singing lessons, under the baritone Emilio de Gogorza, and also received instruction in pianoforte and conducting, the latter from Fritz Reiner. Barber is, then, extremely well-educated musically, and his baritone voice has been put to the service of other people's music as well as his own. His teacher in composition at the Curtis Institute was Rosario Scalero.

Graduating from the Institute in 1932, Barber embarked upon a career as composer. His musical language was so accessible, and his skill in orchestration so assured, that he quickly became successful. Not only was his music liked, he also had a gift for winning prizes, among them the Pulitzer Prize (twice) and the Prix de Rome. He was only twenty-seven when, in 1937, his 'Symphony in One Movement' became the first work by an American composer to be performed at the prestigious Salzburg Festival. The music he wrote in the 1930s could be described as neo-romantic in style, and this is a style which, despite his flirtations with other techniques of composition, Barber has never completely abandoned. The lyrical, yet ardently romantic *Adagio for Strings,* which dates from this period, is Barber's best-known composition. It began as the slow movement of a String Quartet, but was later extracted and orchestrated by the composer. An equally attractive work is *Knoxville: Summer of 1915,* a piece for soprano and orchestra whose words are by James Agee. During the war years, Barber's music began to develop in various directions. His work in the Army Air Corps led him to introduce into his second symphony a tone generator which simulated the sound of a radio beam used for night flying. But when he revised the symphony after the war, Barber removed the tone generator. By this time, he had begun to be interested in ballet, and had provided the score of *Serpent Heart* for Martha Graham's ballet on the subject of Medea.

Barber's later music has not escaped the influence of Stravinsky, but his voice remains an individual one. He is a friend of the opera composer Gian-Carlo Menotti, and it was to a large degree at the instigation of Menotti that Barber turned to opera with *Vanessa,* for which Menotti provided the libretto. *Vanessa* was produced by the Metropolitan Opera, New York, in 1958 and was subsequently staged at the Salzburg Festival in the same year. When the Metropolitan Opera moved to its new home at Lincoln Centre in 1966, Barber was commissioned to compose the opening opera. The result was *Anthony and Cleopatra* which provided Leontyne Price and Jess Thomas with two strong roles well suited to their vocal capabilities. Barber remains one of the most attractive personalities in American music, uninfluenced by current fashions but by no means to be dismissed as old-fashioned.

C.O.

BARTÓK, Béla
(b. Nagyszentmiklós, 25 March 1881; d. New York, 26 Sept 1945)

Mahler's famous complaint that he was 'three times without a country' might have been reiterated, *mutatis mutandis,* by Béla Bartók, Born and brought up in pre-First War Hungary, Bartók watched from his chair at the Budapest Academy of Music as his native land shrank like a puddle in the July sun, leaving every town he had lived in as a child high and dry and, thanks to the barbarity of visas and passports, accessible to him only with difficulty.

After the Treaty of Trianon, by which Hungary was partitioned in 1920, even Bratislava (formerly Pozsony), where Bartók's mother continued to live, could not be visited without formalities. Most of the more remote parts of pre-War Hungary to which Bartók had gone in search of authentic folk music were now cut off. And what the First War had begun the Second continued. When Bartók embarked for the USA in October 1940 it was for the last time. His five remaining years were spent, ironically, cataloguing somebody else's collection of Yugoslavian folk songs and struggling to secure a livelihood against the indifference of the American public and his own rapidly deteriorating health. Unlike Mahler, he never made the return crossing.

Bartók was born in the village of Nagyszentmiklós (now Sânnicolaul-Mare) on the 25th March 1881. It lies near the junction of

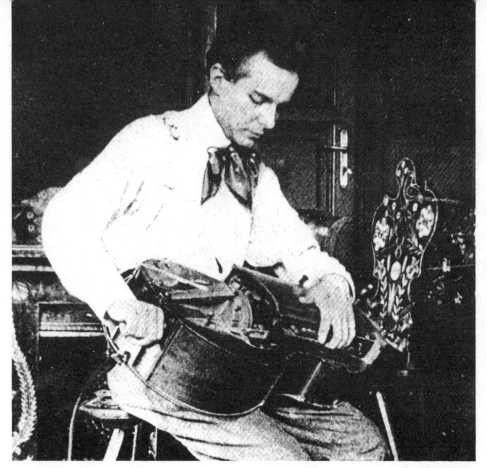

Bartók playing a nyenyere, *a peasant instrument of the hurdy-gurdy family.*

the borders of modern Hungary, Yugoslavia and Romania, and is now in Romania. His father, the director of the local government agricultural college and an accomplished amateur pianist, died when young Béla was seven, after which his early career was guided by his mother, often in the face of real economic, geographical and physical hardship. We can follow their track northwards and westwards, always just outside the fringes of present-day Hungary. At Nagyszöllös, now in the USSR, Paula Bartók taught from 1889 in the elementary school while Béla studied, with conspicuous lack of success, at the Gymnasium in Nagyvárad (now Oradea Mare in Romania). In 1892 the little family, including Béla's younger sister Erzsébet, spent a year's 'sabbatical' in Pozsony to enable Béla to take proper music lessons with László Erkel. Later Paula managed to get a permanent teaching job in Pozsony, and it was there that Béla had

his first real opportunity to hear and make music and to move in musical circles. He met Ernö Dohnányi and succeeded him as organist in the Gymnasium chapel. In 1898, when he was accepted for the Vienna Conservatoire, he followed Dohnányi in preferring Budapest: a fashionable, but in Bartók's case, vital choice.

Bartók's childhood had been seriously affected by ill-health. He was bronchitic, had suffered from pneumonia and been treated for a (wrongly diagnosed) curvature of the spine. These ailments slowed down his physical growth, but could not obstruct his musical ability and intellect. By the time his father died he was picking out tunes on the piano, and at nine he was composing (an activity he called 'remembering'). At ten he appeared at a concert in Nagyszöllös in the dual role of composer/pianist on which his career was later to pivot. But illness continued to dog him. It interrupted his course at the Budapest Academy no less than three times, and may have stopped him composing – though his silence between 1900 and 1902 was probably

Bartók recording Hungarian peasants, 1908.

due to a stylistic impasse which was eventually broken by a performance of Strauss's *Also sprach Zarathustra*. For a time music poured out of him under Strauss's influence, though his biggest work of this period, the *Kossuth* Symphony, is significantly not autobiographical but patriotic and in tune with the vigorous Hungarian separatist movement in the dying years of the Austro-Hungarian empire. *Kossuth* was incidentally Bartók's first work to be heard in England, when Richter conducted it in Manchester in 1904.

A more important event of 1904 was the discovery of Hungarian folk music. Bartók's first recordings of this seem to have been made out of more or less idle curiosity, but in 1905 he began, with Kodály, a systematic survey which took him on collecting trips throughout Hungary, Transylvania and Carpathia and ultimately as far afield as North Africa (1913) and Turkey (1936). Bartók's collation and

editing of this material, though later eclipsed by his own music, was meticulous and scholarly and remains an important contribution to musical ethnology. Moreover, it bore fruit in his music, both in providing actual melodies and in forming the basis of a new and completely individual style. All Bartók's works after the First Quartet (1908) are impregnated with the folk influence.

Meanwhile in 1907 Bartók accepted a teaching post at the Budapest Academy, where he was to remain until 1934. This was, however, the start of a frustrating phase of his career. The Straussian period had been succeeded by a series of more austere and experimental works, including the piano bagatelles, whose modernisms were admired by Busoni, and the First Quartet, which shows the new influence of Debussy. These works encountered growing opposition in Budapest circles, though they were better received abroad. Then came the war of 1914, followed by the abortive Hungarian revolutions of 1918, and the Treaty of Trianon. Throughout this period Bartók worked somewhat hopelessly on collating his folksong collections, teaching his piano students (he refused to teach composition) and writing music of growing rhythmic ebullience and harmonic ferocity. The Second Quartet dates from this period, as does the opera, *Duke Bluebeard's Castle*, the ballets *The Wooden Prince* and *The Miraculous Mandarin* and much piano music. By the early 1920s the future was beginning to look happier for new music. In 1922 Salzburg played host to an international festival of modern music, and the following year this was institutionalised as the festival of the ISCM. Bartók's music featured prominently on these occasions. He was also now an admired international concert pianist, and we owe the first two piano concertos and the great solo piano works of the 1920s (the *Improvisations,* the Sonata, *Out of Doors*) to his Mozartian need to keep his recital programmes fresh. It was as a pianist/composer that Bartók enjoyed a *succès d'estime* in London in 1922 and again in 1923 (each time with a new violin and piano sonata), and paid his first visit to the USA in 1927. The following year the USA paid him a further compliment by awarding a prize to his uncompromisingly difficult Third Quartet.

The closing years of Bartók's life are as melancholy biographically as they are rich musically. To the distractions and exhaustions of a combined creative, performing and teaching career was added the gloom of seeing central Europe fall more and more into Nazi control, and the humiliation of having his own Aryanism investigated (in 1937: he was not, of course, Aryan, but like all pure Hungarians a member of the racially distinct Finno-Ugric stock). The music of this period, however, includes some of the greatest of all 20th-century works: the Fourth and Fifth Quartets, the *Music for Strings, Percussion and Celesta*, and the Sonata for two pianos and percussion. The mellowing of Bartók's style has not at this stage undermined its vigour. But by 1939, the year of the Sixth Quartet and of his mother's death at the age of 82, the strain of regret portends some falling off of creative energy, though this was to be brilliantly but briefly halted in three works of 1943–5, the Concerto for Orchestra (commissioned by the Koussevitzky Foundation), the Sonata for solo violin, and the Third Piano Concerto, all composed in New York.

Bartók is one of the great originals among 20th-century composers. His early chamber works, of which a violin sonata (1903) and a piano quintet (1903–4) have been published

and recorded, still show the influence of Brahms, Strauss and perhaps Liszt. But by 1908, in the bagatelles and the First Quartet, he was writing music which for the most part cannot be traced to any major historical influence except folk music. Bartók's subsequent music presents two significant and opposed aspects of his personality: on the one hand that passionate streak which, according to contemporary accounts, was only evident in the man when he sat at the piano; and on the other hand a fondness for intellectual constructions. In most of Bartók's 'barbaro' writing, from the *Two Romanian Dances* (1910) to the *moto perpetuo* finale of the Concerto for Orchestra (1943) there is some feeling of pent-up emotion bursting out, though he was also undoubtedly influenced by the anti-romantic tendencies of Stravinsky and Prokofiev. Similarly the many 'night-music' movements generate a positively expressionistic tension which seems bound to explode into violence.

This quasi-pathological streak naturally influenced his music at every level. In the violin sonatas of 1922–3 it threatens to unhinge the whole idea of coherent partnership between two instruments, and in the Third and Fourth Quartets it inspires various instrumental effects of a more or less disintegrative nature (including the famous 'Bartók' pizzicato, where the string rebounds harshly against the fingerboard). Such effects were partly influenced by Berg's *Lyric Suite*. But though the Third Quartet is practically non-tonal, Bartók never quite reconciled himself to wholehearted atonality, still less to Schoenberg's twelve-note method. Nevertheless, like Schoenberg, he was a brilliant contrapuntist and moreover probably did arrive quite early at a composing system (based, according to Ernö Lendvai, on the Golden Section). But he never taught or expounded it.

Most of Bartók's music has an expressive urgency in proportion to the lifelong difficulty he experienced in personal communication. As a child he was usually too ill to play normally with other children, and this, together with the early death of his father, seems to have kept back the gregarious side of his nature. Brought up by his mother, he was always happiest in the company of women. He married twice, both times to pupils considerably younger than himself: in 1909 to Marta Ziegler (who was then 16 or 17), and in 1923, after a divorce, to Ditta Pásztory. Most of those who knew him testify to his intensely

Béla Bartók.

private and withdrawn nature, in which there was also a streak of rather proud integrity. When his New York friends wanted to ease his financial worries, they always had to employ subterfuge, since Bartók would never accept straightforward generosity. By the time of his success in the USA, he was too ill to profit by it.

S.W.

BAX, Arnold
(b. London, 8 Nov 1883;
d. Cork, 3 Oct 1953)

An English composer, Bax was also author of literary works under the pseudonym of Dermot O'Byrne. He was trained at the R.A.M. under Tobias Matthay (piano) and Frederick Corder (composition) and travelled widely in youth, particularly to Ireland, to which country – and to the realm of Celtic mythology – he was peculiarly drawn. Being of independent means he was able to devote his life entirely to composition; the only official appointment he ever held was that of Master of the King's Musick (1941–53), for public activities of any kind ill-suited his retiring and hyper-sensitive nature. His was a lavish talent, not restricted to music, as his autobiographical *Farewell my Youth* and pseudonymous poetry make clear. This lavishness with its associated tendencies to prolixity and complexity have certainly hindered thoroughgoing exploration of his work and a just estimate of his stature, which as an 'unabashed romantic' (his own much-quoted phrase) of the 'English Musical Renaissance' is considerable. *Ecstasy* is the keynote of his work; that mystical withdrawal from the daily round and common task which he sought and found in the music of Beethoven, Delius, Sibelius; in Yeats whose poetry came to him as a lightning-flash of illumination, in the Celtic and Nordic mythology in which he was steeped, and to which he gave pantheistic expression in the symphonic poems *In the Faery Hills, Tintagel, The Garden of Fand, The Tale the Pine Trees Knew,* and may earlier large-scale pieces still hardly known (the orchestral *Spring Fire* and *Nympholept, Enchanted Summer* for soloists, orchestra and chorus); in the seven symphonies in which is graven the spiritual odyssey of a lifetime; in the four piano sonatas; in a host of intricately-wrought piano pieces, songs and chamber works. His was a spirit wracked by conflict: the lyric poet of *Summer Music* and *Maytime in Sussex* is also the epic dramatist of the symphonies and a motive force in the strife of the elements in the symphonic poem *November Woods,* the three orchestral *Northern Ballads* and *Winter Legends* for piano and orchestra. Bax emerged almost as a ready-made musical personality; the apprentice-period was unusually short-lived and Gerald Abraham's description of the sources of his style as 'the debris of impressionism' is realistic if accepted in a positive sense. He steered a wholly personal course which came to its appointed end with the Seventh Symphony (1939); thereafter age took a heavy toll on him, although he was still capable of the occasional spirited sally, as in the case of the film-score *Oliver Twist.* After his death his music fell into an oblivion the clouds of which are only just beginning to clear.

C.P.

BEETHOVEN, Ludwig van
(b. Bonn, 15/16 Dec 1770;
d. Vienna, 26 March 1827)

Beethoven was born on the 15th/16th December 1770 at Bonn to a family which originated in Flanders. The particle 'van' does not indicate noble birth of any kind, and it was misleading when the composer translated this to the German 'von'. The composer's grandfather arrived at Bonn in 1733 and evidence has been adduced to show that he had been born at Malines (Mechlin). It might be safe to say that the family rose in Flanders from the social status of workmen to that of *petits bourgeois*. Both the grandfather and the father of the composer served as musicians in the chapel of the Elector, the former eventually becoming *Kapellmeister* and the latter, Johann, a tenor chorister. In 1767 this Johann married Maria Magdalena Keverich, daughter of the chief cook at a neighbouring court and widow of a court valet. Although Johann's father regarded the marriage as a social come-down for his son, there was in fact very little social distinction between musicians and other servants at the princely courts of the day. Of the seven children born to Johann and his wife only three survived infancy: the composer and his two younger brothers, Karl and Johann. The father seems to have been a hard yet feckless character, and his later years were rendered additionally disagreeable for his family by the alcoholism from which his mother had also suffered. As the eldest son, Ludwig was early called upon to direct family affairs, but this was not until his father had attempted to exploit the remarkable musical gifts which the boy showed at an early age. His only education worthy of the name was in the craft of music and he certainly received lessons in pianoforte, organ, violin and viola. Any other schooling had ceased before he was twelve, and although he picked up rudimentary French and a little Italian, his correspondence shows that he always found difficulty in expressing himself clearly in his own language; and he was capable of only the most elementary arithmetic. This total absence of general culture from his home background no doubt explains not only Beethoven's belated attempts at self-education, but also much of his later behaviour, which was put down to natural boorishness when it probably reflected the embarrassment and sense of frustration which he often felt in the company of those more gently brought up than himself. He remem-

Portrait of Beethoven by W. J. Mähler, 1804.

bered his mother with deep affection, but she was unable to do more than mitigate the squalid and penurious circumstances in which the family found itself owing to the father's drinking.

The teacher who exercised the first profound influence on the young Beethoven was C. G. Neefe, who came to Bonn in 1779 and was appointed court organist in 1781. Neefe introduced the eleven-year-old boy to J. S. Bach's *Well-tempered Clavier* and found him so forward that by 1784 Ludwig was officially appointed as Neefe's assistant. When the Elector Max Franz (brother of the Emperor Joseph II and of Queen Marie Antoinette) acceded in the same year, the young Beethoven's duties became less, and he was able to devote more time to study. In 1787 he was sent to Vienna, probably at the expense of Count Waldstein, and according to tradition received a number of lessons from Mozart. After a matter of weeks rather than

A page from the manuscript of the A Sonata *by Beethoven.*

months, however, he was summoned home to attend his mother's death-bed. Two years later his father was dismissed from his post in the choir and at nineteen Beethoven found himself solely responsible for himself, his father and his two brothers. He supplemented his income by giving lessons and also by playing viola in the orchestra of the Opera – an occupation which brought him a first-hand knowledge not only of works by Mozart, Gluck and the Italians Cimarosa and Paisiello but also the masters of the contemporary *opéra comique*, especially Grétry.

The friends which Beethoven made in his youth at Bonn were in many cases to remain intimate with him to the end of his life. They provided a much-needed alternative to a happy family background, and their character and social standing prove that the assistant organist must have possessed altogether exceptional attractions of personality, intelligence and general likeableness. The widowed Frau von Breuning's house, with the children Christoph, Eleonore, Stephan and Lorenz seems to have been a second home to him, and

Eleonore married Franz Gerhard Wegeler who was to be a close friend of the composer's when he moved to Vienna. Stephan von Breuning was a fellow pupil with Beethoven of the violin teacher Franz Anton Ries, who was generous in helping the young composer financially. Also to be mentioned as evidence of Beethoven's ability to transcend social distinctions by sheer character and personality, is his relationship with Count Waldstein, a friend of the Elector's and originally a piano pupil of the composer's but also a real friend and the dedicatee of the piano sonata op. 53. Waldstein may well have been instrumental in arranging Beethoven's removal to Vienna in 1792, either by advising the Elector of its advisability or offering to finance the move, or both. In the same year Haydn passed through Bonn on his return journey from London to Vienna and Beethoven showed him the Funeral Cantata that he had written the previous year on the death of the Emperor Joseph II.

We know that Haydn was impressed, but whether he invited Beethoven to Vienna or played any part in his moving there is uncertain. Certainly by 1795 all Beethoven's family connections with Bonn were severed – his father dead, his brother Carl a music teacher and Johann a chemist's assistant, both in Vienna. Beethoven's instinctive gathering of the remains of his family about him, and his extraordinarily strong feelings of affection and responsibility for them were to have important effects on the course of his life and eventually to determine its emotional direction.

Although life at Bonn had centred round the Electoral Court and social conditions were essentially the same there as elsewhere in Europe before 1789, there was a far more liberal spirit and much greater social mobility there than in Vienna. This was due in part to the nearness of France and the gradual infiltration, rather than any violent imposition, of new revolutionary ideas; and in part also to the genial personality of the Elector Max Franz, who shared many of his brother Joseph's liberal principles and found them more easy to put into practice in a small principality than at the centre of a great empire. The young Beethoven had hitherto been largely spared the personal experience of aristocratic arrogance and of the extreme instances of plebeian disenfranchisement. These soon leaped to his eye in Vienna, where the Imperial Court was surrounded by miniature establishments of the same kind belonging to members of a cosmopolitan – Slav, Magyar, Belgian and Italian as well as Germanic – aristocracy. Music, and in particular instrumental music, played a great part in the entertainments of these, and also lesser households. No doubt Beethoven was assisted by the recommendations of his friend Waldstein (a landowner in the territory of the present Czechoslovakia) and it was not long before he was much in demand first as a performer, then as piano teacher and finally as composer. A mere glance at the dedications of his works over the next 15 years will show how closely engaged he was with the aristocratic world of patronage – Lichnowsky, Lobkowitz, Schwarzenberg, Clary, Keglevics, Kinsky and Liechtenstein were all among the leading families of the old Austro-Hungarian Empire. Many of his patrons recognised in the brilliant, intensely vital yet susceptible young man a genius and a personality that transcended the narrow limits imposed by social caste. Those who did not were liable to get the rough side of Beethoven's tongue, and even a momentary or imaginary slight from those whom he recognised as true friends was apt to receive immediate punishment – 'Lobkowitzer Esel!' or 'Ass of a Lobkowitz!'

Chamber-music, including pianoforte works for his own performance, naturally formed the great part of Beethoven's compositions after his arrival in Vienna. He had already written essays of this kind in Bonn, but it was the stimulus of Viennese demand that accounts for the large production of the ten years following his arrival – the trios, Op. 1, and Op. 9, the Rondino, the violin sonatas Op. 12, the many sets of piano variations on popular operatic melodies of the day, the piano sonatas of Op. 2, 10 and 14 and finally the six string quartets of Op. 18. All these were composed before 1800 and almost all were dedicated to members of one of the princely families mentioned above. The two important exceptions are the piano sonatas Op. 2 dedicated to Haydn and the violin sonatas to Antonio Salieri, both composers of the older

Sketch of Beethoven by Lyser.

A poster announcing a performance of Fidelio, *1814.*

generation; and with them should be mentioned the dedicatee of the first symphony, composed 1799–1800, Baron van Swieten. From Haydn Beethoven had some lessons, but the young man needed more rigorous demands of him and Haydn's nickname for his brilliant pupil, 'The Great Mogul', reflects a certain uneasiness on his side also. Instead Beethoven turned to three very different teachers – Albrechtsberger for the strict counterpoint of the old school, Schenk for theory and Salieri, *Kapellmeister* of the Court, for Italian prosody and vocal writing generally. His living Beethoven earned by playing in aristocratic houses, by composing if not to commission then with the certainty of selling the dedication (a practice considered acceptable at a time when public concerts hardly existed) and by teaching. Among friends who were influential though not belonging to the nobility, the Baron van Swieten was important as the source of Beethoven's knowledge of Handel and both J. S. and C. P. E. Bach. A Dutchman by birth and son of Maria Theresa's favourite doctor, van Swieten had been friendly with Mozart and his patronage of the young Beethoven earned him the dedication of the first symphony. Among the young composer's musician friends were the members of the string quartet attached to

Prince Carl Lichnowsky's establishment – Schuppanzigh, Sina, Weiss and Kraft. His fame as an improviser brought him into professional contact with the leading pianists of the day in the contests, very popular at the time, which set two virtuosos the same theme on which to improvise.

The first two of the piano concertos, in which Beethoven appeared before the public, were written between 1795–7, the third in 1800, the fourth in 1805–6 and the fifth (*Emperor*) in 1809. A much longer period was needed for the nine symphonies, which appeared respectively in 1800, 1802, 1803 (*Eroica*), 1806, 1807, 1808 (*Pastoral*), 1812 (nos. 7 and 8) and 1822. The violin concerto was written at the same time as the fourth symphony (1806), and Beethoven usually followed the practice of working on several different compositions at the same time. The piano sonatas, like the symphonies, cover the whole of his mature working life, the last (Op. 111) appearing in 1822. So too the string quartets after Op. 18, already mentioned – the three *Razumovsky* Op. 59 appearing in 1806, Op. 74 and 95 in 1809–10 and the last five (Op. 127, 130, 131, 132 and 135) between 1824 and 1826. Beethoven remained all his life essentially an instrumental composer, bringing to perfection and further developing the broadly speaking symphonic work of Haydn and Mozart, for both of whose work he had the profoundest admiration. Less at home in vocal music, where his imagination was limited by the physical limitations of the human voice, he composed in 1805–6 a single opera, *Fidelio,* on a text adapted by Joseph Sonnleithner from a French original; and two Masses, the first (C major) in 1807 and the *Missa Solemnis*, the crowning production of his last years, between 1818 and 1823. In each of these fields, except that of the opera, his work reveals a uniquely powerful and original mind which left an unmistakable mark on the history of the genre. *Fidelio,* too, is unique and original, but with a first act strongly influenced by the French *opéra comique* and the final scene approximating a scenic oratorio, the work had no influence on the formal development of opera as a musical genre.

Beethoven was never, even at the height of his fame and in good health, an easy man. He was bitterly aware of the contradiction inherent in the dependence of an artist with his creative gifts on individual caprice and favour. His real charm and obviously exceptional character easily changed to black rage and unmitigated abuse, revealing a deep sense of frustration and resentment. Although he was very attractive to women and had a reputation of success in his affairs, it was not perhaps by chance that all the women with whom he is known to have been in love were unattainable owing to their social position and often to the fact that they were married. Instinctively Beethoven probably knew that, however much he longed for ideal domestic happiness, the overriding importance to him of composition and the total disorder that this often introduced into his daily routine of life were not compatible with marriage. The 'Immortal Beloved' to whom he wrote the strange and moving document which has come down to us has never been satisfactorily identified; but it is interesting to observe that in it Beethoven takes for granted the unhappy ending of their relationship. If the document is correctly dated as belonging to July 1812, the woman was almost certainly Amalie Sebald, a singer from whom he was not separated by any social barrier.

An equally famous and far more important document relating to Beethoven's character is the so-called Heiligenstadt Testament, in which he announced to his two brothers the fact of his incipient deafness and spoke of his interior attitude to this disaster. The letter is dated 1802 and Beethoven had another twenty-five years to live, during which his deafness increased at a pace fluctuating with the state of his general health, which also began to deteriorate early, so that by his middle forties he was almost stone deaf and subject to perpetually recurrent trouble with his stomach, his letters full of references to bronchitis, colic, rheumatism etc. The earlier explanations of Beethoven's deafness and ill-health as the effects of syphilis and alcoholism have recently (1970) been decisively rejected in favour of some form of immunopathic disease, possibly systemic lupus erythematosus. Whatever the explanation, Beethoven was a sick and prematurely aged man when his brother Karl died in 1815; and the legal battle to obtain exclusive control over his nephew (his brother Karl's son, also named Karl) and remove him as far as possible from the influence of his mother, had a disastrous effect on his health. The final blow was struck by Karl himself, whose unsuccessful suicide attempt was no more than a boy's gesture of despair prompted by his uncle's possessiveness and his own inability to satisfy the high standards demanded of his weak, commonplace but in no sense vicious, personality by his guardian-uncle of genius, whose devotion to his nephew dominated his emotional life from 1815 to his death in 1827 and became an obsession recognised by all his friends, as is shown from the conversation-books which the composer's deafness rendered essential. At an age when his creative activity was, except for a single year, increased rather than diminished and ill health had greatly reduced if not quite destroyed his desire for marriage or sexual relations of any kind, all Beethoven's human affections and hopes were centred on this unremarkable son of an unremarkable father. His violent disapproval of the boy's easy-going, feckless mother, whom he pursued through the law-courts and in private, hardly concealed the fact of his jealousy of the boy's affection for her.

It so happened that this new emotional factor in his life appeared at a time when his fame and the estimation of his music in Vienna had waned. With the French occupations of Vienna in 1805 and 1809 and the enormous indemnities demanded by Napoleon the Austrian economy was all but ruined, and of the three patrons who since 1809 had guaranteed him an annual pension – the Archduke Rudolph and the Princes Kinsky and Lobkowitz – only the first was able to maintain payments. The Archduke Rudolph, a brother of the Emperor, was a composition pupil of Beethoven's, and this close link with the royal family most probably saved the composer from the attentions of the secret police, who might otherwise have been less lenient towards his loudly professed republican sentiments. Beethoven's political attitudes were dictated by emotion rather than reason, and a bitter awareness of his own unappreciated worth made him anything but a democrat. He had been deeply disappointed ,in his original enthusiasm for Napoleon, acquired at the French Embassy in Vienna before the First Consul had declared himself Emperor, and had withdrawn the original dedication of the third symphony as a result. The economic collapse of Austria and the increase in taxation, in fact the result of military defeat by Napoleon, were regarded wholly illogically by Beethoven as a personal insult which he attributed to the Emperor Franz. Similarly he regarded the relegation of the lawsuit over his nephew to the common lawcourt, instead of that reserved for the nobility (into which the spurious 'von' in his name had originally obtained his entry) prompted him to the same explosions of indignation and wounded self-esteem as did the treatment that he received from the long succession of servants hired to manage his quite unmanageable bachelor household which shifted from house to house in Vienna with bewildering rapidity.

Beethoven once described himself as someone 'who did everything badly except compose music', and yet he aroused intense personal devotion not only by his music but by his personality, rough and ill-mannered, violent and wrong-headed though his actions often were. The nature of his personality and the fact that he was, outside music, virtually uneducated, gave his musical utterance a simplicity and a sincerity that are without parallel among the great composers; and it is these qualities, coupled with an intense humanity and an inexhaustible power of striving for the ideal, that have earned him his unique place in the affections of ordinary music-lovers. He is the very personification of the quality imagined by Goethe – his antithesis in almost every way – in the line given to the angels in *Faust*: 'wer immer strebend sich bemüht, den können wir erlösen' ('it is the man who never ceases to strive that we can redeem'). Beethoven's religious attitudes and feelings, as we gather them from his music, his chance remarks and the books that he prized, are more significant than his actual beliefs, of which we know little. Brought up as a Roman Catholic, he was not a practising member of any church, though he seems on his deathbed

to have welcomed the administration of the last rites from a Catholic priest. He was a passionate lover of nature, and especially of the countryside round Vienna and the various villages where he spent his summers. His notebooks contain intimate jottings which show that he was intensely aware of the presence of God in the depths of the country. 'Almighty One in the woods,' he wrote, 'I am blissfully happy in the woods; every tree speaks through Thee, O God! what splendour! in such woodlands as these! on the heights is peace to serve Him!' The conception of God as a universal father and all men as His children recurs in the notebooks and is strongly stressed both in the *Missa Solemnis* and the ninth symphony. That he regarded his own vocation as resembling that of a priest is shown by a letter written four years before his death to his pupil the Archduke, himself a priest in Catholic orders. 'There is no loftier mission than to come nearer than other men to the Divinity, and to disseminate the divine rays among mankind'.

Although the last occasion on which Beethoven received public acknowledgment of his genius was during the Congress of Vienna (1814), he continued to receive tributes from all over Europe, and particularly from England, where the Philharmonic Society commissioned the ninth symphony and the firm of Broadwood presented him with a piano (1818); and he was visited by a stream of admirers, many of whom expressed distress at finding him in primitive living-conditions but all of whom, without exception, saw through the rough exterior of the man to the simplicity and nobility within. Much has been made of his supposedly dishonest dealing in selling the *Missa Solemnis* to two different publishers. But apart from the fact that he believed it necessary to make all the money possible for the sake of his nephew, he never showed any understanding of business matters and less still of mathematical calculations, while at this late period of his life his mind was clearly often clouded by the advanced state of his general illness. At the beginning of 1827, when his nephew Karl had sufficiently recovered from the self-inflicted wound of his attempted suicide and could rejoin his regiment, Beethoven was already seriously ill as the result of pneumonia and pleurisy, to which dropsy was soon added. Although by today's medical standards his condition was mishandled by the

Portrait of Beethoven by Kloeber, 1817.

Beethoven's birthplace in Bonn.

doctors, he was surrounded by friends including the thirteen-year-old Gerhard von Breuning, son of his boyhood friend Stephan. He expressed his appreciation of some of Schubert's songs that were shown him and once again his deep admiration for Handel, scores of whose works had been sent him from London. He died on the 26th March 1827 and was buried two days later in the Währing cemetery, from which his body was moved in 1888 to the Central cemetery in Vienna.

M.C.

BELLINI, Vincenzo
(b. Catania, Sicily, 3 Nov 1801;
d. Puteaux, near Paris, 23 Sept 1835)

Although Bellini was born into a musical family (his father was an organist in the Sicilian town of Catania), he took up music as a profession only in the face of severe opposition from his family. Eventually his musical ability simply forced itself on his father's attention, and a number of friends of the family exerted pressure as well. Bellini senior gave in and allowed Vincenzo to study at the Real Conservatorio di Musica in Naples, the costs being met by a Sicilian nobleman who was struck by the child's talent. At the Conservatorium where Donizetti had studied only a few years earlier, and where one of Bellini's fellow-students was Mercadante, the young composer proved a diligent student, and produced his first work for the stage, an opera called *Adelson e Salvini*, while he was still in his final year. *Adelson e Salvini*, written to a highly melodramatic libretto by Andrea Leone Tottola, the librettist of several operas by Rossini and Donizetti, is a tale of friendship, love and jealousy set in 17th-century Ireland. It was performed at the Conservatorium by students in 1825, with such success that the by now twenty-four-year-old composer's examiners invoked a clause in the articles of the San Carlo Opera in Naples, which gave a really promising student the right to have a short work performed in the opera house. Bellini was therefore commissioned by Domenico Barbaia, the manager not only of the San Carlo but also of La Scala, Milan, to write an opera for Naples for the following Carnival season. He chose to compose an opera which, though perhaps short, was to be a full two-act work and not the one-act opera expected.

The subject of *Adelson e Salvini* had probably not been of Bellini's own choosing. Allowed now to decide on his own subject, he turned to one which had its basis in Sicilian history, although by the time it reached the stage the connection with history was remote and confused. Even the opera's title, *Bianca e Fernando*, had to be changed at the demand of the censorship authorities, for Fernando was the name both of the recently dead King of Naples and of his heir apparent. The change, however, was slight, and *Fernando* became *Gernando*. Produced at the San Carlo Theatre on the 30th May 1826, the opera was immediately acclaimed by a fashionable Neapolitan audience. This was no mere apprentice work, but the earliest of Bellini's operas in which his mature musical personality and style are readily apparent. Bianca is one of his great female characters, worthy to stand beside Norma, Adina or Beatrice in his later operas *Norma*, *La Sonnambula* and *Beatrice di Tenda*. In fact, one of Bianca's cabalettas (a cabaletta being the fast, concluding section of an aria) was taken over bodily in *Norma* to become the cabaletta to the eponymous heroine's entrance aria, 'Casta diva'. As well as the general public, several of Bellini's fellow composers praised the opera. After attending the first performance, Donizetti wrote, somewhat inaccurately: '... the first production of our Bellini – bella! bella! bella! – especially as it is the first time he has composed anything.'

An important and immediate consequence of the warm reception accorded to *Bianca e Gernando* in Naples was that Domenico Barbaia commissioned Bellini to compose an opera for La Scala, Milan, then as now Italy's most important and prestigious opera house. When Bellini arrived in Milan to work on the new opera, he was introduced by his old fellow-student Mercadante to the successful and experienced librettist Felice Romani, with whom Bellini was to form a partnership which lasted through several operas. Romani provided him with a libretto for his Scala début, and the work which came of it was *Il pirata*. This was so successful at its Milan premiére in October 1827, that it was immediately accepted for production abroad, in Vienna, Dresden, London, Madrid and elsewhere.

Though *Il pirata* was the opera which both introduced Bellini's name and at the same time established his reputation internationally, it is not, in fact, one of his better works, for in it his particular skill, an ability to write a long, flowing melodic line of grace and suppleness, is exercised only intermittently, and many pages of his score sound as though perfunctorily thrown off. What is not in question, either in *Il pirata* or elsewhere in Bellini's oeuvre, is the soundness and confidence of his technique. His long melodies are said to have influenced, and later perhaps to have been influenced by, Chopin; certainly Bellini's arias and Chopin's nocturnes speak the same language and often convey the same mood. The unadorned simplicity of Bellini's vocal line, though it appealed to a public clearly satiated with the more decorative and decorated style of Rossini, did not always commend itself to Bellini's early interpreters who found it lacking in opportunities for vocal display. Adelaide Tosi, who sang Bianca in the Genoa production of *Bianca e Gernando,* referred contemptuously to one of her arias as 'musica fatta per ragazzi' (children's music), and demanded to have it enlivened and made more difficult, but Bellini, sterner in these matters than either Rossini or Donizetti, insisted on his music being performed as written.

In Milan, Bellini took as his mistress Giuditta Turina, the daughter of one wealthy silk merchant and the wife of another. Their relationship was to last for five years and was useful, to resort to Bellini's own phrase, 'in protecting [him] from marriage', for he was an attractive young man, and much sought after by admiring females.

Bellini's fame was spreading rapidly, and Barbaia hastened to secure his agreement to provide another new opera for La Scala. This was *La straniera*, produced in February 1829.

It proved less immediately successful than its predecessors, though it is an important and significant work, for in it we find Bellini refining his vocal style still further, and placing it more wholeheartedly at the service of the drama than he had earlier been prepared to do. His first audiences and critics found this development disconcerting, and were inclined to consider *La straniera* dull in comparison with *Il pirata*. A contemporary critic refers to Bellini's new method as either 'declaimed song or sung declamation', and asserts that, by attempting to unite the force of declamation with the gentleness of song, the composer has fallen into the trap of confusing the two and producing 'monotony, slowness, disruption and hesitation in the melodic line'. Yet, today, it is these qualities we admire in *La straniera*, which we can clearly see to be a transitional work in its composer's development as a musical dramatist.

A glimpse into Bellini's working relationship with his librettist Romani, and into his musical and dramatic intentions, is afforded by a story told by Bellini's biographer Filippo Cicconetti, whose *Vita di Vincenzo Bellini* was published in 1859. Cicconetti says that, one day, Bellini sat at the piano to compose the final aria for *La straniera*, 'Or sei pago, o ciel tremendo', but found that the verses which Romani had sent failed to move him. When Romani visited him, Bellini asked him to provide fresh verses, and within half an hour Romani did so. Bellini read them, but said nothing. It was only when Bellini rushed to the piano and improvised the melody that had flashed into his mind that Romani's creative spirit responded and he produced the appropriate verses.

Bellini's next opera, *Zaira*, based on Voltaire's tragedy *Zaire*, and first produced in Parma only a few months after the première of *La straniera*, was even less successful than that work. It was written in a hurry, and Bellini was a composer who did not produce his best work under pressure, but slowly, and at his own pace. *I Capuleti ed i Montecchi*, based not on Shakespeare's *Romeo and Juliet* but on one of the earlier Italian sources of the story, did somewhat better when it was first performed at the Teatro La Fenice, Venice, in March 1830, but it was with *La Sonnambula*, composed for the Teatro Carcano, Milan, and produced there in March 1831, that Bellini's reputation took its biggest step forward, and it is *La Sonnambula* which remains today the earliest of Bellini's operas to have established itself in the permanent international repertory.

Bellini and Romani had at first intended to produce for Milan an opera based on Victor Hugo's play, *Hernani*, and indeed several duets and trios were composed before both composer and librettist realised that the political implications of Hugo's play about defiance of tyranny would bring the Austrian censors down on their heads. Bellini put his music aside and used some of it later in *Norma*. A change of subject was made, to the gentle, pastoral romance of *La Sonnambula*, for which Romani produced one of his most poetic libretti, and Bellini his most idyllic and attractive music. The special quality of *La Sonnambula* is unique in Bellini's oeuvre, an appealing and innocent pathos which can hardly fail to be moving, given sympathetic and intelligent interpretation. After the first night, Bellini was able to write to a friend,

> Here you have the happy news of my opera last night at the Carcano. I say nothing about the music, for you will see that in the press. I can only assure you that Rubini and Pasta are two angels who enraptured the entire audience to the verge of madness.

The Russian composer Glinka was in the audience, and he later wrote:

> Pasta and Rubini sang with the most evident enthusiasm to support their favourite composer. In the second act the singers themselves wept, and carried their audience along with them, so that in these happy days of Carnival, tears were continually being wiped away in boxes and stalls alike. Embracing Shterich in the Ambassador's box, I too shed tears of emotion and ecstasy.

Nine months after the première of *La Sonnambula* at the Teatro Carcano, Bellini went back to Milan's more prestigious opera house, La Scala, with his masterpiece *Norma*, which had its first performance on the 26th December 1831. A greater contrast to the pastoral charm of the earlier opera could hardly be imagined, for *Norma* is the tragic story of a Druid priestess who breaks her vows of chastity, and the music Bellini composed for it reveals a greater vigour and energy than anything in his earlier work. The orchestra in *Norma* is given a greater independence than is usual in Bellini's earlier manner, and the choruses are particularly impressive. The opera was received coldly on its first night, but audience enthusiasm increased noticeably at each

Bellini.

succeeding performance, until it became clear that Bellini and his interpreter of Norma, the great Giuditta Pasta, had a triumph on their hands.

Bellini's next opera was *Beatrice di Tenda*, produced at the Teatro La Fenice, Venice, in March 1833. During its composition, Bellini and Romani had quarrelled, principally over Romani's dilatoriness in producing his libretto. The opera was received by the Venice audience politely but without enthusiasm, and Bellini travelled to London where he had been engaged to supervise productions of three of his operas at the King's Theatre. He next made his way to Paris, which was to remain his headquarters for the remaining two years of his life. It was here that he frequently encountered Rossini, living in retirement, and Chopin, playing in the great salons. It was here, too, that he composed his last opera, *I Puritani*, its libretto provided not by Romani but by Count Carlo Pepoli, an Italian political exile in Paris. *I Puritani* was produced at the Théâtre Italien, Paris, in January 1835, with its four principal roles sung by the four leading singers of the day: Giulia Grisi, Rubini, Tamburini and Lablache. The Parisians immediately took it to their hearts: the cold-blooded English were less enthusiastic, for when *I Puritani* was staged later in the year in London, *The Spectator* complained that Bellini's orchestral writing was 'as unskilful as ever, and considerably more noisy than in his former productions'. The tunes, *The Spectator* conceded, were pretty, but hardly turned to proper account due to the composer's lack of skill or knowledge.

Bellini died later in the same year, a few weeks before his thirty-fourth birthday, while staying at the house of an English friend, outside Paris. His death was caused by an acute inflammation of the large intestine, exacerbated by an abscess of the liver. Had Bellini lived a normal span of years, perhaps all those operas up to and including *I Puritani* would now be thought of as his juvenilia. As it is, they are his testament: testament to a unique melodic gift, and to an artistic conscience which, rare in the Italian operatic world of the time, helped to pave the way for his great successor, Verdi, whose earliest operas, especially *Oberto* and *Nabucco*, reveal a strong Bellinian influence.

C.O.

BERG, Alban
(b. Vienna, 9 Feb 1885;
d. Vienna, 24 Dec 1935)

Berg's father Konrad was a well-to-do export merchant who had come to Vienna in 1867 from Nuremberg: his ancestors were officials at the Bavarian court. His mother, Johanna Braun, was Viennese: her father, the court jeweller Franz Xaver Melchior Braun, was gifted both musically and artistically. Alban had two elder brothers, Hermann (1872) and Charley (1882) and a younger sister Smaragda (1887). He spent a pleasant childhood in Vienna and in the summer at the 'Berghof' on Lake Ossiach in Carinthia. His musical talents began to manifest themselves when he was fourteen, stimulated by his sister's excellent piano playing and his brother Charley's singing. His father died in 1900, but help from a rich aunt enabled Alban to continue his studies at the Realschule. His first compositions, three songs, date from this year; on the 23rd

Portrait of Berg by the composer Arnold Schoenberg, 1910.

July he had his first attack of bronchial asthma, an illness which afflicted him throughout his life and made him superstitious about the number 23. By 1902 he had written more than 30 songs and duets. In 1903 he failed his final school examination, and a love affair made him attempt suicide. However, he passed his examination in the follow-

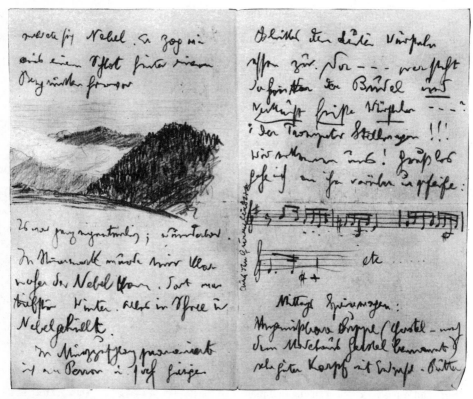

Pages from Berg's notebook, 1924.

ing year and entered the civil service. Shortly afterwards Charley saw an advertisement for pupils by Schoenberg and took some of Alban's songs to him without telling his brother. Schoenberg agreed to take him as a pupil, free to start with, but for a fee when the Berg family came into an inheritance in 1906. The earliest of the songs which Berg later published as Seven Early Songs was written in 1905: in 1906 Berg was able to give up his job and devote himself entirely to music.

He heard a number of Schoenberg's works, including *Verklärte Nacht*, the first string quartet and the chamber symphony. He was deeply impressed by Schoenberg's teaching and his personality, and developed from a dreamy and sensitive boy into a serious artistic personality. The remainder of the Seven Early Songs were written during this period and also the Piano Sonata Op. 1. Some of Berg's early works were performed in concerts of works by Schoenberg's pupils; his style con-

tinued to develop, and he finished the songs Op. 2 in 1909. In the same year he met Oskar Kokoschka and saw a good deal of the poet Peter Altenberg, whose 'picture postcard texts' he set three years later for soprano and orchestra.

In 1907 Berg met Helene Nahowski, who was later to become his wife. His studies with Schoenberg ended in 1910; the String Quartet Op. 3 was the last work written under Schoenberg's guidance. In 1911 the piano sonata and string quartet were performed for the first time but received little attention. On the 3rd May Berg married Helene Nahowski. The Altenberg songs, written in 1912, were first performed in the following year and caused such an uproar in the audience that the concert had to be stopped. Berg wrote the Four Pieces for Clarinet and Piano in the summer, and he planned a large orchestral work for Schoenberg's fortieth birthday on

A scene from Lulu *by Berg with Anna Moffo and Dietrich Fischer-Dieskau.*

the 13th September 1914. He first started a symphony, but later wrote the Three Orchestral Pieces Op. 6. In May 1914 he saw Büchner's play *Woyzeck* at the Vienna Kammerspiele and decided to make it into an opera. From the 1st August 1915, till the end of the war he was called up for military service; he was first trained for active service, and then sent to the War Ministry as unsuitable for the front. He finished his adaptation of the text of *Wozzeck* (as he renamed it) in 1917, and the opera was complete in short score in the autumn of 1920.

The devaluation of the Austrian currency after the war brought problems for Berg, and he was compelled to earn his living by teaching. He also took charge of some of the rehearsals for the Society for Private Musical Performances which Schoenberg founded in November 1918. He finished the scoring of *Wozzeck* in April 1921, and invited subscriptions for the publication of the piano score; in this he was helped by Mahler's widow Alma Maria, and he dedicated the work to her. Copies of the score were sent to the larger German opera houses, but without result. In the summer of 1923 the Orchestral Pieces were performed under Webern for the first time in the Austrian Music Week in Berlin, and the string quartet had a great success at the International Chamber Music Festival in Salzburg. At the same time the conductor Hermann Scherchen persuaded Berg to make a concert suite out of *Wozzeck*, and performed it with enormous success at a music festival in Frankfurt on the 11th June 1924. Meanwhile Erich Kleiber decided to perform the opera in Berlin, and the first performance took place at the Staatsoper on the 14th December 1925. In spite of many attacks on the work its success with the public grew steadily, and by 1936 there had been 166 performances of it in 29 different cities; Berg was able to be present at many of these.

He next returned to chamber music with the Chamber Concerto for violin, piano and thirteen wind instruments (1923–5), dedicated to Schoenberg on his fiftieth birthday and containing themes derived from the musical letters in the names Arnold Schoenberg, Alban Berg and Anton Webern. This was followed by the *Lyric Suite* for string quartet (1925–6); in two of the six movements of this work Berg used the twelve-note method (which Schoenberg had recently developed) and he used it intermittently in his remaining works. The *Lyric Suite* was first performed in Vienna

on the 8th January 1927 by the Kolisch Quartet, who gave it more than 100 performances in eight years. The Chamber Concerto had more or less simultaneous first performances in Berlin, Zürich and Vienna in March 1927.

Berg was now thinking about another opera. On the 30th January 1928 he visited Gerhart Hauptmann in Rapallo to discuss with him an opera based on Hauptmann's *Und Pippa Tanzt*; but in the spring he decided on *Lulu*, based on Frank Wedekind's plays *The Earth Spirit* and *Pandora's Box*, which he had seen in 1905 in Vienna, and began work on it at once. This was interrupted in the spring of 1929 by a request from the singer Ružena Herlinger to write a concert aria with orchestra for her. Berg wrote *Der Wein*, settings of three Baudelaire poems in German translations of Stefan George – though they can also be sung in the original French. This work had several performances at music festivals in the following years. In 1930 he was made a member of the Prussian Academy of Arts, but turned down an invitation to become a professor at the Berlin Music High School. In 1932 he bought a cottage on the south bank of the Wörthersee; but after the rise to power of the Nazis in Germany in 1933 his performances there decreased and so did his income. He worked feverishly on *Lulu*, finishing the short score in April 1934; in order to do this he spent the whole winter of 1933–4 at his country cottage, often in dire financial straits. In spite of his international fame his work was still not appreciated in his native Austria, and he was embittered by this.

The extraordinarily successful performance of the symphony which he had extracted from *Lulu*, given in November 1934 in Berlin under Kleiber, and the many performances of his instrumental works and songs which were given in honour of his fiftieth birthday in February 1935 raised his spirits temporarily; he was working hard on the full score of *Lulu*. He hoped that the first performance of the opera would improve his situation. Meanwhile, in the spring of 1935, he was asked to write a violin concerto by the Russian-American violinist Louis Krasner; the death of Manon Gropius, the eighteen-year-old daughter of Alma Mahler by her second marriage inspired the form of the work, the second movement of which is divided into two parts, 'Catastrophe' and 'Deliverance', the latter being a set of variations on the Bach chorale 'Es ist genug' (It is enough). He finished the score on the 11th

Costume designs for Wozzeck *by Hofmann.*

August, working extremely rapidly, and on the same day he spoke to the musicologist Willi Reich about his plans for future works after the scoring of *Lulu* was finished. He was thinking about a third work for string quartet, chamber music with piano, a symphony, a work specially written for radio, and above all a work for film: his favourite idea was to have a film made of *Wozzeck* which would underline and clarify its dramatic details. But at the beginning of September he received an insect bite which caused an abscess to grow on his back; this was treated by a doctor and healed for the moment. On the 12th November Berg returned from the country to Vienna and was in a feverish condition at the first Viennese performance of the *Lulu* symphony. On the 14th December he corrected the proofs of the piano score of the violin concerto; on the 16th December his abscess burst internally, causing general blood poisoning. He was taken to hospital the next day and operated on at once, but a second operation and a blood transfusion were of no avail and his heart could not stand the strain. He died on the 24th December 1935 in the arms of his wife, in his fifty-first year.

After Berg's death Schoenberg offered to complete the unfinished score of *Lulu*, to the delight of Helene Berg. But after looking through the score he wrote that he was unable to undertake the task, giving as his official reason that the work would be more difficult and would take longer than he had anticipated. In fact he was annoyed by the description in the text of a Jewish character. Webern also felt unable to complete the score, and so the opera has remained a torso: it is only possible to perform the first two acts and the two sections of the third act which Berg orchestrated for the *Lulu* symphony. In this form *Lulu* was given its first performance at the Zürich Stadttheater on the 2nd June 1937. The violin concerto was first performed at the International Society for Contemporary Music's festival in Barcelona on the 19th April 1936, with Louis Krasner as soloist. Webern was to have conducted, but he was so overcome with emotion at the loss of his friend and colleague that he spent the whole of the first rehearsal on the first few bars of the work, and in the end the performance was conducted by Hermann Scherchen.

In his lifetime Berg was the most popular of the so-called 'second Viennese school' (including Schoenberg, Berg and Webern) and it was usually stated that this was because Berg did not follow Schoenberg's methods as strictly as his two colleagues. However time has shown that Berg's music appealed to audiences because of its expressive, lyrical and dramatic qualities, which had nothing to do with technical considerations. Berg used classical forms in his larger works to a great extent; thus the first act of *Wozzeck* is a set of pieces representing the various characters in their relations to Wozzeck himself, consisting of a Suite, a Rhapsody, a Military March and Cradle Song, a Passacaglia and an Andante affettuoso quasi Rondo. Similarly the Second act is a symphony in five movements – a movement in sonata form, Fantasy and Fugue, Largo, Scherzo and Rondo con introduzione, while the third act consists of six Inventions, on a theme, on a note, on a rhythm, on a chord, on a tonality and on a regular rhythmical figure. But little of this is perceptible to the audience in the theatre, who find *Wozzeck* a gripping and moving drama with admirably and indeed overwhelmingly expressive music. Similarly the Chamber Concerto of 1925 adopts some ideas from Schoenberg's recently discovered twelve-note method; thus the first movement is a set of variations in which the second variation presents the theme in mirror form, the third in inversion and the fourth in retrograde inversion. The second half of the slow movement is the mirror form of the first half, while the third is a combination of the material of the two previous movements. Here again these ingenuities are not readily perceptible to the listener, who finds the concerto a very remarkable and exciting work. In the *Lyric Suite* one cannot really distinguish aurally between the movements which use the twelve-note method and those which do not. In *Lulu* each character has his or her own note-series which is derived from the basic series, usually by taking notes at stated intervals from the original series; Berg was evidently afraid of monotony if he based a full-length opera on a single series, but Schoenberg showed in his *Moses and Aron* that this need not be the case. Berg's music is thus a continuation of the Viennese classical and romantic traditions in a new form; it has links with the past, but also looks forward to the future. His two operas are certainly among the greatest of our time – *Lulu* will surely take its place beside *Wozzeck* in the repertory if and when it is possible to complete the score – and his orchestral and chamber works are among the most original and exciting in modern music.

H.S.

BERIO, Luciano
(b. Oneglia, 10 Oct 1925)

Berio's earliest musical studies were with his father. He later attended the Verdi Conservatorium in Milan, where his teacher in composition was Ghedini, and then continued his studies in the United States with Dallapiccola. His early works include *Nones*, a setting of W. H. Auden, and *Mutazioni* (*Mutations*) for chamber orchestra, written in the 1950s. Later, Berio turned his attention to electronic music, and for some time now his compositions have been largely electronic. Other works have been composed especially for performance by his former wife Cathy Berberian, a singer and performer. As founder of the Milan electronic studio in 1955, Berio was instrumental in stimulating Italian interest in this type of composition. At one time, he was considered to be one of the most promising of contemporary composers, but although his music is easier on the untutored ear than much

of what passes for composition in the electronic world he has produced little in recent years to suggest that his music will endure when it ceases to be fashionable.

C.O.

BERLIOZ, Hector
(b. La Côte-Saint-André, 11 Dec 1803; d. Paris, 8 March 1869)

Berlioz was the son of a liberal, free-thinking doctor father and an intensely devout Catholic mother. His father gave him his early education, founding him in the Latin classics and imbuing him with a love of Vergil which was to be lifelong. He also gave the boy elementary medical training with a view to his possibly taking up medicine as a profession. Although given piano lessons by a local teacher, Berlioz preferred the guitar and the flute, the only instruments which he ever mastered. He composed some songs and a quintet, after reading harmony treatises, and these were performed by local amateurs. In 1821 he went to Paris, ostensibly to study medicine since there was no question of his family allowing him to become a professional musician. But he spent much of his time at the Opéra, where he indulged his passion for Gluck's music, and in the library of the Conservatoire, attending medical lectures sporadically and repelled by having to dissect corpses, an occupation he approached in the spirit of a romantic artist in search of the macabre rather than that of a scientific investigator. Life in Paris dangerously inflamed the imagination and distracted the powers of concentration in a young man already at loggerheads with his family and inevitably affected by the contradicting attitudes of his two parents. He managed, however, to enter the Paris Conservatoire where, though he fell foul of the director Cherubini, he found an understanding teacher in Lesueur, an elderly composer of the old school with a great admiration for Gluck. He also studied with Reicha, a learned theorist and a composer of chamber music, a man with an international experience and at one time a friend of the young Beethoven in Vienna. His student days were prolonged by his determination to win the Grand Prix de Rome, for which he first competed in 1827. Between this and his actually winning the prize there elapsed a period of three years which were filled with events for Berlioz.

Caricature by Cham depicting Wagner's debt to Berlioz for Tannhäuser.

As early as 1825 he had had a Mass of his composition performed with an orchestra of 150 players. Lesueur, who remembered the monumental ceremonies of the 1790s, encouraged his young pupil's concern with 'Babylonian' effects and the employing of 'Ninivite' forces to obtain them. The chief experiences in Berlioz's life between 1827 and 1830 were his hearing performances of Beethoven symphonies conducted by Habeneck and seeing performances of Shakespeare plays by an English company at the Odéon. He fell promptly, and as it turned out disastrously, in love with the leading lady, Harriet Smithson, who after many divagations on his part was eventually to become his wife. That, however, was not until 1833. In the meantime he obtained a performance of his *Waverley* overture, wrote *Eight Scenes from Faust* (which he knew in Gérard de Nerval's translation) and a handful of Irish songs. These were in honour of Miss Smithson's country; but at almost the same time he composed his *Symphonie fantastique*, a medley of romantic idealism, pastoral rêverie, macabre visions and deliberately blasphemous scenes of

Berlioz.

witchcraft centred round an *idée fixe* representing the artist's amorous obsession. Berlioz called this work 'Episode in the Life of an Artist' and this title was modelled on De Quincey's 'Confessions of an English Opium-Eater', which Alfred de Musset had recently translated. Berlioz issued an elaborate programme with the music, which had its first performance under Habeneck on the 5th December 1829, and he insisted that the symphony was 'entirely autobiographical in intention'. He now identified Harriet Smithson with his evil genius, though for no apparent reason, and it was not long before he had fallen in love with another woman, Camille Moke, and even became engaged to marry her!

In 1830, the year in which he finally won the Grand Prix de Rome, Berlioz formed part of the Jeune France party which fought the battle unleashed by Victor Hugo's *Hernani*, the play which symbolised the revolt of the young 'Romantic' school against the ancient, and indeed now totally lifeless, 'Classical' pro-

prieties. In Berlioz's case the confusion between life and art became for a time almost total. On arriving in Rome he heard that Camille Moke had deserted him for a member of the piano-making firm of Pleyel, whereupon he tried to commit suicide (very half-heartedly) and then left for Paris, where he intended to kill Camille. Reason reestablished control before he reached his destination and he returned to Rome, where he made the acquaintance of Glinka and, more importantly, Mendelssohn who, however, not unnaturally, thought the young Berlioz in his present state ludicrously conceited and shamefully ignorant of his craft, as by Mendelssohn's standards he was. In fact the ostensibly autobiographical *Lélio,* with which Berlioz returned to Paris, is a very unequal set of musically disconnected pieces precariously linked by a narration which might be a malicious parody of the excesses of the Romantic School. Far more important in Berlioz's development than any musical experiences during this time in Rome, were the scenery of the Campagna, the life of the peasants and the many picturesque spectacles of Italian country life, not excluding the then very common plague of all travellers, highwaymen or *banditi* (real or imaginary), who appealed particularly to young Berlioz's non-conforming, anti-Establishment mentality.

He returned to Paris, after visiting his family in Saint-André, early in November 1832 and in the following month *Lélio* was given its first performance. Almost immediately after this Berlioz met Harriet Smithson again and, after much romantic gesturing which included a threat to poison himself, he persuaded her to marry him, which she did on the 3rd October 1833. Early the following year the violinist Paganini, then at the height of his career, commissioned Berlioz to write a work for viola and orchestra. This was *Harold in Italy*, a four-movement piece in which Berlioz imagined Byron's Childe Harold (represented by the solo instrument) musing over or sympathetically observing scenes of Italian country life such as he had himself lately witnessed – the solitude of the Abruzzi mountains, a procession of pilgrims winding their way past the observer, a mountaineer's serenade and a final 'Orgy' of brigands. The first movement is perhaps the nearest that Berlioz ever approached to the music of Beethoven which he so much admired, while the second forms an interesting contrast to the movement in the *Italian* symphony where Mendelssohn evokes a similar scene. The tumultuous and explosive finale contains reminiscences of the earlier scenes, and the whole work is held together by the theme associated with Harold himself. Unfortunately the solo part offered Paganini nothing that he considered worthy of his bow and at the first performance, in November 1834, the solo part was played by the gifted Chrétien Urhan, a Belgian pupil of Kreutzer and Rode for whom Meyerbeer was soon to write the viola d'amore solo in *Les Huguenots*.

Berlioz had already been reduced, as he felt it, to writing music criticism in order to supplement his income and in 1835 he became the regular critic of the influential *Journal des Débats* as well as writing for the *Gazette Musicale*. His long-standing desire to write an opera was fired by the enormous success of *Les Huguenots* and he had determined on Benvenuto Cellini as a subject, and started work when he received an official commission to write a Requiem Mass. This was planned originally for the annual commemoration of those who had perished in the 1830 Revolution, but was eventually (5th December 1837) used for the office celebrated on the occasion of General Damrémont's death in Algeria. Berlioz conceived the work on the grandest, most romantic and least liturgical scale. This included enormous forces for both orchestra and choir and, in addition, four small brass bands stationed at the four corners of the church of Les Invalides to represent the summoning to the Last Judgment described in the *Tuba mirum* of the *Dies Irae*. At the other extreme lies the orchestration of the *Hostias*, for flutes and trombones, leaving a yawning gulf in the middle register of the orchestral sound. Nothing in the work is conventional, everything highly individual and conceived with the idea of obtaining effects of what the composer himself described as 'overwhelming' and 'of horrifying grandeur'. In fact Berlioz in this work satisfied his romantic ideas of 'Babylonian' immensity achieved by 'Ninivite' forces.

The failure of his opera *Benvenuto Cellini* (10th September 1838) was only partly due to the mediocre libretto based on Cellini's memoirs by Léon de Wailly and Auguste Barbier. There could be no doubt in anyone's mind of Berlioz's dramatic gifts, but these were always better deployed in the concert-hall than in the opera-house, where his imagination was both fatally stimulated by the spectacular nature of contemporary 'grand' opera (Meyerbeer, Halévy) and yet shackled by the need to confine himself to the details of stage-craftsmanship. In the event the work has been best remembered by the overture and the 'Carnaval romain', a brilliant crowd-scene which makes almost as great an effect without the chorus in the concert-hall as it does, in Berlioz's original conception for the stage. His disappointment was mitigated the same year when he received from Paganini, in the most glowing terms, 20,000 francs for a new work of his own choosing. The money enabled Berlioz to pay the debts incurred by a household which now included a small son as well as a wife and to devote himself for a time at least wholly to composition.

Roméo et Juliette is Berlioz's most remarkable tribute to Shakespeare, who shared with Vergil, Gluck and Beethoven the highest place in his pantheon. In the Queen Mab scherzo and Romeo's love music it contains the greatest of all Berlioz's compositions, unflawed by the moments of bathos which too often mar his work and are indeed to be found in other parts of *Roméo* itself and wholly original. The orchestral writing confirms that novel and unique sonorous imagination which made Berlioz, who was to be the author of a treatise (1844) on the subject of instrumentation, the most important single force in developing this aspect of music, a fact at least obliquely admitted by Wagner himself. His next work, *Symphonie funèbre et triomphale* is not comparable in quality, though here again the style is unmistakably personal. During the 1840s he began those increasingly wide-ranging foreign tours on which he conducted his own music. The successes which he obtained in Belgium, Germany Austria and finally Russia made his comparative neglect by his fellow-countrymen all the harder to bear. His marriage had now come to grief, and he had entangled himself with a worse than indifferent singer, Marie Récio, whose presence and performances on his foreign tours were an embarrassment to him. Much of his next work, *La Damnation de Faust* was conceived and written during these foreign travels, and its failure on the 6th December 1846 involved Berlioz in a financial loss only recouped by his subsequent visit to Russia. Like nearly all Berlioz's major works *Faust* suffers from lack of unity of style and moments of bathos, but contains some of his finest music and in Marguerite's 'D'amour l'ardente flamme' one of the greatest of all melodies. The work's hybrid character, well described as *opéra de*

Caricature of Berlioz conducting in 1846.

concert, tells against it but faithfully reflects the composer's instinctive sense of his own gifts and limitations. After a period in London, where he conducted Italian opera at Drury Lane and avoided the revolution of 1848, Berlioz returned to Paris, where his father's death shortly relieved his worst financial worries. In 1852 Liszt put on a Berlioz Week in Weimar, where the composer was fêted; and indeed his increasing fame throughout Germany contrasted ever more starkly with his neglect in France, a situation which has never really changed, though now it is the Anglo-Saxon world that shames the French in performing the music of a composer who, however unequal in performance, eccentric and even uncertain in taste, cannot be refused the name of genius.

The year 1854 saw the death of Berlioz's wife and also the first performance of an unexpected oratorio, *L'Enfance du Christ*, which marks the opening of the final stage in Berlioz's life as a composer and his cultivation of the classical virtues so markedly absent from his earlier music yet surely implicit in his admiration for Gluck and Vergil. It was Vergil's *Aeneid* that inspired the major work of the composer's last years, when his health was poor, his life lonely and his position in French musical life that of a solitary eccentric. He wrote his own libretto for *Les Troyens*, dividing the story into two unequal parts, 'La Prise de Troie' and 'Les Troyens à Carthage'. In form and idiom the work lies uneasily between the severe tradition of Gluck and the lavish, spectacular 'grand opera' of Meyerbeer. One of several great moments is the orchestral 'Royal Hunt and Storm', a tone-poem with obbligato voices but needing no scenery to bring it to life. Another is the septet in which the mutual passion of Dido and Aeneas first makes its full dramatic impact, while Dido's final farewell deserves comparison with the greatest scenes of Gluck's *Alceste* and *Iphigénie*. Berlioz shared with other arch-romantics the characteristic of living entirely through his own feelings, and this was a handicap to him in the musical creation of character. It is neither Dido, nor certainly Aeneas, who gives *Les Troyens* its appeal, but rather Berlioz as he reflects himself and his own sensibilities in such minor roles as Iopas or Hylas, in the mime of Andromache and Astyanax or the Royal Hunt. The second part of *Les Troyens* was given on the 4th November 1863 in Paris, a year after the perverse but often delightful *Béatrice et Bénédict*. The first part of *Les Troyens* was never heard by the composer, having its first performance at Carlsruhe in 1890, 21 years after his death.

The influence of Berlioz's music during his lifetime was chiefly among Russian composers, though Liszt, Wagner and their successors borrowed and developed further his new conception of orchestral timbre and its importance as an integral element of music. Richard Strauss acknowledged his debt in this field, and there are echoes of Berlioz's very individual – and often academically 'incorrect' – melodic and harmonic procedures in such widely different composers as Janáček and Nielsen. For nearly a century after his death his music, with the exception of the *Symphonie fantastique*, was regarded as the preserve of individual conductors, especially Weingartner and in this country Hamilton Harty. Before the centenary celebrations of 1969 there was already a notable revival of interest in his music – his memoirs and other writings were almost universally admired, and often used to throw his music into the shade – and in that year there was launched a scheme for a scholarly edition of his collected works. This had been attempted by Weingartner, but abandoned owing to lack of funds and to the continued, and still all but total, lack of interest among his own countrymen.

M.C.

BERNSTEIN, Leonard
(b. Lawrence, Mass, 25 Aug 1918)

Leonard Bernstein was able to study music privately in his early years and had piano lessons before going to Harvard University where he studied under Walter Piston and Edward Burlingame Hill and developed extraordinary musical abilities. He graduated from Harvard in 1939 and then studied at the Curtis Institute; conducting with Fritz Reiner, orchestration with Randall Thompson and the piano with Isabella Vengerova. He won scholarships which enabled him to attend courses at the Berkshire Music Center in Tanglewood, Massachusetts in 1940 and 1941 where he studied under and became the special protégé of Serge Koussevitzky. He became Koussevitzky's assistant at Tanglewood in 1942 and the following year was appointed assistant conductor to Artur Rodzinski with the New York Philharmonic Orchestra. His memorable début as an orchestral conductor came in November 1943 when he substituted at very short notice for Bruno Walter who had been taken ill. It was a sensational success and thereafter he has pursued a much acclaimed and tremendously active career as a conductor. He became musical director of the New York Philharmonic in 1958. These orchestral activities coupled with an equally accomplished career as a concert pianist have always been something of a divisive factor in the life of a man who would prefer to devote much more time to composing, quite apart from being in demand as a lecturer and writer of entertaining capacities.

Even his career as a composer has experienced dividing loyalties between the separate fields of 'serious' and 'entertainment' music. The first composition to arouse attention was a sonata for clarinet and piano which owed some allegiance to Hindemith. This was written in 1941/2. Almost immediately he found his own vigorous style; strongly lyrical, full of jazz-slanted rhythms, technically accomplished and full of fresh ideas and an unflagging ardour that is part of his Jewish nature. In a sense he is an old-fashioned writer, more concerned with the sweeping effect of the whole than with intricate details, but his style is very much in line with a modern popular idiom. His *Jeremiah* symphony was completed in 1942, a highly romantic work, and the more restrained second symphony *The Age of Anxiety* followed in 1949.

Pre-eminently Bernstein has distinguished himself as a composer who could bridge the gap between the academic and popular worlds of music and provide material for the commercial theatre which had all the merits of experienced craftmanship. His ballet score *Fancy Free* (1944) has remained one of his most popular works, followed by *Facsimile* in 1946. At the end of 1944 the music of *Fancy Free* was expanded into a musical comedy, with book by Betty Comden and Adolph Green, under the title *On the Town*, and was later made into a film musical. This opened a new career in the theatre with *Wonderful Town* in 1953 and the highly successful *West Side Story* in 1957, also equally successful as a film. He also bent these same talents towards more serious opera with the less commercially successful but delightful *Candide* in 1956 and an opera *Trouble in Tahiti* in 1952 – a strange and interesting work for which he wrote his own text. The same adventurous yet memorable vein was caught in his fine choral work *Chichester Psalms* in 1965; and in works as diverse as the third *Kaddish* symphony in 1963 and an excellent film score for *On the Waterfront* in 1954.

P.G.

BERWALD, Franz
(b. Stockholm, 23 July 1796;
d. Stockholm, 3 April 1868)

Berwald was the greatest 19th-century Swedish composer and the finest Scandinavian symphonist before Sibelius. The family came from Germany, settling in Stockholm during the 1770s. His music has strong classical instincts and its many unpredictable touches reflect an exploratory mind, wide in its range of interest and degree of sophistication. This is all the more remarkable when one reflects that

he had no formal education, studying the violin with his father and joining the *Hovkapellet* (the Opera Orchestra) in 1812. He served there either as violinist or violist until 1828, when he obtained a scholarship to study in Berlin. First evidence of any serious creative activity came in 1817 when he composed a concerto for two violins, and a septet. Two quartets followed a year later and in 1819, together with his brother, August, he made a concert tour of Finland and St Petersburg. His works did not always meet with the success they deserved; their modulatory audacities excited hostility in provincial Stockholm and his operatic ambitions were not fulfilled. After unsuccessful attempts to secure performances, he abandoned composition for a while to set up an orthopaedic institute in Berlin, based on Ling's principles as well as his own original thinking. The institute became a great success and flourished for six years.

His orthopaedic venture occupied much of his energies during the 1830s though he still laboured on operatic projects but in 1841 he sold the institute and went to Vienna. The next decade was without question the most productive of his creative career; practically all the works on which his reputation now rests were produced in this single decade. In Vienna two of his tone poems were warmly received and in 1842 he composed two symphonies, the *Sérieuse* and the *Capricieuse*, as well as tone-poems and an opera. His return to Stockholm did not bring him comparable success to that which he had enjoyed in Vienna, and in 1845 his opera, *Modehandlarskan*, proved a fiasco. The two symphonies he wrote in this year, *Sinfonie Singulière* and the Symphony No. 4 in E flat remained unperformed. From 1846 to 1849 he travelled. In Paris he tried to interest French musical circles in his work but without success. In 1847 Jenny Lind took part in a performance of parts of one of his works, and he was made an honorary member of the Salzburg Mozarteum. He returned to Sweden in 1849, the year of his last two string quartets, disappointed with his lack of real success abroad, and two setbacks in Sweden. He had been passed over as Director of Music at Uppsala and later as conductor of the *Hovkapellet*.

In 1850 he became manager of a glass works in Northern Sweden becoming part-owner of the firm in 1853, when he was also active in launching a saw mill. He spent a good deal of the year in Stockholm and composed largely for chamber and instrumental forces; both the piano quintets and three of the piano trios were written in the 1850s. He gave up his business enterprises in the late 1850s and in 1862, the Royal Opera mounted a performance of *Estrella di Soria*, the opera on which he had worked in the 1840s. He was made a Fellow of the Royal Academy of Music in Stockholm in 1864 and Professor of Composition in 1867, only a year before his death. His highly original outlook, particularly in matters of formal layout, prevented his acceptance in the Sweden of his time, and the discovery of his work and its importance is a 20th-century phenomenon.

R.L.

BIZET, Georges
(b. Paris, 25 Oct 1838;
d. Bougival, 3 June 1875)

Bizet was born of musical parents – his father a singing teacher and his mother a gifted pianist whose brother was the fashionable singing teacher Delsarte. He showed an early gift for music and was admitted to the Conservatoire just before his eleventh birthday. He won a first prize in solfège before he was twelve and joined the counterpoint class of Zimmerman, an ageing professor whose place was often taken by Charles Gounod, his son-in-law. The effect of Gounod's influence on Bizet's musical development was traceable to the end of his life, although Bizet soon passed into Halévy's composition class. As a pianist Bizet proved a brilliant pupil of Marmontel, and he was later to earn the praise of Liszt himself. He was already composing songs and piano pieces, and before he was seventeen he had written the Symphony in C major, only discovered and performed for the first time in 1935 and worthy to rank with the finest works written at the same age by Mozart or Mendelssohn. In 1857 he won the Grand Prix de Rome. He greatly enjoyed the Italian climate and countryside, the carefree life and the company which was congenial particularly after the arrival of Ernest Guiraud, prize-winner of 1859 and a lifelong friend. The most important of his Rome compositions was *Don Procopio*, an Italian comedy in the same vein as Donizetti's *Don Pasquale*. But even while he was composing this light-hearted music, he began to undergo a *crise de conscience* occasioned by what he guiltily felt to be his almost indecent facility. He communicated his worries in a letter to Gounod, whose example he determined to imitate, in the belief

that this was an advance on his own spontaneous inspiration. Such a contradiction of his own nature inevitably brought confusion of purpose, and he took up and abandoned many new projects before eventually settling on an ode-symphony based on an incident in Camoens's *Lusiads*. The result, though Bizet himself was pleased with it, proved much less satisfactory than his *Don Procopio*, which he dismissed as feeble.

Bizet left Rome in July 1860, accompanied by Guiraud, and travelled in a leisurely way through Northern Italy to Venice, where he received news of his mother's serious illness. He hurried home, arriving in Paris in September and his mother did not in fact die until the following year. A one-act *opéra comique*, *La Guzla de l'Emir*, was put into rehearsal at the Théâtre Lyrique, but withdrawn before performance in order to qualify Bizet to compete for a handsome prize for a three-act opera by a Rome Prize-winner. This was *Les Pêcheurs de perles*, which probably contains much of the music originally written for the earlier one-acter, and it was given its first performance on the 30th September 1863. The success with the public was very moderate, and the music is in fact uneven, though Berlioz praised the work discriminatingly in what proved to be his last critical article. It is not difficult to identify passages in which Bizet, consciously or unconsciously, imitates Gounod, Verdi and even Mendelssohn, but the opera is still well above the average piece of the day. He spent much of his time in a country cottage built by his father at Le Vésinet, a few miles from Paris in those days, and pleasantly situated on the Seine. His time was taken up to a great extent with hackwork for publishers and piano lessons, unrewarding except financially. An opera *Ivan le Terrible* proved another abortive attempt and the composer must have been glad when he received a commission from the Théâtre Lyrique to compose a libretto based on Walter Scott's 'The Fair Maid of Perth'. This was in July 1866 and the opera had its first performance on the 26th December 1867. It was well received by the press, with the exception of *Le Temps*, to whose critic Bizet wrote acknowledging the justness of many of his adverse criticisms and pledging himself to abandon henceforward 'the school of *flonflons*, trills and falsehoods'.

In 1868 Bizet was thirty and had still achieved nothing that unmistakably bore out the very bright promise of his early years. He seems to have found it impossible to concen-

Bizet by G. Planté, 1860.

trate his energies, partly no doubt owing to the pressing necessity to earn his living; and his prolonged lack of any coherent philosophy of life or aesthetic principles is reflected in the imitative character of much of his music, his repeated abandoning of work on librettos which had at first filled him with enthusiasm and in an easy-going, undemanding way of life reflected in his relationship with the fantastic adventuress Céleste Mogador, his neighbour at Le Vésinet. Many of Bizet's doubts, self-questionings and philosophical speculations are contained in his correspondence with Edmond Galabert, who became his friend and pupil in 1865. In this he appears as a youthful cynic aware of the incompatibility between his cynicism and the ideals in some sense forced upon him by his extraordinary musical gifts and insights. His subscribing to the fashionable Positivism of the day was half-hearted and provided no real solution to his problems. Inasmuch as he reached any such solution it was through the change in his personal life which accompanied his marriage on the 3rd June 1869 to Geneviève Halévy, the daughter of his old composition-master at the Conservatoire. Although he wrote little during the first nine months of this year, a *Fantaisie symphonique – Souvenirs de Rome* was performed in February by Pasdeloup. These three orchestral movements, published in 1880 under the title *Roma*, are in fact pieces written, or at least, begun in Rome and they hardly suggest the quality of the mature Bizet's gifts. After his marriage he settled with his wife in a house shared with some of his wife's relations, including Ludovic Halévy, a librettist well known for his collaboration with Henri Meilhac in pieces for Offenbach. The completion of his late father-in-law's opera *Noé* a work of family piety, took up much of his time; and the rest was occupied with three librettos given him by the Opéra-Comique – *Valendal*, *Grisélidis* and *Clarissa Harlowe*. All three proved abortive, though he was working on them during the summer of 1870, which he spent with his wife at Barbizon. There he was surprised by the outbreak of the Franco-Prussian War (15th July), which brought him and his wife back to Paris. Bizet enlisted in the National Guard and spent the months of the war and the Commune in Paris. The Opéra-Comique turned down *Grisélidis* on the grounds of expense and in compensation one of the directors, Camille du Locle, gave him another libretto, Louis Gallet's *Djamileh* which, after many delays, was performed at the Opéra-Comique on the 22nd May 1872. Although a monstrous miscasting of the title role caused this to fail dismally, it contains music of a new originality which was immediately noticed by two composers, Ernest Reyer and Camille Saint-Saëns. The libretto certainly lacks action but Bizet's lyrical gift, his evocation of a conventional but still highly decorative oriental setting and the exquisite workmanship of the score were to make the work a favourite of Gustav Mahler's. This workmanship was also shown in a small work also written in 1871 – the twelve pieces for piano duet entitled *Jeux d'enfants*, five of which were converted by the composer into a *Petite Suite d'orchestre*. Bizet himself was con-

Carmen *watercolour by Merimée, 1845.*

fident and wrote to Galabert of 'the absolute certainty of having found my path'. In the same letter he announced a new commission from the Opéra-Comique, the setting of a three-act libretto by Halévy and Meilhac. 'It will be gay,' he wrote, 'but with a gaiety that permits style'. The work to which he refers is *Carmen.*

Bizet's son, Jacques, was born on the 10th July 1872 and on the 1st October of the same year Alphonse Daudet's play *L'Arlésienne* was produced at the Vaudeville with incidental music by Bizet. He had an orchestra of only 26 players at his disposal; but this restriction put him on his mettle and his incidental music, which failed dismally at the theatrical performance, was immediately successful six weeks later when a selection from it, rescored by the composer, was performed as an orchestral suite. This was immediately repeated and Bizet now only needed a single large-scale success to establish him as a leading composer in France. When *Carmen* was finally produced

Bizet.

on the 3rd March 1875 a large section of the public was alienated by what they considered the shocking realism of Merimée's story, despite the librettists' attempts to modify this. At the end of the month Bizet was taken seriously ill with the throat infection from which he had suffered intermittently since his student days in Rome, and on the 3rd June he died at Bougival, just as *Carmen* was beginning to receive the acclaim which it has enjoyed ever since. In this last work Bizet, at the age of thirty-seven, fulfilled unambiguously and on a large scale, the fabulous promise of the symphony which he had written some twenty years earlier and his death was the greatest single blow sustained by French music in the 19th century.

M.C.

BLISS, Arthur
(b. London, 2 Aug 1891;
d. London, 27 March 1975)

Although Sir Arthur Bliss was born in London, he had an American father, married an American woman and spent two considerable periods in the United States.

Possibly it was these affiliations that gave him his breezy, adventurous, outlook on life in spite of a conventional upbringing at Rugby, at Pembroke College, Cambridge, and at the Royal College of Music, where he studied under Stanford and Vaughan Williams.

After distinguished war service (1915–18) Bliss produced between 1918–20 the works by which he first became known: *Madam Noy*, *Rhapsody* and *Rout*, all involving solo voices with chamber ensemble. Two years later came his first truly large-scale orchestral work, the well-known *Colour* Symphony. During 1923–5 Bliss made his first extended visit to America, settling down to work at Santa Barbara. Returning to England, he embarked upon a series of vocal works built round anthologies of English texts on an identical theme: the *Pastoral* for chorus and strings (1928), the *Serenade* for baritone and chamber orchestra (1929) and – perhaps his finest work – the choral symphony *Morning Heroes* (1930).

During 1939–41 Bliss made his second visit to America, but on returning to England spent the war years 1941–4 in administrative work at the BBC, becoming director of music. Composition was resumed with *The Olympians*, the 1949 opera for Covent Garden for which J. B. Priestley wrote the libretto. The last twenty-five years of Bliss's life (1950–75) saw public recognition of his work by many honours, including that of Master of the Queen's Musick (1953). His later works include the *John Blow Meditations* for orchestra, the choral *Beatitudes* and the 'Cello Concerto for Rostropovich.

In *Madam Noy* and other early works Bliss trod an unconventional path – always lively, scoring for unusual combinations and showing the influence of the French *Les Six* and early Stravinsky. Later this gave way to a more traditional English outlook, possibly induced by Bliss's admiration for Elgar, as typified in *Morning Heroes*. Other works written at this time – 1930–40 – including the *Music for Strings*, the Clarinet Quintet and the Viola Sonata, are among the finest he wrote.

In the latter part of his life Bliss turned more and more to illustrative music, the prop of a story or situation apparently kindling his imagination more readily than the abstract manipulation of themes in sonata, quartet or symphony. Thus his three ballets – *Checkmate* (1937), *Miracle in the Gorbals* (1944) and *Adam Zero* (1946) – are all first rate, whilst his elaborate film scores such as *Things to Come*

(H. G. Wells) and *Men of Two Worlds* constitute a pioneering achievement in their field. It is by the above-mentioned works, rather than by his later choral and orchestral ones, that Bliss is likely to be remembered.

E.C.

BLOCH, Ernest
(b. Geneva, 24 July 1880;
d. Oregon, 15 July 1959)

Ernest Bloch came from a Jewish family that had been settled in Switzerland for many generations. He was born in Geneva on the 24th July 1880 and among his first musical impressions were the traditional Hebrew chants and melodies sung by his father. An early aptitude for music led to studies in Geneva and other capitals between the ages of fourteen and twenty-two. His principal teachers were the celebrated Ysaÿe for violin and the renowned pedagogue Iwan Knorr, of the Frankfurt Hoch Conservatorium, for composition. Ethnic influences asserted themselves very early with an Oriental Symphony begun when he was fourteen.

Bloch's consciousness of his Jewish background, which had somewhat receded during his foreign studies, was rekindled in the early 1900s. Between 1911 and 1918 he worked on the seven large-scale works constituting his 'Jewish Cycle'. In 1916 Bloch agreed to conduct for an American tour of the dancer Maud Allan but this collapsed after a few weeks. Fortunately he quickly became in demand as a composition teacher and he took American citizenship in 1924. In 1930 an endowment permitted Bloch to return to Europe, and to full-time composing, for eight years. He went back to America in 1938, when he was fifty-eight. The last twenty years of his life were spent largely in composition at Agate Beach, a very quiet place on the coast of Oregon. He died, a week before his seventy-ninth birthday, on the 15th July 1959.

Bloch is usually described as a Jewish nationalist composer. This is an incorrect generalisation. He was, in fact, a constantly developing artist, enriching his work by the steady assimilation of influences, musical and otherwise, from various sources. Only about a quarter of Bloch's seventy published works are Jewish either in musical style or programmatic content. During the last twenty years of his life he wrote only three quite minor essays in this idiom. He was too large a figure to be contained within the limits of national- or any

other 'ism'. His early works were strongly influenced – the Symphony in C sharp minor (1901–2) by Strauss, the orchestral *Hiver–Printemps* (1904–5) by Debussy. But already in the opera *Macbeth*, composed during his twenties, a strong individual voice is apparent. This work has not been staged in Britain, but Andrew Porter, who saw an American production, has described it as 'bold, resolute and masterly . . . at each performance it became more arresting and impressive'.

In the works of the 'Jewish Cycle' (1911–18), such as the dramatic and psychologically penetrating *Schelomo* (*Solomon*), for 'cello and orchestra, the moving Psalm settings for voice and orchestra and the vast Mahlerian-type first String Quartet, Bloch developed a wholly original style, evoking an Old Testament atmosphere and making extensive use of the characteristics of traditional Hebrew melody, although quoting actual tunes quite sparingly. The extent to which Bloch has drawn on these traditional sources has been intensively investigated by Alexander Knapp. Having achieved notable success with the 'Jewish Cycle', what more natural than that Bloch should continue in the same vein? He in fact advanced in a quite new direction in his next three works: the Suite for viola and orchestra or piano (1919), the first Violin Sonata (1920) and the first Piano Quintet (1921). Although these all incorporate the characteristic turns of melody, harmony and rhythm that were first developed in the 'Jewish Cycle' and became permanent features of Bloch's vocabulary, they not only exclude traditional Jewish, middle-Eastern, thematic material but evoke a quite different, more remote, tropical atmosphere. These highly poetic works originated from Bloch's reading of books about Polynesia, Indonesia and Tibet in about 1903.

The burden of full-time teaching during the years 1920–9, necessary to support a growing family, took its toll. The two really large-scale works of this period, the orchestral rhapsody *America* (1926) and the symphonic fresco *Helvetia* (1929), are no more than skilful orchestral documentaries, making extensive use of indigenous folk tunes. Bloch returned to his Jewish style for the *Avodath Hakodesh* (Sacred Service), an extensive choral and orchestral setting of the synagogue Sabbath Morning Service (1930–3). But in seemingly aiming at as wide as possible an appeal, both religious and musical and not only to the Jewish people,

Photograph of Bloch given to the author by the composer.

Bloch adopted a simpler, more traditional, musical vocabulary with unconvincing results. The Service was followed by the Piano Sonata of 1935 in which, conversely, he extended his stylistic frontiers. The notably acerbic harmonic vocabulary, including fierce bitonal clashes of B major and C major in the menacing march-like finale, foreshadowed the coming war. Towards the end of his European stay Bloch wrote a full-scale Violin Concerto (1937–8) that is one of his creative peaks. Kaikhosru Shapurji Sorabji described it as 'a great work . . . crammed with thought and significance, and surrounded with an atmosphere of austere splendour'.

Among the early fruits of Bloch's second American period was the String Quartet No. 2 of 1945. This and other subsequent compositions embody a new technical feature: themes employing all twelve notes of the chromatic scale (in a tonal context). It also incor-porates the cyclic element, with 'motto' themes, employed in much of his music from the 'Jewish Cycle' onward. Ernest Newman described the Quartet No. 2 as 'worthy to stand beside the last quartets of Beethoven' and a work of 'subtle contemplative beauty and torrential power'.

In the 1952 *Sinfonia Breve*, written at the ripe age of seventy-two, Bloch made the most remarkable of all his stylistic advances. A ferocious Varese-like energy and a much higher level of dissonance than before mark this steely, uncompromising, score. Yet as always it remains unmistakably Bloch. The style is largely maintained in the notably fine String Quartets Nos 3, 4 and 5 and other products of the composer's old age, but like the majority of his works they remain virtually unknown. Bloch's output was decidedly variable in quality, more so than that of many lesser masters. The majority of his works are, however, highly original, wide ranging and deeply rewarding to experience.

E.C.

BOÏELDIEU, François Adrien
(b. Rouen, 16 Dec 1775;
d. Jarcy, 8 Oct 1834)

Boïeldieu's father was a clerk in the office of the Archbishop of Rouen's secretary, and his mother was a milliner. He studied music locally, with the organist of Rouen Cathedral who, though an excellent musician and a pupil of Martini, was also a somewhat violent drunkard. When Boïeldieu was eighteen, he composed an opera, *La Fille coupable*, to a libretto by his father, and it was performed at Rouen with some success. Two years later, he and his father collaborated on a second opera, again successfully, as a consequence of which the young composer made his way to Paris in order to further his career. There he met many of the leading composers of the day, among them Cherubini, and did not find it difficult to get commissions. His first opera to be staged in Paris was *La famille Suisse* which was favourably received at the Théâtre Feydeau where it was given a run of thirty performances. Other operas followed, including the enormously successful *Le Calife de Bagdad* which was produced at the Opéra-Comique.

Though immediately popular with the audiences for whom they were written, Boïeldieu's early operas are not among his best, for they lack the style and individuality of his later work. The chamber music which he also composed in his first years in Paris was sufficiently liked for Boieldieu to be appointed professor of pianoforte at the Conservatoire in 1798, but it was not until he began to study counterpoint with Cherubini that his work for the theatre came to exhibit signs of increasing maturity. In 1802 Boïeldieu married a dancer, but the marriage did not last, and the following year he accepted an appointment as conductor of the Imperial Opera in St Petersburg, though not before one of his most attractive operas, *Ma Tante Aurore*, had been staged with great success in Paris at the Théâtre Feydeau.

Boïeldieu stayed in Russia for eight years, composing at least ten operas as well as a vast number of marches for the Tsar's military bands, and then returned to Paris to find that he had not been forgotten and that Paris audiences were keen to hear his new works. *Jean de Paris* was a riotous success in 1812, and it was followed by a number of stage works, most of them written in collaboration with other composers. In 1817, Boïeldieu became professor of composition at the Conservatoire. It was not until 1825 that he produced his finest opera, the charming and tuneful *La Dame*

Portrait of Boïeldieu by Gilbert.

blanche which immediately proved to be his greatest success, and which is still today regarded as one of the masterpieces of French *opéra comique*. Scribe's libretto, put together from Sir Walter Scott's *The Monastery* and *Guy Mannering,* and Boïeldieu's amiable succession of melodies suit each other, and the composer's use of 'Robin Adair' and other Scottish tunes gives the work a unique quasi-Scottish flavour.

La Dame blanche proved to be its composer's last successful work for the stage. His final years were spent in ill-health, though a second marriage, happier than the first, helped to alleviate this and his financial worries. Of his operas, only *La Dame blanche* is performed with any frequency today, but it alone is sufficiently beguiling to keep Boïeldieu's name alive.

C.O.

BOITO, Arrigo
(b. Padua, 24 Feb 1842;
d. Milan, 10 June 1918)

Boito's talent was for both poetry and musical composition. He is remembered today, less for his two operas than for his two libretti, *Otello* and *Falstaff*, written for Verdi. His elder brother Camillo became an architect, and in later life designed for Verdi the Rest Home for Aged Musicians in Milan which the great composer founded. Arrigo Boito at first intended to devote himself to music, and began his studies at the Milan Conservatorium, but soon developed an interest in and a talent for literature as well. After the success of a student work, *Le sorelle d'Italia*, for which Boito wrote the words and half of the music, and his friend Franco Faccio the other half, both composers were given a grant by the Italian government to study in Paris.

After spending some time in Paris where he met Victor Hugo, Verdi, Berlioz and Rossini, Boito travelled to Poland to become acquainted with the relatives of his mother, a Polish Countess, and then made his way via Germany and Belgium to England. Returning to Milan, he became associated with the progressive and reformist groups in Italian music, who tended to admire the Austro-German symphonic school, which was generally ignored by Italians whose tradition was primarily operatic. Boito began to write musical journalism, advocating various reforms, and often attacking contemporary Italian composers. In his mid-twenties, he started work on an opera, *Mefistofele*, for which he provided both libretto and music. But he was torn between composition and criticism, and this indecision, which continued throughout his life, prevented him from completely fulfilling himself in either field. When *Mefistofele* was completed, it was staged at La Scala, Milan, in 1868, and conducted by its composer. It can hardly be said to have been given a fair hearing on that occasion, for the theatre was filled with young progressives determined to make a success of Boito's opera, and traditionalists equally determined that it should fail. The evening ended in a riot both in the theatre and outside in the piazza. After two further performances, and more demonstrations, *Mefistofele* was withdrawn by order of the chief of police.

Though bitterly disappointed by the fate of his first opera, Boito retained his faith in it, and made a number of important revisions to the score and the libretto. When *Mefistofele*

was staged for the second time, in Bologna seven years later, his faith was vindicated. The opera has, in fact, survived in Italy to this day, and is occasionally seen elsewhere. Boito's second opera, *Nerone*, occupied him on and off for the remainder of his life, and in fact was still not entirely complete when, six years after its composer's death, it was performed for the first time, conducted by Toscanini.

Boito's literary output was considerably larger than his slender list of musical compositions. In addition to poetry and criticism, he wrote a number of libretti for other composers, including *La Gioconda* for Ponchielli. By far his finest libretti are the two he wrote for Verdi, based on plays of Shakespeare. Boito had, in his early years, spoken contemptuously of the kind of music Verdi wrote, and for a period the relationship between the two men was distinctly cool. But they were brought together by Verdi's publisher, Tito Ricordi, and although twenty-nine years separated them in age, the youngish Boito and the elderly Verdi found themselves able to collaborate happily. After the success of *Otello* in 1887, Verdi at first felt too old and tired to embark upon another major work, and this time it was Boito who finally persuaded him into undertaking *Falstaff*. By this time a deep and sincere friendship had grown up between the two men, and when Verdi died at the age of eighty-eight, Boito wrote: 'Verdi is dead; he has carried away with him an enormous quantity of light and vital warmth. We had all basked in the sunshine of his Olympian old age.'

Boito's own later years were relatively uneventful. He continued to be interested in politics, and became a Senator in 1912. He died in a nursing home, after having caught a chill during a religious ceremony at the church of Sant' Ambrogio in Milan.

C.O.

BORODIN, Alexander
(b. St Petersburg, 12 Nov 1833;
d. St Petersburg, 27 Feb 1887)

Illegitimate son of a Gedianov prince and the sister of a St Petersburg civil servant, Borodin was given the name of one of his father's servants. He received a mediocre middle-class upbringing which neglected music in favour of his other great passion, chemistry. At seventeen he entered the Academy of Physicians and after graduating he practised medicine for a time, although he had already begun to compose. His interest in music was stimulated by meetings with Mussorgsky, and his musical sympathies broadened to include Schumann and Glinka as well as Mendelssohn. At this period he travelled widely, living and studying abroad for long spells. A momentous event was his meeting with Balakirev in 1862 and his gradual absorption into the Nationalists' circle: for Balakirev persuaded Borodin that his true vocation was composing. Only four years later, however, did his first major opus appear, the First Symphony, and this had to wait until 1869 for a first public performance.

In 1867 Borodin wrote a parody of grand opera entitled *The Valiant Knights* and started work on, but soon abandoned, a serious opera on Mey's *The Tsar's Bride*. Two of his finest ballads, *The Sleeping Princess* and *The Song of the Dark Forest*, were also written during this period, but now, as throughout Borodin's life, a variety of factors combined to reduce systematic effort at composition to a minimum: academic responsibilities and administrative duties (he was now a Professor in the Academy of Physicians), his public status as a scientist and important research chemist, and constant domestic difficulties. Thus the Second Symphony was not finished until 1871, and then only in piano score. The following year he contributed some music to *Mlada*, an opera-ballet composed jointly by members of the 'Mighty Handful', and in 1874 began to work again on his opera *Prince Igor* conceived some four years earlier; in it he incorporated material intended both for *The Tsar's Bride* and the unproduced *Mlada*. Work on the opera progressed fitfully throughout the 1870s, but it remained incomplete at the time of Borodin's death from a burst artery in the heart (as did also the Third Symphony). Rimsky-Korsakov and Glazunov undertook the responsibility of preparing these works for publication and performance. Apart from songs and a *Miniature Suite* for piano, the only other works produced during the last decade were the two string quartets (1877 and 1881) and the orchestral sketch *In the Steppes of Central Asia* (1880).

Borodin's output was slender, due mainly to the peculiarly trying circumstances of his life. It is however doubtful whether he would have wanted to abandon science in favour of music even had he had the opportunity, and it is true that the very breadth and diversity of interests pursued by all the members of the 'Handful' at some stage in their lives – a kind

Borodin.

of inspired dilettantism – was in no small measure responsible for their individuality and for the new nationalist-oriented ways of thinking and feeling musically they helped to inculcate. Borodin outlived the early influence of Mendelssohn and Schumann to produce music distinguished by harmonic and rhythmic originality (chords built of superimposed fourths in the opening 'Allegro' of the First Symphony, added-note harmony in the song *The Queen of the Sea* already close to Delius, almost jazzy syncopations in the 'Polovtsian Dances' in *Prince Igor*); by bright, bold, primary colours in the orchestra; and by melodic beauties of a highly personal flavour which are greatly indebted to the Oriental as well as the Russian folk-melodies. *In the Steppes of Central Asia* epitomises the rift between the languid voluptuousness of the Orient and the long-suffering melancholy of Russia as voiced through their respective folk musics, and the pervasiveness of the Oriental element throughout Borodin's work – Second Symphony, Second String Quartet, the Polovtsian portions of *Prince Igor* – certainly argues the predominance of an Oriental strain in Borodin's lineage. This preoccupation with the exotic was undoubtedly one of the factors which attracted the young Debussy to the work of Borodin and his colleagues, and another pointer to the inbuilt vitality of Borodin's Orientalisms is the great merit and success of the posthumously-contrived musical *Kismet* based almost entirely on themes from his works. On the Russian side both *Prince Igor* and the Second Symphony are outstanding examples of the Russian nationalist aesthetic as given expression on a large canvas in epic terms.

C.P.

BOYCE, William
(b. London, 1711;
d. London, 7 Feb 1779)

William Boyce was the son of a London cabinet-maker. A choirboy at St Paul's, he became the pupil and friend of the cathedral organist, Maurice Greene. He also received musical instruction from Dr Pepusch. Although he became hard of hearing at a comparatively early age, he lived an active musical life, becoming composer to the Chapel Royal, Director of the Three Choirs Festival, and Master of the King's Musick.

Two of his early works were resettings of texts that had already been used for music at the beginning of the century. When Lord Lansdowne's alteration of *The Merchant of Venice* was played at Lincoln's Inn Fields Theatre under the title of *The Jew of Venice* (1701) it contained a masque entitled *Peleus and Thetis*. This text Boyce set in 1747 when the masque was performed in London at the Swan Tavern. Similarly he took Dryden's text for *The Secular Masque*, which had originally been set by Daniel Purcell in 1700, and his version was included, with other compositions by him, in a four-day festival of his music at Cambridge in the summer of 1749 on the occasion of his being awarded a doctorate of music.

About this time Garrick asked Boyce and Arne for two all-sung afterpieces for Drury Lane. Boyce produced *The Chaplet*, a two-act 'musical entertainment', which was enormously successful when produced in 1749. It was played 129 times at Drury Lane until 1773 and reached North America in 1767 when it was given in Philadelphia. (Arne's contribution, *Don Saverio* (1750), does not appear to have been a success.) Another 'musical entertainment' by Boyce – *The Shepherds' Lottery* – was given at Drury Lane in 1751. It was not so much liked as *The Chaplet*, enjoying only twenty-seven performances in three seasons. Full scores of both *The Chaplet* and *The Shepherds' Lottery* were published at the time; and in this connection it is interesting

to note that a licence giving Boyce the right for the sole publishing of his works for the term of fourteen years was prefixed to the full score of *The Chaplet*. An early instance of musical copyright.

In 1760 a collection of Boyce's overtures appeared in parts under the title *Eight Symphonies*. These were rediscovered by Constant Lambert in the 1930s and arranged by him to form the score for a ballet entitled *The Prospect Before Us*, which was produced by the Sadler's Wells Ballet in 1940. In his later years Boyce worked on the completion of Greene's great collection of *Cathedral Music*. When he died, he was buried beneath the dome of St Paul's.

E.W.W.

BRAHMS, Johannes
(b. Hamburg, 7 May 1833;
d. Vienna, 3 April 1897)

Rather than follow in his own innkeeper father's footsteps, Johannes's father, Jakob Brahms, apprenticed himself to near-by town musicians before trying his luck in Hamburg as horn-player in the militia band and double-bass player in casual tavern groups. Though at twenty-four he married a splendid housewife seventeen years his senior, home life for Johannes, his elder sister and his younger brother was humble. But sacrifices were made to give him a good grammar-school education, which kindled his interest in literature, also to send him to an enlightened young teacher, Friedrich Cossel, for piano lessons. At ten, Johannes played well enough for a passing American impresario to propose a tour of the States as a *Wunderkind*. This Cossel forbade, but handed him over to his own teacher, the eminent Eduard Marxsen, who without payment, assumed responsibility for all further tuition in piano and composition, always with strong emphasis on respect for classical tradition.

Despite Jakob's improved position (he eventually played double-bass in Hamburg's Municipal Theatre and Philharmonic Orchestra) Johannes left school at fifteen to augment the family income, once or twice attempting serious recitals but mainly playing in seamy dock-side taverns or else arranging popular

Johann Strauss II with Johannes Brahms.

tunes for publishers. So when early in 1853 a refugee Hungarian violinist, Eduard Reményi, proposed a modest concert tour in nearby places where they had friends, Johannes jumped at the chance of escape.

From Winsen, where as a boy he spent two blissful summer holidays, then Celle, they went on to Hanover to look up Reményi's old student friend, Joseph Joachim, already at twenty-two Konzertmeister to the King. Profoundly impressed by Brahms and some compositions he played, Joachim gave them an introduction to Liszt at Weimar. Though sympathetically received, Brahms felt ill at ease in this grandly organised stronghold of the progressivists of the day, known as the New German School, so much displeasing Reményi for not feigning admiration as to bring their partnership to an end. Fearing similar embarrassments, it was not till late September 1853, that Brahms braced himself to visit the Schumanns in Düsseldorf, again on Joachim's insistence. Here, in a comparatively simple home full of young children, he was immediately happy, the more so when both Robert and Clara Schumann enthused no less that Joachim over his first two sonatas and E flat minor Scherzo for piano, likewise several songs and chamber works. Though now far from well, Schumann even wrote an article for the *Neue Zeitschrift für Musik,* after ten years' silence as a critic, proclaiming Brahms as the outstanding representative of the younger generation for whom the world was waiting.

When news of Schumann's breakdown reached Brahms in Hanover early in 1854, he rushed back to Düsseldorf to help Clara. As hopes of recovery slowly faded, she increasingly relied on him while, to support her family, she resumed her career as a pianist. He in his turn gradually realised he was in love with her, albeit fourteen years his senior and the wife of his greatest champion. Months of anguished conflict sowed the seeds of several major works not completed for many years. Though on Schumann's death in 1856 Brahms and Clara decided to go their separate ways, their friendship remained the deepest emotional anchorage Brahms ever knew.

To pick up the threads of his career he returned to Hamburg, first sharing his parents' flat, then renting rooms of his own in the garden suburb of Hamm. An invitation to spend the last three months of 1857 as pianist and choir conductor at the Court of Detmold proved rewarding enough for him to return

for similar periods the next two years, while in Hamburg he derived much pleasure from a ladies' choral society he founded, conducted and composed for. His main creative energy nevertheless went into a D minor piano concerto conceived during the Schumann crisis, a dramatic, symphonically argued work so misunderstood by the public as to incite hissing when Brahms played it in Leipzig shortly after the Hanover première in January 1859. 1860 brought more trouble when, incensed by an article claiming that everyone of consequence upheld the ideals of the New German School, Brahms and Joachim drew up a protest which they hoped to get signed by a large number of sympathetic friends. But it accidentally found its way into the Berlin *Echo* when only two others had signed besides themselves, humiliating Brahms and casting him as a far more die-hard anti-romanticist than was true. He was still more upset when he was not offered the vacant conductorship of the Hamburg Philharmonic Orchestra, while in his private life friends castigated him for compromising a young amateur singer, Agathe von Siebold, who attracted him strongly and inspired many songs, yet to whom he was unable to 'fetter himself', as he once put it, in matrimony.

A visit to Vienna during the winter of 1862/63 restored self-confidence, especially after an invitation to return as conductor of its Singakademie throughout the 1863/4 season. Old ties with Hamburg were further loosened in 1865 by his mother's death and his father's remarriage, and when in 1872 Jakob Brahms also died and Brahms himself was offered the conductorship of Vienna's renowned Gesellschaft der Musikfreunde, involving orchestra as well as choir, he decided to settle permanently in the Austrian capital, whose gaiety, beauty, and stimulating friendships and musical traditions had begun to mean more to him than anything in his native north Germany.

Besides winning respect on the rostrum, not least for services to his passionately admired Bach, Beethoven, Schubert and Schumann, the première of his own *German Requiem* (inspired by the death of his mother) in Bremen Cathedral on 10th April 1868, at last convinced the world of his true stature as a composer. A spate of other major choral works followed, each to a remarkable degree growing from his own current emotional involvements, whether patriotic, as in the *Triumphlied* (1871), written to celebrate Germany's victory in the Franco-Prussian

Manuscript of the 'Cradle Song' by Brahms.

war, or purely personal, as in the *Alto Rhapsody*, dating from a brief, undeclared and unreciprocated surge of feeling in 1869 for Clara's sweet-natured, frail, third daughter, Julie. Though remaining a bachelor, Brahms's susceptibility to young women, especially singers, remained incurable.

By 1875 his imagination was sufficiently inflamed by orchestral timbre to compel him to resign the conductorship of the Gesellschaft der Musikfreunde to have more time for orchestral composition. In 1876 he completed a first symphony in C minor, sparked off at the time of the Schumann crisis some twenty years earlier, and this he soon followed with a much more genially lyrical second symphony in D and a violin concerto in the same key for Joachim, besides the *Academic Festival* and *Tragic* overtures. Besieged with invitations from all over Europe to conduct as well as play his own music (including an ever-growing number of chamber works and songs) he now found it imperative to escape into the country, preferably amidst mountains and lakes, for long summer breaks to compose. Baden-Baden, where Clara Schumann had a holiday house, was at first a favourite, but Pörtschach, Thun, and Ischl (where Brahms's good friend, Johann Strauss, had a villa) increasingly lured him too. In 1878 his

Viennese friend and champion, the distinguished surgeon, Theodor Billroth, opened up new vistas by taking him to Italy for a holiday, a land he grew to love, equally for its cultural traditions and natural beauty, enough to revisit as often as possible.

Further stimulation for orchestral composition came in 1881 from the conductor, Hans von Bülow, who invited Brahms to use his own exceptionally well trained Meiningen Court Orchestra as a trying-out ground for new works, and also to join the orchestra either as conductor or soloist on its novel, history-making tours. His second piano concerto in B flat (1881) reached a wide public unusually soon in this way, likewise a third symphony in F (1883), once nick-named his 'Eroica' because of its struggle to assert the validity of his life-long F A F motto (*frei aber froh*, in answer to Joachim's *frei aber einsam*, i.e. F A E), and a fourth and last symphony in E minor (1884), ending with a mighty passacaglia on a theme borrowed from Bach. Having reached the peak of his 'architectural' invention here, he only returned to the orchestra once more to write a double concerto for violin and 'cello (1887) as a peace-offering for Joachim after a serious breach in their friendship occasioned by Brahm's sympathy for Joachim's wife at the time of their divorce.

Now sufficiently well off to show exceptional kindness to anyone in need, Brahms nevertheless often upset even his most inti-

At the piano.

mate friends with his gruff plain-speaking. Clara Schumann, more and more bowed down by her own illness and ailing children and grandchildren, perhaps suffered most of all in this respect, also from the knowledge that she now had several other close personal friends whose opinions about music he valued as much as her own. Yet even their worst misunderstandings and estrangements always ended in tender rapprochements, and it was often with Clara in mind that Brahms, increasingly preferring intimate miniatures to larger projects, wrote many of his tender late intermezzos for the piano. In these, as in the clarinet quintet (1891) and other works inspired by the playing of Richard Mühlfeld, first clarinettist in the Meiningen Orchestra, there was an undercurrent of deep nostalgia occasioned by growing awareness of life's transience as those near to him, including his devoted erstwhile pupil, Elisabeth von Herzogenberg, Billroth and Hans von Bülow, all died.

Though still keenly interested in the musical life of Vienna and the activities of every young composer who wanted to visit him, Brahms gradually reduced his own platform activities after turning sixty in 1893. But when Clara died in 1896, an event which though prepared for still shocked him deeply, his waning energy and deteriorating appearance caused such concern that he was reluctantly persuaded to consult doctors. Unbeknown to him, the diagnosis was cancer of the liver, as with his father; by April 1897, he was dead. Though the splendour of his funeral ill-accorded with the simple life-style he had preserved even in mature prosperity, it was as indicative of the esteem in which he was held in establishment circles the world over as the many official decorations and honorary awards showered on him throughout his later years.

Inevitably, younger members of the New German School deplored his rock-like allegiance to those classical principles first implanted in him as a boy by Marxsen. Not interested in current experiments in unity and compression through metamorphosis of a 'motto' theme, Brahms remained faithful to the traditional logic of sonata-form, rondo, passacaglia, fugue and variation (a particular favourite). Nor, because more concerned with design and dialectic than in providing mere *frissons* for the ear, did he find it necessary to include exotic new instruments, like the cor anglais and tuba, in his scores, or to enlarge the existing orchestra by sheer weight of numbers. Loving the bracing, diatonic strength of German folk-song and of themes generated by his arpeggio-type F A F motto, he rarely tried to intensify either his melody or harmony through hyper-exploratory chromaticism.

Above all else he hated wearing his heart on his sleeve in programme-music using sound as a means of painting pictures or telling stories. Yet in a sense Brahms was more romantic than most of those who branded him an anti-romanticist in that nearly every work he wrote – and his large output included almost every genre except opera – grew from his own personal experience. As the late Dr Colles once put it 'There is a story at the back of all Brahms's great works, but it is a personal story, not a dramatic one like the stories of Berlioz and Liszt, and it is told only in music.'

As a craftsman he was a perfectionist, suppressing some works altogether and wrestling with others for years before allowing them to reach the public. 'Go over it again and again until there is not a bar you could improve on', he once counselled a friend. 'Whether it is beautiful also is an entirely different matter, but perfect it must be.' Yet in most of his music, his idiom was very much his own from the start. Time brought new subtleties and refinements, of course, but no steady process of evolution as in Beethoven. In this respect Brahms was one of music's mysteries in 'arriving fully armed, like Athena from the head of Zeus', as Schumann so perciPIently observed in that now famous article of 1853.

J.O.C.

Caricature of Brahms by Bohler.

BRITTEN, Benjamin
(b. Lowestoft, 22 Nov 1913;
d. Aldeburgh, 4 Dec 1976)

Benjamin Britten was born on St Cecilia's Day, 1913. His father was a dental surgeon, his mother a keen amateur singer. Music was an early love; and he started to compose at the age of five. He was taught the piano and viola; and by the time he left his preparatory school, his juvenile output included ten piano sonatas, six string quartets, three suites for piano, an oratorio, and dozens of songs. In 1927 he met the composer Frank Bridge; and it was arranged that he should have composition lessons from him in the school holidays, and piano lessons from Harold Samuel. He spent two years (1928–30) at Gresham's School, Holt, and then, being determined to make music his career, went to the Royal College of Music, having won an open scholarship in composition.

His period as a student seems to have been unsatisfactory and frustrating. He worked under John Ireland for composition and Arthur Benjamin for piano; but during his three years at college (1930–3) only one of his compositions was played there – the *Sinfonietta* – and even that had already been performed at a public concert elsewhere. Residence in London was important insofar as it gave him a chance to attend many concerts, particularly of contemporary music; but he failed to persuade the College Library to buy a copy of the score of Schönberg's *Pierrot Lunaire* and, when he received a small travelling bursary in 1933, he was not allowed to use it as he wished, by going to Vienna to study under Berg.

In 1934, the year in which Holst, Delius, and Elgar died, Britten came of age. He was determined to earn his living by composition. The *Phantasy Quartet* was played at the ISCM Festival at Florence that summer; and a set of choral variations for mixed voices unaccompanied, entitled *A Boy was Born*, was broadcast by the BBC. The following year he joined the GPO Film Unit and in the next five years produced incidental music for numerous documentary films. As soon as his flair for occasional and incidental music was recognised, commissions for theatre and radio work followed.

The GPO Film Unit brought him in touch with the poet W. H. Auden, who was four years his senior, and they worked together on various films including *Night Mail*. This collaboration developed outside the film world.

Britten wrote incidental music for two Auden/Isherwood verse plays; and Auden provided the texts for the first of Britten's song cycles, *On this Island*, and for a symphonic cycle called *Our Hunting Fathers*. His influence on Britten was important, particularly insofar as it brought the composer a deeper appreciation of the beauties of poetry, and an increased awareness of the problems involved in the alliance of words with music.

In 1937, in response to a commission from the Boyd Neel String Orchestra, Britten wrote *Variations on a Theme of Frank Bridge*, which caused a sensation at the Salzburg Festival that summer and helped to establish his international reputation. The following year his Piano Concerto in D major was performed at a Prom, with himself as soloist.

Britten with producer Colin Graham and singer Peter Pears, Aldeburgh 1963.

By 1939 the darkening political situation in Europe led a number of artists to decide to leave England. Auden and Isherwood were among the first to go to the United States, and their example influenced Britten, who (by his own account) was feeling 'muddled, fed-up and looking for work, longing to be used'. He and his friend, Peter Pears the tenor, left England early that summer, going first to Canada, and then to Long Island where they spent the greater part of the next two and a half years. The first major work Britten completed during this American visit was the Violin Concerto in D minor, and this was followed by the *Sinfonia da Requiem* (1940) dedicated to the memory of his parents. Particularly successful were two vocal works: *Les Illuminations* (1939), a setting of some of Rimbaud's poems for high voice and string orchestra, and *Seven Sonnets of Michelangelo* (1940) for tenor and piano, written specially for Peter Pears. Work with Auden was resumed when they collab-

orated on an operetta, *Paul Bunyan*, based on the legend of the giant American pioneer. This was produced at Columbia University, New York, in May 1941 and elicited tepid notices from the critics. Auden also supplied him with the text of a cantata, *Hymn to St Cecilia*.

By 1942 Britten was increasingly homesick and doubtful whether he really wanted to stay on in America. Eventually he made up his mind to return to England; and while he and Peter Pears were waiting on the East Coast for a passage across the Atlantic, he chanced to meet Serge Koussevitzky in Boston, and as a result of this meeting the Koussevitzky Music Foundation offered Britten a commission for a new opera to be dedicated to the memory of Natalie Koussevitzky.

Britten and Pears left America in March 1942, sailing on a small Swedish cargo boat that took more than a month to make the dangerous crossing. During the voyage Britten completed the *Hymn to St Cecilia* and composed *A Ceremony of Carols* for treble voices and harp. As a pacifist by conviction he had to appear before a tribunal shortly after arriving back in England; but in view of his conscientious objections he was exempted from military service and allowed to continue his work of composition, provided he also performed as a pianist at the special wartime concerts that were being promoted by CEMA (Council for the Encouragement of Music and the Arts) all over the country. He returned to his old house at Snape, Suffolk, where he had been living before the war.

The next three years were occupied partly in arranging performances of the works he had brought back from America with him, partly in composing *Rejoice in the Lamb*, a festival cantata to words by Christopher Smart, and the *Serenade* for tenor, horn and strings, but mainly in working on his new opera, *Peter Grimes*, whose hero was based on the eponymous character in George Crabbe's poem *The Borough*. The composition was started in January 1944 and finished thirteen months later. It was agreed that the first performance of *Peter Grimes* (7th June 1945) should mark the return of the Sadler's Wells Opera Company to Sadler's Wells Theatre from which it had been exiled during the war.

The success of *Peter Grimes*, with Peter Pears playing the title role, was immediate and decisive; and Britten's work as an opera composer became a matter of international concern. At the same time dissensions at Sadler's Wells led to a change of operatic policy at that theatre; and some of the artists seceded to form a small-scale company determined to work for Britten. To help launch this company, he agreed to write a new opera for eight singers and twelve instrumentalists. This chamber opera was *The Rape of Lucretia*, which was given at Glyndebourne in the summer of 1946. The following year the company, renamed the English Opera Group, visited Glyndebourne with *Albert Herring*, a new comic opera by Britten, and revived *The Rape of Lucretia*.

In 1947 Britten moved house from Snape to Aldeburgh; and that summer the Group took *The Rape of Lucretia* and *Albert Herring* to two festivals in Europe. It was in the course of this tour that Peter Pears had an inspiration. 'Why not make our own festival', he suggested, 'and have it at home?' The first Aldeburgh Festival was accordingly planned for 1948 and proved so successful that it became an annual event.

Britten's life now began to follow a fairly regular pattern. There was usually a new opera on the stocks, and other compositions to be fitted in; various engagements as conductor or pianist to be carried out, particularly recital tours with Peter Pears; and the annual Aldeburgh Festival to be planned and presented. Three new works of his proved immensely popular. The *Spring Symphony* (1949) for soloists, mixed choir, boys' voices and orchestra, provided a symphonic setting for a miniature anthology of poems about spring. *The Young Person's Guide to the Orchestra* (1946) – variations and fugue on a theme by Purcell – was originally written for a film entitled *Instruments of the Orchestra*, but pursued a vigorous life of its own in the concert-hall. And *Let's Make an Opera!* which might be described as a young person's guide to opera, scored a phenomenal success when presented at the 1949 Aldeburgh Festival.

He frequently received commissions for special occasions. *Billy Budd* was commissioned by the Arts Council for the Festival of Britain, 1951; and *Gloriana* was commissioned for the Coronation of Elizabeth II (1953). Both operas were produced at Covent Garden. *The Turn of the Screw*, a chamber opera, was commissioned by the Venice Biennale of 1954, and *Owen Wingrave* by the BBC for television presentation in 1971. *War Requiem* was written for the Coventry Cathedral Festival (1961) on the occasion of the rededication of that Cathedral.

Towards the end of 1955, Britten and Pears left England on an extended tour that took them to the Far East, where they visited Bali, Japan, and India. On his return Britten wrote the music for *The Prince of the Pagodas*, a full-length ballet, devised and choreographed by John Cranko, which was produced at Covent Garden on the 1st January 1957. Some of its divertissements showed the influence of Javanese gamelan music.

In 1958 the Aldeburgh Festival presented *Noye's Fludde* at Oxford Church. This was the Chester Miracle Play set to music by Britten; and its success led to the presentation of other dramatic works with music for church presentation. In 1964, with the assistance of William Plomer, Britten adapted *Sumidagawa*, a Japanese Noh play, into *Curlew River*, styled 'a parable for church performance', and this was followed by *The Burning Fiery Furnace* (1966) and *The Prodigal Son* (1968), both written to a similar formula, but based on Biblical episodes instead of Noh play material. For these church parables the chamber orchestra was reduced to a group of seven or eight instrumentalists without conductor.

During the 1960s Britten became friendly with a number of Russian musicians. Some of them, particularly Rostropovich and Richter, appeared occasionally at the Aldeburgh Festival; and for Rostropovich he wrote a Symphony for 'Cello and Orchestra (1963) and three suites for 'cello unaccompanied (1965, 1967, and 1971). In 1963 Britten and Pears paid the first of several highly successful visits to the USSR, and two years later they attended a Britten Festival at Yerevan in Armenia.

In early years one of the main difficulties at the Aldeburgh Festival had been how to mount opera productions on the cramped stage of the Jubilee Hall. A chamber opera like *Albert Herring* might just fit; but in 1960 it was only with the greatest difficulty that Britten's *A Midsummer Night's Dream* was squeezed onto it. A solution was found in 1967, when part of the Maltings at Snape was converted into a concert and opera hall. Two years later the building was destroyed by fire. But it was immediately rebuilt; and since then its fine acoustic properties have shown it to be one of the outstanding halls in Europe. It is suitable for the open-platform presentation of opera; and the first performance of Britten's *Death in Venice* was given there (16th June 1973).

In the spring of 1973 Britten was admitted to hospital with a heart lesion. The subsequent operation was only partly successful; and afterwards his activities had to be severely curtailed. Composition continued, though on a more restricted scale than formerly. In 1974 he wrote his fifth canticle, *The Death of Saint Narcissus*, for tenor and harp; and *Phaedra*, an orchestral cantata specially written for Janet Baker, was given at the 1976 Aldeburgh Festival.

Britten always had the knack of knowing how to fit memorable music to carefully chosen words; and this conferred special distinction on all his vocal music, and on his operas too. He knew how to use music to the best effect, whether in the concert-hall, on the stage or in the church. His music possessed qualities of freshness and simplicity that made it easily accessible to the common listener; and he never lost the radiance that came from imaginative understanding of youth.

E.W.W.

BRUCH, Max
(b. Cologne, 6 Jan 1838;
d. Friedenau, 2 Oct 1920)

'In personal appearance, Bruch is by no means as majestic as one would suppose from his works', states that delightful Victorian compendium *Famous Composers and Their Works*, published in 1893. There can be very few modern admirers of the composer who would think anything of the sort. They probably know him by two of his three violin concertos, the *Scottish Fantasy*, and the once-popular *Kol Nidrei*; a few may have heard his second symphony, which receives an occasional broadcast. All these are notable for a flow of melody that occasionally verges on *schmaltz*. In fact, during his own time, Bruch was regarded mainly as a choral composer of genius; and in England, he was admired as a worthy successor of Handel, Haydn, Mendelssohn and Benedict. All that is now forgotten, even in Germany.

Max Bruch was born in Cologne; his family were typical members of the German middle classes, his father being in government employ. His mother's family were musical, and Bruch himself proved to be immensely gifted in this direction. When he was nine years old, some of his compositions were shown to the famous Cologne conductor Ferdinand Hiller, who immediately took charge of the prodigy's education, and trained him so well that he won the Frankfurt Mozart scholarship at the age of fourteen with a string quartet. A generation earlier, Bruch would probably have been rushed all over Europe showing off his skill to aristocratic audiences. Instead, he spent the remainder of his teens studying under such distinguished teachers as Reinecke and Breuning, and travelling at a leisurely pace around Germany's musical centres, learning his trade in the pleasantest possible manner. A comic opera, *Scherz, List und Rache* (based on a rather trivial early comedy of Goethe), was performed when he was twenty, but was only moderately successful; it appeared in due course as his Opus 1. His father died when Bruch was twenty-three, and Bruch set out on another tour of Germany and Austria, finally pausing for four years in Mannheim, where he settled down seriously to composition. A second opera, *The Lorelei* (which Mendelssohn had been working on at the time of his death) proved altogether more successful, although it, too, slipped out of the repertoire.

Bruch was in his twenty-sixth year when he achieved his first undiluted success, a choral work entitled *Frithjof*, based on the Nordic saga of that name. It was an impressive work for male chorus and soprano; much of the music was sombre, and seemed to evoke the great snow-bound forests of the north – a kind of anticipation of Sibelius. This made Bruch famous far beyond Cologne and Mannheim, and he travelled as far as Brussels and Paris to conduct it. This was quickly followed up by the almost equally successful *Schön Ellen*, based on the story of a Scottish girl who heard the bagpipes of the relieving army at the seige of Lucknow, and prevented the garrison from surrendering to the merciless Sepoys. It was all magnificent, stirring stuff of the sort that aroused martial rumbles in the breast of every right-thinking Victorian, and in no time at all Bruch found himself regarded as Mendelssohn's successor and the equal of Brahms. A successor to *Frithjof* followed, based on the same saga, then yet more martial choral works such as *Odysseus*, *Arminius* and *Achilleus*.

In 1866, Bruch produced the work by which he is best known today, the first violin concerto in G minor. It was written for Joachim – for whom Brahms wrote his own concerto a few years later – and the first thing that strikes the listener is its incredible, flowing inventiveness and a lyrical warmth reminiscent of Mendelssohn. In the following year, he be-

came director of the court orchestra at Schwartzburg-Sondershausen, and, like Haydn, the servant of a prince. (Spohr and Weber had been among his predecessors there.) When he left, after three years, Brahms applied – unsuccessfully – for the position. Bruch moved to Berlin for two years, then to Bonn, and his success and fame grew with a series of choral works like *Leonidas* and *Thermopylae*. He even came to Liverpool for three years, as the successor of Sir Julius Benedict, and was tempted to settle in England permanently; but his German accent and teutonic perfectionism caused friction with the chorus and orchestra of the Philharmonic Society, so he moved on to America to conduct more concerts of his music, then returned to Germany. The second violin concerto in D was composed for Sarasate and was almost as successful as the first, although modern audiences rate it far lower. The *Scottish Fantasy* for violin and orchestra, and the *Kol Nidrei* for 'cello and orchestra, were composed during his English residence; the latter is probably responsible for the general (but mistaken) impression that Bruch was Jewish. Bruch also acquired a German wife in England.

Back in Germany – this time in Breslau – his reputation continued to rise until by the mid-1890s, he was generally ranked as one of the major composers of the 19th century. But from then on, his life was all anti-climax. In the age of Mahler, Debussy, Stravinsky, he was still writing and thinking in terms of the age of Mendelssohn. The fashion for choral music evaporated, even in England, and Bruch suffered the same fate as Stainer, Stanford and Parry. A third violin concerto in D was generally judged much inferior to the first two, more prolix and less melodious. The wonderful, soft-flowing melodies of the first two concertos, and the *Kol Nidrei*, kept them in the concert repertoires, but rather as relics of a bygone age. The aggressive German traditionalist Pfitzner tried to revive *The Lorelei* without success. Bruch found this lack of appreciation incomprehensible, and became embittered. He was a rather closed-in personality, inclined to be self-centred and dictatorial – hardly the type to grow old gracefully. The death of his son in World War I plunged him into depression. The music of younger composers like Weill and Hindemith must have struck him as horrible cacophony. He died in 1920 – the year after his wife – at the age of eighty-two, exhausted but still defiant.

C.W.

BRUCKNER, Anton
(b. Ansfelden, 4 Sept 1824;
d. Vienna, 11 Oct 1896)

Rustic, conscientious, cautious, in some ways naïve, Anton Bruckner was well into his thirties before his imagination took full wing, and to the end of his life he remained retiring, reticent, a man of simple tastes, unsure of himself in the intellectual company of Vienna, and something of an enigma. In a sense, his attitude to life and music came from his upbringing. He was born in Upper Austria to a family of schoolmasters, the duties of which included playing the organ in church and teaching music. After his father's death (1837) he was educated as a chorister in the enclosed surroundings of St Florian monastery, where he was taught violin, piano, organ and some rudimentary theory at the Volksschule. Further studies at Linz and elsewhere led to a post as teacher at St Florian and eventually (1848) as organist there. He had already written some organ preludes and a mass, but his duties at St Florian, which became a burden to him, prevented him from developing very fast as a composer. In 1856, he was appointed organist at Linz, a great event in his life as it relieved him of his schoolmasterly duties, and allowed him to devote all his time to music. While at Linz he travelled to Vienna regularly to study counterpoint more fully under the eminent teacher Simon Sechter. Then he went to Otto Kitzler, *Kapellmeister* at Linz, for help with orchestration, so even when well into his thirties, Bruckner still had to gain confidence in his own abilities. His start was both sceptical and tentative. The first mature works, his Mass in D minor and the first symphony, date from this period.

Kitzler's performances of Wagner at Linz turned Bruckner into an ardent Wagnerian. He attended the first performance of *Tristan* at Munich in 1865, when he met the composer, and in 1868 he gave the first public performance of the final scene of *Meistersinger*, with the composer's blessing, conducting the Linz Choral Society in 1868. At about the same time two of his most important early works, the Mass in E minor and the Mass in F minor were written, even though he had had a nervous breakdown through overwork and depression before the F minor was begun. Indeed it was composed against the advice of his doctors, partly as an act of thanks to God and partly as a commission for it had arrived from the Chapel Royal of the Hofburg in Vienna, no less. It was completed shortly

Bruckner.

before Bruckner moved to the capital, but not performed until 1872.

Through the influence of Johann Herbeck, the court conductor in Vienna, Bruckner had been appointed teacher of counterpoint and organ at the Conservatory there in 1868, becoming professor in 1871. He made several pilgrimages to Bayreuth at this time, where he was befriended by Wagner to whom Bruckner dedicated his third symphony – at the instigation of Wagner who told his fellow-composer: 'The work gives me *uncommonly great pleasure.*' As an organist Bruckner visited France and England, where his extraordinary powers of improvisation enthralled his audiences.

In Vienna, he was much lauded by apostles of Wagner, but reviled by many critics, including Hanslick, who was championing Brahms at the time. Bruckner, who never felt entirely himself in the sophisticated milieu of the capital, was hurt by the often-hostile reception of his symphonies. The first performance of the third at Vienna in 1877 was a fiasco. The Vienna Philharmonic, who had at first rejected it, eventually agreed reluctantly to perform it at the behest of a member of parliament. As a result the performance, under Bruckner's direction, was slovenly. There was a good deal of cat-calling from the audience, and by the end only a few adherents of his cause remained to applaud. Hanslick gave it a scathing review. From this point, Bruckner agreed to the revisions of his friends and advocates, such as the conductor Frank Schalk. Simple, shy and humble, Bruckner allowed drastic alterations. Even so, performances of his succeeding symphonies were hard to come by. When the fourth was given at Vienna under Richter in 1881, the public liked it but Hanslick, typically, wrote: 'We are very happy at the success of the work, but we fail to understand it.' The fifth symphony of 1876 had to wait until 1894 for its première, the sixth until after the composer's death for a complete performance.

The seventh marked a turning of the tide – but not in Vienna. Given under Nikisch's direction at Leipzig in 1884, it was widely acclaimed, and the applause lasted a quarter of an hour. Nikisch wrote: 'Since Beethoven there has been nothing that could even approach it . . .', thus swimming against the prevalent Brahmsian tide. Vienna, Hanslick apart, also acclaimed it. The eighth, in 1892,

was also a success, but the ninth was left incomplete, lacking a finale, at the composer's death because Bruckner in his last years was so busy making revisions to his earlier works. These years also saw the completion of the important *Te Deum* and of Psalm 150.

In 1891, Bruckner resigned his post at the Conservatory, which gave him that year an honorary degree of Doctor of Philosophy. His last years were spent in rooms at the Belvedere Palace, granted him by the emperor. In spite of increasing weariness he continued to work on the ninth symphony right up to the day of his death. Shy to the point of awkwardness and consequently not easy to get on with, he led an unhappy and withdrawn private life, but was consoled by his unceasing work on his symphonies and choral works.

When he died, Bruckner was still little known outside German-speaking countries except as an organist, and it was many years until his true stature was realised, for most of the symphonies, even the first performance of the ninth in 1903, were given in unauthentic editions, which often distorted Bruckner's musical image by the pompous reorchestrations of his well-meaning friends. The Bruckner Society began to come to his rescue in the 1930s, and under the editorship of Robert Haas the unadulterated scores at last became available, showing that Bruckner's original orchestration was clearer

Manuscript with writing materials used by Bruckner.

and more individual than the accretions had suggested. In the early days, Bruckner was often misconstrued as a Wagnerian symphonist or a successor of Beethoven, and adversely criticised as such. In fact his music resembles Wagner's only in its long time-scale, and as Robert Simpson has pointed out: 'His peculiar kind of grandeur depends on the apt placing of mass and void', not on an unbroken skein of constantly transformed themes as found in Wagner's music-dramas. Indeed, Bruckner's symphonies present an utterly personal world of expression, and one very different from Wagner's, in spite of some superficial resemblances in thematic material. They are so original in form that any attempt to relate them to Beethoven's is also fruitless and beside the point. Huge masses of material are presented in apparent isolation. The 'voids' are followed by unexpected developments, which seem to be reaching for a climax only to fall away into another void, or into some sudden build-up of a persistent motif. Continuity is not of the essence, but tonal tensions are, and the final effect of Bruckner's structures is a new kind of, and wholly unique, symmetry. In non-musical terms, his symphonies seem related closely to his unshakeable and all-pervading Roman Catholic faith and to his awe before his natural surroundings, while his Scherzo movements almost all reflect the rough dances and folktunes of his native heath. All the elements are held within an organisation that, in spite of the occasional vagaries, has great formal strength. Numbers four and seven have become, by tradition, the most easily assimilated of the set, but numbers six, eight and nine (what we have of it) are arguably Bruckner's most noble edifices.

The symphonies, alike in structure and instrumentation, reflect Bruckner's long hours spent before choirs and in the organ loft. His choral music, naturally enough, is even more closely related to those activities. It draws strongly on the music of the 16th and 17th centuries – the influence can be heard most obviously in the beautiful E minor Mass and the Motets for small choirs – fusing the idioms and spirit of the late Renaissance with 19th-century techniques. The larger works, in particular the F minor Mass and the *Te Deum*, call ideally for church or cathedral acoustics, where the grandeur of concept is much enhanced. When the F minor Mass was first given in Vienna's Augustinerkirche under Bruckner in 1872, a friend ran up to the com-

Silhouette of Bruckner by Schliessmann.

poser at the end of the final rehearsal, calling out, 'I know only two Masses – this one and the *Solemnis* of Beethoven.' The comparison is wholly apt. Bruckner himself regarded the *Te Deum* as his 'finest work' and 'the pride of my life' and dedicated it to God 'in gratitude', as he wryly put it, 'because my persecutors have not yet managed to finish me off'. The numerous liturgical works of his early days are less important, but the string quintet of 1879, too seldom performed, is among his most personal works.

Bruckner is anything but typical of his age. Literature apparently meant nothing to him, nor had he any of the independence of mind of his romantic contemporaries. He had a subservient attitude to colleagues, particularly to the 'dearly beloved Master' – Wagner. He was naïvely pious, right up to his old age, but with the piety went certain psychopathic compulsions and a proclivity for 'pretty little girls' in their early teens. His simplicity may indeed have hid a complex sub-conscious, so that the easy categorising of earlier generations need to be taken with a degree of scepticism. Whatever the man, the music now remains unassailable in its splendour and originality.

A.B.

BUSONI, Ferruccio
(b. Empoli, 1 April 1866;
d. Berlin, 27 July 1924)

Busoni's father was a North Italian clarinet-tist, and his mother an Austrian pianist. For part of the boy's childhood, he was under the care of his grandfather, while his parents were absent on concert tours. Later, both parents gave him piano lessons, and at the age of nine he made his first public appearance playing Mozart's C minor concerto, conducted by his father. In an attempt to exploit Ferruccio's musical talent, his father then took him to Vienna where he studied for a time at the Con-servatorium. Later, he found a congenial teacher, Wilhelm Mayer, in Graz, and it was under Mayer that the young Busoni's musical tastes began to expand and develop. By his mid-teens he had become a pianist of concert standard, and had also begun to compose. In 1883 a cantata of his was favourably com-mented upon by the distinguished composer and librettist Arrigo Boito.

Armed with an introduction from Brahms, Busoni made his way to Leipzig which was then musically a very active city. He remained there for some years, until he went to Helsinki to teach. Here he met the girl he was to marry a year or two later in Moscow, where he had gone to teach. His next teaching post was in the United States, after which Busoni gave up teaching and devoted himself to the life of a

travelling virtuoso. He had become an excep-tionally fine pianist, excelling in a wide range of music, and for the next twenty years, until the outbreak of World War I, he based himself in Berlin, and toured all over the world giving concerts of Bach. During this period his own compositions were neglected. Gradually, however, his thoughts began to turn to opera, and his first completed opera, *Die Brautwahl*, based on one of E. T. A. Hoffmann's stories, was staged in Hamburg in 1912. Too eclectic a piece to establish Busoni as a composer, *Die Brautwahl* is nevertheless a work of subtle inventiveness.

Busoni's next opera, *Turandot* (1917), shares with Puccini its subject, drawn from Carlo Gozzi's fairy-tale, but it is much closer in spirit to Gozzi's original than Puccini's opera is. With *Doktor Faust*, the opera which is Busoni's masterpiece, and on which he worked for nearly fifteen years, Busoni intro-duced his own literary and philosophical ideas into the old German tale. He wrote his own libretto, an austerely intellectual version of the legend which owes little to Goethe, and much to the older German puppet-plays. *Doktor Faust* is the one work of Busoni which

Busoni.

is certain to survive, though it will never be a popular opera. At his death, it was not finished, and the final scene was completed by one of his pupils, Philipp Jarnach.

In 1913, Busoni made a brief return to teaching, when he was invited to become Director of the Liceo Musicale in Bologna. But the administrative work proved irksome, and he soon returned to Berlin. During the war, he refused to perform in any of the warring countries, and retired to Switzerland to compose. When peace was declared he returned to Berlin and to concert-giving, but he was by now in ill health, and died of a kidney disease at the age of fifty-seven. As a pianist, he influenced a younger school of players, while as a composer he trod a solitary path. In the last analysis a minor figure, he is nevertheless an important one.

C.O.

BUXTEHUDE, Diderik
(b. Helsingør, 1637;
d. Lübeck, 9 May 1707)

Buxtehude's father, Hans Jensen Buxtehude (1602–74), was organist of the Olai Church at Helsingør and presumably Diderik's first (and possibly only) teacher in music. Very little is known of his early life apart from the fact that he was appointed organist of St Mary's Church Helsingør in 1660. He must have shown outstanding ability for in April 1688 he succeeded Franz Tunder in the important post of organist at the Marienkirche, Lübeck – one of the best and most lucrative positions in Germany. Here he acquired a tremendous reputation as organist and teacher. Young musicians throughout Northern Europe flocked to hear him, including Nikolaus Bruhns, Georg Böhm and, of course, Bach who made his celebrated two-hundred-mile journey on foot.

Buxtehude instigated a series of concerts – the *Abendmusiken* – at the Marienkirche in 1683. They took place annually on the five Sundays preceding Christmas, following the afternoon service. Programmes included choral, orchestral, and organ music; Buxtehude maintained very high standards and received the loyal support of the townspeople. The concerts were extremely popular and the tradition extended into the early 19th century.

One of the terms of Buxtehude's appointment at the Marienkirche was that he was expected to marry the daughter of his predecessor. This he complied with. Upon his own retirement, well into his sixties, he enforced the same condition, and among the applicants in 1703 were Handel and Mattheson, but both declined the post with its promise of instant domesticity.

Buxtehude as a composer is chiefly remembered for his organ works – toccatas, preludes and fugues, a passacaglia, two ciacconas, and numerous chorale preludes. The designation 'Toccata and Fugue' in Buxtehude does not imply the two-fold division of movements as, for instance, in Bach. Buxtehude's generation preferred a more rhapsodic, multi-sectional format: a toccata flourish (sometimes containing an exacting pedal solo), a fugal section, a 'free' section (often harmonically daring), then another fugal section leading to the finale in toccata style. Unity is often achieved by relating the subjects of the fugues; the Toccata and Fugue in E major, for example, contains three fugal sections – each using a transformation of the same subject.

Of the many types of chorale-based compositions, Buxtehude particularly excelled in two, the extended chorale fantasia, and the ornamented 'cantus firmus' chorale prelude. His fantasias, which treat the chorale lines individually, and make use of a great variety of figuration and texture, frequently summon considerable virtuosity. His chorale preludes are of particular interest as they demonstrate a highly personal interpretation of the chorale, an attitude of writing which found its consummation in Bach.

Buxtehude's clavichord and harpsichord works comprise twenty-nine suites usually of the format: allemande, courante, sarabande, and gigue, and several sets of variations. The melody of the beautiful '*Rofilis*' variations, which is taken from Lully's '*Ballet de l'Impatience*', had already achieved wide circulation in 17th-century Denmark as a hymn tune. There is also an interesting dance suite based on the chorale *Auf meinen lieben Gott*, obviously intended for clavichord or harpsichord, although it appears among the organ music in the complete edition. Mattheson in *Der Vollkommene Kapellmeister* speaks of a collection of seven suites 'in which the nature and character of the planets are agreeably expressed' – but these compositions unfortunately are no longer extant.

Buxtehude's cantatas, in their powerful

subjective insight, exerted a tremendous influence on Bach. They contain neither recitative nor aria, but are written in a vividly pictorial type of accompanied arioso. The brilliant choral writing is clearly of Italianate origin. Sometimes, as in the cantata, *Gott hilf mir*, choir and orchestra exchange roles – the former play the chorale *Durch Adams Fall*, while the singers comment with illustrative figuration. The music which Buxtehude composed especially for the *Abendmusiken* has survived only in part; it is generally more dramatic than the cantatas and, indeed, approaches the nature of oratorio. Much of Buxtehude's remaining instrumental music, including some notable string sonatas, has been published this century; but it is as a composer for the organ that he has achieved lasting recognition.

G.G.

Byrd, from an early engraving.

BYRD, William
(b. Lincolnshire, 1543;
d. Stondon Massey, Essex, 4 July 1623)

William Byrd, one of England's greatest composers, was appointed organist of Lincoln Cathedral on the 27th February 1563, at about the age of twenty. In 1568 he married Juliana Birley, and their two eldest children, Elizabeth and Christopher, were born and baptised in Lincoln. In February 1570, Byrd was appointed Gentleman of the Chapel Royal, succeeding Robert Parsons, but retained his organist's position at Lincoln for a further two years. At the end of 1572, he moved to London and became joint organist of the Chapel Royal with Thomas Tallis. According to Anthony à Wood, Byrd was 'bred up to musick under Thomas Tallis'. We have no means of telling if this was before the Lincoln appointment, but we do know that the composers were closely associated from 1575, the year in which they were jointly granted a virtual monopoly of music printing by licence of Queen Elizabeth. Their first publication was a set of *Cantiones Sacrae*, dedicated to Queen Elizabeth, which appeared in 1575 and contained seventeen motets by each composer. The printing monopoly proved to be less remunerative than they had hoped, and so the composers petitioned again remarking that Tallis was by now 'verie aged' and that Byrd had sacrificed a good living at Lincoln to come to London. The petition was successful, and the Queen granted them a lucrative lease.

In 1577 Byrd moved to Harlington, a village in west Middlesex, and it seems likely that his wife Juliana died while they were living there. He moved from Harlington to Stondon Massey, near Ongar in Essex, in 1593 and remarried at about the same time. His second wife, Ellen, died in 1605. Byrd spent the remainder of his life at Stondon and died on the 4th July 1623. The burial registers have not survived, but there is no reason to think that he died elsewhere.

Throughout his life, Byrd remained committed to the Catholic traditions: we know that his settings were used at recusant services. Father William Weston, in the *Autobiography of an Elizabethan*, writes:

The following day we left the city and went out nearly thirty miles to the home of a catholic gentleman, a close friend of mine. . . . In the house was a chapel, set aside for the celebration of the church's offices. The gentleman was a skilled musician, and there were an organ, other musical instruments, and choristers both male and female. During those eight days it was just as if we were celebrating the octave of some great feast. . . . Mr Byrd the very famous musician and organist was among the company.

Byrd, however, retained his position unmolested at the Chapel Royal, and indeed made a substantial contribution to the music of the English Church, including such masterpieces as *The Great Service* and the anthem *Sing Joyfully*.

Byrd was held in very great respect by his contemporaries – Nicholas Yonge in the Preface for *Musica Transalpina* refers to him as 'A Great Maister of Musicke', and Thomas Morley in his *Plaine and Easie Introduction to Practicall Musicke* insists that Byrd should 'never without reverence be named of the musicians'.

Byrd's compositional output was immense. A great deal of his music has survived in manuscript and several collections of his works were published during his lifetime. The *Cantiones Sacrae* of 1575 were followed by two further collections bearing the same title (in 1589 and 1591 respectively). The volume of *Psalmes, Sonets, and songs of Sadnes and Pietie* of 1588 (the same year as Yonge's *Musica Transalpina*) is particularly valuable for the 'Reasons briefly set downe by th' auctor to perswade eueryone to learne to singe.' We read that 'There is not any Musicke of Instruments whatsoeuer, comparable to that which is made of the voyces of men.' On a slightly less elevated level we learn that singing 'is a singular good remedie for a stutting and stamering in the speech'.

A collection of *Songs of Sundrie natures, some of grauitie and others of mirth* appeared in 1589, and juxtaposes madrigalian pieces with psalms and anthems, the latter including the delightful 'Carowle for Christmas Day', *An Earthly Tree*. The two books of *Gradualia* published in 1605 and 1607 respectively, consist of a complete cycle of motets for the Church's year, and contain some of Byrd's most beautiful music, for instance: *Justorum animae, O Sacrum convivium, Haec Dies* and *Non vos relinquam*. Byrd's final publication *Psalmes, Songs and Sonnets*, which appeared in 1611, is a collection of madrigals and anthems, and also includes two string fantasias. It is not possible to establish the actual date of composition of Byrd's three Latin Masses (to three, four, and five voices). They were published in his lifetime without any title pages, and none of the surviving copies are dated.

Byrd's instrumental music, which is of considerable importance, includes viol fantasias many of which are in the form of 'in nomines', and a large amount of music for the virginals – some one hundred and forty pieces in all. Much of his keyboard music is included in *My Ladye Nevell's Virginal Booke* (1591) and the *Fitzwilliam Virginal Book*. He particularly excelled in dance and song variations, notable examples of which are the *Queenes Alman, Wolsey's Wilde, La Volta*, and the monumental *Quadran Paven* and *Galliard*, all of which may be found in the *Fitzwilliam Virginal Book*.

G.G.

CAVALLI, Pietro Francesco
(b. Crema, 14 Feb 1602; d. Venice, 17 Jan 1676)

Pietro Francesco Cavalli was the son of Giovanni Battista Caletti Bruni, the *maestro di cappella* at the cathedral in the small North Italian town of Crema. His earliest instruction in music naturally was given him by his father, and in his early teens, his singing attracted the attention of the Podestà (the Venetian governor of the town), one Federigo Cavalli, who eventually suggested that the boy should go to Venice to study. In December 1616, he was appointed as a singer in the Doge's chapel, the basilica of St Mark's, at the quite generous salary for his age of 80 ducats. He soon augmented this by becoming the part-time organist of the large church of SS Giovanni e Paolo, and he also attracted the patronage of one of the noble houses of Venice, living in the palazzo of Alvise Mocenigo. In the 1620s he became one of the best known tenors in the city, but he does not seem to have had a great reputation as a composer at this time, although he produced motets and probably larger works for use in the churches in which he was working. The outbreak of the plague of 1630, which carried off a great proportion of the population, caused him to give up his part-time job, and little is known about his life for some years after this, although an examination of his compositions suggests that he was very close to Monteverdi, whose pupil he undoubtedly was.

His fame came quite suddenly. On the opening of the public opera houses in Venice in 1637, he was one of the two or three experienced composers on the spot, and although he seemingly had written no theatre music, he was commissioned to write *Le Nozze di Teti e di Peleo* for the Teatro S Cassiano where it was produced during the carnival season of 1639. This was quickly followed by other operas for various other Venetian houses, until by the mid 1640s he was the most sought after composer of the genre. He owed his success partly to his flair for drama, which he had learned largely from Monteverdi, and partly to his gift

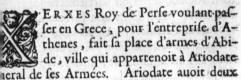

Title page of Xerxes *by Cavalli.*

for melody. His operas gradually increased the number of tuneful arias until they predominate, a fact which helped his works to succeed even when they were given in France and Austria, as happened with several of them. But Cavalli's most powerful pieces are the laments and grand *scenas*, an art in which he developed the basic operatic philosophy of Monteverdi. By the 1650s he became the composer-in-ordinary to the Teatro S Appolinare, for which he wrote at least one opera – sometimes three or four – each year, receiving the ample fee of 400 ducats, for which he had to rehearse and direct the work, as well as compose it in close collaboration with the librettist. All this time he was still in the service of St Mark's, having been promoted to the position of Second Organist in 1640. He published a large volume of church music in 1656, this including the *Messa Concertata*, which has been revived and performed a number of times in recent years, and some Vespers psalms, which however, do not constitute a unified set.

His *Orione* was given under his direction in

Milan in 1653, and his fame was such that seven years later he was asked to compose an opera for the marriage celebrations of Louis XIV, for which he was granted special dispensation from his official duties in St Mark's. He went to Paris in July 1660, with the intention of producing *L'Ercole amante*; this was impeded by a chapter of accidents – the illness and death of Cardinal Mazarin which lead to political intrigues, the difficulties of building a new theatre in the Tuileries, the complexity of the stage machines. In the end an old opera, *Serse*, was given in 1660 and *L'Ercole amante* was delayed until February 1662, when his music received an indifferent reception, although the designer and producer were much praised, and Lully's ballet music proved more to the taste of the audience than did the opera itself.

Cavalli returned to Venice an embittered man, and swore that he would never compose another opera. Nevertheless, within a short time he was tempted by commissions from Venetian theatres and wrote several operas on quasi-historical themes, *Scipione Africano* (1664), *Mutio Scevola* (1665), *Pompeo Magno* (1666), all of which were used by later operatic composers; and there were other productions of works revived from the 1650s. In 1665 he was made First Organist at St Mark's, and then on the death of Giovanni Battista Rovetta (one of his contemporaries and colleagues in the basilica since his earliest days) he became in 1668 *maestro di cappella*, thus directing the musical establishment which he had served since his boyhood. He devoted much of his final period to composing church music, contributing some excellent motets to an anthology assembled by a Bolognese publisher, and then putting together a substantial volume of Vespers music in 1675. In these later years, he seems also to have had some of his opera scores recopied so that they would survive in approved versions; and these volumes form the basis of our knowledge of his work today. Shortly before his death he wrote a Requiem Mass in the solemn old style, especially to be used at his funeral. He died in Venice on the 17th January, 1676. His will shows him to have been comfortably off, and although his wife had died childless many years earlier, he seems to have had many friends and pupils.

His music was known for some time after his death, and historians have always been well aware of his importance in the development of opera, although revivals of his music have become common only in the last twenty years. They show that although Cavalli lacked the sheer genius of his master Monteverdi, he was possessed of charm and fluency; and in his capacity to write motets and opera arias of great emotional strength, he was one of the finest miniaturists of his age.

D.A.

CHABRIER, Emmanuel
(b. Ambert, 18 Jan 1841;
d. Paris, 13 Sept 1894)

Chabrier was born in a little town in the Livradois region of Auvergne in Central France. The family had some inherited wealth and his father was a successful barrister, so Chabrier was brought up in an atmosphere of affluence and culture. His father was determined that he should study the law with a view to a career in the civil service but he was also happy that his son, who showed early musical talent, should study music as an intellectual pastime. He went to a local school and had his first piano lessons when he was six. Two of his early music teachers were Spanish which probably started his lifelong interest in the music of Spain culminating in the brilliant *España* rhapsody of 1883. When Chabrier was sixteen the family moved to Paris where he studied for four years at the Lycée St Louis, eventually obtaining his law degree and entering the Ministry of the Interior as a junior clerk. He was to remain a civil servant for eighteen years but, his work never being particularly arduous, he devoted much spare time to studying music. He had further piano lessons but developed his own composing talents by private study and by laboriously copying the scores of other composers, with a special interest in Wagner whose harmonic example added a piquant element to Chabrier's otherwise elegantly French and occasionally Spanish-tinged scores.

It was an ideal life, that of a comfortably well-off amateur of the arts. He was never under pressure to write and having passed a pleasantly uneventful twenty years in study, the next ten were equally pleasantly occupied with artistic dabblings. He was past thirty when his first work was published and almost forty before he gave up his civil service job to devote himself entirely to music. Both his parents had died when he was twenty-eight.

His interest in the arts was not confined to music where his friends included d'Indy, Fauré, Chausson and Duparc, but also embraced literature where he made friends of eminent writers like Verlaine, Mallarmé, Zola, Daudet and Richepin, and especially painting. In the world of art he enjoyed the friendship of Renoir and Manet (who died in his arms) and had portraits painted by both these masters as well as by Tissot, Degas and several others. In return Chabrier was a great patron of the arts and by the end of his life had acquired a collection of paintings that included eleven Manets, six Renoirs, two Sisleys, a Cézanne and many others, the pièce de resistance being Manet's *Un Bar aux Folies-Bergère* which he bought for 5,850 francs.

His first musical success, while still a civil servant, was with a charming operetta called *L'Étoile* which was performed at Les Bouffes-Parisiens in 1877. The score was commissioned by the librettists Leterrier and Vanloo who had been impressed by some of his early piano music. It made his reputation overnight and two years later he wrote another one-act operetta *Une Education Manquée* of which Poulenc later said that there was 'not a single page which does not bear the imprint of a master's hand'. The success of this piece helped him to make the decision to take up music as a full-time occupation.

A trip to Bayreuth confirmed his decision and when he came to write his operas *Gwendoline* (1886) and *Le Roi malgré lui* (1887) they exhibited their debt to Wagner, although the latter had much of Chabrier's natural French vivacity and good-humour in it. Chabrier's reputation rests on his few orchestral pieces, each a well-considered and expertly-wrought masterpiece full of exhilarating movement and strong melody – *España* (1883); *Joyeuse marche* (1888) both originally written for orchestra and his arrangements of piano pieces – *Habanera* (1885); *Suite pastorale* (1888) and *Bourrée fantasque* (1891). His piano music always exhibited a strong individuality – some being described by César Franck as 'a musical bridge between our own times and those of Couperin and Rameau'. His few songs are as shapely and delightful as one might expect of such a composer.

The end of the story, contrary to its promise, was not a happy one. After a mere ten years or so of composing Chabrier fell into a state of acute melancholia and, verging on insanity, died at the age of fifty-three in Paris. His handful of fine works will always be remembered. He wrote: 'I want my work to be beautiful throughout ... never the same colour, and everywhere variety, shape and, above all, vitality'. This he most certainly achieved.

P.G.

CHAUSSON, Ernest
(b. Paris, 20 Jan 1855;
d. Limay, 10 June 1899)

Chausson was the son of a building contractor who made a fortune in Baron Haussmann's rebuilding of central Paris. Two previous children of his parents had not survived infancy and Ernest was brought up with extreme solicitude and educated by a private tutor rather than allowed to take his chance at a school. He naturally grew up a quiet, considerate and, as he put it, melancholy child. 'The relative solitude of my upbringing and the reading of a few morbid books . . . made me sad without quite knowing why.' To please his parents he took a degree in Law at the University of Paris in 1877; but he had no need to earn his living and could follow his own bent. This seemed at first to be towards either literature or painting and it was probably a visit to Munich in 1879 to hear Wagner's music that finally decided him in favour of music. He entered the Paris Conservatoire as a pupil of Massenet for composition and César Franck for the organ, but within a few months he withdrew from the Conservatoire and enrolled as a private pupil of Franck's. By this time (the autumn of 1880) he had already paid a second visit to Germany and heard *Tristan* for the first time. The so-called 'bande à Franck' was already almost complete, except for the young Belgian Lekeu, and included Vincent d'Indy, Henri Duparc, Pierre de Bréville, Guy Ropartz and Charles Bordes.

In 1881 Chausson competed unsuccessfully for the Prix de Rome, but a trio written the same year was performed in 1882 and a year later the symphonic poem *Viviane*. This was dedicated to Mademoiselle Jeanne Escudier whom Chausson married the same year. She was to prove an excellent wife to him and mother to their five children, an elegant hostess and an excellent companion on the many expeditions abroad which agreeably diversified their life together. In Paris their house in the Boulevard de Courcelles soon became a regular meeting-place for painters and writers as well as musicians. Among the guests were Manet, Degas, Renoir and Rodin; Mallarmé, Henri de Régnier and Gide; Franck, of course, but also Chabrier, Fauré, Koechlin and Satie, Ysaÿe, Thibaud and Cortot. It was a mutual friend, Raymond Bonheur, who introduced the young Debussy, and he and Chausson took an immediate liking to each other. Chausson was already at work on *Le Roi Arthus*, the opera which he did not live to see performed, and Debussy was similarly engaged on his *Pelléas et Mélisande*. Chausson himself, after his early settings of Leconte de Lisle (*Nanny* and *Le Colibri*), and Théophile Gautier (*Les Papillons*) was at this time busy, like Debussy, with texts by Maurice Maeterlinck, which were to appear in the volume of *Serres chaudes*. Maurice Bouchor's *Poème de l'amour et de la mer*, finished in 1892, was an ambitious combination of narrative and lyric, cyclic in form and with an orchestral accompaniment which shows Chausson less at home with the orchestra than in his Symphony in B flat. This was the chief and most characteristic fruit of his three years study with Franck, lively and genuinely symphonic in character but showing something of the stiffness and obedience to (Franckist) convention in its form, which is cyclic. The agonies through which he went in writing this work, and particularly the finale (which is the least satisfactory movement) are described in the correspondance with his brother-in-law Henri Lerolle.

Chausson's discontent with his own music is well expressed in his correspondence with Debussy, who spent much of the summer of 1893 staying with the Chaussons at Luzancy, where they had rented a house. The close and frank-speaking friendship between the two, further cemented by Chausson's characteristic generosity towards a younger colleague often hard pressed for money, was continued during the autumn. Debussy criticises Chausson for his preoccupation with the inner parts of his music, 'something into which we have been led by R. Wagner, so that we think too much of the frame before making certain of the picture'. Other, less friendly disposed critics have spoken of the 'endlessly elegiac atmosphere' of Chausson's music; and this is a valid criticism. The narrowness of emotional range may be explained partly by the too careful upbringing of a sensitive, naturally introspective boy, and the thick textures by the instinct of a man well aware that he might be dismissed as a rich amateur to show his professional ability in complexities not always suited to the simple lyrical nature of his musical ideas. Like all Franck's pupils Chausson also suffered from the standard of 'high seriousness' set by the master and his powerful successor d'Indy, acknowledged as chief of a musical party determined to raise the standard of French music and to compel the public to abandon their hitherto exclusive interest in opera and to interest themselves in symphonic and chamber music. In fact Chausson as a composer was in many ways the victim of his own high-mindedness, and he was chagrined to find that as a musical innovator he was left far behind by his younger colleague and friend. The relationship between him and Debussy as artists has been well compared to that of Verlaine and Rimbaud, in every other way totally dissimilar characters.

In his work on *Le Roi Arthus* Chausson was repeatedly haunted by 'the red spectre of Wagner' or 'that frightful Wagner who is blocking all my paths'. He even shared Wagner's interest in Schopenhauer, a writer calculated to increase Chausson's innate tendency to melancholy and self-distrust. This in its turn was emphasised by the contrast with the easiness of his external existence.

> Good heavens [he wrote] I know only too well that I am what people call fortunate, almost frightfully so. And doubtless I should be too much so, were it not for this wretched, uneasy and violent brain of mine.

He finally completed *Le Roi Arthus* at Fiesole on Christmas Day 1895 and in the following year his Maeterlinck settings, *Serres chaudes* and *Quelques danses* for piano in July. But by far the most important composition of 1896, written in the comparatively short space of time between April and August, was his *Poème* for violin and orchestra. In October of the same year he was in Spain, where he met Granados and Ysaÿe, an old friend who gave the first private performance of *Poème*. Albéniz he already knew, and it was he who persuaded Breitkopf to publish *Poème*, which Ysaÿe played at Nancy in December 1896 and in Paris on the 4th April 1897. When the visiting Berlin Philharmonic Orchestra included his symphony in the programme of their guest-concert in Paris in May 1897 Chausson felt that he had at last established himself as a serious composer.

His increased self-confidence issued in two works, both of which had their first performance in 1898, a piano quartet and a tone-poem

Soir de fête. These and three songs, including *Chanson perpetuelle* with orchestral accompaniment, were Chausson's last compositions. Felix Mottl in Karlsruhe expressed a lively interest in *Le Roi Arthus* and prospects in Brussels were even brighter. In fact it was there, at the Théâtre de la Monnaie, that *Le Roi Arthus* was eventually given its first performance, on the 30th November 1903. But it was too late for Chausson, who was killed in a bicycling accident in 1899 while spending his summer holiday at his house at Limay, near Mantes. His fear of Wagner's overriding influence in the music of *Le Roi Arthus* proved justified in the event; and Chausson's masterpiece, in which his warm imagination, his idealism and the real nobility of his musical mind are most clearly revealed, remains the *Poème* which Ysaÿe played for the first time in London exactly a week after the composer's death.

M.C.

CHERUBINI, Luigi
(b. Florence, 14 Sept 1760,
d. Paris, 15 March 1842)

Maria Luigi Carlo Zenobio Salvatore Cherubini was born in Florence, the son of a musician, and showed an early gift for music. By the age of seventeen he had composed a number of works for the church, including three Masses, and it was on the strength of these that the then Grand Duke of Tuscany (the future Emperor Leopold II) sent him to study with Giuseppe Sarti in Venice. Sarti had already spent two spells of time as composer to the Danish Court in Copenhagen and was later to hold a similar appointment in St Petersburg. Cherubini studied with him while he was director of the Ospedaletto in Venice and seems to have worked exclusively at perfecting his mastery of the traditional contrapuntal style, so-called *alla Palestrina*, still in demand for ecclesiastical works. His first opera, *Quinto Fabio* (1780) was given at Alessandria and was followed two years later by three other pieces all given the same year (1782), one in Leghorn and two in his native Florence. An *opera buffa, Lo sposo di tre, marito di nessuna* was given in Venice (1783); and at the end of the following year, during which he produced *Idalide* (Florence) and *Alessandro nelle Indie* (Mantua), he went to London, where he wrote two *pasticcios* and two operas for the King's Theatre. During the

Portrait of Cherubini by Dubufe.

two years spent in London he attracted the attention of the Prince of Wales and held the post of Composer to the King (George III) for a short time. It was probably this position rather than the popularity of his music that won him an invitation in 1786 to visit Paris, where he stayed for a year; but it was in Italy that he produced his next two operas,(*Didone abbandonata*, Brescia 1786, *Ifigenia in Aulide*, Turin, 1788). The first work that he presented in Paris (December 1788) was *Démophoon*, with a libretto by Marmontel and in a style adapted to that of the prevailing French taste. This meant a cross between the severer, essentially cosmopolitan style of the mature Gluck and the overtly Italian, but still highly dramatic manner popularised by Piccinni and his successors in French favour, Salieri and Sacchini.

When Cherubini settled in Paris, where he was to remain for the rest of his life, he was still under thirty and France was on the very brink of revolution. In the circumstances it seems strange that the Théâtre de Monsieur, where Cherubini conducted an entirely Italian repertory for the next three years (1789–92), had been recently established in the Tuileries by Marie Antoinette's hairdresser Léonard; but the circumstance gives us a good idea of the connection between the Court and the Italian opera and of the similar social rating of

artists and Court servants. Cherubini, however, seems to have been at this period of his life an adaptable young man, for in 1791 he produced the first of a number of operas totally unlike the Metastasio settings of his early days and reflecting, however obliquely, the very different preoccupations of the revolutionary period. The first of these was *Lodokiska*, a 'rescue-opera' with a Polish setting, followed in 1800 by *Les deux Journées*, a *comédie-lyrique* in three acts by J. N. Bouilly, author of that *Léonore, ou l'amour conjugal* which Sonnleithner was to translate for Beethoven's *Fidelio*. The hero of *Les deux Journées* is a peasant, the water-carrier Mikéli, and Bouilly's text is full of priggish sentiments never, fortunately, common in the mouths of any social class.

> Si dans une obscure indigence
> Par le destin je fus jeté,
> Tâchons du moins qu'mon existence
> Soit util à l'humanité!

Mikéli's prosody denotes his social standing, which certainly contributed to the work's success. But the French public, to do them justice, were greatly impressed by Cherubini's new musical style, 'more expressive and more characteristic' than any that they had hitherto heard. Indeed anyone today hearing the overture to his *Démophoon* must immediately be struck by the similarity to the music of Beethoven, at that time (1788) a boy at Bonn; and Beethoven himself was not only greatly struck by Cherubini's music when he heard it in Vienna, but continued to the end of his life to name him as the greatest living opera composer.

Unfortunately for Cherubini Napoleon took a dislike to his unsmiling, perhaps rather schoolmasterly manner; and although he was appointed one of the three Inspecteurs des Études when the Conservatoire was founded in 1795, and married the same year, his life in Paris was complicated by shortness of money. An unexpected return to the world of Gluck, even to the *opera seria*, may well have shown where his own natural tastes continued to lie, and *Médée* (1797) is today regarded as his operatic masterpiece, best appreciated historically if it is remembered that it was written only six years after Mozart's *La Clemenza di Tito*.

The French Embassy in Vienna during the years when Bernadotte was ambassador was an important centre of French musical influence in Austria, and it was there that Beethoven made the acquaintance of the music of Méhul and Cherubini, both of whom he admired. In July 1805 Cherubini arrived in Vienna, where he was present not only at a performance of his own *Les deux Journées* (first given there in 1802) but also on the 20th November at the first performance of Beethoven's *Fidelio*. This was at the Kärntnerthor Theatre where, three months later, Cherubini's own *Faniska* had its first performance, the librettist being the same Sonnleithner who was responsible for the text of *Fidelio*. The two composers met, but seem to have found little in common, least of all perhaps a language that both could use with freedom. In any case war had broken out between Austria and France soon after Cherubini's arrival in Vienna, and on the 13th November 1805, French troops occupied the city. Cherubini found himself obliged to organise and conduct the musical *soirées* which Napoleon gave at Schönbrunn during his stay.

The visit to Vienna, which took place when he was forty-five, seems to have marked the end of a period in Cherubini's creative career. For almost ten years after his return to Paris from Vienna, he wrote comparatively little. An opera based on Rousseau's *Pygmalion* and written for Napoleon's private theatre (1809) and *Les Abencérages* (Opera, 1813) added little to his reputation. He was living in retirement at the château of the Prince de Chimay much of this time, and in 1809 he was persuaded to write a three-part Mass with orchestra for the consecration of a new church in the neighbourhood. This was the first of a number of works written during the next twenty-five years, in which he returned to the world of ecclesiastical music in which he had first distinguished himself, but with all the experience gained meanwhile in the theatre. The finest of these works are two Requiem Masses, in C minor (1817) and D minor, for men's voices only (1836). Cherubini, who had been made a Chevalier of the Légion d'honneur by Napoleon during the Hundred Days, felt much more at home under the Bourbon Restoration. Under Louis XVIII he became a Member of the Institut, musician and superintendent of the King's Chapel and, in 1822, Director of the Conservatoire. The Philharmonic Society of London had already honoured him in 1815 by commissioning a symphony, an overture and a vocal work; and during his long period as Director of the Conservatoire he wrote a number of string

quartets, one quintet, and a number of theoretical works. It was in these rather than in his last three operas (1814, 1821, 1833) that his real interests showed themselves.

Cherubini's portrait by Ingres certainly suggests the dry correctness of an academic establishment-figure, but his brusque and unsympathetic treatment of the young Berlioz and the revenge taken by Berlioz in his Memoirs cast a long and undeserved shadow over a composer who, though often unexpectedly frigid in his music for the theatre, proved himself a master of traditional style, a chaste melodist and, in his middle years, by no means unoriginal handler of harmony and orchestration.

M.C.

CHOPIN, Frédéric
(b. Zelazowa Wola, 1 March 1810; d. Paris, 17 Oct 1849)

Of modest vine-growing background in France, Chopin's father, Nicholas, went to Poland at sixteen, where after working in a tobacco factory and fighting with the National Guard he became tutor to various aristocratic families including the Skarbeks at Zelazowa Wola, one of whose poorer relations he eventually married before settling in Warsaw as French teacher at the Lyceum. Frédéric, second of their four children, was the only boy. From infancy he was acutely susceptible to music, and at seven started piano lessons with Adalbert Zywny, an all-round musician more interested in the classics than the modern virtuoso school. Ordinary lessons were done at home until thirteen, when Chopin entered the Lyceum. Boys who boarded at the Chopin household during term sometimes took him back for holidays on their country estates, where he heard Polish folk-music in its natural surroundings, and started to compose mazurkas and polonaises, as well as variations in the fashionable virtuoso style, all of which greatly enhanced his reputation as a *Wunderkind* when invited to play at Warsaw soirées. At sixteen he entered the newly founded Warsaw Conservatoire to continue composition lessons with its director, the Polish composer, Joseph Elsner who, with his passionate belief in the emergence of a Polish nationalist school allied to profound respect for classical tradition, was an ideal mentor.

Student days past, Chopin set out in the

pianist. But after two appearances early in 1832 he realised with dismay that his delicate style was not to everyone's liking in this city of leonine virtuosity, and would have embarked on a three-year course of technical study with Kalkbrenner but for ardent protests from his parents and Elsner. The situation was saved by an introduction to the wealthy Rothschild family, after which, with his natural elegance of behaviour and dress, he found himself eagerly sought after both to play at soirées and give lessons in the great houses of Paris. New studies, nocturnes and valses for these occasions followed in quick succession, besides many more nationally inspired mazurkas, polonaises and the G minor Ballade. 1835 brought a visit to Karlsbad for a blissful reunion with his parents, then to Dresden to renew acquaintance with his old Polish friends, the Wodzińskis, during which he and their young daughter, Maria, fell in love – and would have married in the course of the next few years had Maria's parents not refused consent because of Chopin's frequent ill-health.

Disconsolate for a time, Chopin was soon in the grips of a more disturbing problem occasioned by his meeting with the notorious, free-living novelist, George Sand, who in the course of 1837 wanted to become his mistress. Dreading gossip in Paris, Chopin eventually agreed to winter with her and her young son and daughter, under cover of reasons of health, on the island of Majorca. Arriving in November 1838, they were idyllically happy until the weather broke and Chopin became ill. With tuberculosis suspected, they were ordered out of their rented villa and compelled to stay in a deserted Carthusian monastery up in the mountains at Valldemosa, where cold, damp, malnutrition and general isolation reduced Chopin to critical weakness. Only an abrupt return to Marseilles and first-class medical care saved his life.

Despite everything, he nevertheless managed to complete his Twenty-four Preludes on Majorca, besides composing the dramatic Scherzo in C sharp minor and tragic Polonaise in C minor. The traumatic winter also left its mark on his Sonata in B flat minor (for which he unearthed an earlier funeral march as slow movement) written during the summer of 1839 at George Sand's country house at Nohant. By the autumn he was well enough to return to Paris, proclaiming his return in one or two recitals. But, hypersensitive as ever, it was not long before he decided only to play at

Chopin, 1826.

summer of 1829 to widen his horizons in Vienna. Introductions included one to the publisher, Haslinger, who agreed to publish his '*Là ci darem*' Variations provided he played them, without fee, at a public concert first. This work and the *Krakowiak* Rondo were enthusiastically enough received for Chopin to plan a much longer return visit. But back in Warsaw he fell in love with a singing student, Constantia Gladkowska. Too shy to declare his passion, he merely poured out his heart in music inspired by her and by Italian opera, including nocturnes and the F minor and E minor Piano Concertos, both of which he introduced to Warsaw before eventually tearing himself away in November 1830. This time the Viennese found him less of a novelty, and he grew disillusioned at their superficiality. So, after a period of acute anguish occasioned by the Polish uprising against the Russians, and his own conflict as to whether to return home to fight (an idea opposed by his family), he decided to make for Paris, eventually arriving at the end of September 1831.

With financial problems now acute, Chopin first tried to attract attention as a concert

Chopin playing for friends by Balestrière.

private soirées, including one performance at the Tuileries Palace for King Louis-Phillippe. Now able to command high fees as well as a private carriage to fetch and return him, he also resumed teaching again, with flexibility of the wrist, unconventional fingering if it aided agility, and beautiful *cantabile* as high priorities in his method. Though well known throughout Paris, he took absolutely no part in 'establishment' musical life. Living close to George Sand, though in a separate apartment for appearance's sake, he preferred the company of cultivated friends from all walks of artistic life, not least those of the Polish Literary Society, with whom he could dine, or visit the theatre or opera, as the mood took him. Every summer he would escape with George Sand to Nohant, where in country peace he devoted himself to composition with an ever-growing desire to strengthen his formal grasp and widen his harmonic vocabulary. The Fantaisie in F minor, the Barcarolle, the Polonaise-Fantaisie, the Sonata in B minor, and the last two Ballades in A flat and F minor all grew from these Nohant retreats. But the idyll was not to last. Like Prince Karol in George Sand's thinly disguised autobiographical novel, *Lucrezia Floriani*, Chopin grew increasingly possessive and moody as her own physical desire waned. With her resentful son and turbulent daughter taking sides in an already faction-ridden household, tension reached breaking-point during 1847. From then on Chopin and George Sand went their separate ways, too proud to speak the healing words for which both secretly longed.

When revolution broke out in Paris early in 1848, Chopin was glad enough to come to London at the invitation of a fond Scottish pupil of forty-four. But despite elegant apartments and immediate acclaim in the highest artistic and aristocratic circles, he was neither happy nor strong enough to make a determined new start. The same was true in the autumn when Jane Stirling, increasingly embarrassing him with a love he could not reciprocate, took him to Scotland to the stately homes of her various relations, in the hope that, as at Nohant, he might work. But, though forcing himself to give a few fund-raising recitals, he was totally unable to compose. As he wrote to an old friend: 'You and I are a couple of old cembalos on which time and circumstances have played out their miserable trills . . . In clumsy hands we cannot give forth new sounds and we stifle within ourselves those things which no one will ever draw from us, and all for lack of a repairer.' Wholly exhausted, he returned to Paris in November 1848. Barely eleven months later he was dead. At his funeral on the 30th October 1849, at the Madeleine, Mozart's *Requiem* was sung, as he had requested; his body was then taken to the cemetery of Père Lachaise.

Except for 17 Polish songs, a piano trio plus a 'cello sonata and a few miniatures for 'cello, Chopin devoted his whole life to enriching the keyboard repertory. Even early sets of vari-

ations and other juvenilia written before leaving Poland have a poetic delicacy and aristocratic finesse of style distinguishing them from the bravura products of the day he used as models. Though sensuous beauty of sound remained a constant ideal, not least in exquisitely embellished Italianate *bel canto* melody, his harmonic idiom grew increasingly chromatic and exploratory over the years.

The only known photograph of Chopin.

Manuscript of the A flat major polonaise by Chopin.

telling. Like Bach and Mozart, whose formal perfection he so much admired, he dissolved every motivating emotion into pure music. Much as he disappointed Elsner by never essaying large-scale nationalist opera, no Pole in history has given more potent voice to racial aspiration. Without a trace of self-conscious, virtuoso flamboyance, he also opened up a whole new world of magical sonority at the keyboard itself. His genius lay in transforming the miniature into great art.

J.O.C.

CILÈA, Francesco
(b. Palmi, 26 July 1866;
d. Verazza, 20 Nov 1950)

It is appropriate that the tender-hearted Cilèa should remain world famous for his *Adriana Lecouvreur*, an opera of delicate sentiment and refined lyricism. The son of a lawyer, he was devoted to music as a child but lacked the force of character to have made his own way. He was fortunately given the necessary encouragement by Francesco Florimo, the friend of Verdi and an influential official of the Naples Conservatoire. His first opera, *Gina*, produced in 1889 towards the end of his student days in Naples, was so highly regarded that he was commissioned to write *La Tilda* for the Teatro Pagliano, Florence, in 1892. The success of these early operas in no way persuaded him to forsake the piano, on which his studies had been concentrated, and he continued to compose prolifically for this instrument. Then in 1897 his opera *L'Arlesiana*, based on the play by Alphonse Daudet, was premièred in Milan, giving the tenor Enrico Caruso his first important success. In the meantime Cilèa had been appointed Professor of Composition at the Reale Istituto Musicale in Florence, enjoying the first taste of academic life that suited his character so well.

Five years after *L'Arlesiana* Cilèa produced the masterpiece which was quickly to become popular all over the world, *Adriana Lecouvreur*. The play by Scribe and Legouve on which the opera is based flagrantly misrepresents the true story of the actress Adrienne Lecouvreur and her ruthlessly ambitious lover Maurice, Comte de Saxe. Adrienne, one of the most distinguished of French tragediennes, reigned for thirteen years as undisputed queen of the Comédie Française, numbering among

Within his own architecturally limited orbit, he also matured to a remarkable degree as a craftsman, hiding seams and developing his themes into longer and more continuous arguments, as notably in the last two, freely self-generating ballades. While a subjective romantic to the core, he abhorred overt story-

her friends half of Louis XV's court and notable men of letters including Voltaire. When she died at the age of thirty-eight it was rumoured, with no real foundation, that she had been poisoned by one of the Comte's other mistresses. The play sentimentalises her character and that of the Comte, and makes a posy of poisoned violets the cause of her death. This romantic treatment of Adrienne's life was tailor-made for Cilèa's individual style, and he wrote exquisitely poignant music for his heroine, the melting melody of her aria 'Io son l'umile ancella' (in which she declares that as an actress she is the servant of the arts) haunting the whole opera. The entire score is constructed with rare ingenuity, providing an endless flow of melody with a highly personal flavour.

Although Cilèa was only thirty-six when he achieved the height of success with *Adriana Lecouvreur*, and was to live another forty-eight years, he composed only one more opera, *Gloria* (1907). He seems to have realised he was not made of sufficiently stern stuff for a career in the turbulent world of opera, choosing instead to take up a succession of professorial appointments and turn his creative talents to chamber and orchestral music. The irony of his life was that he achieved immortality while comparatively young and in return gave immortality to an early 18th-century actress whose name would otherwise be known today only to theatre historians.

F.G.B.

CIMAROSA, Domenico
(b. Aversa, 17 Dec 1749;
d. Venice, 11 Jan 1801)

Although he was born into a very poor family Cimarosa studied in Naples under the finest teachers and scored an immediate success at the age of twenty-two with his first opera, *Le stravaganze del conte*. For the next fifteen years he divided his time between Naples and Rome, composing operas for both cities which were quickly taken up by London, Paris, Vienna and other important centres. Talented, industrious and charming, he won popular success easily and wore it just as lightly. *Opera buffa* was his speciality, for his music bubbles with simple, natural inventiveness, and while its chief attraction lies in the vocal writing the orchestra is always deftly and delicately handled. He quickly became a rival of Paisiello, hitherto Italy's undisputed king of

opera buffa, and the fortunes of the two men were to run parallel courses, though Cimarosa's life was to be much the shorter.

Following in Paisiello's footsteps, Cimarosa left his native Italy in 1787 to become court composer to Catherine II in St Petersburg, where he spent four profitable years writing cantatas and instrumental works in addition to two further operas. His next call came from Vienna, Leopold II offering him the position of *Kapellmeister* to the Austrian court. It was at the Burgtheater in Vienna on the 7th February 1792 that his most enduring work, *Il matrimonio segreto*, was first performed. So sensational was its reception that the Emperor invited all the participants to supper and then commanded a repeat performance of the entire opera. Later in the same year, however, Leopold died, and Cimarosa's conquest of Vienna came to an end with the re-instatement of Salieri as *Kapellmeister*. The silver lining for Cimarosa was the enthusiastic reception he received on his return to Naples, where *Il matrimonio segreto* was given an unbroken run of fifty-seven performances and he was made *maestro di cappella* to the autocratic Ferdinand and music teacher of the princesses. A stream of successful comic operas and less successful serious ones flowed smoothly from his pen, but in 1799 he met his downfall through his sense of social justice. When the French republican army marched into Naples to free the people from the savagery of Ferdinand's rule, Cimarosa made no secret of his revolutionary enthusiasm. A few months later the odious Ferdinand, with the shameful collaboration of Lord Nelson, recaptured his throne and wreaked barbaric vengeance on those who had briefly overthrown him. Only his fame and popularity saved Cimarosa from the executioner: after a period of imprisonment he left Naples for St Petersburg but died in Venice on the first leg of his journey.

History has relegated Cimarosa to minor status because while his music reminds the listener now of Mozart, now of Rossini, it lacks the expressive grace of the former and the glittering panache of the latter. Yet he deserves respect if only for the two charming works which are still revived from time to time: *Il matrimonio segreto*, which influenced *opera buffa* through Rossini and Donizetti up to Verdi's *Falstaff*, and the hilarious one-man show *Il maestro di cappella*.

F.G.B.

COPLAND, Aaron
(b. New York, 14 Nov 1900)

It is arguable that Aaron Copland is the most considerable of American composers to have emerged so far. Whether this means that posterity will regard him as the first great American composer is another matter; it is a question upon which the music departments of most American universities have failed to reach agreement.

Copland's parents were Russian Jews who emigrated to America; the emigration authorities mis-spelt their name, Kaplan – and Copland it remained. His father Harris Copland ran a Brooklyn department store; so the family were comfortably middle-class. None of them cared greatly for music. Aaron came into the world on the 14th November 1900, and grew up in the tough, fast-moving New York that is portrayed in the novels of Dos Passos. His sister Laurine studied the piano, and when Aaron was eleven, he made the discovery that he loved music and would like to be a musician. He began to study harmony and composition with Rubin Goldmark – nephew of the composer – in 1917, and by the age of twenty-one, had scraped together enough money to go to Paris to become Nadia Boulanger's first American pupil. When he returned to America in 1924, he had been thoroughly inoculated with 'modernism'. A Symphony for Organ and Orchestra was conducted by Walter Damrosch in New York in January 1925, and Damrosch remarked flippantly to the audience: 'If a young man at twenty-three can write a symphony like that, in five years time he'll be ready to commit murder.' Critics seemed to regard Copland as a sort of American Prokoviev, chaotic, deafening, bewildering. Jazz influences were heard in *Music For Theatre* (1925) and the Piano Concerto (1926). The Piano Variations of 1930 have been described as a masterpiece; they are also percussive and 'difficult', and convinced Copland's few admirers that he was to pass into realms of non-melodic intellectualism. A *Dance Symphony*, thrown together quickly from an unfinished ballet, *Grohg*, won him a $5,000 prize in 1929; to modern ears, it has a joyful rhythmic vitality that is characteristic of some of his most popular later works. A *Short Symphony* (1931–3), now regarded as one of his finest works, was considered at the time to be too rhythmically complex.

Some time in the mid-1930s, Copland began to worry about the relation between the composer and the public. There had been a

Aaron Copland.

time when audiences rushed to hear the latest symphony, opera or oratorio by a favourite composer; now the best a modern composer can hope for is a clique of academic admirers. Could a modern composer 'reach' a wide audience without cheapening his music? In Copland's case, the answer was yes, for he was a romantic who felt that American music ought to try to express the essence of America. And so a 'difficult' work, *Statements*, was followed by the first of Copland's 'popular' works, *El Salón México*, portraying a smoke-filled dance hall. Its success was immediate. Other 'American' works followed: the ballet *Billy the Kid* (1938), the popular *Outdoor Overture* (1938), *Quiet City* (a suite drawn from his incidental music to a film *The City*), *Rodeo* (1942) – another ballet – and *A Lincoln Portrait* for narrator and orchestra (1942). In 1937 he had also composed an opera for schoolchildren, *The Second Hurricane*, and his music for the film *The Red Pony* was later arranged as a Children's Suite.

By the mid-1940s, Copland was beginning to give the impression of a versatile but rather light-weight composer; his output seemed to lack 'major' works. The ballet, *Appalachian Spring*, which appeared in 1945, seemed to be a step in the right direction; it was thoroughly American, and had a feeling of almost symphonic breadth. It won the Pulitzer Prize and the award of the New York Music Critics. The following year saw the first performance of his longest orchestral work, the Third Symphony, described by Serge Koussevitsky (who commissioned it) as 'the greatest American symphony – it goes from the heart to the heart'. This again won the award of the New York Music Critics. Like so much of Copland's music, the Third Symphony gives the impression of being 'about America'; the first movement might be a description of a kind of glider-flight across the American continent, moving with a Bruckner-like feeling of leisure. The second has a drive reminiscent of Prokoviev. Yet finally, one is inclined to doubt whether this music has sufficient stature to be judged a 'great symphony'. It is attractive rather than impressive. The same comment applies to his other extended work, the opera *The Tender Land* (1954); although it contains some fine music, one gets the final impression that he is too determined to be popular and lyrical and folksy, and falls somewhere midway between opera and the Broadway musical.

On the other hand, two song cycles contain some of the best of Copland. *Twelve Poems of Emily Dickinson* (1949–50) match her bareness and integrity with music that is at once subtle and brilliant. The two-part cycle of *Old American Songs* for voice and piano (1950–2) is completely irresistible in its orchestral version, one of those works that makes an impact on first hearing, yet somehow remains fresh and delightful when one knows every note. Some of its themes are used in the Third Symphony.

Recent years have seen a return to 'difficult' music, with works like *Connotations* (1961–2) and *Inscape* (1967). Now in his mid-seventies, Copland remains best known to the general public for *An Outdoor Overture, Billy the Kid* and *Appalachian Spring*. What emerges basically from his music is a gentle and lovable personality, unashamed of his romanticism. One can imagine that, under different circumstances, he might have settled in Hollywood – like Erich Korngold – and been perfectly happy writing film scores. He seems to have a

natural power of evoking 'the great outdoors'. His final importance may well be that, together with Gershwin, he is the most typically American composer that his country has so far produced.

C.W.

CORELLI, Arcangelo
(b. Fusignano, 17 Feb 1653; d. Rome, 8 Jan 1713)

Corelli was born at Fusignano, a small but ancient town about halfway between Bologna and Ravenna, on the rich plain of the Romagna. His family was one of the best known in the region, among them being lawyers and doctors rich enough to endow a number of churches and to play a notable part in local politics. They seem to have had no tradition of music, and it is a puzzle why Arcangelo should have taken up the art; yet it is clear that his talent revealed itself at an early age. Although his father died before he was born, the family circumstances were comfortable enough, and they sent Arcangelo to study with a priest at the nearby town of Faenza, and then at another, Lugo. From there he went, at the age of about thirteen to Bologna, at that time a musical centre of some consequence, with a great many good instrumentalists who had banded themselves into an Accademia Filarmonica, which was virtually an excellent orchestra. Corelli was admitted to this body in 1670, and later in life he liked to acknowledge himself as a real Bolognese on the title pages of his publications.

It is not known what happened in the next few years but by 1675 he was in Rome, where his fame was to be assured. He may have begun his life there as a theatre violinist; certainly he played in the ensemble of the church of S Luigi dei Francesi on the days of its patron saint, when the gentry were strongly in evidence at High Mass and first Vespers. Starting as a back desk player, he gradually worked himself up to lead the orchestra, and by 1679 he was also directing the orchestra at the Teatro Capranica, apparently earning substantial fees. The seal was set on his reputation by the publication of his Opus 1, a set of trio sonatas, in 1681, dedicating it to one of the most important of Roman patrons, Queen Christina of Sweden, who was also a keen attender at the celebrations of the saint's day at S Luigi dei Francesi; and Corelli directed the music for a grand festival organised by her

Corelli by Howard.

when James II of England sent an emissary to negotiate the (abortive) return of Britain to the Catholic faith in 1687. In that year, he became music master to Cardinal Panfili, in whose palazzo he lived, along with his favourite pupil and a man servant.

By this time he was receiving offers from elsewhere, notably Modena, not very far from his native country and he may even have visited the court there for a short time. Nevertheless, the accession of Alexander VIII to the papacy in 1689, meant that Alexander's nephew, Pietro Ottoboni, became a rich cardinal and could indulge his obsession with music on a more than ample scale. He immediately engaged Corelli to

direct the music of his household, which included a series of Monday concerts famous throughout Italy. Pupils indeed came from as far away as England, since Lord Edgecumbe studied with him and commissioned a portrait; while the nephew of Samuel Pepys, heard him delightedly at a Christmas Eve Mass in 1699. He was honoured by being admitted to the exclusive Accademia dei Arcadi, which included Alessandro Scarlatti and Bernardo Pasquini among its members.

By this period his fame as a composer was at its height. He had published four books of trio sonatas in the years up to 1694 and in 1700 a set of sonatas for solo violin and continuo appeared. Their influence was enormous, and indeed this corpus formed the basic repertoire of the violinists of the next generation, notably Locatelli, Geminiani, Dubourg (Handel's leader for operas and oratorios) and Castrucci. Nevertheless, it seems that in his later years, the younger virtuosi outpassed him in both technique and stylistic knowledge. About 1701 he visited Naples, to be astonished that the players of the royal orchestra could read his concertos at sight almost as well as his own orchestra in Rome could play them after rehearsing, and on the same visit, a passage in a masque by A. Scarlatti which went up to a high F proved too difficult for him – but not for the local leader! There is also the famous story told by Handel's biographer, John Mainwaring, which tells that Corelli, leading the orchestra in the overture to the German's oratorio *The Triumph of Time*, annoyed him so much that Handel snatched the violin from Corelli's hands to show him how it went: to which Corelli replied, 'But, my dear Saxon, this music is in the French style, which I do not understand.' The French style involved double dotting and *notes inégales*, and was now common throughout Europe (Bach frequently used it), so this suggests a by now insular attitude on Corelli's part.

Nevertheless, when an ill-founded rumour circulated in 1708 that he had died, he was mourned by no less a person than one of the Electors of the Holy Roman Emperors. He gave up playing in public about 1710, and two years later became seriously ill. In January 1713, he made his last will, and died on the night of the 8th of that month. He was widely mourned, his patron Cardinal Ottoboni ordering that he should be placed in a triple bier of lead, cypress and chestnut wood and laid in a tomb of marble in the church of the Rotunda in Rome (today known by its former title, the Pantheon). He died a relatively rich man, with a capital of about £6,000 (a substantial sum in the 18th century – according to the estimates of Burney – and a collection of over one hundred paintings, including a Breughel and some landscapes by Poussin. One of his violins may have been a Stradivarius, and he also owned an 'old violoncello', a two-manual harpsichord and a violone. He also left the Concertos of Op. 6 to be published by a pupil, Fornari, and these, his most famous works, were issued in 1714. His compositions were among the most popular of the 18th century and continued in the repertoire, especially in England, for over seventy years.

D.A.

COUPERIN, François
(b. Paris, 10 Nov 1668;
d. Paris, 12 Sept 1733)

Couperin was born into a family in which three brothers in the previous generation – his father and two uncles – had made names for themselves in the musical world. His father died when he was eleven, and although François inherited his father's post as organist of Saint Gervais, Lalande acted as deputy until the boy reached the age of eighteen. In the meantime his musical education, begun by his father, was continued by his uncle François and by Jacques Thomelin, organist of the Chapel Royal. Thomelin was a composer of the old school and it was to him that the young Couperin owed his skill in counterpoint. In 1693 Couperin was chosen by Louis XIV to succeed Thomelin at the Chapel Royal, for although only twenty-five he had already made his name in the musical world. His first organ Masses had not been printed despite the granting of a royal privilege, but Couperin had manuscript copies made with an engraved title-page bearing a 'certificate of merit' from Lalande. This was music in the traditional style, but in 1692 he launched out on a venture which bore witness to his lively, enquiring turn of mind as well as his skill. Fired by the example of Corelli, he wrote a number of trio sonatas 'in the Italian style' and even (as he afterwards revealed) under an assumed Italian name. These were not published until 1726, when he revealed his authorship and his original ruse.

In the meantime Couperin had married, in 1689, Marie-Anne Ansault, who bore him a child in the following year. His duties at Ver-

sailles were shared with three other organists, each working for a three-monthly period, so that Couperin was able to retain his family post at Saint Gervais, which he did not in fact relinquish until 1723. His position at court was confirmed when he was appointed *Maître de Clavecin des Enfants de France* (1694), and this office coincided with Fénelon's period of royal tutorship. Although Couperin's prefaces and titles, and indeed his music, reveal a nice vein of sardonic humour, his ennoblement by the King gave him such pleasure that he designed a coat of arms for himself and a Lateran Order decoration enabled him to sign himself officially 'Le Chevalier Couperin'.

Although he was originally an organist by profession, the fact that the great organ at Versailles was not started until 1702 and not finished in his lifetime explains the virtual absence of organ music from Couperin's output. Officially Jean-Baptiste-Henri d'Anglebert was *Ordinaire de la Musique* at Versailles, having inherited the post from his more famous father in 1674 and retaining it until 1717. After 1700, however, when d'Anglebert's sight began to fail, Couperin was almost certainly in effective charge of the music, and the chamber and harpsichord music composed during the years 1690–1730 were probably all designed initially for the Versailles Concerts du Dimanche and incidental musical occasions at Court. The first to be published were the harpsichord pieces. These eventually took the form of four *Livres de clavecin*, containing between them twenty-seven *ordres*, or sets, each *ordre* containing anything from half a dozen to a dozen pieces. The first book was published in 1713 and the rest followed in 1717, 1722 and 1730. Some of these *ordres* show a certain unity of character, but each piece is given a title of some kind. Many are character-portraits, either general ('L'Evaporée', 'La Galante' or 'L'Enjouée) or particular ('La Princesse de Sens', 'La Montflambert'). There is a portrait-gallery of the virtues in 'Les Folies françoises' of Book 3, which also contains a number of bird-pieces. Some have general dance-titles; and a great many, perhaps the majority, have fantastic names whose allusions may have been topical and are certainly lost today ('Les Culbutes Jxcxbxnxs', 'La Divine Babiche', 'Le Petit-rien'). Probably the great part of these are deliberately fantastic and correspond to the scenes depicted by Couperin's younger contemporary Watteau, demanding no knowledge of contemporary society for their appreciation. Couperin's theoretical work, *L'Art de toucher le clavecin,* published in 1717, is an invaluable source of information on contemporary keyboard practice. The composer himself insisted that his harpsichord music must be played exactly as it is written.

> It is by no means permissible to add whatever embellishments one pleases [he wrote]. I declare that my pieces must be played as they are marked and that they will never make their impression on people of true taste unless all that I have noted is observed to the letter, with nothing added and nothing omitted.

Taken as a whole Couperin's harpsichord pieces present an extraordinarily rich and varied musical picture of French character and life, not only at Court but in both town and countryside. The chamber music includes two sets of 'concerts' published in 1722 and 1724. Here the instrumentation is not specified, but the *Apothéose de Lulli, Le Parnasse, ou l'Apothéose de Corelli* and *Les Nations,* published in 1725–6, are specifically for two violins and harpsichord continuo.

Louis XIV's dislike of long ecclesiastical ceremonies explains the absence from Couperin's work of large-scale settings of the Mass; but his *Leçons des Tenèbres,* written for the Holy Week ceremonies of the church, shows him as master of both the Italian and French vocal styles and furnishes an unmistakable proof that his powers were not confined to the witty, decorative or simply evocative delicacy of the miniature harpsichord-pieces. In his church motets his style contains elements of the solo cantata, as developed by Carissimi, and of the *sonata da chiesa.*

In 1715 Louis XIV died and two years later Couperin became official *Ordinaire de la Musique.* He still held his original post as *Maître de clavecin* to the royal family, and publication of his music continued steadily until 1730, when the last book of harpsichord pieces was published. In the preface to this the composer speaks of his daily diminishing health and his willingness to take the advice of his friends and retire from active life.

> I hope [he adds touchingly] that my family will find among my papers matter which will cause them to regret my death, if indeed such regrets are of any avail to us after death. We must at least cherish this notion

Couperin.

if we are to attempt to deserve that fancied immortality for which almost every man longs.

In 1723 he relinquished his post at Saint Gervais and seven years later gave up all his other offices. He died in 1733 at his handsome new house in the Rue Neuve des Bons Enfants; but although one of his three children, a daughter named Marguerite-Antoinette, was a musician able to take over her father's duties at Versailles until d'Anglebert died two years later, none concerned himself with the publication of the music referred to by the composer in the passage quoted above. Two suites for viols were not discovered until the present century, when they were published by Charles Bouvet.

M.C.

DEBUSSY, Claude
(b. Saint-Germain-en-Laye, 22 Aug 1862; d. Paris, 5 March 1918)

Claude Debussy was born above his parents' china shop where the family lived: he was named Achille-Claude and dropped the first of these names only after he grew up. Manuel

Debussy and his wife appear both to have been rather casual towards their children (the composer later referred to his father as *un vieux galvaudeux* or layabout, though not wholly without affection) but his aunt Clémentine, who kept a dress shop and enjoyed the protection of a wealthy man, Achille Arosa, took an interest in young Claude from the start, she and Arosa becoming his godparents. She went to live at Cannes, marrying in 1871; Debussy visited her there and it was in that southern resort that he received his first piano lessons in 1871. Further lessons followed with a Chopin disciple, Madame Mauté, in Paris.

In 1872, encouraged by Madame Mauté's belief in his future as a musician, Debussy entered the Paris Conservatoire. He was a strange shy boy, with an oddly bulging forehead which embarrassed him and which he tried to cover with his hair. But his teachers found him 'charming', with 'a truly artistic temperament'; while as a pianist capable of playing Chopin's Second Ballade at the age of twelve, he was considered as promising to be 'a virtuoso of the first order'. Later, though, his piano playing became less orthodox: it is odd to learn that this most refined of keyboard composers played 'heavily . . . he appeared to be in a rage with the instrument, puffing noisily in difficult passages.' Finally his sympathetic teacher Marmontel had to conclude, 'He doesn't care much for the piano – but he does love music'.

From about 1876 Debussy had been composing songs mainly, but also pieces for piano, violin and 'cello; but he continued with the piano and was able to earn a little money by playing. In 1880, indeed, he secured a post as pianist in the household of Nadezhda von Meck, Tchaikovsky's wealthy patroness, accompanying her to Switzerland, Italy and finally Moscow. Another patroness, Madame Wilson-Pelouze, together with a young theory teacher called Lavignac, brought him into contact with Wagner's music, and in 1888, with Madame Pelouze, he was to hear *Parsifal* and *Meistersinger* at Bayreuth. But the influence of Russian composers from the von Meck period – Borodin, Rimsky-Korsakov and of course Tchaikovsky – was also important, that of the latter composer perhaps especially in the delicately passionate songs

Photograph of Debussy taken by his wife in 1910.

which belong to this time, including settings of Verlaine. It was in the performance of songs and violin pieces that he made his first public appearance as a composer, on the 12th May 1882: the singer on that occasion, Madame Vasnier, was perhaps the first woman with whom he fell in love. His nature was always strongly sensuous; however, in this particular case no physical relationship has been proved.

In 1884 Debussy won the coveted Prix de Rome for composition with his cantata *L'Enfant prodigue*: It was a triumph of self-discipline for such an un-academic artist: he had schooled himself to write fugues and choral exercises for the preliminary stages of the competition, and even the cantata itself was in a 'safe' style compared to other music he was composing. He left for the prescribed period of residence in Rome early in 1885. He quickly became homesick for Paris, but he composed in Italy and he met and played to Liszt; he also heard Liszt play and liked his subtle pedalling. He enjoyed the music of Lassus and Palestrina which he heard at Liszt's suggestion, austerely visionary religious pieces whose spirit was echoed much later in his piano piece called *The Submerged Cathedral* and his *Saint-Sébastien* incidental music.

Returning to Paris in 1887, Debussy lived with his parents, though they showed some disappointment at their supposedly brilliant son's failure to bring them affluence. He continued a self-educating process, reading extensively and closely associating himself with the growing Wagnerian cult, visiting Bayreuth as well as attending several performances of the operas in Paris. In time, however, he began to react against this influence, so strong that it restricted the growth of many otherwise promising talents. Firstly he decided that Wagner was not 'the birth of a new music'; then he became 'the ghost of old Klingsor . . . the old poisoner'. Even so, *Parsifal* remained a work to which he responded all his life, 'one of the most beautiful monuments ever raised to music', and he once confessed to seeking in his own music to create 'an orchestral colour illuminated as from behind of which there are such wonderful effects in *Parsifal*'.

With his string quartet in 1893, and the *Prélude à l'Après-midi d'un Faune* for orchestra in the following year, Debussy began to reach a wider public at the same time as finding himself as a mature composer. At this time he was living with the green-eyed Gaby Dupont. Finally he left her and married Lilly

Texier in October 1899: they had already lived together and then separated, but suddenly he wished to marry her, threatening suicide if she refused. They moved to a small flat at 58 rue Cardinet; money was short and the composer gave a piano lesson on the wedding morning to pay for the reception. His marriage closely followed that of his nearest friend, the writer Pierre Louÿs, 'the friend I have loved the most'; they were pleased and amused by their new-found domesticity, leaving visiting cards at each other's homes. It looks as if Louÿs, who was wealthy, helped him financially; but his debts increased, and matters were made worse by his wife's poor health. Debussy's love life was plagued with misfortune; in 1904 Lilly attempted suicide when he left her for Emma Bardac, whom he eventually married in 1908 after his divorce and who was the mother of his only child, Claude-Emma, born in 1905.

In 1902 the opera *Pelléas et Mélisande* was produced in Paris: with its text by Maeterlinck, it had fascinated and occupied Debussy over a period of years; now it quickly won him admirers (as well as detractors) and even created a cult of '*debussysme*'. The quasi-bohemian artist whose development had been comparatively slow now received the Légion d'Honneur and was appointed to the advisory board of the Conservatoire. His second wife was well-off; but in any case, ironically, he was henceforth to be financially more stable through the practice of his profession. He was in demand abroad – in Belgium, Holland, England, Austria-Hungary and (in 1913) Russia, where he conducted his own music in Moscow and St Petersburg.

But from this time onwards his health gave him trouble; already in 1909 he suffered from frequent haemorrhages and people remarked on his morbidly sallow complexion. The outbreak of war in 1914 profoundly shocked him: first he could not compose, then he felt that he owed it to his country to do so. In 1915 he underwent an operation for cancer of the rectum. It was fairly successful, but for the rest of his life he had to use a colostomy device: no wonder that he described the act of dressing as like 'one of the twelve labours of Hercules'. Radium and morphine were administered. 'I wonder after all whether this illness isn't incurable,' he wrote, 'in which case I'd better be told. . . .' He was anxious to be reassured about the quality of his recent music, which included three instrumental sonatas and the piano études; but in October 1917 he wrote despairingly, 'Music has quite left me, and I have never forced anyone's love.' By the beginning of the following year he was confined to his room, where he died peacefully on the 25th March 1918: his young daughter wrote that he looked 'happy, oh so happy!' The Minister of Education was present at the funeral, but comparatively few of the composer's friends. A woman stood in a shop doorway in Montmartre and watched the cortège. 'It seems he was a musician', she said.

Debussy is usually called an impressionist composer, and the term links his work with painters like Monet (whose water pictures are akin to Debussy's *Reflets dans l'eau* for piano) and with the poetry of Mallarmé. Indeed it was Debussy's musical evocation of Mallarmé's *L'Après-midi d'un Faune* that helped to establish this style. Often the subjects which inspired him are pictorial and somehow elusive, so that he chose titles like *Brouillards* ('Mists'), *Nuages* ('Clouds'), *Cloches à travers les feuilles* ('Bells heard through the leaves') which are themselves poetic; more 'literary' titles include a *Puck's Dance* and *Homage to Mr Pickwick* which remind us of his attraction to English writers. Yet he remains one of the purest of all musicians. He went back to the mysterious sources of inspiration as few others have done; for him, music was not a mere language to be learned and used, but 'all colours and rhythms'. Preferring suggestion to direct statement, he explored the strange world of waking dreams. He trusted no 'lifeless rules invented by pedants': rather, it was his instinct that he followed, and in the process he brought into music a unique world of sensibility. Thus his music is never intellectual in the sense of elaborately contrived; indeed melody is an important feature always, and this has helped to make Debussy's work genuinely popular. He is perhaps the most subtly and profoundly influential of all the 20th century's composers so far; and his influence, which has reached to a remarkable extent into popular music, appears to be increasing today as musicians once again seek for the essential bases of their art.

C.H.

DELIBES, Léo

(b. Saint-Germain-du-Val, 21 Feb 1836; d. Paris, 16 Jan 1891)

Delibes entered the solfège class at the Paris Conservatoire at the age of twelve and obtained a first prize two years later. During his years as a student he sang in the choirs of several Paris churches, including the Madeleine; and when he was only seventeen he became organist of Saint-Pierre de Chaillot. This was the first of many organist's appointments which ended at Saint-Jean-Saint-François, where he held the post from 1862 to 1871. As a composer Delibes's most influential teacher at the Conservatoire was Adolphe Adam, composer of *Giselle,* and it was through Adam's recommendation that he obtained a post as accompanist at the Théâtre Lyrique in the same year (1853) that he became organist at Saint-Pierre de Chaillot. The Théâtre Lyrique had only been founded in 1851, but under Carvalho's two directorships (1856–60 and 1862–8) it became the most adventurous opera-giving theatre in Paris. While Delibes worked there (1853–63) the new operas given their first performance there included Gounod's *Le Médecin malgré lui, Philemon et Baucis* and *Faust* (*Mireille* and *Roméo et Juliette* were given during Carvalho's second directorship) and Bizet's *Les Pêcheurs de perles.*

Delibes was far from contented with his work as an accompanist, and he filled his time with composition of very varying kinds. During the ten years at the Théâtre Lyrique he wrote seven operettas, five of them for Offenbach's Bouffes Parisiens recently (1855) opened in rivalry with the Théâtre des Folies-Nouvelles, which performed Delibes' first essay of this kind, *Deux Sous de charbon* (1855). The titles of the works written for Offenbach's theatre are a good indication of their character. They include *Dix Demoiselles à marier* and *L'Omelette à la Follembûche.* Not content with this activity Delibes wrote a number of male-voice choruses and a Mass, no doubt for performance by his own parish choir. The traditions of the 18th century were still strong enough for this varied professional activity to be wholly natural. In 1863 Delibes moved from the Théâtre Lyrique to the Opéra, still as an accompanist, but two years later he became second chorus-master under Victor Massé, composer of the enormously popular *Les Noces de Jeannette* (1853), and his cantata *Alger* was performed. In fact his reputation as a composer was now high enough for him to be invited in 1866 to collaborate with one of the regular composers for the ballet, the Viennese-born Léon Minkus, in the score of a new ballet entitled *La Source.* Delibes' music for the second act

and the first scene of Act 3 was notably superior to Minkus's Act 1 and Act 3 scene 2. Minkus's future career lay chiefly in St Petersburg, where in 1869 he wrote the music for Petipa's *Don Quixote*, still in the Bolshoi repertory. Delibes, on the other hand was commissioned to write the complete score for *Coppélia* (1870), and this proved a masterpiece, not only in its rhythmic, 'plastic' and mimetic qualities but by the wealth of its melody, the elegance and inventiveness of the orchestration and the charm of the harmonies, by no means routine in character. Ten years later another ballet, *Sylvia,* confirmed his reputation as a composer for the ballet and was to exercise a notable influence on Tchaikovsky's ballet music and even (as in the trio section of the Valse of No. 5) on his symphonies. Tchaikovsky's statement of his perference for Delibes' music to that of Brahms was later to be reinforced by Stravinsky's inclusion of Delibes in his list of the great melodists, in contrast to Beethoven. If these judgments reflect in both cases a certain anti-Teutonic prejudice (and in Stravinsky's case a mischievous delight in shocking the received opinions of an uncritical public), they are not wholly frivolous.

As an opera composer Delibes was at first less successful. Both his *Jean de Nivelle* (1873) and *Le Roi l'a dit* (1880) were given at the Opéra Comique, but it was not until *Lakmé* (1883) that he scored an operatic success comparable to that of his ballet music. The scene of *Lakmé* is laid in India, and Delibes showed the skill and imagination in conjuring up an exotic atmosphere characteristic of the French composers of the day. Bizet's *Les Pêcheurs de perles*, which had been given at the Théâtre Lyrique when Delibes was accompanist there, was an excellent example, and it was followed by the 'Moorish' *Djamileh* (Opéra Comique, 1872) and three years later by *Carmen*. Delibes must have known both these works when he wrote *Lakmé*; and although he himself was not a composer of Bizet's calibre, the melodic charm of his music and his use of the orchestra show a natural gift and a workmanship of a high order. *Lakmé* is best known by the coloratura 'Bell Song' and Gerald's 'Fantaisie, aux divins mensonges', a fresh and unpretentious lyrical air worthy to stand beside the finest examples in the French repertory. But Delibes's skill and experience are admirably shown in the quintet 'Quand une femme est jolie' and his writing for the chorus, a field in which he had lifelong experience. The characterisation of the fanatical Nilakantha is excellently contrasted with that of the Anglo-Indian 'ladies' and their chaperone, the comic Mistress Bentson (Mrs Benson, presumably).

Neither the cantata *Alger* nor the later *La Mort d'Orphée* (1878) fulfilled Delibes' ambition to write a serious vocal work. As a songwriter, on the other hand, Delibes perfectly expressed a certain light-hearted gaiety unencumbered by the influence of either Italian opera or German *Lieder*. In his best songs, in fact – 'Les Filles de Cadix', 'Avril' or 'Chant de l'Almée' – he avoids Gounod's sentimentality and retains the rare quality of that most typically French form of the solo song, the *chansonette*. If in two of the three songs mentioned this French quality appears in an 'exotic' context, the same might be said of Bizet's 'Adieu de l'hôtesse arabe'. Two of Delibes' best known songs were written as incidental music for plays performed at the Comédie-Française – *Vieille Chanson* (Hugo's *Le Roi s'amuse*) and *Chanson de Barberine* (Musset's *Barberine*). His connection with the theatre was reinforced by his marriage in 1872 to the daughter of a former actress of the Comédie Française, Mademoiselle Denain. He was in many ways a characteristic, almost a 'stage' Frenchman of his day, as is borne out by the story of his attending a performance of *Parsifal* at Bayreuth. He looked forward, he said, to the second act because this brought 'les petites femmes', and they were always amusing. What, one wonders, would have been the reaction of Cosima, let alone the Master himself, to this deeply irreverent description of the Flower Maidens? Not only Delibes' personality but the varied and strictly professional character of his output recall the 18th-century musician, prepared to write a Mass, a ballet, an opera, an operetta, incidental music or drawing-room song to commission and never plaguing himself with questions of aesthetics or dreaming of assuming the priest-like attitude towards his work characteristic of the 19th-century composer.

M.C.

Poster for Lakmé *by Delibes.*

DELIUS, Frederick

(b. Bradford, 29 Jan 1862;
d. Grez-sur-Loing, 10 June 1934)

Delius was the son of a wealthy Prussian industrialist who had settled in Bradford, and was destined by his father for a similar career. Early travel in Europe (particularly in Scandinavia) instigated rebellion, and in 1882 Delius left home to assume control of an orange plantation in Florida. Here he experienced a kind of spiritual awakening crystallised in the form of the sound of close-harmony Negro singing wafting one summer night over the St John River; and Delius realised that music, not grapefruit, was to be his life. For a short time he studied with a local musician from whom he claimed to have learned more in the space of a few months than in the entire three years' systematic instruction at Leipzig which he subsequently undertook. Here, however, he met Grieg, and began to compose prolifically if unoriginally. From 1888 to 1897 he lived in Paris where his circle consisted more of painters, poets and writers (predominantly Scandinavian) than of musicians.

He married a painter, Jelka Rosen, and in 1897 settled permanently in Grez-sur-Loing, a tiny hamlet a few miles from Fontainebleau. For many years, however, he continued to travel widely in Europe and Scandinavia. Only as the composer approached the age of forty, did a definite musical personality begin to assert itself. The derivative water-colourist of the orchestral *Florida Suite*, the opera *Koanga* and a host of songs, orchestral pieces and chamber works (most of negligible interest) suddenly began to paint in oils: the orchestral *Paris – the Song of a Great City* (1899) *Appalachia* (1902) and the opera *A Village Romeo and Juliet* (1901) testify most strikingly to the new accession of creative power. Delius gained much valuable technical knowledge from a concert of his works given at his own expense in London in 1899, but his music began to gain a foothold in England only after the arrival upon the scene of Sir (then Mr) Thomas Beecham in 1907. Meanwhile Germany showed herself particularly receptive, and of the succession of masterworks which flowed from Delius' pen in this the happy prime of his life – *A Mass of Life* (1905), *Seadrift* (1903), *Brigg Fair* (1907), and *In a Summer Garden* (1908) – few failed to find ready performance and acclaim there.

The Deliuses spent the war years in England and Norway, and Delius's music began to grow increasingly Northern or Nordic in inspiration – *A Song of the High Hills* for orchestra and wordless chorus (1911), *Eventyr* for orchestra (1917), *Requiem* (1916) and *Arabesk* (1911) both for chorus and orchestra, and the opera *Fennimore and Gerda* (1910) after a novel by one of Delius's favourite authors, the Danish J. P. Jacobsen (who wrote *Arabesk* and also *Gurrelieder*). From the early 1920s his creative activities were brought gradually to a halt by the onset of blindness and general paralysis, the result of syphilis contracted in the 1890s. With the help of his wife and Percy Grainger he was able to complete the incidental score for the London production of Flecker's *Hassan* in 1920; but in 1928, though totally incapacitated, he was able to resume work through the medium of an extraordinary young Yorkshireman, Eric Fenby, who offered his services as amanuensis. In addition to realising a number of scores left in varying stages of completion (*A Song of Summer, Idyll, Cynara* and others) Fenby also enabled Delius to complete a substantial new work for double chorus and orchestra, the Whitman-inspired *Songs of Farewell* (1931). In 1929 Sir Thomas Beecham organised the first London festival entirely devoted to Delius's works (the second took place in 1946) with the composer in attendance. He died at his home in France but was later disinterred and re-buried in a South of England churchyard.

Delius was one of the few true cosmopolitans in music; many countries and cultures contributed to the making of him, but he never settled in or belonged to any. Rural France became his nominal base, but even here, and even in the heart of Paris where he bade farewell to his youth, he reverted constantly to those scenes which had critically influenced his spiritual development: America (*Appalachia*, the opera *Koanga* completed in 1897,) Norway, the country he loved best of all (*A Song of the High Hills*) the Yorkshire moors of his childhood (*Over the Hills and Far Away*, 1892; *North Country Sketches*, 1914). Although he produced a number of abstract works, particularly in later life (concertos for piano, violin, 'cello, violin and 'cello, three violin sonatas, one 'cello sonata) Delius's overriding

Delius by Augustus John, 1929.

preoccupation throughout his work is nature. He is the supreme poet of nature in her tranquillities; large-scale tone-poems such as *Brigg Fair* and *In a Summer Garden* no less than the exquisite miniatures *On Hearing the First Cuckoo in Spring* and *Summer Night on the River* (1911–12) or the two wordless choruses *To be sung of a summer night on the water* all reflect the idyllic situation of Grez-sur-Loing and the nearby Forest of Fontainebleau, haunts beloved of the Impressionist painters to whom Delius himself was greatly drawn. He has been categorised as a 'romantic of the Impressionist school'; his musical forbears were primarily Chopin, Grieg and Wagner, although less orthodox catalysts (Victorian hymnody and Negro folksong) are also identifiable. In all cases harmonic opulence is the common denominator, and Delius's harmonic language is personal to himself, though frequently imitated. In his literary loves too he was cosmopolitan: his favourites were Nietzsche (*Also sprach Zarathustra* was an all-conditioning influence on Delius's life and mind and the literary basis of his *Mass of Life*) Whitman whom he set in *Sea-drift* and the *Songs of Farewell*, and Jacobsen who has strong affinities with the Swiss Gottfried Keller, begetter of *A Village Romeo and Juliet*.

Delius was a wanderer in sequestered byways, one who had all the time in the world to 'stand and stare', and his was a refined and laser-keen sensibility. His harmonies and colours have been prostituted by many a commercial hack, but nothing can affect the staying-power of the prototype in which the soul of natural beauty and the terrible reality of its impermanence are life-enhancingly juxtaposed.

C.P.

DITTERSDORF, Carl Ditters von
(b. Vienna, 2 Nov 1739;
d. Neuhof, 24 Oct 1799)

Carl Ditters' father was a costumier to the court and the theatre in Danzig; the child Carl was given a good education and soon distinguished himself musically, sufficiently so to be taken up by the Prince Joseph Friedrich von Hildburghausen who engaged the boy for his orchestra. At the outbreak of the Seven Years War in 1758, the nineteen-year-old Ditters and the other members of the orchestra accompanied the Prince on his campaign. When peace came, Ditters attempted to leave the service of the Prince but was arrested and brought back. Later he was dismissed and supported himself by taking a number of engagements. He was befriended by Gluck with whom he travelled over the Alps to Venice. Back in Vienna, he became a friend of Haydn and entered the service of the Austrian Emperor Joseph II, but soon left when refused a rise in salary.

Ditters' next engagement was as *Kapellmeister* to the Bishop of Grosswardein whose palace was near Pressburg (now Bratislava). For the Bishop, Ditters composed a number of orchestral pieces and also oratorios and short operas. The Bishop's worldly life-style led to his being denounced to the Empress Maria Theresa, and this in turn led to his having to dismiss his orchestra. Ditters now set out upon a grand tour, but got only as far as Trieste where he fell in love with a disreputable ballerina from whose clutches his friends had to extricate him. Subsequently, he entered the service of the Prince Bishop of Breslau, which led to his appointment as Chief Forester in the Principality of Neisse. The Prince allowed him to restore a small theatre on his estate, and to collect a company of singers from Vienna, among them a soprano named Nicolini whom Ditters married.

In 1773, again with the help of the Prince, Ditters bought himself into the nobility and became Carl Ditters von Dittersdorf. He continued to compose for the Prince's orchestra and soon the standard of performance and of composition at the Prince's court became much admired. The outbreak of the war of the Bavarian Succession interrupted these activities, and Dittersdorf began now to compose for the public in Vienna. He was also in demand in Vienna as a performer, and it is known that on at least one occasion he participated in a string quartet whose other players were Haydn, Mozart, and the Bohemian composer Vanhal.

Between 1786 and 1791 Dittersdorf composed seven operas, six of which were staged in Vienna, the most popular being his comic opera *Doktor und Apotheke* which is still occasionally performed. Dittersdorf also wrote an autobiography which makes good reading, and in which he says of Mozart's music that 'hardly has the hearer grasped one beautiful thought, when another of greater fascination dispels the first, and this goes on throughout, so that in the end it is impossible to retain any one of these beautiful melodies'.

Dittersdorf's last years were spent in

poverty and ill-health, though he continued to compose operas and symphonies until the end of his life, and to work on his autobiography which was published posthumously in 1801.

C.O.

Variations on a Nursery Song (Op. 25) for piano and orchestra which has endured, and which is still performed in concert programmes throughout the world.

C.O.

DOHNÁNYI, Ernst von
(b. Pressburg [now Bratislava], 27 July 1877; d. New York, 11 Feb 1960)

Born into a Hungarian family in the Austro-Hungarian town of Pressburg, which is now Bratislava and Czechoslovakian, Dohnányi was destined from childhood for a life in music. His father, a professor of mathematics, was a good amateur 'cellist who encouraged his son to study music, and who placed him with the organist of the Pressburg cathedral for lessons in harmony as well as instruction in keyboard instruments. The young Dohnányi had already begun to compose when he left Pressburg at the age of seventeen to enrol at the Budapest Royal Academy of Music. His teacher there, Hans Koessler, also taught Bartók and Kodály. When Dohnányi left the Academy, it was to embark upon a career as a concert pianist, which he did, in Berlin and Vienna, with enormous and immediate success. He played only the Viennese classics, Mozart, Beethoven, Schubert and Brahms, and those who heard him felt convinced of the essential 'rightness' of his performances, in the way that a later generation responded to Otto Klemperer's interpretations of the Beethoven symphonies.

Dohnányi's concert career, however, came to an early end, when he decided to abandon it for teaching and composition. For ten years he taught at the Berlin Hochschule, then returned to Budapest where he became Director of the Academy where he had formerly studied. Though he did not retain this post for long, his life in his native Hungary continued to be one of administrative and public posts. He became the conductor of the Budapest Philharmonic Orchestra, and on his fiftieth birthday in 1927 was awarded a huge grant from the State. Later, he was appointed Director of the Hungarian Broadcasting Service. He survived changes of régime to become, in extreme old age, the Grand Old Man of Hungarian music.

As a composer, Dohnányi was much admired in his own lifetime and in his own country. Some of his early chamber and piano works were liked by Brahms, but it is only the

DONIZETTI, Gaetano
(b. Bergamo, 29 Nov 1797; d. Bergamo, 8 April 1848)

Donizetti came from a large family, his father being a tradesman in the provincial north Italian town of Bergamo, who became porter to the civic Monte di Pietà or pawnshop when Gaetano was eleven years old. There were six children, two of whom, Gaetano and his elder brother Giuseppe, took up musical careers. (Giuseppe became a bandsman in Napoleon's army, and ended his days as Chief of Music to the Ottoman Armies, with the title of Donizetti Pasha.) It seems most likely that the family moved to Bergamo from elsewhere in Lombardy sometime during the 18th century, and that there is no truth in the rather engaging story that Donizetti's grandfather was a Scottish soldier named Donald or Don Izett who drifted to Italy and italianised his name!

When the young Gaetano showed that he had some talent for music, his father allowed him to study at the local Musical Institute in Bergamo. Here he was especially fortunate to have as his first teacher, a distinguished composer, Johann Simon Mayr. Mayr, a Bavarian, was Professor of Composition at the Institute, and had composed a number of highly successful Italian operas, among them *Saffo* (1794), *Ginevra di Scozia* (1801) and *Alonso e Cora* (1803). The young Donizetti came under Mayr's influence, and was to admit his debt to the elder composer for the rest of his life. He was soon sufficiently advanced in his studies to be sent on to the Liceo Filarmonico in Bologna, to complete his studies under another famous teacher, Stanislao Mattei, a composer of church music and himself a pupil of Padre Martini. By the time he was twenty, Donizetti was back in Bergamo, uncertain how next to proceed. His father strongly urged him to take up an academic career, but unwilling to do so he began instead to compose music for a number of local societies, usually amateur. Several string quartets, as well as choral and instrumental pieces, were written at this time.

In 1818, at the age of twenty-one, Donizetti received his first operatic commission. This

Donizetti.

Teatro Argentina in Rome, and produced there in 1822, that Donizetti made his decisive breakthrough into the career of a full-time professional composer of opera, for *Zoraide* was acclaimed with great enthusiasm by its first Roman audiences. After the third performance, Donizetti and his leading tenor left the theatre in a carriage to the accompaniment of a loud military band along a route illuminated with torches in the composer's honour. Of the opera, the weekly *Notizie del giorno* wrote:

> A new and very happy hope is rising for the Italian musical theatre. The young maestro Gaetano Donizetti, a pupil of the most famous professors of music, has launched himself strongly in his *opera* truly *seria*, *Zoraide di Granata*. Unanimous, sincere, universal was the applause that he justly collected from the capacity audience, which decreed a triumph for his work. Every piece was received with particular pleasure.

Other critics praised Donizetti's fluent melodic gift, his knowledge of orchestration, and the confident manner in which he handled his ensembles. His name now became known to opera houses throughout Italy, and invitations to compose operas began to pour in. For the next few years, indeed for the remainder of his active professional life, he produced two, three or even four operas a year, many of them for the Teatro San Carlo in Naples, but others for Rome, Milan, Palermo, Florence, Venice, and in due course Vienna and Paris.

The twenty-six operas which Donizetti composed between *Zoraide di Granata* in 1822 and *Anna Bolena* in 1830 contain very few titles at all familiar to modern audiences. Attempts have been made to revive one or two in Italy, and occasionally elsewhere, but the works themselves have failed to stay alive. It seems safe to say that *Anna Bolena* is the earliest Donizetti opera likely to be encountered in major opera houses today, though small theatres and festivals have been known to mount such works as *L'aio nell' imbarazzo*, *Il borgomastro di Saardam* and *Le convenienze ed inconvenienze teatrali*.

In 1830, the prolific Donizetti composed five operas, of which *Anna Bolena*, based on a libretto by Romani about Henry VIII, Anne Boleyn and Jane Seymour, was the last. Produced in Milan in December of that year, it immediately made Donizetti's name internationally famous. He was able to write to his wife, whom he had married in 1828, that the opera had been given 'a reception which could

came from Paolo Zancla, an impresario who was visiting Bergamo with a touring opera company, and who required a new work for his season at the Teatro San Luca in Venice. To a libretto written for him by his friend and fellow student Bartolomeo Merelli (who was later to become a famous impresario), Donizetti composed an opera, *Enrico di Borgogna*, which, if not an unalloyed triumph in Venice, was at least sufficiently appreciated by its audiences for Zancla subsequently to commission a one-act farce with music by Merelli and Donizetti. This was performed the following month, after which Donizetti returned to Bergamo and to the composition of a great deal of miscellaneous music for various occasions, as well as operas, for he now began to receive commissions from theatres as a result of the Venice operas. It was with one of these, *Zoraide di Granata*, commissioned by the

not possibly have been improved upon. Success, triumph, delirium.' His younger contemporary Bellini had already made his international reputation, and now Italy had a second composer to represent her abroad. *Anna Bolena* was produced in London, Paris, Madrid, Vienna and elsewhere in the following two or three seasons, and for many years to come was regarded as its composer's masterpiece. In London, the bass Lablache had one of his greatest successes as Henry VIII. Among the opera's most enthusiastic admirers was the great republican leader Giuseppe Mazzini, who wrote of it:

The individuality of the characters, so barbarously neglected by the servile imitators of Rossini's lyricism, is painted with rare energy and religiously observed in many of Donizetti's works. Who has not felt in the musical expression of Henry VIII the severe, tyrannical, and artificial language required by the story at that point? And when Lablache fulminates these words: 'Salirà d'Inghilterra sul trono/Altra donna più degna d'affetto' (There will come to the throne of England another woman more worthy of affection), who has not felt his spirit shrink, who has not understood all of tyranny in that moment, who has not seen all the trickery of that Court, which has shown that Anne Boleyn will die? And Anne, furthermore, is the chosen victim, whom the libretto – and history too, whatever others may say – depicts. Her song is a swan song that foresees death, the song of a tired person touched by a sweet memory of love.

Donizetti had now proved himself an all-round composer, as willing to compose farce and *opera buffa* as he was to provide those romantic operas, often on historical subjects, which were enormously popular. His next four operas, three of them written for Naples and one for Milan, include nothing which was able to equal the success of *Anna Bolena*. But in 1832, for the Teatro della Canobbiana, Milan, he composed an opera to a libretto by Romani which was based on a French comedy, *Le Philtre* by Eugène Scribe. This was *L'Elisir d'amore*, which remains to this day one of the most enchanting operas of its kind. Though a comedy, it is not enfeebled by the kind of stock patter music which, it must be confessed, Donizetti was inclined to churn out by the yard in some of his comic operas. The essence of *L'Elisir d'amore* is its warm-hearted melodic generosity. Its characters are credible, and their feelings easy to sympathise with. Even the gullible villagers who listen entranced while the literate heroine reads them the story of Tristan and Isolde, and who queue up to purchase the quack Dulcamara's remedy for all ills, are affectionate caricatures not entirely divorced from reality. Donizetti's gift for romantic and expressive melody was given full play in *L'Elisir d'amore*, and it is hardly surprising that the opera was an immediate success. The *Gazzetta privilegiata di Milano* wrote enthusiastically, 'Everything is beautiful, very beautiful, and was well applauded. To say which number is better than another is not an easy task.' And Donizetti wrote to his old teacher Mayr, 'The *Gazzetta* reviews *L'Elisir d'amore* and says too many good things; too many, believe me, too many!'

Though Donizetti was only thirty-five, he had now composed forty operas. He was never to relax his manic pace of composition, but it is just possible to discern that rather more care was taken with the composition of those from *L'Elisir d'amore* onwards. Certainly, the proportion of successes to failures is higher after 1832. There are, it is true, excellent operas by Donizetti which have not yet come back into the repertoire, but it is unlikely that they include any of those he composed in the 1820s.

Immediately after *L'Elisir d'amore*, Donizetti composed a bloodthirsty melodrama of suicide and attempted filicide, called *Sancia di Castiglia*, which was received with great enthusiasm at its first performance in Naples, the composer and his singers being repeatedly called out and cheered. But the initial enthusiasm soon waned, and eventually *Sancia di Castiglia* disappeared completely from view. Eight weeks after its première, another new Donizetti opera reached the stage, this time in Rome. The opera, *Il furioso all' isola di San Domingo*, based on an episode in Cervantes's *Don Quixote*, was a success: although it has not so far surfaced in the Donizetti revival of the past fifteen years, it is probably well worth the consideration of an enterprising festival, for contemporary reviews speak of the originality of its dramatic characterisation, and it certainly continued to hold the stage for some years. One Roman journal wrote:

It can be said that the music as a whole is compounded of original beauties and is worthy of so distinguished a musician. The concourse of the public, which from the first evening on has never failed to attend in

Bergamo e il suo genio musicale

The caption reads: 'Bergamo and its musical genius'. The music quotation in the beginning of a duet from Lucia di Lammermoor.

large numbers, is the most valid proof for demonstrating this universal approval.

Parisina, based on the poem of that name by Byron, and produced in Florence in 1833, was for many years Donizetti's own favourite among his operas, but *Torquato Tasso*, produced in Rome later the same year, is a considerably more distinguished work. Based loosely on incidents in the life of the great 16th-century epic poet, it manages to combine elements of the old *opera seria* or serious opera with the lightness of touch of comic opera. A semi-professional performance in London in the 1970s revealed *Torquato Tasso* as one of Donizetti's most fascinating scores. 1833 was a vintage year for the composer, for in addition to *Il furioso*, *Parisina* and *Torquato Tasso*, it saw the birth of *Lucrezia Borgia*, in which that notorious member of the Borgia family was given romanticised treatment by Romani, who adapted Victor Hugo's play for Donizetti. Hugo was not pleased with the opera, but the general opinion was that it was one of Donizetti's finest. A discordant note, however, was struck by one of the most influential Roman critics who wrote of the indifferent quality of Romani's libretto, and then went on to say that 'the composer has kept himself hidden, leaving the singers to fabricate the music, so empty is it of inspiration and novelty'.

The year 1834 found Donizetti exploring English history with *Rosamonda d'Inghilterra*, whose heroine is the ill-fated mistress of Henry II, and *Maria Stuarda*, whose heroine is Mary, Queen of Scots, an equally ill-fated victim of Elizabeth I. *Maria Stuarda* is the most impressive of Donizetti's operas based on English history, and has survived to find a place in the modern operatic repertoire. It was, however, with historical fiction from the British Isles, rather than historical fact, that Donizetti was soon to achieve his greatest success, when he composed what is still regarded as his finest opera, *Lucia di Lammermoor*. Based on Sir Walter Scott's novel, *The Bride of Lammermoor*, *Lucia* was composed for the San Carlo Theatre, Naples, and its première was one of the greatest events in the history of that theatre. For most of the evening, many people in the audience were in tears, so great was the expressive intensity of Donizetti's music. Lucia's mad scene, which one might call the apotheosis of the mad scene, is certainly one of the most impressive pieces of bravura vocal writing ever offered to a dramatic coloratura soprano, and its sentimental

melodies have by no means lost their power to affect audiences. *Lucia di Lammermoor* has remained a favourite opera in Italy since its first performance. Its popularity outside Italy has tended to depend upon the availability of a prima donna capable of managing the coloratura passages and of moving an audience in the gentler music.

It was only a week after the première of *Lucia* that the news of Bellini's death at the age of thirty-four reached Naples. Donizetti was deeply shocked by the premature death of his young rival, and composed in his memory a Requiem Mass which, though it is hardly one of his major compositions, is a strangely beguiling piece of music, fittingly operatic in style. While Donizetti was at work on his next opera, his father died. He did not attend the funeral for he was too busy, not only with the composition of *Belisario* but with supervising the first authentic production of *Maria Stuarda* in Milan, for in Naples the libretto had been bowdlerised. In any case, Donizetti's temperament was one which tended to avoid painful experiences. Perhaps, had he faced them, his music would have been the richer for it, but then he would have been a different person. Donizetti shares with Schubert a melodic fecundity, though he lacks the Viennese master's humanity. It is this lack of humanity, rather than differences in form and structure, which also distinguishes Donizetti from his great successor Verdi.

Shortly after *Belisario* had been successfully launched, Donizetti's mother died, and his wife was delivered prematurely of a still-born daughter. He was now teaching at the Conservatorium in Naples, but found time to write both the libretto and the music of a one-act comic opera, *Il campanello di notte*. In May 1837, when the Director of the Conservatorium died, Donizetti hoped to succeed him. Due to various intrigues, however, he could neither get his appointment confirmed nor his resignation accepted. He continued to compose new operas, among them *L'assedio di Calais* (1836), *Pia de' Tolomei* (1837) and, another of his forays into English history, *Roberto Devereux, Conte d'Essex* (1837). *Maria di Rudenz*, written for the Teatro Fenice, Venice in 1838, was a failure, probably because of its gruesome and blood-thirsty plot, and was taken off after two performances.

It was with a comic opera, and in another country, that Donizetti was to prove he had not lost his touch. His wife had died in the process of giving birth to another still-born child, and although he continued to live in Naples for a further two years Donizetti found his life there lonely and without direction or purpose. After another censorship quarrel with the authorities over an opera called *Poliuto*, he began to turn his thoughts towards Paris, having received invitations to compose for the Paris Opera. He took up residence in Paris, adapted *Poliuto* for production in French as *Les Martyrs*, and also worked on *Le Duc d'Albe*, an opera which was not produced until thirty-four years after his death.

The first completely new French opera by Donizetti to be staged was *La fille du régiment*, at the Opéra-Comique in February 1840. Though the first night was sabotaged by organised hostility on the part of French composers and their supporters, and the performance was greeted with a sneering review by Berlioz, nevertheless Donizetti's enchanting and light-hearted comedy proved immensely popular with the public, and continued to hold the stage in France until the end of the century and beyond. As *La figlia del reggimento* it was equally successful in Italy, and even today retains its power to delight.

Some months later, another Donizetti opera, this time a serious work, was produced

in Paris. This was *La favorite*, whose final act, one of the most dramatic and tightly constructed in Donizetti's entire oeuvre, is said to have been composed in less than four hours. After the production of *La favorite*, Donizetti travelled a great deal. For Rome, he composed *Adelia* which was staged in February 1841; for Milan he wrote *Maria Padilla*, produced at La Scala in December of the same year; and in March 1842 he went to Vienna, whose principal opera house was under the management of his old friend and colleague, Merelli. For Vienna Donizetti wrote *Linda di Chamounix*, a romantic opera which had an enormously successful reception. Honours were heaped upon him, and he was appointed *Kapellmeister* to the Austrian Emperor, his acceptance of which post made him several enemies in Italy. Returning to Paris, Donizetti produced another comic opera for that city, but this time an Italian one. *Don Pasquale*, the very epitome of Italian *opera buffa*, was staged at the Théâtre-Italien in January 1843. It quickly established itself in the repertoire, and is as popular today as when it was new. Generally thought of as one of the three greatest Italian comic operas of the 19th century (the others being Rossini's *Barber of Seville* and Verdi's *Falstaff*); *Don Pasquale* is certainly one of Donizetti's most endearing and enduring works.

It was shortly after the triumphant first performances of *Don Pasquale* that the early

Scene from Lucia di Lammermoor.

symptoms of the illness which was to prove fatal to Donizetti began to appear. He had gone to Vienna where his new opera *Maria di Rohan* was staged in June 1843, but he found that recurring bouts of fever prevented him from working with his usual concentration. By November, when he was back in Paris rehearsing *Dom Sébastien* which opened at the Opéra on the 13th November, it was obvious that he was seriously ill, for he would become incoherent in mid-sentence, fly into violent rages for no immediately apparent reason, or exhibit other signs of mental instability. Though he returned to Vienna and continued to work for another year, his condition went on deteriorating until his final collapse into paralysis and insanity, the last stages of a venereal disease. His final two years were spent in an almost comatose condition, until he was taken home to Bergamo to die in 1848.

Donizetti is important as the leading Italian opera composer of the 1830s and 1840s, spanning the gap between Rossini and Bellini whom early retirement and premature death respectively had removed from the scene, and the young Verdi who was, as it were, waiting in the wings. Of Donizetti's more than seventy operas, nine or ten are works which have survived to become a valuable part of the international opera repertory. As the work of reassessment continues, more of the operas of this uneven, prolific composer are being found worthy of revival.

C.O.

DOWLAND, John
(b. London?, 1563;
d. London, 20/21 Jan 1626)

The place of Downland's birth has long been a matter of conjecture. Thomas Fuller in *The History of the Worthies of England* (published in 1662), under the heading 'Worthies of Westminster,' implies that:

> John Douland was (as I have most cause to believe, born in this City; sure I am he had his *longest life* and best livlihood therein, being servant in the Chappel to Queen Elizabeth and King James. He was the *rarest Musician* that his age did behold; having travailed beyond the Seas . . .'

On the other hand, Dowland dedicated the song *From silent night* in his *Pilgrimes Solace*

(1612) 'to my loving contreyman, Mr *John Forster* the younger, merchant of Dublin in Ireland'. The profusion of Dowlinges, Dowlyngs, Doolans and O'Dolans living in Dalkey, Co. Dublin at about the time of Dowland's birth, has given rise to further speculation. All available evidence is discussed fully in Diana Poulton's *John Dowland* (Faber, 1972). In the absence of an actual registration of birth, it seems likely that the problem will remain unsolved. Dowland, himself, gives us the year of his birth. Referring to Hans Gerle's *Tabulatur auft die Laudten* of 1533, he writes 'for myself was born but thirty yeares after Hans Gerles Booke was Printed'.

Nothing is known of Dowland's education. In 1580, at the age of seventeen, he went to Paris as servant of Sir Henry Cobham, the English Ambassador. At this time Dowland converted to Catholicism. He is thought to have returned to England in 1584 and married at about the same time; his son, Robert, being born probably in 1586. On the 5th July 1588, Dowland was admitted B.Mus. at Christ Church, Oxford together with Thomas Morley.

In 1594 Dowland was unsuccessful in his application for the vacant position as one of the Queen's musicians for the Lute, caused by the death of John Johnson; 'my religion was my hindrance; whereupon my mind being troubled, I desired to go beyond the Seas'. He visited the Court of the Duke of Brunswick where he was already known by reputation, 'from thence I had great desire to see Italy and came to Venice and from thence to Florence, where I played before the Duke'. At Brunswick Dowland made the acquaintance of Gregorio Howet the Duke's lutenist, who is mentioned in the preface of the *First Booke of Songs*; at Venice he met Giovanni Croce. Dowland, in visiting Italy, had hoped to meet and study with Luca Marenzio in Rome, but while staying at Florence, he met several English recusants. Alarmed at allowing himself to be in company of men whose intentions were treasonable to the Queen, Dowland

> 'wept heartily to see my fortune so hard that I should become servant to the greatest enemy of my Prince, country, wife, children, and friends, for want. And to make me like themselves, God knoweth I never loved treason nor treachery, nor never knew of any, nor never heard any mass in England, which I find is great abuse of the people, for, on my soul, I understand it not.'

Dowland returned to England via Bologna, Venice and Nuremburg. It was from Nuremburg that he wrote to Sir Robert Cecil the letter from which the above quotations are taken. In 1596 some lute pieces by Dowland appeared in Barley's *New Booke of Tableture*, apparently without his consent. We read in the preface of Dowland's *First Booke of Songs or Ayres of Foure Partes with Tableture for the Lute*, published by Peter Short in 1597, that 'There haue bin diuers Lute – lessons of mine lately printed without my knowledge, falce and vnperfect.' Dowland's *First Booke* was enthusiastically received – a measure of its popularity is given by the fact that in all, five editions were issued by 1613. Richard Barnfield's celebrated sonnet 'to his friend Maister R.L., in Praise of Musique and Poetrie' appeared in 1598 (it has sometimes been attributed to Shakespeare):

If Musique and Sweet Poetrie agree,
As they must needes (the Sister and the Brother),
Then must the love be great, twixt thee and mee,
Because thou lov'st the one, and I the other.
Dowland to thee is deare; whose hevenly tuch
Upon the Lute, doeth ravish humaine sense:
Spenser to mee; whose deepe Conceit is such,
As, passing all Conceit, needs no defence.
Thou lov'st to heare the sweet melodious sounds
The *Phoebus* Lute (the Queen of Musique) makes:
And I deepe Delight am chiefly drowned,
When as himself to singing he betakes.
One God is God of Both (as Poets faigne),
One knight loves Both, and Both in thee remaine.

In November 1598, Dowland was appointed lutenist to Christian IV of Denmark, whose court included a number of distinguished musicians. Dowland received the substantial salary of 500 Daler a year. In 1600 he published his *Second Booke of Songs or Ayres of 2. 4. and 5 Parts* the preface of which is dated 'from Helsingnoure in Denmarke, the first of June'. The following year Dowland, 'at His Majesty's command' visited England to buy musical instruments.

Dowland's *Third and Last Booke of Songs or Aires* appeared in 1603. There is no mention of the composer in the Danish court accounts

for some seventeen months after February 1603, and it seems quite likely that he was in England at this time. *Lachrimae or Seaven Teares figured in seaven passionate Pavans* (for instruments, in five parts) were published by Dowland in April 1604 from his house in Fetter Lane, London. He presumably returned to Denmark later that year, where, from the Court Archives we learn that his conduct was causing concern, particularly with regard to numerous salary advances. He was finally dismissed on the 24th February 1606.

Shortly after returning to London, Dowland issued a translation of *Micrologus* by Andreas Ornithoparcus, the preface of which informs us that he is 'shortly to diuulge a more peculiar worke of mine owne: namely *My Observations and Directions concerning the Art of Lute-Playing*'. The project, however, failed to progress beyond an introductory stage. In 1610 Dowland's son, Robert, published a *Varietie of Lute Lessons . . . Selected out of the best approued Avthors, as well beyond the Seas as of our owne Country*. John Dowland is represented by several already existing compositions (with a certain amount of alteration in the divisions) and by a short treatise on lute-playing. It seems likely that this latter is the total extent of the promised *Observations and Directions*. Robert describes his father as 'being now gray, and like the swan, but singing towards his end'. John Dowland published his last work, *A Pilgrimes Solace*, in 1612. He is here described as lutenist to Lord Walden, and the preface observes that 'I have been long obscured from your sight, because I received a kingly entertainment in a forraine climate, which could not attaine to any (though never so meane) place at home.'

On the 28th October 1612 Dowland was, at last, appointed one of the King's Musicians for the Lutes in place of Richard Pyke, at a salary of 20d a day and £16. 2s. 6d. yearly for livery. His name appears in the accounts as late as 1618 as second musician for the lutes, after Robert Johnson. In 1614 Dowland contributed two sacred songs to Sir William Leighton's *Teares or Lamentacions of a sorrowfull soule*; and a poem to Thomas Ravenscroft's *A Briefe Discourse*. After 1622, he is sometimes referred to as 'Doctor Dowland', although there are no records of his having taken the degree. On the 5th May 1625 he was a member of the Consort that played at the funeral solemnities of James I; Orlando Gibbons, then organist of Westminster Abbey, directed the choir. Dowland himself died the following year and was buried, on the 20th February 1626, at St Anne, Blackfriars (the Register of Burials describing him as Doctor of Music).

Little of Dowland's solo lute music was published during his lifetime, but a large number of pieces have survived in manuscript. Several different versions of the same composition are common, and Dowland frequently revised his music, for example, by adding further divisions; and he sometimes even superimposed a new dedication. The solo lute music includes Fantasies, Pavans, Galliards, Almains, Cornatos, and settings of songs and ballads. Dowland's *Lachrimae* Pavan (No. 15 of the Poulton/Lam Collected Edition, Faber, 1974) achieved immense popularity throughout Europe. He was honoured by English and continental lutenists – the latter including Besardus – who themselves made solo settings of the melody. Byrd, Morley, Farnaby, Sweelinck, and Scheidemann, among others, produced keyboard arrangements; Morley published a further version in his *First Booke of Consort Lessons*. Dowland produced in all three settings of *Lachrimae*, of which the solo lute setting is thought to be the first. The song *Flow my teares* followed (it is contained in the *Second Booke of Songs*, 1600), and finally the arrangement for viols and lute in *Lachrimae or Seaven Teares* (1604). Apart from the many musical acknowledgements, *Lachrimae* received considerable acclaim in the field of literature. Thomas Middleton's *No Wit, no Help like a Woman* (1613) includes the line: 'Now playest Dowland's *Lachrimae* to thy master.' There are numerous similar allusions to the famous melody.

In setting *Go from my Window, My Lord Willoughby's Welcome Home*, and *Robin*, Dowland was in the company of many of his colleagues, including Thomas Robinson who is known to have taught the King of Denmark's daughter, Anne, later James I's Queen. There is no mention of Robinson actually having visited the court of Christian IV. Dowland's style of composition compared with that of Robinson (for instance in their respective settings of *Go from my Window*), shows a far greater emphasis on contrapuntal intricacies, is much more alive rhythmically, and indeed is generally more virtuosic.

Dowland, however, is chiefly remembered as a song composer, and it has been suggested that the exceptional quality of his works in this form places him among the first half-

dozen of the world's song writers. Each of Dowland's four song books contains twenty-one songs and three more were published by Robert Dowland in *A Musicall Banquet* (1610). Dowland's *First Booke of Songs* (1597), as well as instigating a wave of song composition, actually established the printed format of subsequent publications. This allowed for performance either by voice and lute, or four-part consort of voices or instruments. The voice part and the lute tablature were usually printed on the same page in alignment, and an alternative version arranged for A.T.B. so printed that singers or players sitting round a table could all read from the same book (see illustration). Certain songs in Dowland's *First Booke* are known to have been founded on traditional melodies – for example, that of *Now, O now, I needs must part*, which was widely known as the 'frog galliard'. The *Second Booke of Songs* (1600) represented a considerable advance on the 1597 publication, particularly with regard to melodic construction and disposition of the accompaniment. Several of Dowland's best-known songs are to be found here, including *Flow my Teares* (styled *Lacrime*), and *Fine Knacks for Ladies*; the expressive setting of *I saw my Lady Weepe*, bearing the dedication to Anthony Holborne.

Dowland developed a highly individual style – matching music to words, and voice to accompaniment, with great sensitivity and insight – and the perfection which he achieved placed him beyond rival. The profusion of works with sad, melancholic titles indicates an important aspect of the composer's complex and intense personality. *Lachrimae, In Darknesse let Mee Dwell, Forlorne Hope*, and *Weepe you no more sad fountaines* all denote the nature of one who gave as his motto 'Semper Dowland Semper Dolens'.

G.G.

DUPARC, Henri
(b. Paris, 21 Jan 1848;
d. Mont-de-Marsan, 12 Feb 1933)

Marie Eugène Henri Fouques-Duparc came from a comfortable middle-class family which originated in Brittany, but had long been settled in Paris. He was educated at the Jesuit College of Vaugirard, and it was there that he first made the acquaintance of César Franck, music-master of the college and soon to become the young Duparc's master and mentor in the art of composition. He combined his private studies with Franck and his unenthusiastic reading of Law, and before the *Feuilles volantes* for piano, published in 1869, he had already completed a violoncello sonata. This was one of several works which he later destroyed, including two pieces performed by the Société Nationale in 1894, *Laendler* and *Poème nocturne*, of which he preserved part under the title of *Aux étoiles*. Pasdeloup performed Duparc's *Lénore*, written in 1875 and founded on Bürger's poem of the same name, and the respect which this work inspired may be gauged by the fact that it was arranged by Saint-Saëns for two pianos and by Franck himself for piano duet. Duparc formed, with Cahen and Coquard, the original nucleus of enthusiastic Franck-disciples which was be known familiarly as 'la bande à Franck' and was to exercise a strong influence on French musical life between 1870 and 1890. The fellow-student with whom Duparc had most in common was Alexis de Castillon, who died in 1873 from the results of his service in the Franco-Prussian War of 1870–1 and left a handful of remarkable student-works. These show clearly the influence of Beethoven, and it was his Ninth Symphony which served as a revelation to the young Duparc several years before he made the acquaintance of Wagner's music. This was to be an all but overwhelming experience musically, but it is probable that Duparc, who numbered both the poets Leconte de Lisle and Albert Samain among his friends, was already affected by Wagner's reputation among French writers and painters which preceded by almost a decade his influence on French composers. He was a frequent visitor to Germany, going to Weimar in 1869 and meeting Wagner in Liszt's house. His visits to Bayreuth and Munich (one with Chabrier in 1879) deeply affected not only his musical development but also his understanding of the new movements in other arts. He was an early French admirer of Tolstoi and Ibsen, and he must have been one of the very few admirers of Wagner who, even during the composer's lifetime, regretted all realism in the production of his works and looked forward to what Wieland Wagner achieved only sixty years later. When he broached this subject with the composer himself, after a performance of *Die Walküre* in Munich, the discussion became lively. Duparc wanted no flames in the final scene, only the touching of the rock by Wotan's spear. Wagner himself looked forward to 'steam-

jets propelling realistic flames'.

Meanwhile Duparc's literary sympathies showed themselves in the choice of texts for his songs, five of which were published in 1868. He later destroyed three of these, leaving only *Soupir* and *Chanson Triste*. This recurrent impulse to anthologise his own output, leaving only the few works in which he felt that he had really succeeded in doing what he wanted as he wanted, revealed a self-critical faculty developed to an almost morbid degree. Following his master, Franck, Duparc demanded of music before all else a strong emotional prompting. 'Je veux être ému' was the motto which dominated his taste in all the arts and determined the character of his own creation. Is it fanciful to see a link between this extreme emotionalism and the neurasthenia which led him in 1885 to leave Paris and, as it turned out, to abandon composition at the age of thirty-seven?

During the last fifteen years of his life in Paris between 1870 and 1885, he composed a dozen songs; and these, with the earlier *Soupir* and *Chanson*, are the sole works on which his reputation rests. Two are settings of his favourite poet Baudelaire; and *L'Invitation au voyage* may be ranked among the finest of all French songs and, at least until Debussy's Baudelaire settings, uniquely successful in capturing the spirit and quality of a Baudelaire poem. Leconte de Lisle's *Phidylé* inspired one of Duparc's most ambitious songs, which opens with a modal melody worthy of Fauré and closes with a Wagnerian splendour which clearly demands the orchestra. In Théophile Gautier's *Lamento* the basically strophic setting gives the song a unity diversified by Duparc's scrupulous prosody, which allows the text an importance rare even in French song. Jean Lahor's *Extase* prompted Duparc to play a joke on his critics and at the same time produce a masterpiece. As he told his fellow-pupil Bréville, he deliberately imitated in this song the style of *Tristan*; and the harmonies of his setting of Thomas Moore's *Elegy* on the Irish patriot Emmett are in fact equally Wagnerian in character. The hesitant yet forceful accompaniment in his setting of R. de Bonnières' *Le Manoir de Rosemonde* plainly originated in Schumann's *Dichterliebe*, but the obsessive dotted and syncopated rhythm and the explosive violence of the music seem to foreshadow the dramatic miniatures of Hugo Wolf.

In his retirement Duparc consciously sought only solitude and quietness. After

Switzerland he lived in the south-west of France for a time at Pau and at Tarbes. As late as 1894 he wrote to his friend Chausson from Monein, in the Basses Pyrenées, that he was working hard. Three years earlier, in 1891, he confessed to Chausson that the combination of severe rheumatism and a torturing neurasthenia ('a single fly is an agony to me') made him long for death. But instead of dying Duparc lived another forty years, a martyr to his nervous hypersensibility and latterly almost completely blind. At first he worked on a projected *Roussalka*, based on Pushkin, but he eventually burned what he had written. Even his painting, which in 1883 had won the admiration of Harpignies, was to be abandoned and the only record that he left of this long creative silence is to be found in letters to his friends and in a daily journal. In this he noted his reflections on life and, increasingly after his first visit to Lourdes with Claudel and Jammes in 1906, an interior dialogue revealing a profoundly religious nature. His chief correspondent among musicians was Ernest Chausson, the Franck pupil with whom he had most in common. In 1893 he begged Chausson not to concern himself with details of performance in 'the three or four pages of useless music that I have written. It no longer concerns me and I shall not worry about it any more than I should if my poor fat body were also dead and buried.' To Chausson also he confided his difficulty in writing for the piano, speaking of '*pianofortising* the kind of orchestral summary' of his accompaniments. His attitude towards the slow decay of his faculties is perhaps best summed up in this passage from his journal. 'The loss of my sight and the deprivation of what has made my whole life – music and painting, but especially music – is such a grief to me that God could only console me for it by giving me Himself: that is what He has done, and far from regretting anything, I thank Him.' Duparc died in 1933 at Mont-de-Marsan in the Landes.

M.C.

DVOŘÁK, Antonín
(b. Nelahozeves, 8 Sept 1841;
d. Prague, 1 May 1904)

Dvořák is without question the greatest of all Czech composers, and his contribution to the literature both of symphonic and chamber music ranks alongside that of the most com-manding 19th-century masters. He was born in the small Bohemian village of Nelahozeves, on the banks of the Vltava, some fifty or so miles north of Prague. His father served the village both in the capacity of innkeeper and butcher, and Dvořák's son never lost his love of the countryside and its people. Indeed, contact with nature was as vital for him as it was for later artists such as Delius or Sibelius; and his work radiates a richness and generosity of feeling, tempered by a keen musical discipline that almost recalls Haydn. But if in terms of emotional equilibrium he recalls the classical masters, he must be numbered after Schubert, and along with his friend and contemporary, Tchaikovsky, as the most natural melodist of the 19th century. The fund of melodic invention on which he could call seems inexhaustible and its freshness and spontaneity undimmed. Brahms is reported to have come to Dvořák's defence on one occasion, when criticism of his work had been voiced, saying 'I should be glad if something occurred to me as a main idea that occurs to Dvořák only by the way.'

As a small boy he learned the violin, became a chorister in the church of his native village, played for the local orchestra, even composing marches and waltzes for it. When he was twelve, he was sent to the town Zlonice to learn German, and was fortunate enough to find an excellent mentor in the form of his headmaster, Antonín Liehmann, from whom he learned the piano, viola, organ as well as harmony and figured bass. In the autumn of 1857, when he was sixteen, he went to Prague to study at the organ school. Side by side with his studies and his exploration of the classical repertoire, he was succumbing to the spell of Wagner, and by the early 1860s, Smetana, too, was a focal point of his admiration. He spent the bulk of the 1860s as an orchestral player, first in a small band conducted by Karel Komzak, and then later in the Czech National Opera Orchestra, which in the latter half of the decade was conducted by no less a figure than Smetana himself. Dvořák met with very little success at this time, if by success one means recognition, but he composed with energy, ruthlessly consigning the results to the flames. There is an A major String Quintet (1861), a Quartet in A (1862) which escaped destruction, as did the First Symphony in C minor (*The Bells of Zlonice*, 1865).

A Second Symphony in B flat followed a few months later, and even if the obvious models, Beethoven and Schubert, loom large, it is evi-

dent that Dvořák is flexing genuinely symphonic muscle, even if it is far from fully developed. However, neither the symphonies nor the other works (quartets in D major, B flat, the song cycle *Cypresses*, and an early 'cello concerto) were performed in public, and it was not until the 1870s that the tide began to turn in this respect. All this time, the struggling young composer was making his living as a violist with the Opera Orchestra, where he took part in the first performances of a number of Smetana operas including *The Bartered Bride*, *The Brandenburgers in Bohemia* and *Dalibor* under Smetana's own direction, occasions that must have stoked the flames of his own operatic ambitions. These had undoubtedly been fired by contact with Wagner: Dvořák paid numerous visits to the German Theatre in Prague and probably attended virtually every Wagner performance there. He himself composed two operas at the beginning of the 1870s, *Alfred* and *King and Collier*, the overture to which Smetana conducted in 1872. Wagner's influence can be discerned in the two succeeding symphonies, No. 3 in E flat (1873) and No. 4 in D minor (1874).

Already in 1873 Dvořák left the Opera Orchestra to earn his daily bread by less onerous means as the organist of St Adalbert's church, Prague, a post that left him with far more time to compose. He had by now embarked on married life, and his domestic happiness, as well as his growing repute, unleashed a torrent of creative activity. Apart from the two symphonies came three quartets (Op. 9, 12 and 16), a revision of *King and Collier*, a five-act opera called *Vanda*, the famous *Serenade for strings*, the relatively little played but eloquent *Nocturne for strings*, the G major String Quintet, and the marvellous F major Symphony (1875). By the end of the 1870s, the tide was beginning to turn in his affairs. He had already received the Austrian State Prize four years in succession, thanks in no small measure to the efforts of Brahms and Hanslick. Up to this point, recognition had been confined to Prague: Brahms was anxious to widen these boundaries and secure the dissemination of Dvořák's music on the continent at large. Simrock, Brahms' own publisher, was persuaded to take the *Moravian Duets*, Joachim introduced the Op. 48 String Sextet to Berlin, and this together with the *Slavonic Dances* that Simrock commissioned in 1878 carried

Dvořák's name even further than Germany, into England with which country Dvořák was to have a long and fruitful association.

In September 1879 the third *Slavonic Rhapsody* was given in Berlin with great success and two months later, Dvořák went to Vienna to hear Richter conduct it there. As a result of this success he had to promise Richter and the Vienna Philharmonic a new symphony. The result followed in the summer of 1880 when the D major Symphony finally appeared. The D major Symphony is one of the very finest symphonies after Beethoven: its first movement surpasses in breadth and power, and in the naturalness with which ideas are unfolded and grow, almost anything composed between the Great C major Symphony of Schubert and the D major Symphony of Brahms, which had been composed in 1877 and with which the Dvořák symphony naturally invited comparison.

The 1880s saw the composition of such works as the *Scherzo capriccioso* and the Hussite Overture as well as one of his most concentrated chamber works, the F minor Piano Trio. He was also busy writing for the stage and his opera, *Dmitri* (1881–82) was produced in Prague. In 1884 Dvořák made his first visit to London at the invitation of the Royal Philharmonic Society, conducting the D major Symphony, the second *Slavonic Rhapsody* and the *Stabat Mater*. His music has already made headway in England and audiences were enthusiastic, warming both to the new works and to the composer's delightful personality. It was for London that he composed a new symphony in D minor (No. 7) presenting it at St James's Hall in April 1885 when it was immediately acclaimed. Dvořák's relationship with England may be said to dominate the next few years of his life. Between his first visit in 1884 and the first performance of his G major Symphony in 1890, he made no fewer than six trips, and much of his more substantial output was prompted by invitations and commissions from London and the provinces. *The Spectre's Bride* was written for Birmingham in 1885 and *St Ludmilla* followed it only a year later. He was beginning to feel the benefits of his celebrity and by 1884 was sufficiently in funds to buy a small country house, where he spent as much of his ensuing time as he could. His relationship with his publisher was beginning to show signs of strain and cast a shadow over a life, unusually harmonious in character.

Honours were being heaped on him at

Dvořák, 1891.

home: the University of Prague gave him an honorary doctorate of philosophy, and in 1891 he became Professor of composition at the Prague Conservatoire. That same year he made two further visits to England, one to conduct his *Requiem* at the Birmingham Festival and the other to receive an honorary doctorate at Cambridge.

In 1891 he received an invitation to head the recently founded New York National Conservatory of Music, which he at first declined. However, the offer was pursued with energy and persistence by the formidable American matriarch whose fortune had financed the Conservatory. Thus, in September 1892 Dvořák crossed the Atlantic and remained in the United States for the next three years. His vicissitudes in his dealings with Mrs Thurber, who was far from prompt in honouring her financial undertakings, were outweighed by his overwhelming nostalgia for the Czech countryside. His pen was far from idle, and apart from the E minor Symphony (*From the New World*) which was to become his most popular work, he wrote such masterpieces as the 'Cello Concerto, the F major Quartet, Op. 96, and the even finer String Quintet in E flat, Op. 97. In 1895 Dvořák returned to Prague making a visit to London, his ninth, in the following year when the 'Cello Concerto was heard for the first time. Restored to his more congenial environment, Dvořák set to work on a number of symphonic poems including *The Wood Dove*, *The Golden Spinning-Wheel* and *The Noonday Witch* and this period also saw the composition of the last of his string quartets, the G major Op. 106. His closing years were spent largely in operatic activity; *The Devil and Kate* and *Russalka* being the most important of his late stage works. In 1901, when he became sixty, he was appointed Director of the Prague Conservatory and continued his teaching activity. He died in the Czech capital in 1904.

R.L.

ELGAR, Edward William
(b. Broadheath, 2 June 1857;
d. Worcester, 23 Feb 1934)

Elgar was born in a country cottage at Broadheath, westward beyond the River Severn at Worcester. The family had left Worcester to fulfil Mrs Elgar's desire for a country life. She had grown up the daughter of a west-country yeoman farmer, and a gentle strength of char-

acter shone through everything she did. She was a great reader, and found time to write prose and verse of her own while bringing up her large family. A few years before Edward's birth she had become a convert to Roman Catholicism. Her son was later quoted as saying that 'his position was owing to the influence of his mother, and many of the things she said to him he had tried to carry out in his music'.

His father served as organist of Worcester's Catholic Church for nearly forty years, but objected to his wife's raising their children as Catholics. The centre of his professional life was his music shop in Worcester, from which he also carried on a piano-tuning business. In addition he was a competent violinist, and joined generally in the vigorous musical life which flourished in Worcester then. He introduced Edward to the musical society, gentry and clergy, of the Anglican Cathedral which dominated the life of the city – thereby helping to sow the seeds of his son's strong social as well as musical ambition.

When Edward was two years old, his father's growing business compelled the family's return to Worcester to live in rooms over the shop. The deaths of two brothers in 1864 and 1866 left Edward first the family's eldest son, and then their most promising musician. As a boy he was known locally for his playing and extemporising on the piano. (In later years he would disclaim interest in the piano, but used his keyboard extemporising skill nonetheless as a secondary phase in his process of composition.) He learned the organ so as to deputise for his father at the Catholic Church, and at the age of twelve taught himself the violin in order to take part in the orchestral ensembles which thenceforward defined his keenest interest.

This pattern of self-teaching extended to musical composition as well. He himself was later to say:

I am self-taught in the matter of harmony, counterpoint, form, and, in short, the whole of the 'mystery' of music . . . When I resolved to become a musician and found that the exigencies of life would prevent me from getting any tuition, the only thing to do was to teach myself. I read everything, played everything, and heard everything I possibly could.

Those words indicate not only Elgar's juvenile method but the force of his ambition. Yet the ambition, nurtured at first by his mother's interest, was to demand constant encour-

Sir Edward Elgar.

agement from outside himself. Between the ages of twelve and fourteen he drafted his remaining brother and all his sisters into an original musical play. The play (whose music would later be known as *The Wand of Youth*) was to dramatise the idea that children were capable of visionary insight which the 'Two Old People' (the Elgar parents) had lost. It was a theme to which Elgar's later music would return again and again.

His schooling completed at fifteen, Edward spent an unsuccessful year in a lawyer's office before 'arranging' with his mother (as he said) for a career in music. From the age of sixteen until he was past thirty he lived the life of a local musician, taking piano and violin pupils, playing in concerts, and gradually finding op-

portunities to conduct. His most regular conducting engagement was at the nearby lunatic asylum, where a band of players had been recruited from amongst the staff for concerts and dances to entertain the patients. Young Elgar held the conductor's post there from 1879 until 1884. His duties included the writing and scoring of dances for the motley ensembles of instruments produced by the asylum staff. This experience of making an ensemble balance out of almost any instrumental grouping laid the foundations of his later brilliant ability as an orchestrator.

During his twenties Elgar also tried his hand at short orchestral pieces of a more conventional kind. He produced choral music for the Worcester Catholic Church, as well as violin pieces and songs which traced the gradual defining of a highly individual melodic style. Two leading traits of Elgarian melody emerged in the frequent repeating of a figure to make a sequential pattern, and developing not so often toward the customary 'dominant' fifth interval as toward the 'sub-dominant' fourth – the interval commonly associated with returning recapitulation. This played an important part in evoking what his later friend Ernest Newman would describe as 'the sunset quality' of Elgar's music. But the earlier 1880s were still years of waiting, for the encourager who might focus all his talents and energies had not yet appeared.

Elgar's encourager emerged in the person of a lady who suggested two characteristics of his mother: she was decidedly older – by nearly nine years – and she was a writer of considerable prose and verse. But Caroline Alice Roberts (1848–1920) was the daughter of Major-General Sir Henry Roberts, whose retirement to a country house on the southern borders of Worcestershire identified the family as of precisely that 'county' importance which appealed to Elgar through the attitudes of his father. Miss Roberts applied to the younger Elgar for lessons in piano accompaniment in 1886. Just before their engagement in 1888 he wrote his famous *Salut d'amour*, Op. 12. Despite initial family opposition, their marriage in 1889 proved the ideal stimulus to Elgar's creative genius. All his important music appeared during the thirty years of their married life. The only child of the marriage was a daughter Carice (1890–1970), born just as Elgar's first sizeable work of music was to make its appearance.

The goal of Elgar's artistic life was symphonic composition. As he said in 1905, before achieving the goal, 'I hold that the Symphony without a programme is the highest development of art.' His entire career as a composer may be understood as a self-taught pilgrimage toward the achievement of this most traditionally respected form of musical expression. Nonetheless the three decades of his important activity divide into two distinct phases.

Between 1889 and 1906 Elgar's chief energies were devoted to large choral writing. The musical climate of the English Midlands in those years was especially favourable to the production of choral works. But self-teaching could also recognise a real aid to larger expression in the marriage of its music with a plot and libretto which must inevitably shape much of the composer's structure for him. Moreover, the subjects Elgar chose for his early choral works traced a consistent theme of self-reflection: *The Black Knight*, Op. 25

(1889–93), *The Light of Life*, Op. 29 (Worcester Festival, 1896), *Scenes from the Saga of King Olaf*, Op. 30 (North Staffordshire Festival, 1896), and *Caractacus*, Op. 36 (Leeds Festival, 1898). In each case the hero emerged as an outsider attempting to impose his own vision upon an existing order. It is impossible not to identify this succession of heroes with the self-taught provincial, whose music gradually made its composer's way through the ranks of social and academic prejudice to win him the highest honours of any British musician: these were to include a knighthood (1904), the Order of Merit (1911), the Mastership of the King's Musick (1924), and a Baronetcy (1931).

Elgar's choral writing culminated in a long-considered setting of Cardinal Newman's *The Dream of Gerontius*, Op. 38 (Birmingham Festival, 1900), depicting Catholic death and immortality. *The Apostles*, Op. 49 (Birmingham Festival, 1903) began the harvesting of an even older idea – the notion of discipleship, its vision and its difficulty: for the most memorable of Elgar's Apostles is the self-deluded Judas. *The Kingdom*, Op. 51 (Birmingham Festival, 1906) carried on what the composer hoped would become a trilogy of oratorios about the Acts of the Apostles. The project suffered a fatal interruption, however, in the redefining of Elgar's artistic expression which emerged at the time of his fiftieth birthday in 1907. In this, the receding of religious faith – shared by so many of Elgar's generation – played its part. But parallel experiences of musical redefinition emerged also during these very years in the careers of his European contemporaries, Puccini and Richard Strauss.

Not all of Elgar's energies in the first half of his career had gone into choral music. In his orchestral writing between 1890 and 1905 can be seen the developing seeds of his later symphonies and concertos. The earliest of all his larger works was the *Froissart Overture*, Op. 19 (Worcester Festival, 1890), which displayed his orchestral mastery in a very sophisticated sonata-structure. Both of his later overtures – *Cockaigne*, Op. 40 (1901) and *In the South*, Op. 50 (1904) – anticipated four-movement symphonic expression by dividing the central development section into two distinct parts. Both in fact were completed as alternatives to symphonic projects which did not mature: at the time of *Cockaigne*, Elgar's symphonic hopes had attached themselves to a melody which was later on in 1901 to make the famous trio of his *Pomp and Circumstance*

March No. 1, Op. 39 No. 1. Still earlier thoughts of symphony-writing had emerged side by side with the writing of the celebrated Variations on an Original Theme, Op. 36 (1898–9). The theme was labelled 'Enigma'. This Elgar would never explain: 'its "dark saying" [as he wrote] must be left unguessed.' But the variations he built upon it were inspired by the personal traits of a succession of friends. The first evoked his wife, and the last showed the composer himself and what he 'intended to do'. The secret of the work's wide appeal lies in this ability to enact in abstract musical terms a process of artistic self-discovery. That process went farther still in the brilliant Introduction and Allegro for strings, Op. 47 – Elgar's purest expression of abstract music up to the time of its appearance in 1905, and his last considerable instrumental work before the creative crisis of 1907.

The outward manifestation of this crisis came in a reverting to the old *Wand of Youth* music: in two large orchestral suites of 1907–8 based on his own childhood melodies, Elgar in effect surveyed the creative bases of his self-teaching. These suites, Op. 1a and 1b, inaugurated the second phase of the composer's career. There followed directly the achievement of his First Symphony, Op. 55 (1908). Here Elgar applied the technique of variations to achieve a structure unique in symphonic writing. The announcement of the theme makes the symphony's slow introduction; then follows the most remote of all the variations, presented as a primary subject of the main sonata-allegro. The traditional four-movement structure ensues, formed of thematic subjects which are themselves other variations, returning more and more clearly toward the original theme until a final coda brings the inevitable closing of the ring. This symphony created such a success that it was given nearly a hundred performances during its première season. A violin concerto, Op. 61 (1910) seemed at first to duplicate the symphony's success. But Elgar was virtually alone among composers of the major violin concertos in being himself an accomplished violinist as well as a formidable symphonic composer: the length and difficulty of the work he created has not, despite many beauties, encouraged great numbers of players to brave its challenge.

The composer's Second Symphony, Op. 63 (1911) did not at the beginning command any-

thing like the following of the First. And this fact, together with Elgar's extraordinary sensitivity to the mood of his world, began to suggest to him that his day was declining. He completed a final large choral work in *The Music Makers*, Op. 69 (Birmingham Festival, 1912), where new music was joined to thematic ideas ranging back across his creative maturity in an attempt to fix the whole of his achievement in a single vision. The 'Symphonic Study' *Falstaff*, Op. 68 (Leeds Festival, 1913) then emphasised endearing and even creative phases of the old jester's character, side by side with the remorseless rejection that was his fate.

Thus the coming of World War I in 1914 seemed almost to answer the expression of Elgar's later music. The war years saw the appearance of topical songs and recitations with orchestra, as well as the deeply felt choral setting of three poems by Laurence Binyon (including 'For the Fallen') as *The Spirit of England*, Op. 80. But the largest of all his scores then was the incidental music to Algernon Blackwood's fantasy play *The Starlight Express*, Op. 78 (Kingsway Theatre, 1915) which revived again musical and even dramatic themes from *The Wand of Youth*.

In the last year of the war Elgar's music entered its final phase with three works of chamber music (Op. 82, 83, and 84) whose expression pressed further the asceticism already outlined in *Falstaff*. The last of all his major works came in 1919 with the Violoncello Concerto, Op. 85. There the aspiring vision of the earlier music met the later austerity to evoke a survival of older insight into a future of negation. The scoring is the most spare of all Elgar's large works – the orchestra for the most part inhabiting the extremities while the solo instrument wanders alone through an otherwise empty landscape. In the fourteen years which remained after the death of his wife in 1920, Elgar himself often wandered in just that way through the landscapes of his childhood in Worcestershire. But though he tried – and tried hard – for a Third Symphony in 1933, he was never to find again the music which had come with the years of his marriage and triumphant success in the pre-war world.

J.N.M.

FALLA, Manuel de
(b. Cadiz, 23 Nov 1876;
d. Alta Gracia, 14 Nov 1946)

According to Stravinsky, who was a friend of Manuel de Falla for more than twenty years, the Spaniard was 'as modest and withdrawn as an oyster', and he also said of him that his nature was 'the most unpityingly religious' he had ever known. Such comments contrast strangely with the bold colours and often passionate emotional character of much of Falla's music, which has come to represent for us the 'Spanish' spirit at its most ebullient, even though it reflects only a part of the Iberian heritage. Falla was the son of a merchant who could afford a private tutor for his children, and was born at Cadiz, that ancient seaport to the west of Gibraltar, where Andalucia looks out to the Atlantic instead of in to the Mediterranean. The more cosmopolitan character of Cadiz doubtless gave Falla a broader outlook as he began to develop a childhood interest in music with piano lessons, which brought him into a local circle of enthusiastic amateur music-makers, and which led him in due course to his first adolescent compositions.

The family moved to Madrid when Falla was twenty, and although he never formally attended the Conservatory there, he successfully passed seven years of its examinations after only two years' private piano study. During this time he tried his hand at the *zarzuela,* that distinctively Spanish form of operetta. He composed two in collaboration with Amadeo Vives, a well-known *zarzuelista,* and five on his own, but only one was performed – *Los amores de la Inés* in 1902 – and that without much success. After composition studies with Felipe Pedrell, however, Falla achieved an apparent breakthrough when his first opera proper, *La vida breve* (Life is Short), won the first prize in a Madrid competition in 1905. But a competition prize is no guarantee of performance; the opera was still unperformed and the score was in his luggage when, in 1907, he decided to seek wider opportunities in Paris.

Falla spent the next seven years there, becoming a friend of Debussy, Dukas, Ravel and Stravinsky, as well as of other Spanish exiles like Albéniz. He played them *La vida breve* on the piano, and their enthusiasm for it eventually found the opera a publisher and a production – first at Nice in 1913, and later the same year at the Opéra-Comique in Paris. Meanwhile, Falla helped to support himself by giving piano lessons, accompanying singers at soirées and doing translation work. He added to his own works the *Four Spanish Pieces* for piano and some settings of poems by Gautier; started on *Nights in the Gardens of Spain,* and finished the *Seven Spanish Popular Songs* just as the onset of war in 1914 decided him to return home.

Back in Madrid, Falla next achieved three major works which became universally popular. One was *Nights in the Gardens of Spain,* for piano and orchestra, a concerto of haunting poetry more than virtuosity. Another was *El amor brujo* (Love, the Magician), originally conceived as a gypsy ballet for the celebrated flamenco dancer Pastora Imperio and her family, who first performed it at Madrid in 1915. No folk melodies are used in it, but Falla's music evokes the essential character of Andalucian gypsy dance and song in its distinctive blend of tension and languor. It includes the celebrated Ritual Fire Dance, later transcribed for all kinds of probable and improbable instruments, and used for all manner of equally unlikely dances, but which actually derives from an incantation intended to ward off evil spirits while the gypsies were forging their pots and pans.

The third major work of this period was another ballet, *El sombrero de tres picos* (The Three-cornered Hat), written at the instigation of Sergey Diaghilev for his Ballets Russes. Based on a Spanish novel which in turn derived from a humorous folk-tale of a resourceful miller's wife and an importunate town official, the scenario was by Martinez Sierra (the librettist of *La vida breve*). Diaghilev let Falla and Sierra stage this first as a mime-play at Madrid in 1917; the composer then extended his first drafts to meet the requirements of a full-scale ballet. It was eventually premièred in London in the Diaghilev company's first post-war season at the Alhambra Theatre in 1919. Destined to become a classic of its kind, the remarkable original collaboration included choreography by Massine and designs by Picasso (both still used in present-day productions), with Massine and Tamara Karsavina as the Miller and his Wife, and Ernest Ansermet conducting.

All these works are distinctively Andalucian in musical flavour, in the cast of their melodies and in their rhythms and dance-forms, as also is the *Fantasia Baetica*, a piano solo composed in 1919 for Artur Rubinstein. From 1920, however, when Falla actually went to live in Andalucia for the first time

Curtain design by Picasso for De Falla's ballet
The Three Cornered Hat.

since his childhood, and made his home in
Granada, he deliberately turned away from
what he felt to be the excesses of his previous
style. He became friendly with the poet Lorca
and they experimented with puppet plays,
Falla supplying the piano accompaniment.
The outcome was a puppet opera, *Master
Peter's Puppet Show*, based on an episode in

Cervantes' *Don Quixote* and written originally for a puppet theatre – a private one owned by the wealthy Paris hostess, Princesse Edmond de Polignac, where it was given in 1923. Among those who took part was the distinguished harpsichordist, Wanda Landowska, and as a gesture of thanks Falla composed for her the Harpsichord Concerto of 1926. In this the Andalucian flamboyance he discarded is replaced by Castilian restraint and sobriety, in a work which shares with the *Puppet Show* a keener feeling for instrumental texture and sharper colour.

A man of sensitive nature, retiring personality and firm principle, Falla shrank from the horrors of the Civil War in Spain, and succumbed to an illness which bound him to his house for four years. In 1939 he was invited to Buenos Aires for a concert tour and, once in Argentina, he decided to stay, his decision reinforced by medical advice. He settled at Alta Gracia in the Sierra de Córdoba, looked after by an unmarried sister; he composed the *Homenajes* for orchestra but became an increasingly sick man. Most of his available time was spent on a project which had occupied his thoughts since the 1920s – the setting

De Falla.

of an epic Catalan poem by Verdaguer in which the legend of lost Atlantis is the starting-point for a kind of masque of Spanish history. *L'Atlántida* was still unfinished when Falla died on the 14th November 1946; his body was brought back to Spain for burial in the crypt of Cadiz cathedral. A friend and pupil, Ernesto Halffter, completed *L'Atlántida* from the surviving manuscript, and it was eventually heard for the first time at a Barcelona concert in 1961 and was produced as a scenic cantata at La Scala, Milan, the next year. The result, however, added less than Falla must have hoped to a reputation which otherwise remains secure as the foremost Spanish composer of his time.

N.G.

FAURÉ, Gabriel
(b. Pamiers, 12 May 1845;
d. Paris, 4 Nov 1924)

Fauré was born at Pamiers in the Eastern Pyrenean department of Ariège and his father was a village schoolmaster, his mother the daughter of a retired army officer. Fauré's father had been appointed assistant inspector of elementary schools at Pamiers in 1839, but it seems clear that the addition of a sixth child to the family was not particularly welcome, and the small Gabriel was put out to nurse until he was four and never enjoyed much warmth or intimacy in his family as a child. At the age of nine his already marked musical talent was noticed and brought to the attention of Louis Niedermeyer, who had just founded in Paris an 'École de musique religieuse et classique', where he agreed to educate the young Fauré free of charge. He remained at the École Niedermeyer until 1865, and during that time formed a friendship with Camille Saint-Saëns, only ten years his senior but employed as piano-master at the school. Saint-Saëns introduced Fauré to the music of Bach and Liszt and generally helped to fill in the gaps of a musical education consciously weighted towards the ecclesiastical and designed to prepare sound organists and choirmasters. In January 1866 Fauré got his first organist's post, at Rennes, returning to Paris in 1870 and joining a light infantry regiment for the months of the Franco-Prussian War. The years 1871–3 saw him well established as a Parisian organist, with his own church of Saint Honoré d'Eylau and acting as assistant to both Widor at St Sulpice and

Saint-Saëns at the Madeleine; and supplementing his salary by joining the staff of the École Niedermeyer, where Messager was his pupil. At this time he was introduced to Pauline Viardot-Garcia, a famous and successful singer (and sister of 'La Malibran') and an influential figure in Parisian musical life. The young Fauré fell in love with her daughter Marianne who, in 1877, accepted his proposal of marriage but in a short time changed her mind; and it was not until 1883 that Fauré married Marie Fremiet, daughter of a successful sculptor of the day.

His first compositions (Vingt Mélodies Op. 1–8) were written when he first left school, fresh and charming drawing-room melodies with here and there the distinct note of a budding originality, which was to show itself unmistakably in the A major violin sonata of 1876. In the next year Fauré was appointed assistant organist and choirmaster at the Madeleine and he paid his first visit to Germany, being introduced by Saint-Saëns to Liszt at Weimar. In 1878 he went only as far as Cologne, where he heard *Das Rheingold* and *Die Walküre*, but the next year he heard the whole of the *Ring* at Bayreuth. These Wagnerian experiences were reflected in the Ballade for piano and orchestra which he composed in 1881; but Fauré's musical personality never underwent the complete reorientation that Wagner's music caused in Chabrier, d'Indy and Lekeu. The chief effect was to enrich and enlarge his harmonic sense: he was not attracted by the sonority of Wagner's orchestra, by his musico-dramatic theories or his apocalyptic attitude to music generally. As always, Fauré was content to cultivate his own, characteristically French garden; and although he wrote a symphony (performed in 1885 but since lost) it was in the field of chamber music – in the widest sense – that he was to do all his finest work. Even the Requiem, composed in 1886 on the occasion of his father's death, is a work of chamber-music proportions, grave rather than tragic and quite untouched by the grandiose visions and dramatic contrasts of most 19th-century settings of that text.

Of the almost one hundred songs that he wrote during the course of his long life, published at first in sets of three or four and later in so-called 'cycles', some two dozen appeared during the 1880s, following the first twenty which had appeared in 1865 and have already been mentioned. The songs of the 1880s include such minor masterpieces as *Nell, Les*

Berceaux, Les Roses d'Ispahan, Au cimetière and two settings of Verlaine, *Clair de lune* and *Spleen*. The other poets from whom he had chosen his texts included Victor Hugo, Théophile Gautier, Baudelaire, Leconte de Lisle and Sully-Prudhomme but also a number of lesser figures among whom Armand Silvestre is important. In Verlaine Fauré encountered a poet with whom he seems to have felt a unique sympathy, although in personal character and way of living the two were poles apart. During the 1890s he set no fewer than fourteen of Verlaine's poems, and these settings show him at the very height of his powers. The first set (*Cinq Mélodies*), published in 1890, was written in Venice, where the generosity of the future Princesse Edmond de Polignac (an American heiress belonging to the Singer family) enabled him to spend a holiday. These include *Mandoline, En sourdine* and *Green* and they were followed almost immediately by the nine poems collected together as *La Bonne Chanson*, all closely bearing on Verlaine's wooing of his future wife. Fauré's songs never show the acute literary sense, the instinctive reaction to individual words and phrases, that marks Debussy's song-writing. But he comes nearest to it in his Verlaine songs where the piano part ceases to be mere accompaniment to the voice and becomes an integral part of the conception, equal in importance to the voice and developing harmonies and figures which do not simply support but modify the character of the vocal line. Fauré's harmony in these songs is often advanced for the time at which they were written, progressions are elliptical and the sense of tonality is modified by the influence of the church modes, especially at cadences. This modal character is no doubt directly traceable to his musical education at the École Niedermeyer, where the chief emphasis was on ecclesiastical music.

The piano was Fauré's other predominant interest as a composer. The instrument plays a naturally leading role in the two piano quartets (1879 and 1886) in C minor and G minor, but during the 1880s and 1890s Fauré continued to write solo works whose titles – Impromptu, Barcarolle and Nocturne – recall those of Chopin and reveal how strongly the composer felt himself to be a craftsman working within a tradition. In fact these works seem indebted to Schumann rather than to Chopin in their keyboard layout, but they have in common with Chopin a deceptive drawing-room character. Like Chopin, Fauré employed simple, familiar forms and an immediately attractive, though never commonplace, melodic idiom while, as it were, smuggling into the harmonic texture and the elliptical development of his melodies new and personal features. No one could possibly mistake a Nocturne or Impromptu of his for a work by Chopin or Schumann; and even the *Thème et Variations* (1897), which invites immediate comparison with Schumann's *Etudes Symphoniques*, is entirely personal in character. This work forms, with Nocturne No. 6 and Barcarolle No. 5 the crowning point of the composer's maturity as a writer for the piano. After 1896, when Fauré became chief organist at the Madeleine and professor of composition at the Conservatoire, he naturally had less time for composition; and his time was still further reduced when he was appointed Director of the Conservatoire in 1905. Evidence of Fauré's qualities as a teacher ('less a teacher than a guide', as he was described) is provided by the quality of his pupils, who include Maurice Ravel, Koechlin, Schmitt, Roger-Ducasse and Nadia Boulanger. The reforms that he introduced as director were all concerned with broadening the musical basis of the curriculum in order to turn out all-round musicians rather than competent singers and instrumentalists and conventional composers of opera. He met considerable opposition but got his way, which involved Conservatoire pupils in the obligation to become acquainted not simply with the classics of their own field but with music of the remoter past and, more important still, of the present day. Fauré's sympathies with contemporary music were made quite clear when, in 1909, he accepted the presidency of the newly formed 'Société musicale indépendante'.

If official and administrative duties interfered with the volume of Fauré's composition, another important factor determining its character was the deafness which, by 1910, had become a serious handicap. It is altogether natural that any composer in his sixties should reflect in his composition the new balance between senses and intelligence, the increasing domination of the spirit over the flesh, without which old age is an unmitigated disaster. In Fauré's case this balance was tipped further by that gradual isolation from the everyday world which deafness brings. And so his last songs and piano music – the piano quintet No. 2, the piano trio, the violin sonata No. 2, the two 'cello sonatas and the string quartet that he wrote in the last year of his life at the age of eighty – all this music has a certain quality of aloofness from the world expressed in economy of thought and bareness of outline, an increase of that 'quietism' which already marked his Requiem and a certain transparency of texture. It is as though Fauré were catching in his music something of the quality of that Mediterranean light in which he grew up and to which he returned increasingly in his old age when, after his retirement from the Conservatoire in 1920, he spent much of his time with friends who had a house at Annecy in Savoy. This Mediterranean quality, which some commentators have seen as Hellenic, is very strong in his single full-scale opera, *Pénélope* (1913), a much more sympathetic subject than the *Prométhée* for which he had been asked to write music in 1900. Fauré's music is totally untheatrical in character and its drama is essentially interior; the conflicts and struggles, aspirations and fears that find expression there are wholly transmuted into musical terms and demand no physical exteriorisation of gesture or movement, scenery or even orchestral variety. *Pénélope* is essentially a musicians' opera and the singer who takes the title-role needs the intelligence and vocal qualities of a lieder-singer rather than an operatic diva. The four song-cycles written between 1907 and 1922 – *La Chanson d'Eve, Le Jardin clos, Mirages* and *L'Horizon chimérique* – all require this same unostentatious, precise art, a voice capable of infinite nuance rather than grandiose effect and a penetrating, sympathetic intelligence. Fauré is perhaps the most characteristically French of all the 19th-century French composers, and to find a parallel to his art we should turn to the painting of Chardin or Fragonard and the prose of François de Sales or 'La Princesse de Clèves'. He died in Paris in 1924.

M.C.

FIELD, John
(b. Dublin, July 1782;
d. Moscow, 23 Jan 1837)

John Field is a shadowy figure on the musical scene; little is known of his music and even the facts of his life are vaguely documented. He was born in Dublin, probably at some date in July 1782 and was christened on the 5th September. John Field himself was an incurable romantic and helped considerably to confuse his own history by inventing half of it. His father was a violinist and his grandfather a pianist and at the time of his birth both were occupied in teaching music from a house in Golden Lane. The family were constantly on the move, occasionally returning to Golden Lane (probably the grandparent's house) and the subsequent five children of Robert and Grace Field (or Fields as it was sometimes spelt) were mostly born in different temporary residences. When John Field showed early signs of a great musical talent he was thrust forcibly into music with a view to adding to the family's financial resources and was often beaten if he didn't study hard enough. At the age of nine he was sent for further study with an Italian professor Tommaso Giordani who presented his pupil for the first time in public in March 1792 at the Rotunda Assembly Rooms. This was in a varied concert by star pupils in which Field played an arrangement of a Krumpholtz harp concerto on the piano. It was given a glowing review in one Dublin newspaper.

In 1793 Field's father, with Mozartian ambitions for his son in mind, left Dublin for England and the town of Bath, where they remained for a few uneventful months before moving on to London. Here John was apprenticed to Muzio Clementi, one of the leading piano teachers of the day, at a considerable cost to his father. Here he became very much a part of the Clementi household, studied hard and began to build a reputation in an already competitive field that included such rising stars as Dussek, Cramer and Hummel – a favourite pupil of Mozart's. Part of his duties included demonstrating the pianos that Clementi manufactured.

Field had dabbled in composition for some years but began to write seriously around 1796. His first major work was a piano concerto in E flat performed in 1799, which became a popular piece although it was not published for many years. His first published work was a set of three piano sonatas, Op. 1 in 1801. In 1802 Clementi took his best pupil on a trip abroad; first to Paris where he made the acquaintance of Ignaz Pleyel, composer and piano-maker like Clementi, and made a piano arrangement of one of his concertos which Clementi published. Field's skills made a great impression in Paris and they moved on to Vienna where Clementi intended to leave Field to study with Albrechtsberger, the teacher of Beethoven. Field viewed the proposition with dread and persuaded his master

to take him with him on a further trip to St Petersburg. Field made his mark on the St Petersburg musical circles and when Clementi left in 1803, Field remained behind as a sort of Clementi piano ambassador. There was a notable concert in 1804 followed by trips to other Russian cities, and he made his first appearance in Moscow in 1806.

With Clementi out of the way Field blossomed out as a Bohemian dandy and gourmet, swiftly spending the money that he so easily earned. Composing was generally neglected in those years. In 1810 he married Mlle Percheron, a lively and attractive person who failed however to make the composer settle down to an industrious married life. Several important compositions were completed and published at irregular intervals. They returned to St Petersburg just in time to avoid Napoleon's ill-fated march on Moscow. Here Field indulged in various amorous pursuits and had an illegitimate son with a Mlle Charpentier. By 1817 he was at his peak of fame and fortune and a popular teacher – numbering the young Glinka amongst his pupils. With strong rivals such as Moscheles, Kalkbrenner and Hummel active in Europe, Field maintained a steady reputation and made a substantial income from teaching; but between 1824 and 1831, now settled in Moscow, his health was deteriorating, chiefly as a result of his growing addiction to drink and a general liking for self-indulgent pastimes. In 1831 he decided to leave Russia's cold climate for a while so that he could take advantage of better medical facilities in the West (he was already suffering from the cancer that was to kill him ten years later) and to embark on a concert tour. After a short visit to St Petersburg he sailed first for England where he had an operation and was reunited with his mother who scarcely knew him, so old and white-haired had he become. He stayed in London for a year, visited Paris, returned to London, met Clementi just before he died in 1832 and attended his funeral. He toured England, had a further season in Paris, then embarked on a fairly disastrous tour of the rest of Europe including Italy. He returned to Moscow in 1835, now a very sick man and hardly able to play or teach, but he was able to complete some more of his famous nocturnes. He died in Moscow in 1837.

During his life he achieved a great reputation as a player and teacher. Today he is mainly remembered for the nocturnes which were a new concept in romantic piano pieces in his day. Although he never had much praise to offer about Chopin, the Polish composer was a great admirer of Field, teaching his nocturnes to his pupils and, of course, being greatly inspired by them himself. Field played them with a smooth, gliding, cantabile touch. They are basically of simple structure, a melodic right hand with flowing left-hand accompaniment, lightly decorated and full of charming melodies. Their popularity led various publishers to add to the series by making arrangements of movements from other works and calling them nocturnes. The best known piece, the curiously though appropriately Irish-sounding *Midi* rondo (used by Harty in his pleasantly-orchestrated *John Field* suite) is a solo version of a divertissement. The concertos and other works have the same light touch which, at a time when the heavy, virtuoso concerto was on its way to popularity, kept them out of the standard repertoire, though they certainly deserve to be heard occasionally. Much remains to be rediscovered of Field's output; sonatas, fantasias, sets of variations, miscellaneous piano pieces, seven concertos, various chamber works and even a couple of songs. Meanwhile Field remains the delightful 'inventor' of the nocturne.

P.G.

FLOTOW, Friedrich von
(b. Tuetendorf, 26 April 1812;
d. Darmstadt, 24 Jan 1883)

There was no rags-to-riches romance about the career of Friedrich von Flotow. Nobly born in the German duchy of Mecklenburg-Schwerin, he was intended for diplomatic life and sent to Paris to train for that purpose at the age of fifteen. In the French capital, however, he found artistic circles more congenial and quickly became aware of his own musical potential. After a period of serious study he was able to gain a hearing for his music at private soirées in the aristocratic salons so fashionable at the time, frequently in partnership with the equally ambitious but impecunious Offenbach. He came before the wider public in 1839 with *Le Naufrage de la Méduse* at the Théâtre de la Renaissance, and subsequent operas composed for Paris made their way to England and Germany to win him international recognition. None of these early successes, however, has stood the test of time.

The work by which Flotow is still remembered is *Martha*, which began life as a ballet for Paris in 1844 and was then turned into an

opera for Vienna three years later. Skilfully combining gaiety with sentimentality, this finds the composer at his best, pouring out a stream of fresh, spontaneous melody. Its highly unlikely story is set in the reign of Queen Anne and centres on the annual Richmond Fair. The score breathes the unsophisticated charm of the countryside, even incorporating the Irish air 'The last rose of summer', and when produced with taste the opera can still cast a delicate spell. Flotow's lyrical gift is not to be sneered at, and the graceful expertise of his writing for the voice is proved by the fact that tenors of the calibre of Caruso and Gigli chose to appear in the role of Lionel while Sembrich and De los Angeles are numbered among the distinguished sopranos who have appeared as Lady Harriet. Above all, perhaps, *Martha* is famous for Lionel's aria 'Ach, so fromm' (better known in Italian as 'M'appari'), which no leading tenor for generations has left out of his repertoire. For all its use of a German text, an English setting and an Irish folk song, *Martha* reflects its composer's musical training by being essentially French in spirit.

Flotow continued to compose operas, songs and chamber works, but he never recaptured the romantic rapture of *Martha*. Only in that one opera, it seems, did he ever find a story tailor-made for his individual brand of pretty lyricism. He was no work-shy dilettante, however, for in addition to composition he threw himself into the duties of intendant of the court theatre at Schwerin from 1856 to 1863. He spent his later years first in Paris, then near Vienna, and enjoyed the satisfaction of seeing his operas performed as far afield as St Petersburg and Turin. If it appears somewhat sad that a composer who had undoubted talent and the financial means to foster it should leave so little behind, it is no mean reflection on him that the music of *Martha* still exerts its charm almost a century after his death.

F.G.B.

FOSTER, Stephen
(b. Lawrenceville, 4 July 1826;
d. New York, 13 Jan 1864)

The story of Stephen Collins Foster is basically one of an affluent upbringing, early success leading to international acclaim, to be followed by a sad decline, spiritual and physical disintegration and final tragedy. He was born in Lawrenceville, Pennsylvania, a town near Pittsburgh, in 1826. His boyhood was spent in this area and he attended local schools. His father, Colonel William Barclay Foster, was a typical rugged American pioneer who eventually made a successful career in a grocery and hardware firm as head of their shipping department, which often involved perilous journeys from New Orleans to New York either by sea or overland. His wife, Eliza Tomlinson, came from an aristocratic family. Their older children followed a predictable course in life; the eldest son becoming a famous engineer; others going into business. Stephen, who spent his time playing music and jotting down a continual stream of melodies that went through his head, was a puzzle. His father described it as 'a strange talent' but it was beyond the imagination of this highly respectable family to see music as a possible career.

However, Stephen Foster continued to write music, in spite of every effort to turn his steps elsewhere, and he had his first song published when he was sixteen – *Open thy Lattice, Love*. In 1846 he went to Cincinnati to work as book-keeper for one of his brothers and there he became friendly with a music publisher to whom he presented a number of songs including *Uncle Ned* and *Oh! Susannah*. This last song became a popular favourite with the 1849 gold-diggers on their way to California and the publisher is reputed to have made over $10,000 out of these songs. Foster didn't even get his name on the covers.

At this point he became a full-time composer and several songs were commissioned on which he now obtained a royalty agreement. In 1851 when the minstrel craze was growing, the famous minstrel show leader Edward P. Christy offered to publicise some of Foster's songs providing Christy's name was on the cover as composer. Foster kept the publishing rights and was paid a royalty. One of these was the famous *Old Folks at Home*. Others such as *Camptown Races* followed. Following a royalty agreement in 1853 with the firm of Firth, Pond, he published an anthology of tasteful dance arrangements called *The Social Orchestra*. Again, it was many years before Stephen Foster's name was given its due credit on these covers, but at least he was getting an income from them, small though it was by today's standards. *Old Folks at Home* earned him $1,647.46 in its first five and a quarter years (according to the composer's own account book) and *My Old Kentucky Home* earned $1,372.06 in three and

a half years. In the eight years from 1849 onward he was averaging an income of just under $1,200 a year with most of it coming from a mere handful of songs. These monetary considerations are important in Foster's history because it deeply affected his output. In 1860 he sold his royalty interests to various publishers in exchange for an arrangement whereby he received a regular income of around $1,200. His weak character and the increasing reliance upon alcohol made it increasingly impossible for him to write to order. He was always overdrawing on his payments. The agreements fell through and in later life he was reduced to selling songs for anything he could get; perhaps just enough to keep him in food and drink for the day. He formed a partnership with a lyric writer called George Cooper but this was only a temporary encouragement.

Early in 1864 he was taken with a fever and had to stay in his bed at his lodgings in the Bowery. On the third day he was trying to wash himself when he fainted and fell across the wash-basin which broke and cut his neck and face. Cooper was called and found him lying naked on the floor. He told his friend that he was 'done for'. A doctor was called who rendered temporary assistance and then Foster was taken to the Bellevue Hospital where he was also discovered to be suffering from burns. The next day he was dead, the family hearing from Cooper too late to be able to lend any personal or financial assistance. One of his few possessions was a sketch for a song found in his pocket, the first line of which was 'Dear friends and gentle hearts'. In his purse was thirty-eight cents.

Although the last years had been a hand-to-mouth existence with drink taking an increasing hold, he had remained a prolific writer. His wife tried to help him and persuaded him to take several cures. She tried to get him away from New York. She left him briefly but returned when she was told the loneliness was driving him to despair. Finally when he could no longer support her and the children she left him for good. Curiously his last year was one of his most prolific, although most of the songs were insignificant potboilers. The last inspiration was *Beautiful Dreamer*, written a few days before his death and published a few months after.

It is curious too that the majority of the songs that maintain Foster's reputation as a kind of national folk writer are nearly all of the kind of which he was rather ashamed.

Originally he wrote in a letter: 'I had the intention of omitting my name on my Ethiopian songs owing to the prejudice against them by some, which might injure my reputation as a writer of another style of music.' These included *Old Folks at Home; My Old Kentucky Home; Old Black Joe; Massa's in de Cold, Cold Ground; Oh! Susannah* and *Camptown Races.* Having found, as he put it, that 'by my efforts I have done a great deal to build up a taste for the Ethiopian songs among refined people by making the words suitable to their taste, instead of the trashy and really offensive words which belong to songs of that order', he wanted to take full credit for his reputation as 'the best Ethiopian writer'. Christy's name continued to appear on *Old Folks at Home* until as late as 1873.

Beyond these Foster was always on the point of lapsing into sheer Victorian sentimentality and bathos. There were other good songs: *Nelly was a Lady; Old Uncle Ned; Nelly Bligh; Old Dog Tray; Jeannie with the Light Brown Hair; Some Folks Do; Ring, Ring de Banjo; De Glendy Burke; Come Where My Love Lies Dreaming* and *Beautiful Dreamer.* Some of his 'good time coming' sort of songs have stirring qualities, but there are many poor ones out of the total of around two hundred. It is apparent from what he himself said and from these facts that Foster had little idea of his true merits. Even his reputation as a composer of true 'black' songs is over-exaggerated. Of the thirty or so that he wrote in this idiom, many of the best were written before he had any real contact with the genuine item beyond the minstrel shows. In his brief and tragic life, Foster discovered a melodic vein of universal appeal, but the pressures and prejudices of society of the time led his weak steps astray. There should have been at least one folk opera from such a natural songwriter.

P.G.

FRANCK, César
(b. Liège, 10 Dec 1822;
d. Paris, 8 Nov 1890)

Franck's father was of Flemish stock and belonged to a family who had worked for more than a century as directors or superintendents in the mines of the Walloon district of the modern Belgium. Both César and his brother Joseph showed marked musical gifts and were sent at a tender age to the Liège Conservatoire. When César himself was twelve, he had already completed his first tour as an infant prodigy with his brother Joseph, who was a violinist. The ambitious father now removed the whole family to Paris, where César first studied privately with Reicha, an admirable musician and author of a number of theoretical works as well as much well-written and attractive chamber-music. In 1837 he entered the Paris Conservatoire, where his feats of transposition and contrapuntal improvisation when competing for the pianoforte and organ prizes became legendary. His father, however, anxious to exploit his talents financially, removed him from the Conservatoire before he had time to compete for the Prix de Rome. César spent the years 1842–3 travelling on concert tours with his brother and composing, in the first place showy piano-pieces for his own repertory, but much more interestingly four piano trios which won him an enviable reputation as the list of subscribers shows. This included the names of Liszt and Chopin as well as the internationally famous opera composers Meyerbeer, Spontini and Donizetti and such gods of the Conservatoire as Adam, Auber, Halévy and the rare French chamber-music composer Onslow. Franck's first orchestral composition, a biblical oratorio entitled *Ruth*, had its first performance in 1846, at the Conservatoire.

César Franck was already resentful of his father's insistence on his continuing the most financially rewarding side of his musical career, but in 1846 this resentment was intensified when he became engaged to a young woman whose mother was the actress Desmousseaux. The conventional Franck family were horrified by this alliance, but after a wedding celebrated at the height of the 1848 revolution Franck settled down to earn his living not by concert-giving but by teaching. This involved him for almost the whole of the rest of his life in an unceasing round of drudgery, since it meant travelling all over Paris to the houses of his pupils, while at week-ends he was taken up with his work as organist and choirmaster at a succession of Paris churches – Notre Dame de Lorette, St Jean-au-Marais and finally St Clotilde.

His position at the Conservatoire, where he was eventually made Professor of the Organ in 1872, was complicated paradoxically by the extreme simplicity, even naïveté, of the man himself. He confronted the many intrigues for position and pupils among his colleagues by a disconcerting innocence which won him the dislike and distrust of the majority, but the

Franck as schoolmaster with pupils Dupaic, d'Indy,
Leken, Chausson, Pierné, etc.

whole-hearted admiration, amounting in some cases almost to adoration, of the few. What was officially an organ class came to be known among the students as in fact the class in which much more general musical problems were discussed in the light of contemporary musical ideas, most notably those of Wagner which were *tabu* with the professors of composition. Before the Franco-Prussian War of 1870–1 Franck already had a number of private composition pupils, including Henri Duparc and Alexis de Castillon, who were instrumental in attracting some of the most gifted and musically inquisitive of the younger composers. These included, during the 1870s and 1880s, Vincent d'Indy, Pierre de Bréville, Charles Bordes, Ernest Chausson and the Belgian Guillaume Lekeu. In d'Indy Franck found not only an extremely gifted musician but a man of ambition and determination with all the gifts for organisation and propaganda that he himself lacked. This group of young composers, known as 'la bande à Franck' soon became a force to be reckoned with in French musical life, which had received in the war and the Commune a salutary shock. While the Conservatoire retained much of its old complacency and continued to train musicians chiefly for the opera or the *opéra comique*, Franck and his pupils devoted themselves to symphonic and chamber-music.

Franck himself continued until the mid-1870s to write music either for the church itself, or of a distinctly ecclesiastical nature; notably the two oratorios *Rédemption* (1873) and *Les Béatitudes*, written between 1870 and 1880. The first of three symphonic poems, in which the influence of Liszt was immediately noticeable, was *Les Eolides* (1877), and this was followed by *Le Chasseur maudit* (1883) and *Les Djinns* (1884), which contained an important part for solo pianoforte. In 1885 Franck produced another work for orchestra and pianoforte, *Variations symphoniques*, which many consider his masterpiece. Indeed, during the 1880s, when the composer was already in his sixties, Franck produced a large body of work incomparably more interesting and original than any that he had composed earlier. A piano quintet was followed by the monumental *Prélude, choral et fugue* and the hardly less ambitious *Prélude, aria et final*, both for pianoforte; and a symphony in D minor and a string quartet in D major completed the tally of this extraordinary 'second spring'. Two operas written during the same

period, *Hulda* and *Ghisèle* witness to his phenomenal productiveness at this time, although they reveal no real gift for the theatre.

Although Franck obtained little or no official recognition for his music during his lifetime, he was idolised by his pupils and no less a personage than Liszt was willing to attest to the superb musical character of his organ improvisations. The organ remains in many ways the key to his musical personality, and the *Trois pièces pour grand orgue* (1878) and *Trois chorals* (1890) were unique in the organ literature of the day. In his use of the orchestra he often betrays a taste for the sonorities characteristic of organ 'mixtures', while the frequent antiphonal passages standing between dramatic rests or fermatas reflect the physical habits of the organist moving from one manual to another or altering registration. Even the strongly chromatic character of his harmony, though no doubt derived ultimately from the music of Liszt and Wagner, suggests the action of the organist's fingers or feet executing a sliding semitonal descent on the keys or pedals. The note of high-pitched idealism or rapturous adoration, frequent in his music, is not always set off by a corresponding forcefulness of the same musical quality; and it was not without reason that he was charged with an inability to give musical expression to more mundane or negative moods. Even his mature pianoforte music occasionally reflects the showiness and facility of his early virtuoso music; and none of his works achieve the sustained grandeur and solemnity of his Austrian contemporary and, in many ways counterpart, Anton Bruckner. The violin sonata, which he wrote in 1886, for his fellow-Belgian Eugène Ysaye, is perhaps his finest monument, alone worthy to be set by the side of the *Variations symphoniques*.

Like many other men of his temperament, Franck unfortunately chose as his wife a woman who quickly succeeded to the position hitherto occupied in his life by his parents; and he only exchanged one set of tyrants, anxious to exploit his gifts financially, for another. He found consolation for this not only in the affection and respect of his pupils in general, but in the devotion of one in particular, the Franco-Irish Augusta Holmès. Although Franck died in 1890, chiefly as the result of being knocked over by an omnibus, his spirit was the guiding force in the formation a few years later of the Schola Cantorum under the direction of two of his favourite pupils

Charles Bordes and then Vincent d'Indy, whose biography did much to present the idealised picture of Franck and his music which inevitably led in time to a reaction and a consequent under-valuing of Franck's music itself and of his influence in the development of French music.

M.C.

FRESCOBALDI, Girolamo
(b. Ferrara, Sept 1583;
d. Rome, 1 March 1643)

Girolamo Frescobaldi, the greatest Italian organist of the 17th century, was born in Ferrara in 1583 and studied with Luzzasco Luzzaschi, the Cathedral organist. Frescobaldi is known to have had a beautiful singing voice, and it is certain that as a young man he enjoyed a considerable reputation both as singer and organist. He is sometimes also referred to as an accomplished lutenist.

In January or February 1607 he was appointed organist at the Church of Santa Maria in Trastevere, Rome, but the appointment was short-lived and during the summer of that year he journeyed to the Netherlands where Sweelinck was, by now, at the height of his powers. Frescobaldi remained in the Low Countries for a year (the preface of the First Book of five-part madrigals is signed 'Antwerp, 1608') but returned to Italy presumably in the autumn of 1608 when the second book of his *Fantasie a 4* was published in Milan.

On the 1st November 1608, Frescobaldi became organist of St Peter's in Rome, and his first performance there is said to have attracted an audience of thirty thousand. He remained at St Peter's until 1628 when he accepted an invitation to become organist to the Grand Duke of Tuscany, Ferdinando de' Medici, in Florence. Eventually social and political uncertainties obliged him to leave, and on the 1st May 1634 he was reinstated as organist of St Peter's, Rome – a position which he occupied until his death. Frescobaldi's great art of organ playing was passed on to other schools through his numerous pupils, the most notable of whom was Froberger who lived in Rome between 1637 and 1641.

Frescobaldi is chiefly remembered today as a composer of keyboard music – his vocal works are rarely heard. His keyboard compositions, which include toccatas, ricercari,

canzoni and variations, were published in a series of ten volumes (though there is a certain amount of duplication, revision and enlargement). The music was published in score in *Fiori Musicali* complete with a recommendation in the preface from Frescobaldi that:

> I consider it of great importance for the player to practise playing from score, not only because I think it necessary for those who wish to intensively study the form of these compositions, but particularly also because it is a test which distinguishes the genuine artist from the ignorant.

The pedagogic value of open score was likewise fully appreciated by Bach as we know from the *Art of Fugue*. Frescobaldi transformed the style of the toccata inherited from Merulo; his bold understanding of harmonic effect infused considerable dramatic contrast – indeed, tension. The toccatas had several functions – as preludes to larger pieces, as complete compositions in their own right and, of course, they were used at certain points in

Frescobaldi by Mellan.

the Mass (the Elevation of the Host). The 'alternatim' practice (substituting organ for choir in alternate verses of plainsong) required contrapuntal treatment of the chant; the 'cantus firmus' may appear in a web of counterpoint, or act as the subject of a fugal paraphrase. Frescobaldi demonstrates both these methods to perfection in the *Fiori Musicale* which appeared in 1635 and later made such an impression on Bach that he copied it out in full.

Complete contrapuntal understanding is also apparent in the strictly fugal ricercari, of which the 'Ricercare Cromatico' is a particularly notable example. Frescobaldi enlarged the scope of the canzona by introducing variation technique – where contrasting sections are unified by transformation of a single theme. Among his most popular, and brilliant, keyboard works are the variations or 'Partitas' as they were called – particularly 'Romanesca', 'Ruggiero', and 'La Follia'. Frescobaldi often prefixed his publications with an introduction to the performer, extremely valuable today for the light thrown on contemporary 17th-century performance style. Precise indications are given for the correct interpretation of certain phrases, yet on the other hand, in the preface to *Fiori Musicali* we learn that 'Some Kyries may be played vivace, others slowly, whichever the player considers correct.'

Frescobaldi, as an organist, was fully aware of the practicalities of service accompaniment – that the music required might differ widely in terms of duration, according to individual circumstances. Thus we are told that:

In the Toccatas I have not only paid regard to the fact that they are rich in varied passages and ornaments but also that the individual sections may be played separately from one another, in order to enable the player to make a conclusion at will, without having to end the Toccata. (Preface to *Toccate d'intavolatura di Cimbalo et Organo . . . Libro Primo, 1637*)

G.G.

GABRIELI, Andrea
(b. Venice, *c* 1520;
d. Venice, 1586)

GABRIELI, Giovanni
(b. Venice, 1557?;
d. Venice, 12 Aug 1612)

Although relatively little is known about their lives, the two Gabrielis, Andrea and Giovanni, were among the finest composers of church music in the 16th century, especially in the grand manner for which the Venetian school was renowned and of which they were the most famous members.

Andrea was born in the part of Venice known as Cannareggio (nowadays the area near the railway station) probably between 1510 and 1520. Nothing is known about his early life, though he may have been a singer at St Mark's, and was certainly the organist of the Venetian church of S Geremia (now S Lucia) in 1558. Shortly after this date, he went to Munich, where he became involved in the group of musicians around Lassus, and travelled widely in southern Germany in 1562, when he attended the celebrations at the coronation of Maximilian II as Holy Roman Emperor. This period in Germany seems to have acted as a catalyst, for from being a total nonentity before it, on his return to Venice about 1566, he became one of the most productive and best-liked composers of his time.

Title page of Andrea Gabrielli's Canto Chori in Musica.

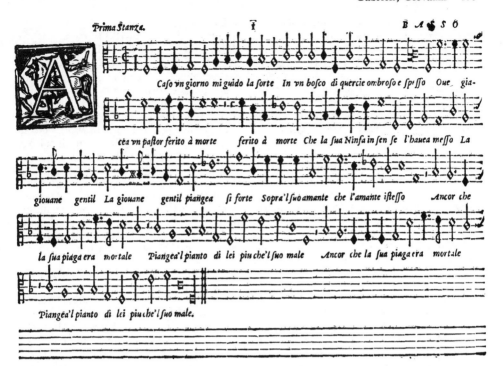

Page of manuscript by Giovanni Gabrieli.

He was appointed one of the organists of St Mark's in September of that year, and almost immediately began publishing music of all kinds. Naturally some of it was church music – masses and motets; but remarkably his secular music was of equal importance. His madrigals were very popular, as were his *giustinianae* – comic portrayals of Venetian eccentrics showing a keen eye for caricature. It was probably in the 1570s that he began writing for the large forces then being built up in St Mark's, adopting that style known as *cori spezzati*, whereby different groups of musicians were stationed in the various galleries of the basilica, so that the sound came from widely separated places. He also was one of the pioneers in using instruments not just to double the voices but to add depth (and height) to the ensemble. Some of this music is among the most brilliant of its time and reflects the glory of the Venetian Republic, whose visitors it was meant to impress. Andrea's grandest music was not published until after his death in 1586, when it was collected and edited by his nephew, Giovanni Gabrieli, whose music was to be even more renowned than his own.

Giovanni was born about the middle of the 1550s (the usually given year is 1557, but this is not certain) and studied with his uncle. He too went to Munich to work with Lassus, arriving there about 1575, and serving as a musician at the Bavarian court for several years. Like his uncle, he was unknown when he went there, but within months of his arrival he published some madrigals and gradually became well known as a composer. He returned to Venice some time before 1584, in which year Andrea arranged for him to act as temporary replacement of the other organist, Merulo, who had left quite suddenly. This led to his permanent appointment from the 1st January, 1585 and he was in the service of St Mark's until his death. The two Gabrielis were colleagues for only a short time, but after Andrea's death, Giovanni took his place as the principal composer of grand ceremonial music. He also held the post as part-time organist to the Scuola Grande di San Rocco, a religious confraternity which prided itself on the sumptuous music performed on the day of its patron saint. This further allowed Giovanni scope as a composer of large-scale music, a role which he fulfilled splendidly for twenty-five years.

In the earlier years after his return to Venice, he wrote some madrigals, mainly for publisher's anthologies, but partly in response to the demand for music in plays which were performed in front of the Doge at various festivities. His greatest efforts, however, were in the field of church music, where he developed many of his uncle's techniques, notably those in the use of *cori spezzati* and in the idiomatic writing for instruments. He went further than Andrea in this, composing music for a large ensemble of instruments – mainly cornetts, violins and sackbuts – without voices, his most famous piece being the *Sonata pian e forte*, not in fact the first to use expression marks or to specify the actual orchestration, as has sometimes been maintained, but a fine work meant probably to express the mystery of the reincarnation at the Elevation of the Host in the Mass.

He collected much of his music in a publication of *Sacrae Symphoniae* (1597). By this time he was extremely well known, more especially in Germany, from where he began to receive a number of pupils. He wrote some works for the court at Graz, and seems to have had connections with people at Augsburg and Nuremberg, amongst other places. He set his pupils the task of writing madrigals in a mannerist style, and his own work reflects his interest in the forward-looking music of Monteverdi, for he composed a number of highly emotional motets, full of strange dissonance and melody, expressing the fear of death and damnation. But other works show his flair for the grand manner, in which he now used solo voices, the chorus and a veritable orchestra in a way anticipating the music of Purcell and others. He had some financial troubles in these later years and suffered from a kidney stone. He died in 1612. Among his last pupils was Schütz, to whom he gave his ring on his death bed. He left many of his works unpublished, but they were collected by one of his pupils and also his confessor, who saw them through the press in 1615. Manuscript copies are also to be found in the collection of the court at Kassel, where Schütz worked for many years, and it was in Germany that his main influence was continued. In Venice he was soon forgotten; but Schütz remembered him forty years later with these words: 'Giovanni Gabrieli – what a man was he.'

D.A.

GERSHWIN, George
(b. New York, 26 Sept 1898;
d. Hollywood, 11 July 1937)

Gershwin's father was a Russian Jew who left St Petersburg and emigrated to the United States of America in the early 1890s – the exact date appears to be unknown. His name was Moishe Gershovitz which he had changed, by the time his sons were born, to Morris Gershvin. In 1895 he married Rose Bruskin, also an immigrant. At that time he was a foreman in a factory making the upper parts of lady's shoes. He was a restless, ambitious but mainly unsuccessful man who nevertheless managed to maintain his family in reasonable comfort; though it is recorded that by 1916 the family had moved house twenty-eight times while the head of the household had tried almost as many occupations.

Into this migratory establishment, the eldest son Ira (christened Israel and generally called Izzy) was born on the 8th December 1896; the second son George (christened Jacob) was born on the 26th September 1898; and a daughter Frances on the 6th December 1906. There seems to have been a rather casual attitude toward names in the Gershwin family. George changed his name to Gershwin when he became a professional musician but other variants of it were used from time to time. George Gershwin described his father as an 'easy-going, humorous philosopher', his mother (generally known as Rosa) as 'nervous, ambitious and purposeful'.

In his early schooldays Gershwin had no interest in music. Then one day in 1904 on 125th Street in Harlem he heard an automatic piano playing Rubinstein's *Melody in F*. It had a strange fascination for him. After this he heard all the music he could and was particularly attracted by the art of a ragtime pianist on Coney Island. The music was obviously sinking in, for on the day in 1910 that the family bought and installed a piano (intended for Ira), George sat down at it and immediately played some of the popular songs of the day. He had lessons with the local lady teacher, progressing to a more advanced tutor soon after, and learned all he could about music by attending regular concerts. He played with a local musical society and then, in 1913, went to the teacher whom he described as 'the first great musical influence in my life' – Charles Hambitzer. By 1913 he was studying with the possible intent of becoming a concert pianist but his real interest was in popular music and jazz and in May 1914 he

George Gershwin.

left school, aged fifteen, and became a staff pianist with the Tin Pan Alley firm of Jerome H. Remick & Co. Accompanying song-pluggers was not a very satisfying task particularly as, when he started writing songs, the company turned them down. His first published song was the lengthily titled 'When you want 'em, you can't get 'em; when you've got 'em, you don't want 'em' which was issued by the Harry Von Tilzer Music Publishing Company in 1916.

Influenced by the music of composers like Jerome Kern and Irving Berlin, Gershwin gradually built himself a reputation as a composer for the theatre. His first successes were songs interpolated into other people's scores; his first full-scale musical was *La La Lucille* in

1919. His reputation was established with songs like 'Swanee' used in the Al Jolson show *Sinbad*, 'I'll build a stairway to Paradise' used in George White's *Scandals of 1922* and 'Somebody loves me' in the *Scandals of 1924*. In January 1924, while Gershwin was working on a show called *Sweet Little Devil,* he read in a newspaper an announcement by Paul Whiteman that Gershwin was working on a jazz concerto for a forthcoming concert at the Aeolian Hall. In fact, he had discussed the possibilities with Whiteman but nothing further. However, Whiteman was persuasive and Gershwin's *Rhapsody in Blue* (orchestrated by Ferde Grofé, Whiteman's arranger and first heard on the 12th February 1924), aroused tremendous interest and variable opinions. It was successful enough to lead to further 'serious' commissions and in 1925 he produced his Piano Concerto in F, which he orchestrated himself.

The show *Lady Be Good* starring the Astaires, coincided with a European trip, and he was in London for its British première. In spite of a now established reputation, Gershwin never relinquished a desire to study music more deeply. He asked both Ravel and Nadia Boulanger to take him on as a pupil but both refused, believing that it was wrong to try to impose their ideas on his natural genius. In his last years he studied for a time with Joseph Schillinger.

Throughout his career Gershwin maintained a remarkable partnership with his brother Ira who was one of the most talented lyric-writers in popular music. It was a true combination of talents rather than mere brotherhood and Ira's ingenious words were the obvious inspiration of many an intricate Gershwin melody. They both went to Hollywood in 1930 and completed some excellent film-scores, starting with *Delicious*. In May 1931 he wrote his *Second Rhapsody* and in 1932, after a trip to Havana, he wrote his *Cuban Overture*. In Hollywood, in the last years of his life, he spoke of plans for a string quartet, a symphony, a ballet and a cantata based on the Gettysburg address. The brain tumour that cut short his life at thirty-eight robbed the world of many Gershwin masterpieces – for surely he would have gone to greater heights. The final proof of this is to be found in his ambitious folk opera *Porgy and Bess*, written after many years of sporadic effort and first produced on the 30th September 1935. Its full acceptance was to come after Gershwin's death. His last works of note were some fine songs for the films *Shall We Dance* and *Damsel in Distress*.

A proper assessment of Gershwin's merits in terms commensurate with those applied to academic musicianship has always proved difficult to make. There is still an unwillingness to accept that anything written in a popular or jazz idiom can be taken seriously. It can be given a nod but cannot be wholeheartedly commended. So *Rhapsody in Blue*, in spite of unabating performances, is sneered at by the highbrow for its lack of form and serious development and by the jazz critic (who is full of blind prejudice) for not being jazz. It is, in fact, a well-contained and shapely rhapsody which exploits and widens the range of the popular song. Any one of its themes could have been a Gershwin song; the composer gives them the strength to stand in purely instrumental terms. It is certainly memorable and effective if you accept the Tin Pan Alley

idiom – even inspired. *An American in Paris* has even more to offer by way of rhapsodic ingenuity but, being more expansive, is less memorable. It has been pointed out that Gershwin's Piano Concerto, which was commissioned by Walter Damrosch, is the most often played of any American concerto and its regular revival and the serious attention it gets from reputable players counters the condescending and uncomprehending sort of remarks that Eric Blom allowed Gershwin in the 1954 Grove. The concerto's themes can stand comparison with those of the Rachmaninov concertos.

The potential ingenuity and imagination of Gershwin is most clearly indicated in the very effective piano transcriptions of his songs, in the three Preludes and the *I Got Rhythm* variations. As a song-writer he came at the right time in America's history. Greatly inspired by Jerome Kern, whose music bridged the gap between the 'straight' and the 'jazz' ages of popular song, he showed to what heights of elegance and literacy the art of Tin Pan Alley could go, particularly when spiced with the preservative jazz idiom. In *Porgy and Bess* (whether it is accepted as an opera or not) he showed that his songs were capable of rising to much greater heights than usually achieved in musical comedy. It could be rated as at least the *Die Fledermaus* of American light opera.

There is no sign of any decline in Gershwin's reputation; indeed it seems to improve steadily and he has been given more literary attention than any other American composer. The approval, once so reluctantly given, is now more or less universal.

P.G.

GIBBONS, Orlando
(b. Oxford, 1583;
d. Canterbury, 5 June 1625)

Orlando Gibbons was born in Oxford and baptised at St Martin's Church on Christmas Day, 1583. The family moved to Cambridge in 1588, and in 1596 Orlando entered the choir of King's College, where his brother, Edward, was then Master of the Choristers. He matriculated in 1598 as 'a sizar from King's' and the 'Mundum' account books show that in 1602 and 1603 he received reimbursement for music composed for special occasions. In March 1605, at the age of twenty-one, Gibbons was appointed organist of the Chapel Royal – a position he held for the remainder of his life. The following year he proceeded to the degree of B.Mus. at Cambridge. At about this time he married Elizabeth, daughter of John Patten of Westminster. Gibbons and his wife lived in the Woolstaple, Westminster, and their seven children were born there and baptised at St Margaret's Church.

In addition to his appointment at the Chapel Royal, Gibbons enjoyed considerable Royal patronage – in 1619, for instance, he succeeded Walter Earle as one of the 'musicians for the virginalls to attend in his hignes privie chamber' at a salary of £46. On the 17th May 1622, Gibbons received the degree of D.Mus. at Oxford. In 1623, he succeeded John Parsons as organist of Westminster Abbey, where, on the 5th April 1625, he was responsible for conducting the music at the state funeral of James I. Two months later the new King, Charles I, summoned the Chapel Royal to Canterbury to await the arrival of his queen, Henrietta Maria, from France. On Wednesday the 5th June, before the queen arrived, Gibbons suffered an apoplectic fit and died. He was buried the next day in Canterbury Cathedral, and a memorial tablet surmounted by his bust and coat of arms, was placed on the north wall of the nave. A copy of a contemporary portrait of Gibbons is in the Faculty of Music at Oxford. The original is unfortunately lost.

Gibbons wrote no music for the Latin rite of the church so far as is known, his great reputation is founded on his English Church music, secular vocal music and instrumental music. His church music includes a full service, a verse service, some forty anthems, two sets of preces, and seventeen hymn-tunes – most of which are found in the collection of *Hymnes and Songs of the Church* published by George Wither in 1623. Very little of Gibbons' music was published in his lifetime – a set of *Madrigals and Mottets of 5 Parts: apt for Viols and Voyces* appeared in 1612, some keyboard pieces in *Parthenia (n.d.)*, and two sacred songs were included in Leighton's *Teares and Lamentacions* (1612).

Gibbons' 'Short' Service is exceptionally tuneful, a quality which secured the work immediate and lasting popularity. The 'Verse' Service stands among the finest of such settings. Of the large-scale full anthems, *Hosanna to the Son of David*, *O clap your Hands*, and *Lift up your heads*, are particularly impressive, To this list must be added the peni-

tential six-part anthem *O Lord in Thy wrath*, a work of solemn intensity. In contrast to the magnificently rhetorical anthems, Gibbons proved himself to be a master of small design, as in the beautiful four-part setting of *Almighty and everlasting God*. A work of similar proportions, the anthem *O Lord, increase my faith*, long attributed to Gibbons, is now known to have been composed by Henry Loosemore, who was organist of King's College, Cambridge. A high proportion of Gibbons' anthems favour the verse structure – alternating passages for solo voice, with choir. Many have accompaniments for viols instead of organ. *This is the record of John* is Gibbons' most popular verse anthem, and clearly demonstrates his absolute mastery of the medium. His sensitive understanding of the declamatory features of the solo voice are fully exploited here and in another superb verse anthem *See, see the Word is incarnate*. He is often said to have experimented with the form and in effect to have prepared it for consolidation in the hands of Blow, Humfrey and Purcell. Gibbons regarded the solo voice more as part of the contrapuntal texture, with constant interplay of idea between voice and instrument resulting in an essentially polyphonic form – a completely different attitude to the Restoration composers.

Gibbons' ever-popular madrigal *The silver swan* (which is in a form closely akin to the 'ayre') is contained in the 1612 publication of *Madrigals and Mottets*. This important collection includes works which rank with the greatest music of the age: for instance, *Now each flowry bank*, *What is our life*, and *Dainty fine bird that art encaged*.

A performer of great accomplishment, Gibbons was described by a contemporary as having 'the best hand in England'. Yet his own keyboard compositions are noticeably restrained. Excluding some of the variations and dances, there are very few instances of the brilliant flourishes which colour so much keyboard music of the period. The Earl of Salisbury's Pavan and Galliard are acknowledged masterpieces among virginal music, and although the magnificent four-part *Fantasia* seems likely to have been intended for the organ, it was included in *Parthenia*, 'the first musicke that ever was printed for the virginalls'. The collection also includes five other keyboard pieces by Gibbons, which in total represents all that were published during the composer's lifetime. *A Fancy For a Double Orgaine*, the sole source of which is Benjamin

Cosyn's Virginal Book of 1620, is the earliest extant example of the form which later became known as the 'double' voluntary. It gives us a glimpse of the qualities of Gibbons' organ playing which commanded such wide respect. Among his string compositions are a set of nine fantasias, the first music ever to be 'cut on copper'. A complete edition of Gibbons' keyboard music was published in 1967 by Professor Gerald Hendrie in the 'Musica Britannica' series.

G.G.

GIORDANO, Umberto
(b. Foggia, 27 Aug 1867;
d. Milan, 12 Nov 1948)

The son of a chemist, Giordano was intended to take up the same profession, but when he displayed an early talent for music his father generously allowed him to study locally. Thanks to the help of a wealthy neighbour he was sent in 1881 for more advanced studies to the Naples Conservatoire, where at the age of twenty-two he wrote his first opera, *Marina*, for the competition promoted by the publisher Sonzogno which was won by Mascagni with *Cavalleria Rusticana*. His meeting with both publisher and fellow-composer played an important part in his later career. Sonzogno commissioned an opera, *Mala Vita*, which was premièred in Rome in 1892 with considerable success, its blatant *verismo* qualities pleasing the taste of the day. Giordano at once abandoned this type of opera dealing with everyday life, however, turning to more romantic subjects for all his later works. He suffered a setback in 1894 when *Regina Diaz* proved a dismal failure at its first performance in Naples, though it was of some value to him in that its music was a necessary step forward to *Andrea Chénier*, the most enduring of all his operas, which made his name internationally two years later.

During these two years Giordano eked out a precarious living in Milan on the small allowance sent to him each month by Sonzogno, who still had faith in him. The composer's own faith in himself was kept alive by his work on the libretto of *Andrea Chénier* which Luigi Illica had provided. 'This *Chénier* will change everything for us,' he wrote to his father, 'and then you will bless the sacrifices you have made for me.' The letter was typical of an unusually modest composer who always appreciated the kindness shown to him by his family and friends, and who behaved in turn with unfailing kindness to those less fortunate than himself. At one point there was a quarrel between composer and librettist, which ended in Giordano visiting Illica and threatening him with a toy pistol. The terrified Illica promised to do anything Giordano asked, then as soon as the latter confessed the weapon was only a toy both men burst out laughing and remained good friends ever afterwards. The opera, duly completed on time for the Scala season, was suddenly withdrawn when one of Sonzogno's advisers told him it was no good. Giordano was then in Florence attending a season of operas by Mascagni, who agreed to meet him to discuss the unexpected action of La Scala. Because of this meeting Mascagni missed the opening ceremony for the city's new transport system, at which the tram he should have been riding in with other distinguished passengers crashed, killing and injuring several people. Believing that Giordano had saved his life, Mascagni went at once to Milan, where he successfully persuaded the management to change its mind about *Andrea Chénier*. The opera was the success of the season, and immediately the cheering was over the composer sent a telegram to Mascagni consisting of the one word, 'Prophet!' *Andrea Chénier* was soon given throughout Italy, reached New York later the same year, and was produced in Moscow the following season. It is interesting that the year 1896 also saw the première of Puccini's *La Bohème*, but whereas Puccini was to go on from strength to strength, Giordano was to join the band of Italian opera composers remembered in most parts of the world only for one youthful success.

The story of Marie-André Chénier, the French poet who became both champion and victim of the French Revolution, was an ideal operatic subject, and by making him fall in love with a member of the aristocracy he so hated in itself the drama was given personal as well as political conflict. Giordano rose magnificently to the challenge, providing lyrical arias for Chénier the poet balanced by equally rewarding heroic outbursts for Chénier the revolutionary. The music of the opera as a whole is most skilfully paced, gathering momentum and intensity all the way from the opening party scene through the grim trial of Chénier to the terror of the prison scene and the exit to the guillotine. The characters are drawn in bold strokes which are matched by music of expressively virile power, with contrasting tender moments which show that Giordano was capable of a light touch when necessary. There is an intriguing parallel between Chénier and the vengeful Gérard in this opera and Cavaradossi and Scarpia in *Tosca*, which was to come four years later and suggest that Puccini had learned something from *Andrea Chénier*. What Giordano lacked, and could never learn from Puccini, was poetic delicacy and subtlety of both vocal and instrumental writing.

Giordano's next success was *Fedora*, premièred in 1898, a highly romantic story of a Russian Princess in love with a Nihilist which takes the audience on a Cook's tour of Paris, Switzerland and St Petersburg. The tenor role of Loris was created by the young Enrico Caruso, whose reputation it established as one of the world's greatest singers. After *Fedora* Giordano composed several operas which enjoyed a measure of success at the time, notably the attractively romantic *Madame Sans-Gêne*, premièred at the Metropolitan in New York in 1915 with Geraldine Farrar as the likeable earthy heroine, and the satirical *La Cena delle Beffe*, brilliantly produced at La Scala, Milan, in 1924 with Toscanini conducting. All failed to keep a place in the repertoire, however, so Giordano is today remembered in Italy as the composer of *Andrea Chénier* and *Fedora*, and in the rest of the world only by the former.

A simple man with a warm sense of humour, Giordano was content with what he had achieved. Was not Chénier the favourite role of Beniamino Gigli and one which most leading tenors fought for? He knew he was no innovator, that his music lacked profundity, but he could console himself with the thought that he had used his modest talents well. He enjoyed the limelight from time to time, but for the most part he preferred to stay at home, spending several hours each day playing the piano. A popular man throughout his life, he was universally mourned in Italy when he died in 1948. He would have appreciated the last tribute paid to him at the funeral: when the cortège came to La Scala on its way to the cemetery the coffin was placed in the open doorway while the orchestra played 'Amor ti vieta', the celebrated tenor aria from *Fedora*. Few composers have left the world to such a fitting gesture.

F.G.B.

GLAZUNOV, Alexander
(b. St Petersburg, 29 July 1865)
d. Paris, 21 March 1936)

It seems to be a strange law of art that those composers whose rise to success is smooth, and whose subsequent career is free of violent perturbations, suffer an abrupt decline in reputation the moment they are safely underground. It was so with Mendelssohn, Gounod, Massenet, Saint-Saëns, Bruch – all regarded nowadays with a lack of reverence that would have puzzled their contemporaries. As to Alexander Glazunov, once accepted as the spiritual heir of Glinka, Tchaikovsky and the 'Kuchka' – the 'mighty five' – he has not even been accorded the dubious immortality of one overwhelmingly popular work like the *Ave Maria* or *Danse Macabre*. It is true that the ballet music of *Raymonda* and *The Seasons* have maintained their place in the gramophone catalogues since the earliest days of the LP; but it would be a highly knowledgeable music lover who could whistle a few bars of either.

From the beginning, Alexander Glazunov was a darling of fate. He was born in St Petersburg on the 29th July 1865, son of a successful publisher. His mother was a good amateur pianist, and studied with Balakirev. At the age of twelve, Glazunov enrolled in the *Realschule* and dropped piano lessons for a while; but Balakirev influenced him to return to music, even suggesting that the boy should go to Mme Glazunova's teacher – a young musician, whom he himself had recommended, called Rimsky-Korsakov. Glazunov became Rimsky's favourite pupil; he and Balakirev encouraged the youth to compose, and when Glazunov produced a symphony in E flat major, they saw to it that it was performed. Glazunov was then sixteen. At this concert, a wealthy timber merchant named Belayev was present, at Rimsky's invitation. He liked the work so much that he travelled to Moscow to hear it performed for a second time. Belayev and Glazunov developed a close friendship, and the timber merchant decided to form a music publishing house to bring the young Russian composers to the attention of the public. A Second Symphony and a tone poem, *Stenka Razin*, were immediately successful. That open-hearted publicist Franz Liszt conducted the First Symphony at Weimar, and the Second Symphony was heard, together with *Stenka Razin*, at the Paris Exhibition of 1899, in a series of Russian concerts arranged by Belayev. In the same year, Glazunov was

Glazunov.

appointed professor at the St Petersburg Conservatory; in 1905, he was elected Director. He made no secret of being a musical conservative, and walked out of a performance of an early Prokoviev work. It must be added that, in spite of his distaste for Prokoviev's discords, he encouraged the young student and secured a performance of his original First Symphony (later destroyed).

Glazunov's fame increased steadily; by 1902 he was well known in England, and his name appeared regularly on American concert programmes. He travelled in Europe and conducted his own music. His one-act ballet *The Seasons* figured prominently in Pavlova's programmes. His eight symphonies were held in high esteem, and regarded as – next to Tchaikovsky's six – the most substantial contribution to the Russian symphonic repertoire.

Glazunov felt no love for the new order that came to power after 1917; nevertheless, he remained in Leningrad until 1928, bringing a valuable sense of continuity to the Conservatory. In that year he left for Paris. He composed little in his last years, and died in 1936, feeling – like many Russian exiles – that fate had played him a disagreeable trick.

It is difficult to know whether Glazunov's music will one day achieve a revival. As one listens to his symphonies – mostly available in Russian recordings – it is easy to see why they were popular. And why the *Violin Concerto* still is. You might be listening to Tchaikovsky or Rimsky-Korsakov – or Taneiev or Liadov, for that matter; but there are none of the surges of emotion that characterise Tchaikovsky, and none of Rimsky's orchestral fireworks. His friend Stasov, the most powerful music critic of the age, said of him: '[His music] is characterised by its incredibly large sweep, power, inspiration, optimism, marvellous beauty, rich imagination, humour, sentimentality and passion. . . .' But a typical modern evaluation – from R. A. Leonard's *History of Russian Music*, comments on Glazunov's generation: 'Neither as a group nor individually were they genuinely creative. Instead they worked chiefly with formulas, which they evolved either by imitating the Nationalist works of their great predecessors or the standard procedures of the West.' To the modern ear, this sounds more accurate than Stasov's biased assessment.

At the same time, it is worth bearing in mind James Bakst's comment that Glazunov was basically an 'objective' composer, whose music has a quality of serenity and objective contemplation 'from a distance'. Before composing this article, the writer listened his way through most of five symphonies, two piano concertos, the violin concerto, two piano sonatas, *Stenka Razin*, *The Seasons*, *Raymonda* and the Third String Quartet. The rather obvious use of the Volga Boat Song in *Stenka Razin* aroused a certain irritation. But the surging climax of the Fourth Symphony, the gaiety and vitality of the opening movement of the Fifth, arrested any inclination to dismiss Glazunov as a feeble, imitative composer. He may be no innovator, but he is a true musician, whose work often has the power to move the emotions – even if only to nostalgia,

as in the Second Piano Concerto. It is significant that Glazunov was labelled 'the little Glinka' at the beginning of his career, and later became known as 'the Russian Mendelssohn'. He has something in common with both composers, as well as with Liszt. In such company, he cannot complain.

C.W.

GLINKA, Mikhail
(b. Novospasskoye, 1 June 1804; d. Berlin, 15 Feb 1857)

It is ironical that the composer generally regarded as the 'father of Russian music', a national school remarkable for its earthy and virile style, should have been a pampered, cosmopolitan dilettante. Mikhail Ivanovich Glinka did not so much achieve greatness as have it thrust upon him by later generations of Russian composers of richer talents who were never more eloquent than when declaring their indebtedness to his trail-blazing. All of them treated with reverence a man who has remained a somewhat shadowy figure to Western eyes and whose two uneven operas, *A Life for the Tsar* and *Ruslan and Ludmilla*, have found no very wide favour outside Russia. Glinka's own *Memoirs* tell us a good deal about the man himself, but throw little light on his creative ideals or practices, while the reminiscences of his sister and others who knew him tend merely to gossip or romanticise over him. It is difficult to place Glinka in proper perspective, because while he was undoubtedly a composer of originality and vision, he was not a positive genius in the sense that Beethoven, Verdi or Wagner were. Perhaps Tchaikovsky summed him up most accurately: he admired Glinka's music so much that he could compare him with Mozart, yet he once wrote that 'Glinka is a talented Russian gentleman of his time, pettily proud, little developed, full of vanity and self-adoration.' Even so, Tchaikovsky regarded Glinka as 'the acorn from which the oak of Russian music sprang'.

To understand Glinka we need to know something about his family and social background and also about the general state of Russian music before he came on the scene. He suffered all his life from a childhood spent in the care of his maternal grandmother, who brought him up, physically and morally, in an enervating hothouse atmosphere. Born in the year when Napoleon became emperor, he lived through a period of tremendous political, social and intellectual upheaval to which he never made any positive response. He enjoyed financial security all his life, working for only two brief periods – first in the Ministry of Communications, then as Master of the Imperial Chapel – because it was always an easy matter for him to exploit the generosity of his doting mother. He was attracted to pretty teenage girls, and if they were empty-headed, so much the better. The one he married, to whom he was consistently unfaithful, finally turned the tables by marrying someone else without taking the trouble to divorce him first. Admittedly he suffered from weak health, but he exaggerated it to provide an excuse for regular travels to warmer climates.

Russia at that time had its own highly individual liturgical music and folk song, but foreign influences dominated in the concert hall and opera house. Curiously, it was the amiable, weak-willed Glinka, whose youthful facility was not developed at the time, who finally threw off these influences and created a true Russian style. This was a slow process, however, his earliest songs and chamber compositions (later discarded) following conventional patterns, and his first real studies taking place on his visit to Italy in 1830 when he was twenty-six years old. During this three-year period he worked with Italian teachers, meeting Bellini, Donizetti and, more briefly, Mendelssohn. More serious studies followed in Berlin, and when he eventually returned home in 1834 on the death of his father he was already resolved to compose a national opera. The result was *A Life for the Tsar* (known in Russia today under the title *Ivan Sussanin*), which was premièred in the presence of the imperial family in St Petersburg on the 9th December 1836. It proved a wild success, admired on the immediate level for its freshness and patriotic appeal while more perceptive critics and fellow-musicians appreciated it as something radically new, a work which could well establish a genuine school of Russian opera. The vocal writing may owe a great deal to Italian influences, which is not surprising since, on his own admission, he had 'shed copious floods of tears of emotion' over Bellini's *La Sonnambula*; but the imaginatively-varied orchestration represented a considerable advance on his Italian models and was to influence all the later Russian nationalist composers including Rimsky-Korsakov. The story of Russia's defeat of an invading Polish army, with Ivan

Susasin as the hero who sacrifices his own life by leading the Poles on a false trail, gave Glinka scope to bring in music of strongly contrasted Polish and Russian character. *A Life for the Tsar* also pioneered the use of leitmotifs long before Wagner began to elaborate this system of giving unity to a dramatic score. Sussanin's final aria, one of the glories of the opera, is in fact made up of themes already heard in earlier scenes.

Six years later Glinka completed his second opera, *Ruslan and Ludmilla,* a fantastic tale of magical plot and counter-plot adapted from a poem by Pushkin. Curiously, Glinka abandoned the leitmotif system that he had used with such skill and imagination in *A Life for the Tsar*, but in other respects he established stylistic patterns that his successors were all to continue. The opera combines heroic declamatory writing with more lyrical flowerings which are distinctively Russian in flavour. It also abounds in unusual harmonies which effectively express the supernatural elements of the story, as well as incorporating authentic oriental themes to create the fantasy atmosphere which Rimsky-Korsakov, in particular, was later to favour so much. Finally, he provided a variety of exotically scored dances and choruses which anticipated those of Borodin's *Prince Igor* and other Russian operas. At times, however, he would slip back into florid arias in slavish imitation of the Italian school. *Ruslan and Ludmilla,* therefore, was not wholly original or purely Russian in style, but considering that Glinka was virtually working in a vacuum it is a miracle that he was able to progress as far as he did along a new road. Without his two operas, uneven as they are, it is unlikely that Mussorgsky could have composed *Boris Godunov,* or Tchaikovsky *Eugene Onegin.* The failure of *Ruslan and Ludmilla* to please the public threw Glinka into the deepest despair, and his last years were sadly unproductive. He continued to produce occasional orchestral, choral and chamber works, as he had done before during his major effort to establish himself as a composer of opera, but his inspiration had lost momentum.

For most of the last thirteen years of his life Glinka travelled around Europe, spending considerable periods of time in Paris, Berlin, Madrid and Seville. In Spain he made a close study of the *cante jondo* as well as the local dark-eyed beauties. Occasionally he returned to Russia, but always the more sophisticated capital cities lured him back, and it was in

Berlin that he died and was originally buried. Four months later, with cultured Russians paying extravagant tributes to the composer they had neglected to their loss, the remains of the 'father' of their national music were taken from Berlin to be reinterred in St Petersburg.

F.G.B.

GLUCK, Christoph Willibald
(b. Erasbach, 2 July 1714;
d. Vienna, 15 Nov 1787)

Gluck was born at Erasbach in the Upper Palatinate (Oberpfalz), the sun of a huntsman and forester of German-Bohemian birth. Three years later his father was appointed ranger to Count Kaunitz and the family moved to Neuschloss, near the then Böhmisch Leipa, in the modern Czechoslovakia. In 1722 they moved again, to Böhmisch Kamnitz, where Gluck's father became a forester to Count Kinsky and in 1724 to Reichstadt, as forester to the Duchess of Tuscany. The year following, when the boy was still only eleven, his father re-entered the Kinsky service and returned to Böhmisch Kamnitz. Whether, as seems probable, the young Gluck spent the years 1726–8 at the Jesuit school in Komotau is uncertain, as is the tradition that he entered as a student at Prague University in 1732. We know that he was in Prague between 1732 and 1736, earning money by teaching and performing music (violin, violoncello and keyboard instruments); that he acted as assistant organist at the Teinkirche and St James' church in Prague and that he had some lessons from Černohorsky. Probably in 1729 his father once again moved, to become head forester to Prince Lobkowitz, and it was no doubt this connection that eventually brought the young Gluck to Vienna as a chamber musician in the Lobkowitz household. This was in 1736. A year later he was heard by a Prince Melzi, a civil servant in the Austrian administration of Lombardy, who took him to Milan, where for the next three years he studied with Sammartini. Between 1741–5 Gluck produced his first operas in Milan, Venice, Bologna, Crema and Turin and with such success that he received an invitation to visit London, where he went with his original patron, Prince Lobkowitz, during the late summer of 1745. The party stayed in Paris en route and here Gluck heard a number of French operas, including Rameau's.

The political situation in London immedi-

ately after the Jacobite rebellion of 1745 was not favourable to the arts, but Gluck made a hasty *pasticcio* for a topical text and *La caduta dei giganti* was produced in London on the 7th January 1746. Another *pasticcio* followed in March and before leaving London in the autumn Gluck met Arne and also Handel, who liked him but thought him a poor contrapuntist. Six trio sonatas of his were published in London that November. For the next three years Gluck worked as conductor to Pietro Mingotti's travelling Italian opera company, visiting Leipzig, Dresden, Hamburg, Copenhagen and eventually Holland. During this time he returned to Vienna for the production of his *Semiramide riconosciuta* (May 1748) and in Copenhagen he appeared, as he had in London, as a soloist on 'the glasses' or glass harmonica. Back in Vienna in 1749 he met a well-to-do banker, Joseph Pergin, whose daughter he asked in marriage. The request was refused, but Pergin died the following year and Gluck married Marianne Pergin and settled comfortably in Vienna on his wife's considerable fortune.

Marriage did not interrupt for long the nomadic existence characteristic of a successful opera-composer in the mid-18th century. In 1751 he was in Prague for his *Ezio* and again a few months later for *Issipile*, and his visit to Naples for the production of *La Clemenza di Tito* took up most of the second half of 1752. He returned to Vienna in December and very soon afterwards obtained the post of conductor for the private orchestra of Prince Hildburghausen, one of the spectacularly unsuccessful Austrian commanders in the war with Turkey which ended in the disastrous Peace of Belgrade. It was through this position that Gluck became known at the court of the Empress Maria Theresa, whom Hildburghausen entertained at his summer palace in 1754. *Le Cinesi*, presented on that occasion, so pleased the Emperor Francis I that he arranged for its performance in Vienna; and Gluck himself was engaged the same year as musical director to the court by Count Durazzo, director of the imperial theatres.

Gluck was now forty. He had written at least twenty operas, *pasticci* or similar *feste teatrali* without arousing much more than general satisfaction. In Durazzo, however, he met an intelligent man who had long been interested in the 'reform' of Italian opera on what could be called French lines – the redressing of the balance, that is to say, be-

Gluck.

tween music and drama; the elimination of the castrati; and the unification of music, drama, scenery and production into a single coherent complex. In Vienna the master-librettist of the old unreformed *opera seria*, Pietro Metastasio, was still poet laureate, but there was a growing opposition to the ideals which he represented, and Durazzo was a leading member of this opposition. Another Italian, the dancer Gasparo Angiolini, was keenly interested in a similar reform of the ballet and in 1761 there arrived in Vienna Ranieri Calzabigi who, beside running a lottery organised in Paris by Madame de Pompadour and indulging in financial speculation on a large scale, was a man of learning and wit and (on Casanova's own evidence) 'a great lover of women'. It was such a character as this that the anti-Metastasio faction needed, a bold intriguer and strategist as well as a poet. Calzabigi himself says that he 'chose' Gluck as the composer best suited to give musical expression to the new operatic ideals and it happened that between 1755 and 1760 Gluck had indeed had experiences that had enlarged his purely professional attitude and made him think about the nature of opera. In the first place he had met the antiquarian and aesthete Winckelmann on a visit to Rome for the production of his *Antigono* (1756) and in the second he had been commissioned by the court to adapt, or to imitate, the French *opéras comiques* which the Austrian ambassador in Paris relayed among the examples of the latest fashions.

The first work of the 'reform' group to which Gluck wrote the music was not an opera but a ballet, *Don Juan* (October 1761); but this caused nothing like the excitement, and eventual enthusiasm, aroused by *Orfeo ed Euridice* on the 5th October 1762. The libretto, by Calzabigi, contains beside the two lovers only the god of Love and the various choruses (mourners, demons and blessed spirits) to which the new theorists attached especial importance. The title-role, it is true, was still sung by a castrato and the overture, instead of initiating the drama, is hardly more than a prolonged fanfare to obtain silence before the work opens. If *Orfeo*, therefore, was something of a transitional work, it was *Alceste* (1767) that not only showed the principles of the reform complete and unambiguous, but also stated them in the preface written by the composer. In the intervening years Gluck had paid a visit to Italy with the composer Dittersdorf and had produced his *Tionfo di Clelia* – a traditional setting of a Metastasio text – at Bologna. It would be wrong to imagine Gluck like Wagner, a conscious revolutionary dedicated to his new ideals. He was, and always remained, a professional composer of the

18th-century type, ready to compose to commission in any style suited to the occasion. In 1764 he even produced a comedy *La Rencontre imprévue*; and in the same year he visited Paris, where *Orfeo* was published though not yet performed, and Frankfurt, where it was given with the original cast and the fifteen-year-old Goethe in the audience. That he was still on good terms with Metastasio is shown by the fact that the old poet wrote a special libretto ('Il Parnaso confuso') for Gluck to set to celebrate the second marriage of the future emperor Joseph II. This same year he also wrote a *Telemacco* which contains music that he was to use again in the future. It is probable that the Vienna performance of Traetta's *Ifigenia in Tauride*, which Gluck conducted, was not without its influence on him, since Traetta had already written Italian operas very much in the 'reform' spirit for the Bourbon court at Parma.

Gluck was now a rich man and able in 1768 to buy a handsome house, but his marriage was childless and in 1769 he and his wife adopted his ten-year-old niece, Marianna Hedler, who had already shown musical talent and was to become a fine singer. Another opera in the spirit of the reform and with a libretto by Calzabigi, *Paride ed Elena*, was given in Vienna in 1770, but Gluck had retired from his court appointment at the same time as Durazzo, in 1764, and his future lay not in Vienna but in Paris, which he visited in 1773 with his wife and adopted daughter. A member of the French Embassy in Vienna, François du Roullet, had already approached him with a libretto, *Iphigénie en Aulide,* and in 1773 Gluck undertook to write five operas for Paris. The first of these was *Iphigénie en Aulide*, given in Paris on the 19th April, 1774 after long rehearsals with the composer, who found much to correct in the traditional style of production. This had hardly changed since the days of Lully, since Rameau had concentrated all the interest of his operas on the music and introduced few innovations in their dramatic presentation. Gluck's former singing-pupil, the Austrian princess Marie-Antoinette, was married to the Dauphin (the future Louis XVI) and did much to forward the cause of her old teacher's music, which caused an uproar in the French musical world. The brilliant journalists who played a large part in French intellectual life at this time organised cabals for and against Gluck's music, and his opponents not only organised a hostile claque at the performance of a French version of *Alceste* (1776), but also engaged an Italian composer hitherto known for comic opera, Niccola Piccinni, to write works in opposition to Gluck. Although Gluck's Paris successes were acknowledged officially when he was appointed Imperial Court Composer in Vienna, his life was greatly saddened by the death of his adopted daughter in 1776.

The production of Piccinni's *Roland* (January 1778) only inflamed the quarrel between Gluckists and Piccinists, in which the Gluckists had already scored another major success in the preceding September, when Gluck's *Armide* was given. The two composers felt no animosity towards each other, and Piccinni was to show a touching and sensible willingness to learn from his much greater rival without sacrificing the natural Italian character of his own music. Vienna and Paris were now the two poles of Gluck's existence and he was perpetually travelling from one to the other. On one of these he visited Voltaire, living in exile at Ferney, a few weeks before the old man died (1778). Between March and November that year Gluck was in Vienna composing his *Iphigénie en Tauride*, to a libretto by Nicolas-François Guillard, a work that was to crown his career; and also the much slighter *Echo et Narcisse*, with a libretto by the Baron Tschudi. *Iphigénie en Tauride* had its first performance at the Opera on the 18th May 1779, and succeeded as it deserved to do; but the second work failed when it was produced in September and Gluck, who was now sixty-five, decided to abandon the French scene and retire to Vienna. He must have been influenced in this decision by considerations of health, as he had already had several 'apoplectic seizures' (perhaps minor thromboses) when he left Paris at the end of October. A more serious stroke partly paralysed him in 1781 and forced him to give up work on the operatic setting of Klopstock's *Hermannschlacht* which he had had in mind ever since 1771, when he set a number of Klopstock's odes to music and paid the poet two visits in 1774 and 1775. In Vienna he gave his paternal support to Salieri, who had spent much time there since 1766 and was to become Court Kapellmeister in 1780; and he was delighted by a performance of Mozart's *Entführung* specially given for him in 1782 and by a concert the following year at which Mozart improvised variations on a theme from the old man's *La Rencontre imprévue*. It was to Salieri that Gluck gave the manuscript of a *De Profundis* which he wrote in 1782 and Salieri whom he recommended to the Paris Opéra. When Salieri's *Les Danaïdes* was produced in Paris (1784), Gluck's name stood with his on the programme, and this caused Calzabigi to make a public protest over Gluck's treatment of him, since the libretto of *Les Danaides* was identical with Calzabigi's *Ipermestra*, which Gluck had undertaken to compose in 1778. Gluck died of a final stroke in November 1787 after entertaining two friends from Paris to lunch.

Gluck's importance in the history of opera far outweighs that which attaches to his name in the history of music generally. Italian composers before him (including, as we have seen, Traetta; and also Jommelli) had begun to work towards the ideal which was eventurlly embodied in the six 'reform' operas written by Gluck between 1762 and 1779. No other composer, however, showed himself able to understand and assimilate the aesthetic ideals of Winckelmann, one of the main sources of the Neo-Classical movement; the plastic ideas embodied in the new ballet initiated by Noverre; and the concentrated drama of the texts supplied by Calzabigi. Gluck was before all else a great man of the theatre, and his music makes little effect outside its dramatic setting. He himself liked to compare the work of the opera-composer to that of the ceiling-painter, who must be able to calculate exactly the effect of his work when seen from below and at a distance. Gluck's music owes much of its greatness to its austerity of design, the refusal of all the dramatically inessential musical ornament that characterises the operas of Rameau, far more interesting from a purely musical point of view, but too often enfeebled dramatically by decorative passages. Gluck sought a unity which develops, without interruption, from the overture onwards; a pathos and a magnificence to which the orchestra and the chorus contribute almost as much as the solo singers; and that truth to Nature which was the ideal of J. J. Rousseau and the philosophers of Diderot's great Encyclopaedia. Yet paradoxically his operas look backwards rather than forwards. They are still conceived if not for the court, at least for a minority of connoisseurs. It is interesting to observe that Mozart's operas in the old Italian manner – *Idomeneo* in his youth and *La Clemenza di Tito* at the end of his life – are nowhere indebted in any way to Gluck, whose only influence on future composers is to be found in those of the French school, and most notably in Berlioz, whose admiration for Gluck's music was hardly this side of idolatry.

Three lines sum up his position and his affinities among his contemporaries and successors:

Lessing der Oper, die durch Göttergunst
Bald auch in Mozart ihren Goethe fand;
Der grösste nicht, doch ehrenwert vor allen

(The Lessing of the opera, which by heaven's grace
Soon found in Mozart its Goethe:
Not the greatest among musicians, but worthy of honour before all)

M.C.

GOLDMARK, Carl
(b. Keszthely, 18 May 1830;
d. Vienna, 2 Jan 1915)

Goldmark is one of those composers whose posthumous reputation rests almost entirely upon one work. In his own day, however, a large number of his compositions were highly regarded. He was born into a Jewish family in the old Austro-Hungary, his father being the cantor at the synagogue in their Hungarian village. The child was taught music by the village schoolmaster, and it was early discovered that he was especially gifted as a violinist. At the age of fourteen, he was sent to Vienna where he studied violin at the Conservatorium, and also took lessons in harmony. When the Conservatorium was closed during the 1848 revolution, the now eighteen-year-old Goldmark took a job in the theatre orchestra in the Hungarian provincial town of Györ. It was while he was there that he was one day arrested and was about to be shot as a rebel when the mistake was discovered just in time.

On his return to Vienna in 1850, Goldmark began to compose in earnest: chamber music, songs and other small pieces. Later he went to Budapest to study, but by 1860 he was back in Vienna teaching piano. His symphony, subtitled *Ländliche Hochzeit* or *Rustic Wedding,* the work by which his name is known today, was first performed in 1876. It is in five movements, instead of the usual four, which led the Viennese critics to wonder whether it could properly be described as a symphony. Brahms, who was a close friend of Goldmark (the two men used to go hiking together in the mountains), pointed out that the question depended not on the number of movements but on whether the composition had the char-

acteristics of a symphony and was constructed as such. The piece is, in fact, symphonic in construction, and is orchestrated with an almost Brahmsian warmth.

For several years, Goldmark played in the orchestra of the Carl Theatre in Vienna. The knowledge and experience he gained playing a wide variety of theatre music obviously stood him in good stead when he came to compose operas. His first, *Die Königin von Saba* (*The Queen of Sheba*) took him nearly ten years to compose. When it was staged at the Vienna Opera in 1875, it was immediately successful, and was produced in several other German and Austrian theatres as well as in New York. For years, Goldmark was known for this one work, though it is but rarely performed today. None of his other five operas rivalled it in popularity. They include *Das Heimchen am Herd*, based on *The Cricket on the Hearth* by Charles Dickens, and *Ein Wintermärchen*, based on Shakespeare's *A Winter's Tale*. This latter work was composed when Goldmark was nearly eighty.

C.O.

GOUNOD, Charles
(b. Paris, 18 June 1818;
d. Saint-Cloud, 18 Oct 1893)

Gounod was born in Paris, where his father was a painter of some talent, having won a second Grand Prix de Rome in 1783. Early piano lessons from his mother, who was a daughter of a Conservatoire professor of the piano, Pierre Zimmermann, were followed by a full classical education at the Lycée Saint Louis, so that when Gounod entered the Conservatoire in 1836 he was already a Bachelor of Arts. His further musical education had begun privately some time before, so that he won a second Prix de Rome in 1837 and the Grand Prix de Rome itself in 1839. His masters were Paer and Lesueur (who also taught Berlioz) for composition and Halévy for counterpoint. Unlike Berlioz, he found in Rome itself musical experiences that were to influence his whole life and development. These were the performances of Palestrina in the Sistine Chapel, which prompted the young composer to try his own hand at the austere polyphonic style of church music then totally out of fashion. In May 1841 his three-part Mass with orchestra was performed at the French church in Rome, San Luigi ai Francesi, and a Requiem and unaccompanied three-part Mass composed shortly afterwards were performed in Vienna, where Gounod stayed some time on his way home from Rome to Paris. In Rome he had met Fanny Henselt, Mendelssohn's sister, and he now met Mendelssohn, heard the Leipzig Gewandhaus orchestra, then the best in Europe, and made the acquaintance of Schumann's music. In fact, on his return to Paris Gounod was almost unique among French composers of the day in his knowledge of the latest contemporary music and the standards of performance outside France.

His friendships in Rome and the influence of the Dominican preacher Père Lacordaire, as well as temperamental inclination, determined the course of Gounod's career on his return to Paris. He accepted the post of organist and choirmaster in the church of the Missions Etrangères in the Rue du Bac, where

he attempted to introduce music, including that of Palestrina, very different from the existing repertory of sentimental and operatic works common in Catholic churches at this time. But his religious enthusiasm went further and led him eventually (1846) to become an external student at the seminary of Saint Sulpice. Between 1845 and 1850 there were no performances of new works by him except two Masses for men's voices only, but in 1851 numbers from his *Messe Solennelle à Sainte Cecile* were given in one of Hullah's concerts at St Martin's Hall, London and won glowing notices.

Gounod's vocation to the priesthood, however, proved no more than a passing phase in the life of a man whose subsequent career proved him to be wholly dominated by his emotions. A friendship with the singer Pauline Viardot (who was for many years the mistress of the Russian novelist Turgeniev) led not only to an engagement to one of her daughters, but also to an interest in the opera, the most common and certainly the most lucra-

Gounod at work.

tive field for French composers at this time. The engagement fell through, but Pauline Viardot sang the title role in Gounod's first opera, *Sapho* (Paris Opéra, 1851), which was praised by Berlioz and became the foundation of Gounod's reputation in the theatre. His life-long interest in choral singing found expression in the choruses written for Ponsard's play *Ulysse* (1852), and in the same year he was appointed conductor of the Paris 'Orphéon', a men's choral society for which he was to write his second Mass for men's voices only (1870). His second opera, based on Lewis's *Monk*, and entitled *La Nonne Sanglante* was a failure in 1854, but the much more modest *Le Médecin malgré lui*, based on Molière (1857), showed him at the height of his powers as a craftsman and lyricist and untouched by the grandiosity and theatrical pretentiousness of the current operatic style popularised by Meyerbeer.

With *Faust* (1859), written in a comparable style with spoken dialogue and no ballet, he achieved his first resounding success which also proved in many ways his undoing. Asked to write sung recitatives for a performance in Strasbourg, he complied and ten years later, with ballet added, the present familiar version of the work was given at the Paris Opéra. During those ten years Gounod also wrote the modest and delightful *Philémon et Baucis* and *La Colombe*, both of which had their first performance in 1860, and a year later the much more pretentious and Meyerbeerian *La Reine de Saba* (Opéra, 1862). A Provençal opera based on Mistral's *Miréio* (*Mireille*, 1864) proved over-long and was cut from five acts to three, but again shows Gounod's charming if limited melodic gift and a nice sense of atmosphere. This was given at the Théâtre Lyrique, where *Faust* was first presented, and so was his next opera, *Roméo et Juliette*. The two librettists, Barbier and Carré, who were already responsible for the texts of *Le Médecin malgré lui*, *Faust*, *Philémon et Baucis*, *La Colombe* and *La Reine de Saba*, constructed on this occasion a skilful and on the whole remarkably faithful version of Shakespeare's play, and *Roméo et Juliette* is arguably Gounod's finest work for the stage. The prevalence of the love interest gave the composer almost unlimited opportunity to exploit his lyrical vein, but Juliet's waltz-song, the Queen Mab music and the page Stephano's provocative 'Que fais-tu, blanche tourterelle?' are also in the very finest French operatic tradition. Although much admired by Sir Thomas Beecham *Roméo et*

Juliette has not won favour comparable to that of *Faust* in this country, but it is still regularly given in France.

The outbreak of the Franco-Prussian war in 1870 found Gounod holidaying by the seaside with his wife, whom he had married in 1864. With a number of other French artists, including Pauline Viardot, he fled to London and this change of scene brought about a great change in his musical interests as well as in his private life. The fact that his stay in England was prolonged until 1875, long after the end of the war, was due to his close relationship with a gifted, influential but eccentric and psychologically unstable woman, Mrs Augusta Weldon, separated from her husband and wholly devoted to the cause of musical education and to furthering her own career as a singer. He returned to Paris in 1871 for the first performance of his patriotic cantata *Gallia*, but his chief musical concerns during these years in London were conducting the Philharmonic, the Crystal Palace and other concerts and the formation of a choir named first after himself, then the Albert Hall Choral Society and eventually the Royal Choral Society. Abandoning the opera, he turned his attention again to choral music often with liturgical texts (*Missa brevis, Messe des anges gardiens, Messe brève pour les morts*) but also indulged to the full that vein of saccharine piosity already familiar from *Jésus de Nazareth* and *Bethléem*, both written during the 1850s, and exploited in England with only a minimal variation to suit the Protestant rather than the Catholic ethos. Most important of all was his experience of large English choirs, whose performances were a revelation to him as they had been to Handel and Haydn; and it was this experience that prompted him to compose the two 'sacred trilogies' which were his most important works of the 1880s – *La Rédemption* (1881) and *Mors et vita* (1884).

Gounod's affair with Mrs Weldon, who was rapidly moving towards the state of mental disintegration which made the last years of her life a nightmare of litigation and even involved her in a prison sentence, dragged on interminably with quarrels, reconciliations and even a lawsuit, which naturally caused havoc in his family circle. Of the three operas that he wrote after his return from England only *Polyeucte* (Opéra, 1878) had at least a *succès d'estime*. In this he tried to apply to dramatic music the principles which had for long guided him in composing for the

church – a minimum of modulation, a maximum of rhythmic simplicity and a recitative not far removed from liturgical monotone. The suavely platitudinous result failed to interest the public. Gounod called it 'la fresque musicale' – musical fresco-work – and there are many examples of it in *La Rédemption* and *Mors et vita*, as well as in the nine Masses that he wrote between 1882 and his death in 1893.

Many years earlier, while he was engaged in writing *Roméo et Juliette*, he had written to a friend, 'In the midst of this silence I seem to hear an interior voice speaking to me of something very great, very clear, very simple and very childlike.' His detractors might well suggest that this was no more than flatulence, and there is no doubt that Gounod was unable to distinguish the sublimely simple from the simply banal in his own music. He is among the composers who is at his best when he does not aim too high, as is shown not only by the less pretentious of his operas but by a number of charming drawing-room songs and the *Petite Symphonie* for wind instruments written five years before his death. His bland, suave lyrical line had a deep influence on French opera composers of the next generation after his own, most notably Bizet (Micaela's music in *Carmen* is almost pure Gounod) and Massenet, who was nicknamed 'la fille de Gounod'; and also on English composers of church music, among whom he succeeded to the position earlier held by Mendelssohn.

Gounod's music has a great purity of line and an immaculately transparent texture. What he lacked was the ability to sustain a melody without frequent cadences, and any deep reserves of either thought or imagination. It is essentially an art of the surface, a fact suggested by Wagner who spoke of Gounod's as 'face-powder music', which is unjust as a general judgment but an apt image of its weakness.

M.C.

Title page of Gounod's Faust.

GRANADOS, Enrique
(b. Lérida, 27 July 1867;
d. at sea, 24 March 1916)

Granados belongs by heritage to a different Spain from either Albéniz or Falla. His father was from Cuba, an officer serving in the Spanish army, and his mother was a Montañesan from Santander in the north, lying remote beyond Castile. A delicate child, he showed musical aptitude very early and undertook piano studies when his family moved to Barcelona, where he won a competition at sixteen and studied with Felipe Pedrell, supporting himself as a café pianist. Private patronage enabled him to go to Paris in 1887, but illness kept him from the Conservatoire's entry examinations and he studied the piano privately for two years before returning to Barcelona, where he settled and married. Here he acquired a fine reputation as a pianist, shared concerts with Casals, Crickboom, Thibaud and other leading artists of their time, and founded his own piano school, the Academia Granados, in 1901.

By this time he had begun to compose some of the early *Danzas españolas* for piano, which still retain their popular appeal, and of which he also made some orchestral versions. He was attracted to the theatre, and scored a popular success in 1898 with his first opera, *Maria del Carmen*, a zarzuela grande which owed much of its appeal to the distinctive Murcian regional flavour of its music. In five subsequent operas, his lyric gift was led astray by unsuitable libretti, and his feeling for the voice found its best expression in collections of songs, many of which were composed after the style of the 18th-century *tonadillas*. His love for this period of Spanish history was combined with a serious study of Domenico Scarlatti in his two books of *Goyescas* – in which the art of Goya provides subject-matter for piano pieces of outstanding poetic imagination and vivid yet elegant pictorial character.

Except in the operas, and in an overblown Lisztian symphonic poem on Dante's *Divina commedia*, Granados sought modesty and simplicity of form, but indulged a supple melodic line and a tendency to over-ornamentation – traits characteristic of the music of Montañesa. These qualities are given a deeper expressive character in his later *Canciones amatorias*, settings of the best classic Spanish poets, which have been justly compared to Schumann's *Dichterliebe* in beauty of style and poetic sensibility. His talent also extended to exuberant improvisation, much

Enrique Granados.

GRÉTRY, André
(b. Liège, 11 Feb 1741;
d. Montmorency, 29 Sept 1813)

Grétry received his early musical training first as a chorister at St Denis, Liège, and then as a pupil of Nicolas Renekin and Henri Moreau, both local musicians. His early compositions (symphonies, masses and motets) evidenced sufficient talent to win him a grant allowing him to study for a period in Italy. From 1760 to the beginning of 1766 he was attached to the Liège College in Rome; here he engaged in a thorough, if highly conservative, course in compositional techniques under G. B. Casali, *maestro di capella* at St John Lateran. Afterwards he took the examination of the *Accademia dei Filarmonici* in Bologna (supervised by Padre Martini) qualifying himself for a church post. However, his future was to lie in an entirely different direction.

His interest in the theatre received its first real encouragement with the success of *Le Vendemmiatrice*, an intermezzo commissioned for and performed during the Roman carnival in 1765. Grétry moved next to Geneva, where he composed the music for the comedy *Isabelle et Gertrude* (1767); again a success. After this, on the advice of Voltaire, he decided to try his luck in Paris. But *Les Mariages samnites* (1768) was a disaster. It offended Parisian taste. To please a French audience, Grétry had to learn to handle French declamation in the approved style, to study the manner in which his *dramatis personae* might be presented with deeper psychological insight, and to be prepared to simplify his musical inventiveness, to make it fully the servant of dramatic events. He needed only a year: in 1768 he produced *Le Huron* (libretto by Marmontel) at the Théâtre des Italiens; it enjoyed an immediate and resounding success.

Le Huron was the first of a long series of stage works with which Grétry established and maintained his position in Paris as the leading composer of *opéra comique* during the latter part of the 18th century. His attempts at tragédie, for example in *Andromaque* (1780), did not meet with the same success. His muse was not suited to that genre. Operas such as *Lucile* (1769), *Le Tableau parlant* (1769), *Sylvain* (1770), and *Zémire et Azor* (1771) revealed the strengths of Grétry's genius, and those aspects upon which he was to build. *Lucile*, by its tenderness and simplicity, found a particularly responsive resonance in the naïve sensibilities of the Parisian public; *Le*

enjoyed by his friends and reflected for us in the *Allegro de Concierto* for piano, which became a permanent set piece for the Madrid Conservatory diploma. He made a version of *Goyescas* as a short opera, with a narrative libretto by Fernando Periquet fitted to existing music, but the outbreak of war in 1914 prevented its intended production at the Paris Opéra. It was given instead at the New York Metropolitan Opera in 1916 with some success, and with a newly-composed Intermezzo which became widely popular on its own account. Granados and his wife attended the première, but on the return journey their ship, the *Sussex*, was torpedoed by a German submarine while crossing from Folkestone to Dieppe. According to the master, who brought his crippled ship into port, Granados drowned in going to the aid of his wife, who perished with him.

N.G.

Grétry.

Tableau parlant, in its open humour, radiated unaffected joy; *Zémire et Azor*, through the richness of Grétry's invention, added oriental splendour to the fantasy of Marmontel's libretto. In these works Grétry derived from Italian sources his melodic freshness and sense of line; from French sources his simple declamatory style. He endeared himself to the *philosophes* by his natural grace and simplicity, and yet remained close enough to his Italian roots to earn himself the title 'The French Pergolesi'.

Of his operas after *Zémire et Azor*, the three he wrote on libretti by d'Hele (alias Hales), *Le Jugement de Midas* (1778), *L'Amant jaloux* (1778), and *Les Evénements imprévus* (1779), were among his most popular, combining in equal measure charm and good humour. But we have to wait for the works of the 1780s, and in particular *Richard-Coeur-de-Lion* (1784), to reach the summit of his career.

Grétry continued to compose for the stage after the overthrow of the French monarchy, but of course on subjects near to Republican ideals (*Guillaume Tell*, 1791; *Denis le Tyran*, 1794; etc.), but it is clear that the composer's heart was not in his work. As he wrote less and less as a musician, so he took to literary activities, publishing his *Mémoires* (1789–97) and engaging on other works of a general philosophical nature, such as *De la Vérité* (Paris, 1800/1) and *Réflexions d'un Solitaire* (MS). Having lost all three of his daughters and his wife, he spent his declining years in isolation in the former hermitage of J. J. Rousseau at Montmorency. Here he died in comparative obscurity in 1813.

E.H.

GRIEG, Edvard
(b. Bergen, 15 June 1843;
d. Bergen, 4 Sept 1907)

Norway's most famous composer, Edvard (Hagerup) Grieg was actually of Scottish descent on his father's side. His great-grandfather had left Scotland after the Battle of Culloden in 1746 to settle in the port of Bergen, where he took citizenship but maintained the link with his native country by becoming British consul, as did his son and grandson after him. It was from his mother that the future composer inherited his musical talent: an accomplished pianist, and a regular performer at local concerts, she gave him his first piano lessons at the age of six. He must have been a responsive pupil, for he composed his first piece, a set of variations, only three years later. He was sent at fifteen to the Leipzig Conservatoire, where he came under the influence of Schumann. The strength of this influence can be clearly seen in the Piano Concerto, his best-known work, which owed much of its inspiration and form to that of the German composer. He heard Clara Schumann play her husband's concerto at Leipzig, where one of his fellow-students was Arthur Sullivan, and where he also attended several performances of *Tannhäuser* even though he had little liking for the music of Wagner. He was to find the most important influence on his musical development in Copenhagen, where he first went to live for a time in 1863.

Copenhagen was at that time the chief centre of Norwegian as well as Danish cultural activity, and his brief residence in the city made Grieg aware all at once of his Scandinavian heritage. 'For the first time', he wrote in an autobiographical sketch, 'I learned to know the northern folk tunes and my own nature.' For the next three years he divided his time between Denmark and Norway, finally coming to grips with the latter's folk music which he was subsequently to draw upon so consistently for his own compositions. Ironically, it was on a visit to Rome in 1865 that he first met his great compatriot Henrik Ibsen, for whose drama *Peer Gynt* he later composed incidental music. These were principally years of continued study in an attempt to find his true creative personality, but at the same time he was establishing himself as a composer with groups of songs and piano pieces, including his only Piano Sonata and the Violin Sonata No. 1. He finally settled in Norway in 1866, busying himself by promoting concerts and founding the Norwegian Academy of Music, which opened the following year. This was also the year of his marriage to his cousin, Nina Hagerup, a talented singer who had also been born in Bergen but brought up in Denmark. It was the beginning of what was to be a fairly settled life for a composer, his work as both creative and performing artist, augmented by state bursaries, ensuring him freedom from financial worries. He continued to suffer all his life, however, from frequent bouts of ill-health resulting from a severe attack of pleurisy at the age of seventeen. A man of determination and courage, he made annual concert tours in spite of this handicap, not so much to promote his own work as to bring the music of Norwegian composers in general to the attention of audiences abroad.

For the world as a whole, however, Grieg remains *the* Norwegian composer, and even so he is popularly regarded solely as the composer of the Piano Concerto in A minor. This is a grave underestimation of his true stature, though it cannot be gainsaid that the concerto is his only successful large-scale work. It is surprising, perhaps, that this most impressive and successful of all his works should have been composed when he was twenty-five and had thirty-nine active years ahead of him. The explanation is that Grieg was by nature a miniaturist, albeit of the highest order, with an inclination towards musical ideas which are potent in themselves but unsuitable for lengthy extension, and his fondness for folk-style music further restricted him. The Piano Concerto is the exception that proves the rule, a work of the utmost freshness and considerable originality for which he produced themes capable of development in traditional form. He revised the scoring many times, completing the version we are so familiar with today only in the last year of his life. He made sketches for a second concerto in 1883, but soon gave up the attempt, realising all too clearly that his talent was for works on a smaller scale.

Leaving aside his unsuccessful youthful attempt at a symphony, Greig's orchestral music consists mainly of arrangements of piano works and the incidental music for Ibsen's *Peer Gynt* and Bjornson's *Sigurd Jorsalfar*. The original music for *Peer Gynt* consisted of twenty-two pieces for stage performances of the play, but the composer later arranged from them the two well-known suites. From original piano works he made the popular orchestral Norwegian Dances and Holberg Suite. His orchestral writing is rich and varied in colour,

Grieg accompanies his wife at the piano.

though not in the sense of local colour such as we might expect of a strongly nationalist composer. There is much to be admired also in his small output of chamber works, though none of them exhibits the mastery of formal construction to be found in the Piano Concerto. The Violin Sonata No. 3 and the 'Cello Sonata are to be enjoyed rather for the attractive qualities of their individual parts rather than for the sum of those parts. His String Quartet in G minor, which has the distinction of influencing Debussy's, also has sufficient passages of charm and imagination to compensate for some weakness in its over-all construction.

As a song-writer Grieg stands much higher, thanks to his unusually sensitive response to the words he was setting, to his gift for ex-

pressive melody and to the original and poetic piano accompaniments that he provided. Well over a hundred songs spanned the whole course of his creative life, and they show him at his best as a natural melodist completely free from pretension. It has often been said, and is still believed by many people today, that Grieg used actual folk tunes for his Norwegian songs, but this is not so. He was influenced by folk style, but he did not use traditional melodies, except for one song. 'Out of all my songs', he wrote to a friend towards the end of his life, 'only one, Solveig's song [for *Peer Gynt*], has borrowed a tune – no more.' It was his great achievement in his songs to give the spirit of Norway to the world in an international musical language. His music for solo piano is also highly individual, especially in the impressionistic miniatures of his later years. Again the spirit of his country is expressed in wholly original melodies, except for certain arrangements of folk tunes when the intention was made quite clear.

As a man Grieg was essentially a lonely figure, though he could show a delightful sense of humour in company and was a witty after-dinner speaker. A republican in politics, he was not greatly impressed by the honours bestowed on him by royalty, though he confessed: 'Orders and medals are most useful to me in the top layers of my trunks: the Customs officials are always so kind to me at the sight of them.' This is typical of a man of even temper – except when he rounded on critics whom he believed had unfairly attacked a fellow-composer – who spiced his general modesty with frequent pinches of wit.

F.G.B.

HANDEL, George Frideric
(b. Halle, 23 Feb 1685;
d. London, 14 April 1759)

George Frideric Handel was born in 1685, son of an elderly Halle barber-surgeon, Georg Handel, by his second wife, Dorothea. The elder Handel was a rather severe man, and when George Frideric began to show an interest in music he discouraged him – recommending that the boy should follow a more serious pursuit such as law. Georg (Sr) held the appointment of barber-surgeon at Saxe-Weissenfels and in 1693 young George accompanied him on a visit. Whilst they were there the Duke overheard the young Handel playing the organ in the chapel and urged his father to permit him to study music seriously. Georg rather grudgingly agreed, but was still determined that his son should pursue a legal career. The boy was placed with Friedrich Wilhelm Zachau, organist of St Michael's Church, Halle, and under him studied composition, oboe, violin, as well as organ and harpsichord. Progress was rapid. Zachau had quite an extensive musical library containing French and Italian music as well as German, so the boy was able to become acquainted with the various national styles at an early age.

In 1695 Handel was taken on a trip to Berlin where he met the eminent composers Ariosti and Bononcini, whom he was to meet again in later years. Shortly after returning to Halle, Handel's father died – but the old man's influence persisted and in 1702 George Frideric entered the University of Halle to study law.

Music obviously had a stronger appeal and soon he became organist of Halle Cathedral. The appointment was short-lived, and he moved on to Hamburg where there was a famous Opera House 'on the Goosemarket'. Handel was given employment firstly as one of the *ripieno* violinists and later as harpsichordist. The composer, singer and harpsichordist Johann Mattheson was a colleague of Handel's at the opera house; the two young men became firm friends and travelled to Lübeck together where the ageing organist Dietrich Buxtehude was contemplating retirement. On their arrival they discovered that one of the conditions of succeeding to Buxtehude's position entailed marrying Buxtehude's daughter. Both men beat a hasty retreat.

A year or so after returning to Hamburg, Handel and Mattheson quarrelled – Handel refusing to allow Mattheson to take over the direction of one of the latter's operas. They drew swords, and an angry duel was fought in the Goosemarket. Mattheson in later years commented that the result might have been disastrous, 'Had not God's guidance graciously ordained that my blade thrusting against the broad metallic coat button of my opponent should be shattered.' The two quickly forgave each other and Mattheson attended the rehearsals of Handel's first opera *Almira*, which was produced with great success on the 8th January 1705. A second opera *Nerone* produced six weeks later was less successful. Handel then made the decision to travel to Italy, at that time the European centre of opera. How he got to Italy or exactly when he arrived there, we do not know. He was certainly in Florence in the summer of 1706, and is supposed to have written the opera *Rodrigo* for performance there. From then on Handel astonished the Italians with his virtuosity in organ playing, and Domenico Scarlatti was his only possible rival as a harpsichordist. Handel met Scarlatti in 1708, and the story of a (musical!) contest between the two is recounted in the article on Domenico Scarlatti in the present volume. The contest took place at the palace of Cardinal Ottoboni in Rome, in whose service was the eminent violinist Arcangelo Corelli. Handel would also have met Alessandro Scarlatti at this time.

Portrait of Handel by Thomas Hudson, 1756.

Several of Handel's compositions on Latin texts date from this period – the Dixit Dominus, Laudate pueri, and Gloria patri; although Handel rigidly adhered to his Protestant faith. He visited Venice probably in the autumn of 1707, but returned to Rome where he composed a splendid oratorio *La Resurrezione* which was performed on Easter Day 1708, with Corelli leading the orchestra. By June 1708 Handel was in Naples where his serenata *Aci, Galatea e Polifemo* was performed, and which must undoubtedly have suggested the later English version *Acis and Galatea*. He was back in Rome during the spring of 1709 where he may have met the composer–diplomat Agostino Steffani. He was commissioned to write an opera for Venice, and his *Agrippina* was produced there on the 26th December 1709. Whilst in Venice he met Prince Ernst of Hanover, younger brother of the Elector, who invited him to Hanover. So after four years Handel left Italy and returned to Germany where he was appointed *Kapellmeister* to the Court of Hanover. Handel did not remain in Germany for long, he received an invitation to visit England, and after obtaining leave of absence, set off for London.

Handel arrived in London late in 1710 and found a flourishing musical environment which for fifteen years since the death of Henry Purcell had lacked a leader. The aristocracy craved for Italian opera as Handel's first biographer Mainwaring wrote:

At this time, operas were a sort of new acquaintance, but began to be established in the affections of the nobility, many of whom had heard and admired performances of this kind in the country which gave them birth. But the conduct of them here, all that regards the drama, or plan, including also the machinery, scenes and decorations, were foolish and absurd almost beyond imagination. . . . The arrival of Handel put an end to this reign of nonsense.

Handel composed *Rinaldo* in a fortnight, and the work, first produced at the Queen's Theatre in the Haymarket on the 24th February 1711, was a tremendous success – indeed it secured Handel's British reputation for ever. The London publisher Walsh made so much money by printing songs from it that Handel rather dryly remarked that Walsh had better write the next opera and he, Handel, would publish it. Fêted everywhere, it was probably with some reluctance that Handel, aware of his responsibilities in Hanover, returned to Germany. The lure of success in London was too great and in the spring of 1712 he left once more for England, having promised to return to Hanover 'in reasonable time'.

Il Pastor Fido was performed at the Haymarket on the 22nd November 1712 and was followed by *Teseo* in January 1713, neither of which matched the success of *Rinaldo*. For Queen Anne's birthday on the 6th February 1713 he composed a delightful Birthday Ode (the first time that he had set English words), and his grand *Te Deum* for the peace of Utrecht was sung at St Paul's Cathedral on the 7th July. The Queen was an ailing woman and could not attend the Cathedral ceremony, but had the music repeated privately. Such was Her Majesty's pleasure that she awarded Handel a royal pension of £200 per annum. Handel was by now well established, and remained in London, ignoring his promise to return to Hanover within a 'reasonable time'.

Queen Anne died in 1714, and Handel's employer the Elector of Hanover succeeded her as King George I of England. He arrived in Britain on the 18th September, and ten days later the new King attended a service in the Chapel Royal at St James's during which Handel's *Te Deum* was sung. It was presumably at this time that the reconciliation took place, and not, as popular legend would have us believe, through the composition of *Water Music*, which dates from 1717. Indeed, in 1716 the King took Handel with him when he visited Germany. At this time Handel seems to have persuaded his old friend Johann Christoph Schmidt of Ansbach to return with him to London, where as John Christopher Smith he became Handel's scribe and amanuensis. Back in London, Handel revived *Rinaldo* and *Amadigi*. It was at this time that the famous *Water Music* was performed at a royal water party on the Thames. The event, which took place on the 17th July 1717, was chronicled by Bonet, the Prussian resident in London, who reported to Berlin that:

A few weeks ago the King expressed to Baron Kilmanseck his desire to have a concert on the river, by subscription, similar to the masquerades this winter which the King never failed to attend. The Baron accordingly applied to Heidecker – a Swiss by origin, but the cleverest purveyor of entertainments to the nobility. The latter replied that, much as he would wish to comply with His Majesty's desires, he must reserve sub-

Page of manuscript of Handel's Salve Regina.

scriptions for the great events, namely the masquerades, each of which bring him in three or four hundred guineas net. Observing His Majesty's chagrin at these difficulties, M. de Kilmanseck undertook to provide the concert on the river at his own expense. The necessary orders were given and the entertainment took place the day before yesterday. At about eight in the evening the King repaired to his barge, into which were admitted the Duchess of Bolton, Countess Godolphin, Madame de Kilmanseck, Mrs Were and the Earl of Orkney, the Gentlemen of the Bedchamber in Waiting. Next to the King's barge was that of the musicians, about 50 in number, who played on all kinds of instruments, to wit trumpets, horns, hautboys, bassoons, German flutes, French flutes [recorders], violins and basses; but there were no singers. The music had been composed specially by the famous Handel, a native of Halle, and His Majesty's principal Court Composer. His Majesty approved of it so greatly that he caused it to be repeated three times in all, although each performance lasted an hour – namely twice before and once after supper. The evening was all that could be desired for the festivity, the number of barges and above all of boats filled with people desirous of hearing was beyond counting.

Handel became composer-in-residence to the Duke of Chandos at Cannons – he did not replace Dr Pepusch the music director, as is sometimes said. Here Handel composed his twelve *Chandos Anthems* which contain some of his finest church music. *Acis and Galatea*, one of the most enchanting of all his works, dates from this period. Handel left Cannons in the early spring of 1719 – having decided to start a new Italian opera company to be called the Royal Academy of Music, and which would centre around the King's Theatre in the Haymarket. On the 21st February, *The Original Weekly Journal* reported that: 'Mr Hendle, a famous Master of Musick, is gone beyond the Sea, by Order of His Majesty, to collect a Company of the choicest Singers in Europe, for the Opera in the Haymarket.'

The Academy opened its first season in the spring of 1720 with a performance of an opera by Porta, *Il numitore*. Handel produced his opera *Radamisto*, and it was a great success. In November 1720 Handel published his first collection of harpsichord lessons, the *Suites de Pieces pour le Clavecin*, which included an air and variations which posterity has styled 'The Harmonious Blacksmith'. The opera project continued to flourish. One of his greatest masterpieces *Giulio Cesare* was produced in February 1724, and *Tamerlano, Rodelinda, Scipione*, and *Alessandro* followed in quick succession. In 1727 Handel applied success-

A scene from John Gay's Beggar's Opera.

fully for naturalisation as a British subject. King George I died in June 1727 and Handel busily prepared anthems for the coronation of King George II on the 11th October. Four magnificent anthems were the result including the magnificent *Zadok the Priest*, which has been heard at practically all British coronations since.

In January 1728, John Gay produced his *Beggar's Opera* at John Rich's Theatre in Lincoln's Inn Fields. It was immensely successful, in fact one of the greatest theatrical successes of all time. No longer was opera the sole preserve of the aristocracy; Gay's English 'folk' opera appealed to a far wider audience. Within six months, Handel's Academy was bankrupt. Undeterred, a new subscription was soon proposed and Handel once again set off for the continent to collect singers. The new company opened with Handel's *Lotario* in December 1729, but the work was a failure. Handel revived several of his early successes – *Giulio Cesare, Rinaldo* and *Rodelinda* – while still continuing to write Italian opera. Elsewhere, Bernard Gates, Master of the Children of the Chapel Royal, revived *Haman and Mordecai* as the 'oratorio' or religious opera *Esther*, and the Arne family presented *Acis and Galatea* as 'an English opera'. Handel, however, still chose in the main to favour Italian opera. Handel's audiences were enticed away by a rival Italian opera group called

Opera of the Nobility, directed at first by his old rival Bononcini.

Handel turned to English oratorio: *Deborah* was performed on the 13th March 1733, and the following month Handel himself revived *Esther*, and at the same time instigated the tradition of playing organ concertos between the acts. *Athalia* was performed in Oxford in the summer of 1733. The Opera of the Nobility acquired the use of the King's Theatre, so Handel entered into an agreement with John Rich to perform operas at Covent Garden. Rich had enlisted the services of the celebrated French ballerina Mlle Marie Sallé, and many of the operas which Handel composed in the mid-1730s for Covent Garden contain beautiful *entrées de ballet*. By 1735, both opera companies had suffered great financial losses.

Handel had a change of fortune: his setting of Dryden's *Ode for St Cecelia's Day*, under the title *Alexander's Feast*, was a huge success. Handel continued to compose Italian operas despite the fact that the public was becoming increasingly indifferent. Handel's health suffered, and in the autumn of 1737, he went to Aix-la-Chapelle 'to take the waters'. The cure would appear to have been effective, and Handel returned to London where he applied himself once again to Italian opera. *Faramondo* was followed by *Serse* which contains the melody 'Ombra mai fu', which has become widely known as Handel's 'Largo'. (The tempo indication of the original, incidentally, is larghetto!).

In the summer of 1738 Handel began working on his great oratorio *Saul*, on a text by Charles Jennens. His Six Organ Concertos Op. 4 were published, and by November another large-scale oratorio *Israel in Egypt* was complete. The Twelve *Concerti Grossi* Op. 6 followed in 1739: the publisher advertising a subscription list even before the last concerto had been finished. Handel's setting of Milton's English poem with an Italian title *L' Allegro ed il Penseroso ed il Moderato* appeared in 1740. His last two Italian operas were *Imeneo* and *Deidamia*, the latter receiving only three performances. Handel was now obliged to turn his attention to English oratorio; scarcely had he finished *Messiah* when he commenced another great work, *Samson*. Handel travelled to Ireland in 1741 and it was in Dublin that *Messiah* received its first performance. It was an instantaneous success. Handel remained in Ireland for ten months. On returning to London he continued his Lenten oratorio series with *Samson*. *Messiah* initially failed to summon the response that it had received in Dublin, but it soon grew in public esteem to such an extent that it became the most popular of Handel's oratorios, even during the composer's lifetime. Numerous other oratorios followed including *Semele, Belshazzar, Hercules, Susanna, Solomon* and *Judas Maccabeus*. The Stuart rising called forth the *Occasional Oratorio*. On the 27th November 1743 the *Dettingen Te Deum* was performed in the Chapel Royal in commemoration of the victory of the English troops, and some six years later the celebrations of the Peace of Aix-la-Chapelle prompted the composition of the *Musick for the Royal Fireworks*.

The success of the oratorios had fully reimbursed Handel for the losses he suffered in the opera house, and he spent his last years in complete financial security. He became one of the Governors of the Foundling Hospital, and greatly increased its revenue by his annual charity performances of *Messiah* in the Chapel there; he also donated an organ for the Chapel. Gradually his sight began to fail him, an operation was only temporarily successful, and eventually he became totally blind. He still continued to give concerts, aided by John Christopher Smith the son of his old amanuensis, playing organ concertos from memory and extemporising. Dr Burney speaks of seeing him 'led to the organ. . . at upwards of seventy years of age, and then conducted towards the audience to make his customary obeisance. . . .' On the 6th April 1759 he directed a performance of *Messiah* at Covent Garden, from the organ. He was taken ill upon returning to his home in Brook Street, and retired to his bed. He died on the 14th April, the day after Good Friday, and was buried in Westminster Abbey during the evening of the 20th April. Handel had asked to be buried privately, but his wish was not granted – some 3,000 persons attended, and the choirs of Westminster Abbey, St Paul's Cathedral and the Gentlemen of the Chapel Royal took part in the service. Handel requested that a monument be erected to his memory, and this wish was granted. The French sculptor Roubiliac was commissioned to produce a statue of Handel which was duly placed in Westminster Abbey.

Sir John Hawkins aptly remarked that Handel's works are so 'multifarious that they elude all but general criticism'. Whilst Handel started life as essentially a Germanic com-

Handel (right) directing a performance.

poser, his period of residence in Italy was of immense importance, and his compositional style became very Italianate. But through his long residence in England he has almost become recognised as a British composer and, of course, was afforded a state funeral in Westminster Abbey. Yet, at the same time, he always remained a thoroughly eclectic composer, drawing his inspiration from many sources.

His music is characterised by the excellence of its melodic quality, its memorability, impact and superb technical mastery, which seems, paradoxically, to have been achieved by the easiest means. It is acknowledged that Handel plagiarised other composer's works, but as his near-contemporary Dr Boyce remarked, Handel 'took other men's pebbles and polished them into diamonds'. But it is not surprising to discover that he sometimes resorted to borrowing other people's tunes, when one appreciates the pressure under which he worked. *Messiah* is reputed to have been written in twenty-three days, and such was the speed of his invention that, for instance, in the organ concertos whole passages were left to be improvised during performance. Indeed, it has been said that Handel's music is 'magnificent improvisation'.

G. G.

HAYDN, (Franz) Joseph
(b. Rohrau, 31 March 1732;
d. Vienna, 31 May 1809)

Franz Joseph Haydn was born at Rohrau, lower Austria, second son of the wheelwright Matthias Haydn. Like Handel, Joseph Haydn seems to have had no notable musical ancestry. He received his first musical training from his cousin Johann Mathias Franck, and at the age of eight was admitted as a chorister at St Stephen's Cathedral in Vienna where he remained until 1748. *Kapellmeister* Georg Reutter took little interest in Haydn, and when his voice had broken he was dismissed from the choir and obliged to live on his own resources. He experienced great poverty at this time, yet managed to obtain and study some important theoretical works (Fux's *Gradus ad Parnassum*, for instance) and so gradually build up his technique as a composer. He also received a few lessons from Nicola Porpora, the famous Italian composer and singing teacher then living in Vienna.

Haydn's early compositions, which include string quartets, divertimenti, cassations and the Mass in F, gained him increasing recognition. In 1759 he was appointed *Musikdirektor* to Count Morzin who maintained a small private orchestra at Lucaveč near Plzeň. Haydn's salary of 200 florins a year, though small, granted security, and in November 1760 he married Maria Anna Keller. The marriage was ill-fated. The following year Count Morzin was compelled to disband his musical establishment and Haydn was obliged to seek employment elsewhere. The then reigning Prince, Paul Anton Esterházy, had heard several of Haydn's works when visiting Morzin and was quick to secure the services of the young composer as a second *Kapellmeister* under the then ageing Werner. He took up the appointment in May 1761 and remained in the full employment of the enormously wealthy Esterházy's until 1790. Eisenstadt, the country seat of his employer, possessed an orchestra, chorus and solo singers who took part in the church services, concerts and sometimes operas. Haydn's enthusiasm added great impetus to the Eisenstadt musical life, and in return the excellence of the resident musicians was a powerful source of inspiration. Haydn became sole *Kapellmeister* at Werner's death in 1766; Prince Paul Anton had died four years earlier and was succeeded by his brother Nicolaus 'the Magnificent' who was one of the greatest benefactors of the arts in the whole of the Age of Patronage. A new Palace –

Esterház – was built near Süttör, beside the Neusiedlersee, and its splendours were said to compare with Versailles. Provisions for music included a sumptuous opera theatre, a second theatre, and two concert halls; the orchestra was selected from the house musicians and directed by Haydn. Visiting companies were often engaged, and travelling virtuosi often performed with the orchestra. Special periods were set aside for chamber music. Haydn was highly respected by his musicians, and he himself was on the best of terms with his employer – his salary was generous, and he was given every encouragement to write as he felt and as he wished. In his own words:

As a conductor of an orchestra I could make experiments, observe what produced an effect and what weakened it, and was thus in a position to improve, alter, make additions or omissions, and be as bold as I pleased; I was cut off from the world, there was no one to confuse or torment me, and I was forced to become original.

Haydn's contract with the Esterházys had initially forbidden him to sell or give away any of his compositions, but these provisions were soon relaxed; in the early 1770s his works were appearing in print in London and Amsterdam.

Prince Nicolaus frequently entertained distinguished guests at Esterház. The Empress Maria Theresa was there in September 1773, and heard, among other works, a new symphony by Haydn (No. 48, which now bears her name). The Prince took great pleasure in Esterház and he was reluctant to leave it; he rarely visited Eisenstadt, and journeys elsewhere were often curtailed. Consequently, his musicians were frequently obliged to remain at Esterház for long periods – many of them not allowed to bring their families. Haydn's *Farewell* Symphony (No. 45, 1772) discreetly drew the Prince's attention to the matter and achieved a satisfactory solution: 'If all go,' said the Prince, 'we may as well go too.'

During his visits to Vienna between 1780 and 1790, Haydn met a number of artists including Paisiello and Sarti, and three visitors from London: Nancy and Stephen Storace and Thomas Attwood. But by far the most important meeting of all was with Mozart. It is thought that they first met during the winter of 1781/2 during the court festivities in honour of Grand Duke Paul, though there is no documentary evidence to support this. The Irish singer and actor Michael Kelly, in his *Reminiscences*, comments on a quartet party

The castle at Esterhazy.

held in the home of Stephen Storace. He remarks humorously that:

> The players were tolerable, not one of them excelled in the instrument he played; but there was a science among them, which I dare say will be acknowledged when I name them: The First Violin, Haydn; Second Violin, Baron Dittersdorf; Violoncello, Vanhall; Tenor, Mozart. The poet Casti and Paesiello formed part of the audience. I was there, and a greater treat or a more remarkable one cannot be imagined.

Although Haydn made only brief annual visits to Vienna until 1790, and Mozart did not visit Eisenstadt, the two composers held each other in very high esteem. In 1785 Mozart composed a set of six quartets which he dedicated to Haydn. After a performance of one of these, Haydn made his now-famous remark to Mozart's father: 'I tell before God and as an honest man, that your son is the greatest composer I know, personally or by reputation, he has taste and apart from that the greatest possible knowledge of composition.'

During the late 1780s Haydn received several invitations to travel abroad, but declined all of them, probably because of a strong sense of allegiance to Prince Nicolaus. On the 28th September 1790, Prince Nicolaus died leaving Haydn an annual pension of 1000 florins while he remained *Kapellmeister*. The new Prince, Anton, added another 400 florins but then dismissed the whole musical establishment. Haydn moved to Vienna.

The well-known London impressario and violinist Johann Peter Salomon, on hearing of Prince Nicolaus's death, immediately went to Vienna to try to persuade Haydn to visit London. He succeeded, and on Wednesday the 15th December 1790, they set off for London arriving on New Year's Day 1791. Haydn was afforded great acclaim; he received visits from the aristocracy, and was surrounded by a host of distinguished artists. He was constantly in demand at public functions ranging from musical societies to Lord Mayors' Banquets.

Salomon, before leaving Vienna, had commissioned Haydn to compose six symphonies, which were now performed in a series of extremely successful subscription concerts. Such was the immediate appeal of these works that the Adagio of the symphony heard during the first concert (No. 93), was encored – a very unusual occurrence. On the 8th July 1791 Oxford University conferred on Haydn the honorary degree of Doctor of Music. During the celebrations, the previously-composed *Oxford*

Symphony (No. 92) was performed with Haydn directing from the organ. He returned to London to find that the directors of the 'Professional Concerts', hoping to establish themselves as rivals of Salomon, had invited his former pupil Ignaz Pleyel to conduct their concerts. Master and pupil remained the best of friends, without the slightest hint of rivalry. Haydn continued to produce symphonies, concerti, divertimenti and arias for his concerts in great quantity, and all were received with tremendous enthusiasm. After the concert season had finished, he visited Windsor, Ascot races, and Slough where he met the famous astronomer Sir William Herschel. In 1791 he attended the meeting of Charity Children in St Paul's Cathedral, and as his diary relates, was greatly impressed with their singing. The same year he was present at a performance of *Messiah* given during the Handel Commemoration in Westminster Abbey; overwhelmed by the 'Hallelujah' chorus, Haydn exclaimed, 'He is the master of us all.'

Towards the end of June 1792, Haydn returned to Vienna by way of Bonn where he met Beethoven. The Viennese audiences had been eagerly awaiting hearing the London symphonies and they were not disappointed. In December 1792 Beethoven journeyed to Vienna and became a pupil of Haydn until the latter left in 1794 on his second journey to England, again at the instigation of Salomon. The second London visit followed very much the same format as the first. Haydn was again asked to provide six new symphonies, which included the *Military* Symphony (No. 100), whose array of 'Turkish' percussion instruments enthralled the London audiences. There was ample opportunity for Haydn to further his acquaintance with Handel's music as regular performances of the oratorios were held in Lent both at Covent Garden and Drury Lane. Salomon was unable to continue his concerts after January 1795, and Haydn subsequently became associated with the 'Opera Concert' series at the King's Theatre in the Haymarket where he was joined by Clementi, Dussek, Cramer and Salomon.

At the end of his stay in London, Haydn was a frequent guest of the Royal family, some of whom were accomplished musicians. The King and Queen invited him to spend the summer at Windsor, but Haydn declined, being unwilling to completely abandon Prince Esterházy. Haydn returned to Vienna in 1798. His second visit to England had been as strenuous as the first, and equally as remunerative.

His concerts, lessons and compositions had again realised the substantial sum of £1200.

He spent his last years in Vienna composing as rapidly as ever. In January 1797, Haydn provided the Austrian people with their national anthem, the *Austrian Hymn*. The Masses and grand Te Deum had already demonstrated Handel's powerful influence on Haydn's choral music, and the two oratorios – *The Creation* (1797/8) and *The Seasons* (1801) – proved this beyond doubt. Both were immensely successful, and did much to establish the important position of oratorio in 19th-century musical life.

By now the infirmities of old age were becoming evident. Prince Nicolaus II supplemented Haydn's pension to 2300 florins and paid all his medical bills, thus removing any financial burden from the composer. Haydn died on the 31st May 1809 and was buried in the Hundsturm Churchyard. His

Silhouette of Haydn by Rossini.

remains were later exhumed, by command of Prince Esterházy, and reinterred in the upper parish church at Eisenstadt. At his death, Haydn's genius was acknowledged throughout Europe, and he was honoured by all.

It is often asserted that Haydn invented the symphony and string quartet. The symphony was a flourishing form long before Haydn began to compose. Johann Stamitz, the greatest of the famous Mannheim School, wrote several dozen symphonies before his death in 1757, and 1757 has been established as the very earliest date for Haydn's first symphony. Haydn turned to the examples of the Viennese composers, Wagenseil and Monn, not perhaps so much the Mannheim School, and between 1759 and 1769 produced his first forty-nine symphonies. The early symphonies are in the galante style, easy to listen to, even somewhat superficial. With Symphony No. 49 *La Passione*, composed in 1768, the music becomes more emotional, the direct result of the influence of *Sturm und Drang*; Haydn had become more aware of the possibilities of the form. He now displayed a greater interest in the question of musical architecture – which became one of the chief constituents of the continuous link between late Haydn and early Beethoven. With the *Oxford* Symphony, No. 92 (1788)

Haydn reached full maturity as a symphonic composer, and from then on – with the *London* symphonies – demonstrates complete assurance in handling the form. The *London* symphonies represent the culmination of his art as a symphonist; they synthesize all that he had done in the field, and in many ways anticipate the symphonic works of Beethoven, Schubert, Schumann and Mendelssohn.

Although we do not know exactly how the string quartet began, we do know that Haydn was directly responsible for establishing the form. The Op. 20 *Sun* quartets, dating from 1771, mark the beginning of the string quartet repertoire. A notable feature of these quartets is the growing independence of instruments; viola and 'cello begin to share the melodic interest, and were not simply retained for purposes of accompaniment. The Op. 33 *Russian* quartets written 'in an entirely new and special manner' did not appear until 1781. They show considerable advances on the *Sun* Quartets, particularly in their mastery of thematic development. Mozart was greatly impressed by these works, they came as an artistic shock to him, and certainly affected a lot of his music. Haydn's last quartets include Op. 76 (a collection of six, 1797) and the two quartets of Op.

Haydn and Mozart.

Announcement of the first performance of The Creation.

77, the second of which is probably his greatest work in this form. These quartets represent the highest sophistication of his use of sonata form, and in their liberation of instruments clearly foreshadow Beethoven.

Haydn's keyboard sonatas date from a wide span of the composer's life, from 1760 to 1794. They demonstrate a great variety of styles and vary also as to the intended medium for performance: clavichord, harpsichord, or piano. The music is marvellously unpredictable – he loved the unexpected – compared with the more formalised manner of Mozart. Haydn dedicated his last three sonatas to the brilliant pianist Theresa Jansen, whom he met in London during his second visit. These three works may be regarded as the summit of Haydn's achievement in writing for the piano; the drama and vigour of the E flat major sonata, for instance, points directly towards Beethoven.

As we have seen, the symphonies composed for London were immensely successful. Surprisingly, they were the last that he wrote, although he did continue to compose instrumental music. He returned to the large-scale orchestral Mass, using its extended length in a symphonic manner; the late Mass settings are in reality symphonies for voice and orchestra using the Mass text. His early Masses, of which the Mass in F is an excellent example, are written in a bright rococo manner typical of the late 1750s. During the 1770s the passions of *Sturm und Drang* effected a change in Haydn's church music comparable with that in his instrumental works, and prompted a new interest in intensity through rhythmic counterpoint. The *Stabat Mater* is a perfect example of this transformation: chromaticism, sighs, syncopations and sforzandi (essentially the language of C. P. E. Bach) beautifully underline the text.

The last six Masses are masterpieces. They were written for Prince Nicolaus Esterházy (II) who took a great interest in sacred music. The works were conceived on a large scale, and pay eloquent tribute to the great Handel oratorios which had so greatly impressed Haydn in London. The *Missa in Tempore Belli* or *Paukenmesse* of 1796, and the *Missa in Angustiis* or *Nelson Mass* of 1798 are excellent examples of the breadth of design and dignity of these works, and together with the *Harmoniemesse* of 1802, reflect much of the character of the instrumentation of the *London* symphonies. The cheerfulness which pervades Haydn's Mass settings does not arise from

The house in Vienna in which Haydn died.

frivolity: the composer himself acknowledged that 'at the thought of God his heart leaped for joy, and he could not help his music doing the same'.

Handel's influence is also felt in the two Viennese oratorios *The Creation* and *The Seasons*. No sooner had the score of *The Creation* been engraved than the work was performed everywhere – indeed, its popularity for a long time equalled *Messiah*. The text Haydn used was an 18th-century English fusion of the First Book of Genesis and the seventh book of Milton's *Paradise Lost*, abridged and translated into German by Haydn's friend Baron Gottfried von Swieten. The work, as *Messiah*, falls into three sections, and is notable for its vivid musical descriptions of the various stages of the evolution of order from chaos. Haydn's last major work, *The Seasons*, appeared in 1801, but did not achieve the same lasting popularity as *The Creation*. The work suffers from a relative weakness of musical contrast, and an apparent lack of any compelling dramatic core. It is for this reason that the last six Masses have proved generally more popular than *The Seasons*. The same criticism – a lack of dramatic impetus – is often levelled against the twenty-five or so operas which Haydn composed for performance at Esterház.

Nothing has been said of Haydn's concertos, or certain aspects of his chamber music, because these works are relatively less important in his total output. It was as a composer of symphonies and string quartets that he exerted the greatest influence on the subsequent course of music. In the words of Mozart: 'There is no one who can do it all – to joke and to terrify, to evoke laughter and profound sentiment – and all equally well: except Joseph Haydn.'

G.G.

HAYDN, (Johann) Michael
(b. Rohrau, 14 Sept 1737;
d. Salzburg, 10 Aug 1806)

Johann Michael Haydn, younger brother of Joseph Haydn, was born in Rohrau, Lower Austria. He was a chorister at St Stephen's Cathedral, Vienna, from 1745 until 1754, and succeeded his brother as principal soloist. He became proficient on the violin, and his skill in organ playing soon enabled him to act as deputy organist of St Stephen's. He showed greater aptitude for academic work than Joseph, and became something of a leader among his circle of friends, forming a club for the detection of plagiarism in their musical work! He taught himself composition from Fux's *Gradus ad Parnassum*, which he copied out in full in 1757. The same year, he was appointed *Kapellmeister* to the Bishop of Grosswardien, and in 1762 succeeded Johann Ernst Eberlin as conductor of the Salzburg court orchestra. He also became organist of the churches of Holy Trinity and St Peter in 1777, succeeding Anton Adlgasser. His salary, at first 30 florins with board and lodging, was afterwards doubled, but still remained a modest income. In August 1768 he married the Salzburg court singer Maria Magdalena Lipp, daughter of the second organist of the Cathedral; Maria is known to have taken the principal soprano parts in several of Mozart's early operas. The couple settled in Salzburg; their one child, a daughter born in 1770, died in infancy. Michael turned to drink, quite often to the detriment of his organ playing. During a performance of a Te Deum he was, as Leopold Mozart relates, a 'little drunk, and head and hands could not get together'.

In 1798, Michael visited Vienna where he met his brother who had recently returned from his second enormously successful visit to England. Among the other composers he met were Süssmayr and Hummel. In December 1800, Salzburg was taken by the French, and Michael's property was seized. Joseph sent some money and a gold watch to help him recover his loss, and the Empress Maria Theresa commissioned a Mass setting and later a Requiem. At about the same time Michael Haydn and his friend Rittensteiner visited

Joseph at Eisenstadt. Prince Esterházy commissioned Michael to compose a Mass setting and Vespers, and also offered him the appointment of second *Kapellmeister* which he refused, hoping that the conditions of his employment at Salzburg would improve. Soon afterwards he was elected a member of the Stockholm Academy, an indication of the extent of his reputation. He completed his last Mass in December 1805, and continued working on the Requiem commissioned by the Empress. This remained unfinished at his death, which occurred on the 10th August 1806. He was buried in St Peter's Church, and a fine monument was erected in his memory. After visiting the church in 1825, Schubert wrote:

> Here is to be found, as you know, M. Haydn's monument. It is rather pretty, though not well placed. . . . It hovers round me – I thought to myself – thou tranquil, clear spirit, thou good Haydn, and if I cannot myself be so tranquil and clear, there is no one in the world, surely, who reveres thee so deeply as I.

Leopold Mozart, writing to his son, remarks that 'Herr Haydn is a man whose merit you will be forced to acknowledge.' We know that Wolfgang did: he copied out and studied a number of Michael's works. In 1767, Mozart made his first contribution as a composer to the Archiepiscopal court, collaborating with Adlgasser and Michael Haydn in writing a dramatic oratorio entitled *Die Schuldigkeit des ersten und fürnehmsten Gebotes*. The Archbishop commissioned Michael to compose two duets for violin and viola: we know that because of indisposition, these were actually written by Mozart, and submitted under Haydn's name. The Symphony in G (No. 16) was formerly thought to be entirely the work of Mozart (and actually numbered as his Symphony 37, K444), but we now know that Mozart's authorship extends merely to the introduction of the first movement, the remainder being by Michael Haydn. The *Toy Symphony*, long ascribed to Joseph Haydn, is now thought to be the work of Leopold Mozart or Michael Haydn, and possibly even a compilation of both.

As a composer, Michael Haydn was overshadowed by his brother. Yet contemporaries regarded his church music as better than Joseph's. Indeed the latter professed that in earnestness, severity of style, and sustained power, Michael's church music was superior to his own – a view shared by

E. T. A. Hoffmann in his collection of essays entitled *Old and New Church Music* (1814). Michael's church music has tremendous dignity, reflecting his study of Fux's treatise, and this is admirably demonstrated in the Mass in D minor and the *Lauda Sion*. The Requiem in C minor (1771) in matters of structure vividly foreshadows Mozart's great work of twenty years later.

The instrumental music includes symphonies, concerti, serenades, marches and minuets for full orchestra; and various chamber works including a set of three divertimento-like string quintets, which together with those of Boccherini, antedate Mozart's essays in this form. There has been a considerable revival of interest in Michael Haydn's concerti and symphonies in recent years – the Trumpet Concerto, and the Concerto for Viola and Organ are notable examples, – but the operas have remained more or less unknown. Suites of instrumental extracts are sometimes heard, and there exists an interesting suite of 'Turkish' music. The instrumental music generally reflects a typically Viennese lyricism and good humour: qualities which sometimes also pervade his choral music, for example, the delightful Christmas *pastorella*, *Lauft, ihr Hirten allzugleich*.

G. G.

HENZE, Hans Werner
(b. Gütersloh, 1 July 1926)

Hans Werner Henze was born in Westphalia, in 1926. His father was a schoolteacher in that town. He himself went to school in Bielefeld and later in Brunswick, where he attended the State Music School. But his musical education was severely interrupted by the war. In 1944 he was conscripted, and taken prisoner by the British Army. Resuming his studies after the war, he worked with Fortner in Heidelberg and then, most significantly, with the dodecaphonic pedagogue, René Leibowitz, in Paris. Henze's earliest works, dating from immediately after the war, and including the Symphony No. 1 and the Chamber Concerto, are neoclassical in style, indebted to Stravinsky and Hindemith, as well as to Fortner and his German contemporary Boris Blacher. But he soon began to write serial music, at first using the method in a fairly orthodox manner, later diluting it with allusions to other, less rigorous techniques and styles. After his first opera, *Das Wunder-theater* (1949), this 'freeing off'

process was quite rapid. Thus *Boulevard Solitude* (1952) is a highly eclectic 'number' opera, while *König Hirsch* (1956 but later revised as *Il re cervo*) veers towards an Italianate lyricism, though still within a textural language derived from serialism. In 1952 Henze had emigrated from Germany to Italy (living successively in Ischia, Naples and Rome), partly, he claimed, out of distaste for the materialism of post-war Germany. Most of his music of the late 1950s and early 1960s is impregnated by a certain lyric sensuality which is normally if perhaps naïvely attributed to this change of scene. It includes four more operas (*Der Prinz von Homburg, Elegy for Young Lovers, Der junge Lord* and *The Bassarids*), the fourth and fifth symphonies and many smaller chamber and vocal works in which the blend of classical structure and romantic melody is particularly striking.

After *The Bassarids*, first produced at the Salzburg Festival in 1966, Henze underwent a second major change of direction. Again he claims to have been disgusted by the materialism within the stratum of society to which his music mainly appealed (that is, the rich bourgeoisie). He became a Marxist and wrote music exclusively committed to that ideology. Furthermore, most of these works have adopted avant-garde techniques which would previously have been thought quite alien to Henze's nature. A preoccupation with Cuba and its social problems has thrown off a massive sixth symphony, a symphonic poem, *Heliogabalus Imperator*, and a dazzling, if musically slender, song-cycle, *El Cimarrón*, based on the adventures of a runaway Cuban slave. Other major works of this period are *The Raft of the Medusa*, a cantata derived from Géricault's painting, which caused a political riot at its (attempted) first performance in Hamburg in December 1968, concertos for violin and viola (both of a highly unconventional, even, in the case of the viola concerto, anarchic, design), a further 'song-cycle', *Voices*, and a music-theatre work, *The Tedious Journey to Natasha Ungeheuer's*.

The politicisation of Henze's recent works was in a way so unexpected that it is easy to exaggerate its musical significance. Musically, he seemed to awaken from a dream. It is hardly surprising therefore that his work should again have become as eclectic as it was in the early 1950s. But while the social message of these works is sometimes naïve, their content and execution are not less brilliant than before. In *The Raft of the Medusa* we still feel the rich imagination and instinctive theatrical sense of the earlier Henze, strengthened perhaps by a more outgoing humanity. The Sixth Symphony shows him as gifted as ever at extended musical thought. *Voices* is as devastating a synthesis of received idioms as *Boulevard Solitude*. There remains, no doubt, some lack of fusion, due in part to the anomalous position of the progressive socialist artist. But Henze, still in early middle age, is of living composers probably the best-equipped to solve such problems.

S. W.

HINDEMITH, Paul
(b. Hanau, 16 Nov 1895;
d. Frankfurt, 28 Dec 1963)

Paul Hindemith was born in Hanau in 1895. Among the formative composers of 20th-century music he was thus the youngest. As a child he was a gifted violinist and violist, while his younger brother Rudolf played the 'cello, and his sister Toni the violin. There is some evidence that their father treated them rather as Leopold Mozart treated his children. Their musical education was forced, and they appeared in public when still very young as child prodigies, collectively billed as the Frankfurter Kindertrio. At thirteen, Paul entered the Hoch Conservatorium in Frankfurt-am-Main, where he studied composition with Arnold Mendelssohn and Bernard Sekles.

A certain confusion has surrounded his activities at the start of the war in 1914. He himself was not conscripted until 1917, after which he served for eighteen months in the German army, while the Hindemith who went to the front in 1915 was his father, Robert Rudolph, who volunteered and was killed in action in Flanders in the summer of that year. Paul meanwhile (June 1915) had accepted the post of principal violinist in the Frankfurt Opera orchestra, and this he held, with the break for military service, until 1923. He was also by this time composing, and from his time in the army date his earliest published works, the Three Pieces for 'cello and piano, Op. 8, the String Quartet Op. 10, and the first two violin sonatas of Op. 11. After the war he adopted for a while a certain satirical tone, in the one-act opera *Das Nusch-Nuschi* and the *Kammermusik No. 1*, which contains jazz parody. But although Hindemith's *enfant terrible* phase lasted some years (until *Neues vom Tage* in 1929) it was never for him a crucial or

productive strain. Of greater importance are the many instrumental works of this period, which include the earliest of his so-called *Gebrauchsmusik* – that is, useful music – mainly for instruments and designed to form a ready and painless introduction to the mysteries of modern music for performers of amateur or professional ability. In these works we find Hindemith developing new harmonic and contrapuntal techniques on which he was later to publish an important treatise ('The Craft of Musical Composition', published 1937 and 1939). The basis of the style was a linear counterpoint of a mildly Bachian cut which was promptly dubbed 'Back-to-Bach' and was held to align Hindemith firmly with the neoclassical 'school' of Stravinsky *et al*, though Hindemith's aesthetic was quite unrelated to Stravinsky's. The characteristic work of the period is the song-cycle, *Das Marienleben* (1923, but drastically revised in 1948). But throughout the 1920s Hindemith produced a series of smaller instrumental masterpieces

Hindemith's sketch for the title-page of his Klaviersuite, 1922.

which, being serious, technically solid and above all craftsmanlike, attracted less attention. In 1929 his theories about the function of music brought about a collaboration with Brecht (*Lehrstück*), but this was not a success.

Hindemith meanwhile was continuing his career as a performer, plus a new career as teacher. In 1921 the first Donauschingen Festival of contemporary music included a string quartet of his, and for this performance a quartet was specially formed, the Amar Quartet, with Hindemith as violist. In due course the Amar was to become one of the celebrated quartets of the day. In 1927 he moved from Frankfurt to Berlin to be Professor of Composition at the Hochschule. But after 1933 he was soon a casualty of the Nazi propaganda machine. Early skirmishes were followed by a major scandal over Hindemith's opera, *Mathis der Maler*, though apparently not on account of its political content (its central incident is the Peasants' Revolt of 1524). Despite the intervention of Furtwängler, who conducted the symphony based on the opera in Berlin in March 1934, the authorities refused to allow the opera to be performed, alleging among other things that Hindemith had made defamatory remarks about Hitler, was an associate of Jewish musicians (this was undoubtedly true), and belonged at heart to the 'decadent' phase in German music of which *Das Nusch-Nuschi* was a typical excrescence. In 1935 Hindemith left Germany for the last time until after the war.

He went first to Turkey, where he spent a year organising the country's musical life, then made a series of three tours to the USA, the last of which was to be permanent, owing to the outbreak of war in Europe. In 1940 he joined the music staff at Yale, and in 1946 became an American citizen. Nevertheless, when the war was over, he soon toured Europe, visiting Germany as a conductor in 1949. In 1948 he was appointed to the music faculty at Zürich University, but not until 1953 did he at last decide to resettle in Europe, choosing Switzerland as the most natural and convenient country of residence. He continued conducting, without ever establishing himself (as he would have liked) as a repertory conductor. His health, however, declined rapidly in the 1960s, and he died of a stroke in Frankfurt in 1963.

After the war Hindemith took many years

Hindemith with the singer Jennie Tourel, sketch by Dolbin.

to live down his failure to pursue the 'progressive' paths of his youth, which were, as we can now see, largely a digression. The mainstream of his music is represented by the instrumental works of the 1920s leading up to the operas *Cardillac* (1926) and *Mathis der Maler*, by which time the Hindemithian style, with its characteristic fourth-based harmonies, its compound rhythms and rapid-flowing polyphony, is established. This style is milder than that of certain earlier works, which approach atonality. But Hindemith was never attracted by Schoenberg's theories or, it seems, by his music, and the later works, with their warm, comparatively opulent textures and generous rhetorical gestures, though far from the studiedly unpretentious world of the early *Gebrauchsmusik* pieces, are the natural outcome of his technical theories and of his views about the artist's role in society.

These, both as expressed in *Mathis der Maler* and as carried out in his own life, are effectively that the artist should cultivate his gifts and not meddle in politics. His dealings with the Nazis, which at times have a dangerously pragmatic appearance, were probably no more than the logical result of his fundamentally apolitical temperament. Music he considered had a duty to be useful first and beautiful second. He was deeply serious about art, but a child of his time in deploring naked aestheticism. Nevertheless in due course he became a great and individual artist in spite of himself, and his finest works, from the early sonatas, through *Das Marienleben, Cardillac, Mathis der Maler* (especially the Symphony), *Nobilissima Visione*, the *Konzertmusik* for strings and brass, the Cello Concerto, and the *Symphonic Metamorphoses*, to the late opera *Die Harmonie der Welt*, form an oeuvre to which many of Hindemith's contemporaries would be happy to put their name.

S. W.

HOLST, Gustav
(b. Cheltenham, 21 Sept 1874; d. London, 25 May 1934)

Of Swedish descent, Gustav Holst was born in Cheltenham, Gloucestershire, in 1874. His father taught music and his mother was a pianist. Much of his youth was spent in music-making: he played the organ in a local church and conducted for a choral society. But he was especially drawn to composition and studied

this at the Royal College of Music in London, where his main teacher was Stanford; a fellow-pupil, Vaughan Williams, became a lifelong friend. He also studied the piano, organ and trombone, and after leaving the College he earned his living mainly as an orchestral trombonist.

In 1903, approaching thirty, he changed direction and became a teacher, remaining so for the rest of his life. His two main posts were the musical directorships of St Paul's Girls' School and Morley College, an adult institution; both of these were in London. He also taught composition at the Royal College of Music from 1919 to 1923. In February 1923 he had a fall and suffered slight concussion. This seems to have weakened his constitution, never very robust, and his health during the remaining eleven years of his life was poor. Yet it was at this time that his reputation as a composer consolidated itself. In 1923 he visited the USA to conduct his own music at Michigan University; he went again to the USA subsequently, and though he refused the honorary degrees offered him there he accepted (in 1930) the Gold Medal of the Royal Philharmonic Society in London.

Holst does not seem to have enjoyed his eminence. He took little interest in public affairs and, save to a few close friends, mainly musical ones, he seemed a remote figure though not an unkindly one. His daughter Imogen, herself a musician and teacher who has written about him with sympathy and insight, tells us that at times he sank into a 'cold region of utter despair . . . a grey isolation'. He felt he had lost touch with the human warmth which makes music lovable. But he did not cease to compose: his last music dates from 1933, the year before his death in London.

Holst today is a well-known name largely on the strength of one work, the colourful and brilliantly scored orchestral suite *The Planets* (1916). This astrologically-inspired piece symbolises his interest in Eastern mysticism, as do his settings of hymns from the Hindu *Rig-Veda* (1908–12), the austerely beautiful opera *Sàvitri* (1908) and the choral-orchestral *Hymn of Jesus* (1917). Here his visionary qualities are unmistakable. A more homely, folk-inspired side of the composer is to be found in his *Somerset Rhapsody* for orchestra (1907), dedicated to Cecil Sharp, and the Shakespearean opera *At the Boar's Head* (1924), in both of which he used folk melody. The keen

Holst by Sir William Rothenstein.

teacher and amateur music-maker may be seen behind the composition of some attractive military band music, and he also wrote some children's songs.

Nevertheless, to come fully to terms with Holst's genius one should know such music as the *Ode to Death* (to Whitman's words, 1919) and the Choral Symphony with its text by Keats (1924); the neo-classical and/or polytonal music such as the *Fugal Overture* (1922) and Concerto for two violins (1929); the Four Songs for voice and violin (1917) and the masterly Twelve Songs to poems by Humbert Wolfe (1929) – in these, his last songs, the music recalls late Debussy in its combination of restraint and intense feeling. Holst's own favourite work, which he considered his best, was the orchestral tone-poem *Egdon Heath* (1927), inspired by a description in a Hardy novel. 'Haggard Egdon', Hardy wrote, 'appealed to a subtler and scarcer instinct . . . than that which responds to the sort of beauty called charming and fair.' The same may perhaps be said of some of Holst's music: it makes few concessions to popularity, but seems likely to endure.

C.H.

HONEGGER, Arthur
(b. Le Havre, 10 March 1892; d. Paris, 27 Nov 1955)

Arthur Honegger was born in Le Havre, in northern France, but his parents were Swiss from Zürich and Honegger retained his Swiss citizenship throughout his life, most of which he spent in France. His mother was a keen amateur pianist, and the boy was trained as a musician from an early age. At eighteen he went for two years to the Zürich Conservatory, and then returned to Paris for a further course in the Conservatoire there. This was interrupted by military service in Switzerland in 1914. Nevertheless by 1916 Honegger was already producing works which were to make him a considerable reputation in Parisian musical circles, some time before the wider notoriety arising from his association with 'Les Six' after the war. A group of songs, 'Quatre Poèmes', given in Paris in 1916, the first string quartet in 1917, and in 1918 the first violin sonata, with Honegger himself as violinist partnered by Andrée Vaurabourg, whom he later (1926) married.

The episode of 'Les Six' was for Honegger more or less accidental. He can have had little

Curtain by Léger for the ballet Skating Rink *with music by Honegger, 1922.*

sympathy with the more whimsical or deflating objects of that so-called group, invented by the critic Henri Collet in 1920, fathered by Erik Satie, mothered by Jean Cocteau, but soon dispersed by the sheer triviality of its artistic creed. As Honegger's own music was already demonstrating his nature was serious, religious, conservative, and by no means devoid of that rhetoric which 'Les Six' were supposed to despise. Only the Piano Concertino (1924) survives as a document of his short trip up a blind alley. Far more characteristic are the oratorio *Le Roi David*, first performed at Mézières in Switzerland in June 1921, *Judith* (1926: another oratorio, though intended to be staged as a 'biblical opera'), the 'mimed symphony' *Horace Victorieux* (1921),

and the Symphony No. 1 (1930). Honegger's most interesting essays in modernism are less satirical than impressionistic: the 'mouvements symphoniques' *Pacific 231* (a portrait of a steam engine in motion) and *Rugby*, which was actually first performed in a football stadium, owe something aesthetically to the futurists Carrá and Russolo, and musically to Stravinsky's early ballets. But the idiom itself is not particularly advanced.

By the 1930s Honegger had firmly renounced any association with *enfant terriblisme*. Two more large-scale oratorios, *Jeanne d'Arc au bûcher* (1934–5, first performed in Basle in 1938) and *La Danse des Morts* (1939) are the most significant and typical products of these years. Honegger spent the war in occupied Paris, and his Second Symphony (for strings but with a phoenix-like trumpet solo in the last movement) records something of the tension and austerity of that period. After the war Honegger wrote three more symphonies, two of them intensely serious in style and content: No. 3, the *Liturgique* (1946), and No. 5, *Di tre re* (1951). By this time, however, he was suffering from heart disease, to which he eventually succumbed in Paris in 1955.

Honegger's music is sometimes underrated, partly one must assume through his known connection with 'Les Six', whose work has a reputation for being both trivial and dated. In fact, as we have seen, Honegger was a serious and ambitious artist. His early works show the conventional influences of the day, Ravel, Debussy and later Stravinsky and Prokofiev, but never Satie, whose aesthetic was completely alien to him. Later on he developed a reasonably individual style of a faintly neo-classical cut, based on polyphony and dense bitonal harmony but always propelled by muscular rhythms. The oratorios and biblical operas also reveal a taste for melodrama and even for heavy religious symbolism. Sometimes the effect is turgid, but it can also be original and inspired, as in *Jeanne d'Arc au bûcher*, where the novel idea of telling Joan of Arc's story as a series of flashbacks as she waits to be burned at the stake is finely rendered in music of great vividness and resource. The episodic character of this work is typical of Honegger. Even so he was capable of more extended musical thought, as the Second and Fifth Symphonies, in particular, show.

S.W.

Honegger.

HUMPERDINCK, Engelbert
(b. Sieburg, 1 Sept 1854;
d. Neusterlitz, 27 Sept 1921)

It is one of music's little ironies that the only opera by which Engelbert Humperdinck is widely remembered today, *Hänsel und Gretel*, was composed almost by accident. He was a composition student of outstanding promise both in Cologne and Munich, and in 1879 his winning the Mendelssohn Prize gave him the funds to travel to Italy. There he met Richard Wagner, who invited him to Bayreuth to assist him in the preparation of *Parsifal*. Helping to write out the orchestral parts of this sacred festival drama, then serving as stage manager for its première, Humperdinck inevitably fell under Wagner's influence to some extent. Soon he was on his travels again, however, having won a further scholarship which allowed him to go back to Italy, then on to France and Spain, where he became a professor at the Barcelona Conservatoire in 1885. Two years later he returned to his native Germany, taking up teaching again in Frankfurt.

His career as composer began in 1880 with a Humoresque for orchestra and some choral works which were also well received. Then his sister, who had written a play for children based on the Grimm fairy-tale *Hänsel und Gretel*, asked him to supply a little music for it. Humperdinck complied with some reluctance, but later became so fascinated by the story that he extended the simple music he had already composed into a full-length opera. He sent the manuscript to Richard Strauss, who wrote back, 'This is truly a masterpiece of the first rank', and arranged for its première in Weimar on the 23rd December 1893. The familiar story of Hansel and Gretel, who successfully turn the tables on the evil witch who catches them in the woods at night, is told with admirable directness, the somewhat heavy, Wagnerian-style orchestral writing leavened by the catchy children's songs scattered through the score. The opera quickly became popular, arriving in London at Daly's Theatre in an English translation on the Boxing Day of the following year, then at Covent Garden in 1896. It became a favourite Christmas entertainment the whole world over, winning the distinction of being the first complete opera ever to be broadcast in both Europe (1923) and the United States (1931). It was a success that Humperdinck was never to repeat, so that he was obliged to return to academic life in 1900 as Director of the Berlin Meisterschule of Composition.

Fortunately this did not entirely mark the end of the road for Humperdinck the composer. After several operatic failures he turned his hand to writing incidental music for various dramatic productions, notably of Shakespeare's *As You Like It, The Merchant of Venice, The Winter's Tale* and *The Tempest,* though he gained the widest recognition in this field with his music for Max Reinhardt's production of *The Miracle* in 1911. The previous year he had come close to a second operatic success with *Königskinder* (The Royal Children) at the Metropolitan in New York, but this is now virtually unknown outside Germany. While there are still people in the world who are young in heart, however, Humperdinck will be remembered as the composer of *Hänsel und Gretel.*

F.G.B.

INDY, Vincent d'
(b. Paris, 27 March 1851;
d. Paris, 2 Dec 1931)

At one time, d'Indy was one of the most noted and respected composers in Western Europe and, until World War I, was a force to be reckoned with, his influence rivalling Debussy's for a short time. Now he is largely forgotten and his works are seldom performed, mainly because of their somewhat extravagant demands for very large forces.

Descended from a noble family, d'Indy received a strict and ruthless upbringing from his paternal grandmother, whose influence coloured his whole life. It was she who first taught him the piano, later passing him onto the great pianist, Marmontel. D'Indy was a remarkable prodigy, and at fourteen began to study harmony under Albert Lavignac, one of Debussy's future masters. After a courageous participation in the Franco-Prussian War (1870–1) he threw himself into the musical milieu of Paris, where, through the conductor Jules Pasdeloup, he met, among others, Saint-Saëns, Massenet, Bizet and de Castillon. Pasdeloup performed one of d'Indy's early works, *Symphonie Italienne,* which was well received, and d'Indy sent some of these works to César Franck who wrote back: 'You have ideas but cannot do anything!' This led to d'Indy studying counterpoint, fugue and composition with Franck, as well as organ, at the Paris Conservatoire.

On a Summer tour of Germany and Austria d'Indy met Brahms, and also Liszt,

whose method of teaching strongly influenced him. In 1876, he attended the première of *The Ring* at Bayreuth, and subsequently became an ardent Wagnerian. By 1880, he was a sincere and dedicated composer and from this period come his greatest compositions: *Le Chant de la Cloche,* a vast vocal and orchestral work comparable with Berlioz' *Faust; Symphonie Cévenole,* an intense nationalist work based on a simple folk song; *Istar,* a set of variations written in reverse order, with the theme at the end; two string quartets, and a large scale music-drama, *Fervaal.*

After leading the Societé Nationale de Musique, under Franck, d'Indy formed the Schola Cantorum and, as its principal and chief lecturer, influenced the French school considerably. More works followed, including *Souvenirs,* a large symphonic poem depicting the death of his wife, *Jour d'été a la montagne* a vast symphonic poem which utilised French folk song and Gregorian chant, a Second Symphony in B flat (the first was never published or performed) and the Piano Sonata in E minor, a work of great beauty which elevated the mounting Debussy–d'Indy rivalry into wholesale war. D'Indy's last great work of any significance was the opera *La Légende de Saint Christophe,* an extraordinary work which couples an anti-semitic fervour with Roman Catholic fanaticism, the whole tinged with a sensual paganism which made it the scandal of 1920, when it received its first and only performance in Paris. D'Indy was still working and composing, when he died peacefully aged eighty in 1931.

Today, the neglect of this composer seems inexplicable when one considers the depth and unusual style of his music. It is a strange, yet beguiling combination of Wagnerian eroticism and the purity of texture one finds in Berlioz. Forgotten now, he may one day be properly re-evaluated for what he is – a neglected master.

B.G.C.

IRELAND, John
(b. Bowdon, 13 Aug 1879;
d. Sussex, June 1962)

John Ireland was born in Cheshire, in 1879. His father's family came from Fifeshire and his mother's from Cumberland; both were writers, and his mother was an authority on

Jane Welsh Carlyle. Carlyle and Emerson often came to their house as well as other writers. Ireland's sisters used to play the piano, and his mother took a keen interest in music. Both Ireland's parents died when he was about fourteen, and he came to London in 1893 to study at the Royal College of Music, earning his living as an organist. For four years he studied piano with Frederick Cliffe and theory with James Higgs: in 1897 Stanford took him as a composition pupil. He was a contemporary of Vaughan Williams and Holst, and later of Frank Bridge. He had already begun to write music before going to the College, but in later years he discarded all his works written before 1908.

After leaving the College in 1901 he lived mainly in London, with occasional visits to West Sussex and the Channel Islands. He took his degree of Bachelor of Music at Durham University in 1905, and from 1904 until 1926 he was organist of St Luke's, Chelsea. He also taught composition students for many years at the Royal College of Music, and his pupils included E. J. Moeran, Alan Bush, Benjamin Britten (who was sent to him by Frank Bridge), Richard Arnell and the present writer. His music, to some extent inspired by French models – though much of his chromatic harmony is nearer to Scriabin – helped to liberate English music from its previous Teutonic domination. Ireland mainly made his reputation in his early days by his chamber music, beginning with the Phantasy Trio of 1908, piano music and songs; his setting of John Masefield's *Sea Fever* became immensely popular and was included in a London variety programme at one time. His first orchestral work, *The Forgotten Rite* of 1913, was one of several works in which Ireland sought to evoke in music the mysteries and rituals of ancient British civilisations: in this he was considerably influenced by the writings of Arthur Machen.

Ireland's most successful period dates from the first performance of his second violin sonata of 1917; from this time onwards he was considered as one of the leading British composers, and the 1920s he produced a number of important works, including the symphonic rhapsody *Mai Dun* (1921), inspired by the ruined Maiden Castle in Dorset, the piano concerto of 1930, which rapidly became popular and still remains in the repertoire, and the *Legend* for piano and orchestra (1933), suggested by an old track, leading to the ruin of an ancient church, which was reserved exclusively for lepers. He also wrote several song cycles, subtle and sensitive settings of English poems, of which *The Land of Lost Content* and *We'll to the Woods No More* (Housman) and two sets of Thomas Hardy songs strike an individual note in British music. In 1937 he was commissioned to write a choral work in honour of the Coronation of King George VI, and set John Addington Symonds' 'These Things Shall Be', a Utopian poem in praise of the brotherhood of man; the score contains a concealed quotation from the *Internationale*. Most of Ireland's many sets of piano pieces – he was an excellent pianist himself – date from the inter-war period.

Ireland was in the Channel Islands when World War II broke out; he managed to escape before the German occupation in 1940, and after a period of living in Essex he returned to London after the war. His later works include the lyrical Fantasy Sonata for clarinet and piano (1943) and the amusing overture *Satyricon* (1946). He spent his last years in a windmill in Sussex, dying there in June 1962 in his eighty-second year. All who knew him remember him with affection.

H.S.

IVES, Charles
(b. Danbury, Conn., 20 Oct 1874;
d. New York, 19 May 1954)

Charles Ives is a unique figure, not only in American music but in the whole musical history of the last hundred years. American music, indeed, owes its existence as a separate phenomenon to his work. But just as Ives had no real predecessors, he has had no successful imitators either. His influence has been less wide than has sometimes been supposed; and where an influence can be traced – for instance, in Cage or Carter or Copland – it is either partial or misunderstood. Ives's true importance lies in having given American music self respect; this is clear from the frequency with which present-day American composers of every hue quote his music as the source of their own. As for Ives's modernisms, these were not influential since his music was mostly not known until long after the devices with which he happened to experiment had become common currency for other reasons. In any case, such techniques were for Ives a symptom of his peculiar place in history: he was a primitive working from a powerful conviction as to the ethical force of art, in a primitive environment. Without these basic circumstances, repetition of his techniques has seemed little more than mannerism.

Ives was born in Danbury, Connecticut, on the 20th October 1874. Throughout his life he cleaved to New England: its countryside colours his music, and its characteristic philosophy (that of Emerson and Thoreau) seems to have influenced his technique. His father was quite a well-known bandmaster, first in the civil war, later as founder and conductor of the Danbury Town Band, in which Charles played the cornet and which in 1888 gave the first documented performance of one of his works (a *Holiday Quick Step*). George Ives, the father, exerted an important musical influence on his son. Naturally experimental himself, he constantly encouraged Charles to tinker with unfamiliar sounds, to investigate, as it were, what music *could* do rather than what it merely had done. Ives later maintained that many of the more startling effects in his music were aural memories from his childhood: memories of hymn-tunes wrongly harmonised, or of accidental coincidences of sound in a small-town environment. The main point is that Ives's earliest musical training was almost entirely unconventional. When he went to Yale in 1894 he tried hard to absorb an academic training, but failed. His First Symphony, a student work, is a curious hotchpotch of European influences with little personal impulse. His Second Symphony, completed in 1901, mixes these same European influences (notably Beethoven and Dvořák) with indigenous American material. But the effect is still that of a snapshot album, recording people and things in the photographer's life but leaving out the photographer.

On leaving Yale in 1898 Ives started selling insurance in New York. In 1906 he was co-founder of an insurance firm which became successful and gave Ives a comfortable income for the rest of his life. From the first he believed that an artist should never be dependent on art for his living. Knowing that his music had no hope of commercial success, or even of performance, he never courted publication and, when performances began to take place, tended to regard them with indifference. Thus, while working daily in an insurance office in downtown New York, Ives was composing some of the most extraordinary music ever written though his office colleagues were largely ignorant of his connection with anything more aesthetic than actuarial statistics. From this period (1901–28) date the Third and Fourth Symphonies, the *Concord* Sonata for piano, *Three Places in New England,* the *Holidays* Symphony, the four violin sonatas, the *Tone Roads* for small orchestra, and various smaller orchestral works. In 1928 Ives was forced by illness to give up composition, and in 1930 he retired from insurance and thereafter spent all his time at his farm in Connecticut. He became diabetic and suffered from heart disease. Nevertheless he lived until 1954, dying on the 19th May of that year, aged seventy-nine.

Even after his retirement his music made its way very slowly. The earliest publications were at his own expense: of the Concord Sonata in 1919 and of the 114 Songs in 1922, copies being distributed free to the composer's friends. Later in the 1920s and 1930s a few scattered performances were put on. But the major works remained practically unknown until the 1950s. The Third Symphony won a Pulitzer Prize in 1947, but the Fourth Symphony was not played at all until 1965, the Second Symphony not until 1951.

Ives has since been something of a vogue figure. But his achievement is indeed quite uneven. His best works imaginatively are the miniatures, including some of the songs, tiny instrumental 'poems' like 'In the Cage', or visionary impressions like 'The Housatonic at Stockbridge', in the *Three Places*. His longer works suffer from the usual faults of a primitive style. The development and contrapuntal texture are apt to sound amateurish and to extend the structure without in any way supporting it. Also one finds grotesque inconsistencies of style, as in the Fourth Symphony, where the massive second movement collage of musical Americana – perhaps the most brilliant extravaganza in music before 1920 – is followed by a naïve sentimental fugue on a hymn-tune subject, in an entirely diatonic idiom. Such things are justified philosophically by their basic 'truth to experience'. Ives's nature was open, receptive and completely unaffected and without pretension. However, the lack of assimilation marks this art as an early and, though often exciting, largely unformed growth.

The modernisms in Ives's style are impressive precisely because they arise from philosophy rather than aesthetic theory. Where the bitonality of the post-war French school is an in-joke at the expense of an earlier tonality and therefore seems artificial and without expressive point, Ives's polytonality and polyrhythms have a genuine and infectious exuberance which springs from a real contact with life. The fact that they are also much earlier in date is interesting but not of great significance. The same is true of Ives's borrowings from sentimental music, hymntunes, popular American songs, patriotic songs, and even of his drawing-room parodies, where the attack is as much social as aesthetic. Ives was a musical pioneer who felt a moral obligation to explore and who consequently despised the agreeable music-making of the 19th-century salon. In this he represents young America as against old Europe to whom the United States were still a cultural province. And this has been the source of his strength and powers of renewal since his death.

S.W.

JANÁČEK, Leoš
(b. Hukvaldy, 3 July 1854;
d. Prague, 12 Aug 1928)

It is interesting that we tend to think of Janáček as a more-or-less modern composer – let us say, as a contemporary of Schoenberg and Stravinsky. For he was born in 1854. If he had died at the age of fifty, he would now be regarded as one of the good minor Czech composers, like Novák or Fibich. The remaining twenty-four years of his life produced works that place him beside Dvořák and Smetana as one of his country's greatest composers.

This late harvest is made all the more surprising in view of Janáček's early musical development. Born in the village of Hukvaldy, in eastern Moravia, Leoš Janáček was singing in village festivals at the age of six, and became a music student at the age of eleven. His family was poor – he was the ninth of fourteen children – but the surrounding scenery was magnificent, with mountains, forests, open fields, even a ruined castle overlooking the village. When he was eleven, Janáček's father – the village schoolmaster – was unable to make up his mind whether the boy should be trained as a teacher or a musician. It was decided that Leoš should attend the monastery school in Old Brno; the choirmaster there was Pavel Křižkovský, a well-known composer of choral music and a friend and protegé of Janáček senior. Janáček found the life lonely, but he learned a great deal about music from

singing in the choir; he even took part in a performance of Meyerbeer's *Le Prophète*. At the age of fourteen, Janáček entered the Imperial and Royal Teachers Training Institute, on a state scholarship (this had been his father's last wish before his death) and spent three years there. Then, having passed his examinations with honours, it was back to the monastery as a teacher and unpaid deputy choir master. His earliest attempts at composing organ and choral works date from this period; but, as might be expected, they show little individuality. Having now determined that his career should be in music, Janáček felt the necessity for the academic qualifications that could only be gained in Prague. He obtained a year's leave, borrowed a little money from a friend, and moved to the capital. There his enthusiasm was so intense that he was able to cram a three-year course into a single year, and left the Organ School with the necessary certificates. Back in Brno, after more exams, he became a music teacher at the Teacher's Training School, returned to conducting the monastery choir, and in due course became Director of the Philharmonic Society. Oddly enough, his great ambition was to found a music college of his own. So although he was now engaged to one of his piano pupils, Zdenka Schulz, he decided to spend the winter of 1879 and the spring of 1880 at the Leipzig Music Conservatoire. The remainder of his year's leave of absence was spent at the Vienna Conservatoire, studying composition. When his professor there criticised a violin sonata of Janáček's as too academic, Janáček left Vienna without even waiting for his diploma. It was not his first disagreement with academic authorities on the subject of music, and it confirmed him in his desire to found his own school. His own theories about music were unorthodox; he was convinced that it should follow the rhythms of the human voice and of animal and bird noises.

Back in Brno, Janáček married Zdenka, and it was an exceptionally happy marriage. He was twenty-seven, and his head was full of dreams: of a new national music; of turning Brno into a musical centre on a level with Prague; of new teaching methods. And for the next twenty years, Janáček was absorbed in teaching, in studying folk music, and in writing male voice choruses, a couple of abortive operas, and some immature orchestral works, like the *Lach Dances*. Janáček had still not found his own voice. This was not to happen until his late forties, when he began to com-

Portrait of Janáček by Sichana, 1882.

pose his opera *Jenůfa*, sub-titled *The Step Daughter*, and based on a play by Gabriela Preissova. His twenty-one-year-old daughter Olga died while he was completing the opera – the second of Janáček's children to die – and traces of his sorrow can be found in the music of the second and third acts.

Jenůfa was performed in Brno in 1904, Janáček's fiftieth year, and was a triumph. Yet the triumph failed to spread beyond Brno. Janáček was, indeed, known in Prague, and

that was partly the trouble: he was known as a folklorist with some odd musical theories. And, incredibly, enemies in Prague succeeded in blocking all efforts to get *Jenůfa* considered for the National Theatre. It would take twelve more years to reach Prague.

The story of how this happened is told by Janáček's friend (and Kafka's) Max Brod, who declared that a certain writer heard a peasant woman singing an air from *Jenůfa* as she sat working at her front door. He was so impressed that he telephoned the director of the National Opera, and arranged for Janáček to send a score. The director turned it down.

The writer was so irritated that he brought the peasant woman to Prague and had her sing the melodies to the board, who were finally convinced. The story seems to be slightly touched-up. The 'peasant woman' was actually a singer, and a close friend of Janáček's enthusiastic supporter, Dr Veselý, and the writer, Karel Sípec was approached in the normal way. Still, what followed was romantic enough: the première, on the 26th May 1916, was again a triumph; at sixty-two Janáček at last became famous, and *Jenůfa* was soon being sung in half the opera houses of Europe. Janáček's career had finally started.

During the years between the first Brno performance and the Prague triumph, Janáček had not ceased to compose. In 1914 there was a delightful work, *Mr Brouček's Excursions*, in which the hero visits the moon in a dream. This contains some music – in the last scene, for example – which is even more typical of Janáček than *Jenůfa*. It is highly romantic and warm, yet at the same time, astringent. The music often seems to move forward in jerks, like someone driving a fast car and clapping on the brakes every few seconds, but in between the 'jerks' it surges forward with tremendous rhythmic vitality. There is something unmistakably modern about it, reminiscent of the angular periods of Stravinsky's *Les Noces*, yet it combines this with a touch of classical coldness, almost as in Gregorian chant, and with an overall feeling of romanticism and delight in nature. Almost any single bar is immediately recognisable as Janáček.

In the twelve years of life that remained to him after the success of *Jenůfa*, Janáček produced four great operas, several magnificent pieces of choral music, including the *Glagolitic Mass*, one great song cycle, the *Diary of a Man Who Disappeared*, a *Sinfonietta*, and a number of piano and chamber works including two remarkable string quartets, and a sextet, *Youth*. It would be only a slight exaggeration to say that every work of this later period is a masterpiece. At least, lovers of Janáček would be unwilling to be without any single one of them.

Janáček was now an international figure, and his post-war fame coincided happily with Czech political freedom, the aim that had been so dear to the heart of Smetana. He had another reason for flinging himself into creative activity. During the war, a friendly antique dealer named David Stössl had been able to obtain food for the Janáčeks, and in return, Janáček was later able to help to save

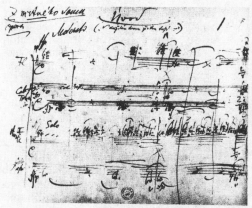

Announcement of Viennese performance of Janáček's From the House of the Dead, *with a section of manuscript.*

him from being expelled as an alien. In 1918, he met Stössl's wife Kamila, a pretty, temperamental, gypsy-like girl, with whom he had already corresponded; he promptly became infatuated with her. Janáček's wife, though admirable, was thoroughly middle class – she has been compared to Wagner's first wife Minna – and this lack of adaptability had occasionally caused friction between husband and wife. Kamila was no Mathilde Wesendonck; she did not reciprocate Janáček's feelings. All the same, she made the ageing composer dream. And the dreams overflowed in operas like *Katya Kabanová* (1919) based on Ostrovsky's gloomy domestic drama *The Storm,* and *The Makropoulos Affair* (1923–5) about a magical three-hundred-year-old woman; in two astonishing string quartets sub-titled respectively the *Kreutzer* (inspired by Tolstoy's novel *The Kreutzer Sonata*) and *Intimate Pages*. (The latter was to have been called *Love Letters*.) Most of all, perhaps, they overflowed into the song cycle *Diary of a Man Who Disappeared*, based on the case of a young farmer who abandoned his home and inheritance, and eloped with a gypsy girl. This is one of Janáček's most moving works, and is probably the ideal introduction to the composer. (For English listeners, the version sung in English makes a far greater impact than the original Czech.)

Janáček never grew old. At the age of seventy, he wrote one of his most delightful works, the wind sextet *Youth*. And his health and creative abilities were still undiminished when he caught a cold during an over-long walk in the woods near his home village; it turned to bronchial pneumonia, and he died in 1928, aged seventy-four. His last opera, *The House of the Dead*, shows no falling off in creative power; on the contrary, it is one of his most original works. This setting of Dostoevsky's gloomy novel of Siberian prison life attempts to portray human suffering in music; Janáček deliberately sets out to create an 'alien' quality. The 'overture' is simply a repeated phrase, which suggests at the same time the sort of exoticism found in *Prince Igor* and the cold detachment of Gregorian chant. The opera itself – much of it choral – has these same qualities of fire and ice. Janáček is the only composer so far to have translated Dostoevsky's world of spiritual torment into music that does not trivialise it. If greatness is to be judged by the depth of its seriousness, then Janáček is Czechoslovakia's greatest composer.

C.W.

IOSQVINVS PRATENS

Josquin Desprez.

JOSQUIN DESPREZ (or des Prez)
(b. ? Picardy, c. 1440;
d. Condé-sur-l'Escaut, 27 Aug 1521)

This composer's family name occurs in many forms, in one word or two but with 'z' rather than 's', is thought to be the one he himself favoured, since it occurs as an anagram in the text of one of his motets, *Illibata dei virgo nutrix*. He was in any case most often referred to during his lifetime, as since, by his rather unusual first name, a Picard diminutive of Josse (Joseph). This perhaps indicates his exceptional standing among the composers of his generation, a generation which includes

such famous names as Obrecht, Isaac, Brumel and Pierre de la Rue, but which he effortlessly dominates by the variety, breadth and intensity of his music.

Considering his prominence it is surprising that we do not know precisely when or where he was born. If the Josquin who is documented as a singer at Milan Cathedral from 1459 was indeed the composer, as is now generally accepted, he can hardly have been born much later than 1440, nor, since he is known to have died in 1521, much earlier; eighty years is an exceptional life-span for the period. Various traditions and scraps of evidence put his birthplace in Picardy, in the county of Hainault, in the county of Vermandois (around St Quentin) and in the diocese of Cambrai, in which he was ordained. All that can be said with certainty is that he came from the general area of Cambrai, which was then an episcopal city within the Holy Roman Empire, but probably from the French side of the nearby border.

There are various indications that Josquin held Johannes Ockeghem and his music in particular respect, and it is tempting to postulate a period of service under Ockeghem in the French royal chapel, but no direct evidence for this has yet been found. Josquin was at any rate almost certainly at Milan by 1459, and in

1473 was accepted into the personal chapel of the new duke, Galeazzo Maria Sforza, a passionate music-lover who declared his intention of assembling the best chapel in Europe and was prepared to recruit singers for it from as far away as England. After Galeazzo's assassination (22th September 1476) this group of singers was allowed to decline. Many of its members took service at the nearby court of Ferrara or in the Papal Chapel at Rome. Josquin himself joined this latter group, but not until 1486; in the interval it seems likely that he spent some time at least in the service of Galeazzo's younger brother, Cardinal Ascanio Sforza, who became the Milanese dynasty's political representative at the court of Rome. Josquin's presence in the Papal Chapel is documented (with a two-year gap between 1487 and 1489) from September 1486 until at least November 1494; he thus served two popes, Innocent VIII and his more celebrated successor Alexander VI (Rodrigo Borgia), at the height of Rome's late-medieval magnificence and corruption, and witnessed the first of the French invasions which were to reshape the political map of Italy.

After another gap in the evidence Josquin reappears north of the Alps in 1502, this time in the orbit of the court of Louis XII of France, with whom he is connected by various anecdotes, unfortunately undated. He was also in communication with the court of Ferrara, and was employed there at a very handsome salary from April 1503 to April 1504 as the aged Duke Ercole I's *maestro di cappella*. In the following month he had already returned north once more, by now as Provost of the collegiate church of Notre Dame at Condé-sur-l'Escaut. Condé is now in France but lay at that time within the borders of Hainault and thus of the Empire; it may well have been due to Josquin's influence that its collegiate church apparently maintained a more sumptuous level of ecclesiastical ceremony than any of its more richly endowed neighbours. Here Josquin spent, so far as is known, the last years of his long life, though he may have had some contact with the French court and that of the Archduchess Margaret of Austria, the Regent of the Low Countries. He died on the 27th August 1521 according to his epitaph; this is preserved in a manuscript at Lille, but his tomb, together with his church, was destroyed at the French Revolution.

That Josquin was regarded as towering over his contemporaries even during his lifetime is proved not only by flattering references in the writings of theorists and of such diverse literary figures as Castiglione, Rabelais and Luther, but by the fact that Ottaviano dei Petrucci, the inventor of music-printing and the first music-publisher, devoted three volumes to his masses (1502, 1505, 1514) and no more than one to those of any other composer. This high reputation lasted throughout the 16th century, particularly in Germany, but went into eclipse thereafter. In the late 18th century Charles Burney began to re-establish Josquin's place in his history of music, but the real foundations of his present recognition were laid by the musicologist A. W. Ambros (1868). Since then a complete edition of his music has appeared (ed. Smijers and Antonowycz), and the work of many scholars has contributed to analysing and endorsing his greatness as a composer.

The bulk of Josquin's surviving work is sacred: some eighteen masses and about eighty motets (many inauthentic works in both categories have been attributed to him by unscrupulous publishers and careless collectors over the centuries); there are also a number of instrumental pieces and settings of secular French texts. One of Josquin's achievements was to take the largely linear art of Dufay and Ockeghem and to infuse it with a stronger sense of harmonic direction, a greater expressive power. This is particularly conspicuous in the motets, in which he sets a wider variety of texts, liturgical and non-liturgical, than any of his contemporaries, and with a new sensitivity both to the rhythm of the words and to their expressive meaning that is entirely characteristic of the Renaissance. The radiant tenderness of *Ave Maria . . . virgo serena*, the pathos of *Huc me sydereo* or *Absalom fili mi*, the austere grandeur of *Pater noster* are all immediately recognisable to a 20th-century listener. Less immediately obvious, perhaps, is the constructive strength and imaginative vitality displayed in the masses, where Josquin's mastery of contrapuntal technique (especially every form of canonic writing) combines with his subtle sense of rhythm and texture and his ability to spin apparently self-generating melodies to fill the broadest canvas of his day with no trace of monotony. It is above all his ability to infuse rationally controlled musical structures with the breath of individual fantasy that makes Josquin the supreme representative of the high Renaissance in music.

J.N.

KHACHATURIAN, Aram
(b. Tiflis, 6 June 1903)

Prior to the 1939–45 war, the work of the younger Soviet composers was virtually unknown in the West. It was only after the war that the name of Khachaturian became known, at first through the brashly though excitingly scored 'Sabre Dance'. The son of an Armenian bookbinder in Tiflis (now Tbilisi), Khatchaturian appears to have shown no particular interest in music until the age of nineteen when he approached the composer and teacher Gnesin with a request to be taught composition, for he wanted to be a composer and knew nothing about music. Gnesin, himself a pupil of Rimsky-Korsakov, soon discovered that his young pupil had an instinctive gift for composition, and within two years Khachaturian was taking his first hesitant steps towards actual composition. He was only twenty-two when his *Dance* for violin and piano was accepted for publication by the Armenian State Publishing House; a year later his *Poem for Piano* was also accepted.

These, and other early works of Khachaturian, have a decidedly oriental character. Although, as he progressed towards maturity, Khachaturian used Armenian–oriental colouring more sparingly, he never completely lost that exotic touch which makes his scoring so distinctive among that of other modern Soviet musicians. In 1929, he entered the Moscow Conservatorium and joined the composition class of Myaskovsky who exercised a strong influence upon him. During his five years at the Conservatorium, Khachaturian perfected his technical skills, and also deepened his interest in the folk music of his native Armenia, recognising that in this music lay his real heritage and one which would be of immense use to him.

In 1934, Khachaturian completed a full-scale Symphony in three movements, which Russian critics of the time found satisfactorily nationalistic in form, whatever that may mean. It is certainly a work of firm achievement and even greater promise, and the Piano Concerto which followed it is, of its kind, excellent. This is the work by Khachaturian which is best known to British and American audiences, and which has been taken up by a number of Western pianists. The Violin Concerto of 1940 won the Stalin Prize and also the advocacy of the great Soviet violinist, David Oistrakh. Khachaturian is a prolific composer, but much of his patriotic music is no better than it should be. His scores for the ballet lean even more heavily on Armenian tunes than his orchestral and chamber music, but are enjoyable theatre music, and always skilfully scored.

C.O.

KODÁLY, Zoltán
(b. Kecskemét, 16 Dec 1882;
d. Budapest, 6 March 1967)

Zoltán Kodály was born in Kecskemét in central Hungary. Both his parents were musical, his father being a violinist and his mother a pianist, so that from the first the boy was brought into contact with living music. He often heard chamber music at home, and later took up the 'cello himself to help his father make up a quartet. Like Bartók's family, the Kodálys moved house several times during Zoltán's childhood: they lived successively in Szob, Galánta and Nagyyszombat, before Zoltán went to Budapest in 1900 to study at the Academy of Music. He had already begun to compose, but without, it seems, any marked sense of aim. At the Academy, he came across Brahm's music for the first time, and most of his student works (like those of his older contemporary, Dohnányi) sound more or less Brahmsian. Later, he came under the influence of Debussy. But, as with Bartók again, the determining influence of this period was Hungarian folk music, which Kodály began by researching academically and then, in 1905, by field research with recording cylinders. His early collecting expeditions were undertaken with Bartók, and their joint publications, starting in 1907, were the most systematic and scholarly of their kind to that date. Meanwhile, late in 1906, Kodály visited Berlin, going on to Paris early in 1907, but returning to Budapest later that year to take up a teaching post at the Academy. From then until his death sixty years later teaching was to remain a major activity for Kodály.

By the time war broke out in 1914, he had also written a good deal of music, though nothing as momentous as Bartók's best works of that period. The first mature orchestral work, *Summer Evening*, dates from 1906, and after this come a number of works for small instrumental groups, the First Quartet (1909), the Sonata for 'cello and piano (1910), and some piano pieces, Op. 3, whose advanced idiom provoked discussion when they were played in Paris by Tivadar Szántó in 1910.

Kodály.

During the war further chamber works appeared: a Second String Quartet (1918), and the Sonata for solo 'cello (1915). All these works were heard in Budapest but created no stir, and after the war Kodály's reputation was not sufficient to protect him against suspension from the Academy by the bureaucratic regime which succeeded the brief revolutionary phase of 1919. He was eventually reinstated in 1922. The following year he was commissioned, with Bartók and Dohnányi, to supply a new work for a concert in honour of the 50th anniversary of the unification of Pest and Buda. His contribution was the *Psalmus Hungaricus*, the first of a series of large-scale religious choral works which were at last to bring Kodály a genuinely international reputation. For a similar occasion in 1936 – the 250th anniversary of the expulsion of the

Turks from Buda – he wrote the so-called *Budavári Te Deum*. By this time he was a national hero, a kind of Hungarian Sibelius, and his work had become an aspect of the nation's identity, in sharp contrast with that of Bartók, who was already drawing away from a direct involvement in Hungarian musical life. Significantly, Kodály felt able to stay in Hungary during World War II, while Bartók fled in 1940 to the USA. But this is not to say that Kodály collaborated with the Germans or their puppet government. He seems, on the contrary, to have behaved with dignity and courage, particularly during the Russian siege of Budapest in 1944. He had resigned from his professorship at the Academy in 1941. In 1944 he completed his *Missa Brevis*, in its version for chorus and orchestra. When the war ended it was inevitable that Kodály would be regarded as a national institution and, musically, as practically an oracle.

Between 1945 and his death on the 6th March 1967 his power within Hungarian music was almost total. His music-teaching system, based on singing, was adopted throughout the country. His presence unquestionably stimulated new music, though his own increasing conservatism of taste made it hard for *really* new music to get official approval, even after the 1956 revolution, when official control of music began to relax. He himself composed rather little. By far his most substantial post-war work is the Symphony in C, completed in 1961. But this is not comparable in quality with the best orchestral works of the pre-war years including the Suite from the opera *Háry János* (1925), the two sets of dances from Marosszék (1930) and Galánta (1933), the *Peacock Variations* (1939), or the short but impressive Concerto for Orchestra (1940). He travelled a good deal, especially to the USA, and at home is said to have kept fit by long walks interspersed with short, sharp sprints. This austere regime, so far as it went, must greatly have reinforced his popular image in Hungary as a Christ-like figure, bearded, benign but resolute, humble but omniscient, a suitable guide for his people through the tangled and bewildering complexities of post-war music.

It is Kodály, rather than Bartók, who most closely resembles the great 'national-monument' composers of the 20th century: Vaughan Williams, Sibelius, Neilsen. Like Vaughan Williams his style was mainly formed from contact with folk music and ancient church music, and unlike Bartók he avoided 'distorting' this material into an obscure or introspective personal style. Kodály's idiom remains open, diatonic, based on melody and ornament, lyrical with epic connotations, rhapsodic. Before the war, in particular, he composed quantities of simple choral works intended as an extension of music-education. Indeed, he practically invented the idea of the choral festival in Hungary, modelling it, it has been said, on the Three Choirs' Festival in England. Of his three operas, *The Spinning-Room* (definitive version 1931), is based exclusively on folk tunes, while *Háry János* contains so much undigested folk music mixed up with long stretches of dialogue as seriously to inhibit its success as music drama. On the other hand Kodály's original music for this opera, much of which is in the well-known suite, is masterly and characteristic and enshrines the best features of his style: its picturesque tunefulness and colour (like the twanging of the cimbalom in the Intermezzo), its rigorous use of fourths as a basis for both melody and harmony, its swinging sense of rhythm, its piquant use of dissonance (a remnant, perhaps, of Debussy's influence), its tender lyricism. A certain whimsicality seems to anticipate the Prokofiev of *Lieutenant Kijé*. On the other hand, the music remains slightly objective and lacks a strong personal impulse, which may be why Kodály's more elaborate instrumental works, like the Solo 'Cello Sonata or the *Peacock Variations*, have a tendency to hang fire. This could also explain why, since his death, Kodály's musical influence in Hungary has been less than might have been predicted, while that of Bartók has grown and grown.

S.W.

KŘENEK, Ernst
(b. Vienna, 23 Aug 1900)

Though nearly half of his life has been spent in the United States to which he emigrated when Hitler invaded Austria, Ernst Křenek is very much part of the Austrian musical tradition. In his native Vienna, he studied composition with Franz Schreker at the Academy of Music, and when Schreker, himself a remarkable composer, became Director of the Berlin Academy of Music in 1920, Křenek followed him and continued his studies there. In the Prussian capital he broadened his musical and artistic horizons through his meetings with

Křenek.

Busoni, Artur Schnabel and others, and finally parted company from his old teacher in 1923, by which time he had already built up an impressive list of compositions which were predominantly late-romantic in style. Schreker had kept his young pupil away from the music and influence of Schoenberg and his experiments in atonality, and it was only during his Berlin years that Křenek began cautiously to explore Schoenberg's world. Křenek himself has said that at this time he also became attracted to the music of Bartók, 'and began to write music that dispensed rather cavalierly with the respectability of tonal relationships, and was rich in dissonant polyphony and rhythmic insistence on protracted ostinatos.' His early string quartets, written during this period in Berlin, certainly betray Bartókian leanings, though his first Symphony, also composed in 1921, already reveals Křenek as being a continuer of the Austrian symphonic tradition whose last great representative had been Gustav Mahler. In 1922, Křenek married Mahler's daughter, Anna.

Opera was to play an important part in Křenek's oeuvre, and his first steps in this direction were taken in Germany, where his one-act opera *Die Zwingburg* and his full-length comic opera, *Der Sprung über den Schatten,* whose style encompasses jazz and atonality, were produced in Berlin and Frankfurt. During the 1920s he worked in opera houses at Cassel and Wiesbaden, and it was at Cassel that his next opera, *Orpheus und Eurydike*, composed on a libretto by the painter Kokoschka, was produced. While he was at Wiesbaden, Křenek composed the opera which was to make him famous. This was *Jonny spielt auf* (Johnny strikes up), whose libretto he also wrote. The story of a black jazz violinist and his involvements with white women, *Jonny spielt auf* again utilised a mixture of musical styles. Its Leipzig première in 1927 attracted a great deal of attention, and the opera soon achieved a kind of notoriety when the German Nazis decided it was offensive to their ideals of racial purity. Soon, *Jonny spielt auf* had achieved production in more than a hundred opera houses, and its composer from then on was able to live in comfortable independence and devote his time to composition. When his first marriage broke up, he married an actress, Berta Herrmann, and returned to Vienna. The next years, until the Anschluss of 1938, Křenek spent composing, and visiting other countries as conductor or performer of his own music. The satirical operas he wrote immediately after *Jonny* failed to duplicate the success of that work, nor did his tragic opera, *Leben des Orest* (Life of Orestes) fare better, and much of Křenek's music written in the 1930s returned to that mood of nostalgic *Sennsucht* to which every Viennese composer, from Schubert through Johann Strauss to Mahler and Berg, has access. One of the most attractive of Křenek's works in this vein is his song-cycle, *Reisebuch aus den österreichischen Alpen,* for which the composer wrote the words: a set of sentimental, ironic and philosophical sketches in praise of the Austrian Alps, but clearly modelled on Schubert's *Die Winterreise.*

It was in Vienna in the 1930s, however, that Křenek first seriously came to grips with the new Viennese school, and with the music and theories of Schoenberg's disciples, Berg and Webern. His last years in Vienna were spent acquiring a new technique of composition, and also lecturing and writing. One of the first fruits of his involvement with serial technique was his huge play with music, *Karl V*, produced in Prague in 1938. After his emigration to America, where he undertook several academic engagements before finally making his way to the West Coast, Křenek plunged into composition, producing chamber operas, choral works, and symphonies. If the music of his mature years has failed to engage the public attention as forcefully as those works he composed in Europe, Křenek has nevertheless continued to tread his own path, and to refuse to be deflected from it by fashion. In recent years, he has written a great deal about music, most notably in *Exploring Music* (1966) and *Horizons circled* (1974). A recent large-scale work which proved that, in his seventh decade, Křenek's creative forces are undiminished, is the opera *Sardakai* (1969).

C.O.

LALO, Édouard
(b. Lille, 27 Jan 1823;
d. Paris, 22 April 1892)

Although Lalo is usually remembered for the wrong reason, for his *Symphonie espagnole* rather than for his operatic masterpiece, *Le Roi d'Ys*, there is this to be said in its favour: it reminds us that the composer was prominent among those who helped restore orchestral music to its rightful place in the Paris of the 1870s and 1880s.

A year younger than César Franck, and like him a provincial who found fame in Paris, Lalo was born in Lille in 1823. (His family was by origin Spanish though long domiciled in France.) Trained as a string player at the local Conservatoire, the young musician defied his soldier father by embarking for Paris where he joined Habeneck's violin class at the Conservatoire and studied composition privately. At first he made no particular impression and apart from producing some songs and chamber music (for which there was little market anyway), he made his living as an instrumentalist and teacher and, as a member of the Armigaud–Jacquard String Quartet, acquired an excellent knowledge of the classical chamber music repertory. By nature retiring and contemplative his career might have remained in the doldrums but for his marriage in 1865 to a singer, Mlle de Maligny, who encouraged him to write for the stage. His first attempts were discouraging. His opera *Fiesque*, based on Schiller, only won third prize in a government-sponsored competition. The director of

the Théâtre Lyrique procrastinated and then the outbreak of Franco-Prussian war made its production impossible. The set-back was however only temporary, for Saint-Saëns' recently founded Société Nationale de Musique provided an outlet for new French orchestral music.

Inspired by the great Spanish violinist Sarasate, who launched both works, Lalo introduced his Concerto in F in 1874 followed by his *Symphonie espagnole* in 1875. They made his name. Meanwhile, he was engaged upon another opera, *Le Roi d'Ys*, based on a Breton legend, extracts from which were heard at the Colonne Concerts in 1876. Two years later the opera was complete, but is production was postponed and he was asked instead to write a ballet for the Opéra – to be ready in four months. The time was short, the task outside his experience. The effort of composing *Namouna* brought on nervous prostration and the scoring had to be finished by Gounod. Despite the vociferous enthusiasm of the young avant-garde composers the combination of a hostile claque and a hostile press ensured its failure. It was said to be 'symphonic' and 'Wagnerian', reproaches no longer valid when suites from it were successfully performed in the concert hall.

Apart from the *Norwegian Rhapsody* and the 'Russian' Violin Concerto, the next major work was his admirable G minor Symphony (1887) in which German procedures were crossed with the piquant distinctiveness of his melodies and scoring. When eventually *Le Roi d'Ys* was staged at the Opéra in 1888, it confounded its ill-wishers by becoming a best seller. It proved that Wagner's musical methods could be exploited without recourse to his literary–philosophical preoccupations. Lalo had a taste for the picturesque and the exotic but his real claim to fame was his ability to synthesise the best of the French and German traditions.

C.G.

Title-page of Le Roi d'Ys *by Lalo.*

LE ROI D'YS

POËME DE EDOUARD BLAU

MVSIQVE DE: E. LALO

PARIS, G. HARTMANN ET Cie

LANNER, Josef
(b. Vienna, 12 April 1801;
d. Vienna, 14 April 1843)

Together with his friend and colleague Johann Strauss (father of the 'waltz king'), Lanner was largely responsible for introducing the waltz to Vienna. His father was a glove-maker, and young Lanner had to teach himself music. By the time he was twelve he was sufficiently proficient on the violin to obtain an engagement with Pamer's dance orchestra, which was popular in the taverns and dance halls of Vienna. Michael Pamer was a composer of dance tunes, and his orchestra played these and other light music for dancing. At the age of seventeen, Lanner left to form his own group which consisted of two violins, viola, 'cello and guitar, the viola played by Johann Strauss the elder, who had also defected from Pamer's orchestra. Lanner's ensemble, which was enlarged as time went by, soon established itself as the leading orchestra of its kind, playing in the coffee houses and taverns, and in the Prater, the huge amusement park in Vienna. Such was its popularity that Lanner eventually split the orchestra into two, directing one ensemble himself, and entrusting the other to Strauss. In 1825 the colleagues separated, and Strauss formed his own orchestra. Lanner marked the occasion by composing a 'Trennungswalzer' or 'Parting Waltz'.

Now Vienna had two splendid orchestras to dance to, and, delighting in the rivalry between the rival composer–conductors, the Viennese paid homage to them both, playing them off against each other. The two former friends who had, as youths, shared lodgings, girls and even shirts, now became professional rivals, though in due course they resumed their friendship, and would meet to play each other's music. When Chopin came to Vienna to give concerts in 1830, he wrote that he found it difficult to interest people in his music, for 'Lanner, Strauss and their waltzes dominate everything'.

In 1829 Lanner was appointed *Hofball-musikdirektor* or director of music for all court balls. Unlike Strauss, however, he did not achieve great fame outside Austria, or even outside Vienna, for he had no love of travel or fame, preferring to live quietly in the Viennese suburb of Döbling, composing his gentle, almost Schubertian waltzes and Ländler for his fellow Viennese to dance to. He was fond, too, of the Viennese new wine, the 'Heuriger'; perhaps over-fond for there was one occasion

when he was conducting in the presence of the Emperor who, noticing that Lanner was swaying rather dangerously as he conducted, asked his Master of Ceremonies to 'take Lanner out, or he might fall off the platform and hurt himself.'

Lanner's music, gentle, sensuous, but imbued with that melancholy which is as quintessentially Viennese as their gaiety and charm, contrasts quite clearly with that of Strauss. As the Viennese saying has it, 'With Lanner, it's "Please, dance, I beg you", but with Strauss it's "You must dance, I command you".' The genuine vein of poetry which co-exists in Lanner with his melodic fecundity has kept his music alive and is perhaps responsible for a renewed interest in him in recent years. He composed more than a hundred waltzes, including such real masterpieces of the genre as *Die Werber*, *Abendsterne* and *Die Schönbrünner*.

C.O.

LEHÁR, Franz
(b. Komárom, 30 April 1870;
d. Bad Ischl, 24 Oct 1948)

For many generations, the Lehár family lived in a village called Lesnitz, in what was then part of Austria, but is now Czechoslovakian. They were glaziers, until one of them Franz Lehár the elder, showed some musical promise and was allowed to study. By the time he was twenty-four, Lehár had become Bandmaster of an Austrian Regiment, the youngest Bandmaster in the Imperial Austrian Army. After the war with Italy, in 1869, the Regiment was sent to a small town in Hungary, where Bandmaster Lehár married a local girl. A year later, their son Franz was born.

Franz, it was eventually discovered, had inherited his father's musical ability. While the family was kept continually on the move with the Regiment, the child had to study as best he could. By the time he was twelve, however, he had won a scholarship to the Music Academy in Prague where he stayed for six years. He had already begun to compose, and had also become a very proficient performer on the violin. When he showed some of his student pieces to Dvořák, the eminent composer said 'You know what, my lad? You should hang up your fiddle, and concentrate on composing music.' And when Brahms

Lehár.

visited Dvořák in Prague, he too encouraged the young Lehár.

After leaving the Academy, Lehár took a job as first violinist in a small German theatre, but after a year of this decided to follow his father into the Army as a musician. 'I obtained the post of Bandmaster', he said later, 'with a Regiment stationed in a Hungarian village. At twenty, I was the youngest Bandmaster ever appointed in the entire Army, beating my father's record by four years.' Soon he had written an opera, *Kukuschka*, and when a Viennese publisher expressed interest in it Lehár impulsively gave up his Army post to become a full-time composer. His opera, in the style of Mascagni, whose *Cavalleria Rusticana* Lehár had very much admired, was produced in Leipzig and later in Budapest. It was rejected by Mahler at the Vienna Opera, but was produced in Vienna a few years later at the Volksoper. By the time of the Volksoper production, however, Lehár had turned his attention to operetta, had moved to Vienna, and had begun to make a name for himself with *Wiener Frauen* (Viennese Women) at the Theater an der Wien, and *Der Rastelbinder* (The Tinker) at the Carl Theater. Then Lehár set to work on the operetta which was to make him famous throughout the world, *Die Lustige Witwe* (The Merry Widow), which was produced at the Theater an der Wien in 1905.

Seventy years of productions all over the world, in a variety of languages, and as often as not performed by not very talented amateurs, have failed to dim the brilliance of Lehár's score for *The Merry Widow*, a masterpiece which revitalised the genre of Viennese operetta, whose great founding figure, Johann Strauss II, had died in Vienna six years earlier. The music of *The Merry Widow* is brilliantly written for the orchestra and the voices, and covers an incredibly wide range of feeling. The Camille–Valencienne duet in Act II, 'Sieh dort den kleinen Pavillon', has an undercurrent of eroticism that makes it Lehár's equivalent of the *Tristan und Isolde* love duet.

The success of *The Merry Widow* released a flood of creative energy in Lehár. In less than a year he composed three operettas which ran simultaneously in Vienna: *The Prince's Child*, *Gypsy Love* and *The Count of Luxembourg*. *The Count of Luxembourg*, the finest of the three, is a continuation of the musical style of *The Merry Widow*, with elegant and sophisticated characters and those heady, sensuous waltzes which seemed to come so easily to Lehár.

From the very first, it was a success with audiences and critics, as was Lehár's next operetta, *Eva*, for which Lehár accepted from his librettists Willner and Bodanzky a story somewhat more down to earth than the usual operetta plot, a story which claimed to have some contemporary social awareness, or so the Viennese press rumoured in advance. These rumours upset the impresario of the Theater an der Wien who feared he was about to become involved in political arguments. In the event, Lehár was praised for the rich and fascinating sound of his orchestra, and also for the splendid music he had written for the heroine.

After *Eva*, it seemed for a time that Lehár's run of luck was deserting him. *The Ideal Wife* (1913) was a re-working of an earlier operetta, and was only moderately successful. It was followed by *Endlich Allein* (Alone at last), which was unusual in that one entire act consisted of an extended love duet for two young people alone on top of a mountain. It failed to please: critics spoke mockingly of it as Lehár's *Tristan* and called it pretentious. Lehár himself remained convinced that this second act with its Alpine scenery was one of the finest things he had written, and whenever the question of re-adapting the operetta came up he was always insistent that no change should be made to the structure of that particular act.

Lehár had married, and had bought a splendid villa in Bad Ischl, the attractive spa resort in the Salzkammergut, where the Emperor Franz Josef used to spend every summer at his hunting lodge. During the years of World War I, Lehár and his wife Sophie remained in Vienna, where his next operetta, *The Stargazer* was produced in 1916. It and its successor, *Where the Lark Sings*, failed to attract the public. The war was now in its final stages, and the citizens of Vienna were weary and dispirited. The old Emperor died, and so did their favourite comedian Giradi. Public transport broke down, and theatre performances were given only in the afternoons. But, after the war, the Viennese flocked again to the Theater an der Wien for a special occasion. Lehár was fifty, and was celebrating with a new operetta, *The Blue Mazurka*. On the first night, the lovely old theatre was covered in bouquets and garlands of flowers, and the government and well-wishers from many countries paid tribute to 'the world's most famous Austrian'.

It was while he was composing his next operetta, *Frasquita*, that Lehár met the great Mozart tenor and Lieder singer, Richard

Tauber, whose later career was to be so bound up with his. Lehár played him one or two of the songs from *Frasquita*, Tauber was enchanted with them, and the following year in Vienna he sang the leading tenor role in the operetta. From then on, every Lehár operetta was written for Richard Tauber, and the Tauberlied in each work became the moment of highest excitement, as the great tenor sang the melodies fashioned to suit his voice, his range, and his temperament. The first work of the composer–singer collaboration was *Paganini*, whose leading character was the famous 19th-century violinist, and whose big Tauber song was 'Gern hab' ich die Frauen geküsst' or, in its English version, 'Girls were made to love and kiss'.

Lehár's next operetta, *The Tsarevich*, was based on a Polish play about a Russian Crown Prince who, to the dismay of those concerned with the future of the monarchy, appears to be allergic to women. In order to accustom him to the company of the opposite sex, the Tsar's ministers introduce him to a girl disguised as a boy. The cure works only too well, and the young couple fall in love. But destiny calls, the Crown Prince cannot be allowed to marry a commoner, and the ending is inevitably an unhappy one. Lehár, having at first expressed his enthusiasm for the plot, later decided that the idea of the heroine disguised as a boy was indecent, and refused to proceed with the project. The authors then sold the libretto to Mascagni who failed to produce a single bar of music for it. They next offered it to another operetta composer, Eduard Künnecke, who had already composed the first act when Lehár, persuaded by Tauber, changed his mind and agreed to compose *The Tsarevich* himself. Künnecke behaved with great generosity and understanding, handing back the libretto with the remark that it was a pleasure for him to have helped Lehár towards the production of a new masterpiece. And a masterpiece, or at least a great success, it turned out to be. Tauber sang the title-role, and the composer conducted at the Berlin permière.

The series of Lehár–Tauber operettas continued with *Friederike*, and *Das Land des Lächelns* (The Land of Smiles). In box-office terms, *The Land of Smiles* was Lehár's most successful work since *The Merry Widow* of a quarter of a century earlier. It was to prove his last great success. His librettists next provided Lehár with a plot concerning an Army captain and his passion for a labourer's wife, a passion which destroys both of them. When Tauber heard the score, his enthusiasm was such that he insisted the work was more opera than operetta, and that it must have its première at the Vienna Opera. Lehár at first laughed at the idea, but it began to grow on him. To have one of his works performed in the famous opera house whose director of thirty years earlier, Gustav Mahler, had rejected Lehár's opera, would be the crowning success of his career. And he, the composer, would conduct the famous Vienna Philharmonic, which played, and still plays, for the Opera.

The first night of *Giuditta* at the Vienna Opera in January 1934 was a glittering affair, though the work proved somewhat uneven, as though unsure of its status. No one then could have guessed that they were witnessing Lehár's last new work for the stage, but the times were changing. Some weeks after the première, the Austrian Chancellor Dollfuss was murdered by the Nazis. Lehár became involved in bothersome litigation with a woman who claimed that the libretto of *Giuditta* plagiarised a fairy-tale she had written; almost simultaneously his weakness for the ladies led the ageing composer into the hands of blackmailers. As the Nazi menace spread, many of his friends and collaborators left Europe for the New World, Tauber became *persona non grata* in Germany, and when Hitler marched into Austria he fled to England. Lehár and his Jewish wife Sophie retired to their villa in Bad Ischl where they spent the six years of the war. One day the Gestapo arrived at the villa to take Lehár's wife away, but a frantic phone call from the composer to the local Nazi chief saved her. When the war ended, and American troops arrived in Bad Ischl, they too turned up at the Lehár villa to pay their respects to the seventy-five-year-old composer, and to request his autograph. Late in 1947, Sophie Lehár died. A few months later, just after he had sung a superb Ottavio in *Don Giovanni* at the Royal Opera House, Covent Garden, Richard Tauber died in London. And some months after that, Lehár died in Bad Ischl. His fame as the last of the great composers of Viennese operetta is secure, and *The Merry Widow* will continue to be produced, well and badly, all over the world, for many years to come.

C.O.

LEONCAVALLO, Ruggiero
(b. Naples, 8 March 1858;
d. Montacatani, 9 Aug 1919)

The fact that Ruggiero Leoncavallo was the son of a magistrate is of some importance, because his father was the judge at the trial in Montalto of an actor in a touring theatre company who had murdered his wife after a performance. It was on this tragic incident that the composer based the libretto of *Pagliacci*, the opera for which he is still famous the world over. This was first produced at the Teatro dal Verme in Milan on the 21st May 1892, winning him overnight success, but before that he had studied and worked hard to no avail. Having shown musical ability at an early age he was admitted to the Naples Conservatoire as a student of piano and composition, leaving at the age of eighteen with the diploma of 'maestro' to begin work straight away on an opera on the story of the ill-fated English poet Thomas Chatterton, his inspiration fired by the drama by Alfred de Vigny. He completed the opera at Bologna and arranged for its production, but the unscrupulous impresario vanished just before the première, leaving Leoncavallo almost penniless and in despair. He was obliged to earn a livelihood by giving piano and singing lessons, from which he graduated to accompanying soloists at café concerts. As a menial accompanist he began to travel widely, not only going to France, Holland, Germany and England but venturing as far as Cairo.

Returning at last to Italy, Leoncavallo embarked on an ambitious operatic trilogy covering the events of the Renaissance in his native country, but after waiting in vain for a performance of the first of these operas, *I Medici*, he set to work on the short two-act *Pagliacci*. (He had wanted to enter this for the competition which was won in 1890 by Mascagni's *Cavalleria Rusticana*, but it was ineligible since the Sonzogno competition was for one-act operas only.) Throughout his life Leoncavallo seems to have set his sights on a plane above the *verismo* melodrama of *Pagliacci*, though it soon became clear that this is where his natural talent lay. He had no reason to feel his popular opera was in any way inferior, because it is a masterpiece of its kind. The Prologue, partly instrumental and partly vocal, is indeed a stroke of genius, still capable of striking the opera-goer of today as a *tour de force* in spite of its familiarity. The melodies flow with natural ease and are always perfectly tailored to character and situation, while the orchestration is both vivid and subtle. The music for the play within the play is skilfully designed to stand apart from that which depicts the characters' real emotions, of which the arias for the broken-hearted clown are particularly expressive. By one of the few benevolent tricks which fate has played on composers, *Pagliacci* made the ideal companion-piece for *Cavalleria Rusticana*, so that both operas became assured of immortality as a double bill.

Leoncavallo was never to repeat this first triumph. In 1893 his originally spurned *I Medici* was finally staged, but it proved such a failure that the composer gave up any thought of completing his grand trilogy. The earlier *Chatterton* was tried out three years later, but the Roman public gave it the thumbs down. Leoncavallo scored a near-hit in 1897 with *La Bohème* at the Teatro la Fenice, but though this adaptation of Henri Mürger's novel was quite well received it was overshadowed by Puccini's more appealing opera on the same subject, which had been premièred in Turin a few months earlier and was then sending audiences at a rival theatre in Venice into ecstasies. It is possible, indeed, that Leoncavallo's *Bohème* might still have a place in the popular repertoire today had Puccini not beaten him to the post. After *Pagliacci* Leoncavallo's most successful opera was *Zazà*, also cast in the *verismo* mould, which started life in Milan in 1900 with Arturo Toscanini conducting a star cast. It can still prove an effective piece when a gifted singing actress performs the title-role of a Parisian music-hall singer who finally sees the folly of her affair with a married man and returns to her previous lover. Although the opera enjoyed some international success at the time, it is now rarely revived outside Italy. More operas followed, some tragic and others comic, and also two operettas, but Leoncavallo was forced to realise in the end that he would be remembered by posterity simply as the composer of *Pagliacci*, and that even this powerful work would only survive in perpetual tandem with Mascagni's *Cavalleria Rusticana*.

F.G.B.

Caricature of Liszt, Marie d'Agoult and Pictet, by George Sand.

LISZT, Franz
(b. Raiding, 22 Oct 1811;
d. Bayreuth, 31 July 1886)

Franz (Ferencz) Liszt was born at Raiding near
Sopron in Hungary. His father Adam
(1776–1827) was an official in the service of
Prince Nicholas Eszterházy; his mother Anna
Laager (1788–1866) was of south German
origin. Many prominent musicians, including
Haydn, Cherubini and Hummel, visited the
palace of Eszterháza; Adam Liszt was a
talented amateur musician who played the
'cello in the court orchestra – he had also been
a Franciscan novice for two years at the age of
nineteen. Adam soon perceived his son's
talent and gave him piano lessons from the age
of seven onwards; the young Liszt appeared in
concerts at Sopron and Poszony when he was
nine. After this a group of Hungarian mag-
nates set up a fund for the boy's education,
and in 1821 the family moved to Vienna,
where Franz had piano lessons with
Beethoven's pupil Karl Czerny and composition lessons with Salieri, the musical
director of the Viennese court. Franz gave
successful concerts in Vienna and met Beethoven and Schubert; he also contributed a variation on a waltz by the publisher Diabelli to a
symposium in which fifty Austrian composers
took part – Beethoven wrote his set of thirty-
three variations on the same theme.

In the autumn of 1833 the Liszt family
moved to Paris; Franz was refused admission
to the Conservatoire by Cherubini as he was a
foreigner. Instead he studied theory with
Anton Reicha and composition with Ferdinando Paer. He played at many fashionable
concerts in Paris and also visited England in
1824 and 1825; he was hailed as a successor to
Mozart as an infant prodigy. In October 1825
his one-act opera *Don Sanche* was performed
at the Paris Opéra; in the following year he
wrote the *Étude en Douze Exercices*, the original version of the Transcendental Studies.
But the continual touring was beginning to
affect his health, and he expressed a wish to
give up the concert platform and become a
priest – he had been deeply religious since his
earliest days. He went with his father to Boulogne to recover, and there Adam suddenly
died of typhoid fever. Liszt returned to Paris,
where he earned his living by teaching the

piano. Next year he fell in love with one of his pupils, Caroline de Saint-Cricq, the daughter of the Minister of Commerce; when her father insisted that the attachment be broken off Liszt again became ill and went through a long period of religious doubt and pessimism. He had many discussions with his 'spiritual father', the Abbé de Lamennais, and also became interested in the ideas of the Saint-Simonians.

The revolution of July 1830 shook him out of his lethargy; he sketched out a *Revolutionary* symphony, began to read widely, to make up for his lack of general education, and met many artists including the three composers who were to influence him most greatly – Berlioz, Paganini and Chopin. From Berlioz he learnt the command of the modern orchestra which he was to show in his later orchestral works, and also a feeling of diabolism which remained with him all his life; he was staggered by Paganini's virtuoso technique and was determined to transfer his extraordinary effects to the piano, while Chopin influenced the lyrical and poetical side of his writing.

In 1834 Liszt met the Comtesse Marie d'Agoult, and they began an affair; next year she left her husband and family and joined Liszt in Geneva, where their first daughter Blandine was born on the 18th December. Liszt and the Comtesse lived together for the next four years, mainly in Switzerland and Italy, with occasional visits to Paris. On one of these the celebrated 'pianistic duel' occurred in which Liszt defeated his rival Sigismond Thalberg at Princess Belgiojoso's house. During this period Liszt wrote the first and most difficult version of the Transcendental and Paganini Studies and also the first two books of the *Années de Pèlerinage*, lyrical evocations of his travels with the Comtesse. Their second daughter Cosima was born near Lake Como on the 25th December, and their son Daniel on the 9th May 1839 in Rome, but in the autumn their relations became strained, and when Liszt heard that the proposal to build a Beethoven monument in Bonn was liable to collapse through lack of funds he decided to raise the money by returning to the life of a travelling virtuoso. The Comtesse went back to Paris with the children while Liszt gave six concerts in Vienna. He also visited Hungary for the first time since his boyhood, and again heard the music of the gypsies, which had fascinated him in his youth. He began a series of compositions based on their music which later became the Hungarian Rhapsodies; he was also presented with a poem of homage by the Hungarian poet Vörösmarty.

Until 1847 Liszt continued to tour the whole of Europe from Ireland and Portugal to Turkey and Russia. He spent the summer holidays with the Comtesse and their children on the island of Nonnenwerth in the Rhine until 1844, when they finally separated and Liszt took the children to live with his mother in Paris. This was the period of his greatest brilliance as a pianist; he was lionised everywhere, was showered with honours, and had numerous mistresses, including the original 'Dame aux Camellias' and the dancer Lola Montes. However he continued to compose, now writing songs and choral music as well as piano works; he wrote his first Beethoven Cantata for the celebrations in Bonn in 1845, his first work for chorus and orchestra. In February 1847 he played in Kiev and there met Princess Carolyne Sayn-Wittgenstein, who was to be associated with him for the rest of his life. She persuaded him to give up his career as a virtuoso and to concentrate on composition. He spent the following winter with the Princess on her estate at Woronince, and in February 1848 he settled in Weimar, where he had been Director of Music Extraordinary since 1842; the Princess joined him there in the following year. Now began the period of his greatest production; during the next twelve years he wrote the first twelve symphonic poems, the *Faust* and *Dante* symphonies, the final versions of the two piano concertos and the *Totentanz* for a piano and orchestra, the piano sonata and other major piano works, including revised versions of the Transcendental and Paganini Studies and the first two books of the *Années de Pèlerinage*, the *Gran Mass* and other choral works and songs. He also conducted a number of works by contemporary composers, including Wagner's *Tannhäuser* and the first performance of his *Lohengrin,* Schumann's *Genoveva* and *Manfred,* Berlioz' *Benvenuto Cellini* and operas by Verdi and Donizetti. He also taught numerous pupils, including Hans von Bülow and Carl Tausig. Unfortunately his support of the avant-garde aroused opposition, and when Liszt conducted the première of *The Barber of Bagdad* by his pupil Peter Cornelius in 1858 the audience made a demonstration which he took to be directed against himself; he resigned his post.

Liszt remained in Weimar till 1861; his son Daniel died in 1859 at the age of only twenty,

Liszt's birthplace.

and his elder daughter Blandine died in 1862. Liszt had hoped to marry the Princess in Rome in 1861, but at the last moment the Pope revoked his sanction of her divorce. Liszt remained in Rome and devoted himself mainly to writing religious music; he took the four minor orders of the Catholic Church in 1865, but never became a priest. In 1869 he was invited back to Weimar to give master classes in piano playing, and from 1871 he was asked to do the same in Budapest: from then till the end of his life he made regular journeys between Rome, Weimar and Budapest – his 'vie trifurquée'. His second daughter Cosima, who had married von Bülow in 1857, had now begun an affair with Wagner and bore him two illegitimate children; this led to a quarrel between the two composers which was not patched up till 1872. During this period Liszt received visits from many of the younger generation of composers, including Borodin, Fauré, Saint-Saëns and Debussy, to all of whom he gave help and advice; among his pupils were Eugen d'Albert, Felix Weingartner, Frederic Lamond, Moriz

Rosenthal, Emil von Sauer and Jose Vianna da Motta. In 1886 Liszt made his last tour, visiting Budapest, Liège, Paris and London, where works of his were performed and he was received enthusiastically. In July he visited Bayreuth for the festival, but he was now ill from dropsy which developed into pneumonia, and he died there on the 31st July.

Liszt was the greatest pianist of his age and possibly of all time. His compositions for the piano revolutionised keyboard technique, and he was the first pianist to give a complete 'recital' lasting a whole evening. He also prompted works by Bach, Beethoven and Schubert at a time when they were by no means popular, and he helped his contemporaries such as Berlioz and Wagner by performing their works. His invention of the one-movement symphonic poem created a new musical form, and he expanded the harmonic language of his time – his later works even anticipate the methods of Debussy, Bartók and Schoenberg. His idea of 'transformation of themes', in which all the motifs in one work are derived from a single basic idea also anticipates Schoenberg's twelve-note technique in essence, and was also the foundation of Wagner's system of *leitmotivs*. And Liszt's music at its best is always original, expressive and colourful: he was certainly one of the major composers of the 19th century.

H.S.

LOEWE, Carl
(b. Loebejuen, nr. Halle, 30 Nov 1796;
d. Kiel, 20 April 1869)

Loewe, the son of a schoolmaster, was the youngest of twelve children. He was taught music by his father, and at the age of eleven had become a sufficiently good singer to be offered a place in the court chapel choir at Cöthen. After spending two years in the choir, he went on to a high school in Halle whose head was also conductor of the Halle choral society in whose choir Loewe therefore sang. An annuity he received at this time made it possible for the youth to devote himself full-time to the study of music, and to become proficient as a pianist. He also learned French and Italian: he was already attracted to poetry and presumably wanted to be able to range in his reading beyond the German language. In his teens, he began to compose songs, the first of them being 'Klothar' (Op. 1) and 'Das Gebet des Herrn und die Einsetzungsworte des Abendmahls' (Op. 2).

When the war of 1812–13 broke out, the Chancellor of the Gymnasium or high school at Halle helped Loewe to enter the University as a theological student. When a Singakademie was founded in Halle, Loewe joined that as well. In 1818, he began to compose the first of the ballads which made him famous: 'Edward' and 'Der Erlkönig'. Goethe's 'Erlkönig' had already been set by the eighteen-year-old Schubert three years earlier, though Schubert did not publish his song until after Loewe's. In 1821 Loewe married a girl he had met in the Singakademie, but she died three years later. Meanwhile, his musical and academic career flourished. After some years as Professor of Music at Stettin, he was elected a member of the Academy of Berlin. Several opportunities for travel presented themselves, and thus he went to Vienna in 1844, London in 1847, Scandinavia in 1851 and France in 1857. He continued to compose his songs quite prolifically until in 1864 when he suffered the first onslaught of the illness which killed him three years later.

Loewe composed not only songs but five operas, only one of which was performed, and numerous symphonies and concertos, but it is for his songs alone that he is remembered. At one time there was a great vogue for Loewe in Germany, particularly on the level of domestic music-making, but his work is less frequently encountered in recital programmes nowadays. Loewe was no Schubert, but he was certainly gifted, though his gift was a somewhat specialised one. Of his songs – and there are nearly four hundred of them – the majority are ballads. The ballad-poems which inspired Loewe, and indeed Schubert, derive from the Scottish and English narrative ballads, many of which were translated into German. The form was eagerly taken up in the 18th century, even by poets of the stature of Goethe and Schiller. Generally speaking, in Loewe's ballads the music tends to follow the mood and form of the words in a fairly simple and subservient way, underlining and thus emphasising the form's narrative importance. Loewe's setting of Goethe's 'Erlkönig', for instance, obeys these unwritten rules in a way that Schubert's does not. But he has his own distinctive narrative style, which sets him apart from the other ballad composers of his day. His tunes are sweetly sentimental or highly dramatic, his accompaniments relatively simple. The best of his songs are rewarding both to perform and to hear.

C.O.

LORTZING, Albert
(b. Berlin, 23 Oct 1801;
d. Berlin, 21 Jan 1851)

The theatre certainly ran in the blood of (Gustav) Albert Lortzing, who became in turn actor, singer, producer, librettist and opera composer. His parents were amateur actors at the time of his birth, but when he was twelve they turned professional and he shared their wandering life touring Germany as a boy actor. He inherited his musical gift from his mother, but was largely self-taught as pianist, 'cellist and composer. Curiously perhaps, his earliest compositions were instrumental, but after his marriage to an actress in 1823 he devoted all his energies to the lyric theatre and family life, producing fourteen operas and eleven children. Ali Pascha von Janina, composed in 1824, met with little success, and he was forced to continue acting like the rest of his family: he appeared in Cologne, incidentally, with his wife and parents in the Schlegel translation of Shakespeare's *Romeo and Juliet*. Later, at the court theatre of Detmold, he composed incidental music for plays in addition to acting, singing and occasionally playing the 'cello in the orchestra. It was with his subsequent move to the municipal theatre in Leipzig that he launched himself into comic opera, the field in which he was to prove most at home.

The opera for which Lortzing is most widely remembered today was his fourth, *Zar und Zimmerman*, composed and performed in Leipzig in 1837. This story of Peter the Great of Russia, disguised as a carpenter, and the real carpenter Peter Ivanov, involves a series of mistaken identities leading to comic situations of a naïve yet theatrically effective kind. The score is full of light, engaging melodies ideally suited to the tone of the libretto, written by the composer himself after a French play. The success of the opera was established with its Berlin production two years later, and it has remained a highly popular work throughout Germany and one revived not infrequently in other countries. Less popular, but musically more refined, is *Der Wildschütz* (*The Poacher*), which followed five years later and was also premièred in Leipzig. The characterisation here is more subtle, the melodies more elegant and the ensembles constructed with greater care and finesse. The opera breathes the good humour and contentment of Lortzing himself, who for all his unsettled life as a touring actor was essentially a genial bourgeois German of his time. His romantic operas, of which only *Undine* (1845) can be considered satisfactory, found him lacking in both depth and invention. Comedy tinged with sentiment was his strong suit.

Although his more successful operas were given many performances during his lifetime and brought him considerable fame, Lortzing made very little money from them and was obliged to work in ill-paid posts as theatre conductor. At a time when four of his operas were being played to full houses in Berlin he and his family were on the brink of starvation. He was too ill to attend the première of his last opera, the one-act *Die Opernprobe* (The Opera Rehearsal), at Frankfurt on the 20th January 1851, dying in Berlin the following morning before the news of its success could reach him. As we would say today, that's show business.

F.G.B.

LULLY, Jean-Baptiste
(b. Florence, 29 Nov 1632;
d. Paris, 22 March 1687)

To relate Jean-Baptiste Lully's life and achievements is to relate a story almost without parallel in the history of music. From the most obscure of beginnings (he was the son of a Florentine miller) he rose to become not only the foremost French composer of his day, and certainly the richest, but also an intimate of Louis XIV, and in time one of his *secretaires* (a position reserved for the king's most eminent and trusted advisors). Such was the giddy pace of Lully's ascent in Fortune's wheel that his detractors (he had many) ascribed much of his success to base intrigue. Lully seems to have owed it more to luck, opportunism, and not least to talent.

He was born in Florence in 1632. It was the Chevalier de Guise who led him to France, and into the service of his cousin Mlle de Montpensier, who sought an Italian for conversation in that language. Lully was fourteen when he became her *valet de la chambre*. Between his arrival in France and 1652, he clearly studied music and composition, but we know very little besides the fact that he took lessons from François Roberday (1624–c. 1672), Nicolas Gigault (1627–1707), and Nicolas Métru (dates unknown). In 1652 he left de Montpensier for the court, where he soon made his mark, not only as a musician but also as a dancer. Early in 1653 he danced in the *Ballet de la nuit* alongside the king, and by the 16th March of that year he had found such favour that he was appointed *compositeur de la musique instrumentale*.

This appointment was clearly no idle gesture of Louis XIV's: from 1653 Lully produced a steady stream of ballet music for the court which continued unbroken until 1671. His first important test came in 1656 with *La Galanterie du Temps* for which he had written most (if not all) of the music. The production of this ballet was also marked by the first appearance of Lully's own orchestra, the 'Petits Violons', a group he had formed to rival the established '24 Violons du Roi'. The court was not slow in recognising the superiority of Lully's band, nor the excellence of his music. His popularity rapidly increased; by how much and in what little space of time may be judged from the accounts of the production at court of Cavalli's *Serse* in 1660, when *entrées* Lully had composed for the ballet completely outshone Cavalli's much more substantial contribution.

When Jean de Cambefort died in 1661, there could be little doubt concerning his successor as *Surintendant de la musique de la chambre du roi*: on the 16th May, Lully was nominated; in December of the same year he became a naturalised Frenchman, and in 1662 he married the only daughter of the celebrated court composer Michel Lambert. Clearly Lully had decided to make Paris his home. The 1660s were also the years of his comédies-ballets, in which he and Molière worked together to produce some of their most admired entertainments, culminating in *Les Amans Magnifiques* (1669) and *Le Bourgeois Gentilhomme* (1670).

Whilst these works were immensely popular at court, and brought Lully much fame, he could not fail to notice the success of a new venture begun by Robert Cambert (*c.*

1627–77) and Pierre Perrin under a licence from the King allowing them to establish in Paris an 'Académie Royale de Musique'. Their presentation of *Pomone* in 1671 showed that the Parisian public had a taste for serious musico-dramatic entertainment. Lully was not slow in reacting. The following year, 1672, he purchased the licence from Perrin whilst the latter was languishing in jail – the victim of unscrupulous entrepreneurs – and then

(right) Title-page of Armide *by Lully.*

Page of manuscript of Lully's Acis et Galatée.

LE
TRIOMPHE
DE
L'AMOVR

Daniel Marot Sculp

pressed for a series of patents and ordinances from the king with the object of preventing any rivalry within the domain of the Parisian theatre. He severed his connections with Molière, rewarding him cruelly with another series of repressive patents in 1673 forbidding comedians to use more than two singers and six violins in their productions. In effect Lully established a monopoly of theatre music, a monopoly which he continued to exercise until his death.

But not only did 1673 mark the beginning of Lully's domination of the Parisian theatre, it also marked, with the production of the tragédie-lyrique *Cadmus et Hermione* at the 'Académie Royale', the beginning of French national opera. Works such as the comédie-ballet *Les Amans Magnifiques* had led the way towards a more dramatically unified spectacle. The tragédie-ballet *Psyché* (1671) was very close to the tragédie-lyrique genre, as its revision of 1678 shows. In *Cadmus* the various strands of courtly entertainment (ballet, the pastoral, the comédie-ballet, and not least Italian opera) are pulled together and submitted to a dramatic unity, and the whole articulated by a newly-evolved recitative style.

Cadmus was but the first of a long series of stage works in this vein. Each year brought a new work and almost always a fresh triumph: *Alceste* (1674), *Thésée* (1675), *Atys* (1676), *Isis* (1677), *Pysché* (1678), *Bellérophon* (1679), *Prosperine* (1680), *Persée* (1682), *Phaéton* (1683), *Amadis* (1684), *Roland* (1685) and *Armide* (1686). In all but *Psyché* and *Bellérophon* Lully collaborated with the poet Philippe Quinault. These tragédie-lyriques steadily increased in stature reaching what was universally considered to be Lully's masterpiece in *Armide*. Lully had Paris, and that meant France, at his feet. He allowed no infringement of his monopoly, but nor did he abuse this privilege. The public were well rewarded for their compliance.

Lully died as a result of an infection got from stabbing his foot with a cane whilst conducting. He was directing a Te Deum in celebration of the recovery of the King from a grave illness the previous year. Nothing could more eloquently testify to Lully's assiduity in pleasing the monarch, nor more clearly point to the nature of the relationship which existed

Title-page of Le Triomphe de l'Amour *by Lully.*

between these two absolute dictators. On the one side Louis required magnificent theatrical entertainments, spectacles to reflect and enhance the splendour of his own person, his realm, and his deeds. He also needed to divert his court. On the other side Lully saw in the King's favour the means of realising his ambition: pre-eminence in the world of French music.

After his death, Lully became an institution, his style a touchstone for all that was considered admirable in French music. The latter he set on a new course, his works showing a gradual excision of contrapuntal science and harmonic adventurism. He aimed at the natural, the simple. In his looks far from fair, in his private life far from exemplary, in his business affairs far from ingenuous, Lully the musician nevertheless fully earned the admiration of those of his contemporaries who were sensible to music's charms.

E.H.

MAHLER, Gustav
(b. Kaliště, 7 July 1860; d. Vienna, 18 May 1911)

'Whoever listens to my music intelligently', Mahler once said 'will see my life transparently revealed.' It is a true and telling statement, for Mahler drew on personal experience and on his own complex cultural heritage more consciously and more cogently than most artists would dare. With Mahler the music and the life are interdependent. He wrote symphonies as Proust wrote novels and as Yeats wrote poems – not as independent, separately conceived offerings but as an envolving exploration, rich in natural imagery, of his own and his age's consciousness.

He was born in the village of Kaliště, on the borders of Bohemia and Moravia. His father was an enterprising, self-educated man who had transcended his humble origins (Mahler's grandmother had been an itinerant ribbon-seller) and acquired respectability and success as owner of a small brandy distillery. Times were buoyant, socially and economically. Reform was in the air and there had been every opportunity for this 'coachbox scholar' – Jewish, German-speaking (a necessary attribute in the towns) but a peasant at heart – to make his way in the world. He had married well. His wife was the well-to-do daughter of a soap manufacturer, sensitive and long-

suffering, and the children – those who survived child-birth – were also sensitive and full
of promise. It must have been quite a feather
in the cap of Bernhard Mahler, now successfully established in the German-speaking
community of Iglau, when his ten-year-old
son set the town talking after a remarkable
solo piano recital. And he must have been
prouder still when, in September 1875, Gustav
left Iglau to be enrolled as a student at the

Conservatoire in Vienna (to come back, at the
end of the year, laden with honours). In later
life Mahler frequently and publicly discredited his father. His parents, he claimed, had
been as ill-matched as fire and water; his
mother had been a martyr to the whims of a
brutal and ambitious man. Perhaps so: but
Mahler's early career would not have been
possible without Bernhard Mahler's drive
and pertinacity; and Mahler himself, in later
life, though he revered his mother (and
even, it's said, affected her limp), revealed a
practical shrewdness, a tireless, unflagging

Mahler at the Vienna Opera, 1907.

energy that must have derived in no small measure from his father's example.

As a child Mahler seems to have lived in a dream world, isolating himself, as children can, from family tensions, from the ceaseless strivings on his behalf, from brutality, and from death. Of the twelve children born to the Mahlers, five died in infancy. Mahler's beloved younger brother, Ernst, died at the age of thirteen; Otto committed suicide at twenty-five. From his earliest years, the future composer of the *Kindertotenlieder* and *Das Lied von der Erde* was caught between an acute, sensuous love of the world and an equally acute consciousness of death, the beautiful earth where, in Keats's words, 'Youth grows pale, and spectre-thin, and dies.' In a famous letter of 1879 Mahler wrote:

I have stood high on the mountains where the spirit of God breathes; I have walked in the meadows, lulled by the sound of cowbells. But I have been unable to flee from my destiny . . . the pale figures of my life pass before me like the shadows of a long-lost happiness, and the song of longing sounds again in my ears.

Other things from his childhood haunted him too. In an interview with Freud towards the end of his life, Mahler told how a particularly painful family row was linked in his mind with the sound of a hurdy-gurdy playing a popular Viennese song outside the window. There is, as Noel Coward once said, a potency about cheap music; in Mahler's consciousness cheap music was irreversibly linked with deep personal tragedy, with a sense of the tragic ambivalence of things. And there was more besides. The Mahlers lived near a military barracks. Thus the sound of marches and reveilles, images of death and destructive conflict, permeate his music, from the haunting soldiers' tales of the *Des knaben Wunderhorn* songs to the marches and counter-marches of the symphonies, seemingly prophetic of the coming Armageddon. There were nature sounds too; and for anyone who has noted the haunting purity of even Mahler's most sensuous melodies there is the significant moment in Prague (where Mahler was briefly sent after the success of the Iglau concert) when the eleven-year-old boy witnessed a brutal rape. In his creative mind sensual gratification and human suffering were closely linked. In fine, Mahler's childhood taught him that he had genius and special awareness; but it also

taught him that the world was a glorious birth in which pain and suffering are inextricably mixed. Out of these images he made his music.

In spite of success at the Conservatoire (and Vienna in the 1870s was an exceptionally lively place, fervidly Wagnerian, stimulating to radical minds like Mahler's and that of his friend Hugo Wolf) Mahler soon realised that he could not earn a living as a composer. When he failed to win the Beethoven Prize and the money that went with it he turned to conducting, first in Bad Hall in Austria (a short summer engagement) and then in Laibach, his first permanent position. Wherever he went he worked assiduously, unsparingly. Comfortable traditions were questioned and usually overturned (even in the halcyon days of his rule in Vienna he was accused of loving change for change's sake). Local opinion was amazed, shocked, outraged and delighted in more or less equal measure, as much by his personal habits (he refused beer, wine and meat and lived on water, fruit and spinach) as by his prodigious energy and obvious musical acumen. Engaged in opera, Mahler's early work as a composer is largely vocal and quasi-operatic. The work which he later dignified with the designation 'Op. 1', his *Das klagende Lied*, is a dramatic cantata, the tale of a woodland minstrel, a magic singing bone, murder, incest and the collapse of a corrupt court as dramatically (and as spaciously) conceived as the fall of Valhalla. But the cantata, like the *Lieder eines fahrenden Gesellen*, intensely wrought, beautifully scored orchestral songs written under the spell of a turbulent romance in the early 1880s, merely provides the language and the musical images for the larger goal – music dramas shaped to the demands of what was to Mahler the purest and most august of musical forms: the instrumental symphony.

Success breeds success, and by the mid-1880s Mahler's services were being widely sought. For a time he worked in uneasy harness with the gifted young conductor, Artur Nikisch, in Leipzig. In one season in Leipzig he conducted over 200 performances, edited an unfinished Weber opera, *Die drei Pintos*, fell in love with the wife of the composer's grandson and, amid the turbulence, completed his First Symphony. The symphony is a work full of energy, irony and ingeniously wrought nature music; a work – and this was a significant departure – which renders in symphonic form two ideas we first meet in the *Lieder eines fahrenden Gesellen*.

From Leipzig Mahler moved to the Royal Hungarian Opera, Budapest, his own master again. In Budapest he created a genuinely national opera, an ensemble built round Hungarian singers and musicians, a gloriously indigenous growth. 'To hear the true *Don Giovanni*', wrote an admiring Brahms at this time 'go to Budapest'. From Budapest he went to Hamburg, the preserve of the great impresario Pollini who had long been angling for Mahler's services. Again there were major successes: early performances of Puccini's *Manon Lescaut* and Verdi's *Falstaff*, and an *Eugene Onegin* which Tchaikovsky happily allowed Mahler to direct in his stead. 'The conductor here is not of the usual kind, but a man of genius who would give his life to conduct the first performance', wrote Tchaikovsky to a friend.

Only one great musician barred Mahler's way during this triumphant decade and that was Hans von Bülow, conductor in Munich and Meiningen, pianist and close friend of Wagner and Brahms. In the early 1880s von Bülow had failed even to acknowledge an effusive letter of self-recommendation from the young Mahler. Later, when Mahler had made von Bülow's acquaintance and played to him some passages from his projected Second Symphony, von Bülow remarked dismissively, 'If this is still music, I know nothing of music.' Much has been made of the fact that the idea for the incorporation of Klopstock's 'Resurrection Ode' in the Second Symphony came to Mahler during von Bülow's funeral service. Certainly the death of the man who had once so firmly barred Mahler's way as a composer coincides with a great new creative surge, a surge which now flows unabated until Mahler's death in 1911.

New patterns also start to emerge in Mahler's life at this time. With the death of both his parents in 1889 Mahler had assumed responsibility for the family. He established an annual routine with, always, a long summer vacation spent amid mountain and lakeland scenery. Here he would compose; and it was in such a setting at Steinbach on the Attersee between 1893 and 1896 that Mahler worked on his Third Symphony. It was to be 'a gigantic hymn to the glory of every aspect of creation'. It evokes, wrote Mahler 'the victorious appearance of Helios and the miracle of Spring, thanks to which all things live, breathe, flower, sing and ripen; after which appear those imperfect beings who have participated in this miracle – man.' It is an extra-

The summer-house at Toblach (now Dobbiaco) in which Mahler composed Das Lied von der Erde.

ordinary work which begins with primitive surges of energy, nature brute in the crucible, and ends with an instrumental hymn of joy to the creator. And in between (for writing a symphony was to Mahler an all-embracing gesture) blue-denimed workers march through the Prater in Vienna, wind and sun stir the forest depths, posthorns call across the shimmering Austrian summer landscape, children sing of the joys of heaven and an alto contemplates the world's depths in a passage Mahler drew from Nietzsche's newly-published *Also sprach Zarathustra*. The critics, as Mahler predicted, were dizzied by Mahler's audacity, by the symphony's wealth of imagery, its consciously-contrived banality, its breadth of view, a view which was conjured out of the silences of Mahler's lakeside hut at Steinbach. (They were real silences, incidentally; for when Mahler was composing cows were stripped of their bells, dogs and cats enticed into far away places, chickens cooped up, harvesters forbidden to sharpen their scythes.)

In 1897 Mahler, who had by now tactfully but sincerely espoused the Catholic faith, was invited to Vienna to conduct Wagner's *Lohengrin*. Later that year he was appointed artistic director of the Vienna Court Opera. The Vienna Philharmonic soon followed suit; Hans Richter, doyen of the Viennese musical scene, left for the Hallé in Manchester, and there began a new age of musical and operatic achievement perhaps unequalled in Vienna's history since the time of Beethoven. Mahler had arrived at a new peak. For a summer retreat he now bought land at Maiernigg on the Wörthersee. The Fourth Symphony, the last of the so-called *Wunderhorn* symphonies, and one of the most original and ineffably lovely of all symphonic creations, was created at this time.

Moving now in a large and influential circle of artists and writers, Mahler became associated with the avant-garde 'Secessionist' movement in Vienna, a movement led by men like Gustav Klimt and the artist Carl Moll. A favourite meeting place was the house of Carl Moll, and it was Moll's step-daughter, Alma Maria Schindler, whom Mahler met and immediately fell in love with in 1901. Alma was both beautiful and accomplished, well read and a fine musician (she had studied composition with Schoenberg's teacher von Zemlinsky.) During a long walk in the snow in December 1901 – Mahler was an insatiable walker – he announced to Alma that she was to be his wife; and it appears that the marriage, which took place officially on the 9th February 1902, was consummated that same day. 'We were certain, why wait', Alma later remarked. It was a remarkable marriage but not an easy one. The 'small fidgety man with a fine head', as Alma once described him, made great demands. He required total freedom; Alma must be subservient to his every whim; she must give up her own composing. He once told her that her face was insufficiently marked with suffering, a clear reference to his mother. In fine, she was to be mother, wife and amanuensis. (Interestingly, Justine, Mahler's sister to whom he had confided everything since his mother's death in 1889, married a distinguished Viennese musician at the same time as Gustav married Alma.) Only towards the end of his life, when he mistakenly opened a love-letter from Walter Gropius to Alma, did Mahler realise – and then with a terrible, lacerating insight – what he had demanded, and what he was in danger of losing.

The first five years of Mahler's marriage saw him at a zenith, immensely productive, deeply happy. His two daughters were born, he created his great central symphonic tryptych, the purely instrumental Fifth, Sixth and Seventh Symphonies (20th-century works, deploying harmony and polyphony with a new and brilliant resourcefulness), and he took the Vienna Court Opera to new heights of artistic achievement. As in Budapest, Mahler's aim was the creation of an operatic ensemble of the highest quality. Great singers were nurtured and moulded to fit the ensemble; the orchestral playing became at once more disciplined and more flexibly expressive; the audience was cajoled, tyrannised, disciplined (Mahler was impatient of applause and forbade latecomers). Above all, every aspect of opera production was supervised by Mahler. Working with a great stage designer, Alfred Roller, he experimented with space and light and a complementary structuring of musical and scenic values in ways which predicted the work of Wieland Wagner and the new Bayreuth of the 1950s. Here at last Mahler was able to realise the Wagnerian ideal that had haunted him in years gone by, though it was perhaps his great Mozart cycle of 1906 and his last production of all, Gluck's *Iphigénie en Aulide,* heard in 1907, which were the real crowning glories of his reign in Vienna. So much change, so much imaginative energy, inevitably alienated conservative opinion in Vienna; but Mahler (and here one harks back to his father's acumen) was a practical man; under him the Vienna Opera made a profit. Whatever 'artistic' misgivings the court bureaucracy might have had, they supported him to the hilt.

When Mahler left Vienna in 1907 many were pleased to see him go. He left in an increasingly troubled situation but at a peak (it was at this time that he conceived and wrote the Eighth Symphony, the 'Symphony of a Thousand', his massive setting of the great Pentecostal hymn 'Veni, Creator' and the final scene of Goethe's *Faust*). His exit was a dignified one. A decade was, he knew, enough for one man to hold such a post (Karajan, whose reign in Vienna in some ways resembled Mahler's, survived only seven). But 1907 was not to be a happy year for him. The spectre of death had never left him. He had already written the *Kindertotenlieder,* much to Alma Mahler's horror; and the Sixth Symphony, with its stultifying hammerblows, is a tragic, near apocalyptic piece. Then in 1907 he lost his eldest daughter and found that his own life was hanging in a precarious balance; a chronic heart condition, inherited from his mother, was diagnosed by a local doctor. The year brought him only one slender thread of consolation. Whilst staying in Schluderbach, Mahler came across a volume of a newly-translated volume of poems from the ancient T'Ang dynasty of China. The world of Chinese art, with its crafted fineness, its delicate sense of the transcience of things, its pessimism tinged with gaiety ('a gaiety transfiguring all that dread' as W. B. Yeats expresses it in his great 'Chinese' poem 'Lapis Lazuli') chimed with Mahler's mood. Here were the images he so clearly needed. And given the images, Mahler, since the Seventh Symphony, had the language with which to clothe them. What emerged was *Das Lied von der Erde*, a marvellous distillation of Mahler's imaginative world, with a purity of colour and a severe beauty of line that reminds one of the work of Dante and William Blake. Although the Ninth Symphony and the uncompleted Tenth take us even further into the traumas of the 20th century (for as Leonard Bernstein has observed 'ours is a century of death and Mahler is its spiritual prophet') it is *Das Lied von der Erde,* and perhaps the Adagio of the Ninth Symphony, which best sum up the mingled wonder and sadness of a death-haunted man who, contrary to common supposition, truly mistrusted what he called 'all cloudy, sunless passions'.

Not that Mahler's career was over. In 1907 he travelled to America and was overwhelmed ('Fortissimo at last!', he is said to have exclaimed when he first saw Niagara Falls). With Toscanini also in New York Mahler's opportunities in the opera house were limited; but he was happier, as it turns out, forging a new career as a symphonic conductor. Although, as always, Mahler was ruthless in his methods of administrating the orchestra (cruel-to-be-kind to players long past their prime whom he immediately spotted, exposed and dismissed) his music-making, according to those who still remember playing under him, was informed with a vibrance and a beauty, with that subtle, living pulse which had always been its distinguishing feature from earliest days. In the summer he would return to Europe. In September 1910 he supervised the enormously successful première of the Eighth Symphony in Munich. 'Imagine the whole world beginning to sound and rejoice', he said. It did, and the work was an overwhelming success, even if nowadays it seems strangely anachronistic alongside the achievement of the late instrumental symphonies and *Das Lied von der Erde*.

Early in 1911 Mahler was taken ill in New York. He returned to Europe, to Neuilly near Paris, but his condition was beyond hope and treatment only seemed to worsen the malady. Haunted by the spectre of losing Alma, gloomily aware, as he had been now for many months, of omens of death and destruction, he survived until the May of 1911 – a dying man haunted by the world and the future course of his friends' lives (of Schoenberg's life and career above all). Of his last days, Alma Mahler has written 'I can never forget his dying hours and the greatness of his face as death drew nearer. His battle for eternal values, his elevation above trivial things and his unflinching devotion to truth are an example of the saintly life.'

Mahler asked for no monument (his tomb bears nothing but his name) nor, as he himself implied, does analysis help to define his achievement, fascinating as it is to ponder the magical, fibrous growth of his works, the rich succession of musical images, and the wonder of orchestration, so complex, so vibrant, so clear – which pointed the way for men like Berg, Webern, Schoenberg and Shostakovich. Mahler straddled many worlds in his symphonies, but perhaps his music speaks most potently of a specifically modern tragedy – of a loss of innocence and wonder, of the transmutation of beauty, in the 20th-century context, into something death-ridden and elusive to the grasp. Like Fitzgerald's Gatsby, Mahler was the creator of a dream. Like Gatsby he dreamt of 'the orgastic future that year by year recedes before us'. Mahler never lost his sense of wonder. He retained a romantic hope, even in the face of death. 'Tomorrow we will run faster, stretch out our arms further. . . . And one fine morning –.' Only if we are prepared to contemplate such ideas, and conceive of such images, can we hope properly to understand the nature of Mahler's achievement.

R.O.

MALIPIERO, Gian Francesco
(b. Venice, 18 March 1882;
d. Treviso, 1 Aug 1973)

Malipiero comes from a long line of Venetians, one of his ancestors having been a 12th-century Doge of Venice. The composer's grandfather was a 19th-century composer, and considered locally a second Verdi. His father, too, was a musician. The young Gian Francesco was given music lessons, though as a child he appeared to be more interested in painting than in music. When the family moved for a time to Berlin and Vienna, the fourteen-year-old lad began to take a more active interest in his musical studies, and attended a class in harmony at the Vienna Conservatorium. His studies continued on his return to Venice, and it was then that he began to concentrate upon composition. Two key influences upon him as a young man were his first hearing of Wagner's *Die Meister-singer von Nürnberg* and his discovery of a number of 17th- and 18th-century musical manuscripts in a Venetian library. It was from this latter experience that his love for the old Italian music derived. He was later to become a great authority on Italian music of the pre-classical period, and this music also left its mark upon his compositions.

In 1910, Malipiero married the daughter of a Venetian artist, and settled down to the life of a composer. He had already toyed with opera, but had destroyed his first opera as unsatisfactory. When he visited Paris in 1913, and attended the now legendary first performance of Stravinsky's *Rite of Spring*, he realised that his own musical horizons had been too narrow, and thereafter took steps to broaden them and to take a greater interest in the music of his own day. During World War I, he retired to the village of Asolo to compose, but was forced to flee when the village was overrun by the retreating Italian army. It took him some considerable time to recover from the war period, for his temperament was hypersensitive, perhaps bordering on the psychopathic. During this time, he composed his ballet suite, *Pantea*, an extremely gloomy work, and then turned his attention again to opera. The first, and perhaps most important, fruit of this is the work called *Sette Canzoni* or Seven Songs, based on seven human episodes observed by the composer in his daily life. The stories are mimed by actors, while the singers, hidden like the orchestra, perform Malipiero's settings of appropriate poems.

Malipiero composed several operas, all to his own libretti, before meeting the great Italian poet and dramatist Luigi Pirandello. When Pirandello invited him to set his *Favola del Figlio Cambiato* to music, Malipiero responded enthusiastically, and the work was successfully staged in Germany. The Rome performances in 1933 were disrupted by the fascists, and the opera was formally banned by Mussolini. Malipiero turned to safer subjects, and composed successful operas on Shakespeare plays: *Julius Caesar* (1936) and *Antony and Cleopatra* (1938). His later operas and orchestral pieces were all respectfully received. Malipiero's last years were spent privately, in the study of old music, and in work on a complete edition of the works of Monteverdi. His own words admirably sum up his musical temperament:

> We live in a century of noise, and noise is the negation of music. If we mount towards the sources of antique musical art we shall be able to project ourselves with greater strength into the future, avoiding the abyss of the chaotic present.

C.O.

MARTINŮ, Bohuslav
(b. Polička, 8 Dec 1890;
d. Liestal, Switz., 28 Aug 1959)

There is something at once tragic and irritating about the creative life of Bohuslav Martinů the most important Czech composer since Janáček. Driven from Europe – like Bartók and Schoenberg – by the advance of Nazism, his finest music expresses the strength of the human spirit in the face of chaos. The irritating thing is that so little of his music is of his best. Like Hindemith and Milhaud, he wrote a vast amount of 'bread and butter music', even if he never used this phrase. The consequence is that if you buy a gramophone record of some hitherto unrecorded work of Martinů (and the Czech Supraphon label has served him well), you never know whether it will be some powerful, brilliant composition, or so commonplace that it might be by half a dozen other composers.

Bohuslav Jan Martinů was born in the small Czech town of Polička in 1890, the son of a cobbler. His father was also Keeper of the Church Tower, and Martinů was actually born in it, and spent the first eleven years of his life there, with a magnificent view of the surrounding countryside. His early years parallel, in many ways, those of his older contemporary Janáček: the straitened childhood, early signs of musical talent, involvement in folk festivals. Martinů's talent as a violinist was so remarkable that a group of citizens banded together to send him to study at the Prague Conservatory. Again, like Janáček, Martinů clashed with academics, both at the Conservatory and at the Organ School, where he enrolled after being expelled from the former institution. The disaster had its positive side; he managed to persuade his parents to keep up a small allowance, and lived a bohemian life in Prague, composing prolifically, and spending much time at the theatre and at rehearsals of the Czech Philharmonic. When the war came in 1914, he was placed on the reserve list, and worked on in Polička. He succeeded in passing teaching exams on his second attempt (the first was a disaster) and became a violin teacher in his home town in 1916. After the war, he played in the Czech Philharmonic, under Vaclav Talich, and even re-entered the Prague Conservatoire; it took him less than a year to discover that he still loathed academic discipline. It was Talich who conducted Martinů's ballet *Istar* in 1922. By this time, Martinů was showing the influence of various French composers, notably Debussy and Ravel. He was, in fact, moving roughly in the same direction as 'Les Six', or Kurt Weill in Germany. The ballet *Who Is the Most Powerful Man in the World?* contains an amusing fox-trot, while the slightly later *Revue de Cuisine* – about kitchen utensils coming to life – contains some of the best spoof-jazz ever written by a serious composer.

Paris was obviously the place where his heart lay; accordingly, he went there in 1923, and was to remain there until the coming of the Nazis drove him to America in 1940. International fame finally arrived in 1927, with the first performance of *La Bagarre* (meaning 'The Tumult'), written to celebrate Lindbergh's flight across the Atlantic; it made much the same kind of impact as Honneger's *Pacific 231*, and may well have been inspired by that work, which came out in 1924. Koussevitsky gave the work its first performance in Boston; Talich performed it all over Europe.

The next decade saw the production of a few masterpieces, and a large amount of 'bread and butter music' of admirable craftsmanship but slight inspiration. The ballet *Špalíček* has gaiety and vitality – passages are reminiscent of Poulenc – combined with a distinctly Czech inspiration, and its *Dance of the Maids of Honour* is memorably delightful. The opera *Julietta*, dating from the mid-1930s, is one of Martinů's key works, a kind of dreamplay full of nostalgia and symbolism. A harpsichord concerto dating from 1935 is full of his characteristic driving, astringent lyricism. The *Fifth String Quartet*, whose manuscript vanished from 1938 until 1953, is one of his finest works in this medium. The *Double Concerto* for piano and two string orchestras was also completed in 1938, and is generally considered Martinů's greatest work; melodically, it has some of the same qualities as Frank Martin's *Petite Symphonie Concertante* and Bartók's *Music for Strings, Percussion and Celesta*; it reflects the emotional turmoil created by the rise of Nazism, and in the last movement, we seem to hear its inexorable advance across Europe. 1940, the year Martinů left Paris, also saw the composition of one of his most enjoyable works, the *Sinfonietta Giacosa* for piano and orchestra, whose gaiety is reminiscent of Shostakovich's first Piano Concerto. The *Field Mass* of the same period is one of his most powerful and compelling works. America was already familiar with Martinů's music, so he enjoyed his stay there rather more than Bartók or Schoenberg did. Yet although the American period saw the composition of many major works, including a vast cantata on the *Epic of Gilgamesh*, an opera on Kazantzakis's novel *The Greek Passion*, and six symphonies, Martinů made no conquests in the field of musical creativity. The Fourth Symphony has some of the joy and inventiveness of the *Sinfonietta Giacosa*; the long introduction to the last movement of the Fifth has some of the tragic power of the *Double Concerto*. The Sixth was originally called *New Symphonie Fantastique*, a title Martinů wisely dropped – it hardly bears comparison with Berlióz – in favour of *Fantasie Symphonique*. It contains some brilliant orchestral effects, and has been much admired by many critics; to the present writer it lacks a sense of inner compulsion and is characteristic of Martinů at his rather-less-than-best, a comment that applies to all too much of his music.

After the war, Martinů was invited back to the Prague Conservatoire as a professor, but refused, probably recalling old quarrels; but it must have pleased him to know that the tower he was born in was now a Martinů museum, and that the main square of Polička was called Martinů Square. The last work before his death in 1959 (of a stomach cancer) was a sombre cantata *Prophesies of Isiah*, a fine work that reminds us again that, for reasons that are difficult to fathom, Martinů somehow failed to become the great Czech composer of the mid-20th century.

C.W.

MASCAGNI, Pietro
(b. Leghorn, 7 Dec 1863;
d. Rome, 2 Aug 1945)

The ups and downs of the career of Pietro Mascagni could well be made the subject of the *verismo* style of opera that he created. Forbidden by his father, a baker, to take up the study of music, he entered himself secretly as a pupil of the Istituto Luigi Cherubini. His father, who intended him to take up the more secure profession of lawyer, eventually discovered what he was doing, which might have brought young Pietro's musical career to an end had not a sympathetic uncle adopted him and taken him into his own house. Now able to study openly, he made such rapid progress that he composed a symphony and a Kyrie which were both performed in 1879, when he was only sixteen. The success of a cantata, *In Filanda*, two years later reconciled his father to his way of thinking, and the young composer returned home free to follow his chosen path. A setting of Schiller's *Ode to Joy* was so successful that a wealthy aristocrat offered to pay for him to go to the Milan Conservatoire, where he became a student of Ponchielli, the composer of *La Gioconda*, who was also the teacher of Puccini. Mascagni, however, hated formal studies so much that he fled from fugue and counterpoint to take up a post as conductor with a travelling opera company. This gave him valuable experience for a time until he married and settled down at the small town of Cerignola to manage the municipal school of music and give piano lessons.

In 1889 he rose from obscurity in a single leap by winning the first prize in a competition promoted by the publisher Sonzogno with his one-act *Cavalleria Rusticana*, which received its triumphant première in Rome the following year. Within two years it had been produced virtually everywhere, its composer finding himself something of a national hero and acclaimed the successor of Verdi. It has become fashionable in academic circles to sneer at this vivid melodrama of Sicilian life based on the famous story by Giovanni Verga, but to the unprejudiced opera-goer it should rank as a minor masterpiece. (At the time it must have appealed to audiences grown weary of romanticism on the one hand and Wagnerian grandeur on the other.) Verga's story is concise and brutally true to Sicilian life: Turiddu, the swaggering idol of the village girls, deserts his fiancée Santuzza for Lola, whose husband kills him in a fight when he learns the truth. Mascagni's music is equally direct in its impact, alive with broad, warmhearted melodies and orchestral colouring that is always emphatically bold. There are several strokes of originality, among them Turiddu's serenade behind the scenes in the middle of the orchestral prelude, but few of any great subtlety. To look for subtlety here, however, is to misunderstand Mascagni's intention – and his remarkable achievement too. The opera's very vigour and relentless intensity hold the attention from first to last, the composer having learned from his touring experience exactly what qualities gripped the general opera-goer and provided them in *Cavalleria Rusticana* without a single bar of padding. When Boito played the opera from the piano score to the seventy-year-old Verdi the great master stopped him after a time with the words: 'Enough, enough. I understand.' An eminently practical man of the theatre, Verdi saw at once why the new work was such a success. No doubt he also realised why Mascagni would never reach greater heights.

In later life Mascagni once remarked: 'It was a pity I wrote *Cavalleria* first. I was crowned before I was king.' There was much truth, as well as a trace of bitterness, in this self-judgment, for he was never to match the success of his first opera with any of the fourteen which followed. It is surprising, and considerably to his credit, that he did not continue to follow the same pattern but tried out one new stylistic path after another. His second opera *L'Amico Fritz*, for instance, is a delicate comedy about a wealthy young man whose avowal never to marry is overcome by the machinations of his match-making friend, the rabbi David. (When Mussolini adopted Hitler's racial laws in 1938, the rabbi was changed into a doctor, a practice still followed in some Italian productions of the opera today.) Premièred in Rome in 1891, *L'Amico Fritz* was enthusiastically acclaimed even though the audience had expected another *Cavalleria*, and it was quickly taken up abroad. Gustav Mahler, who conducted it in Hamburg in 1892, considered it a marked advance on the earlier opera. The music is beautifully tailored for the pastoral mood of

Mascagni.

the story, with orchestral colours in pastel shades and arias of tender appeal. The neglect of *L'Amico Fritz* outside Italy is as surprising as it is unjustified.

After this there followed romantic tragedies like *Guglielmo Ratcliff* and *Parisina*, the symbolic music-drama *Iris* (in which the heroine drowns herself in a sewer), the commedia dell'arte *Le Maschere*, the operetta *Sì*, the grandiose *Nerone* composed as a tribute to Mussolini, and other operas in a variety of styles. Sadly they revealed a steady decline in inspiration and judgment, for which Mascagni's lack of self-discipline and self-criticism was largely to blame. His music, as he grew older, became increasingly banal. He seemed to realise that he would be remembered by posterity only as the composer of *Cavalleria Rusticana* (to be paired eternally with Leoncavallo's *Pagliacci*) and sought compensation by pursuing a career as conductor, in which he proved highly successful with tours throughout Europe and America. For a time he was also musical director of La

Scala when Toscanini relinquished the post in 1929.

Perhaps Mascagni's greatest mistake was to embrace fascism when Mussolini came to power. When he threw himself all too eagerly into composing choral and orchestral works to glorify political occasions, thus making himself the musical mouthpiece of fascist Italy, most of his fellow musicians turned their backs on him in open contempt. It is true that he owed the eventual production of *Nerone* at La Scala, which had spurned it for some considerable time, to the personal intervention of the Duce, but he was later to pay a high price for his political activities. When Mussolini was finally overthrown Mascagni was stripped of his property and honours, and he passed his last years in comparative poverty and complete disgrace in a small hotel room in Rome. It would be wrong, however, to allow dislike of the man to affect our judgment of his work, so we should remember Mascagni with respect and gratitude for giving to the world in *Cavalleria Rusticana* one of those relatively rare works which exert their magic on all sections of the opera-going public from the connoisseur to the least sophisticated.

F.G.B.

MASSENET, Jules
(b. Montaud, 12 May 1842; d. Paris, 13 Aug 1912)

Jules Massenet was born at Montaud, near St Etienne to an ironmaster and his second wife, who bore him three other children all musically gifted. When the boy was six, the family moved to Paris and, their financial circumstances deteriorating owing to his father's ill-health, his mother started taking piano pupils. She also taught Jules so well that at eleven he was able to enter the Paris Conservatoire. He was still a student when his family moved from Paris to Chambéry, but Jules remained in Paris with a married member of M. Massenet's family by his first wife. At the age of seventeen he entered Réber's harmony class and his master for composition was Ambroise Thomas, who was shortly to make his name with the opera *Mignon*. During his student years Massenet earned pocket money, and gained experience of orchestration, by helping out the percussion section at the Théâtre du Gymnase and the Théâtre-Lyrique; and he was thus able

to orchestrate a Mass for military band by Adolphe Adam (composer of *Giselle*). He won a first prize for piano, and in 1863 the coveted Prix de Rome, which took him to the Villa Medici. While in Rome he met Liszt, and it was through him that he was introduced to a Mme Sainte-Marie, to whose daughter he gave piano lessons. Before he returned to Paris in 1866 she had become his wife.

Massenet was a favourite pupil of Thomas, and it was his influence that obtained a performance of the young man's *La Grand' Tante* at the Opéra-Comique (1867) and the performance by Pasdeloup of his first orchestral suite. Before 1870 two song-cycles, *Poème d'avril* and *Poème du souvenir* had been published. The Franco-Prussian War of 1870–1 gave young French composers a new feeling of national solidarity and Gounod's prolonged absence in England (1870–5) left a gap among opera composers, which was further widened by Bizet's death in 1875. Massenet was admirably suited to fill this gap. All his life he was an indefatigable worker; and this, combined with his strong instinctive desire to please and to succeed, enabled him to cater for the taste of the French public of the day in a succession of operas which opened with *Le Roi de Lahore* (1877) and continued unbroken until his death in 1912. His first major success, however, was an oratorio, *Marie Magdeleine* (1872), in which the title role was sung by one of the most famous singers of the day, Pauline Viardot-Garcia, sister of 'La Malibran' and for many years mistress of the Russian novelist Turgeniev. The opera *Hérodiade*, a melodramatic treatment of the same story as Strauss's *Salome*, was successfully given in Brussels in 1881, but Massenet's greatest triumph came three years later with *Manon*. In this and all his succeeding operas Massenet struck the desired middle point between conventionality and daring. His operas have been well described as a portrait gallery of *amoureuses*, and in all of them the discreetly erotic note is dominant, but set off either by charming genre-scenes or spectacle, alternately glittering (as in *Esclarmonde*, 1889, *Thaïs*, 1894 and *Cendrillon*, 1899) and, more frequently intimate. *Manon*'s seduction of des Grieux in the sacristy of St Sulpice, the Christmas preparations at the opening of *Werther* (1892) and the death of the tumbler in *Le Jongleur de Notre Dame* (1902) show Massenet's affinity as a musician with the art of the late 19th-century illustrators, the painters of academy prize-winning pictures which

Massenet.

lightly touch the emotions and the senses but have little appeal to either the intellect or the specifically aesthetic sense. His music performed for the French bourgeoisie very much the same service as Puccini and Strauss performed for the same class in Italy and Germany.

Werther, based on Goethe, was first performed in Vienna, but its appeal was by no means confined to German-speaking countries. As in *Manon* the erotic obsession of the title-character forms the centre of the picture, beautifully and distinctly drawn by Massenet and framed with exemplary taste and care, so that the listener shall never be compelled to take the story too much to heart. Massenet, like Puccini later, was quite aware of the avant-garde music of his day, which was in his case that of Wagner, borrowing what suited him from the new style without any fundamental revision of his musical ideals. With all French composers this meant little more than giving added prominence to the brass instruments of the orchestra and ear-

marking the chief characters by an easily recognised *leitmotif*. If the emotionalism and over-heated idealism of Goethe's hero is unmistakably German, Massenet's *Werther* is profuse in emotional outbursts of an unmistakably French character ('O spectacle idéal', as he observes Charlotte with her younger brothers and sisters) and it is hard to think that Tchaikovsky did not know the music of the climactic scene of Werther's suicide.

Massenet was indeed only continuing in the path of Gounod's *Faust* when he insisted on the live humanity and intimate feelings of his characters in reaction against Meyerbeer's cardboard historical characters, whose chief function is to look magnificent and to dazzle by their vocal powers. Massenet's melody is comparatively informal and flexible, often closer in character as in form to the salon or the boudoir than to the theatre (cf. Manon's 'Adieu, notre petite table' and Charlotte's 'Qui m'aurait dit la place que dans mon coeur il occupe aujourd'hui', as she goes through Werther's letters).

On occasion Massenet could return to the more formal style of Meyerbeer's operas, as in the Alexandrian scenes of *Thaïs,* where the elaborate ballet movements form another link with earlier days. The quasi-religious interest, which had paid such high dividends when blended with the erotic in *Marie Magdeleine*, was consciously exploited by Massenet, who was himself a complete sceptic. He borrowed much in this field from Gounod, so much that he was dubbed 'la fille de Gounod', a reflection both of this particular debt and of the essential femininity of Massenet's music. *Le Jongleur de Notre Dame*, on the other hand, was an exception, for this is perhaps the only case before Britten's *Billy Budd* of an opera with no feminine role. The monastic setting included a scene which is one of the composer's most effective genre-pictures, the rehearsal of a new motet.

A characteristically shrewd essay in the new taste for realism in opera, started by Mascagni's *Cavalleria Rusticana* (1890), was *La Navarraise*, which had its first performance in 1894, at Covent Garden. Equally skilful but considerably more subtle, *Thérèse* (1907), is a simple love-story only mildly flavoured by the political interest inherent in the French Revolutionary setting. Here the composer introduced the unfamiliar harpsichord with considerable dramatic effect. *Sapho* (1897), based on a novel by Alphonse Daudet, exploits the same contrast between conventional bourgeois life and the Bohemian existence of the Paris demi-monde that had inspired Verdi in *La Traviata*, and Massenet contrived to make both life-styles convincing and attractive without committing himself to any awkward moral judgment between the two.

Mention should be made of the part played in Massenet's career by the young American soprano Sibyl Sanderson, whom he regarded as the ideal interpreter of the title-role in *Manon*. For her he wrote both *Esclarmonde* and *Thaïs*, a part in which he found her 'unforgettable'. It was for another singer, Fyodor Chaliapin, that he wrote the last of his operas which has remained in the present repertory – *Don Quichotte* (1910). This was the fourth of his operas to have its first performance at Monte Carlo, where the impresario Raoul Gunsbourg remained faithful to the composers of an earlier generation long after Debussy's *Pelléas et Mélisande* (1902) had initiated a new operatic taste in Paris. Massenet, now in his sixties, was Gunsbourg's favourite and *Le Jongleur de Notre Dame, Thérèse* and *Don Quichotte* were followed by *Roma* (1912) and two posthumous works, *Cléopâtre* and

Amadis. All these were perfectly suited to the tastes of the princely family and the rich cosmopolitan visitors who between them determined the success or failure of the opera-house at Monte Carlo.

Although his music was cordially detested by the younger generation of French composers, for whom it became synonymous with the superficial artistic tastes of the philistine bourgeoisie of the era between the two wars with Germany (1870–1914), Massenet's unfailing invention of a charming, short-breathed melody redolent of the salon and his shrewd understanding of the theatre cannot be so easily dismissed. *Manon* and *Werther* are masterpieces of their own strictly limited kind, and it was one of Massenet's great virtues as an artist that he never attempted any subject that was beyond his range. With suitable casts at least half a dozen of his other operas have shown themselves worth at least occasional revival. Though *Thaïs* and *La Navarraise* have recently proved successful among opera-lovers, *Le Jongleur de Notre Dame* and *Thérèse* contain better music than either. The Belgrade Opera has shown that a great bass-singer can easily justify the retention of *Don Quichotte* in the operatic repertory.

All these works were designed, and retain their appeal for those of the musical public who enjoy opera as such and are not likely to be found at concerts whose programmes contain works by either Beethoven or Boulez. Massenet's operas do not challenge comparison with those operas which are also, sometimes incidentally, great music; but they can hold their own among the many works in the operatic repertory which continue to exert their attraction if really well sung and produced. *Manon* can even survive translation, always a severe test for French opera, in which the language itself plays an exceptionally important part.

Massenet's life was almost entirely devoted to work and to enjoying the very considerable financial fruits of his labours. From 1878 onwards he was Professor of Composition at the Paris Conservatoire, where his pupils included Alfred Bruneau, Gabriel Pierné and Gustave Charpentier. He seems to have been a charming and adaptable teacher, not intolerant of pupils whose ideals and methods of composition differed from his own. Those who were temperamentally unfitted to learn from him found different teaching-methods and a totally different conception of music at the Schola Cantorum, where Vincent d'Indy and his picked staff dispensed a Wagnerian and post-Wagnerian musical gospel. Massenet's influence, however, was by no means restricted to those who actually studied with him. The early music of Debussy shows clear traces of Massenet's influence; and Romain Rolland, speaking of *Pelléas et Mélisande* in his musical novel *Jean Christophe*, shrewdly pointed to passages in that work where, as he put it, 'the Massenet who slumbers at the heart of every Frenchman awakes and waxes eloquent.'

M.C.

MENDELSSOHN, Felix
(b. Hamburg, 3 Feb 1809;
d. Leipzig, 4 Nov 1847)

Few composers have been born into such congenial and unworrying circumstances as Felix Mendelssohn. He came into the world, son of the banker Abraham on the 13th February 1809, and he was never wanting for material needs, yet even if he had not had these advantages his natural talent would surely have brought him to prominence. He had a liberal education, encompassing many subjects, and later commented that he got into music 'he hardly knew how'. His mother Lea, who was a motivating influence on his life as he later averred, gave him the rudiments of music; then, when the family was in Paris, the eleven-year-old boy received important instruction from various excellent teachers. Back in Berlin, he made his debut as a pianist in 1818. In the meantime he had begun to compose prolifically, and his early works include pieces for all kinds of voices and instruments. They were a product of a hardworking day, which began, at his father's behest, seldom later than 5 a.m., a discipline that may have affected his health in later years.

About this time, Mendelssohn first met Goethe and received further intellectual instruction while delighting the poet by playing him the fugues of Bach, and by his own gift for extemporisation. Comparisons were already being made with Mozart, whom Mendelssohn certainly resembled in adolescent skill and fecundity of playing and composition. At Sunday-morning concerts *chez* the Mendelssohns, Felix, his accomplished pianist-sister Fanny, his brother Paul ('cello) and his other sister Rebecca (a singer) entertained the cream of Berlin's intellectual society. During 1824, Felix added to his own talents by learning the violin, which soon helped him in his work on his string quartets. His violin teacher was Edward Rietz, whose copy of Bach's *St Matthew Passion* was given to Mendelssohn by his grandmother, and proved a seminal influence.

Back in Paris in 1825 with his father, he widened his musical knowledge by his acquaintanceship with such figures as Moscheles, Hummel, Cherubini and Rossini. His lively correspondence to Fanny show that his reverence for his seniors was more than a little tinged with astute and far from reverential criticism. Cherubini was most aware of the youth's talents, and his high opinion of Mendelssohn's attainments persuaded Abraham to let his son continue in a purely musical career. The latter part of 1825 saw the production of the Octet, generally acknowledged then and now as a work of prodigious talent and unending delight. It was followed the next year by the overture to *A Midsummer Night's Dream*, which confirmed Mendelssohn's arrival on the musical scene as a major composer.

However, his education was by no means complete. Philosophy instruction at the foot of Hegel at the University of Berlin and lectures in geography supplemented his continuing musical studies; so did friendships with poets, among them Heine, and visits to Heidelberg and Frankfurt. The Sunday-morning concerts were now augmented by ones on Saturday evening, when Mendelssohn rehearsed a choir in the *Matthew Passion,* which after some trials and tribulations was presented, an historic occasion, under Mendelssohn's direction at the Singakademie in Berlin on the 11th March 1829 – the work's first performance since Bach's own time. In the meantime he had written more works, including *Calm Sea and Prosperous Voyage* and the Quartets, Op. 12 and 13.

In the spring of 1829, he visited England for the first time, going on to Scotland in the summer 'with a rake for folksongs, and an ear for the beautiful, fragrant countryside, and a heart for the bare legs of the natives'. He met Sir Walter Scott, then visited the Hebrides, where he derived inspiration for one of his best-known pieces. The winter was spent back in Berlin after which he began a thorough Grand Tour, taking in Austria, Switzerland, Italy, Germany and France, before returning to London in 1832. There, he conducted the now-completed *Hebrides* overture, and the first volume of *Songs Without Words* (for piano) was finished. A year later he directed the first performance of the *Italian* symphony at a Philharmonic Society concert.

Meanwhile in Germany he had been made conductor of the important Lower Rhine Festival, at which he revived neglected works such as Beethoven's *Pastoral* symphony and Handel's *Israel in Egypt*. He managed with great energy to run affairs at Düsseldorf while continuing to compose avidly. As well as many other works, his first oratorio, *St Paul*, was already on the stocks, and it was given at Düsseldorf in 1836, the year he met his future wife Cécile Jeanrenaud, daughter of a French Protestant clergyman. They were married on the 28th March 1837. Fanny wrote of her new sister-in-law: 'She is amiable, childlike' – ten years younger than Mendelssohn, and so still in her teens – 'fresh, bright and even-tempered and I consider Felix most fortunate. . . .' They had five children, and she became an efficient housewife.

In 1835, he accepted an invitation to conduct the Leipzig Gewandhaus and became its musical director. He improved its standard of playing, increased its repertory, and promoted an advance in musical education in the city, which became the musical capital of Germany. Mendelssohn's commanding presence was felt coursing through every aspect of musical affairs there. He made many friends, among them Schumann and Chopin, and a few enemies. He still found time for plenty of composition. These years saw the Op. 44 quartets, the second piano concerto, *St Paul* and *Ruy Blas* completed, and the violin concerto was begun. On further journeys to England, he played the organ in London and conducted *St Paul* at Birmingham in 1837, and the *Hymn of Praise* at Birmingham in 1840. Indeed in Britain he was considered the leading composer of the day, eventually becoming a favourite of Queen Victoria and Prince Albert; his *Scottish* symphony (1842) is dedicated to Victoria.

While continuing his connection with Leipzig, Mendelssohn took the post of *Kapellmeister* in Berlin in 1841 at the behest of Frederick William IV. This was just another commitment to add to his many others, and not surprisingly the strain on his health was beginning to tell, yet he still managed to find time to compose between caring for the needs of the Prussian and British royal families. In 1843, he gave a series of concerts at Berlin by royal command. In the summer of that year he took tea at Buckingham Palace and played some of his *Songs Without Words*. A concert he conducted for the Philharmonic Society was attended by Sir Robert Peel. In spite of all this pomp and circumstance, he still seemed to prefer his work at Leipzig to all else, and he was instrumental in the founding of the Conservatory there in 1843. This was one of his most cherished schemes to improve the musical standards in Germany, and for it he had the cooperation of the Schumanns, Robert and Clara, and many other musicians of the time.

The success of *St Paul* in 1836 had led Mendelssohn to look for another suitable subject to set as an oratorio. The libretto for *Elijah* was by the clergyman Julius Schubring, with whom he corresponded at length to make certain the work had the dramatic impact he wished. The work was eventually completed shortly before its first performance, at Birmingham on the 26th August 1846. He was elevated by the work's undoubted success – 'Not less than four choruses and four solos were encored, and not a single mistake occurred in the first part . . .' – but he returned to Leipzig in a state of exhaustion, which was exacerbated by the death of his beloved sister Fanny in May of the following year. Although he at times seemed to show a will to live on and write more music, his condition gradually declined, and after a final visit to Berlin to supervise the first performance there of *Elijah*, he returned to Leipzig, suffered several severe fits, and died on the 4th November 1847, mourned throughout the musical world of Europe.

As a composer, Mendelssohn's reputation remained high throughout Victorian times. With the decline in respect for the ideals of those times, his music was less revered, less played. In recent times, a compromise has been found between the often unthinking adulation of his near-contemporaries and the breaking of his fame in the middle decades of this century. Certain works have survived whatever the state of his reputation. The fresh lyrical impulse of the *Midsummer Night's Dream* music, particularly the overture, the skill and lightness of the early Octet, the illustrative poetry of the *Hebrides* overture, the youthful brio of the *Italian* symphony, the religious optimism of *Elijah* have never lost their appeal with the public, nor has the marvellous violin concerto which, with its fine combination of the classical and romantic, tempers reason with imagination to an extraordinary degree, and is notable for its warmth and vivacity.

Mendelssohn.

All these works show Mendelssohn's genius for orchestration, but he could excel equally in the purer forms of piano music and the string quartet, and in these fields he is perhaps still underrated. His eight books of *Songs Without Words* for piano have been overawed by the more obviously virtuoso works of his contemporaries. They, and the *Variations Sérieuses*, show Mendelssohn's undemonstrative eloquence in writing for the piano. Below the calm surface of many of the movements in the quartets there is often an intellectual strength and emotional commitment, occasionally a profundity, that recalls Mozart and Schubert in this field, if not reaching the extreme concentration of late Beethoven. The Adagio of Op. 44, No. 3 and of Op. 80 (written under the tragic influence of Fanny's death) are only the most potent examples of Mendelssohn's strengths in this genre.

The symphonies, other than the *Italian*, the two piano concertos, *St Paul*, the organ works and the songs may reach such exalted levels more intermittently, but none is devoid of the command of means and of expressive integrity that distinguishes the greatest of his pieces. His contribution to musical development and to the needs of scholarship must also weigh in the favourable balance. In his music we must not seek the breast-beating of the romantics, who were his contemporaries, nor the extroverted expression of emotions, but feeling is there, even when it sometimes takes second place to the composer's desire merely to please.

A.B.

MENOTTI, Gian-Carlo
(b. Cadegliano, 7 July 1911)

The fact that Menotti has been a permanent resident in the United States since 1927 without giving up his Italian citizenship is not without significance: his musical roots are clearly Italian, while at the same time his outlook has been influenced by the American theatre. Several of his operas have in fact enjoyed profitable runs on Broadway, and he has twice won the annual New York Drama Critics Award. This duality is also reflected in the Festival of Two Worlds which he founded in 1958, for though it takes place every summer at Spoleto in the Umbrian hills, it is largely a platform for American art and artists. There is a similar ambiguity in his artistic achievement: his operas have reached a wider public than those of any other composer of his time, yet their durability is questionable. They rely for their success rather on their theatrical effectiveness than on their actual musical qualities, and Menotti, who writes his own librettos, has always been inclined to follow popular trends in the theatre which might easily become dated beyond redemption. It is here that he differs so fundamentally from Puccini, whose melodic style he has often tried to copy, for while Puccini's operas may be based on a type of drama which is now as dead as the dodo, the memorability and blazing genius of his music should ensure their immortality. Menotti's music, on the other hand, is rarely strong enough in itself to provide more than a background to the drama.

Menotti set out along the traditional path, beginning his studies at the age of twelve at the Verdo Conservatoire in Milan, then continuing at the Curtis Institute of Music in Philadelphia. He was only twenty-five when he scored his first mature success with the one-act *Amelia al Ballo*, which was premièred in Philadelphia in an English translation as *Amelia Goes to the Ball*. In 1939 he experimented with radio opera, composing *The Old Maid and the Thief* for the National Broadcasting Company of America. Three years later he made a more ambitious bid with *The Island God* at the Metropolitan Opera in New York, suffering the only failure of his career. Official musical circles fortunately showed their faith in him by awarding him substantial grants, and a commission from the Ditson Fund of Columbia University resulted in *The Medium*, a macabre offspring of the 19th-century *verismo* movement. This proved so successful there that it was taken up for a Broadway run in 1947, with *The Telephone*, perhaps best described as a revue sketch with music, as a curtain-raiser. *The Medium* was brought to London's Aldwych Theatre the following year with an American cast, and it appeared in a film version directed by the composer in 1951, winning a special citation at the Cannes Festival. In subsequent years it has been given in many opera houses.

In the meantime Menotti was busily engaged on what remains his most consistent and substantial opera, *The Consul*, which was given its première in Philadelphia on the 1st March 1950 prior to a six months' run on Broadway. Later the same year it became the

Menotti by Dolbin.

first American-composed opera to be given at La Scala, Milan. Its grim story of repression under political dictatorship gripped the imagination of audiences throughout free Europe, and the simplicity and directness of the music ensured its appeal to a wider audience than that which usually goes to the opera. *The Consul* kept its place for several seasons in the repertoire of the then Sadler's Wells Opera. It has failed to establish itself, however, as a latter-day *Tosca*, and for the simple reason that the music does not add a sufficiently strong new dimension to the melodramatic text.

Ever prepared to tackle any new medium, Menotti composed the first television opera, *Amahl and the Night Visitors*, for transmission on the Christmas Eve of 1951. This treats the story of a crippled boy, Amahl, who offers the Three Wise Men his crutches as a gift to the infant Jesus, and becomes miraculously healed. Here Menotti makes effective use of dramatic recitatives alternating with lyrical ensembles. The work was presented over the NBC network each Christmas for more than a decade, the practice being discontinued only when the composer insisted on a new production which the television company refused to provide. Several performances by BBC Television have made it the most widely known of Menotti's works in Britain. The BBC also introduced *The Saint of Bleeker Street* to Britain after this equally sentimental religious work had been staged first on Broadway in 1954, then at La Scala, Milan, and other opera houses. The subject matter of this tragedy is alien to English tastes, which also rejected *Maria Golovin*, a three-act stage opera which was premièred in Brussels during the 1958 World's Fair, subsequently presented on Broadway and finally taken up by the New York City Opera. It reached London in 1976, directed by the composer for the Camden Festival, when its music was generally considered too insubstantial to carry its story of a blind man in love with a woman whose husband, long held a prisoner of war, finally comes back to her. More recent operas have been *The Last Savage*, given its première in a French translation at the Opéra-Comique in 1963, the 'operatic riddle' *Labyrinth* written for television the same year, and *Martin's Lie*, a work similar in form to Britten's church parables, commissioned for the Bath Festival of 1964.

Menotti, who also supplied the libretto for Samuel Barber's *Vanessa*, has composed a number of non-operatic works. These include concertos for piano and violin, a Fantasia for 'cello and orchestra, the ballet *Sebastian* and a song cycle, *Centi della Lontananza*, written for and first perfomed by Elisabeth Schwarzkopf. Essentially, however, he is a man of the theatre, his works for which reveal versatility and undoubted flair. He has shown a remarkable gift for tailoring pieces of musical theatre to please the popular taste of the moment. It remains to be seen whether this facility for achieving instant success also carries within it the seed of ephemerality.

F.G.B.

MERCADANTE, Saverio
(b. Altamura, Sept 1795;
d. Naples, 17 Dec 1870)

Nothing is known of Mercadante's family. The boy was brought to Naples at the age of thirteen where he studied the violin, flute and other instruments. In 1818 he wrote the music for three ballets, and in the following year his first opera, *L'Apoteosi d'Ercole* was produced at the Teatro San Carlo with enormous success. Thereafter, he continued to produce operas to commission, often at the rate of three or four a year. Mercadante saw himself as a revolutionary, avant-garde composer. 'I have varied the forms,' he wrote, 'abolished trivial cabalettas, exiled the crescendos.' But his sixty operas, though widely acclaimed in his own day, have failed to survive. It is true that his treatment of the orchestra is often almost Verdian, and indeed anticipates Verdi, but his music lacks individual character. The most successful of his operas include *Il giuramento* (1837), *La vestale* (1840) and *Gli Orazi ed i Curiazi* (1846).

In 1840, Mercadante became Director of the Naples Conservatorium, and retained this post until his death. He became totally blind in 1862, but continued to compose. He himself was somewhat embittered at having been eclipsed by Verdi, and his more enthusiastic admirers spread the story that Verdi plagiarised him and then denigrated him. Though this is obviously untrue, Verdi was certainly influenced by Mercadante, as well as by his more distinguished predecessors, Rossini, Bellini and Donizetti. In recent years, there have been occasional attempts to revive operas by Mercadante, but so far none has found its way back into the general repertory.

C.O.

MESSIAEN, Olivier
(b. Avignon, 10 Dec 1908)

Messiaen was born into a literary family: his father was a professor of literature and a translator of Shakespeare, and his mother the poet, Cécile Sauvage. His interest in and talent for music revealed itself early, for at the age of eight he began to teach himself the piano, and to compose. He was still only eleven when he entered the Paris Conservatoire, where he studied for the following eleven years, his teachers including the composer Paul Dukas and the distinguished organist Marcel Dupré. During those years Messiaen won a number of prizes, for counterpoint and fugue, accompaniment, organ and improvisation, history of music, and composition. In his spare time he also studied plainsong, Hindu music, microtonal music and birdsong.

Upon leaving the Conservatoire, Messiaen became organist at the Trinité in Paris, a post he held for over twenty years, and in the same year, 1931, had his first orchestral work, *Les Offrandes oubliées*, performed in Paris. Five years later he helped to found the Jeune France group of young French avant-garde composers, and also became a professor at the École Normale. His first visit to London was made in 1938 when he took part in an International Society for Contemporary Music Festival and played part of his organ work, *La Nativité du Seigneur*.

During the war, Messiaen served in the French forces, was captured by the Germans and taken to a prisoner-of-war camp where he managed to compose his *Quatuor pour la fin du temps* for violin, clarinet, 'cello and piano. The quartet was given its first performance in the camp in 1941. Soon after, Messiaen was repatriated and in 1942 became Professor of Harmony at the Paris Conservatoire. His work first became known to more than a small circle of admirers when he visited London on several occasions after the war, often with the pianist Yvonne Loriod, and gave performances of many new works, among them the *Visions de l'amen* for two pianos. His huge symphony, *Turangalîla,* was commissioned by Serge Kussevitsky, and given its first performance by the Boston Symphony Orchestra under the young Leonard Bernstein.

Messiaen's music has always been placed at the service of his religious beliefs. In 1938 he issued a manifesto which attempted to describe the kind of music he wrote, and why he wrote it. His main interest was in 'the emotion and sincerity of musical work' and he stressed that in his case it would always be at the service of the dogmas of Catholic theology. This sincerity would be expressed 'by melodic and harmonic means: the gradual augmentation of intervals, the chord of the dominant, pedal points, expanded ornaments and appoggiaturas'. The manifesto ends: 'The subject theological? The best, for it comprises all subjects. And the abundance of technical means allows the heart to expand freely.'

The abundance of technical means is certainly an important element in Messiaen's music, with its rhythms and harmonies taken from Hindu music, from bird-song and a variety of other sources, and with its obsessive, hypnotic interest in states of mystical prayer. One of his most important works, the *Vingt Regards sur l'Enfant-Jésus*, is written for solo piano and lasts nearly two and a half hours in performance. It is based on motto themes which have a theological significance for the composer. Messiaen is clearly not in the main-stream of contemporary composition, wherever that stream may be wandering, but has made a safe place for himself in one of its backwaters.

C.O.

MEYERBEER, Giacomo
(b. Berlin, 5 Sept 1791;
d. Paris, 2 May 1864)

Meyerbeer was born in Berlin, the eldest son of a highly successful Jewish banker, Herz Beer, and he started his career as Jakob Liebmann Beer. 'Meyer' was added at the wish of an uncle, and Jakob became Giacomo during the period which he spent in Italy. His family belonged to the group of rich and highly cultivated Jewish bankers settled in Berlin and Hamburg which included the families of the poet Heine and the composer Mendelssohn. His early musical studies were with Zelter, the friend of Goethe and his adviser on all musical matters, but he spent three years between 1810 and 1813 at Darmstadt with the eccentric but original 'Abbé' Vogler. The composer Weber was a fellow student and a friendship formed at this time lasted, though not without qualifications, until Weber's death.

Meyerbeer's first stage-work was a biblical *Jephtha's Vow*, with a German text, given at Munich in 1812, and in the following year he produced at Stuttgart a comedy known at different times as *Host and Guest, The Two Caliphs* and *Alimelek*. This was successful enough to interest a Vienna management and in 1814 Meyerbeer travelled there to oversee the production. The work, given in October 1814, was unsuccessful, but the Viennese visit was a turning-point in Meyerbeer's early life. He was already a more than competent pianist, but after attending a concert given by Hummel he decided to embark on a new period of study. An encounter with Beethoven, in a performance of whose *Battle of Vittoria* he played the bass drum, earned him one of the composer's gruffer comments. 'Young Meyerbeer', he said, 'never had the pluck to come in at the right time.' Salieri, whom he also met in Vienna, advised him to try his luck in Italy, and after spending six months in Paris he crossed the Alps in the spring of 1816.

He found Italy under the spell of the half dozen works which the young Rossini had presented between 1812 and 1815, and Meyerbeer fell so completely under this same spell that, with the facility of a chameleon, he transformed himself in a few months into an Italian composer indistinguishable from any other imitator of Rossini. Of the six operas which he wrote between 1817 and 1824 one, *Emma di Resburgo*, was also successfully produced in Dresden, where Weber commented ruefully on the spectacle of 'a composer of creative ability stopping to become an imitator in order to win the favour of the crowd'. The fate of the last of these Italian operas, *The Crusader in Egypt*, was to confirm Meyerbeer in his determination to win popularity with the public. Its success first in Venice and then in Naples took *The Crusader* first to London, then to Munich and in September 1825 to Paris, where Rossini gave it at the Théâtre Louvois. In Paris Meyerbeer met the man who more than any other helped him to realise his ambitions. This was the playwright Eugène Scribe, who was already successful as a librettist to Auber.

In 1826 the death of his father recalled Meyerbeer to Berlin, but he took with him a libretto by Scribe which, after many transpositions, was eventually to become *Robert le Diable*. Now, however, Meyerbeer was to experience a severe check in his hitherto easy-flowing career. The death of Weber in 1826 was no doubt a grief to him, following on that of his father, but neither of these could compare with the loss of both the children of his marriage to a cousin, Minna Mosson, which had taken place in 1826. It was not until after

the July Revolution of 1830 that he was to return to Paris.

It must not be forgotten that Meyerbeer's wealth gave him an advantage over other composers such as we today may find it hard to imagine. He used it unscrupulously to obtain the very best possible conditions of performance, for publicity purposes and every smallest detail that could further his career. It may be argued that no amount of financial support will make up for lack of talent. But Meyerbeer had great talents and it was on the presentation of his music that he spent his money, with the same need for reassurance that he was to show in his neurotic demand for ever more rehearsals and his badgering all and sundry for advice and suggestions as to possible improvements. There can, I think, be no doubt that part at least of Meyerbeer's insecurity, like that of Heine, came directly from the humiliating fact that, however rich and successful he might be, no Jew could at that time hope ever to be accepted on equal terms in Gentile society.

However that may be, when Meyerbeer returned to Paris with the score of *Robert le Diable* he found an entirely new régime at the Opéra and one which was exceedingly favourable to him. After the July Revolution the new Director, Louis Véron, set out to attract a new public of recently enriched bourgeois and cosmopolitan visitors to the Opéra. He spent enormous sums on magnificent scenery and sumptuous productions, made a special feature of new and ingenious lighting (which he entrusted to Daguerre, inventor of the daguerrotype) and laid particular emphasis on the ballet, which was led by Taglioni and Fanny Elssler. He profited from Rossini's training of a new generation of singers to collect star-studded casts for the new, popular style of operas designed to attract the public. These were in the first place magnificent spectacles, historical pageants on the largest scale, in which one breathtaking tableau succeeded another and music was only one of the many arts employed to dazzle the audience. To ensure success on the widest front Véron maintained a well-paid *claque* of hired supporters at each performance and bribed the Press generously. Those who are interested in the background of this whole period have only to read Balzac's novels of Parisian life to obtain a very clear picture. Already before Véron's time the Opéra had enjoyed huge successes with works of this description, Auber's *La Muette de Portici* and Rossini's *Guillaume*

Scene from Meyerbeer's Robert le Diable.

Tell. It was two years after the latter of these, in 1831, that Meyerbeer's *Robert le Diable* had its first performance, after five months of rehearsals. Meyerbeer was leaving nothing to chance.

Scribe produced in *Robert*, as in the three subsequent librettos that he wrote for Meyerbeer, – *Les Huguenots* (1836), *Le Prophète* (1849) and *L'Africaine* (1865) – a libretto perfectly calculated for both composer and audience. Frequent and highly contrasted changes of scenery included a ballet of spectral nuns in *Robert*; scenes of Renaissance splendour including a ballet of bathing beauties, the 'blessing of the daggers' and the massacre of St Bartholomew in *Huguenots*; a skating ballet, a coronation and a huge explosion in *Le Prophète*. Vast crowd scenes, often contrasted with ensembles of five or six soloists, gave Meyerbeer an opportunity to deploy his forces in almost symphonic style and to create the tableau-finale which became a regular feature of 'French grand opera' and was taken over by Wagner in *Rienzi* and by Verdi in all the operas which he wrote either for Paris or under the influence of Meyerbeer's example. Character-drawing is virtually non-existent in these works, and singers were given music designed in the first place to exhibit their virtuosity. The orchestra is entrusted with a wholly new importance, used often with originality and always with dramatic effect in a manner that owed much to Berlioz's example. Brilliance and complexity are cleverly contrasted with extreme simplicity, and Meyerbeer flattered French taste by perpetuating characters and even music reminiscent of the popular *opéra comique*. The rough old Huguenot soldier, Marcel, in *Les Huguenots* and the pathetic Fides in *Le Prophète* are outstanding examples. In fact, as Mendelssohn commented after seeing *Robert*, every taste is catered for, every means of holding the attention of a musically uneducated public is employed; but as Mendelssohn added, there is little to engage the heart. Scribe's characters are flat, two-dimensional pasteboard puppets and the drama is always one of situation rather than of human personality. Yet there is no denying the effectiveness of these works in terms of the theatre, and Meyerbeer played an important part in the history of 19th-century opera. Verdi's debt, already mentioned, is most noticeable of all in his *Aida*, where he borrows many ideas from the opera which Meyerbeer never lived to see performed, *L'Africaine*. Here the melodic interest of the music, which is secondary in Meyerbeer's other operas, is notably greater and in Vasco's 'O paradis, sorti de l'onde', he left a melody which has survived the otherwise almost total eclipse of his music.

The enormous popularity of his operas in Paris, and no doubt the wealth and influence of his family, earned him the post of General-musikdirektor in Berlin, which he held from 1842 to 1849, during which period he performed his old friend Weber's *Euryanthe* and Wagner's *Rienzi*. Wagner repaid Meyerbeer's kindness to him as a struggling composer in Paris by pillorying him in his anti-Semitic essay *Das Judentum in der Musik* (Jewishness in Music) just as Heine mocked him in his occasional verses. In spite of Meyerbeer's phenomenal success, which included the honour of representing Germany at the London International Exhibition of 1862, and the devotion of two of the century's greatest singers – Jenny Lind and Pauline Viardot – to his music, his later years were clouded by hypochondria and by the obsessive anxiety which prevented him from producing a final version of *L'Africaine*, which did not have its first performance until the year following his death.

M.C.

MILHAUD, Darius
(b. Aix-en-Provence, 4 Sept 1892; d. Geneva, 22 June 1974)

Darius Milhaud was born in 1892, of Jewish parents, at Aix-en-Provence. He was a musical child, and by the time he left Aix for Paris at the age of seventeen he was an accomplished violinist and pianist, had composed a sonata for those instruments and was already

Milhaud.

acquainted with the music of Debussy. It was intended that at the Paris Conservatoire he should study to be a professional violinist. But his creative gifts soon asserted themselves. While still a student he wrote his first string quartet, a further violin sonata (the earliest work he later acknowledged), and his first opera, *La Brebis Égarée*. Even at this early stage his immense facility is apparent.

Like most artists of his generation, Milhaud was held up in his career by the outbreak of war in 1914. Though he was rejected for military service on medical grounds, the war terminated his studies. No doubt they were in any case nearing the end of their usefulness, for Milhaud was by now hard at work as a practising composer. In 1912 he had struck up a friendship with Paul Claudel, and by 1915 had written music for two parts (*Agamemnon* and *Les Choéphores*) of Claudel's *L'Orestie* trilogy. In 1916 Claudel was appointed French ambassador in Brazil, and Milhaud

Léger's decor for Milhaud's ballet, La Creation du Monde.

travelled with him, staying in Brazil from early 1917 to the end of 1918 when he returned to France via the USA. In Paris he found himself almost willy-nilly associated with the anti-establishment activities of Les Six, and some of his works of this period (though not the

haps the best known of these works. But Milhaud also wrote more ambitious works both using Latin-American and jazz material (*La Création du monde*, 1923) and using avantgarde harmonic and rhythmic techniques in straight instrumental music. His output at this period is astonishing. By 1922 he had written his sixth quartet (the eventual total was 19) and his fifth symphony, and the Cocteau opera, *Le Pauvre Matelot*, written in 1926, is his fourth opera and his fourteenth stage work, counting ballets and incidental music.

Milhaud continued to turn out music at something like the same rate until the 1960s. But after the 1920s he fades somewhat from the historian's view. His later career is punctuated at regular intervals by large-scale operas, starting with the ambitious and still experimental *Christophe Colombe* (1930, libretto by Claudel) and ending with *La Mère Coupable* (1966, a setting of Beaumarchais' third and last Figaro play). In 1940 Milhaud and his wife (his cousin Madeleine, whom he married in 1925) left France for the USA, where Milhaud took an appointment at the music faculty of Mills College, Oakland, California. But after the war he returned to France and subsequently divided his time between America and Paris, where he became Professor of Composition at the Conservatoire in 1947. Though severely arthritic since before the war, he remained active and continued to conduct.

Like the other members of Les Six (notably Honegger) Milhaud was undoubtedly damaged in the eyes of later critics by his association with that vacuous and futile movement. Certainly his gifts were peculiarly suited to an empty-headed aesthetic. He was incredibly fluent, could write simple, memorable tunes in various popular styles, and had a definite taste for experiment of a whimsical kind (typical of this are his string quartets Nos 14 and 15, composed in 1948–9, which can also be played together as an octet).

But Milhaud's importance is not only historical. One of the first composers to experiment with bitonality (in *Les Choéphores* of 1915) he later put this device to vigorous and inventive, if occasionally arbitrary, use in his music of the 1920s and 1930s. His use of jazz and Latin rhythms was seminal, and still sounds fresh and piquant when both devices might seem to have been done to death by lesser composers. After World War II Milhaud was also influenced by Hebrew folk music, in several works culminating in the opera, *David* (1954). Sifting through his work

most important) reflect Cocteau's popularist aesthetic, for which Milhaud's Brazilian experiences, and later (after a tour of the USA in 1922) his interest in jazz, provided plenty of material. The *Saudades do Brasil* (1921) and the ballet *Le Boeuf sur le toit* (1919) are per-as a whole we can still find much to delight and refresh, if not so much as he might have hoped to impress or overwhelm.

S.W.

MONTEVERDI, Claudio
(b. Cremona, May 1567;
d. Venice, 29 Nov 1643)

Claudio Monteverdi was born in May 1567, the son of a barber surgeon-cum-chemist and his third wife, in Cremona, a small town in the rich Po Valley, some forty-five miles from Milan. It was seemingly a musical family since Claudio's younger brother, Giulio Cesare, also became a professional musician, but there is no reason to assume that their father had any specialised knowledge which would have helped them. However, his shop was near to the Cathedral, and Claudio's earliest studies were with its *maestro di cappella*, Marc'Antonio Ingegneri, a sound musician of a rather conservative nature. His pupil was distinctly talented, and at the age of fifteen had already written a group of short religious pieces worthy of publication by a famous Venetian publisher. A year later Claudio had composed some religious madrigals and he soon followed this up with some attractive canzonettas, so that before he was out of his teens, he was already an accomplished composer. His next two books of madrigals, conventional but pleasant in style, set the seal on his youthful reputation.

By his early twenties he was beginning to look for a post in a more fruitful town than Cremona, and was accepting freelance engagements as a string player (it is not certain whether of viols or the more modern violin) and when he was almost twenty-four he gained a job in the musical establishment of the Gonzagas, at Mantua, the nearest of the opulent courts of the north Italian plain. Here he met some notable musicians, of whom the greatest was the director of music, a Netherlander called Giaches de Wert, from whom he learned a great deal, and within a short time he produced a revolutionary madrigal book in a quite novel style. He had some difficulty in following this up, and did not publish anything for eleven years. Even so, he was clearly esteemed by the Duke, his employer, who took him on an expedition against the Turks in Hungary, Monteverdi being in charge of a small group of musicians who spent several months away from home. A few years later he went in the Duke's retinue to the watering place, Spa, in Flanders, where his master was taking a cure, both these trips helping to broaden his musical horizons.

Shortly before this trip in 1599 and just before his thirty-second birthday, Monteverdi married Claudia Cattaneo, one of the virtuoso singers in the Duke's musical establishment, and in the next five years they had three children – two sons, and a daughter who seems to have died in infancy. They could afford the family because Monteverdi had been promoted *maestro di cappella* in 1602, and his wife went on working (or at least receiving her stipend). And he was becoming famous outside Mantua, for a conservative theorist, Giovanni Maria Artusi, a Bolognese monk, devoted serious attention to some of Monteverdi's as yet unpublished madrigals, accusing him of various offences against the rules of composition. This may have stimulated him to publish the music, and his next madrigal book (the fourth) came out in 1604 and was quickly followed by yet another, this one containing a preface defending his new style on the grounds that although it was not conventional by traditional standards, nevertheless it was built 'on the foundations of truth', and reflected the ideas of the Greek theorists so greatly respected by Renaissance writers. This caused a further condemnation by Artusi, which in turn provoked a reply, this time from Monteverdi's brother, who amplified the preface to the fifth madrigal book. The publicity apparently did Monteverdi nothing but good; his former madrigal books were quickly reprinted and by the age of forty, he was one of the most famous composers in Europe. In 1607, he wrote his first opera, *Orfeo*, its première taking place before the Mantuan courtiers. Nothing is known about its reception, but it is significant that it was published a couple of years later and also received at least partial performances elsewhere.

At the height of his success and fame, disaster struck: his wife died in September 1607, and as they had been very close, Monteverdi suffered a profound depression which lasted for several years. He was in despair, living at his father's home in Cremona, when he was summoned back to court to compose a new opera, *Arianna*, meant for the celebrations for the wedding between the heir apparent and a princess of the house of Savoy. When it was in rehearsal, yet another disaster happened, the prima donna destined to 'create' the title role dying of smallpox. Nevertheless, another singer was found, and the opera was the greatest success of its time, and as it was given before one of the most distinguished audiences possible, Monteverdi's reputation reached a new apex. Yet he was now more deeply depressed than ever, and for the next two years composed little, quarrelling with the Mantuan authorities, and requesting permission to leave. It was in this period that he composed some if not all of the *Vespers* published in 1610, and the volume may indeed have been an attempt to obtain a church appointment in Rome or Venice. In this it was not successful and two years later, when the Duke of Mantua died, Monteverdi was suddenly dismissed, apparently at the whim of the new duke, who sacked a number of other artists at the same time. For a year he was unemployed and was supported by his father at Cremona. Then, out of the blue, came an invitation to become *maestro di cappella* at St

Mark's in Venice; he accepted and moved with his two sons to Venice, being robbed on the way by highwaymen in August 1613.

Here he had a much calmer life. He was paid well – and regularly (which had not always been the case at Mantua). He was also honoured by the city at large and his employers in particular, who gradually raised his salary to a level far beyond that of his predecessors. He turned out to be an efficient administrator, expanding the musical establishment of the basilica and generally improving its standards after a bad patch. There being no opera in Venice, he responded to commissions from elsewhere (mainly from Mantua where he was now very much persona grata) for various kinds of dramatic works. His sons caused him a certain amount of trouble, both becoming students at Bologna University, the elder eventually giving up law and taking to singing as a career (he was a member of the choir of St Mark's), the younger studying medicine was even arrested by the Inquisition as a heretic for reading forbidden books (his father had to rescue him by means of influence and intrigue). But by and large, Monteverdi was happy during these years, developing various ideas on the composition of theatre music, which resulted in the *Combattimento di Tancredi e Clorinda*, produced in a Venetian nobleman's palace in 1624. He also occasionally went to other cities to supervise productions of his works, notably to Parma in 1628, where his music for a spectacle was actually rained off, in spite of long rehearsals.

The major event of this period was the outbreak of the plague, which arrived in Venice in 1630, killing off thousands of people and causing a total interruption of musical and social life for several months. He became a priest shortly after this, and wrote a great Mass of thanksgiving for the cessation of the disease. He published little in the next few years, but assembled a grand retrospective volume of all kinds of secular music, issued under the title of *Madrigali guerrieri et amorosi* (Madrigals of war and love) in 1638, and another of church music two years later. But then, just as he was seemingly an old man who was finished with active life, he had, like Verdi, an Indian Summer. The first public opera house opened in Venice in 1637 and as the one experienced native composer in the genre, he was naturally invited to contribute to their repertoire. *Arianna* was revived in 1639; in 1641 he wrote two operas, one of which was *Il ritorno*

A page of Monteverdi's Lamento d'Ariana.

VERDE ✻ CLAVDIO MONTE

FIORI POETICI
Raccolti nel Funerale
DEL MOLTO ILLVSTRE,
E Molto Reuerendo
SIGNOR CLAVDIO
Monte verde
Maestro di Cappella della Du-
cale di S. Marco.
Consecrati
DA D. GIO: BATTISTA
Marinoni, det. Giove:
Maestro di Cappella del Do-
mo di Padoua
ALL' ILLVSTRSSIMI
& Ecc eilentissimi
SIG. PROCVRATORI
Di Chiesa di S. Marco.

In VENETIA, Presso Francesco Miloco.
Con Lic. de Sup.   MDCXLIV.

Title-page of Monteverdi's Fiori Poetici.

d'Ulisse in patria, as well as a ballet for a court entertainment at Piacenza. In the following year he wrote his final masterpiece *L'Incoronazione di Poppea*, a work of astonishing energy and sustained power for a man of seventy-five. In 1643, he decided to visit his old haunts, travelling to both Cremona and Mantua in the Spring. He returned to Venice, where he died on the 29th November. He was much honoured, and was buried in the church of S Maria Gloriosa dei Frari, where a memorial plaque can be found in one of the chapels to the north of the high altar.

D.A.

MORLEY, Thomas
(b. London?, 1557;
d. London, Oct 1602)

Thomas Morley was a chorister at St Paul's Cathedral and probably a pupil of Sebastian Westcote the Cathedral organist. He left the St Paul's choir in 1573 and at about the same time became a pupil of William Byrd. Morley was choirmaster at Norwich Cathedral from 1583 to 1587. He graduated B.Mus. at Oxford in 1588 and is thought to have been organist of St Giles, Cripplegate at the same time. He is said to have become organist of St Paul's Cathedral in 1589 and was certainly there in 1591 when he was implicated as, of all things, a political agent. Writing from the Low Countries on the 3rd October 1591 a Roman Catholic intriguer by the name of Paget expounds:

Ther is one Morley that playeth on the orgaines in poules that was with me in my house. He semed here to be a good Catholicke and was reconsiled, but not-withstanding suspecting his behaviour I entercepted letters that Mr Nowell wrote to him, whereby I discovered enoughe to have hanged him. Nevertheles he shewing with teares great repentaunce, and asking on his knees forgivenes, I was content to let him goe.

In 1592 Morley was sworn a Gentleman of the Chapel Royal, and between 1596 and 1601 he was living in the Parish of Little St Helen's, Bishopsgate – the same parish as Shakespeare. Indeed, it seems likely that the two were on personal terms; Shakespeare, of course, borrowed Morley's lute-song setting of *It Was a Lover and His Lass* for *As You Like It*. In 1598 Morley was granted a printing monopoly which replaced the one formerly held by Byrd. His health was by now beginning to fail – he complained of the 'solitarie life which I lead (being compelled to keepe at home)' – and in 1602 he resigned his position in the Chapel Royal and was replaced by George Woodson. The actual date of Morley's death is not known. In 1601 he edited the famous collection of madrigals *The Triumphes of Oriana* which was not published until 1603, a fact giving rise to much confusion among biographers. In all probability he died in the autumn of 1602.

Although the biographical details of Morley's life are somewhat inconclusive, there can be few composers who have made a more influential contribution to the musical life of their time. The important series of madrigals composed or edited between 1593 and 1601 established the form (madrigal, canzonet, ballet) used by Gibbons, Weelkes, Wilbye and the other Jacobeans. Morley's book of *Madrigalls to Foure Voyces* (1594) was the first completely English publication of its kind. Madrigal singing had by now become extremely fashionable. If a man could not sing a part at sight, according to Morley, it was considered a sign of poor education.

Morley excelled in the lighter forms of ballet, a form which he introduced into England, and canzonet. Both show obvious signs of Italian origin (particularly in the works of Gastoldi and Anerio), but in the hands of Morley became infused with an instinctive sense of tunefulness and cheerfulness. Morley's church compositions are no less masterly. There now remains a complete Morning, Communion and Evening Service set in the 'verse' manner, a five-part and a 'short' setting of the Evening Canticles together with versicles and responses and a set of festal psalms. His motet *Nolo mortem peccatoris*, on a macaronic English/Latin text, is widely known, as is the verse anthem *Out of the Deep*. Burney comments at length on Morley's setting of the Burial Service which he heard sung at the funeral of George II in Westminster Abbey in 1760.

Morley's *First Booke of Consort Lessons* (1599) was the first printed book of ensemble

Ptolomeus

Marinus

VIRESCIT VVLNERE VERITAS

Strabo

Aratus

Polibius

Hipparchus

A
PLAINE AND
EASIE INTRODVCTI-
ON TO PRACTICALL
MVSICKE,
Set downe in forme of a dialogue
Deuided into three partes,
The first teacheth to sing with all
things necessary for the knowledge of
prickt song.
The second treateth of descante
and to sing two parts in one upon a plainsong or
ground, with other things necessary
for a descanter.
The third and last part, entreateth of com
position of three, foure, fiue or more parts with
many profitable rules to that effect
With new songs of.1.3.6. and .5 parts.

Astronomia

Geometria

By Thomas Morley, Batcheler of musick, &
one of the gent. of hir Maiesties Royall Chappell.
Imprinted at London by Peter Short dwelling on
Breedstreet hill at the signe of the Starre. 1597.

Musica

Arithmetica

MERCVRIVS

music in England, and also the first to specify exact instrumentation. He also composed music for viol consort and for lute. Morley's surviving keyboard music, consisting of pavans, galliards, song variations and a fantasia, is often reminiscent of Byrd. In 1597 Morley published *A Plaine and Easie Introduction to Practicall Musicke*, an extremely comprehensive survey of the theory and practice of music. Written in the form of a dialogue, which often charmingly reflects on contemporary musical life, it is one of the most important musical treatises ever published.

G.G.

MOZART, Wolfgang Amadeus
(b. Salzburg, 27 Jan 1756;
d. Vienna, 5 Dec 1791)

It is probable that more people have visited the birthplace of Mozart in Salzburg than that of any other composer. His father, Leopold, was a violinist and composer in the service of the Prince Archbishop of Salzburg, and had written an important treatise on the violin which was published a few months after the birth of Wolfgang, the seventh and last of his children. Leopold's ambition was to become, in due course, Kapellmeister or leading musician in the Archbishop court. It was an ambition he was never to achieve. By the time young Wolfgang had reached his eighth year, Leopold had become Vice-Kapellmeister, a post he occupied until his death. But by now his ambition had altered, for he had discovered young Wolfgang to be a musical prodigy. He and his sister Maria Anna, the only survivors of the seven children, were both musically talented. The three-year-old Wolfgang liked to sit at the keyboard, picking out thirds, and showing obvious delight at the harmonies thus produced. In his fourth year, Leopold began to teach him simple pieces, and, as his sister was to recall many years later, 'he learned a piece in an hour, and a minuet in half an hour, so that he could play it faultlessly and with the greatest delicacy, and keeping exactly

Mozart with his father and sister, by Carmontelle, Paris, 1763

in time. He made such progress that by the age of five he was already composing little pieces.'

Leopold was so excited by his youngest child's precocious musicianship that he became determined to make a famous musician of the boy. Doubtless his motives were impure: a child prodigy must have represented an enormous financial advantage to a hard-pressed family, and Leopold was to squeeze the utmost commercial advantage out of his son's genius while he was still a child and thus a phenomenon. But it is also true that he believed his son's gifts to be God-given, and saw it as his duty to make them known to the world. The obvious way to do this was to introduce the boy to the various courts of Europe, and so Leopold and both children set off from Salzburg in January 1762, shortly before Wolfgang's sixth birthday, for a three-week stay in Munich, performing at the court of the Bavarian Elector. Later in the year, this

Mozart with his father and sister (and a portrait of his mother) by della Croce, Salzburg, 1780.

time with the children's mother as well, they travelled to Vienna where Wolfgang and 'Nannerl', as his sister was called, played at the palace of Schoenbrunn before the Empress Maria Theresa and her family, including the seven-year-old Marie Antoinette. The Vienna visit was so successful that, after a mere six months at home in Salzburg, the entire family set out again on a tour of Europe which was to last three and a half years. In the course of this tour they visited London where they stayed for several months, giving concerts to which the general public flocked, and playing for royalty. At most of the courts they visited, the Mozarts would be given expensive presents, which was how the enterprise was financed. On the way back to Salzburg, both children became quite seriously ill, but in due

course they arrived home, in November 1766. Early the following year, Mozart was given the opportunity to write his first work for the stage, *Apollo et Hyacinthus*, a musical intermezzo which was performed between the acts of a Latin play in the Great Hall of Salzburg University. A year or two later, at the instigation of the Emperor Joseph II, Wolfgang received a commission to write a full-length opera for Vienna. This was *La finta semplice* which reached the stage only after a series of intrigues by jealous Viennese musicians had been dealt with, and then not in Vienna but in Salzburg.

In December 1769, Wolfgang and his father set out on their travels again, this time south to Italy. In Milan, Wolfgang was fêted, and also obtained a commission to compose the opera to open the following season. In Bologna they met the famous old composer Martini who tested Wolfgang's musical knowledge and spoke of him with admiration. More concerts and receptions followed in Florence, Rome and Naples. In Rome, Pope Clement XIV awarded Wolfgang the Order of the Golden Spur, and gave him an audience. The Mozarts remained in Italy long enough for Wolfgang to write his opera, *Mitridate, Rè di Ponto*, and to conduct its first performance from the cembalo. It was a great triumph, with cries of 'Evviva il maestro' and demands for encores. The travellers arrived back in Salzburg in March 1771, but within months they were back in Italy for Wolfgang's success had led to further commissions. When Salzburg received a new Prince-Archbishop, the worldly Colloredo, Wolfgang composed a dramatic serenade, *Il sogno di Scipione*, in his

Act IV of Le nozze di Figaro, *engraving by Beguinet.*

honour. During the next years in Salzburg, he composed symphonies and divertimentos to order, as well as the operas *Lucio Silla*, and *La finta giardiniera*, the former commissioned for performance in Milan, and the latter for Munich. Important non-operatic works which date from Mozart's teen-age years in Salzburg include the violin concertos, and a number of Masses, divertimenti and serenades, including the popular *Haffner* Serenade. But, increasingly discontented with life under Archbishop Colloredo, and encouraged by his father to embark upon another tour, Mozart set out in 1777 for Paris, accompanied this time by his mother.

Their progress was leisurely, and indeed it had to be, for the journey could be financed only by fees and gifts received for performances given *en route*. The first stop was

Munich, where the Elector of Bavaria praised the young performer–composer to the skies, but claimed he had no vacancy in his court for another musician. In Augsburg, Mozart delighted in the company of his cousin Maria Anna who shared his robust sense of humour, and of whom he was very fond. But it was in Mannheim that he fell in love for the first time, with Aloysia, second of the four daughters of a music copyist, Fridolin Weber. Leopold Mozart was horrified to receive a letter from Wolfgang proposing a change of plans. Instead of proceeding to Paris, he and his mother would accompany the Weber family on a visit to Italy. Leopold put his foot down firmly, which was something Mozart's mother was temperamentally incapable of doing, and eventually, in March 1778, mother and son continued on to Paris.

The months spent in Paris were hardly fruitful ones for Mozart. Several projected works and commissions came to nothing, though he did compose the music for a ballet, *Les petits riens*. His mother became ill, and died in Paris on the 3rd July. Though he dearly loved her, the twenty-two-year-old Wolfgang reacted to the tragedy with a remarkable composure. He even wrote to his father immediately after his mother died, merely warning him that she had been taken ill, and preparing him for the shock of her death. There was now nothing for Mozart to do but return to Salzburg, though he dawdled for some time in Munich where the Weber family was now living. Aloysia, however, had recovered from her infatuation with him, and Mozart was forced to console himself by flirting with his cousin. Eventually, in January of the following year, he returned home to Salzburg.

The next two years were spent performing and composing music to order in Salzburg. But a commission to provide an opera for the opening of the carnival season in Munich in 1781 led to the composition of *Idomeneo*, the first of Mozart's indisputably great operas. To a libretto by a Salzburg colleague set at the time of the Trojan war, Mozart wrote his mag-

Title-page of a piano score of Die Entführung aus dem Serail.

nificent farewell to opera seria, a work of great power and artistic maturity. Immediately after the opera's first performance in Munich, he was called to Vienna, as part of the Archbishop of Salzburg's entourage. The letters he wrote home to his father reveal how frustrated and discontented Mozart had become in the Archbishop's service. Smarting from the indignities heaped upon him as little better than a servant in Colloredo's employ, he angrily offered his resignation. At his last interview, he was literally kicked out of the Archbishop's Vienna residence by his Steward.

Determined to make a career for himself in Vienna as composer, performer and teacher, Mozart took lodgings with his old friends the Weber family, who had moved from Bavaria to Vienna. Having failed with Aloysia who was now married, he now fell in love with her younger sister, Constanze. Against the wishes of his father, and to a certain extent bullied into it by the girl's mother, Wolfgang married Constanze. Their first child, Raimund Leopold (who did not long survive) was born nine months after the wedding.

Constanze was affectionate by nature, somewhat flighty, and no good as a housekeeper. For a time, the young couple were happy enough in Vienna, though money was scarce. The favourable reception of Mozart's German-language opera, *Die Entführung aus dem Serail*, and of several instrumental compositions, led to his procuring a few pupils. But this precarious source of income soon dried up, and the Court appointment that he was always hoping for failed to materialise. It was at about this time that Mozart joined the Society of Freemasons, then a powerful underground organisation and an implacable enemy of the Roman Catholic Church.

Some of the most beautiful and individual of Mozart's piano concertos were composed during the early years of his residence in Vienna, as were the six string quartets dedicated to Haydn. When he met the Italian Jewish poet and librettist, Lorenzo da Ponte, who had recently arrived in Vienna and been appointed Court Poet by the Emperor, Mozart invited Da Ponte to provide him with a libretto. Their choice fell upon the play, *Les noces de Figaro* by Beaumarchais. Although the play had been banned in Vienna because of its revolutionary sentiment, Da Ponte obtained the Emperor's permission to adapt it for operatic purposes on the understanding that any passages offensive to the monarchy

would be omitted. In the event, Da Ponte produced a libretto which, while it certainly does underplay the class warfare of Beaumarchais' original, is in its own right a witty and engaging comedy. Mozart composed upon it an opera which is today one of the best-loved in the entire operatic repertoire. The characters of the quick-witted Figaro, the wise and loving Susanna, the formidable Count and the unhappy Countess spring to life in the music. Just as the old opera seria was raised to new heights in *Idomeneo*, so was the Italian comic opera formula transcended in *Le nozze di Figaro*.

The opera was produced in Vienna on the 1st May 1786. Michael Kelly, the Irish tenor who sang the roles of Basilio and Curzio, has left in his Memoirs a lively description of the first performance, and of the audience's enthusiastic applause for Mozart at the end of Act I. *Le nozze di Figaro* was an enormous success in Vienna, and was even more rapturously received when it was staged in Prague. Indeed, the Prague performances led to a commission for Mozart to compose a new opera for that city, and thus it was that Mozart and Da Ponte set to work on *Don Giovanni*, which had its première in Prague in October 1787, and was an even more resounding success than *Figaro*.

Leopold Mozart had died earlier that year, in May. The relationship between Mozart and his father may have cooled temporarily at the time of Wolfgang's marriage, but father and son had become close to each other again, and Wolfgang felt his father's death very keenly. To his sorrow was added an increasing desperation, for despite the success of his operas no lucrative commissions came his way, teaching was becoming more of a drudgery, and pupils in any case harder to get. Unable to support his wife and children adequately, Mozart began to borrow from the wealthier of his fellow Masons, in particular from Michael Puchberg, a Viennese merchant. Mozart's importuning letters to him are still distressing to read, and Puchberg's generous response is extremely moving. It is difficult to comprehend how, during this period of extreme financial need, Mozart was able to compose his three greatest symphonies, those in E flat (No. 39), G minor (No. 40) and C (No. 41, the so-called *Jupiter* Symphony).

In May of 1788, *Don Giovanni* was staged in Vienna in a version which differed slightly from that performed in Prague. (For instance, since the Viennese Ottavio found 'Il mio tesoro' too difficult, Mozart wrote him a new aria, 'Dalla sua pace'.) The opera failed to repeat its Prague success, and Mozart's financial situation worsened. By now he had been appointed Court Composer to the Emperor, but at a purely nominal salary. In 1789 he visited Berlin where he played for the Prussian Emperor who offered him the post of Kapellmeister at a generous salary. But Mozart was apparently unwilling to contemplate moving from Vienna to Berlin. Despite the difficulties he encountered there, he loved Vienna.

The story of Mozart's last years is one of increasing poverty and distress. When Constanze became ill, doctors' fees were added to the family's burden of expenses. A third opera written in collaboration with Da Ponte, *Così fan tutte*, was staged in Vienna in January 1790, but although it is a masterpiece it did nothing to alleviate the composer's situation. When, later in the year, an opportunity arose for him to go to England, Mozart declined the offer. Da Ponte had already established himself in London, and it is fascinating to speculate on what the course of English opera in the 19th century might have been had Mozart survived and he and Da Ponte continued their operatic partnership in London. But Mozart did not survive. He wrote two more operas in the few months that were left to him: the sublime pantomime-opera *Die Zauberflöte* for his old friend Schikaneder's Viennese suburban theatre, and *La clemenza di Tito* for coronation festivities in Prague. The latter was a late

return to *opera seria* which he thought he had finished with, years earlier, in *Idomeneo*. Mozart's heart was not in this final Prague commission, though the opera does contain some lovely music.

When a mysterious stranger visited Mozart to ask him to compose a Requiem Mass, the composer, now ill and despondent, fancied that his visitor had come from another world, and that the Requiem would be for the repose of his own soul. The visitor had come, not from another world, but from an eccentric nobleman; nevertheless, the Requiem was, in a sense, Mozart's own, for he died on the 5th December 1791, before he had managed to complete it. His funeral service at St Stephen's Cathedral was attended by a few friends, but not by Constanze who was too ill and griefstricken. He was buried in an unmarked grave in the churchyard of St Mark's, and within a short time the exact location of his grave had been forgotten, for the day of the funeral had been bitterly cold and wet, and not one of the mourners in the cathedral followed the coffin all the way to St Mark's. Mozart's mortal remains are lost; his music remains among the most cherished possessions of the civilised world.

C.O.

A room in the Villa Bertramka, Prague, where Mozart composed much of Don Giovanni.

MUSSORGSKY, Modeste
(b. Karev, 21 March 1839;
d. St Petersburg, 28 March 1881)

'Another friend and pupil of Balakirev was Modeste Mussorgsky. He wrote song, pianoforte pieces and three operas, one of which, *Boris Godunov*, attained to considerable popularity.' These are the few lines devoted to Modeste Mussorgsky by Harry T. Finck in *Famous Composers and Their Works*, published twelve years after Mussorgsky's death in 1881. And in Arthur Pougin's *History of Russian Music* (1915), we read: 'If Borodin can be called a master of technique one cannot say the same of Mussorgsky, that strange, incomplete composer, musically only half-educated, who was clumsy in the expression of his ideas from sheer lack of musical knowledge. . . .' It is amusing to speculate on what Finck and Pougin would have said if someone had told them that in a few years' time, Mussorgsky would be classified far above Balakirev and Borodin, and that *Boris* would be regarded as the greatest of all Russian operas.

It was fitting that Mussorgsky and Rimsky-Korsakov should become close friends and fellow-lodgers in the Petersburg of the 1870s; their backgrounds and early careers display some astonishing parallels. Both were sons of landowners; both were originally intended for military rather than musical careers; both were lured into composition by a meeting with Balakirev. Mussorgsky was five years Rimsky's senior, being born in 1839. He studied the piano as a child, and was so naturally talented that at the age of eleven he played a John Field piano concerto in front of a large audience. Yet still no one suspected that he was destined for a musical career – least of all Mussorgsky himself. Perhaps this was because he found discipline so irksome, and rebelled against most of his piano teachers.

At the age of ten, his family moved to St Petersburg, and Modeste entered the military academy. From Father Krupsky, one of his teachers, Mussorgsky acquired a thorough knowledge of old church music. Then, at the age of seventeen, he entered the Preobrajensky Regiment, a famous old Guards regiment; and there he learned the art of heavy drinking that ruined his health and eventually killed him. It was at this period that he met Borodin, and the future composer of *Prince Igor* commented on Mussorgsky's good looks, elegance, and on the demand for his pianistic skills in the *salons*. Soon Mussorgsky was acquainted with the rest of the Petersburg

Chaliapin as Mussorgsky's Boris Godunov, *by Golovin.*

group of composers – Dargomizhky, Cui and Balakirev, and the critic Stasov. Mussorgsky began to take lessons from the highly dominant Balakirev, who introduced him to the work of all the major composers of the 19th century. Mussorgsky began to compose. Two piano sonatas (which have disappeared) and an abandoned symphony were stiff and academic. But half a dozen early songs – which also vanished for many years – show definite originality in their key contrasts and chord constructions. It was such innovations that convinced his contemporaries that he was clumsy and unskilled.

It took only two years for Mussorgsky to decide he was not intended for the army. He was romantic, morbid, introspective, oversensitive. Byron's *Manfred* became his Bible.

And as his inner being unfolded, he found it increasingly difficult to deal with the external world. He developed a defensive self-mockery and a bizarre sense of humour. Stasov described him irritably as 'flabby and colourless' and as a 'perfect idiot'. In 1863, when he was twenty-five, the blow fell: the Tsar Alexander I liberated the serfs, and Mussorgsky's family became impoverished. Mussorgsky had to take a job as a government clerk. Anyone who has read Gogol or Dostoevsky will know how dreary this could be. Mussorgsky remained a clerk for most of the remainder of his life.

Shortly before this, Mussorgsky had moved into a flat with five other young men who regarded themselves as fellow artists and intellectuals; there he began work on a second opera – an earlier attempt to set Hugo's *Hans of Iceland* had been scrapped – based on Flaubert's *Salmmbô*; this was finally abandoned, and some of its music transferred into *Boris*. In 1865 came Mussorgsky's first collapse from alcoholism, complete with delirium tremens. He left the 'commune' and moved in with his brother, where he soon recovered, and launched himself into the composition of some of the most

remarkable and original songs that have ever come out of Russia. They give him a secure place, together with Schubert and Wolf, among the greatest of European song composers. When his brother had to leave Petersburg, he moved into the house of a friend, Alexander Opochinin, and launched into a third opera, based on Gogol's *The Marriage*. This follows Dagomizhky's method of moulding the music to the words, and abjuring songs and arias; it is, on the whole, a dull piece of work. But it prepared him for the composition of *Boris Godunov*, based on the Pushkin play. He worked so fast that it was completed in the autumn of 1869. It was submitted to the Imperial Opera, who found its realism baffling and rejected it. Mussorgsky settled down to re-modelling it and making it more conventional, throwing in some arias and a love duet. By now, he and Rimsky-Korsakov were sharing a room – Rimsky had been introduced to the Balakirev group ten years earlier, in 1861 – and taking it in turns to use the piano. The Imperial Opera rejected the

Title-page of Boris Godunov.

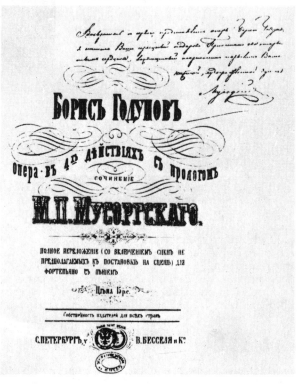

re-modelled *Boris* in 1872. Mussorgsky took the disappointment lightly, since he was now absorbed in a new opera, *Khovanschina*. In 1873, his luck began to change. Three scenes from *Boris* were performed at a benefit performance, and their success led a publisher to acquire the rights. But Mussorgsky's own weakness betrayed him. He plunged back into heavy drinking, sold his belongings, and sometimes vanished for days on end.

In the autumn of 1873, a singer who had taken part in the benefit performance of *Boris* insisted that the opera should be presented for her own benefit performance. It was not an overwhelming success, yet in spite of hostile criticism, it continued to be performed once or twice a year for many years. But the story of the remainder of his life is of struggles to complete *Kovanschina* and a new opera, *Sorochintsy Fair* (based on Gogol), and debilitating bouts of drunkenness. (Riepin's famous portrait, with its bleary eyes and red nose, makes him look rather like a bearded Dylan Thomas.) In 1879, he went on a tour of southern Russia as accompanist of the singer Daria Leonova, and seemed to gain a new lease on life. Then he was dismissed from his clerical post for drunkenness, and he became accompanist in Leonova's singing classes, a position that his friends regarded as degrading. Money was raised to help him complete the two operas, and he worked heroically. But in February 1881, he was thrown out of his lodgings, and suffered an epileptic fit. He lived for another month in a military hospital, sometimes raving, sometimes lucid, and died on the 28th March shortly after his forty-second birthday.

Rimsky-Korsakov, convinced that his friend's 'clumsiness and illiteracy' obscured his genius, proceeded to rewrite most of his works, including *Boris*. His 'improvements' could be compared to adding liberal doses of sugared water to a harsh Burgundy. But at least they achieved their purpose, and the Rimsky-ised *Boris* went on to conquer the world. The unfortunate Rimsky-Korsakov has brought down showers of critical execration on his own head, and caused the value of his own music to be underrated. Yet in the 1920s, critics began to recognise the harsh originality of Mussorgsky's original orchestrations, and in our own time, the *ur*-text is at least as well known as the Rimsky revisions. In the end, it has all worked out for the best – at least, for Mussorgsky.

C.W.

Mussorgsky, 1876.

NIELSEN, Carl
(b. Nørre Lyndelse, 9 June 1865; d. Copenhagen, 2 Oct 1931)

Nielsen was born the son of a peasant labourer on the island of Fyn. At fourteen he became a military bandsman in Odense and soon thereafter began to compose chamber music. In 1884 he entered the Conservatorium at Copenhagen and from 1889 to 1905 played second violin in the Royal Theatre Orchestra which in 1894 gave the première of his First Symphony under Johan Svendsen. In 1902 Nielsen himself directed the first performance of his opera *Saul and David* and of his Second Symphony (*The Four Temperaments*), and in 1905 that of one of his greatest successes, the opera *Maskarade*. From 1908 to 1914 he was conductor of the Royal Theatre Orchestra, but found his appointment with the Music Society of Copenhagen (1915–27) more congenial, mainly because it allowed him greater freedom to compose. He visited London in 1924 to conduct a concert of his works at the

Queen's Hall, and in the same year his sixtieth birthday was celebrated in Denmark as a national event. Heart trouble affected him increasingly from 1929 onwards, yet he undertook the Directorship of the Copenhagen Conservatorium in 1931. He died of a heart attack in October of that year.

Nielsen's primitive feeling for nature implanted in him during his childhood years on Fyn – which he described in a minor classic among autobiographical writings, *My Childhood on Fyn* – gave him a sense of identity with the Danish soil and an ability to distil the essence of the Danish temperament in music; he is considered the Danish composer *par excellence*, although recognition outside Denmark has come belatedly. The Danishness consists not so much in linguistic features derived from folk song (though these, fully absorbed into the bloodstream, are regularly to be found) as in the hardy Danish characteristics which inform all his best work – unsentimental directness of expression, discipline, constructive clarity, humanity and warmth. The cycle of six symphonies forms the cornerstone of his creative output; Brahms is the rock on which they are built although Nos. 4, 5, and 6 all move away from classical precedent and all six are governed by the composer's concept of 'progressive tonality'. No. 3, the *Sinfonia Espansiva*, sounds the authoritative Danish note most positively, while the essence of No. 4, *The Inextinguishable,* and No. 5 – now a universally recognised masterpiece – is conflict. Non-symphonic orchestral works of moment include *Pan and Syrinx: a nature-scene, Saga-drøm*, the *Helios* overture, concerti for violin, flute, clarinet. The choral repertoire is enriched primarily by the *Hymnus Amoris* to a Latin text, and by *Springtime on Fyn* a 'lyric humoresque'; the solo songs, a large corpus of work, show Nielsen's mastery of the Danish folk-idiom at its most basic, whilst among the keyboard works the Op. 45 *Suite* for piano and the composer's last work *Commotio* for organ reign supreme. Of the two operas the second, *Maskarade*, is the Danish *Meistersinger*.

C.P.

OFFENBACH, Jacques
(b. Cologne, 20 June 1819;
d. Paris, 4 Oct 1880)

Offenbach's father was a Jewish cantor, musician, author and bookbinder from the town of Offenbach-on-Main, whose original name was Isaac Juda Eberst. Known amongst his acquaintances as 'Der Offenbacher', when he settled in the Cologne area at the age of twenty, he adoped the name of Offenbach. His son Jacques (or Jacob Levy as he was originally christened) was born in Cologne the year after the family had moved there and his father had become cantor of the local syna-

gogue. Jacques was the seventh child and was taught the violin by his father, who supplemented his income by giving music lessons. The whole family were musical and often enjoyed evenings of chamber-music. Jacques found that the 'cello was his favourite instrument and began to study with a local teacher, giving his first concert at the age of twelve. He had already begun to compose music when he was six.

In November 1833 he was accepted at the Paris Conservatoire after impressing the Director Cherubini with his youthful talents and he studied the 'cello under Vaslin. After an

The Bacchanale from Offenbach's Orpheus in the Underworld *by Gustave Doré.*

undistinguished and not particularly hard-working year he left the Conservatoire and took a couple of minor orchestral jobs before becoming a 'cellist in the orchestra of the Opéra-Comique. One of his extra tasks was to do some copying for the young composer Friedrich Flotow (1812–83) and the two joined forces in writing two albums of 'cello pieces, Offenbach providing melodies that already bear his distinctive traits and Flotow writing the piano part, which they played in recitals together.

Offenbach's earliest essay as a theatre composer was in writing incidental music for Bourgeois's *Pascal et Chambord* at the Palais Royal in 1839. He also wrote many songs, but, for a time, he was able to make a better income as a fashionable salon 'cellist. An interesting and handsome young man, full of typical Jewish vitality, he had highly successful tours in France and Germany and came to London in 1844 where he played at a 'grand morning concert' at Her Majesty's Theatre directed by Michael Costa and Julius Benedict. He made several London appearances and played before Queen Victoria and Prince Albert who presented him with a valuable diamond ring. He returned to Paris affluent enough to be able to devote himself at last to musical composition, became a Roman Catholic and married a Spanish lady called Herminie de Alcain. His one ambition was to succeed with a comic opera, but his setting of *L'Alcôve* only got a performance at the Salle de la Tour d'Auvergne and was politely declined by the directors of the Opéra-Comique. He continued to write and had achieved at least some instrumental success with his *Musette* (1843), described as an 'Air de Ballet du 17e Siècle' which had the honour of being included in a critical journal in a series 'Well-Known Violoncello Solo: How to Play Them' by E. van der Straeten. Offenbach himself generally brought the house down with this piece by a clever imitation of the bagpipes.

1848 was the year of the Revolution and Offenbach returned for a time to Cologne where his one-act operetta *Marietta* (later rewritten as *Madame l'Archiduc*) was produced in 1849. The following year he was appointed conductor of the Comédie Française at a salary of about £240 a year which gave him ample opportunity to use his own pieces as incidental music. One which became very popular was his 'Chanson de Fortunio' which was used in Alfred de Musset's *Le Chandelier*. He remained in this post for five years and gained much practical experience of theatre orchestration. He had three minor performances of operettas and, in his frustration at being denied the stage of the Opéra-Comique often thought of founding his own theatre. In 1855 he took the plunge and leased a tiny theatre in the Champs-Elysées which was nicknamed the 'Bonbonnière' and produced there *Les Deux Aveugles, Le Violoneux* and other works whose scope was confined by licence to no more than four speaking parts. In December he moved to the Théâtre des Jeunes Elèves in the Rue Choiseul and, under the name of Théâtre des Bouffes-Parisiens, proceeded to build its reputation and to entertain Paris with an ever-changing feast of humour, dance and song in such pieces as *Ba-ta-Clan* and *Tromb-al-Cazar*. Everything went his way and he gained much praise for encouraging young composers by a competition for setting a libretto called *Docteur Miracle* which was jointly won by Lecocq and Bizet.

Part of Offenbach's success was due to his collaboration with such up-and-coming writers as Meilhac, Halévy, Nuitter and Scribe; part through a bright young singing star he discovered called Hortense Schneider; part through the infectious tunefulness and gaiety of his rapidly written scores. There were anything from three to seven productions each year, many of which were exported straight to the London theatres as soon as they had made their mark in Paris, and Offenbach came over to conduct them in 1857. In 1858 came his first big success with the original two-act version of *Orphée aux Enfers* which gained such a bad reputation for its saucy dances and its biting satirical wit that lampooned many prominent figures of the day that everyone flocked to see it.

As a theatre director he was never successful, having no money sense and spending over-lavishly on costumes and sets. As a composer his reputation soared. Among the subsequent successes were *La Chanson de Fortunio; La Belle Hélène; La Vie Parisienne*; his greatest success of all *La Grande-Duchesse de Gérolstein* which gave Hortense Schneider her most celebrated part; *La Périchole; Les Brigands* and *Geneviève de Brabant* which took London by storm with its two Gendarmes and Emily Soldene in the title part. He visited London as a conductor again in 1866 and in 1870 on a private visit; made many trips to Vienna where the legend has it that he persuaded Johann Strauss to venture into operettas (and he certainly influenced many composers including Suppé); and in 1875 he made a disastrous trip to America where his diminutive and mild appearance and subdued orchestral concerts disappointed the Americans, while the long, tempestuous sea-voyage nearly killed him. He wrote a book about his

Offenbach by Gustave Doré.

experiences called *Notes d'un Musicien en Voyage* which was published in 1877. Like most light musicians Offenbach nourished an ambition to write and produce a grand opera. By now a sick man, soon to die of gout of the heart, he spent several months writing his *Les Contes d'Hoffmann* but he died before he could see it produced. It had 101 performances after its production in 1881. His widow died in 1887.

The musical world has been unstinting in its praise of Offenbach with praises like Rossini's 'the Mozart of the Champs-Elysées'. He is acknowledged as the father of operetta and influenced light opera all over the world, including Gilbert & Sullivan. And yet his works are comparatively neglected beyond a well-known half dozen or so. Even these are often unfaithfully produced and robbed of their true flavour. The satire and humour in many of his works lies in the librettos which, however, do not survive translation and have nothing in them as inspired or as memorable as Gilbert was to write for Sullivan. Offenbach was a much more confined writer than Sullivan, but achieved polish, an unmistakable style and a genuine vein of comic music by comparatively simple means. His best songs were either immensely vivacious patter songs or gracious and lightly sentimental waltzes like the famous 'Letter song' from *La Périchole*. In a world overwhelmingly committed to the heavily romantic in music, Offenbach's frivolous gaiety and sparse classical lines are savoured by a minority and much of his work stays unknown alongside most of the gems of the French *opéra comique* school.

Like many an opera composer he is best-remembered by his sparkling overtures, by a few isolated songs from the operettas, and certainly by one irrepressible can-can. There is certainly much to be explored and rediscovered in his non-theatrical writings but when we consider that he wrote almost a hundred operettas there is no question that these are curiously neglected though many of them are slight and insignificant. Of his ballets *Le Papillon* is remembered by one splendid waltz and has been revived, while his curiously theatrical 'cello music should certainly be explored. What is needed to successfully revive Offenbach is a writer who could refurbish the dated old librettos and a translator to put them into lifelike English. Then Offenbach's melodic gift may be given its full chance to flourish once again.

P.G.

ORFF, Carl
(b. Munich, 10 July 1895)

Carl Orff was born in Munich into a family with strong connections with the Bavarian Army. After normal schooling he went to the Akademie der Tonkust in 1913 having already had private lessons in playing the piano, the organ and the 'cello. Of an original turn of mind from his earliest days he was writing songs as a child and had his first story published in 1905. He didn't take kindly to instruction either as a composer or pianist and much preferred to improvise and to develop his musical ideas through imitation of earlier composers. There was plenty of music at home, the whole family being musical, and his mother helped him with his first songs. His first works were published when he was sixteen, all vocal. He always wrote prolifically and during the first half of 1911 set some fifty texts by various authors. In 1912 he completed his first full-scale choral work *Also sprach Zarathustra*. All this was before he had any proper academic training.

In 1913 he wrote an opera *Gisei, das Opfer* on a Japanese theme and the last of his immature compositions was an orchestral work, *Tanzende Faune*. By 1914 he was beginning to be influenced by Schoenberg but he was also indebted to Richard Strauss and he wrote works in the style of both of these composers. This phase passed and he began to feel that his future style might come from earlier models. From 1915 to 1917 he was gaining practical experience as repetiteur and conductor of the Munich Kammerspiele and developing a growing interest in the theatre. In 1917 he joined the Army and returned to the theatre in Mannheim and Darmstadt after the end of World War I. He wrote several suites of incidental music, found himself again much attracted by the writings of Richard Strauss and composed many more songs. But his music had still not found its future strong individuality.

One of the important turning points in his career came when he met Dorothee Günther with whom he founded, in 1924, the Günther Schule which taught gymnastic dancing. He was beginning to find his true aims in music – 'reviving the natural unity of music and movement . . . which arise from a single source'. From this point he maintained a strong interest in musical education, creating a whole new range of percussion instruments and working on his influential *Schulwerk* which was to be published in 1930. Here we find the germ of

Orff.

Orff's obsession with primitive and evocative rhythms. The other element of his work, its simple, formal melody, grew from a new interest in Monteverdi and adapting his stage works for the National Theatre of Mannheim. Choral works and songs written before 1930 all begin to show the characteristics of Orff's best-known works. In 1930 he went to Italy for further study of Monteverdi and the music of the Renaissance and on his return home at the end of the year he wrote *Catulli Carmina*, seven settings of Latin texts for unaccompanied choir, which was published in 1931. Another influence developed when he was appointed conductor of the Bach Society of Munich. Some imaginative stagings of Bach and Schütz led to him writing *Carmina Burana*, first performed in June 1937. At this point Orff said that he would willingly have all his previous works destroyed – 'With *Carmina Burana*, my collected works begin.'

Carmina Burana is the work the public knows and loves. It has all his trademarks. It is spiritually a work of the modern age yet its literary message is ages old. Its rhythmic and harmonic devices are traditional and yet made modern by the sheer animal vivacity and strength of the ostinato phrases, repetitive, motor rhythms; allying themselves both to ancient folk and modern jazz characteristics. Orff's music remains in the mind as being percussive, but his use of percussion varies from one bass drum in *Antigonae* to a battery of sound. The most insistent percussive effect is often supplied by the voices. An acquaintance with *Carmina Burana* leads to an instant appreciation of his operas *Der Mond* (1937/8) and *Die Kluge* (1941/2); less so to the other sections of the *Trionfi* – *Catulli Carmina* (1931) and *Trionfo di Afrodite* (1950/1) which are more refined. It must be remembered that *Carmina Burana* was designed to be seen as well as heard. Many of Orff's important mature works are not often performed and remain unrecorded, and a full appreciation has yet to come. The popularity of *Carmina Burana* and the practical effects of his *Schulwerk* are indications that, given the opportunity to hear them, Orff's works have potential appeal for a very wide and mixed audience.

P.G.

PAGANINI, Niccolò
(b. Genoa, 17 Oct 1782;
d. Nice, 27 May 1840)

In every age, there are certain men and women who become legends, because they seem to embody the dreams, or nightmares, of their contemporaries. Perhaps the most interesting are those who manage to embody both – like the god Dionysus, half miracle-worker, half demon. Niccolò Paganini is one of the few musicians to have occupied this dubious eminence.

He was born in Genoa in 1782. None of the reference books seem quite sure about his father's occupation, which is variously described as a packer and a negotiator of cargoes in the port. All that seems certain is that his fortunes fluctuated between poverty and relative affluence, and that he played the mandoline. Paganini's mother had a dream in which an angel told her that her unborn child would be the world's greatest violinist, and the father took this sufficiently seriously to make the child begin practising the fiddle as soon as he could hold it. The severity of the training undermined the child's health, but had turned him into a virtuoso by the time he was eleven. It was then that he gave his first public concert, during which he played his own variations on the French patriotic song *La Carmagnole* and aroused the audience to intense enthusiasm. Two years later, in 1795, he raised the money for a journey to Parma with a benefit concert, and presented himself at the house of the celebrated teacher and composer Signor Rollo. The story has it that Rollo told his wife to say he was ill in bed. Paganini and his father were left in the study, where Rollo's violin, and his latest composition, lay on the table. Paganini's father told the boy to play it at sight. The amazed Rollo sent out to ask the name of the professor he had just heard; when told it was a thirteen-year-old boy he said: 'I have nothing to teach him.' Nevertheless, he *did* teach him for a few months, before Paganini moved on to another famous teacher, Ghiretti. In his mid-teens he gave a number of concerts throughout Lombardy and Tuscany, and soon ceased to be poverty-stricken. But

success made him unstable; he began to gamble and drink so heavily that it seemed fairly certain that he would be dead before he was twenty. But when he was nineteen, a noble lady transported him off to her country estate and cared for him for the next three years. His health recovered and he spent the time practising the violin and inventing incredible new techniques. She also taught him something of the arts of love, for which he eventually became as famous as for his playing. Her name is still unknown.

When he was twenty-three, he resumed his concerts, and from this point onward, his life becomes an almost monotonous story of triumph. He became organiser of music at the court of Napoleon's sister, Elisa Bacciochi, in Lucca, as much for the opportunity for love affairs as for the meagre salary. He showed his virtuosity by writing a *Scène Amoureuse* for

Paganini. playing in the Tyrol.

two strings only, followed up by a *Military Sonata* for Napoleon on only one string. A warm friendship with Rossini gave both of them the opportunity to indulge their love of practical jokes and noisy misbehaviour. In 1824, these indulgences caused another breakdown in health. This may explain why, for the next four years, he remained faithful to the same woman, the singer Antonia Bianchi, who bore him a son to whom he remained passionately devoted. Antonia proved a virago and they separated in 1827. There followed triumphant tours in Austria, Germany and France, and in Westphalia he was made a baron. And by this time, he moved in an atmosphere of legend, which he may or may not have encouraged. It was widely believed that he had learned to play the violin during a long spell in prison for the murder of his mistress (the period in question was, in fact, the three years on the noble lady's estate). And almost equally persistent was the story that he had acquired his incredible virtuosity in a pact with the devil. His concert performances seemed to give substance to the story; his skill seemed more than human. And, of course, the legend produced an agreeable *frisson* in his breathless audiences. He seemed to be accompanied by a smell of brimstone. He helped Berlioz out of financial difficulties by commissioning a viola concerto – *Harold in Italy* – but never played it because there was not enough demand for sheer virtuosity in the soloist's part. And a tour of England, Ireland and Scotland was as wildly successful as everything else he undertook.

In the late 1830s, his health, and his luck, began to fail. He bought an estate near Parma, where he hoped to spend the rest of his life in peaceful retirement. His source of income was to be a Paris gambling casino where Paganini would occasionally give concerts. The casino failed to gain a licence, and Paganini lost a vast sum of money. He moved to Marseilles, then to Nice (an Italian possession at the time), where he finally succumbed to a disease of the larynx on the 27th May 1840. He spent his last hours improvising on the violin, and legend naturally asserts that it was the greatest performance of his whole life. Even after death, the legend continued to snowball; the church authorities refused to allow him to be buried in consecrated ground because he had not received final absolution. His body continued to be moved around from one churchyard to another until as late as 1926.

The only works by Paganini that the modern listener is likely to know are some caprices and the violin concertos – of the six only the first two are at all well known. The concertos are full of technical fireworks, but are thin in the kind of melodic invention we have become accustomed to expect in our romantic violin concertos. The Paganini theme best known to most music lovers is the one used as the basis of various sets of variations, by Brahms, Rachmaninov and Lutoslavski, and that gives a fairly accurate idea of the average Paganini tune – clever and impressive rather than beguiling. Yet if his compositions are flashy and rather shallow, his influence on the history of European violin playing remains incalculable. Inspired by the devil or not, he was a one-man revolution.

C.W.

PAISIELLO, Giovanni
(b. Taranto, 8 May 1740;
d. Naples, 5 June 1816)

Although his name features but rarely in the modern opera house or concert hall, Giovanni Paisiello was one of the most famous and the most successful of late 18th-century Italian composers. Born in Taranto in 1740, educated by the Jesuits and intended for the law, his precocious musical gifts led to his admittance to the Conservatorio di San' Onorio in Naples in 1754. There his teachers included the illustrious Durante. A preliminary preoccupation with church music was shelved on his discovery that his true métier was opera, largely but not exclusively *opera buffa*. After early successes in Parma, Bologna and Rome he settled down in Naples where his reputation soon rivalled that of such established masters as Piccini and Guglielmo. His renown spread throughout Europe and by 1776 he was in a position to turn down invitations from London and Paris in favour of the highly-paid Inspectorship of Italian opera at the court of Catherine the Great in St Petersburg. (Italian opera had been established there in 1734, sponsored by the Empress Anne.)

During the next eight years he revived earlier operas of his and produced a succession of major new works, including *Il re Teodoro* and *Il barbiere di Siviglia*. Although Beaumarchais's play had already been exploited by two other composers, Paisiello's version (1782) held the stage triumphantly for about thirty years until it was gradually superseded by Rossini's masterpiece. In 1784, he returned to Naples via Vienna, where he dedicated twelve symphonies to Joseph II, in order to become *maestro di capella* to Ferdinand IV. His position was brilliant, his prestige at its zenith, and it was during that halcyon period that he brought out *Pirro, Nina* and *La Molinara* (Beethoven based a set of piano variations on its aria, 'Nel cor più non mi sento'). In the volatile political situation in Naples at the turn of the century, Paisiello's opportunist manoeuvres were however ultimately to prove his undoing. His temporary Directorship of National Music under the Republic and the two years he spent in Paris as *Maître de Chapelle* to his admirer Napoleon (for whose Coronation he wrote the music) went against him on his return to Naples in 1804. Discredited, spitefully jealous of competition and growing out of date, his star had set.

Though his output included symphonies, harpsichord concertos, string quartets, cantatas, masses and a Passion, it was his hundred or so operas that his contemporaries valued so highly. They relished in particular his 'elegant and simple melodies' (Burney), his graceful powers of characterisation, the vividness of his scoring and his evolution of the elaborate ensemble finale. Yet despite those significant virtues, posterity has preferred the operas of Cimarosa or, in a wider European context, those of Mozart.

C.G.

PALESTRINA, Giovanni Pierluigi da
(b. Palestrina, *c.* 1525;
d. Rome, 2 Feb 1594)

Giovanni Pierluigi da Palestrina was born in 1525 or 1526 and takes his surname from the small hill-town near Rome in which he was born. He was a chorister at the Cathedral of Sant' Agapit, and in 1537, joined the choir school of Santa Maria Maggiore, Rome. He returned to Palestrina in the autumn of 1544 as *organista e maestro di canto* of the Cathedral, where he remained until 1551. He married Lucia Gori and received a substantial dowry; their two sons, Rodolfo and Angelo were born at this time. In 1551, Palestrina was appointed master of the *Capella Juliana*, the choir which sang the services at St Peter's; his motet *Ecce sacerdos magnus* dates from this time and was dedicated to Pope Julius. At his death in 1555, Pope Julius was succeeded by

Pope Marcellus who, voicing disapproval at the way in which the Good Friday services were sung, summoned his singers and decreed that the music 'must be sung in a fitting manner, with properly modulated voices, so that everything may be heard and understood'. Palestrina began work on a new Mass composed in this manner – the *Missa Papae Marcelli* – but the Pope did not live to hear it performed. His successor, Pope Paul IV, instigated a spirit of reform, and among these was his disapproval of married men singing the services. Palestrina left, and soon succeeded Orlando di Lasso as musical director of St John Lateran where he remained for the next five or so years, installing his son Rodolfo in the choir school. In 1561 he moved to Santa Maria Maggiore, and from 1565 to 1571 taught at the recently established Jesuit seminary in Rome.

He twice considered offers of employment outside Rome, one for the Emperor in 1568, and another for the Duke of Mantua in 1583, but declined them both. He did however compose a number of Mass settings for the Duke. In 1570 he was reinstated to his old appointment as director of the Julian choir – with increased salary. The plagues which swept Italy at this time claimed the lives of his wife and two sons. Palestrina decided to enter the priesthood, and was ordained priest *ad titulam magisterii Capelle Musices Basilice*. Shortly after taking up an appointment in a benefice belonging to the Cathedral of Ferrentina, Palestrina suddenly re-married and presumably renounced his religious vows. His second wife, Virginia Dormuli, was in possession of a modest fortune gained from a successful fur-trading company, and Palestrina is known to have taken an active part in the running of the business, yet still managed to find time to compose regularly. The Masses *Assumpta est Maria* and *Ecce ego Joannes* were both composed at this time.

Palestrina's fame was by now widespread: his church compositions were heard in Munich under Lassus, and four madrigals were included in Yonge's *Musica Transalpina* issued in England in 1588. The composer's later years were spent in complete financial security (Pope Clement VIII ensured that he was adequately reimbursed for his services) and he eventually contemplated retirement to his native town. His relative and pupil Giovanni Veccia was organist and choirmaster there until his death in 1593 when Palestrina agreed to take temporary charge. As he pre-

Palestrina, 1578, engraving by Ghezzi.

pared to leave Rome, in January 1594, he was taken ill, and on the 2nd February he died. The funeral service, which included the singing of the response *Libera me*, was 'attended by a great number of musicians and others.' The coffin bore the inscription 'Princeps Musicae'.

Palestrina is regarded as one of the greatest composers of all time. He wrote predominantly for the Church, demonstrating a clear affinity with the Roman preference for *a capella* singing. It must be remembered that the style of performance in Palestrina's day would permit extensive ornamentation of the melodic lines – and examples of such *abbilmenti* have survived. It is generally thought that there is no instrumental music by Palestrina, but a set of keyboard *Ricercari* is extant. Although many of the works contained in the two books of madrigals may justly be compared with Lassus or de Monte, they are not important in the development of the form. In a dedicatory address to Pope Gregory in 1584, Palestrina apologised for the subject material of his secular madrigals.

Palestrina composed over one hundred Mass settings which may be divided into their respective compositional groups. The 'Parody' masses include *Veni Sponsa Christe* and the sublime *Assumpta est Maria*, perhaps the finest of all his masses, especially notable for its qualities of vocal 'orchestration'. There are thirty-four paraphrase Masses and eight which use 'cantus firmus' technique (for example, the first of the two settings of *L'Homme armé*). Five Masses are canonic throughout, the *Missa ad Fugam* (published in the Second Book of Masses, 1567) demonstrates his flawless contrapuntal mastery. The 'free Masses' include the *Missa Papae Marcelli* and the *Missa Brevis* which was very popular in Palestrina's own lifetime, and still is. The motets are remarkable for their range of expression; the Easter motet *Sicut cervus* contains folk-like, almost madrigalian features, which contrasts sharply with the deeply moving penitential *Super fluma Babylonis*. Particularly notable is the great six-part Pentecostal motet *Dum Complerentur* a work of resounding festive brilliance. The *Stabat Mater* (1589/90) for double choir, is one of Palestrina's finest compositions; in its use of antiphony, the work reflects Venetian influences. Written for the Papal choir, the *Stabat Mater* was sung every year at High Mass on Palm Sunday. It was known in England in the late 18th century in an edition by Dr Charles Burney, and was later taken up by Samuel Wesley. Richard Wagner, who admired the 'sublimity, richness, and indescribable depth of expression' of Palestrina's music, published an edition of the *Stabat Mater* in 1877.

Dr Burney, in his *General History of Music*, observes that 'In a general *History of Ancient Poetry*, Homer would doubtless occupy the most ample and honourable place; and Palestrina, the Homer of the most *Ancient Music* that has been preserved, merits all the reverence and attention which it is in a musical historian's power to bestow.'

G.G.

PFITZNER, Hans
(b. Moscow, 5 May 1869;
d. Salzburg, 22 May 1949)

In Germanic countries Pfitzner is regarded as a figure ranking in importance not far below Richard Strauss. People who have seen his opera *Palestrina* speak of it with genuine enthusiasm. But outside Germany and Austria Pfitzner remains an almost unknown quantity. True, we hear an occasional broadcast of one or the other of his many works yet without receiving a lasting impression; and Pfitzner has never figured in our public orchestral concerts. You may say that, being too narrowly German in spirit, his music is not for export. Even in his own country he now appears, for all his great name and reputation, a somewhat neglected composer. It may be that in marked contrast to the extraversion and hedonism of his rival Strauss, the Nordic austerity and reticence, the introversion and ultimately the pessimism of much of Pfitzner's music militate against its wider acceptance. Yet musicians who have seriously studied his work agree that within his limitations Pfitzner is an inspired and to some extent an original creator endowed with a sovereign technical command.

Hans Pfitzner comes of a musical family. Both his grandfather and father were professional musicians, the latter a violinist who worked for some time in Moscow where Pfitzner was born in 1869. In 1872 the family returned to Germany, and Pfitzner entered the Hoch'sche Conservatoire in Frankfurt. By the time he finished his studies (1890) he had already a small number of substantial works to his name such as the fine 'Cello Sonata Op. 1 and incidental music for Ibsen's *Feast on Solhaug* which marks the threshold to his maturity. His first opera was the Wagnerian music drama, *Der arme Heinrich*, and to achieve a performance of it Pfitzner accepted the post of an unpaid conductor at the Mainz Theatre where it was given in 1899. In his second opera, *Die Rose vom Liebesgarten*, subtitled 'A romantic opera' (Elberfeld, 1901), he began to come away from the Wagnerian leitmotive technique and altogether aimed at more sustained lyrical writing. In 1899 he eloped with Mimi Kwast, the daughter of his Frankfurt piano teacher, and married her, much against her father's will, in Canterbury. In 1906 Pfitzner became conductor of the renowned Kaim Orchester in Munich where he wrote the music for a play, *Das Christelflein* (1906) which in 1917 he turned into a two-act comic opera. Pfitzner's most important appointment was at Strasbourg (1910–18) where he was director of both the opera and the conservatoire and conductor of the symphony concerts. It was at Strasbourg that Pfitzner wrote his operatic masterpiece, *Palestrina* (Munich, 1917) which he called 'A musical legend' and which in Germany ranks in importance next to Wagner's *The Mastersingers*. In the period after World

War I Pfitzner was Professor of Composition in Berlin and, later, Munich where he composed his great cantata, *Von deutscher Seele* (1922), to verses by Eichendorff, a German romantic poet whose imagery struck a deep chord in the composer's artistic personality. The death of his wife (1926) resulted in a four-year-long interruption of his creative activity. In the ensuing period Pfitzner produced a number of instrumental works and his last opera, *Das Herz: A Drama for Music* (Munich, 1931). Though an ardent nationalist, he was at loggerheads with the Nazi regime and for a long time was ostracised by it. Pfitzner died at Salzburg in 1949. At the instigation of the Vienna Philharmonic Orchestra he was buried in the Vienna Zentralfriedhof.

Pfitzner called himself the 'last romantic' standing at the end of the line Schumann–Brahms–Wagner. This statement is not entirely true, for technically he pointed to the future as in the floating tonality and the linear counterpoint of his later works, a parallel case to the late Mahler. But he expressed a profound longing for Germany's romantic past and, as already indicated, much of his music is permeated by a pessimism perhaps not surprising in a composer who was so deeply steeped in Schopenhauer. Significantly, a quotation from Schopenhauer heads the score of his *Palestrina* which is an expression of Pfitzner's pessimistic view of life and is at the same time an autobiographical work. Compared with *The Mastersingers*, 'the apotheosis of the new' in *Palestrina* 'everything inclines to the past, there reigns in it compassion with death', Pfitzner said. As to its autobiographical character, just as Palestrina was the last great master of polyphony before the advent of monody, so Pfitzner regarded himself as the last great composer to defend the tonal heritage against the iconoclasts of the 1920s and 1930s. Like *The Mastersingers* and Hindemith's *Mathis der Maler*, Pfitzner's opera is an artist's drama showing him in his spiritual isolation and idealism (Acts I and III) against the background of worldly intrigues and cabals (Act II). The text, which treats the historical events in a free manner, is Pfitzner's own and is of a literary quality acclaimed by even so critical a judge of the German language as Thomas Mann. Pfitzner believed that opera was his chief domain. This is not quite the case since he also cultivated virtually every genre of instrumental and choral music and wrote some 150-odd songs. He was not a born opera composer like Wagner and Strauss, because in his stage-works the inner drama fails to be sufficiently strongly and effectively exteriorised. It is states of mood rather than conflict of characters that the composer projects.

Pfitzner strongly believed in the primacy of the *Einfall*, the inspired musical idea from which the whole work has to grow, be it a short song or a whole operatic act. Hence his emphasis on pure melody which, he felt, tends to be destroyed or at any rate suffer through the application of Wagner's leitmotive technique. Also in his instrumental works there is an abundance of sustained lyrical writing which is not confined to the slow movements only; his often dense contrapuntal thinking – the 'Gothic' element in Pfitzner's style – somehow impairs the effect of his melody.

Pfitzner was a fertile and brilliant essayist and engaged in fierce polemics with some of his German contemporaries, such as Busoni, against whom he wrote his pamphlet *Futuristengefahr* (1917), and the music critic, Paul Bekker, whom he castigated for the cerebral element of his Beethoven book in *The New Aesthetic of the Musical Importence* (1919). Berg wrote an elegant and caustically satirical reply to it in his *The Musical Impotence of the 'New Aesthetic' of Hans Pfitzner*.

Mos.C.

PONCHIELLI, Amilcare
(b. Paderno Fasolaro, Cremona, 1 Sept 1834; d. Milan, 17 Jan 1886)

Providence and musicologists alike have dealt unkindly with Amilcare Ponchielli, the former by allowing him to be born only five years before Verdi launched his first opera and then to die before the première of the older composer's *Otello*, the latter by consistently sneering at his one resounding success, *La Gioconda*. Overshadowed by Verdi throughout his lifetime, he was eclipsed a few years after his death by one of his own pupils, Puccini. It would be wrong to dismiss Ponchielli, however, for the popularity of *La Gioconda* is assured so long as there are singers to do justice to its flamboyant arias and audiences who appreciate a powerful melodrama that is expertly tailored.

The son of a small shopkeeper, Ponchielli grew up in humiliating poverty and it was only thanks to the remarkable talent he showed as

a boy that he was able to study at the Milan Conservatoire from the age of nine. His first opera, *I promessi sposi*, based on Manzoni's celebrated novel, was performed when he was twenty-two in Cremona, where it was enthusiastically received as the work of a local organist. It opened no doors for the ambitious composer, however, who moved on to become bandmaster in Piacenza, a form of drudgery relieved only temporarily by the local success of his second opera, *Roderico*, in 1863. Fortune smiled on him at last in 1872, when he was commissioned to write an opera for the opening of the Teatro dal Verme in Milan. He offered a drastically revised version of *I promessi sposi* for the occasion and was rewarded with immediate success and the request to compose a ballet for La Scala, which led to his opera *I Lituana* being staged there in 1874.

Ponchielli reached the peak of his career in 1876 when *La Gioconda* was premièred at La Scala, its libretto the work of the distinguished composer and poet Arrigo Boito after Victor Hugo's play *Angelo, tyran de Padoue*. Its plot, set in 17th-century Venice, concerns the rivalry of two women in love with the same man which is complicated by the machinations of a spy of the Inquisition. Ponchielli, who sought only popular and commercial success, wisely ignored the literary pretensions of the libretto and provided music which compensated in vigorous lyrical abandon for its lack of subtlety. Successive generations of the world's finest singers have been attracted by the rewarding music of its five main roles. *La Gioconda* swept triumphantly round the world within a few years and is still immensely popular in Italy and the United States. The composer's eight other operas, like his sacred works and the cantatas in memory of Donizetti and Garibaldi, have passed into oblivion. During the last ten years of his life he rested on the laurels of *La Gioconda* and filled the posts of *maestro di cappella* of Bergamo Cathedral and Professor of Composition at the Milan Conservatoire.

F.G.B.

POULENC, Francis
(b. Paris, 7 Jan 1899; d. Paris, 30 Jan 1963)

Poulenc was the son of a father with big interests in chemical products and a music-loving mother, who gave him his first piano lessons. His father, whose family came from the southern department of Aveyron, was a devout Catholic, while his wholly Parisian mother had less interest in religious matters. She came of a family which had been noted cabinet-makers, or *ébénistes*. At the age of fifteen the boy had made such progress as a pianist that, while still at the Lycée Condorcet, he started piano lessons with Ricardo Viñes, the Spanish-born pianist who did much to make Debussy's piano works known and was regarded as their ideal interpreter. A year later, in 1916, the young Poulenc met Erik Satie and his own contemporary Georges Auric, whose astonishingly wide culture made a great impression on him. Satie's *Parade* (1917) was the beginning of a friendship later to be interrupted, and in December Poulenc's own *Rhapsodie nègre* made him known overnight in smart avant-garde circles, musical and social. In the same year he met Honegger, Durey and Tailleferre who with Milhaud – then in Brazil with Claudel – were to form the so-called 'Groupe des Six'. Meanwhile Poulenc was aware of lacking the formal musical training provided by the Conservatoire, and approached Paul Dukas in the hope of receiving lessons from him. In this he was disappointed, and when a further attempt to find a master failed ignominiously (he was virtually shown the door by Paul Vidal to whom he had submitted his *Rhapsodie nègre*) Poulenc took Satie's advice and decided to dispense with formal education for the time being.

Meanwhile he was called up in 1918 and spent the months from July to October on the Vosges front, where he composed *Mouvements perpetuels* for piano, and a year later the settings of poems from Guillaume Apollinaire's *Bestiaire*. Although he was not demobilised until 1921, his work at the Air Ministry allowed him time to compose (settings of Jean Cocteau's *Cocardes* date from this period) and to lead the social life which he enjoyed in Paris. Between 1921 and 1924 he had lessons with Charles Koechlin, an original composer ideally suited to guide rather than instruct a fellow-artist of Poulenc's temperament and gifts. His musical horizons were widened at the same time by a visit with Milhaud to Vienna, with the express purpose of meeting Schoenberg, Berg and Webern. On his return his position as a composer was finally established by the ballet which Diaghilev commissioned from him in collaboration with the painter Marie Laurencin (*Les Biches*, 1924) and it was at this time that a perspica-cious critic, Roland-Manuel, neatly summed up Poulenc's music as 'sometimes verging on triviality but never falling into vulgarity'. This is a good description of the *Chansons gaillardes* which had their first performance, with a new trio for oboe, bassoon and pianoforte, in May 1926. The singer on that occasion was Pierre Bernac, but it was another nine years before Bernac became the singer for whom Poulenc was to compose all his songs. In the meanwhile his harpsichord *Concert champêtre* (1929) was written for Wanda Landowska; and three years later the cantata *Bal masqué* (to a text by Max Jacob) and the Concerto for Two Pianos were commissioned by the Noailles and Princesse de Polignac respectively. Poulenc was in fact not only welcomed by the French *haut monde* for his wit, his gifts and his droll appearance (Cocteau compared him to a young dog) but had himself bought an attractive house, 'Le Grand Coteau' at Noizay in Touraine. After his father's death in 1917 his religious promptings and practice had declined, but in 1936 a visit to the shrine of Notre Dame de Rocmadour undertaken by chance at the same time as the sudden death of his friend Octave Ferround (biographer of Florent Schmitt) brought about a strong reversion in his religious attitudes reflected in the unaccompanied *Litanies à la Vierge Noire de Rocmadour* (1936), a Mass in G major (1937) and the *Quatre Motets pour un temps de pénitence* (1939), to which should perhaps be added the Organ Concerto (1938). The religious vein was to recur, formally or informally, throughout the rest of Poulenc's life; and between this and his strong appetite for the pleasures and amusements of the world as between two poles, his art, like his life, developed. He described his Catholic faith as 'that of a country priest', no doubt something of an exaggeration in so sophisticated and characteristic a Parisian. One of his friends described his personality as '*moitié moine, moitié voyou*' (half monk, half guttersnipe), which is nearer the mark and answers well to his physical appearance.

The revivifying of Poulenc's religious faith was reflected not only in his setting of overtly religious texts. After Apollinaire and Jacob it was Paul Eluard whose poems most appealed to him and the nine songs of *Tel jour telle nuit* (1937) mark a new and more serious departure in his song-writing. The sinister and doom-laden atmosphere of the years immediately preceding the outbreak of war in September 1939 clearly marks much of this music, but

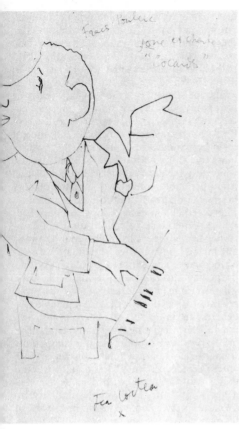

Poulenc by Cocteau.

that Poulenc's high-spirited and witty other side remained unimpaired is shown by the Vilmorin settings *Fiançailles pour rire* (1939), *Banalités* (Apollinaire, 1940) and *Chansons villageoises* (Fombeure, 1942), with orchestral accompaniment. The two Aragon settings (*Deux Poèmes*, 1943) include the 'C' which is perhaps one of Poulenc's finest and most characteristic songs. His collaboration with Pierre Bernac, begun in 1935, no doubt occasioned and determined the character of many of these songs, which are as it were 'tailored' for Bernac's light, flexible high baritone voice, sensitive musicianship and, perhaps most important of all, that sense of humour and of the ridiculous which he shared with the composer. The last and most tragic of Poulenc's works prompted by the war and the German occupation of France, *La Figure Humaine* (text by Eluard), though written in 1943, had its first performance in London in

1945, when it was given by the BBC Singers under Leslie Woodgate. In a totally different mood, and the extreme expression of the composer's joker-nature, was his first attempt at opera, *Les Mamelles de Tirésias*, based on Apollinaire and first given at the Opéra-Comique on the 3rd June 1947. This outdoes both Offenbach and Satie in its farcical fancifulness and desire to *épater le bourgeois*. It is characteristic of both the man and the work that the singer he chose for the main role of Thérèse, Denise Duval, had in fact been performing at the Folies Bergère, though in the event she was to show herself capable of very different roles from the hilarious one of Thérèse.

In 1949 and again in 1952 Poulenc visited the USA with Bernac, and in 1950 the Boston Symphony Orchestra commissioned a piano concerto from him. The speed and ease with which Poulenc wrote, his remarkable adaptability and chameleon-like versatility, made it inevitable that even his best music should be marked by spontaneity and individuality of invention rather than by a uniformly high standard. As a composer he could, to quote Oscar Wilde's words in another context, resist anything but temptation, and in his case it was his natural facility against which he seemed helpless. A song-cycle *La Fraîcheur et le feu* and a setting of the *Stabat Mater*, first given at Salzburg in 1951, are among the most carefully worked and finest productions of these years, when he was at the height of his powers. The subject of his one serious opera, *Dialogue des Carmélites*, was suggested to him by Ricordi and the work had its first performance on the 26th January 1957 at La Scala, Milan. Bernanos based his work on a German original, Gertrud von Lefort's *Die Letzte am Schafott*, and Poulenc found an easy and effective style in which to carry forward without monotony the scenes of convent life; and the final scene, in which the nuns walk in procession to the guillotine chanting the 'Salve Regina', has undeniable dramatic force. As a whole, however, the music fails to maintain the emotional tension and to communicate the full moral significance of the issues involved, and Poulenc seems too easily satisfied with that overall rhythmic pattern of two bar repetitions which was the bane of French music. After the opera Poulenc's one major work was the setting of Cocteau's *La Voix Humaine*, a dramatic work for a single singer and brilliantly interpreted by Denise Duval, who was also the composer's ideal interpreter of the part of Blanche de la Force when *Dialogues* was given in Paris. His final works were *Sept Répons des ténèbres* and two sonatas – one for oboe in memory of Prokofiev and the other for clarinet in memory of Honegger. His own death took place suddenly and without any previous warning in Paris on the 30th January 1963. He will be remembered as a master in music of that *esprit gaulois* that he so much admired in Chabrier's music; for the high spirits and charm of his piano music and many songs; and for the touching innocence and genuine simplicity of his best religious music.

M.C.

PROKOFIEV, Sergei
(b. Sontzovka, 23 April 1891;
d. Moscow, 7 March 1953)

Sergei Prokofiev is one of the most attractive and interesting figures in 20th-century music. This is not simply because he was one of the few outstanding creative musicians to combine a genuinely modern idiom with a strong and individual melodic impulse, but also because he achieved this synthesis with a minimum of artistic or intellectual posturing, with wit and humanity and without false pathos. Above all he seems to have possessed an innate musicality greater than any composer of his time or since, with the possible exception of Britten. Twentieth-century music has been so full of attitudes, so self-conscious, so often a vehicle for ideas, feelings and manifestos which themselves have nothing to do with music, that it is peculiarly refreshing and reassuring to come back to a composer who wrote music simply out of an instinctive and irrepressible feeling for that medium.

Prokofiev was born at Sontzovka in the Ukraine. His parents were well off, his father being a successful business man and his mother an accomplished amateur pianist, and the boy seems to have enjoyed an untroubled and exceptionally active childhood. In music, he was a child prodigy. He wrote his first music at the age of five, and his first opera at nine, by which time he was also showing outstanding talent as a pianist. At thirteen he entered the St Petersburg Conservatory, studying composition with Rimsky-Korsakov, Tcherepnin and Liadov and piano with Annette Essipov. He was to remain at the Conservatory until shortly before the outbreak of war in 1914. But long

before then he had become one of the best-known, not to say notorious, composers in Russia, and had firmly adopted a modernistic stance. His first two piano concertos (1912 and 1913 respectively) had been received with mixed feelings, the general view being that Prokofiev's talent was so obvious that one could only condone the more outrageous features of the music, its strange juxtapositions of keys, its pugnacious rhythms and violent melodic gymnastics. To us today the most remarkable thing about these 'student' works, which also include the First Piano Sonata and a number of other piano works, is their highly original and already well-formed personality. Like several composers of his generation Prokofiev seems to have arrived quite spontaneously at such ideas as multi-tonal harmony and melody, a percussive, rhythmic treatment of the piano, and ostinato ('motor') rhythms propelling the form as a whole. Naturally, when he came into contact with the new western music after the war these fashionable tendencies became even stronger in his own music. The interesting thing is that later on, in his Soviet period, when he was supposedly trying to get rid of such devices, they are still much in evidence, though less dominant. That they steadfastly refused to disappear is evidence, both of their quintessentiality to Prokofiev's style and, no less impressively, of his own basic artistic honesty.

At the outbreak of war in 1914 Prokofiev found himself in London, but he returned to Russia, there to work not on the war effort (from which he was exempted by being the only son of a widow) but on a ballet commission from Diaghilev, which was to produce Prokofiev's most aggressively modern score to date, the *Scythian Suite*. Diaghilev rejected that work, but later took up another ballet score of the same period, *Chout* (eventually staged by the Ballet Russe in May 1921). Other wartime works include the *Classical Symphony* (1917), Prokofiev's one and only flirtation with neo-classicism (again apparently quite spontaneous), the First Violin Concerto (1917) and the piano suite *Visions fugitives* (1915–17). In 1917 Prokofiev was still in Russia. In May of the following year, however, he embarked on his first US tour, perhaps scarcely dreaming that he would not see Russia again for nine years and not return

Prokofiev by Matisse, 1920.

there to live for fifteen. In America his success as a pianist was offset by the hostility created by his music, which was ironically enough regarded as a characteristic expression of Bolshevism. The opera, *The Love of Three Oranges*, commissioned by the Chicago Opera, was badly received in Chicago and New York in 1921–2, and the much more accessible Third Piano Concerto (completed in 1921) hardly fared better. But back in Europe in 1922 Prokofiev found himself more in tune with the fashionable music. At that period the Parisian vogue for Russian art was at its height, and Prokofiev responded by writing, for the only time in his life, music of self-conscious modernism. The spirit of alienation is dominant in his music of the 1920s, notably in the Second Symphony (1925), a work rather curiously modelled on Beethoven's C minor Piano Sonata, Op. 111, and in the ballet *Le Pas d'acier*, which deliberately and without irony equates Soviet life with the most avant-garde musical idiom. The Third Symphony (1928, but derived from the opera *The Fiery Angel*, completed the previous year) the Fourth Symphony (1930, from the ballet *The Prodigal Son* of 1928), and the Fourth and Fifth Piano Concertos (1931–2) are all extensions of this avant-garde phase. But there is already some evidence of mellowing. In *The Fiery Angel* expressionism frequently dissolves into lyricism, while in *The Prodigal Son* and the Fifth Concerto simplicity and clarity of texture and form begin to reassert themselves. By the time Prokofiev returned finally to Russia in 1934 (he had toured there in 1927) his idiom had already matured in a way which suited the artistic doctrine of socialist realism as applied to music in the 1930s.

That Prokofiev did not need to falsify his approach in the first instance is obvious from the quality of the music he wrote during his first fifteen years back in Russia. From this period date his three great film scores, *Lieutenant Kijé* (1934), *Alexander Nevsky* (1939, later adapted as a cantata), and *Ivan the Terrible* (1945), his two great classical ballets *Romeo and Juliet* (1936) and *Cinderella* (1944), the Second Violin Concerto (1935), *Peter and the Wolf* (1936), the Fifth Symphony (1944), the Sixth Symphony (1947), the Seventh, Eighth and Ninth Piano Sonatas (1942–7), the Second String Quartet (1941) and the opera *War and Peace* (1942). Most of these works are of a more popular cast than their predecessors, but for quality of invention and vitality of execution they have hardly been surpassed

in the 20th century. It seems reasonable to conclude that Prokofiev (unlike Shostakovich) relished the excuse to write simply and with the accent on melody and rhythm, his two master-cards. If so, then the artificiality we may discern in the more modernistic works of the 1920s is easier to understand and explain.

Even so, Prokofiev was doomed to fall foul of the regime. Along with several other major Soviet artists he was hauled up in front of Zhdanov's Central Committee in 1948 and accused of 'formalistic deviations and anti-democratic musical tendencies'. The Sixth Symphony and, after its production late in 1948, the opera *The Story of a Real Man*, were fiercely criticised. The composer seems at first to have behaved less submissively than his colleagues, but eventually, in failing health and clearly anxious for his own future, he wrote a letter admitting his mistakes and acknowledging the justice of the official criticism. His subsequent work nearly all betrays the anxiety of these final years. The Seventh Symphony (1952) is both less ambitious and less assured than its two immediate predecessors. And though Prokofiev was in due course restored to official favour, winning a Stalin Prize in 1951, his creative will seems to have been permanently undermined. He died only two years later on the 7th March 1953.

Seen as a whole Prokofiev's Soviet period stands out as an illustration of the possibilities of a vigorous and popular strain of modern music, and it is truly astonishing that the Soviet authorities should themselves have attacked this growth instead of publicising it as a demonstration of their theories. However, they were evidently disconcerted by lingering 'modernisms' in Prokofiev's style, by its distinctive and sometimes quirkish personality, and by its aggressive energy. For his part, Prokofiev clearly never quite understood what the official critics were getting at, and in the end ran for cover, like so many of his colleagues, by writing music which was nothing in particular and therefore (presumably) could not be 'wrong'. Until 1948 his music had the best possible qualities of a living popular art. Though melodious, it was never bland, and though always strongly rhythmic it was never crude or blatant. In form and texture it was much simpler than the work of his Parisian period, but this was certainly an improvement, Prokofiev being a true Russian composer to whom contrapuntal elaboration was essentially foreign and likely to produce a purely artificial complexity. Finally, Prokofiev had discarded an earlier tendency to overscore and moved on to a phase in which instrumentation precisely served the direct lyrical aims of the music. The scoring of works like *Romeo and Juliet* and the Fifth Symphony is as original in its way as Prokofiev's melodic and rhythmic idiom. And nobody who could write such music should have had to apologise for his art, either to progressive critics or to obscurantists.

S.W.

PUCCINI, Giacomo
(b. Lucca, 22 Dec 1858;
d. Brussels, 29 Nov 1924)

Puccini and his brother Michele, a singing teacher who died young, represent the fifth generation of a musical dynasty living and working at Lucca in Tuscany. All the previous Puccinis were, in the main, church composers and organists at Lucca's Cathedral San Martino. Giacomo, the fifth of seven children, was expected to follow in the footsteps of his forefathers and thus continue the long family tradition. A visit, however, to nearby Pisa in 1876 to see *Aida* revealed to him in a flash that his true vocation was for opera and opera only. He completed his studies at Lucca's Conservatorio Pacini in the summer of 1880 with a Mass, and then went to Milan, which on account of its renowned Teatro alla Scala was the Mecca for all budding opera composers. For three years (1880–3) Puccini continued his studies at the Conservatorio Reale under Bazzini and Ponchielli, the composer of the once famous *La Gioconda*, and wrote as a 'leaving exercise' an orchestral piece, *Capriccio sinfonico*, which achieved great success at its performance by the students' orchestra under Franco Faccio. It revealed two of Puccini's characteristic gifts – a marked sense of melody and colourful orchestration.

In the preceding April the music publishing firm of Edoardo Sonzogno announced the first of several competitions for a one-act opera (Mascagni's *Cavalleria Rusticana* was discovered in this way in 1889) and Puccini, then still a pupil of the Conservatorio, decided with Ponchielli's encouragement to take part in it. Ponchielli also found him a librettist, a young journalist named Ferdinando Fontana, who suggested to the young composer *Le Villi*

– the legend of brides, deserted by their lovers and turned into spectres, dancing the loved one to death. Such subjects were then in vogue in Italy in the wake of the German romantic operas of Weber, Marschner and the early Wagner. When the result of the competition was announced early in 1884, Puccini's name was not even mentioned. At a party at the home of a wealthy art-lover (Marco Sala) where Arrigo Boito (the librettist of Verdi's *Otello* and *Falstaff*) and other influential persons of the world of music and literature were present, Puccini was invited to play and sing from the opera at the piano and won such acclaim that it was decided to stage the work at the Teatro dal Verme where it was first given on the 31st May 1884, and achieved an immense success. The result was that the great Milanese music publisher, Giulio Ricordi, acquired the rights of *Le Villi* and on his advice Puccini expanded the opera into two acts. Furthermore, Ricordi commissioned from him a new opera, again with Fontana as the librettist. This marked the beginning of Puccini's life-long association with the House of Ricordi in whose head he found a fatherly friend and wise mentor. The new opera, *Edgar*, based on a turgid verse drama by Alfred de Musset and containing a Carmen-like character (Tigrana), was a subject wholly unsuited to Puccini's gifts. Its first performance (Milan, La Scala, 25th April 1889) was coolly received. Puccini compressed its four acts into three (Ferrara, 1892) and made further revision in 1901 and 1905, but the opera has not survived. In the composer's words it was a 'cantonata' – 'a blunder'. Into the time of work on *Edgar* falls the beginning of his association with Elvira Gemignani, the wife of a Lucchese wholesale merchant, who in 1886 bore him an only son, Antonio. Italy being then a rigidly Catholic country, a divorce was impossible, and it was not until the death of Elvira's husband in 1904 that the union could be legalised in church.

It was the world success of Massenet's *Manon* (Paris, 1884), based on the famous and largely autobiographical novel by the Abbé Prévost, which induced Puccini to choose the same subject for his next opera, *Manon Lescaut*. Its plot, the characters and the atmosphere, he felt, were eminently suited to his particular genius. The genesis of the libretto is a story by itself; suffice it to say that it was fashioned by no fewer than five different authors – first Leoncavallo, then Marco Praga and Domenico Oliva and finally Luigi Illica and Giuseppe Giacosa, with Ricordi advising them and Puccini controlling the whole operation. It was the first time that he took an active part in the shaping of a libretto which to him was as important as its musical setting. Because of its multiple paternity *Manon Lescaut* was published without the names of the librettists, surely a curiosity in operatic history. The first performance of the opera (Turin, 1 Feb 1893) in which Puccini speaks for the first time with his own individual voice, achieved a success such as he was never to repeat again with any of his subsequent and mature operas. Overnight his name was known all over Italy and beyond. After its first London production (1894) G. B. Shaw, then a music critic, wrote the prophetic words: 'Puccini looks to me more like the heir of Verdi than any of his rivals.' While still at work on the opera, Puccini acquired a house in 1891 in a simple village, Torre del Lago by the lake of Massaciuccoli near the Maremma. He chose it because it allowed him to indulge his love of

Tosca *by Erté.*

LA TOSCA

shooting waterfowl. With the exception of *Turandot*, all his other operas were composed at Torre del Lago.

For his next three operas which are Puccini's most popular stageworks – *La Bohème, Tosca* and *Madama Butterfly* – he had as librettists Illica and Giacosa. There was clear division of labour between the two. Illica would draw up the scenario and invent picturesque details while Giacosa would look after the poetic side and do the versification of the prose text. There were innumerable quarrels and clashes between them and Puccini, who was a hard taskmaster, with Giacosa threatening to resign a number of times. Yet, in the end, Puccini's will prevailed for he possessed a quite extraordinary sense of the stage and its imponderables and knew instinctively what would make an impact from the dramatic point of view. From a mere hint in Prévost's novel he developed the Embarkation scene of *Manon Lescaut*, a scene unique in all opera; he invented the spine-chilling man hunt in *La Fanciulla del West*, and created the character of the slave girl Liù and the scene of her suicide in *Turandot*. Added to this, there is his gift of inventing a liquescent, melting melody – the morbidezza of the typically Puccinian cantilena is irresistible in its effect; there is his magisterial treatment of the singing voice and there is his masterly exploitation of harmonic, rhythmic and orchestral devices. Technically he always kept abreast of the innovations of his time, with Wagner, Debussy and Stravinsky as his main guides. It is the accumulation of such gifts which makes Puccini the most important Italian opera composer since Verdi. The fact that nearly always his heroines are more important than his heroes (seven of his twelve stageworks are called after the name of the heroine) and that he treats them with a most subtly calculated mixture of true affection and refined sadism – all this may be traced to primitive drives and fantasies in his unconscious.

La Bohème (Turin, 1st February 1896) was at first not well received by the critics who had come expecting an opera in the rich romantic vein of *Manon Lescaut*, whereas the new work was for the most part in a light conversational style, touching on realism and displaying a quasi impressionist language in its harmonic and orchestral texture. For many musicians of today the opera ranks as the composer's masterpiece. *Tosca* (Rome, 14th January 1900) was Puccini's first excursion into pure *verismo* or realism, which was a short-lived movement in Italian opera initiated by *Cavalleria Rusticana* and Leoncavallo's *Pagliacci* as a reaction against the symbol-laden mythological music-drama of Wagner and taking its cue from the French realists (Zola, Merimée) and Bizet's *Carmen*. *Tosca* has recently been called a 'shabby little shocker'. The fact, however, remains that it is music theatre *par excellence* and that Puccini was able to pour an astonishing amount of sheer lyricism into Sardou's melodrama. In *Madama Butterfly* (Milan, 17th February 1904), based on David Belasco's one-act play after a magazine story by John Luther Long, which in its turn is based on a real incident, Puccini was most strongly attracted by the character of the heroine – the very image of a typically Puccinian 'little woman' with most intense feeling; and the exotic atmosphere fascinated him. It is the first opera of his in which he used authentic (Japanese) folk tunes. The first performance at La Scala was a fiasco almost unique in the annals of opera and we are now certain that it

was engineered by Puccini's many rivals. But after a revision in which the second and final act was divided into two parts, with an interval between, and various other excisions and alterations, *Madama Butterfly* achieved an enormous success at Brescia a few months later (May 1904).

In January 1909 there occurred a tragedy in the Puccini household the consequences of which affected the composer to such an extent that for some time to come his creative power and desire to work was seriously impaired. Their maid, Doria, completely unnerved and made distraught by the persecution of Puccini's wife who suspected her, wrongly, of being the composer's mistress, committed suicide.

After his latest opera, Puccini wanted to turn his back on *tragédie larmoyante* and attempt something of a harder, more virile fibre such as he had done in *Tosca*. This he found in Belasco's Wild West melodrama, *The Girl of the Golden West*, which plays among the miners in the Californian gold rush round 1849. Its mixture of stark realism and sentimentality appealed to the composer, and since the opera takes place in America it was appro-

Puccini in his villa at Torre del Lago.

Scene from Puccini's Turandot, *by Steven Spurrier.*

priately first produced at the Metropolitan (New York, December 1910). Caruso and Destinn sang the leading roles and Toscanini conducted, and it was a *succès fou* with the public but not with the critics. In all technical respects, notably in its Debussian harmony and Straussian orchestration, the opera is a masterpiece in which Puccini also made pointed use of American and Red Indian tunes. But it lacks sufficient lyrical incandescence, which is probably the reason that outside Italy it has never established itself in the regular repertory.

Serious differences with Giulio Ricordi's son Tito, who after his father's death (1912) became head of the great publishing firm, was the chief reason for Puccini accepting the offer of two Viennese theatre directors to write an operetta for them. The first subject submitted to him he rejected out of hand, but another subject was turned into an acceptable libretto by Giuseppe Adami, a young playwright and the work was called *La Rondine* (*The Swallow*, Monte Carlo, 27th March 1917). The fact, however, that the libretto hovers uneasily be-

tween opera and operetta impeded Puccini's invention and with the exception of the waltz music in Act II, there is little in *La Rondine* to hold the attention. Yet perfectionist as he was, Puccini treated the score with the same technical excellence he displayed in his other operas. It is ironical that the least successful of the composer's mature works should have involved him in a big political scandal – by the time of its first production (in Monte Carlo) Italy was already fighting on the side of the Allies against the Central Powers – in which his patriotism was seriously questioned. Not only had he written what he called an 'Austrian opera'; he was also reported to have said that as far as he was concerned the Germans could not capture Paris too soon!

In the following *Trittico* (New York, 14th December 1918; Rome, 11th January 1919) Puccini adopted the scheme of the Parisian *Grand Guignol* in which on one evening a horrific episode was followed by a sentimental tragedy and ended with a comedy or farce. *Il Tabarro*, the first of Puccini's triptych, has a libretto adapted by Adami from Didier Gold's *La Houppelande*, while *Suor Angelica* and *Gianni Schicchi* have libretti by Giovacchino Forzano who developed the comedy from a few lines in Canto XXX of the *Inferno* in Dante's *Divina Commedia*. The most frequently played of these three one-act operas is *Gianni Schicchi* which displays a quite unsuspected *vis comica* in Puccini and provides a parallel with Verdi's *Falstaff*. Latterly *Il Tabarro* has come into its own, for it is most remarkable for its sombre atmosphere painting and concentrated drama. Occasional productions of the entire *Trittico*, as was always Puccini's wish, have proved the theatrical viability of his conception.

Puccini had now arrived at the point where he wanted 'tentar vie non battute' – 'to strike out on new paths' and the result of this change of direction was *Turandot* (Milan, 25th April 1926), after a fable of Carlo Gozzi adapted for him by Adami and Renato Simoni. This opera is indeed wholly different from all he had written before and represents his greatest masterpiece in which are combined the heroic (Turandot and Calaf), the lyrical–sentimental (Liù), the comic–grotesque (the three Masks who go back to the ancient *Commedia dell'arte*) and the exotic. Thus, the wide range and diversity of Puccini's operatic vision is defined at one end by *La Bohème*, and at the other by *Turandot*. Puccini, who in December 1921 moved from his beloved Torre del Lago to Viareggio, died of cancer of the throat on the 19th November 1924 leaving the last two scenes of the opera unfinished. They were completed from his sketches by Franco Alfano. At its first performance at La Scala conducted by Toscanini, the opera closed with the death of Liù which was as far as the composer had completed the work. The next evening it was played with Alfano's ending.

Mos.C.

PURCELL, Henry
(b. London, 1659;
.d. London, 21 Nov 1695)

In the second half of the 17th century, various members of the Purcell family became known for their musical abilities. At the first performance of William Davenant's representation, *The Siege of Rhodes* (1656), a 'Henry Persill' played Mustapha. It is uncertain whether this was the father or uncle of Henry Purcell the composer who was born in London in 1659. At an early age the young Henry became a chorister in the Chapel Royal; and this brought him under the care of Captain Henry Cooke, who had sung Solyman in *The Siege of Rhodes* and composed the music for two of the five entries. When Cooke died in 1672, his place was taken by Pelham Humphrey; but Humphrey himself died two years later at the early age of twenty-seven and was succeeded by John Blow. Cooke, Humphrey, and Blow – these were Purcell's masters. When Matthew Locke died in 1677, Purcell was appointed to his position in the Chapel Royal as composer in ordinary for the violins. Two years later he became organist of Westminster Abbey.

His compositions are numerous and include important works in every category of music practised in his time. He wrote 'welcome songs' for Charles II and James II, and odes for various occasions including Queen Mary's birthday and St Cecilia's Day; anthems, services, and miscellaneous vocal pieces with religious words; songs, duets, trios, and catches with secular words; sonatas for strings and keyboard, fantasias in three, four, five, six, and seven parts, and pieces for organ and for harpsichord. Of special interest is his music for theatre.

After the lean years of the Commonwealth, the London theatre scene burst into lively activity after the Restoration of Charles II. Important theatre patents were granted to Thomas Killigrew and Davenant; and when Purcell came of age (in 1680) Killigrew's company was active at Drury Lane and Davenant's company at Dorset Garden. Shortly afterwards the two companies united; but in 1695 the actor Thomas Betterton led a secessionist group of 'old stagers' from Drury Lane to the theatre in Lincoln's Inn Fields. It was here and in Dorset Garden that Purcell found a market for his talent as a composer of theatre music. His first essay in this direction was Nathaniel Lee's play *Theodosius* (Dorset Garden, 1680) for which he wrote 'several entertainments of singing'. The success of his incidental music was so pronounced that in the next sixteen years he wrote music for a further forty-three plays. Many of these enjoyed a continuing popularity and were revived from time to time, particularly *The Libertine Destroyed* (1692), *Oedipus* (1692), *The Old Bachelor* (1693), *Don Quixote* (1694), *Timon of Athens* (1694), and *Oroonoko* (1696). Some of this theatre music was published by Purcell's widow shortly after his death, in *A Collection of Ayres* (1697) and the two volumes of *Orpheus Britannicus* (1698 and 1702).

It seemed inevitable that sooner or later Purcell's talents would be deployed in the direction of 'opera', though at that moment no one in London can have been quite sure what that Italian term meant. Occasionally there were private performances of small-scale 'masques' that used music, singing and dancing; and some years previously Davenant had experimented with plays that were embellished by the addition of musical entertainments. Later on these came to be known as 'dramatic operas'.

About 1682 Blow composed a little masque called *Venus and Adonis*, which was played privately at Whitehall. It seems almost certain that Purcell attended a performance; and it certainly influenced him when a few years later he was invited by Josias Priest, who ran a boarding-school for 'gentlewomen' in Chelsea, to write an entertainment for performance there. The subject chosen was Dido and Aeneas; the libretto written by Nahum Tate; and, remembering that Priest was a dancing-master, Purcell supplied seventeen different dances for the girls. *Dido and Aeneas* was produced some time in 1689, shortly after the accession of William III and Mary. Though most of the performers are likely to have been amateurs, the collaboration of Purcell and Priest was considered so remarkable that they were immediately invited by Betterton to work on a professional production for Dorset Garden.

The Prophetess, or, The History of Dioclesian by John Fletcher was the play chosen for this purpose. Music was introduced at key dramatic points such as the celebration of Diocles's slaying of the Boar and his investment as Emperor; some special dances were featured – including a dance of Furies, a Chair Dance, a dance of Butterflies, and a Country Dance; and at the end of the play there was an entertainment in the form of a masque. None of the music was sung by any of the dramatis personae: so a double cast of players and singers had to be engaged. *The Prophetess* enjoyed a great success when produced at Dorset Garden in 1690; and Purcell's score was published later that year in a handsome folio volume.

The Prophetess was followed by *King Arthur*. This time Purcell collaborated with John Dryden, who some years previously had drafted a libretto for a dramatic opera and allowed Louis Grabu to make a separate setting of its allegorical prologue under the title of *Albion and Albanius* (1684). Dryden now offered Purcell the text of the dramatic opera proper. He seems to have been fully alive to Purcell's genius and even agreed to adapt his verses to meet the composer's wishes. An interesting feature of *King Arthur* (Dorset Garden, 1691) was the fact that two of the dramatis personae are singers, *viz.* Philidel, an Airy Spirit, and Grimbald, an Earthy Spirit. This helped to ease the transition on the stage from natural action to supernatural, and back again. Purcell's next dramatic opera, however, did not consolidate this advance.

The libretto of *The Fairy Queen*, which is anonymous, is thought to have been written by Elkanah Settle, who took the text of Shakespeare's *A Midsummer Night's Dream*, shortened it, and then introduced four separate entertainments of singing and dancing into Acts II, III, IV, and V. None of the dramatis personae were singers. There were more dances (ten in all) than there had been in *The Prophetess* or *King Arthur*. The production of *The Fairy Queen* was a magnificent one (Dorset Garden, 2nd May 1692); but it proved so expensive that the management was unable to consider mounting a new dramatic opera from Purcell and Priest for 1693. Instead, a revised version of *The Fairy Queen* was produced with alterations and additions. In 1695, at the time of the secession of Betterton and the 'old stagers', Purcell worked on

two new dramatic operas for the 'young stagers' at Drury Lane – *Bonduca* and *The Indian Queen*. At one time it was thought that a new musical score for *The Tempest* was by him and dated from this period; but modern scholarship has shown that it was probably written by John Weldon about 1710.

Purcell died on the 21st November 1695. Five days later he was buried in Westminster Abbey; and the music he had composed for Queen Mary's funeral the previous year was performed at his own funeral service. His comparatively early death – he was only thirty-six – caused widespread grief. The year after his death, his younger brother, Daniel, who had been the organist at Magdalen College, Oxford, for some years, had his first dramatic opera, *Cinthia and Endimion,* produced in London, and he became extremely active as a theatre composer during the next five years or so.

As for Henry Purcell, his reputation continued to flourish. In the years immediately following his death, *The Indian Queen* and *The Prophetess* were given at Drury Lane (or, occasionally, Dorset Garden). *King Arthur* was revived in 1698; but *The Fairy Queen* was no longer played, perhaps because of the mysterious disappearance of the theatre score (which fortunately reappeared over a century later). In 1700 Charles Gildon decided to adapt Shakespeare's *Measure for Measure* as a dramatic opera. Cuts were made in Acts I, II, III, and V for the insertion of musical entertainments (as in *The Fairy Queen*); but in this case the four entertainments were the three acts of *Dido and Aeneas* followed by its prologue. This strange gallimaufry was given at Lincoln's Inn Fields in 1700. Four years later Purcell's opera was rescued, revived independently as *The Masque of Aeneas and Dido*, and played as an afterpiece at the same theatre. By the end of the first decade of the 18th century the Purcell boom was beginning to fade. Public taste was beginning to veer towards the import of Italian *opera seria*, and the time was ripe for the advent of Handel.

E.W.W.

RACHMANINOV, Sergei

(b. Oneg, 1 April 1873;
d. Beverly Hills, 28 March 1943)

Sergei Vassilyevich Rachmaninov was born on the estate of Oneg in the province of Novgorod, between present-day Leningrad and

Moscow. His family was aristocratic and landowning: at the time of the future composer's birth, however, its fortunes were steadily declining. Indeed the situation was not unlike that described by Russian dramatists of the period. Decline was not resisted by prudent measures, and Sergei's father Vassili was extravagant, speculative and expensively amorous, though possessing considerable charm and, besides this, a notable talent as a pianist. The composer was the fifth of six children, and showed an early interest in the piano; the talent was doubtless inherited from his father, but it was his mother who was to nurture it. For when he was nine, the family estate had to be sold and his parents separated. As an aristocrat Sergei could not have taken up music professionally; now without property and expectations, living with his brothers and sisters with his mother in St Petersburg, he was launched upon a serious study of the subject.

In 1883 Rachmaninov entered the St Petersburg Conservatoire, where he studied harmony and impressed fellow-students with his gift of absolute pitch. He also accompanied his eldest sister, Helena, a promising singer who unfortunately died just at the start of her professional career; with her, he came to love the Tchaikovsky songs for which he played the piano parts. His maternal grandmother, now living with the family, took him to hear a good deal of music, often the choral singing of the St Petersburg churches; she also took the family each year, during the three months of summer vacation, to her country house on the banks of the River Volchov, near Lake Ilmen, not very far from their original home. A love of rivers and boats stayed with the composer for the rest of his life; when he was in his sixties, his favourite relaxation was that of touring the Lake of Lucerne in his speedboat.

In 1885 Rachmaninov entered the Moscow Conservatoire on the advice of his cousin, a gifted young pianist called Alexander Siloti who had studied with both Tchaikovsky and Liszt. Siloti recommended that Sergei should join the 'school' of another of his former teachers, Sverev, who actually took his pupils into his home and supervised them thoroughly. Rachmaninov, with two other boys, shared a bedroom and the use of the piano, taking it in turns to practise for three hours at a stretch. Sverev was a disciplinarian, but he had wide interests, encouraging his charges to discuss music and not merely play it, taking them regularly to the theatre (where he occu-

pied the best box) and allowing them to mix with the artistic celebrities whom he invited to his house. The only omission in Rachmaninov's curriculum of work was composition: in spite of his brilliant powers of improvisation, it does not appear to have occurred to Sverev that he should receive serious training in the creative side of music. However a meeting with a harmony teacher during a holiday with Sverev led him to a swift mastery of elementary techniques and qualified him to enter Arensky's advanced harmony and composition class at the Conservatoire. His progress there was rapid, and Sverev was so impressed with a piano Study in F sharp minor which the boy showed him that he took the manuscript to Tchaikovsky; the older composer started to take an interest in the boy and was instrumental in his being granted entry to the special composers' course. There his principal teacher of counterpoint was Taneyev, though studies with Arensky continued also.

A somewhat difficult period began at around this time. Taneyev's strict teaching was little to the young student's taste (where was the heart and inspiration in all this paperwork?) and he grew restive under Sverev's kindly but somewhat authoritarian rule. In 1889 he asked Sverev if he could have a room of his own with a hired piano for his exclusive use; the older man took offence and in the end Rachmaninov left his house and moved in with a fellow-student from the Conservatoire. He decided to hurry the remainder of his course there and asked for permission to sit the final piano examination a year ahead of time; he was allowed to do this, played movements from Beethoven's *Waldstein* and Chopin's B minor Sonatas, and passed with honours. He still had to finish his course in composition, however, and a bad bout of malaria weakened his health for over a year. Still, he managed also to take his final composition examination early and gained a Gold Medal with a symphony, a one-act opera and some songs. Old Sverev was delighted to see his former student gain the highest award Russia's academic musical world could offer; all quarrels forgotten, he gave Rachmaninov his prized gold watch, a memento which the composer carried with him thereafter.

It was now 1892. As well as the works already mentioned, Rachmaninov had also composed his First Piano Concerto, in F sharp minor, though he was to revise this later, in 1917. The year 1892 also saw the composition of the group of Five Pieces, Op. 3, dedicated to Arensky, which include the celebrated piano Prelude in C sharp minor and the lively *Polichinelle*. He was lucky in finding a publisher, Gutheil, who evidently accepted the early works of the young composer because he felt that this talent would develop into the finest since Tchaikovsky's. The one-act opera, *Aleko*, was performed in Moscow in 1893 and made a considerable impression (several arias were encored) and at the same time Rachmaninov began appearing as a pianist. This was also the time of the First Suite for Two Pianos, dedicated to Tchaikovsky; the composer's death in 1893 grieved and shocked him, and an *Elegiac Trio* in D minor was immediately written in his memory.

But isolated successes did not bring much in the way of regular income. He undertook some routine playing as an accompanist, little to his taste; teaching, of which he did a fair amount, suited him even less. He was now composing a new symphony: for two years or so he worked at the score, sometimes with fervour and yet at other times with self-doubt. He submitted it to the Society of Russian Symphony Concerts in St Petersburg, and it was performed there on the 27th March 1897 under Glazunov's baton. It was a disastrous failure; the twenty-three-year-old composer recognised that it had been poorly conducted, but he knew also that the work itself was less than adequate. Later he said: 'Its defects were revealed to me with a terrible distinctness . . . something within me snapped and all my self-confidence collapsed. When the indescribable torture of the performance finally ended, I was a different man.' He did not publish the symphony and even destroyed the manuscript. (It was not heard again until 1945, after reconstruction from the orchestral parts and piano reduction.) The music now hardly seems to deserve the scorn poured upon it by its first critics; perhaps the performance was truly very bad. Months went by without his recovering fully from this psychological blow; during this time he sought refuge with his family. Then a wealthy friend came to the rescue with the offer of a second conductorship in a Moscow opera house. By 1898, having gained some useful experience there, he felt able to compose again and wrote a few songs and piano pieces. An invitation to London (perhaps thanks to Siloti, who had introduced his music to England) was a piece of good fortune; he appeared for the Philharmonic

Rachmaninov.

Society as composer, pianist and conductor, directing among other things his tone poem *The Rock* (1893) and playing his famous Prelude in C sharp minor. He was so successful that he was invited back for the 1899–1900 season, and he decided to write a new piano concerto for this tour.

Yet on his return to Russia he found his depression returning and work on the new concerto came to a halt. For three months in 1900 Rachmaninov went to a psychologist called Dr Dahl for treatment designed to restore his confidence. The doctor's suggestion – 'You will start writing, and the work will be excellent' – had its effect. The dedication of the work to 'Monsieur N. Dahl' was his reward. Another happy event was that Siloti agreed to give him financial support for two years so that he might devote himself to composition. Finally, on the 29th April 1902, Rachmaninov married Natalie Satin, to whom he was related on his father's side; the marriage was happy, blessed with children, and long-lasting: indeed his wife outlived him by some years.

For a while, Rachmaninov's career seemed steady and settled. He composed regularly if not prolifically, and further experience as an operatic conductor led him to write the operas called *The Miserly Knight* and *Francesca da*

Rimini, produced as a double bill in 1906. But it proved impossible to find sufficient time for composition in Moscow, where he was in constant demand as a conductor or pianist. He moved with his family to Dresden in Germany in late 1906, living there for two years and composing his Second Symphony, First Piano Sonata and the tone poem called *The Isle of the Dead*. He then returned to Moscow, but this was merely a stopping-place, since he had agreed to visit America and take part in twenty concerts there. He composed a Third Piano Concerto for this tour, arrived in the United States in the autumn of 1909 and played it twice in New York, on the second occasion under Mahler, whose musical insight and careful preparation of the score greatly impressed him. Returning to Russia in February 1910, he accepted the post of Vice-President of the Imperial Music Society, a body responsible for all higher musical education; he did important work in developing conservatoire teaching in provincial towns hitherto badly served. He conducted the Moscow Philharmonic Concerts from 1911 to 1914, and these years saw the composition of more piano music and songs as well as the choral work *The Bells*. More foreign travel, on concert tours or holidays, seems to have prepared him for his quarter-century of exile from Russia following upon the War and the 1917 Revolution.

In November 1917 Rachmaninov, with his family, left Russia for a Scandinavian tour; he carried only a little money and only such possessions as were portable, but he did not expect any early return to a country where his birth and upbringing made him a stranger to the new political system. Finding a home was difficult, but eventually Rachmaninov responded to repeated offers from America and sailed with his family for the New World on the 1st November 1918. Now came the years of concert playing, which were to continue with few interruptions until the time of his death in 1943. His repertory was not large by modern standards: he played relatively little music before Beethoven and little truly modern music. In fact he specialised in the kind of music that his audience wanted to hear, the romantics such as Chopin, Schumann and Liszt – and of course, his own music. He made many recordings, sometimes more than one version of the same piece: it is a thousand pities however that he was never asked to record substantial sets of his own music; say the Preludes or Études-Tableaux.

He did, fortunately, record all four of his piano concertos – the Fourth (1927, later revised) is an uneven work though by no means negligible – and his *Paganini Rhapsody* (1934). He also conducted recorded performances of his Third Symphony (1936) and *The Isle of the Dead*.

In 1931 Rachmaninov bought a house on Lake Lucerne in Switzerland and thenceforward he enjoyed some peaceful stays in Europe, delighting in the possession of a powerful car and speedboat. He often visited England and in 1932 was awarded the Royal Philharmonic Society's Gold Medal. In private he continued to send large sums of money to worthy causes in Russia; and he was greatly heartened when the Soviet authorities, having for many years considered his music 'bourgeois' and decadent, changed their minds in 1939 and invited him to send scores to Russia for performance. But gradually composition had become more difficult for him. He said as much to a friend: 'How can I compose without melody?'. It was cancer that struck him down finally: ignoring the symptoms of severe back pains, he continued to play in public. His last recital was in February 1943; on the 28th March he died, and was buried in the Kensico Cemetery near New York.

Rachmaninov's achievement is perhaps difficult to assess, in view of his popularity with the concert-going public on the one hand and his poor reputation with some critical writers on the other. He is the heir of Tchaikovsky, rather as Puccini is the heir of Verdi: a lesser figure in historical importance, doubtless, but an enormously attractive one whose personality is unmistakable and of unique value. Like Liszt, Rachmaninov has often been admired (and also disliked) for pieces which do not represent him at his deepest or most subtle. Not until his religious choral music (say the *Vesper Mass* of 1915) and his songs and purely orchestral works are more familiar will western critics be able to arrive at a balanced evaluation; but in the Soviet Union today he is regarded as a major composer whose achievement links the generation of Tchaikovsky with that of Prokofiev. Most of his music – for he was very self-critical and maintained a high standard – has an inner vitality and spontaneity that makes an immediate impact upon a receptive listener.

C.H.

RAMEAU, Jean-Philippe
(b. Dijon, 25 Sept 1683;
d. Paris, 12 Sept 1764)

Rameau was the seventh child of the eleven born to the church organist Jean Rameau and his wife Claudine (Demartinécourt) at Dijon. He was baptised on the 25th September 1683 and was therefore almost certainly born earlier that month. His father wanted him to be a lawyer, but the boy showed such aptitude when instructed by his father in keyboard playing and musical theory that he was allowed to leave the Jesuit College of Dijon with his education only half completed and despatched to find his own musical education in Italy. It seems that his school record was so poor that the Fathers were not sorry to lose him, and in an age when clarity of expression and a modest elegance of style were by no means rare, Rameau's use of the French language was to the end exceptionally clumsy.

In Italy he reached Milan but seems to have gone no further, and there is a story that he joined a troupe of travelling musicians as their first violin. He was almost certainly in France between 1698 and 1702, the year in which we next have definite information about him. That January he was made temporary organist at Avignon cathedral and in May of the same year he took a similar post at Clermont-Ferrand. By 1706 at the latest he was in Paris, almost certainly spending much time if not actually studying with the greatest French organist of the day, Louis Marchand, and acting as organist at two Paris churches. In the same year he competed for the organist's post at La Madeleine, but although successful appears never to have taken up the work. In this same year also appeared his first book of harpsichord pieces.

In fact Rameau in his youth seems to have found it difficult to put down his roots anywhere. In March 1709 he succeeded to his father's old post as organist in Dijon, but he did not remain there for the stipulated six years and in July 1713 he was at Lyon, organising the musical side of the town's celebrations of the Treaty of Utrecht. How long he was in Lyon, and exactly how he was employed, is uncertain; but when his *Traité de l'harmonie* was published in 1722, the author is described as cathedral organist at Clermont-Ferrand. There is a probably apocryphal story of the canons of Clermont refusing him permission to go to Paris as he wished, and his revenging himself on them by either absenting himself from offices where he was expected or 'pulling out all the most unpleasing stops and adding every imaginable discord'.

However that may be, Rameau was a man of nearly forty when he finally arrived in Paris, in either late 1722 or early 1723. The *Traité de l'harmonie*, followed in 1726 by his *Nouveau système de musique théorique* won him a reputation as a theoretician, but his second book of harpsichord pieces (1724) bears no address. All we know for certain of his activities is that he cooperated with a fellow Dijonnais in producing music for the entertainments at the big annual fairs where the French *opéra comique* originated. At the age of forty-two, in February 1726, he married a girl of nineteen, Marie-Louise Mangot. She belonged to a family of musicians from Lyon, and her father is described in her marriage settlement as 'symphoniste du roi'. In spite of the difference in age and Rameau's difficult character the marriage appears to have been successful, and his wife bore him two sons and two daughters.

Hitherto Rameau had composed harpsichord pieces and cantatas, but the *Traité* shows that he had already given his mind to the principles of dramatic composition. Prob-

Rameau, by Greuze.

ably through Piron he was introduced to a rich
and influential *fermier général*, or tax-
gatherer, who was also a considerable patron
of the arts. This was Le Riche de la
Pouplinière, at whose house Rameau met Voltaire on some occasion in the late 1720s and
there was a long-drawn-out but eventually
abortive attempt at collaboration in a 'sacred'
opera. In Voltaire's stead Rameau had
recourse to another librettist, the Abbé Pelle-
grin, an experienced writer for the theatre, and
their joint work, *Hippolyte et Aricie*, was given
privately at La Pouplinière's in March or
April 1733 and on the 1st October of the same
year a few days after Rameau's fiftieth birthday.

During the next thirty years Rameau produced some thirty pieces designed for the
theatre in one form or another. Many of these
were not operas in our sense of the word but
either a comédie-ballet like *La Princesse de
Navarre* (with Voltaire, 1745), pastorale
héroïque, ballet allégorique, ballet héroïque or
simply fête. These were often given their first
performances at Versailles or Fontainebleau.
The only ballet héroïque that has survived, because it contains some of Rameau's finest
music, is *Les Indes galantes* (Opéra, 1735). The
operas proper, which are entitled simply
tragédie, were all given at the Opéra, and the
greatest are *Castor et Pollux* (1737), *Dardanus*
(1739) and *Zoroastre* (1749). To these should
be added, if only for the quality of its music,
the comédie-ballet *Platée* (Versailles, 1745).
Rameau was not greatly interested in changing or developing the form of the *tragédie
lyrique* as he inherited it from Lully, its inventor who had died in 1687. He was concerned
first and last with music, and the moulds into
which it was cast were of quite secondary interest to him. In this he was the exact opposite
of Gluck, for whom the drama was of primary
importance; and it is the dramatic quality of
Gluck's masterpieces that have ensured their
performance up to the present day while
Rameau's, for all their superior musical interest, are seldom performed in France and virtually never elsewhere. Rameau's operas are
unmistakably court pieces and the drama is
repeatedly interrupted by ballets and other
divertissements which betray the French preference for spectacle to music proper. Even his
chamber music, contained in five 'concerts'
for harpsichord with violin or flute and viol or
second violin, betrays this need for extra-
musical interest by the titles frequently given
to the constituent movements, either 'por-

Décor for Act II of Rameau's Dardanus.

traits' like *La Pouplinière*, or dance pieces
(menuet or tambourin) and the same is true of
the harpsichord pieces, which contain a number of type-portraits such as *La Villageoise*,
La Joyeuse and *La Boiteuse*.

Beneath all this apparent frivolity or conventionality, however, Rameau remained a
powerful and essentially 'learned' composer, a
bold experimenter in harmony based on his
theoretical writings and a master of orchestration. It was in this light that he was seen by
his contemporaries, who found the orchestral
storm-pieces in his operas not only terrifying
but deafening and all his music alarmingly
complex and demanding, quite unlike the
charming dance-pieces, the ariettes and the
little programmatic works to which they were
accustomed. It is in the choruses of his operas
that Rameau showed most clearly his quality

as a musician, qualities which won him unique distinction among French composers of the 18th century. Rameau wrote nothing of importance between *Zoroastre* (1749) and his death in 1764. In his old age he seems to have been crotchety and mean, but much of the adverse comment on his character can be traced to Diderot's fascinating *Le Neveu de Rameau*, which is a novel and does not pretend to be a faithful portrait of the composer.

M.C.

RAVEL, Maurice
(b. Ciboure, 7 March 1875;
d. Paris, 28 Dec 1937)

This most quintessentially French of composers was of Swiss descent on his father's side and Basque on his mother's. Pierre-Joseph Ravel was an engineer involved in the construction of the Spanish railways when he met Marie Delouart in 1873 in Castile; they married in the following year and Maurice Ravel was born on the 7th March 1875 at Ciboure, now part of Saint-Jean-de-Luz on the Atlantic coast of France to the south of Bayonne. Three months later the family moved to Paris; a younger son, Edouard, was born in 1878. Both boys were musical, and their father encouraged their interest. Maurice began piano lessons in May 1882 with Henri Ghys, who wrote in his diary: 'Today I started teaching a young pupil, Maurice Ravel, who appears to be an intelligent boy. . . .' The Spanish lullabies which his mother sang attracted him more than the piano, however, and his father had to allow him fifty centimes for each half-hour spent usefully at the keyboard.

From 1887, Ravel studied harmony as well as the piano, and his first exercises in composition impressed his teacher by their spontaneity and originality. Then in 1889 he enrolled at the Paris Conservatoire, where his principal teachers were André Gédalge and Fauré: later he was to say that he owed them much, in technique and art respectively. He remained a student for some ten years. Even beyond that period he stayed within the academic framework in order to try and win the coveted Prix de Rome (gained previously by Berlioz, Bizet and Debussy among other distinguished names): he got as far as a second prize in 1901, but attempts in subsequent years were less successful. Finally in 1905 he was eliminated by the academic jury even before the final stage of the competition. By this time he had already composed his *Jeux*

d'Eau for piano, his String Quartet and the three songs with orchestra called *Shéhérazade*; he was recognised as an artist of distinction and several important musicians protested against the jury's humiliating decision. The Director of the Conservatoire resigned, and Fauré took his place. Ravel himself said little and hid whatever embarrassment and hurt he felt, going off with friends for a sailing trip in Holland. Significantly, though, he vehemently refused the Légion d'honneur decoration in 1920, even though his name had already appeared in the lists and its withdrawal caused something of a scandal. He seems to have agreed with Baudelaire that to accept honours is to recognise that the government has the right to judge you. But even as a young man he manifested a certain reserve, and this quasi-haughtiness of spirit prevented even his closest friends from becoming wholly intimate. He never married, and his inner emotional life has remained the secret that he evidently wished it to be.

Accordingly, any account of Ravel's life is to a large extent a list of external events. He remained very close to his parents and brother and was greatly saddened by their deaths in 1908 and 1917; even after that the family home was not broken up, and he lived for two further years with his brother. In the meantime, however, he had travelled, for he was not a stay-at-home. He worked with Stravinsky in Switzerland in 1913, on a commission from Diaghilev to revise Mussorgsky's unfinished opera *Khovanshchina*. And of course the war came in 1914; he tried to volunteer but his very light weight (about seven stones) disqualified him medically. In 1916, however, he went to the front at Verdun as a driver. 'I'm a peaceful person,' he wrote, 'I've never been brave – yet I'm eager to have adventures. . . . I ate a meal here with a family who have been evacuated and made paper hens and breadcrumb ducks for the kids. . . .'

It was an illness, dysentery, which brought him back to Paris in time to be with his mother when she died in January 1917. Though he had always been sensitive about his small stature, little over five feet, his health had been fairly good until now. But in the months after the war ended he suffered from insomnia and what he called nervous debility. The insomnia was to remain with him for the rest of his life. But his career went smoothly and well. He bought a small villa, Le Belvédère, at Montfort-l'Amaury about thirty miles to the south-west of Paris: it had one storey in front, facing a road which descended towards the little town, and three at the back, where the garden offered a magnificent view. Ravel furnished the rooms carefully and even painted some of the decorations himself; there were innumerable small ornaments and mechanical toys such as he lovingly collected and exhibited to friends, as well as the grand piano at which he composed. He travelled to Vienna, Stockholm and London in 1920–2, to Italy and Scandinavia and the United States in 1923–8. In October 1928 he received an honorary doctorate from Oxford University: a photograph taken on that occasion shows that the academic robes seem long for his diminutive figure. He was in demand everywhere (this was the year of the orchestral *Boléro* and its phenomenal success) and more concert tours followed: sometimes he played the piano, sometimes he conducted his music, fulfilling both roles with reasonable though not exceptional skill.

His health still gave him cause for anxiety, and because he slept badly he liked to take long nocturnal walks, or alternatively sit endlessly over coffee or wine in a café with congenial company. His appetite was good, though, both for gourmet and simple cooking, and he enjoyed smoking his favourite strong cigarettes, even slipping out of concerts for what he called a 'life-saving' puff or two. He liked swimming as well as walking, and his hair, although white towards the end of his life, remained quite thick and wavy. The first indication of serious illness came in 1933. He noticed while swimming at Saint-Jean-de-Luz that he could no longer perform certain movements. His doctor ordered rest; but gradually his powers of gesture and articulation became more affected, so that he found it difficult even to write. His intelligence remained clear, but physically he felt himself to be 'living in a fog'. He spent hours gazing out from his balcony at Montfort, and when he was asked what he was doing he replied simply, 'Waiting'. Friends tried to divert him with travel, but his disease steadily worsened. Sometimes, as on one occasion after hearing his own *Daphnis et Chloé* in July 1937, he was in tears: 'I've still so much music in my head.' Eventually an operation was decided on, and this was performed on the 19th December 1937. There was no sign of a brain tumour. He lingered on, unconscious save for a brief moment when he opened his eyes and called for his brother;

Ravel, by Benois, 1914.

Décor by Bakst for Act I of Ravel's ballet, Daphnis et Chloé.

finally death released him early on the 28th December.

'All music, after his, seems imperfect', wrote the critic Romain Rolland after Ravel's death. Yet the dazzling precision of the technique has sometimes given rise to an image of the composer as dandyish, ironical, dry and detached, artificial rather than warmly human. This is unfair. He himself said: 'Great music must always come from the heart. Music made only with technique and intellect is not worth the paper it is written on, for it loses its special quality as the expression of human feeling. Music should always be first emotional and only after that intellectual.' His technique was a means to an end, never an end in itself, and his music reveals all the passion and tenderness which he seemed able only cautiously to show in his personal life. Such a work as the ballet *Daphnis et Chloé* (1912) is beautiful by any standards with its shapely melody, harmonic

richness, rhythmic vitality and iridescent orchestral sound; but it is much more than this, stirring the emotions of a sympathetic listener to an almost unbearable degree. The humour, and the human warmth, of the songs and the two operas – *L'Heure espagnole* (1907) and *L'Enfant et les Sortilèges* (1925) – are a constant delight. But personal reactions to music must remain subjective. What can never be doubted is the presence in Ravel's art of a marvellous skill. It was Debussy who once said of him that he possessed 'the finest ear that ever existed'.

C.H.

REGER, Max
(b. Brand, 19 March 1873;
d. Leipzig, 11 May 1916)

The son of a teacher in Brand, Bavaria, Reger showed early musical promise and became a pupil of Hugo Riemann, first at Sonderhausen then at Wiesbaden. In 1901, already with copious compositions to his credit, he went to

Munich where he established himself as pianist, teacher and composer, although his music met with widespread critical opposition on account of its supposedly radical nature. In 1907 he became· a professor at the Leipzig Conservatory, a post he retained to the end of his life; and the list of his compositions in all genres grew longer by the day. In 1911 he was appointed Director of the court orchestra at Meiningen, but in 1914 he retired to the intellectual centre of Jena in order to devote himself to composition. He undermined his constitution through excessive indulgence in food and drink, and succumbed to a heart attack in a Leipzig hotel at the age of forty-three.

To describe Reger as a prolific composer would be an understatement: works for chorus, organ, piano, solo voice, solo instruments and the chamber medium all flowed from his pen in indiscriminate profusion. Only his organ music has remained permanently in the repertoire, although certain chamber, vocal and orchestral works are occasionally revived with some success. Reger was a German composer through and through and basically a traditionalist: he took his bearings from Bach and the Lutheran chorale, as the titles and textures of many of his most celebrated organ works made clear (*Fantasy and Fugue on B.A.C.H.*, numerous fantasies on chorales, two volumes of chorale preludes, the *Introduction, Passacaglia and Fugue* in E minor). He was not however a reactionary or conservative: like Schoenberg he took the labyrinthine chromatic entanglements of *Parsifal* a stage further, but his music never acquired that exclusively linear orientation which resulted elsewhere in the demolition of tonality. Indeed he was always rather furtively responsive to the essentially un-German blandishments of impressionist harmonic colour and timbre (e.g., in the orchestral *Vier Tondichtungen nach Böcklin*) although the absence of a genuinely lyrical impulse renders the effect of many a gargantuan harmonic–polyphonic complex null and void. Those who cannot adjust to the aggressive (and to some minds unpalatably oppressive) Teutonism of such a work as the *Variations and Fugue on a theme of Hiller* for orchestra – which features one of the most thrilling climaxes in the modern orchestral repertoire – are best directed to the many sets of charming songs and miniature piano pieces which disclose and unexpected vein of poetic sensitivity.

C.P.

RESPIGHI, Ottorino
(b. Bologna, 9 July 1879;
d. Rome, 18 April 1936)

Respighi was born in Bologna and studied there at the Liceo Musicale under Federico Sarti (violin and viola) and Guiseppe Martucci (composition). In 1900 he went to St Petersburg as first violist in the Opera orchestra, where he took lessons in composition and orchestration from Rimsky-Korsakov who was to prove a cardinal influence on the development of his musical personality. In 1902 he spent a period in Berlin working with Max Bruch, and in the same year his early Piano Concerto was performed in Bologna; nevertheless until 1908 his career was that of soloist and violinist in the Mugellini Quintet. After the performance of his operas *Re Enzo* and *Semirama* his reputation was such as to cause him to be appointed a professor of composition at the Conservatorio Santa Cecilia in Rome. In 1923 he was made Director of that institution, but resigned in 1926 in order to devote himself to composition and concert-giving. He died in Rome after a long illness.

In terms of instrumental music rather than operatic, Respighi alone brought his country back before the widest public, chiefly by means of his two symphonic poems *The Fountains of Rome* (generally considered his best work) and *The Pines of Rome.* Less well-known are *Brazilian Impressions, Church Windows* and the third of the 'Roman' triptych, *Roman Festivals.* The idiom is pleasantly, even lusciously, eclectic if lacking in strong individuality and may be defined as 'romantic-impressionist'. His orchestration is masterly with beauty of sound ever a major preoccupation; but the musical substance is derived from such composers as Rimsky-Korsakov, Strauss, Debussy and to some extent Puccini. His artistic temperament has been likened to that of d'Annunzio, and certainly the 'medievalism' of those works based on Gregorian chant (*Concerto Gregoriano* for violin, *Quartetto dorico* for strings) is no more authentic than that of the English Pre-Raphaelites. On the other hand his many transcriptions of Italian music of the 17th and 18th centuries (three sets of *Ancient Airs and Dances for the lute*) and of other 'old' music (e.g., *The Birds*) are models of their kind, likewise the ballet *La Boutique Fantasque* after Rossini. Respighi also wrote nine operas and a realisation of Monteverdi's *Orfeo*, songs and a quantity of unfairly-neglected choral and vocal music.

C.P.

RIMSKY-KORSAKOV, Nicolai
(b. Tikhvin, 6 March 1844;
d. St Petersburg, 21 June 1908)

In 1936, the late Gerald Abraham wrote an excellent history of Russian music that was subtitled *Rimsky-Korsakov and his Contemporaries*; it devoted a chapter to Glinka, one to Tchaikovsky, one to Mussorgsky, and seven to Rimsky-Korsakov. The perspective strikes us as a little odd, and it is worth recalling for that reason. In the period between the wars, no critic need have felt any misgivings in assessing Tchaikovsky and Mussorgsky as less important than Rimsky – or the other way round, for that matter. It was largely a matter of how you felt. Nowadays, of course, we take it for granted that Tchaikovsky and Mussorgsky are the major Russian composers of their period, and that Rimsky belongs on a lower step, with Balakirev and Borodin; but there is no absolute certainty that we are right. It is worth bearing in mind that every music lover is familiar with the major works of Tchaikovsky and Mussorgsky. How many of us are familiar with even one of Rimsky-Korsakov's operas, which he himself regarded as the essence of his achievement?

Nikolai Andreevich Rimsky-Korsakov was born at Tikhvin, near Novgorod; his father was a retired civil Governor and a landed proprietor. The whole family was fond of music – the mother had once been a pianist – and when the child began to take piano lessons, it was discovered that he had perfect pitch. But no one thought of him as a future musician; he was a lively and mischievous child whose ambition was to become a sailor, like a much-admired elder brother.

At the age of twelve he entered Naval College in St Petersburg. Friends of his brother took him to the opera; he heard Meyerbeer's *Robert the Devil* (the opera that bowled Wagner over), Donizetti's *Lucia* and Glinka's *Life for the Tsar* and *Ruslan*. The Persian music from the latter so enchanted him that he arranged it for 'cello and piano and played it repeatedly with a friend. For the next four years, he continued to study piano, still with no intention of making a career of music. Then he began to take lessons from a teacher named Canillé, whose love of music stirred the teenager to enthusiasm, so that his efforts at composition grew more ambitious. It was Canillé who introduced the boy to his friend Mily Balakirev, another lover of the music of Glinka, and one of the most influential – and

despotic – members of the group known as the Kuchka. The other members were Cui, Borodin, and Mussorgsky. With the arrival of Rimsky-Korsakov, the four became 'The Five.'

Balakirev immediately suggested (a better word may be 'ordered') that his young disciple should try writing a symphony in E flat. One early reference book states that this was the first Russian symphony; but this honour should probably go to Balakirev who had then been working on his own symphony for some time. And it was at about this time, in 1862, that Borodin began his own first symphony. While Rimsky was still working on his symphony, he had to abandon music for the navy; in spite of Balakirev's pleas, his brother flatly refused to be swayed. So Rimsky sailed off for three years on the *Almaz*. At least, it gave him the opportunity to hear music at Covent Garden and in New York.

He was twenty-one when he arrived back in St Petersburg, old enough to decide on his own future. The performance of his First Symphony at one of Balakirev's Free School concerts may have made the decision easier. Life was not too bad for the young man. In musical circles he was regarded as a moderately talented amateur; but among his brother's friends, he was accepted as a brilliant pianist (which he was not) and a knowledgeable music critic. It was good for the ego; and he tinkered about with composition. He and Mussorgsky became close friends. Mussorgsky liked a song Rimsky had written called *Oriental Fantasy*, and encouraged him to try a larger work in the same manner; the symphonic poem *Sadko* resulted. When Berlioz came to St Petersburg, he conducted a number of Free School concerts, alternating with Balakirev, and Rimsky had the pleasure of hearing his own music under the baton of the great romantic. Rimsky came to be regarded as a disciple of Berlioz and Liszt, and a critic violently attacked *Sadko* for its 'modernist' tendencies. (Mussorgsky, in turn, wrote a little satirical song called 'The Classicist' in which *Sadko* is quoted.)

The First Symphony had been a fairly classical work, free of anything that could be called exoticism or modernism. A second symphony in the same manner was soon abandoned, on criticism from Balakirev; instead, Rimsky wrote the symphonic poem *Antar*, with an oriental programme, and this became Symphony No. 2. He was also struggling with an opera, based on a play called *The Maid of Pskov*, but inspiration was lacking. Then, in

Nijinsky and Ida Rubinstein in Scheherazade, *the
ballet to Rimsky-Korsakov's music. By Barbier, 1912*

LE COQ D'OR

Geologi Polkin — Paysan — Persane — L'un des Fils de Roi Dodon — Demoiselle d'Honneur — Paysanne — Paysan — Le Roi Dodon

1er Acte — Le Roi Dodón s'endort tranquille puisque le Coq d'Or veille.
3me Acte — Le Roi Dodón ramène en son Palais la Reine de Chemákha.

Maquettes de Mlle Nathalie Gontcharova, pour les Décors et Costumes du " COQ D'OR ".

Designs by Nathalie Gontcharova for Rimsky-Korsakov's The Golden Cockerel.

the summer of 1868, he spent some time with Borodin on a country estate in Tver province. The Russian countryside and the peasant dances were just the inspiration he needed, and the opera began to move forward at a greater speed. It was further delayed when Cui asked Rimsky to help him orchestrate an unfinished opera by the recently deceased Dargomizky, *The Stone Guest*; but the incidental lesson in dramatic construction and orchestration was probably as valuable as the time he lost.

His fame continued to spread. He was twenty-seven when, to his astonishment, he was offered a job as Professor of Composition and Instrumentation at the Petersburg Conservatory. He accepted, then settled down to the serious study of technique. He and Mussorgsky shared a lodging during this period. A Third Symphony reverted to the academic manner. He was still officially in the navy, and in 1873, he was appointed Inspector of Military bands, a job that stirred him to further intense study of orchestration. Eventually, the self-taught amateur was to become the greatest master of the orchestra in Europe next to Berlioz.

The remainder of Rimsky-Korsakov's life is a history of his music and of his influence as a teacher, rather than of external events. In 1875, he began a collection of *A Hundred Russian Folk Songs*, which confirmed his tendency to nationalism in music. The first fruit of this re-awakening was the Gogol opera *May Night*, followed by *The Snow Maiden*. His basic characteristics had now emerged: nationalism, orientalism, and an interest in magic and fairy tales which no doubt amounted to 'escapism'. Mussorgsky's death from drink in 1881 left Rimsky with the task of completing and orchestrating the unfinished *Boris Godunov*. In 1888, he completed three of his most famous compositions: the *Spanish Capriccio*, *Scheherazade* and the

Russian Easter Overture. In the following year, he had a chance to hear Wagner's music when a German opera company visited St Petersburg; the results of his fascination with Wagner can be heard in the orchestration of his next opera *Mlada*.

Overwork caused a period of nervous exhaustion; he hovered on the edge of total breakdown from the age of forty-five to forty-seven. Then there was another burst of creative activity which produced the operas *Christmas Eve, Sadko, Mozart and Salieri, The Tsar's Bride, Tsar Saltan* and *Servilia*. Now the most famous member of 'The Five', Rimsky was virtually dictator of musical life in Petersburg. Yet surprisingly enough, this established figure took the side of revolutionary students who criticised the conservatism of the academic authorities in the stormy year 1905, and he was actually dismissed. He immediately became – as might be expected – a popular hero. In spite of this upheaval, he completed work on his strange, mystical opera *The Invisible City of Kitezh*. His favourite pupil Glazunov resigned from the Conservatory in protest; when he was recalled, as Director, he promptly reinstated Rimsky. The political upheavals may have influenced his choice of subject for his last

Rimsky-Korsakov, by Repin.

opera, *The Golden Cockerel*, about a stupid Tsar and his moronic officials. The censor banned it, and the composer was never destined to see it performed. He died of angina pectoris in June 1908.

We might conclude by returning to the speculation with which we began. Ever since his death, Rimsky-Korsakov has been known to concert audiences mainly through *Scheherazade, The Flight of the Bumble Bee* and a few overtures and suites. It is only in recent years that music lovers have been able to make the acquaintance of the majority of his operas on gramophone record, mainly imports from Russia. *May Night, Tsar Saltan, Sadko, Mlada, The Tsar's Bride* and *Christmas Eve* prove to have as much fine music in them as any opera by Tchaikovsky, and two of them, *The Invisible City of Kitezh* and *The Golden Cockerel* are masterpieces. If Rimsky had been a Czech like Smetana, or a Pole like Moniusko, his fellow countrymen would have built a national opera house for the regular performance of his works. It would be absurd to claim that, as a body of work, they could hold their own beside Wagner or Verdi; yet they certainly emerge with honours in a comparison with Smetana or Fibich or Moniusko. Then how do we account for their relative neglect in Russia when compared, say, with Tchaikovsky, or even Rachmaninov? The answer must be that the times have so far been unpropitious for their large-scale revival. During its first fifty years, Soviet Russia was busy turning its back on escapism and Gogolian nostalgia for 'old time landowners' and water sprites and magic horses. But now the 19th century is far enough behind them, and nostalgia creeps back into fashion, it becomes increasingly likely that the Soviet government might one day decide that the operas of Rimsky-Korsakov are one of their great national assets.

C.W.

ROSSINI, Gioacchino
(b. Pesaro, 29 Feb 1792;
d. Passy, 13 Nov 1868)

Rossini, whose father was municipal trumpeter in the small town of Pesaro, revealed his own musical ability at a very early age, and by his early teens was proficient not only on the piano but also on the viola and the horn. He was also much in demand locally as a boy soprano, and soon began to compose music, including a number of arias and some duets for horn which he wrote for his father and himself to perform. When Rossini senior was dismissed from his ill-paid municipal post because of his political opinions, he and his wife who was a singer accepted engagements in a number of theatres in the vicinity. While they were touring, the young Gioacchino was left in Pesaro in the care of his aunt and his grandmother. Eventually his parents settled in Bologna, and young Rossini was then able to procure at the Liceo Musicale the kind of musical tuition which had been lacking in Pes-

aro. His teacher in Bologna, Mattei, had been a pupil of Padre Martini, and gave Rossini the basic grounding in strict counterpoint which was to stand him in good stead in later years. He was eighteen when he left the Lieco, by which time he had won a prize for counter-point and had also composed a great deal of music, for instance five string quartets which are more than mere juvenilia. Soon after leaving the Liceo, he was invited to write a one-act opera for Venice.

The Venice opera, *La cambiale di matri-monio,* was successful enough to lead to several other commissions for one-act comic pieces, but the first really important Rossini opera is the full-length *opera seria, Tancredi,* based on the tragedy by Voltaire. Though the standard

Teresa Berganza (Rosina) and Geraint Evans (Bartolo) in The Barber of Seville.

of its musical invention is uneven, *Tancredi* was highly acclaimed by its first audiences in Venice, and one of its arias, 'Di tanti palpiti', became so popular that it was hummed and whistled in the streets and alleyways of Venice from morning till night. Less than three months after the première of *Tancredi*, the now twenty-one-year-old composer scored an even greater success, again in Venice, this time with a comic opera, *L'Italiana in Algeri*. This opera, still performed today, is the kind of sparkling, brittle and unsentimental comic piece which we most associate with the name of Rossini. Its tunes are basically simple, though embellished to give the singers opportunities for display, and its orchestration is attractive and imaginative.

With *L'Italiana in Algeri*, Rossini suddenly found himself famous throughout Italy. He was now invited to write operas for Milan, but his next real success came in Naples in 1815 with *Elisabetta, Regina d'Inghilterra*, whose leading character, Queen Elizabeth I of England, was sung by the famous prima donna Isabella Colbran. It was with *Elisabetta* that Rossini began his practice of writing out fully the decorations and embellishments to his melodies, rather than leave them to the uncertain taste of his performers. In November 1815, Rossini temporarily forsook Naples for Rome, whither he had been called to provide a new opera for the Teatro Argentina. The opera which he composed in less than a fortnight is the one generally regarded to be his masterpiece, *Il barbiere di Siviglia* (The Barber of Seville). The statement that it was written in less than a fortnight must be slightly modified, for Rossini was a great borrower from himself, and most of his operatic scores contain at least one number lifted from an earlier work. Some of the music of *Il barbiere* had already been heard in *Elisabetta*, but by far the greater part of the opera is original, and the quality of invention throughout is remarkably high. *The Barber of Seville* is one of the wittiest and most immediately appealing comic operas in the repertoire today, and as fresh to the ear now as when it first burst upon its Roman audiences in 1816. The first night in Rome was actually something of a fiasco, to some extent due to the fact that the audience wanted to remain loyal to Paisiello, whose own *Barber of Seville* had held the stage for many years. But from the second performance onwards Rome forgot Paisiello and worshipped Rossini.

Based now mainly in Naples where he was conducting an affair with the prima donna

Isabella Colbran, who had formerly been the mistress of the Naples impresario Barbaia, Rossini began to turn out operas in quick succession. *Otello* (1816) contains much beautiful music. Though it is lacking in dramatic impetus, it held the stage in Italy until Verdi's towering masterpiece in 1887 dealt it a death blow. *La cenerentola* (1817), a comic opera based on the Cinderella fairy-tale, though by no means the equal of *The Barber of Seville*, is an entertaining work which is

Caricature of Rossini by Dantan.

still quite frequently staged. *Mosè* (1818), *La donna del lago* (1819) and *Maometto II* (1820) are more uneven, and *La gazza ladra* (*The Thieving Magpie*, 1817) is a curious piece which attempts to combine elements of both serious and comic opera. Rarely staged, it is known to most opera lovers today only by its overture.

Rossini's last opera for Naples was *Zelmira* in 1822, after which he spent four months in Vienna with Isabella Colbran, whom he had now married. *Zelmira* was staged at the Kärntnertor Theater in Vienna, which was under the management of Colbran's ex-lover, Barbaia. During his time there, Rossini was fêted by the Viennese. He managed to meet the somewhat reclusive Beethoven whom he greatly admired, and though he did not meet Schubert his music certainly made a deep impression on the young Viennese composer. Rossini's next opera of any consequence was *Semiramide*, which was first performed in Venice in 1823. Later in that year he was invited to London where, instead of composing the opera which was expected of him, he led a lively social life. He even sang duets with George IV.

In August 1824, Rossini left London for Paris where he was welcomed with open arms as one of the most celebrated of living composers, and given the general management of the Théâtre Italien, the Parisian theatre in which Italian operas were performed in Italian. But, with his sights set on the Paris Opéra, Rossini produced French-language versions of his *Maometto II* (*Le Siège de Corinthe*) and *Mosè* (*Moïse*), forerunners of the Meyerbeerian Grand Opera, and then turned again to *opéra comique* with *Le Comte Ory* (1828), an elegant and charming comedy. His most important and influential opera for Paris, however, was *Guillaume Tell*, based on Schiller's play about the Swiss patriot William Tell. A large-scale work of great originality and power, *Guillaume Tell*, which was produced at the Opéra in 1829, came in due course to influence an entire generation of French composers.

Curiously, Rossini wrote no more works for the stage after *Guillaume Tell*, although he was only thirty-seven years of age and at the height of his creative powers. He was to live on to the age of seventy-six, producing virtually no new music at all. Many writers have speculated on the reasons for his absurdly early retirement: it seems likely that, at first, he intended to continue his career but merely wished first to take an ex-

tended holiday from composition. However, as the years wore on he became more remote from the new music and the new, post-1830 society, and he had also made sufficient money from his earlier works to be able to live comfortably. He occupied his time in lavish entertaining and in travelling. After separating from Isabella, he took up with Olympe Pélissier, a celebrated Parisian beauty whom he married after Isabella's death in 1845. Though his physical health remained generally good, his mental health did not. His nervous condition worsened over the years, and it was not until, after years of living in Italy, he and Olympe returned to Paris, that he recovered somewhat. In his old age he began to compose again, short trifling piano pieces and songs for performance at his own famous Saturday evening parties. Near the end of his life, however, he composed the Petite Messe Solennelle, which is neither especially short nor in the slightest degree solemn. After a short illness he died in November 1868, and was buried in the Paris cemetery of Père Lachaise. Nineteen years later his remains were removed to Italy, to the Church of Santa Croce in Florence.

C.O.

SAINT-SAËNS, Camille
(b. Paris, 9 Oct 1835;
d. Algiers, 16 Dec 1921)

Saint-Saëns was born in Paris, to a family of peasant origin from the neighbourhood of Dieppe, while his mother's family (Collin) were petits bourgeois from the Champagne district. There is no truth in the often-stated Jewish affiliations of either family. Owing to grave concern for his health, caused by the recent deaths of several members of his family and very soon by that of his father, the child was brought up for the first two years by foster-parents at Corbeil; and during his later youth every summer was spent with his mother's relations in Champagne. His musical gifts, which showed themselves very early, were accompanied by an exceptional intellectual liveliness in all fields and a fondness for what most children regard as work. He was brought up by his mother, a pupil of the rose-painter Redouté, and her aunt who had brought her up; and from the first his exceptional gifts were recognised and fostered in this exclusively feminine environment.

At seven he started piano lessons with the

Greco-French Stamaty, who had recently returned from studying in Germany with Mendelssohn and had brought back with him much Viennese classical music then largely unfamiliar in France. It was not surprising therefore that at the age of ten he appeared as pianist in a performance of a Beethoven violin sonata with the Belgian Bessems. He had given a piano recital in the Salle Erard before going to the Paris Conservatoire (1848), and in 1851 he entered Halévy's composition class. He had already met, and impressed, the great singer Pauline Viardot and now met Liszt, whose compositions and playing made a deep impression on him, and with both of these he was to remain on mutually cordial terms. He surprisingly failed to win the Grand Prix de Rome (1852), but an *Ode à Sainte Cécile* won him a prize the same year, and at seventeen he was plainly on the threshold of a great career both as composer and performer. Appointed organist at Saint-Merry in 1853, he moved from there to the Madeleine in 1857, thus achieving at twenty-two the most coveted organist's post in France. His first and second symphonies were performed in 1853 and 1857 respectively, and showed immediately an exceptional and effortless mastery of traditional symphonic writing, owing much to Mozart and early Beethoven in manner and to Mendelssohn in mood. His piano-playing was marked both now and for the rest of his life by an apparently effortless technical facility, unfailingly limpid tone and that scrupulous articulation which has always marked the French school. (He practised scales daily, with the newspaper propped in front of him.) The only period of his life during which he devoted himself to teaching was 1861–5, when Fauré and Messager were his piano pupils at the École Niedermeyer.

Not dismayed by a second failure to obtain the Prix de Rome (1864), probably due less to personal prejudice in the examiners than to the essentially undramatic nature of his gifts, Saint-Saëns now embarked on the first of the twelve operas he was eventually to write and only one of which, *Samson et Dalilah*, was ever to succeed. This was his third opera and was first given (1877) not in Paris but at Weimar, where Liszt's influence obtained a hearing for this awkward but often effective hybrid obtained by crossing oratorio with Meyerbeerian 'grand' opera. More in accordance with his real gifts, which were for symphonic music and almost unique in France at that time, was the series of concertos which

opened in 1858–9, with one each for piano and violin. Ten years later came a group which has remained in the international repertory, consisting of the second (G minor) piano concerto and the *Introduction et rondo capriccioso* for violin and orchestra, to which should be added the third (E flat major) piano concerto, still performed in France today.

During the 1860s Saint-Saëns had on several occasions met Wagner, who was amazed at the young pianist's ability to read at sight scores which included that of *Tristan*; and according to Saint-Saëns himself, he acted as Wagner's accompanist when the composer sang passages from *Das Rheingold* at the Austrian Embassy. Saint-Saëns's first violin concerto had been played by Sarasate and his second piano concerto by Anton Rubinstein; Berlioz, Liszt, Gounod and Ferdinand Hiller attended his piano recitals; and he was an habitué in the salon of the most powerful figure in the French art world, Princesse Mathilde, who was not only a member of the Imperial family but also for many years the mistress of the Ministre des Beaux Arts, Nieuwerkerke. In 1868, aged only thirty-three, he was decorated with the Légion d'Honneur. In Germany he had the honour of playing his third (E flat major) piano concerto with the Leipzig Gewandhaus orchestra (1869) and a year later Liszt invited him to take part in the Beethoven Centenary celebrations at Weimar.

Saint-Saëns was thus one of the most famous musicians in France when the Franco-Prussian war broke out in 1870. During the war itself he gave charity recitals, but when the Commune threatened to disrupt the whole of French life, he was despatched to London by his anxious family, who themselves felt old and unimportant enough to risk remaining in Paris. During his few weeks in London Saint-Saëns gave an organ recital at the Crystal Palace, and in 1875 he undertook the first of many triumphant foreign tours, visiting Russia as well as Austria. As a composer he formed during the 1870s in France part of the Lisztian rather than the Wagnerian avant-garde, writing four orchestral poems of which the best known are *Le Rouet d'Omphale* and *Danse Macabre*. He had joined in 1871 the newly formed Société Nationale de Musique for the support and propagation of music by contemporary French composers; and while the fourth (C minor) piano concerto confirmed his reputation in more conservative circles, the tone-poems and later (1886) the immaculately written but very uneven C minor symphony (No. 3) showed his sympathy with rather newer ideas. The first 'cello concerto (1873) and second violin concerto (1880) both reveal the same very individual mixture of symphonic seriousness and that salon prettiness or Parisian wit which are to be found in their purest state in the *Havanaise* for violin and piano and the *Carnaval des animaux* respectively. The C minor symphony shows unmistakably a sympathy with the chromatic harmonies and the chorales which formed characteristic features of César Franck's music and that of his disciples.

Although Saint-Saëns's pronounced and well publicised views on French–German relations after the war involved him in a public scandal on a visit to Berlin in 1886, his popularity in this country may be gauged by the fact that he appeared here regularly as a soloist from 1874 onwards and in 1887 played all four of his then existing piano concertos at a single concert. Cambridge awarded him an honorary Doctorate of Music (with Tchaikovsky, Boito and Grieg) and in 1913 a Jubilee Festival of his music was held in London. After 1890, however, he wrote little of consequence, continuing to produce unsuccessful operas, while a fifth piano concerto (1895) contained some of those exotic (in this case Egyptian) evocations which marked his increasing fondness for foreign travel. He was a great lover of the sun, which he had found first in Algeria, then in many visits to the Canary Islands and even as far afield as Colombo and Saigon. His literary gifts found expression in neat verses and also in music criticism, which became increasingly ill-natured as his own compositions became thinner and less appreciated, and music itself moved into a phase which he viewed with mixed incredulity and indignation. The most important of his writings are to be found in *Portraits et souvenirs* (1899), the least acceptable perhaps in *Germanophilie* (1916). More interesting in any case was his work as editor of 17th- and 18th-century music including M. A. Charpentier's incidental music for Moliere's *Le Malade imaginaire*, Gluck's *Echo et Narcisse* and the music of Rameau, of whose complete works he was the general editor. His last compositions which bear the opus number 168 and were written in the year of his death, are three sonatas for oboe, clarinet and bassoon respectively. He died in 1921 at Algiers. The effortless craftsmanship and frequently all too facile invention of his music ally Saint-Saëns to composers of the 18th

Saint-Saëns conducting at the Théâtre des Champs-Elysées, 1913.

rather than the 19th century; and indeed his alert, sceptical, witty personality and wide general information and interests ally him to the *philosophes* who collaborated with Diderot in producing the Grande Encyclopédie in the years immediately before the revolution of 1789.

M.C.

SATIE, Erik
(b. Houfleur, 17 May 1866;
d. Paris, 1 July 1925)

One of the most ambiguous and controversial musicians of the whole modern period, Erik Satie, was born at Honfleur in northern France, on the 17th May 1866. One of his early music teachers was the local organist, one Vinot, who introduced the boy to, among other things, medieval chant. Plainsong, together with a certain ambience of remote, mystical devotion, was to exert an abiding influence on Satie, but especially during the ten years or so between the mid-1880s and the mid-1890s when he was under the spell of the Rosicrucian philosopher-playwright, Joséphin Péladan. A popular misconception about Satie is that he came to music late in life. This is the reverse of the truth. He entered the Paris Conservatoire in 1879, but spent only a year there, finding himself at odds with the academic routine he was required to follow. His earliest piano pieces date from the mid-1880s, and already embody certain characteristic ideas which were later to give him quasi-revolutionary status among Parisian composers. In the *Sarabandes* of 1887 and the *Gymnopédies* of the following year we already find that non-functional use of unresolved dissonance whose invention is generally attributed to Debussy (it has never been quite clear whether Satie was aware of Debussy's reputation at the Conservatoire for eccentric chordal doodling). The fragile simplicity and unpretentious grace of these pieces were also to remain distinctively Satiesque qualities. And his taste for whimsical schoolboy humour, which survives in the titles of his later piano pieces, is already expressed in the labelling of his earliest published work, a pair of waltzes issued in 1887, as Op. 62.

In 1886 Satie briefly did military service, and it was at this period that he came under the influence of the Rosicrucians. His music of the time is peculiarly redolent of medieval church music and chant, but nevertheless advanced in its continued use of non-evolving, non-functional dissonance (for instance, the *Messe des pauvres* of 1895). In 1891 he met Debussy and at once impressed the older composer with his views on the direction French music should be taking. This, so to speak, reverse influence by a young and unknown composer on an older and better established one is curious, particularly in the light of Satie's unpretentious nature. The tendency is to attribute it, along with Satie's later reputation with Cocteau and 'Les Six', to the French taste for paradox and anti-heroism. But the significance of Satie's ideas should not be underrated simply because he himself was at this stage a composer of decidedly limited attainments. Not only his fascination with novel technical devices, but his broader distaste for the whole concept of the Romantic artist, was ahead of his time, and though out of tune with the then fashionable aesthetic movement, was

sufficiently perceptive of underlying and incipient tendencies to be immediately grasped as important by an artist of Debussy's stature. Satie, as it happens, was beginning to be conscious of his technical shortcomings, and in 1905 he enrolled in the Schola Cantorum for study with d'Indy and Roussel. The music immediately preceding this step, including the well-known music-hall songs and some of the most eccentric piano pieces, is perhaps inexpert and short-winded. But the staccato forms are not solely the result of technical inadequacies, but carry through into Satie's more famous and assured later works, where they become a key part of a whole new movement in favour of mosaic designs.

From this period of study dates Satie's more concrete association with the tendencies in modern art which his earlier work had foreshadowed. Among younger French composers he became a revered figure. He made friends with Cocteau and Picasso, and with Diaghilev, whose company presented Satie's most famous work, the ballet *Parade*, at the Ballet Russe de Monte Carlo in Paris in May 1917. Somewhat unwillingly he became the centre of various artistic groupings: the 'Nouveaux Jeunes' and their offspring, 'Les Six', and the abortive 'École d'Arcueil' (Arcueil being the Parisian suburb where Satie lived, always

Satie by Picabia, 1924.

in circumstances of extreme indigence). Satie's last works were thus willy-nilly objects of fashionable badinage. The ballets *Mercure* and *Relâche* were both produced in Paris in 1924, the year before his death. The austere and enigmatic *Socrate* was also heard in Paris in 1920, and in the same year Satie pioneered another far-reaching experiment, the so-called *musique d'ameublement* – 'furniture music', a forerunner of modern background and incidental music. By this time Satie had acquired a theoretical apologia, in Cocteau's *Le Coq et l'Arlequin*, an abstraction of aesthetic tenets which was supposed to be the manifesto for 'Les Six'. But Satie himself never seems to have theorised systematically, and he remained to the end a somewhat reclusive, non-factious, detached individual, preoccupied with his own music.

The controversy surrounding Satie's work has always hinged on the discrepancy between his obvious imaginative flair and his allegedly defective technique. His importance is beyond dispute. His use of non-functional dissonance, of ostinato and of bare, economical textures, his borrowings from popular music, and his apparently whimsical antinomianism: these things all foreshadowed later movements which were, however, scarcely in the air at the time. Later, in *Parade*, Satie produced what is conceivably the one masterpiece of musical Dada, with its strange, mosaic form, its popular *objets trouvés* (notably ragtime), and its disjointed yet intriguing and satisfying harmonies. But, though anti-romantic, Satie was far from advocating mere imbecile debunking. As David Drew has written, there is in these strange and seemingly insignificant formal sequences the distinct flavour of a private, enigmatic but profoundly disturbing personal expression. And Satie was certainly never less than serious about art as such.

Picabia's décor for Satie's ballet, Relâche, *1924.*

On the other hand his music is undoubtedly uneven. This creative imagination was (*pace* some of his critics) essentially musical. But it was not always well supported by his intellect or technique. By a miracle of the kind which so often infuses new art, his best music has an intuitive coherence. But where this failed Satie did not truly know how to supply the deficiency. His worst pieces are almost unbelievably trivial, and his 'classical' simplicity and avoidance of rhetoric are little more than dullness. His personality, however, is always unmistakable, and this is perhaps his surest entitlement to be considered a genius, however minor.

S.W.

SCARLATTI, Alessandro
(b. Palermo, 2 May 1660;
d. Naples, 24 Oct 1725)

Alessandro Scarlatti was born in 1660, eldest son of Pietro Scarlata, a native of Trapani who had settled in Palermo and married Eleonora D'Amato there in May 1658. Very little is known of Alessandro's early life – he is said to have studied with Carissimi in Rome, although that master died when Scarlatti was in his early teens. An entry in the archives of the Archiconfraternità del SS Crosifisso, Rome, under the 27th January 1679 mentions that 'il Scarlattino alias al Siciliano' was commissioned to compose a Lenten oratorio.

Alessandro married Antonia Anzalone, a native of Rome, in April 1678. They had a large family which, of course, included the celebrated Domenico born in 1685. Alessandro's first opera *Gli equivoci nel sembiante* was first produced during February 1679 at the Teatro Capranica, Rome. Among the audience was Queen Christina of Sweden, who subsequently favoured Scarlatti with royal patronage. In the libretto of his second opera *L'honestà negli amori* he is described as *maestro di cappella* to Queen Christina.

In December 1683 a new opera *Psiche* was given at the royal palace Naples, and during February of the following year Alessandro was appointed *maestro di cappella* of the royal chapel. In June 1702 he was granted a spell of absence from Naples and with Domenico, journeyed to Florence where they enjoyed the patronage of Prince Ferdinando de' Medici, who had a great love of music. The Prince was unable to offer a permanent appointment, and eventually Scarlatti travelled to Rome where

his friend and patron, Cardinal Ottoboni, secured for him the appointment of assistant *maestro di cappella* at the church of Santa Maria Maggiore. The Cardinal, a great benefactor of music and the arts, appointed Scarlatti his private *maestro di cappella*. In May 1707, Antonio Fogga died, and Alessandro succeeded him as principal *maestro* at Santa Maria Maggiore. Many of his most beautiful chamber cantatas, and several of his operas date from this time. In 1707 he wrote two operas *Mitridate Eupatore* and *Il trionfo della libertà* for Venice, and travelled there to direct them in person. In April, he was in Urbino where his eldest son, Pietro was *maestro* at the Cathedral. In the autumn of 1707 Alessandro returned to Naples, and two years later was restored to the appointment of *maestro di cappella* at the royal chapel at an increased salary. At this time, Scarlatti was at the height of his powers, producing operas such as *Tigrone* (1715), a work on a magnificent scale. He received civic recognition in the form of a knighthood; the libretto of *Carlo, re d'Alemagna* (1716), is believed to be the first instance where he is styled 'cavalier'. In October 1717 Scarlatti was granted leave to visit Rome where his final series of operas was produced. These works of his artistic maturity include *Telemaco* (1718), *Marco Attilo Regolo* (1719) and finally *Griselda* of 1721, his 114th and last full-scale opera. A good deal of church music dates from this time including a magnificent orchestral Mass for St Cecilia's Day. In 1721, Clement XI was succeeded by Innocent XIII and Scarlatti composed a pastoral for the formal entrance of Pope Innocent to the Vatican. Scarlatti returned to Naples in 1722 or 1723.

An important teacher, Scarlatti expounded his ideas on accompaniment in a treatise *Regole per Principianti*. One of his most notable pupils was Johann Adolf Hasse, who having quarrelled with his previous teacher Porpora, joined Scarlatti in 1724. The following year Johann Joachim Quantz visited Naples and, meeting Hasse, begged him to arrange an introduction with Scarlatti. The old man is said to have replied to Hasse's request: 'My son, you know that I cannot endure players of wind instruments, for they all blow out of tune.' Eventually, however, a meeting was arranged and Quantz heard Scarlatti play the harpsichord 'in a learned manner'. Scarlatti, indeed, composed a couple of flute pieces for him and accompanied him in a solo.

Alessandro Scarlatti died in 1725, and was buried in the church of Montesanto. During his lifetime he had become the most renowned composer of opera and cantatas. He is remembered chiefly as the leading figure of the Neapolitan Opera School which achieved widespread importance, influencing among others, Handel. Scarlatti's own earlier works show the influence of Carissimi, Rossi, Legrenzi, and Stradella. Whereas his concerti and sinfonie may be regardèd as 'retrospective in attitude', the operas are truly progressive – like those of Monteverdi, Lotti and Marcello. Scarlatti established the Da Capo aria as the definitive aria type, avoiding rigidity through his great melodic gifts. Quite often melodic figurations are included which resemble those of instrumental concerti – Corelli, for instance. Scarlatti introduced the 'Italian' overture, establishing the format which, despite development by subsequent composers, remained for decades. As his style matured he adopted a more 'modern' approach to the orchestra, avoiding the rather angular alternations of orchestra and continuo which characterise the late 17th-century

Alessandro Scarlatti.

opera. The final period operas unite brilliant orchestral perception with a deepened emotional response, which had hitherto been found only in the cantatas.

Alessandro Scarlatti's instrumental music is of less importance. In 1715 he composed a set of twelve magnificent sinfonias in all probability for the Royal Chapel at Naples, and of his noble sonata-based *Concerti Grossi* Dr Charles Burney wrote that they were possibly too severe to be played 'anywhere except in a church' although they have been quite acceptably performed as concert pieces in our own times. His keyboard music is of little consequence when compared with that of his son Domenico. The Toccatas are rather patchy, but there is a superbly effective set of variations on the *Folia*.

There are nearly seven hundred surviving cantatas by Alessandro, all for varying combinations of voices and instruments. As with 18th-century chamber cantatas in general, the greater number have a pastoral subject with stock characters from antiquity, such as *Floro e Tirsi* (1707). One of the most beautiful of Scarlatti's cantatas is the delightful *Cantata pastorale per la natività*, first performed in Rome in 1695 at the Palazzo Apostolico. Dr Burney, writing in the late 18th century, considered Alessandro Scarlatti 'the most voluminous and most original composer of cantatas that has ever existed.' He continues 'indeed, this master's genius was truly creative; and I find part of his property among the stolen goods of all the best composers of the first forty or fifty years of the present century.' More recent writers have expanded this opinion to include the whole of Classical music.

G.G.

SCARLATTI, Domenico
(b. Naples, 26 Oct 1685;
d. Madrid, 23 July 1757)

Domenico, sixth son of Alessandro Scarlatti's ten children, was born in 1685 in Naples. Domenico's home environment was saturated with music, and he received his early musical training from his father. On the 13th September 1701 Domenico became organist and composer at the royal chapel, of which Alessandro was *maestro di cappella*. In June 1702, he was given leave to travel with his father to Florence, but a few months later returned on his own to Naples where, following in his father's footsteps, he turned his attention to opera composition. *Ottavia ristituta al trono* was produced at the Teatro San Bartolomeo in 1703, and was followed by *Giustina* produced later that year, and *Irene* in 1704. Alessandro then living in Rome, observed in a letter to Ferdinando de Medici, dated the 30th May 1705: 'My son is an eagle whose wings are grown; he ought not to stay idle in the nest.' Alessandro's hopes for a court appointment for Domenico at Florence did not however materialise, and in 1708 Domenico journeyed to Venice where he became a pupil of Gasparini.

At this time Scarlatti became acquainted with a number of young foreign musicians who had travelled to Italy, attracted by its pre-eminence in opera. One of these was Thomas Roseingrave who, according to Dr Burney:

Being arrived in Venice in his way to Rome, as he himself told me, he was invited, as a stranger and a virtuoso, to an accademia at the house of a nobleman, where, among others, he was requested to sit down to the harpsichord and favour the company with a toccata, as a specimen *della sua virtù*. And, says he 'finding myself rather better in courage and finger than usual, I exerted myself . . . and fancied by the applause I received, that my performance had made some impression on the company. . . . After a cantata had been sung by a scholar of Fr. Gasparini, who was there to accompany her, a grave young man dressed in black and in a black wig, who had stood in one corner of the room, very quiet and attentive while Roseingrave played, being asked to sit down to the harpsichord, when he began to play, Rosy said, he thought that ten hundred d – – –'s had been at the instrument; he never had heard such passages of execution and effect before. The performance so far surpassed his own, and every degree of perfection to which he thought it possible he should ever arrive, that, if he had been in sight of any instrument with which to have done the deed, he would have cut off his own fingers. Upon enquiring the name of this extraordinary performer, has told it was Domenico Scarlatti, son of the celebrated Cavalier Alessandro Scarlatti.

Roseingrave's subsequent relationship with Scarlatti was of considerable importance and was largely responsible for the development of what was later known in England as the 'Scarlatti sect'.

In 1708 whilst still in Venice, Scarlatti met Handel, and the two became firm friends. They journeyed to Rome together where, early in 1709, Cardinal Ottoboni the great benefactor of music and the arts arranged a contest at one of his *Accademie Poetico Musicali*. John Mainwaring takes up the story:

The issue of the trial on the harpsichord hath been differently reported. It has been said that some gave the preference to Scarlatti. However, when they came to the Organ there was not the least pretence for doubting to which of them it belonged. Scarlatti himself declared the superiority of his antagonist, and owned ingenuously, that till he had heard him upon this instrument, he had no conception of its powers. . . . Handel used often to speak of this person [Scarlatti] with great satisfaction, and indeed there was reason for it; for besides his great talent as an artist he had the sweetest temper and the genteelest behaviour. On the other hand, it was mentioned . . . that Scarlatti as oft as he was admired for his great execution would mention Handel, and cross himself in veneration.

Other famous musicians whom Domenico would have heard at Cardinal Ottoboni's Palace, apart from his own father, would include Pasquini and Corelli. In 1709 Domenico entered the service of Maria Casimira, Queen of Poland, and composed several operas for her including *La Sylvia* (1710), *Orlando* and *Tolomeo e Alessandro* (1711) and *Amor d'un' ombra* (1714). Roseingrave produced this latter opera in London in 1720 under the title *Narciso*, adding several movements of his own.

In 1714 the Queen left Rome, and Scarlatti became *maestro di cappella* to the Portuguese Ambassador, and in January 1715 he also became *maestro* of the Cappella Giuliana in the Vatican where Palestrina had once held the same office some one hundred and fifty years earlier. Among the church music composed by Scarlatti at this time are two *Misereres* and the impressive ten-part *Stabat Mater*. In August 1719 he resigned from his post at the Vatican and the manuscript diary of Francesco Colignani states that 'Sig. Scarlatti having left for England, Sig. Ottavio Pitoni, who was at San Giovanni in Laterano, was made *maestro*.' From this time until his arrival in Portugal (the date of which is uncertain) Domenico's movements are impossible to trace. No evidence has yet been found to prove that Scarlatti ever visited England. He is sometimes said to have visited Ireland in 1740/1, but the Scarlatti in question is now known to have been Francesco, Domenico's uncle.

The date usually given for Scarlatti's appointment as *maestro* at the royal chapel at Lisbon is 1720 or 1721, although documentary proof is lacking. In addition to his duties as chapel master, Scarlatti was responsible for the musical instruction of Don Antonio, younger brother of the King, and of the King's daughter, Maria Barbara, later Queen of Spain. Scarlatti returned to Italy in 1724 and Quantz in his autobiography remembered meeting him in Rome. Four years later he was back in Italy and on the 15th May 1728 married Maria Catalina Gentili in Rome. Scarlatti and his bride presumably returned to Portugal. Maria Barbara herself was married in January 1729 and upon moving to the Spanish Court at Madrid, took her music-master with her. Scarlatti was to spend the remaining years of his life in service in Madrid. Maria Barbara's gratitude for this life-long devotion was manifest in her will when she bequeathed a ring and two-thousand doubloons to 'dn. Domigo Escarlati, my music-master, who has followed me with great diligence and loyalty'. Further recognition of Scarlatti's royal favour is provided by the knighthood which he received in April 1738. Scarlatti's first wife died on the 6th May 1739 leaving five children. He remarried, some time later, Anastasia Maxarti, who bore him four more children. A glimpse of Scarlatti's life at the Spanish Court is provided by an article which Dr Burney contributed to Rees' *Cyclopoedia*. Reporting a conversation which he had with Farinelli, who was also in the service of the Spanish court, we learn that Scarlatti, 'an agreeable man in society, was so much addicted to play, that he was frequently ruined, and as frequently relieved in his distress by his royal patroness, the Queen of Spain, who was constant in admiration of his original genius and incomparable talents.' It is believed that Scarlatti's last composition was the beautiful *Salve Regina*. He died on the 23rd July 1757 and was buried in the Convento de San Norberto.

Following his father Domenico Scarlatti composed operas, cantatas, and church music, but it is for his harpsichord music that he is best known today. It is surprising, then, to find that he was more than fifty before any of his sonatas were published, and that more than half of his total output of these works – some 555 in all – were apparently composed during the last six years of his life.

Domenico Scarlatti.

The *Essercizi per Gravicembalo* dedicated to the King of Portugal, were published in London in 1738. The following year Thomas Roseingrave published his edition of *XLII Suites de Piéces pour le Clavecin ... Composées par Domenico Scarlatti*, which sparked off the English 'Scarlatti Sect'. The greatest concentration of Scarlatti's sonatas is, however, to be found in two large manuscript collections. The first, numbering some thirteen volumes, was copied out for the use of Queen Maria Barbara between 1752 and 1757. Two earlier volumes, copied out in 1742 and in 1749, were added to the series. All fifteen volumes were sumptuously bound in red morocco and the combined arms of Spain and Portugal were inlaid in gold on the covers. They are now to be found in the Biblioteca Manciana, in Venice. A further collection of fifteen volumes, largely duplicating the Queen's volumes, were copied out from 1752 to 1757 and bound in plain leather. They are now housed in the Conservatorio Arigio Boito at Parma – and are now usually referred to as the 'Parma' manuscripts. These two collections form the principal sources of all but a few of the 555 known sonatas. No autograph manuscripts of the keyboard music are known to exist. Recent research has shown that most of the sonatas in the Venice and Parma manuscripts were copied out and intended to be performed in pairs, thus conforming with contemporary Italian practice. (It is believed, however, that the sonatas of Paradies were meant to be grouped in threes.)

Scarlatti's sonatas are bounded in the main by binary structure from which the composer was able to draw seemingly unending variety and flexibility of expression. Some are virtuoso pieces of extreme difficulty, while others are quiet and restrained. There are numerous reminiscences of national idioms and instruments – Italian, Portuguese and Spanish dance rhythms abound – and yet all are completely idiomatically conceived for the harpsichord. Exciting rhythms and brilliant execution are complemented by an equally virtuosic command of harmony. Scarlatti's unpredictable harmonic sequences and chord formations prompted Dr Burney to recall that in his youth 'Scarlatti's were not only the pieces with which every young performer displayed his powers of execution, but were the wonder and delight of every hearer who had a spark of enthusiasm about him, and could feel new and bold effects intrepidly produced by the breach of almost all the old and established rules of composition.'

Scarlatti's harpsichord music ranks him as probably the most original genius of the 18th century.

G.G.

SCHMIDT, Franz
(b. Bratislava, 22 Dec 1874; d. Vienna, 11 Feb 1939)

Franz Schmidt's father was of German stock; his mother's family came from the Slovak countryside. He was educated in Bratislava, where he heard Liszt play as a boy. His musical talent developed early, and he was given instruction by the cathedral organist Rudolf Mader and the Franciscan Father Felician. In 1888 the family moved to Vienna, and Schmidt earned his living by playing the piano in dance schools. He also had some piano lessons with Leschetitzky and wrote two youthful piano sonatas. In 1890 he entered the Vienna Conservatory, studying composition for a short time with Bruckner and later with Fuchs; he also studied the 'cello with Hellmesberger and Udel. At this time he wrote four pieces for 'cello and piano on Hungarian themes and also a cadenza for Haydn's D major 'cello concerto which

attracted the attention of Brahms in 1896. In the same year he obtained a position as 'cellist in the Vienna Court Opera orchestra, a post he held for fourteen years. From 1901 onwards he taught the 'cello at the Vienna Conservatory: after leaving the orchestra he was offered the post of professor of piano at the Vienna Academy, and became a professor of composition there as well in 1922. From 1925 to 1927 he was Director of the Academy, and from 1927 to 1931 Rector of the Musikhochschule. He was a man of great energy, and continued to perform as a 'cellist and pianist in addition to his activities as a composer and teacher.

His first symphony won the Beethoven Prize of the Vienna Gesellschaft der Musikfreunde in 1902. In the same year he began an opera, *Notre Dame de Paris*, based on Victor Hugo's *The Hunchback of Notre Dame*; the subject was suggested to Schmidt by a visit of his orchestra to Paris under Mahler. The opera was not finished till 1914. In the 1920s Schmidt was considerably helped by several commissions from Paul Wittgenstein, the pianist who had lost his right arm in World War I, and asked a number of composers, including Britten, Prokofiev, Ravel, Schmidt and Strauss, to write piano works for the left hand for him. Schmidt's compositions seem to have pleased him more than those of some of the others, and Schmidt wrote two concertos for him (1924 and 1934), a piano quintet (1926) and two quintets for piano, clarinet, violin, viola and 'cello (1932 and 1938). In 1928 Schmidt's third symphony won a prize in the Columbia Graphophone Company's Schubert centenary competition; but his life was clouded about this time by the deaths of his first wife and their only daughter, apart from his own illness; his fourth symphony of 1934 is a kind of requiem for his daughter. He was given many honours in his last years. In 1937 disease compelled him to give up his teaching activities and confine himself to composition, and in 1938 he produced what is perhaps his greatest work, the oratorio *The Book with the Seven Seals*. He died in Vienna in 1939, leaving an unfinished cantata which was later completed by R. Wagner. His second wife Margarethe survived him.

Schmidt was considered the most important composer in Austria during his lifetime, a period when the music of Schoenberg and his school was unappreciated by the Austrian public. His music continues the tradition of Wagner and Strauss; it is rich and strongly melodic, but does not attempt to be avant-garde, though it has an individual flavour. Schmidt wrote a second opera, *Fredegundis*, in 1922 and also a number of works for organ.

H.S.

SCHOENBERG, Arnold
(b. Vienna, 13 Sept 1874;
d. Los Angeles, 13 July 1951)

Arnold Schoenberg's parents came from German Jewish communities in Central Europe; his father, Samuel Schoenberg had come to Vienna from Bratislava and his mother Pauline, née Nachod, from Prague. Both parents were interested in music; Samuel Schoenberg sang in a choral society and several members of the Nachod family became professional singers. Samuel Schoenberg supported his family by running a shoe shop. At the age of six Arnold entered the Volksschule in the Leopoldstadt district of Vienna, where the family lived, and moved to the Realschule in 1885. There seems to have been no music-making in the Schoenberg household, and they did not possess a piano, but Arnold learnt to play the violin and viola as a child and made music with his friend Oskar Adler, eventually mastering the 'cello as well. Samuel Schoenberg died at the end of 1890, so Arnold had to take a job in a bank in order to support his mother and sister, who was two years younger than himself. He did not enjoy this employment, and the director of the bank complained that he was covering all his papers with music. His earliest surviving compositions from this period are three piano pieces dated 1894, strongly influenced by Brahms.

Schoenberg seems to have left the bank in 1895, and from then onwards earned his living as a musician. He obtained work as a chorus master with some workers' choral societies, and through this met Alexander von Zemlinsky (1872–1942), the composer. Together with other young musicians they formed the 'Polyhymnia' orchestral society, where they were able to play their own works. Schoenberg played the 'cello in this ensemble. Zemlinsky introduced him to Wagner's music, which exerted a strong influence on him from then onwards, and also gave him the only formal musical training which he had in the whole of his life. About this time Schoenberg wrote a string quartet in D major which was performed in Vienna on the 17th March 1898

by the Fitzner Quartet. Four days later he left the Jewish faith of his father and entered the Protestant community, influenced by his friend the opera singer Walter Pieau. He also wrote the songs which were later published as Op. 1–3, and was able to earn a living by orchestrating operettas. In 1899 he wrote his first really important work, the string sextet *Verklärte Nacht*, and in 1900 he began work on the colossal *Gurrelieder*, which however he was not able to finish till 1911 owing to the necessity of earning a living. In 1901 he married his friend's sister, Mathilde von Zemlinsky, and the couple moved to Berlin, where Schoenberg had been engaged as conductor at Ernst von Wolzogen's 'Überbrettl', a kind of intellectual cabaret; he also wrote some songs for this theatre. He was helped by Richard Strauss, who obtained the Liszt Scholarship for him. While in Berlin Schoenberg wrote the symphonic poem *Pelleas und Melisande*, at the same time and without any knowledge of Debussy's opera: Strauss had suggested the idea to him, and the music is somewhat influenced by Strauss. Schoenberg's eldest daughter Trudi was born in Berlin in 1902; she later married the composer Felix Greissle. Wolzogen left the 'Überbrettl' in 1903 and Schoenberg returned to Vienna.

Here Zemlinsky was able to obtain 'bread and butter work' for him, and he also began his long career as a teacher; among his first pupils were Alban Berg and Anton von Webern. Meanwhile *Verklärte Nacht* had been performed in both Vienna and Berlin, arousing considerable attention, and in 1904 Schoenberg conducted the first performance of *Pelleas und Melisande* at the newly-founded Society of Contemporary Musicians in Vienna. His next important works were the First String Quartet, still tonal but very complex in texture (1905) and the First Chamber Symphony (1906), in which tonality is stretched to its limits. Schoenberg also became friendly with, and was helped by, Mahler, and the latter's departure from Vienna at the end of 1907 was a severe blow to him. About this time he began to be interested in painting, and he and his wife took lessons from a young painter, Richard Gerstl, who was living in the same house. Schoenberg's marriage had been unhappy since the birth of his son Georg in September 1906, and in the summer of 1908 Mathilde Schoenberg ran off with Gerstl. Mutual friends, especially Webern, persuaded her to return, but Gerstl could not bear to break with the Schoenbergs,

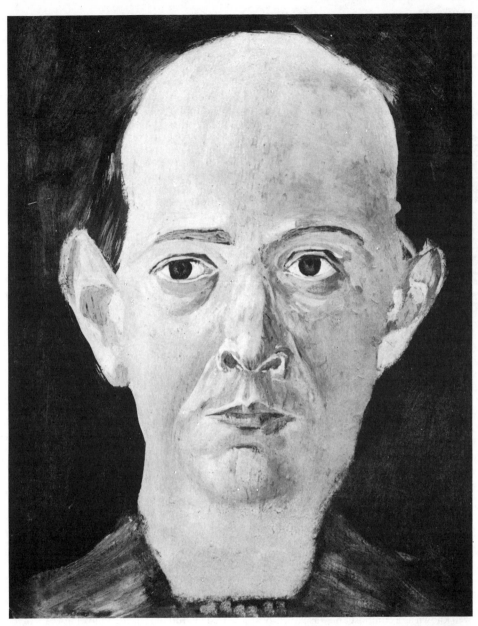

Schoenberg, a self-portrait.

and on the 4th November 1908 he committed suicide at the age of twenty-five. This event is reflected in a curious passage in the scherzo of Schoenberg's Second String Quartet, which he was writing at this time; the folk song *O du lieber Augustin* is played by the second violin over a parodistic accompaniment in the other instruments; the significance lies in the words of the song 'Alles ist hin' (All is lost), not only referring to Schoenberg's domestic situation but implying some kind of musical surrender.

But Schoenberg soon recovered from his depression: the final movement of the quartet, which he dedicated to his wife, contains passages which go beyond the bounds of tonality, and on the 27th September 1908 he wrote the

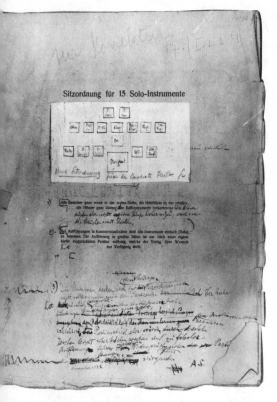

A page of the Chamber Symphony, Op. 5, with corrections by Schoenberg.

first piece in which tonality is completely suspended, the song *Du lehnest wider eine Silberweide* from the song-cycle *The Book of the Hanging Gardens.* During the next five years Schoenberg poured out the first 'atonal' compositions by which he is chiefly known (he disliked the term himself) the Piano Pieces Op. 11 and 19, the Orchestral Pieces Op. 16, the two dramas *Erwartung* and *Die Glückliche Hand*, *Pierrot Lunaire*, *Herzgewächse* and the Orchestral Songs Op. 22. But though he was now well known as a composer he was violently attacked both orally and in print. Concerts at which works by his pupils, including Webern and Berg, were performed, were used to discredit him as a teacher, which naturally affected his income. In addition he was subjected to political anti-semitic attacks when it became known that he was to be offered a professorship at the Vienna Academy of Music, where he was working as a private teacher. During this period he also completed the *Har-*

monielehre, an important treatise on classical and romantic harmony up to Debussy, Bartók and his own early works. But in view of his difficult financial situation he decided to move to Berlin, where he was able to teach at the Stern Conservatorium; Strauss had recommended him for this position. He went there in the autumn of 1911 after a summer spent on the Starnberg Lake in Bavaria – he had fled there in August after an engineer living in the same house as the Schoenbergs in Vienna made a murderous attack on him.

In Berlin things went better and Schoenberg obtained greater recognition. Busoni was helpful to him, and he conducted *Pierrot Lunaire* in many German and Austrian cities. In 1912 Sir Henry Wood gave the first performance of the Five Orchestral Pieces at a Promenade concert in London, and in 1913 the first performance of the *Gurrelieder* took place in Vienna under Franz Schreker. It was Schoenberg's first real popular success. Schoenberg conducted *Pelleas* in St Petersburg in the 1912–13 season, and in 1914 he conducted the *Gurrelieder* in Leipzig and the Five Orchestral Pieces in Amsterdam and London. Further plans were upset by the outbreak of war, and in 1915 Schoenberg moved back to Vienna; towards the end of the year he was called up for military service. Surprisingly enough he was a very patriotic soldier in this war, and even wrote a march, The Iron Brigade, for a regimental concert. He was given leave in the autumn of 1916, and next year he began composing the oratorio *Jacob's Ladder*, which was left unfinished. Late in the summer he was called up again, but was finally released towards the end of the year as physically unfit.

In January 1918 Schoenberg settled in Mödling near Vienna; he continued his teaching, and in the autumn he founded the Society for Private Musical Performances, which gave contemporary works under ideal conditions. In 1920 he conducted the *Gurrelieder* at the Vienna Opera and also conducted and lectured in Holland. In the following years there were several foreign tours by the Vienna *Pierrot* ensemble. During this time the 'twelve-note method' began to mature; it first appeared in the last of the Five Piano Pieces, Op. 23. Schoenberg, who had written little music since 1914, apart from the sketches of *Jacob's Ladder*, now composed a number of works employing this method, including the Suite for Piano Op. 25 (1921–3), the Wind Quintet (1923–4) and the Suite for seven instruments,

Op. 29 (1925). On the death of Busoni in 1924 Schoenberg was offered the position of director of a master class in cc nposition at the Prussian Academy of Arts in Berlin. He moved there in January 1926. His first wife had died in 1923, and in 1924 he married Gertrud, the sister of the violinist Rudolf Kolisch, who was a faithful interpreter of his works for many years. She bore him three children, Nuria, Ronald, and Lawrence in the 1930s. This was probably the most successful part of Schoenberg's life; his financial worries were less, and he was able to write a number of important works, including the Third String Quartet (1927), the Variations for Orchestra (1926–8), the one-act opera *Von Heute auf Morgen* (1928–9) and the first two acts of *Moses und Aron* (1930–2). But the climate of Berlin did not agree with his health, and he had to spend some time in Switzerland and Spain.

The advent of the Nazis to power in 1933 led the President of the Academy to announce that 'the Jewish influence at the Academy must be eliminated'. Schoenberg promptly resigned his post and left Berlin on the 17th May. He went to France, returning to the Jewish faith in Paris on the 24th July, but failed to find work there, and as the Berlin Academy had illegally terminated his contract he accepted an offer from the Malkin Conservatory in Boston, arriving in New York on the 31st October. At first he taught in Boston and New York, but his health was so poor that he moved to Hollywood in the following year. He began by teaching privately, but later lectured at the University of Southern California, and in 1936 he was appointed Professor of Music at the University of California, Los Angeles. His principal works of this period were the Fourth String Quartet and the Violin Concerto, both written in 1936. He became an American citizen in 1941; in 1944, on reaching his seventieth birthday, he was compelled to retire from his university post and return to private teaching, as the pension was so small. In 1946 he had an almost fatal illness in which his heart actually stopped beating; he described this experience in the String Trio of that year. Other late works include the Fantasy for violin with piano accompaniment and some choral works. His health continued to decline and he died on the 13th July 1951.

Though many composers such as Bartók, Busoni, Reger and Scriabin were writing highly chromatic music in the first decade of this century, Schoenberg was the first to draw the logical conclusion from this tendency and to suspend tonality or key-feeling altogether. His later 'method of composition with twelve notes related only to one another' gave his works a basis of organisation and enabled him to write in larger instrumental forms. Both these innovations were attacked at the time as making music unintelligible or 'mathematical', but Schoenberg himself said: 'In the formula, the method of composition with twelve tones, the accent is not so much on the twelve tones as on the art of composing'. In fact he was very much an instinctive composer who usually wrote very quickly; if he could not finish a work at once he often abandoned it altogether. In spite of his long life he only wrote fifty works with opus numbers and another ten without, apart from arrangements. At the best his music is highly expressive and dramatic, as in *Pierrot Lunaire*, *Erwartung* and *Moses und Aron*, for instance, and it has intellectual power without becoming academic. And his innovations have influenced a whole epoch and have spread all over the world, so that he can truly be regarded as the father of modern music. Schoenberg also wrote numerous books and articles which were highly stimulating, and his many pupils have carried on his work. Though his music has not even now become 'popular' in the way Stravinsky's has, it is the kind of music which will be appreciated more and more with increasing acquaintance.

H.S.

SCHREKER, Franz
(b. Monaco, 23 March 1878;
d. Berlin, 21 March 1934)

Though Austrian, Schreker was, in fact, born in Monaco. He was a student at the Vienna Konservatorium from 1892 to 1900; he studied violin and composition, the latter with Fuchs. It was not until 1908 that Schreker achieved his first big success, with the performance of his ballet *Der Geburtstag der Infantin*. In the same year he founded the Philharmonic Choir, which he conducted until 1920 and which was instrumental in bringing to performance many modern works, notably Schoenberg's *Gurrelieder*. On the strength of his growing reputation, Schreker was in 1912 appointed to a teaching post in composition at the Vienna *Akademie für Musik*. On the 18th August 1912 the première of his opera *Der ferne Klang* (*c.* 1901–10) in Frankfurt-am-Main established Schreker as one of the most progressive composers of his time. The première of his next opera, *Das Spielwerk und die Prinzessin*, was given in 1913 simultaneously in Frankfurt, where it had a *succès d'estime*, and in Vienna, where it caused a scandal. This was the first and last of Schreker's mature operas to receive its première in his own country. His next two operas, *Die Gezeichneten* and *Der Schatzgräber*, consolidated the reputation already gained by *Der ferne Klang*. They received their premières in Frankfurt, in 1918 and 1920 respectively.

In 1920 Schreker gained the Directorship of the Berlin *Hochschule für Musik*, which he held until 1932. For the next ten years his fame was at its peak. His later operas were *Irrelohe* (première 1924, Cologne), *Der singende Teufel* (1928, Berlin), *Christophorus* (withdrawn before its première under threat of Nazi disruption), and *Der Schmied von Gent*, whose première (1932, Berlin) was marred by Nazi demonstrations. In the same year Schreker was forced to resign from the Directorship of the *Hochschule*, and he took over a master-class in composition at the Prussian Academy of Arts, from which he was dismissed at the end of 1933. The shock of his dismissal caused a severe heart-attack, from which he died on the 21st March 1934.

Nowadays Schreker is remembered mostly for his influence on Alban Berg's *Wozzeck*. Berg made the vocal score of *Der ferne Klang* in 1911 and thus knew Schreker's opera in every detail. Act II of Schreker's opera, with its skilful dovetailing of on-stage instrumental groups with the main orchestra, undoubtedly had a decisive influence on the fourth scene of Act II of *Wozzeck*. In addition, Schreker's act is cast, albeit somewhat loosely, in the form of a symphony: Berg's Act II is cast in the same form, though much more strictly so.

Schreker's earlier operas, on which his fame largely rested before his eclipse in the 1930s, can be said to combine a Straussian richness of orchestration with an impressionistic tendency towards non-functional harmony and pointillistic scoring. These characteristics, allied to an almost Puccinian theatrical instinct, probably account for Schreker's tremendous popularity between the two world wars. In his later years, perhaps conscious that his hyper-romantic style was in danger of becoming obsolete, he moved towards the neo-classical ideal: his last opera, *Der Schmied von Gent*, shows a preoccupation with dissonant, linear counterpoint and with 'closed' forms such as fugue and passacaglia that presents a startling contrast to his earlier manner.

N.C.

SCHUBERT, Franz
(b. Vienna, 31 Jan 1797;
d. Vienna, 19 Nov 1828)

Schubert, most quintessentially Viennese of the great Viennese composers, was born, lived and died in the city which, in his day, was the world capital of music. The Schuberts had eleven children, of whom only three, including Franz, survived infancy. Schubert senior was a schoolmaster in a Viennese suburb, and a keen amateur musician. He himself taught young Franz the violin, and the boy's elder brother Ignaz taught him the piano. When he was ten he began to have more formal musical tuition from the organist of the parish church. That the boy was possessed of more than ordinary talent for music was very soon evident. In 1808 he was accepted as a choir-boy in the court chapel, which gave him automatic admission to the principal boarding-school in Vienna, the *Stadtkonvikt*. Before long he was the leading violinist in the school orchestra, and was occasionally allowed to conduct it. His musical tutors at the *Stadtkonvikt* included Salieri, Mozart's old rival.

Schubert made quick progress both in his musical and non-musical studies, and although he was shy he appears to have made friends easily through the gentle nature of his temperament. His first compositions date from his years at school: most significant among them was his first song, 'Hagars Klage' which he wrote at the age of fourteen. Though he was to write in most of the accepted forms – symphony, quartet, sonata, even opera with which he had surprisingly little success – it is primarily as a writer of songs that Schubert is still loved today. These first childhood settings already reveal his extraordinarily fluent melodic gift and his own personal lyrical style.

In 1812 Schubert's mother died, and the following year his father married again. 1813 was Franz's last year at school, and although he would have preferred to attempt to find a career in music immediately he bowed to the inevitable and to his father's wishes. After a

Schubert by Rieder, 1825.

few months at a teachers' training school, he took up a position as assistant teacher in his father's school, and continued to compose in his spare time. He had been reading Goethe's *Faust*, and his setting of Gretchen's 'Meine Ruh' ist hin', the song known as 'Gretchen am Spinnrade', which he wrote one day in October 1814, is his first masterpiece. Many other songs followed, several to poems by Johann Mayrhofer, a minor Viennese poet with whom Schubert had become friends. Symphonies, dances for social gatherings, sonatas, choral music, and always more songs continued to flow from his pen in 1814 and

1815. In the latter year he also turned his attention to the theatre, and composed five operas, in quick succession. He composed a hundred and fifty songs in this same year, among them the astonishing 'Erlkönig', his masterly setting of Goethe's popular ballad. The story is told, and is well documented, of how 'Der Erlkönig' was composed at white heat in almost no more time than it took Schubert to read the poem.

In 1816, Schubert made the acquaintance of Franz von Schober, a law student and amateur poet, and formed another deep friendship. In the rooms shared by two other friends, there were often convivial evenings with music by Schubert, occasions which the circle of friends called Schubertiads. It was for these domestic surroundings that many of

Schubert's most delightful occasional pieces were composed. The composer himself, a stocky young man whose height was no more than five feet two inches, sat and played at the piano, frequently improvising waltzes and other dances, some of which he would later put on paper.

At the end of the year, Schubert moved into rooms in the house of Schober's mother where he remained for some months. Temporarily leaving his teaching job, he concentrated for a time upon composition, and in March 1817, Schober introduced him to the famous opera singer, the baritone Johann Michael Vogl. Vogl was then nearly fifty and approaching the end of his operatic career. Struck by Schubert's genius in song, he devoted himself to singing and popularising the songs, not only at the Schubertiads but in his public concerts as well. 'When Vogl sings and I accompany him', Schubert wrote to his brother Ferdinand, 'we seem for the moment to be one, which strikes the good people here as

something quite unheard of.' Though Schober was a mediocre poet, posterity remembers him with profound gratitude for it was to a poem of his that, in 1817, Schubert composed one of his most beautiful and deeply felt songs, his testament to his own art, 'An die Musik'. Other famous and greatly loved songs composed during that year were 'Der Tod und das Mädchen' and 'Die Forelle'. In December Schubert returned for a time to teaching and to the bosom of his family, but he was restless and when, in July 1818, he was offered the position of music teacher to the children of Count Esterházy, he accepted, and moved to the Count's castle at Zseliz in Hungary, about a hundred miles from Vienna. But he missed his friends and the musical and social delights of Vienna. By November he was back, and living with Mayrhofer. His music was beginning to be known beyond the immediate circle of his admirers, and Schubert himself began to embark upon journeys in the company of Vogl. In the summer of 1819 they spent three months in Steyr, ninety miles from Vienna, in countryside which Schubert found 'inconceivably lovely'. It was here that Schubert began to compose the popular 'Trout' Quintet. Back in Vienna, he continued his prolific pace of

A Schubertiad by Moritz von Schwind. Schubert at the piano, with the singer Vogl on his right.

Schubert (right) with his Graz acquaintances Johann Jenger and Anselm Hüttenbrenner.

composition. In 1820, two of Schubert's operas or operettas were produced in Vienna: *Die Zwillingsbrüder*, with Vogl doubling the roles of the twin brothers, and *Die Zauberharfe*. Neither was very well received, and none of Schubert's other works for the theatre were performed during his lifetime.

1820 and 1821 saw the completion of several more masterpieces of song and of chamber music, and also saw Schubert extending the range of his friendships. Through the Esterházys he met Baron von Schönstein, who had a fine baritone voice and who made Schubert's songs more widely known. (It was Von Schönstein who, in later years, introduced Liszt to the songs.) Schubert now began to change his lodgings rather more frequently, usually for no apparent reason. It became his habit to compose in the mornings, meet his friends in the afternoons in the coffee houses of Vienna, and perform at the sociable Schubertiads in the evenings. He also began to earn money from the publication of several of his songs.

The friendship with Schober deepened. In the summer of 1821 the two men and several other friends spent a month in the country at Atzenbrugg, and Schubert produced some delightful dance music for their parties. In the autumn he and Schober collaborated on an opera, *Alfonso und Estrella*, some of it written in beautiful surroundings near St Pölten, at a castle owned by Schober's uncle, the Bishop of St Pölten. At the beginning of 1822, the two men took rooms together in Vienna in the Spiegelgasse. By now the young artist Moritz von Schwind, later to become famous, and the playwright Eduard Bauernfeld had been added to the circle of friends. This year a number of songs were composed to poems by Mayrhofer, and also the 'Wanderer' Fantasy for piano.

Schubert's most popular non-vocal work, his Symphony No. 8 in B minor, was also begun in the autumn of 1822: begun, but never finished, for it is the work still known as the 'Unfinished Symphony'. The two movements which exist show that it was intended to be a larger-scale work than the earlier symphonies. In its truncated state, however, it is the work's lyrical qualities which are emphasised. It is one of Schubert's most beautiful creations,

The house in Vienna in which Schubert died.

and the fact that he broke off work on it because he became ill with syphilis is a sad irony. By the beginning of 1823, Schubert was very ill, and had moved to his father's house. In May he was admitted to the General Hospital in Vienna, and it may have been here that he began to compose his sweetly sentimental cycle of songs, *Die schöne Müllerin,* to poems by Wilhelm Müller.

In the summer, Schubert went to Linz and Steyr to recuperate, and to work on another opera, *Fierrabras.* But he was never completely rid of his disease, for which in those days there was no real cure, and there can be no doubt that it was a major contributary cause of his death at the tragically early age of thirty-one. In the five years that remained to him, he suffered intermittent bouts of illness and depression, which radically affected his intrinsically sunny disposition. For the production, in December 1823, of *Rosamunde,* a romantic drama by Helmina von Chézy, he composed incidental music. The play was a miserable failure, but Schubert's music remains deservedly popular in concert performance.

A number of fine instrumental works date from the early part of 1824, among them the Quartets in A minor and D minor (with one movement a set of variations on 'Der Tod und das Mädchen') and the delightful Octet. But this is also the year in which the Schubertian circle of friends began to break up and to reform. Schubert's mood was one of misery and despair, and he looked back nostalgically to the happy days of ten years past. In the summer he went to tutor the Esterházy children again, but wrote to Schober of his loneliness 'in the depths of the Hungarian country whither I unfortunately let myself be enticed'. He longed to be back in Vienna, and finally returned in September. Having lost some of his earlier acquaintances, he became closer than ever to Moritz von Schwind and Bauernfeld. He went to live in rooms next door to Schwind, and was soon composing new songs which he performed with Vogl in various houses. Early in 1825 the great A minor Piano Sonata was composed, and the songs from poems in Sir Walter Scott's *The Lady of the Lake,* among them 'Ave Maria'.

From the end of May to the beginning of October, 1825, Schubert and Vogl travelled through the beautiful mountains and lakes of Upper Austria, staying at Steyr, Gmunden, Linz, and Badgastein. This was a particularly productive tour for Schubert. Not only did he and Vogl perform his songs wherever they went; Schubert also composed some of his loveliest music, inspired by the beauty and grandeur of the landscape around him. At Gastein he finished the D major Piano Sonata and one of his most magnificent songs, 'Die Allmacht'.

In the autumn in Vienna, Schober, who had been absent for some time in Breslau, rejoined the circle of Schubertians and for a time the conviviality of earlier days returned. The following January Schubert composed some of his finest Goethe settings and completed his D minor String Quartet. More works were published, though none of them brought a great deal of income to their composer. In April Schubert petitioned the Emperor for the position of Vice Musical Director to the Court Chapel. But he was unsuccessful, and the appointment went to Josef Weigl. Schubert is said to have remarked, 'Much as I should have liked to receive this appointment, I shall have to make the best of the matter since it was given to so worthy a man as Weigl.'

In February of 1827, the first part of *Die Winterreise* was composed: twelve of the twenty-four songs which go to make up this profound song cycle, which many regard as Schubert's greatest achievement. In May, the still young composer visited the dying Beethoven and a few days later acted as one of the torch-bearers in Beethoven's funeral procession. Schubert's reputation had by now spread beyond Austria to Germany, and performances of his songs were increasingly frequent. In June he was honoured by being made a representative to the Vienna Philharmonic Society, and in the autumn he visited Graz where, for the inevitable Schubertiads, he composed some of his most charming dance music. But he was in ill-health and depressed again when he returned to Vienna and to the completion of the *Winterreise* songs. The two piano trios, favourite works, were also composed in the autumn of 1827, and most of the piano Impromptus.

Schubert embarked upon his last year in poor health and spirits, yet miraculously he produced during that year his great C major Symphony, the ineffably beautiful Quintet in the same key, the final three piano sonatas and the fourteen songs which go to make up the *Schwanengesang*. He succumbed to typhoid, and died after an illness of three weeks. On his death-bed he corrected the proofs of *Die Winterreise*.

Franz Schubert, most lovable and accessible of the great Viennese composers, was for many years after his death neglected and forgotten. But he is now recognised as the equal of and the successor to Haydn, Mozart and Beethoven, and as a strong link in the chain which leads from them to Bruckner, Mahler and the second Viennese school of Schoenberg, Berg and Webern. Some of his music reaches exalted heights, some of it is content to inhabit more sociable earthly domains. He is one of those few composers who are for all moods, and for all seasons.

C.O.

SCHUMANN, Robert
(b. Zwickau, 8 June 1810;
d. Endenich, nr. Bonn, 29 July 1856)

Schumann is a key figure in the romantic movement, an artist who, not only in his music, expressed vividly and subtly the romantic's peculiar obsession with individual fantasy, but who also understood and tried to disseminate the deeper-rooted philosophy of romanticism, its literary origins, its connections with liberal thought, and its glorification of feeling and passion over reflection and self-control. But perhaps most important, Schumann exemplifies the anomalies of romanticism. Though an admirer of the

fantastic elements in Jean Paul and E. T. A. Hoffmann, he was himself of conservative temperament and rather taciturn: except when young and in private, the least flamboyant of men. When he married he soon became domesticated and, by romantic standards, boring. (Liszt and Wagner both found him personally dull.) His own music, particularly early on, is marvellously whimsical and spontaneous, but he himself, in respecting the formal classical styles of writing, thought that the greatest honour was to write a good symphony, and while at the same time looking forward to 'the music of the future', almost completely failed to understand the two most progressive musicians of his day, Liszt and Wagner. Romantically enough, he died in a lunatic asylum, having for most of his life suffered premonitions of just such an end. But medical opinion now tells us that his symptoms were probably caused by syphilis, contracted before his marriage. There could be no more sordid kick-back from the romantic indulgence of passion.

Schumann was born in 1810. He was exceptionally lucky in his circumstances. His parents were well-to-do, and since his father was a bookseller and publisher, the boy had ready access to books and enjoyed the other advantages of a bookish, literary, quietly cultivated ambience. While still at school, at the Zwickau Lyceum, he got to know Shakespeare, Goethe, Schiller, Jean Paul, and a wide range of classical authors, Latin and Greek. At one time he himself aspired to be a writer. In his late teens his letters have that flowery, rather affected literariness much cultivated in the dawning age of self-expression. They are, nevertheless, well written; scenes and people are vividly described, and one feels the personal glow and enthusiasm of the writer. At this period he also enjoyed intense, romantic friendships: there was a boy called Emil Flechsig, with whom he shared an overweaning admiration for Jean Paul and with whom he exchanged Jean-Paulesque letters full of extravagant imagery; and a certain Gisbert Rosen, a fellow law-student whom Schumann accompanied on a tour of Germany and eventually followed to Heidelberg University.

Neither of Schumann's parents was musical, but his own musical gifts were encouraged from the start. He took piano lessons at school, and was soon showing outstanding ability. A strong early impression was of the playing of Moscheles, whom his father took him to hear at Carlsbad one day in 1819. It seems likely that if the father had not died when Schumann was sixteen (partly from shock at the suicide of Robert's elder sister Emilie) Robert might have embarked on a pianistic career earlier than he did. As it was his mother, distrusting music as a livelihood, directed him towards law, and in 1828 Schumann enrolled in the faculty at Leipzig University. From the outset his interest in the subject was minimal, and when, later that year, he put forward the distinguished law professor at Heidelberg, Anton Friedrich Thibaut, as an argument for his proceeding to that more distant university, he was certainly influenced by the fact that Thibaut was also a well-known musical aesthetician. Gradually, and with a good deal of sensitivity, Schumann persuaded his mother, and his guardian Gottlob Rudel, that he ought to take up music. He named the well-known piano teacher Friedrich Wieck, whom he had met in Leipzig during his tour with Rosen, as a guarantor of his musical potential. And, when he finally got his way in 1830, it was to Wieck that he went for tuition, board and lodging.

1830 also marks roughly the beginning of Schumann's mature career as a composer. Before that he had written isolated pieces, notably songs, and had poured hours of piano music into the atmosphere in the form of improvisation. For some years the piano had been, in his own description, a diary of his thoughts and feelings. And so it was to remain. For a decade he wrote little but piano music. At first he pursued diligently Wieck's course of instruction. But at some time around 1832 he suffered an accident to his right hand, perhaps as a result of experimenting with a device for making his fingers more independent, or perhaps (a recent and very speculative theory) as a side-effect of the then normal mercury treatment for syphilis. In any case his right hand was permanently crippled, and he had to give up the idea of a virtuoso career. Instead he applied himself to that of a composer. Piano music flowed from his pen: *Carnaval*, the *Symphonic Studies*, the *Fantasy in C*, the *Davidsbündler-Tänze*, the three sonatas, plus many smaller pieces, all date, in conception at least, from this time. In 1834 he also embarked on a secondary career as a writer on music. He helped found the *Neue Zeitschrift für Musik*, and when, later in the year, his collaborators dropped out for various reasons, he took over sole editorship, which he retained until 1844. He soon became one of the best and best-known music critics

of the day. Though sometimes wayward in his judgement, he did much to establish certain criteria of criticism, such as the recognition of imaginative excellence and an appreciation of technical detail, which we now accept without question but which were by no means general in the 1830s. In true romantic spirit, Schumann saw himself as a crusader defending the great tradition of German art against the encroachments of philistinism. He attacked empty virtuosity and jejune prettiness and the mere parroting of classical formulae. He was the first German critic to recognise Chopin, one of the first to admire Berlioz, and the first to predict Brahms's greatness. He collaborated with Mendelssohn in reviving the music of Bach, and was vociferous in defence of Beethoven and Schubert (whose Great C major Symphony he unearthed in Vienna in 1838). Above all he wrote expertly and colourfully, but always seriously and with studied fairness, seldom allowing personal bias to influence his musical judgement. Thus his literary background had, in the end, a practical outlet.

At Wieck's, Schumann slowly became intimate with the teacher's young daughter Clara (1819–96), who was herself already one of the best pianists in Germany and her father's star pupil. Their relationship had one serious interruption, in 1834–5 when Schumann was briefly engaged to a fellow pupil, Ernestine von Fricken (the *Symphonic Studies* are variations on a theme by her adoptive father). But thereafter the only obstacle to their love and eventual union was Clara's father, who as soon as he became aware of it objected violently to the affair and refused to agree to the marriage. The dispute is one of the most distasteful in the whole annals of music. Wieck forced the couple to separate, opened their letters, and eventually embarked on a campaign of personal vilification which ended with a law-suit and judgement against him. Robert and Clara were finally married on the 12th September 1840, the day before Clara's 21st birthday.

His marriage introduced a completely new phase in Schumann's creative work, part of which may be traced to Clara's personal influence. Among wives, she belonged to the type that wish their husbands to conquer the highest summits, however unsuited to their climbing gifts, and she soon brought pressure to bear on her husband to do what, to tell the truth, he had himself often dreamed of doing, namely write symphonies. Already the piano no longer seemed adequate to express the

Schumann by Bendemann.

complex of feelings which welled up as Schumann's life came to its crisis. 1840 is supremely his song year (the *Liederkreis*, Op. 24 and 39, *Dichterliebe, Frauenliebe und leben,* and many other famous songs, some 140 in all), and though mostly these were written before his marriage, the influence of that impending event was clearly important. He then turned to the symphony and, in 1842, to chamber music. Clara meanwhile endeavoured to keep up her playing, but found it hard to practise when Robert had to have silence for composing. He for his part found it galling to take a back seat when he ac-

companied her on tour. He even came home before her from a tour of Russia in 1844, apparently for this reason. His health began to cause alarm. He suffered from many symptoms of nervous breakdown, but above all experienced aural hallucinations which are now seen as evidence of his previously quiescent syphilis. He resigned from the teaching post Mendelssohn had created for him in 1843 in the new Leipzig Conservatory, and at the end of 1844 the couple moved to Dresden, in the hope that a quieter life would restore Robert's health.

For a time the hope was fulfilled. Dresden was dull, conservative, and undemanding, despite the presence of the young Wagner, with whom Schumann struck up what can only be called a misunderstanding. He was able to compose. The Piano Concerto was completed (1845) and the Second Symphony written (1845–6; it is strictly No. 3). Also, perhaps in emulation of Wagner, Schumann began writing for the theatre: *Genoveva*, his only opera (1847–8) and incidental music for Byron's *Manfred* (1848–9). He reverted to song and to solo piano music, and wrote a whole series of partsongs for the local choral society, whose conductor he became in 1847. But the years in Dresden still read unhappily. True they mark a resting-place on the downward slope. But already Schumann seems careworn and blunted. There is something symbolic in his escaping from a press-gang in the 1849 revolution through the back door of his house, while Wagner, only three years younger, is designing barricades. Schumann must have been relieved to accept, the following year, the post of Director of Music in Düsseldorf.

The Rhineland town, home of a famous festival, welcomed him feverishly. But it was to regret its choice. The directorship involved conducting both choir and orchestra, and for this, as it proved, Schumann had no talent. Worse, neither he nor Clara seemed able to recognise the fact. After a good start relations quickly deteriorated, there were resignations, and finally, after a particularly disastrous concert in October 1853, Schumann was himself forced to resign. Though he had never shown ability as a conductor, his competence was by now definitely impaired by mental decline. Naturally reserved, he had become completely introverted, unable to communicate, and often unaware of his surroundings. His poor stick technique was not offset by personal magnetism. A dying shaft of lucidity had, in September 1853, illuminated the coming genius of the young Brahms, about whom Schumann wrote a famous article for the *Neue Zeitschrift*. By February 1854 he was severely assailed by hallucinations, incessant aural noise, and the imagined ministrations of angels and demons. On the 27th he threw himself into the Rhine, but was rescued and taken to the asylum at Endenich, near Bonn. There, after two and a half years of misery, he at last died, on the 29th July 1856.

Schumann's incontrovertible greatness rests on his early music, up to 1840, and on two or three later works. The long series of piano works 1830–40 are a major contribution to the romantic keyboard literature, and the songs of 1840, especially those of the *Lieder-*

Clara Schumann.

kreis, Op. 39 (poems by Eichendorff) and *Dichterliebe* and the many other settings of Heine, rank among the greatest lieder after Schubert. The two oeuvres really belong together. Schumann's genius as a lyricist is already evident in the piano works with their accumulation of tiny characteristic pieces. Going over to song, he made a crucial innovation in treating the piano as an equal partner with the voice, whose line, in some of the earliest songs, duplicates lines in the piano part. This intimate marriage of voice and accompaniment was to influence Wolf profoundly. The tone is also unique and original. Where Chopin offers a rich, passionate emotion tempered by an exquisitely refined and decorative piano style, in Schumann the feeling is elusive, enigmatic and often semi-humorous. A certain secretness reminds one of Schumann's love of codes, acrostics and double meanings. Of all early romantic music, his is the wittiest, the most tinged with irony and mockery, the least self-important, though often painfully beautiful, as throughout *Dichterliebe*, or at the start of the F sharp minor Sonata.

His attempts to expand this sketch-pad style into the dialectical context of the symphony and string quartet have always provoked disagreement. The symphonies, long neglected, have recently come into their own. Their imaginative qualities are undoubtedly great, they show a novel and nearly always successful formal balance, and are by no means as badly scored as is sometimes made out, though their Allegro scoring tends to be undifferentiated and wearisome to play. The chamber music is also ineptly scored and awkward to bring off. But in an expert performance a work like the A major Quartet (1842) can still leave one marvelling at Schumann's fertility of invention. Of the later works this is less consistently true. About 1845 Schumann began to study Bach, but though the influence had some interesting effects (for instance, in the strange, linear textures of the last songs) it was never completely absorbed, any more than that of Wagner, whose sense of the theatre is completely absent from *Genoveva*. However, the familiar argument that Schumann's creative powers were in decline along with his mental health from as early as 1844 is hard to sustain against the evidence of works like the Second and Third Symphonies (1846 and 1850), the 'Cello Concerto (1850), the *Faust* music (1844–53) or the D minor Piano Trio (1847). Probably after 1850 Schumann was becoming too disjointed to sustain the effort of concentration necessary for good composition. But before that his faults, such as they were, were mainly technical.

S.W.

SCHÜTZ, Heinrich
(b. Köstritz, 8 Oct 1585;
d. Dresden, 6 Nov 1672)

Heinrich Schütz, the most eminent German composer before J. S. Bach, was born at Köstritz in Saxony in 1585. In 1599 he became a chorister at the chapel of the Landgrave of Hesse-Kassel, and received a thorough musical and general education. In 1608 he entered the University of Marburg, with the intention of taking up law as a career. On a visit to Marburg, the Landgrave marked in his *protégé* a leaning towards music, and paid for him to go to Venice, where his teacher was Giovanni Gabrieli. He remained there from 1609 to 1612, and during that time composed his first music, some five-part madrigals. For a while he returned to his law studies, now at Leipzig, but they were finally abandoned when he was appointed organist to the Landgrave.

In 1613 he visited Dresden with the Landgrave, and helped the following year to prepare the music for the christening of the son of the Elector of Saxony, who appointed him to the Electoral chapel in 1615. There he reorganised the electoral music along Italian lines, sending musicians to Italy to imbibe the new concerted style. In 1619 he married Magdalene Wildeck, who bore him two daughters, but their life together was all too short: she died in 1625. To distract himself from his sorrow, and to gain fresh impetus for his work, he went back to Italy in 1628 to familiarise himself with the music of Claudio Monteverdi. (q.v.). Back in Saxony, he found that the turmoils occasioned by the Thirty Years War were upsetting the tempo of normal life, music included. He was given leave to become *Kapellmeister* at the Danish Court in Copenhagen from 1633 to 1635. He returned there from time to time afterwards, but Dresden became his unwilling base again from 1641. He was dissatisfied with the organisation at the electoral court and with non-payment of musicians, but his resignation was consistently turned down by the Elector, and he continued with his work there intermittently right down to the time of his death. In 1657 he moved to Wessenfels to live with his sister. In his later years, his powers began to fail, and he could hear only with difficulty. He spent most of his days reading the scriptures. He died at Dresden in 1672.

Almost all Schütz's music consists of vocal settings of sacred texts. They are uniquely important in bringing to German music of the time the fertilising influence of the Italian school. One of the first to show this is the *Psalmen Davids* of 1619, which gave to his master Giovanni Gabrieli's polychoral methods a distinctly German flavour, and did much to establish Schütz's reputation outside Dresden. They are typical in their sensitivity to accurate word-setting and painting within the framework of a solemn gravity of style. Two, three and four choirs of voices and instruments combine to give all the splendour of which the style is capable, and each one explores a different sonority. 'Zion spricht' is possibly the gem of this series, conceived on the most lavish scale and contrasting different timbres.

The other wing, the austere one, of Schütz's achievement is first represented by his next major work, the *Historia der Auferstehung Jesu Christi*, published in 1623. Apart from the opening and closing chorus, there is little choral writing. The narration of the Evangelist, which is accompanied by four violi da gamba, fluctuates between free and measured declaration, and the whole Easter story is told with the utmost simplicity, yet interest is sustained by the use of vocal duets and trios for the characters other than Jesus. Monody here supersedes polyphony. With the *Cantiones Sacrae* of 1626, he returns to elaborate contrapuntal writing. This is a collection of motets to Latin texts for four voices and continuo, although the instrumental bass is not essential. Here Schütz marries the dramatic madrigal style with that of the polyphonic motet, and produces with his daring harmonic twists choral writing of emotional intensity.

In 1627, Schütz produced his opera *Dafne*, the music of which is sadly lost. His next major offering, the first set of *Symphoniae Sacrae* of 1629, shows the influence of his second visit to Italy and so of Monteverdi in the use of solo singers and instruments. The lines are more florid, the declamation more passionate, the harmony richer than heretofore in his music. With the wartime upheavals, Schütz composed little in the succeeding years until the *Musikalische Exequien* of 1636 for soloists and choir, a large-scale, three-part work described as a 'concert in the form of a German funeral mass' and combining Italian and German methods, solo and choral sections. The *Kleine geistliche Konzerte* (1636) showed the way in simplicity of style to the *Seven Words from the Cross* (1645?), restrained and intimate in its phraseology while maintaining dramatic impetus in its narration.

The second set of *Symphoniae Sacrae* (1647), now with Schütz's favoured German, rather than the previous Latin texts, are restrained in manner, usually employing only three solo voices and few instruments in contrast to the third set of 1650, where more sumptuous forces are used in much more elaborate forms. Among these pieces is the exceedingly dramatic *Saul, Saul was verfolgst du mich?*, telling of Saul's conversion on the road to Damascus.

After a decade in which he composed little, there was a remarkable resurgence of inspiration in Schütz's old age when he wrote *The Christmas Story* (1664) in which all the participants are wonderfully characterised with their own, individual scoring while the Evangelist tells the story accompanied only by a continuo. Finally came several austere settings of the Passion, in which Schütz pared down his

Schütz, by Christian Romstet, 1672.

style, achieving his dramatic aims through unaccompanied choruses, plainsong intonation, and syllabic recitative. All inessentials are refined away, as if Schütz wanted to produce a simple, pure music, a distillation of all he had created in the past. With these, as much as with his more approachable early works, his place in musical history as a composer of extraordinary ingenuity and imagination is now secure.

A.B.

SCRIABIN, Alexander
(b. Moscow, 6 Jan 1872;
d. Moscow, 27 April 1915)

Scriabin's mother died soon after he was born, and he was reared largely by relatives. During the nine years he spent in the Moscow Army Cadet Corps his musical studies were guided largely by Taneiev, and when he entered the Moscow Conservatoire in 1888 he joined the piano class of Safonov. He made little headway with Arensky, however, and left the Conservatoire without a composer's diploma. Nonetheless a career as composer–pianist soon opened up for him under the aegis of the rich publisher Belaiev, who sponsored his first European concert-tour in 1895/6. In 1898 he became a Professor of Piano at the Moscow Conservatoire, a post he found uncongenial and from which he resigned in 1903 in order to devote himself to composition. He took up residence in Switzerland and there produced his Third Symphony, *The Divine Poem,* a turning-point in that it marked the beginning of the composer's obsession with theosophic mysticism, one which vitally determined the character of later milestones such as the *Poem of Ecstasy, Prometheus* and the later piano sonatas. Scriabin spent most of the 1900s in Europe touring and composing, and returned in 1909 to a Moscow increasingly sympathetic to his works. In 1910 he made a successful tour of the Volga with Koussevitsky and travelled extensively elsewhere, pondering the while his 'Mystery' – a proposed world-cataclysm in which he, the new Messiah, would induce a moment of collective, creative ecstasy after which the physical plane of consciousness would dissolve and a new world-order begin. But only the text and a few rough musical jottings for the Initial Act were committed to paper, for at Eastertide 1915 Scriabin died suddenly of a tumour on the lip.

A vision of some kind Scriabin certainly had, though he was critically mistaken as to its true nature. Basically he sought ecstasy through the senses (*Prometheus* is designed to be complemented by a continuous play of colours) and, through ecstasy, Truth. We may see in him today, with minds neither overawed or antagonised by all the mystico-theosophic paraphernalia (by which, it was once argued, he merely sought to camouflage the absence of any positive creative talent) a prophet of multi-media expression, science-fiction and space-travel (the ending of Stanley Kubrick's film *2001 – A Space Odyssey* is pure *Prometheus*), mass pot-induced euphoria. The development of his highly personal style was inextricably linked with 'ideas', and though the influence of romantic composers such as Chopin, Liszt, Franck and Wagner is strong in earlier works they are all quickly assimilated and outgrown as Scriabin, fanned by the supernatural exhalations of such contemporary artists and poets as Balmont, Blok, Roerich and Kandinsky, aspired ever further towards his supreme final ecstasy. His works number five symphonies, ten piano sonatas and numerous smaller pieces for piano, behind nearly every one of which there burns a flame. A fascinating 'sport' whose peculiar brand of erotic mysticism finds later expression only in the music of Olivier Messaien, Scriabin either thrills or appals, but never bores.

C.P.

SHOSTAKOVICH, Dmitri
(b. St Petersburg, 25 Sept 1906; d. Moscow, 9 Aug 1975)

Dmitri Shostakovich was born in Podolskaya Street in St Petersburg, now Leningrad. His parents were both musical, as he wrote in an autobiographical note of 1956: 'My mother, Sophia Vasilyevna, studied for some years at the Conservatoire and was a good pianist; my father, Dmitri Boleslavovich, was a great lover of music and sang well.' It was an intellectual family, reasonably well-off: his father, a chemical engineer, considered music to be an essential part of his children's education, and when Shostakovich was about nine years old his mother started him off on the piano. His talent developed so rapidly that after about a year he was taken to play to the Director of the St Petersburg Conservatoire, Glazunov, who heard him not only in repertory piano pieces but also in some of his own first compositions. As a result he entered the Conservatoire and studied piano and composition, the latter subject with Maximilian Steinberg. He graduated from the Conservatoire in 1923.

He had become an outstanding pianist.

Shostakovich by Rémusat.

'After finishing the Conservatoire I faced the problem: should I be a pianist or a composer? The latter won. If the truth be told I should have been both.' After about 1930 he appeared as a performer only in his own compositions, though as late in his life as 1974 he looked back with pride on his achievement as an executant – 'I've been a performer, a pianist myself', he told an interviewer, emphasising the necessity for a creative musician to remain in real contact with his audience. As it happened, his composing career did not begin easily: shortly after his graduation he became dissatisfied with his music and destroyed nearly all his student work. However this difficult time quickly passed. His First Symphony was performed in Leningrad in May 1926, when he was still under twenty: it possessed great fluency, personality and youthful vitality and achieved performance as far afield as Germany and (under Stokowski and Toscanini) the United States, winning early recognition for its composer.

At this time it seemed that Shostakovich was firmly launched upon a distinguished career. Even in political terms he appeared to be strongly placed as the first wholly Soviet – that is, post-revolutionary – composer to make an international reputation. But by about 1927 he found himself in a new creative phase which was to disturb his progress for nearly a decade: in that year he composed a set of ten piano pieces called *Aphorisms* which he later described as representing 'abstract experimentation' and an erroneous striving for originality. His natural interest in his Western contemporaries, including his compatriots resident abroad, Prokofiev and Stravinsky, had led him into a conscious modernity of style that brought him into growing conflict with the Soviet establishment. Like everything else in the Soviet Union, music was to be seen in political terms: the musicologist Asafiev had written in 1924 that the new Russia awaited 'a composer whose melodies will touch the hearts of all sections of the population and the breath of whose music will not only warm the concert hall but the streets and fields as well, because it will be music with roots deep in Russian life and . . . will grow to reach genuine majesty and beauty.' But Shostakovich did not heed the warning signs. In the severe words of his Soviet biographer Rabinovich, he and some other young composers 'raced recklessly forward, as they thought, and very soon found themselves in a *cul-de-sac.*'

The problem was not easily to be solved; for a composer writes from inner compulsion as well as in response to external stimuli and to interfere with his creative freedom is seriously to risk stunting his growth. Schoenberg might have written scornfully that 'if it is for All, it is not Art'; but on the other hand a great Russian, Tolstoy, had required art to communicate to the wide lay public to qualify as such. Shostakovich's opera *The Nose* (1929), based on Gogol, was enjoyed by cultivated audiences because it matched bright modernity of style to the grotesque humour of the story; however there were grumblings that this was a 'malignant ridicule' of operatic tradition, and the work did not remain long in the repertory. The real storm broke some time after the production in 1934 of a second opera, *Lady Macbeth of Mtsensk*. Here the subject was serious, even sordid: the chief character, Katerina Ismailova, commits a series of murders and finally drowns herself. But it was genuinely tragic too; and despite the uncompromising modernity of the music the opera had considerable success both in the Soviet Union and abroad. Two years later, however, an article appeared in the official newspaper *Pravda* called 'Confusion in place of music': it bitterly attacked the opera, accusing the composer of adopting the worst of decadent Western manners and so producing an art that was offensive, not to say harmful, to Soviet citizens.

Shostakovich reacted quickly. He went so far as to withdraw his Fourth Symphony (1936) which was being rehearsed in Leningrad: it was not performed until 1961, when it proved to be highly original in structure and feeling, while clearly remaining the work of a master. (Long after, in 1974, the composer replied to a question about his reaction to this early harsh criticism of his work, saying that he thought some of it was justified, 'despite its excessive emotion and abuse.' He added, significantly: 'I think art should be addressed to the people. They must be able to love and understand it; that's altogether essential. I try to use clear language – sometimes I succeed, sometimes not.') After this crisis, the thirty-year-old musician changed artistic direction with a heroic effort of will. His Fifth Symphony (1937) is headed with the words 'A Soviet artist's response to just criticism'. It is clear in structure, straightforward in rhythmic and melodic style; yet it is a response, not a humiliating or insincere recantation, and its fine dramatic character makes its direct impact without descending to the commonplace.

It is worth reminding ourselves at this point that the changes of style that took place in Shostakovich's work at this time were not wholly imposed from outside, or even simply dictated by the artist's own political (rather than musical) ideals. His First Symphony had shown his inborn capacity for noble utterance as well as direct tunefulness and charm; so had his 'Cello Sonata (1934). The film and theatre music which he had written since 1928 was often abundantly simple and broad in style; indeed the knockabout humour of such pieces as the ballet called *The Bolt* (1931) is so demotic as to make an Elgar march or an early Verdi chorus seem austere. What may seem vulgar or banal to a Western ear in Shostakovich, almost cynical in its apparent facility, has had to be accepted as a lasting aspect of the composer's musical personality. Perhaps it is not unfair to link it, certainly in his later career, to works of deliberately popular and political intent. For example there is the Twelfth Symphony (1961), celebrating the Revolution and dedicated to Lenin's memory: its ideas seem crude and they receive inflated and repetitious treatment.

Throughout World War II, Shostakovich remained in the forefront of Soviet musical life. He was awarded a Stalin Prize for his Piano Quintet (1940), while his *Leningrad Symphony*, composed during the following year under severe conditions while he was serving as a fire-fighter in beleaguered Leningrad, became a national song of defiance and heroism. He came in some senses to be considered as an artistic war hero (he had volunteered for active service but was rejected because of his poor eyesight); and he only left Leningrad with his wife and young son and daughter when he was ordered to do so by the authorities, concerned for his safety.

In 1942 Shostakovich was in Moscow, where he had settled with his family and taken up a post as teacher of composition at the Conservatoire. He seems to have been an inspiring teacher, a friend as well as a guide to his pupils: some of these, like Sviridov and Vainberg, have become successful Soviet composers without, however, achieving fuller recognition abroad. Yet it is sad to relate that gradually the critical clouds gathered once again, and in 1948 a now notorious conference of the Composers' Union was convened by Stalin's right-hand man Zhdanov: Russia's leading composers, especially Prokofiev and Shostakovich, were taken to task for their

failure to remember their duties towards the Soviet people and reminded that their work should afford inspiration and relaxation. Shostakovich defended himself with some dignity, while accepting the political ideology behind these strictures. He composed 'acceptable' works such as the patriotic oratorio *The Song of the Forests* (1949) and the cantata *The Sun Shines Over Our Land* (1952). But at the same time he continued to produce more private pieces like his string quartets, Twenty-four Preludes and Fugues for piano (1951), the tragic Tenth Symphony (1953) – surely among his finest – and the Violin Concerto No. 1 (1955). From this time onwards, he seems to have written this 'personal', often introspective and dark-coloured music quite freely alongside the public works expected of him, among which were the massive Eleventh (*The Year 1905*) Symphony, which won him a Lenin Prize following on its Moscow première in October 1957, and the patriotic Twelfth Symphony of 1961, already mentioned above.

In 1954 Shostakovich's first wife died; two years later he married a young teacher, Margarita Andreyevna Kainova. His son Maxim, born in 1938, was at this time studying for a musical career: he has since become a conductor and a noted interpreter of his father's works. The composer, now fifty, travelled quite frequently from Moscow to his native Leningrad; he went outside Russia less often, though he made a long trip abroad in 1958 and in that year received an honorary doctorate from Oxford University. Travel for its own sake seems to have interested him little; however, a lifelong interest in sport took him to innumerable football matches at home and elsewhere. In the 1960s his health began to give serious cause for anxiety, and serious heart trouble was diagnosed. The flow of his music was not halted or even significantly slowed; nevertheless it became clear that from now on he intended to follow a wholly personal creative path. Thus the last four of his string quartets (Nos. 12–15, composed from 1968 onwards) and the Fourteenth and Fifteenth Symphonies (1969 and 1971) are among his boldest yet most enigmatic works: the Fourteenth Symphony, for two solo voices and chamber orchestra, has death as its theme. Many people anticipated that this would be his last symphony; perhaps the composer himself felt as much. In fact the Fifteenth Symphony is quite different, by no means humourless and with several quotations from the *William Tell* Overture as well as Wagner's *Ring* and Shostakovich's own works. He came to London in 1972 for its first English performance, but appeared rather frail as he acknowledged the applause from a box in London's Royal Festival Hall: the conductor was Maxim Shostakovich. The decline in his health continued slowly. On the 9th August 1975, he died in a Moscow hospital.

Shostakovich has been called 'the only Soviet composer with an indisputable claim to genius'. An obituary in *The Times* newspaper described him as beyond doubt 'the last great symphonist'. He is the heir to Tchaikovsky and Mahler, both of whom he admired; but his style is also indebted to his compatriots of one generation before him, Prokofiev and (though less obviously) Stravinsky. His often-displayed impish humour, such as we find in the Ninth Symphony, has troubled solemn-minded Soviet critics although it is clearly in a great Russian tradition. Such critics are happier with the epic qualities of the Fifth, Seventh ('Leningrad') and Eleventh Symphonies; the Tenth, though equally impressive in scope, is for these musicians uncomfortably pessimistic, and indeed Shostakovich has perhaps looked with more courage into the abyss of despair than any other 20th-century composer. He believed, he declared, in writing 'good, beautiful, inspired music'; but his art is truthful. After his death, his colleague Khachaturian described him as 'the conscience of Soviet music'.

C.H.

SIBELIUS, Jean
(b. Hämeenlinna, 8 Dec 1865;
d. Järvenpää, 20 Sept 1957)

Sibelius is the only Finnish composer of commanding international stature. His close identification with the cause of Finnish nationalism and his pre-occupation with mythology gives him a special place in the development of Scandinavian music, and a dominant one in Finnish musical life. Seen in a wider context, it was his highly developed instinct for form and his powerful originality as a symphonic thinker that have ensured him a special place in the history of western music.

Johan Julius Christian Sibelius was born into a middle-class Swedish-speaking family in Hämeenlinna, a small town in south central Finland. (He adopted the name, Jean, when he came across a set of visiting cards used by a sea-faring uncle who had gallicised the name, Johan, on his travels abroad). His father was a doctor, who died during the cholera epidemic of 1867–8 while the boy was still in his infancy, and he was brought up by his mother and grandmother. During this period, Finland was a Grand Duchy of Tsarist Russia and was largely governed by the Swedish-speaking minority. Sibelius himself was enrolled in the first Finnish-language grammar school, and though he spoke some Finnish from about the age of eight onwards, he did not attain complete proficiency in the language until he was a young man. His first effort at composing, a simple piece for violin and 'cello called *Water Drops*, comes from his tenth year and was followed by a large number of juvenilia, all chamber works, including a Piano Trio in A minor (1881–2), a Piano Quartet in E minor and a string trio. For a long time he nourished ambitions to be a violinist and in his twenties became a pupil first of Mitrofan Wasilyeff and later of Hermann Csillag: he was advanced enough to manage two movements of the Mendelssohn concerto, and the E minor concerto of Félicien David. Even as late as 1891 he auditioned for the strings of the Vienna Philharmonic!

His early chamber compositions reveal three basic influences: first, the Viennese classics (Haydn, Beethoven, Mozart); secondly, the music of Grieg, who served as a model for the Violin Sonata in F (1889), and thirdly, Tchaikovsky whose harmonic language exerted a strong appeal.

Like many other composers he began his university years by studying law at Helsinki, but soon turned to music, becoming a pupil of Martin Wegelius. On the staff at Helsinki during this period was Ferruccio Busoni for whom Sibelius formed a lifelong friendship.

After graduating, Sibelius went to Berlin in 1889 for further studies with Albert Becker, a contrapuntist of the strictest school, and a year later to Vienna, which he found more congenial. Armed with a letter of introduction to Brahms from Busoni, he ended up as a pupil of Goldmark, for whom he wrote his first orchestral essay, an Overture. It was after his return to Finland in 1891 that he embarked on his first major orchestral composition, the five-movement *Kullervo* Symphony, an am-

Sibelius by Callen, 1894.

bitious score of Mahlerian proportions with two soloists and a male chorus, based on the *Kalevala*. It was the performance of this score in 1892 that established him as Finland's most important composer virtually overnight. A commission from Robert Kajanus, the leading Finnish conductor and himself a composer, came immediately and the result was *En Saga*. During the remainder of this decade Sibelius consolidated the position he had won with *Kullervo*, and subsequent works such as the *Lemminkäinen Suite* showed how enormously powerful an impact Finnish national mythology had made on his consciousness. He was disappointed in 1897 at being passed over as the director of music at the University in favour of Kajanus, but consolation soon came in the form of a small life-pension voted by the Finnish Senate. During the 1890s and particularly with the series of tableaux composed for an historical pageant to mark the Press Celebrations of 1899, which included *Finlandia*, he became increasingly identified with the movement towards Finnish nationalism that had grown in direct consequence of the tightening of the Tsarist hold on Finland.

In 1899 came the first of his seven symphonies which set the seal on his success in Finland. If the late 1890s had seen his consolidation at home, the first decade of the present century was to see the growth of his reputation on the continent. In 1898 he had acquired a continental publisher, Breitkopf and Härtel. To them Sibelius was later to sell the rights of *Valse triste* for the derisory sum of 300 marks. It made Breitkopf a fortune. In 1900 Robert Kajanus took the Helsinki Orchestra, which he had founded in the 1880s, on an European tour culminating at the Paris World Exhibition. *The Swan of Tuonela*, *Lemminkäinen's Return*, *Finlandia* and the First Symphony were all well received; in 1901 Sibelius was invited to Heidelberg to conduct his music, and in the following year he went to Berlin to conduct the revised and definitive version of *En Saga* at one of Busoni's New Music Concerts. Busoni also secured the first performance of the Second Symphony in Berlin in 1905. His fame was also beginning to spread in England: Henry Wood conducted the *King Christian* Suite at a 1901 Prom, and Bantock introduced the First Symphony a few years later: Hans Richter presented No. 2 at a Hallé concert in 1905.

This period sees the end of the 'national romantic' phase of his development. After the

Violin Concerto (1903 rev. 1905), his art assumes a more deeply individual character. Although his personal life was beset by pressing financial worries (he was in debt from the 1890s through to the post-1914–18 war period, and heavy drinking posed its problems too), his artistic life was entering a particularly productive period. The next few years found him turning away from the increasing complexity of language and richness of palette that characterised many of his contemporaries such as Strauss, Scriabin, Mahler (whom he met when he came to Helsinki in 1907) and Ravel. Indeed the Third Symphony (1904–07) evinces a remarkable neo-classicism both in terms of content and form. The greater concentration that the outer movement of the symphony show can also be seen in *Pohjola's Daughter* (1906) in which the symphonic and programmatic elements are superbly balanced. Some of his finest music for the theatre, the incidental music to Maeterlinck's *Pelléas et Mélisande* and Hjalmar Procopé's *Belshazzer's Feast* date from this period.

A serious illness developed in 1908 and Sibelius had to undergo a series of operations in both Helsinki and Berlin for suspected cancer of the throat. For a number of years he was forced to abjure his lifelong addiction to cigars and alcohol, and the bleak possibilities that the illness opened up, may well account for the austerity, concentration and depth of the works that followed in its wake: the Fourth Symphony, *The Bard* and *Luonnotar*. With the Fourth Symphony (1911) his language is more elliptic and in his extensive use of the tritone, he comes closer to indeterminate tonality than in any other of his major works. Sibelius was a keen traveller, making several visits to England, Italy, Germany and France, conducting his works in most major musical centres. It may fairly be said that his activities as a conductor were compensation for his failure to achieve his ambitions as a violinist. In 1912 he was offered the Chair of Composition at the Imperial Academy of Music in Vienna and two years later he was given an honorary doctorate at Yale, as a climax of his visit to the United States. If the first decade had marked his conquest of Germany and England, the second established his reputation in the United States. On this 1914 visit he conducted a number of his works and presented *The Oceanides* for the first time.

The first world war deprived him of his contact with the major musical centres of Europe and also cut him off from his royalties. As a result (and in the absence of conducting commitments abroad) he wrote large quantities of trivial piano works for the domestic market. The only major composition of the war years was his Fifth Symphony, finished in time for his fiftieth birthday celebrations on the 8th December 1915, an event treated almost as a national holiday. After the October Revolution, Finland proclaimed its independence, but early in 1918 it was plunged into civil war as a result of an attempted *coup d'état* on the part of the Red Guards. Sibelius fled from his home, which since 1904 had been in Järvenpää as his sympathies were with the Whites. The Fifth Symphony was in four movements originally and, like so much of Sibelius's music, was subjected to a thorough revision: a second version appeared in 1916 and the definitive score was completed some three years later.

Apart from some light music, the *Suite mignonne* and the *Suite champetre* and a handful of other pieces, the post-war years saw only four major works: the Sixth and Seventh Symphonies, the symphonic poem, *Tapiola* and the incidental music for the 1926 Copenhagen production of Shakespeare's *The Tempest*. He visited London for the last time in 1921 when he was reunited with Busoni, and made a number of other visits before retiring from the world in the mid-1920s. A promised Eighth Symphony never materialised, although it was almost certainly completed. Part of it was sent for copying in the early 1930s but with the growth of his international reputation (and his always lively powers of self-criticism) he withheld and then subsequently destroyed the score. His last years were spent quietly in Järvenpää, honoured as an elder statesman of music and revered as a national figure. His reputation, secure in the Anglo-Saxon world until his death of cerebral haemmorhage on September 20, 1957, made the customary decline but his achievement as a symphonist is secure.

R.L.

SMETANA, Bedřich
(b. Litomyšl, 2 March 1824;
d. Prague, 12 May 1884)

The 'father' of Czech music, Bedřich Smetana was fortunate that his own father was a keen amateur musician as well as a successful brewer. He was given a sufficient grounding in

practical music at home to be able to play first violin in a Haydn string quartet at the age of five and make his first public appearance as a pianist a year later. It is curious that after this promising start he should subsequently receive so little formal education in music. In other subjects too he was a quick, bright pupil, but as a result of either laziness or bad behaviour he was sent from one grammar school to another over the years. At seventeen, in Pilsen, he seems to have spent his time playing the piano in the homes of the wealthier citizens. 'I wish to become a Mozart in composition and a Liszt in technique', he wrote rather grandly in his diary at this time. When schooldays came to an end he decided to go to Prague in 1843 to achieve these ambitions, even though his father, whose musical enthusiasm had evaporated along with his business success, was unable to give any appreciable financial assistance.

With no specific training or achievement behind him, the nineteen-year-old Smetana soon discovered that Prague was not impressed, and he was completely frustrated until Kateřina Kolářová, a girl with whom he had fallen precociously in love in Pilsen, persuaded her own professor to give him lessons in composition and theory. A simultaneous stroke of good fortune came with his appointment as resident piano teacher to the large family of Count Leopold Thun. During the next two years he made rapid progress in his studies and composed several promising piano pieces when holidaying with his patron at his hunting lodge. He met Berlioz about this time, who was visiting Prague to conduct his *Symphonie Fantastique*, also Robert and Clara Schumann. In 1847, having failed in his bid to establish himself as a piano virtuoso, Smetana decided to open his own music school. He wrote to Liszt for advice and a loan, enclosing his *Six Characteristic Pieces* for piano suitably dedicated to his idol – a gesture which was later to be handsomely repaid. Liszt provided him with advice and a promise to find a publisher for the young composer, but ignored the plea for a loan. Undeterred, Smetana went ahead with his plans, duly opening his school in 1848, the Year of Revolution.

Although there was a Czech language, there was of course no Czechoslovakia in Smetana's day: the lands of Bohemia simply constituted a part of the Austrian Empire. During the 18th century the prevailing social and political conditions had become intolerable to musicians, almost all of whom migrated to Vienna, London, Paris or some other capital city. A strong nationalist movement developed in the 19th century, culminating in the revolt which broke out in Prague on the 11th June 1848. Up to this time Smetana had not shown any great interest in nationalism, even though his early piano pieces had what might be called a Bohemian accent, and he had in fact been brought up to speak exclusively in German. (He did not attempt to write a letter in Czech until 1856.) The short-lived revolution, however, sparked off his nationalist fervour to the extent that he helped to man the barricades in Prague. For eight years after the brutal suppression of the uprising Smetana made little progress either as composer or performer, and though he married his Kateřina in 1849 this was to bring little but grief: of their four daughters only Zofie survived, while Kateřina herself began to show symptoms of tuberculosis in 1855. Depressed by domestic misfortune, and feeling there could be no future for him in Prague, he moved in 1856 to Göteborg in Sweden, where as well as securing a conductorship and an enthusiastic stream of pupils he at last won fame as a concert pianist. Returning from a visit to Prague the following year he broke his journey at Weimar to see Liszt, who charmingly repaid his compliment of ten years previously. A Viennese conductor taunted Smetana with belonging to a race which had produced some fine violinists but not a single composer capable of writing worthwhile Czech music. Liszt at once sat at the piano, played the *Six Characteristic Pieces* to the admiring assembly, then declared: 'Here is a composer with a genuine Czech heart, an artist by the grace of God.'

The orchestral works composed by Smetana during his five years in Sweden were symphonic poems showing the strong influence that Liszt exerted on him. Their titles alone, *Richard III*, *Wallenstein's Camp* and *Haakon Jarl*, make it clear that Smetana had not yet turned his mind towards expressing his nationalist ideals in his music. What they *do* show is a steadily growing mastery of symphonic writing, a Wagnerian use of *leitmotif*, and a strong feeling for drama. His life itself took a dramatic turn during his stay in Sweden: Kateřina died in 1859, and a year later Smetana married Bettina Ferdinandová, a sister-in-law of his brother Karl. It would seem he desperately needed a wife by his side while having to live in a foreign land. Fortunately the political situation in Prague sud-

denly changed for the better, so he returned to settle there in May 1861. It may not have been a hero's return, but it was as a mature composer ready to give Czech music a voice of its own at last.

Prague, unfortunately, was not ready for a composer of such strong individuality as Smetana. His work was criticised as being too Wagnerian, and he was also under constant attack from an opposition group of conductors and opera house administrators. His first opera, *The Brandenburgers in Bohemia*, though completed in 1863, was not performed at the Provisional Theatre until the beginning of 1866. Thanks to its patriotic story and flashes of genius which nobody could deny, it

Smetana.

enjoyed a triumph which temporarily confounded his critics. (It also won for him the chief conductorship of the Provisional Theatre, a post he held for eight years.) Then only four months later, on the 30th May 1866, came *The Bartered Bride*. The première of this now most popular of all Smetana's operas did not set the Vltava on fire, but this was due, not to any musical consideration, but to the unsettled political atmosphere on the eve of the Austro-Prussian war. The situation was so serious that Smetana himself thought it prudent to leave Prague before the Prussian troops arrived, and for a month he lived in the sanctuary of the countryside. A few weeks later, however, it became a riotous success and never looked back (reaching its two-thousandth performance at the Prague National Theatre alone by 1952). Three revisions of the original score, which had employed spoken dialogue instead of the recitative we know today, were made by 1870. Its story is a slice of simple Bohemian village life, but the music has subtlety and consummate artistry, combining warmth with sparkle, vigour with refinement. Its high spirits never descend into farce, its characters are drawn in the most skilful musical terms, and there are many passages of almost Mozartian grace. Smetana kept the pulse of Czech folk music racing through the score, yet he never drew on actual folk material. In later years he came almost to resent its popularity, because he considered it a lesser work than some of its successors which the public received with comparative coolness.

In *Dalibor*, for example, first heard on the occasion of the laying of the foundation stone of the Prague National Theatre in 1868, Smetana paid a truly noble tribute to a legendary Czech hero personifying every national virtue. The public, however, presumably expecting another *Bartered Bride*, were bewildered by the progressive music, and the critics saw the spectre of Wagner hovering behind the score. It is true that there are Wagnerian influences in this music for a story bearing a certain resemblance to *Fidelio*, but basically it is pure Smetana. It was rarely given in the composer's lifetime, so that he died thinking that it would never be understood. Two years after his death, however, it returned to the Prague repertoire and has held a place of honour there ever since.

In spite of much official hostility and the deafness that overtook him in 1874, Smetana went on to complete five more operas whose different styles reveal remarkable versatility. *The Two Widows* (1874) is a comedy composed as a 'conversation piece' of great originality and charm, which incidentally became such a favourite opera of Richard Strauss that he always made sure it was in the repertoire when he made visits to Prague. (Strauss's own *Intermezzo* shows how strongly *The Two Widows* impressed him with its intimate style.) *The Kiss* (1876) and *The Secret* (1878) return to the idyllic countryside of *The Bartered Bride*, but *The Kiss* shows a new mastery of character realisation while *The Secret* reveals the composer's increasing command of orchestral writing with an unbroken flow. Both operas, which remain highly popular in Czechoslovakia, have been unjustly neglected in other countries. Then in 1881, the intensely patriotic *Libuše*, composed eight years earlier but kept in hand until a suitable occasion arose, was performed at the opening of the new National Theatre. This is a grandiose work extolling the greatness of the Czech nation, solemn in style and relying heavily on powerful declamation – though the composer's natural lyricism keeps breaking through. Smetana, now completely deaf and suffering serious ill-health, was shabbily treated by the theatre's directors at this première but was rousingly acclaimed by the audience. Finally came *The Devil's Wall*, subtitled by Smetana a 'comic–romantic opera' and incorporating an element of parody within its lyrical framework. The remarkable thing is that the composer's invention never flagged through these later years when, afflicted by various symptoms of the syphilis from which he was to die, he lived in the country with his daughter Zofie and her husband.

Smetana's music is not confined to opera, though it is for his stage works that he is best known. His cycle of symphonic poems with the general title *Má Vlast* (My Country) is his greatest orchestral achievement, two of them, *Vltava*, an epic musical picture of the river which flows through Prague on its course from the forests to join the Elbe, and *From Bohemia's Fields and Forests*, having found a permanent place in concert halls the world over. Never attracted to purely abstract music, Smetana is both descriptive and subjective in his major chamber works, the Piano Trio (1855) being an elegy on the death of his first daughter, the First String Quartet (1876) inspired by reflections on his youth and the Second (1883) reflecting the suffering brought on by his deafness. His piano music has Lisztian virtuosity, the many polkas doing for this Bohemian dance-form something of what Chopin did for the Polish mazurka. For the Czechs all Smetana's music is the supreme expression of their national feelings and aspirations.

F.G.B.

SPOHR, Ludwig
(b. Brunswick, 5 April 1784;
d. Cassel, 22 Oct 1859)

Ludwig Spohr, or Louis Spohr as he was commonly called, was born in Brunswick in 1784. Few other musicians of his time enjoyed a more varied or successful career. He combined in equal measure the life of a violin virtuoso, a conductor, and a composer. If now we refer to him as the leading *minor* German composer of the first half of the 19th century, in his own day he enjoyed an international reputation fully the equal of that belonging to Beethoven, Schubert, Schumann, Weber, and Berlioz.

He gained employment as a violinist at the court of the Duke of Brunswick when he was still in his teens. He showed such talent that the Duke felt disposed to find him a teacher of standing. The choice fell on Franz Eck. At the expense of the Duke, Spohr accompanied Eck on his next concert tour (as far as Russia), taking lessons from the master as occasions presented themselves. Spohr clearly worked hard at his technique during this period (1802–3), and when he returned to Brunswick, he returned a fully equipped virtuoso.

Spohr's career now unfolded itself before him. Directed as much by his ability as a violinist as by his talents as a composer, it began with a concert tour of Germany (1804–5). Subsequent tours which he made with his first wife Dorette Scheilder (a concert harpist), went further afield, including Switzerland and Italy (1815–17), and England and France (1820–1). He was to visit England several times, establishing himself, along with Mendelssohn, as a firm favourite both in London and the provinces. Spohr wrote much music specifically for these tours, including pieces for violin and harp, and the famous concerto for violin 'in modo d'una scena cantante' for his Italian visit. These pieces won him as much applause as his playing.

Spohr also held several appointments. The first of these was at the court of Gotha (1805–12). He moved subsequently to Vienna where for two years he was musical director of the Theater an der Wein, and where he composed *Faust* (first performance Prague, 1816), with E. T. A. Hoffmann's *Undine* the first truly Romantic opera. From 1817 to 1819, on his return from Italy, he directed the opera at Frankfurt-am-Main. He took up his last permanent appointment in 1822 when he became director of music at the court of Cassel. Here he wrote his famous opera *Jessonda* (1823) (*Der Berggeist, Pietro von Albano* and *Der Alchymist* also date from this period, but none achieved the success of *Jessonda*), completed his *Violinschule* (published in Vienna in 1832), conducted performances of *Die fliegende Holländer* and *Tannhäuser* in 1842 and 1853 respectively, and undertook commissions for English patrons, visiting England again in 1843, 1847, 1852 and 1853. Life at Cassel, however, was not made easy by the petty despotism of the elector. Spohr experienced increasing difficulties, having finally made no secret of his support for freedom and tolerance in the newly emerging German nation. In 1857 he was retired against his will. He died peaceably at Cassel in 1859.

Spohr's output includes 11 operas, several oratorios, including *The Last Judgement*; 9 symphonies, amongst them: *Die Weihe der Töne* (No. 4), *The Historical Symphony* (No. 6), and *The Seasons* (No. 9); 15 concerti for the violin; songs; and chamber music, of particular interest being the Octet (Op. 32) and Nonet (Op. 31) written in Vienna, and the 4 Double String Quartets. Spohr was a lifelong admirer of Mozart. He also championed the first period works of Beethoven, but could never bring himself to like much else of his music with the same unqualified zeal. His style was essentially lyrical, rich in chromaticism, fluent in invention, but too often derivative and facile: not only as a performer was he willing to accommodate audiences which sought as a rule entertainment rather than edification. Of all the German Romantic composers he comes closest to Mendelssohn, though he never matched the latter's stature as a composer.

E.H.

SPONTINI, Gasparo
(b. Majolati, 14 Nov 1774;
d. Majolati, 24 Jan 1851)

Gasparo Luigi Pacifico Spontini spent the larger part of his life in Paris and Berlin pursuing a career as a composer of opera and conductor. He owed to Italy, however, his early musical training (at the Conservatorio della Pietà de' Turchini in Naples), and to Italian impresarios his first operatic successes, beginning with *Li Puntigli delle donne* (first produced in Rome in 1796). Other works of his Italian period include *L'eroismo ridicolo* (1798) and *La fuga in maschera* (1800), both produced in Naples. He also received tuition from Picinni during this period.

In 1802, Spontini left Italy for Paris, which he made his home for a number of years (1803–19), eventually taking French nationality and marrying a French bride (Mlle Erard). He also found favour with the Empress Josephine, becoming her *compositeur particulier*. With the Parisians he experienced a reception not uncommon among Italian-trained musicians invading for the first time the domain of French *opéra comique*. *La Petite Maison* (1804) and *Julie* (1805) were both greeted with outright hostility. But with *La Vestale* (1807) Spontini finally conquered the French public, following this triumph with *Fernand Cortez* (1809), and much later *Olympie* (1819). Meanwhile he had been appointed conductor of the Théâtre italien in 1810 (he was dismissed shortly afterwards in 1812), and had duly celebrated the restoration of the monarchy with *Pélage, ou le Roi de la Paix* (1814).

One of Spontini's admirers during the 1810s was King Frederick William III of Prussia, who during a visit to Paris in 1814 had been deeply impressed with his operas. On his return to Berlin he embarked upon plans to attract Spontini into his service. These finally came to fruition in 1820 when Spontini moved to Berlin to occupy the post of chief *Kapellmeister* at his court, with the task of providing two operas every three years. Even in his Parisian days Spontini had shown a considerable slowing down in his speed of composition: in the twenty or so years he spent at Berlin he completed only three new stage works, *Nurmahal* (1822), *Alcidor* (1825) and *Agnes von Hohenstaufen* (1829). He nevertheless retained the support of the King, albeit against a rising tide of opposition among the adherents of German national opera, grouped around Weber. The latter faction saw in Spontini's work only superficial charms, gained largely through lavish effects. These rivalries increasingly soured Spontini's relations with the court, German musicians and the public. Matters came to a head in 1841 in legal proceedings connected with an article Spontini had written attacking his critics. So high ran the tide of public feeling by this time that a performance of Mozart's *Don Giovanni* was abandoned when Spontini (who was conducting) was hissed out of the theatre.

Spontini finally left Berlin in 1842, but not without a handsome pension. He settled in Paris to a distinguished retirement, but achieved nothing artistically. His final years were saddened by deafness. He returned to Italy and in 1850 to his birthplace, exercising himself in good works. He died in Majolati in 1851.

Spontini's increasing lack of fluency after his departure from Italy contains within it the key to understanding his musical personality. He was at root an Italian. Where he was able to adapt himself to Imperial France, and to stage works that caught some of the high drama of Napoleon's exploits, he clearly never came to an instinctive understanding of the early 19th-century German temperament. Partly as a result of this, Spontini became ever more fastidious, finally it seems frightening his muse away completely.

E.H.

STOCKHAUSEN, Karlheinz
(b. Mödrath, 22 Aug 1928)

Stockhausen was born near Cologne in 1928. His education was interrupted by World War II, and between 1944 and the end of the war he worked in a military hospital close to the front line. After the war he spent three years at the Musikhochschule in Cologne, leavening his studies—as he has himself recorded—by playing in bars and dancing classes, and as accompanist to a travelling conjuror. He then worked for a time with Frank Martin before going to Paris, where Milhaud and, more significantly, Messiaen were his main teachers. His earliest surviving works, which date from this period, already show the influence of Messiaen's 'Mode de valeurs', the source work of multi-dimensional serialism, and include *Kreuzspiel* (1951), *Kontrapunkte* (1953) and the first nine piano pieces (1952–4). But Stockhausen was already under the spell of Pierre Schaeffer, the inventor of *musique concrète* and an authority on the as yet primitive techniques of electronic composition. Stockhausen undertook a close study of these techniques, and soon composed some of the earliest works using exclusively synthesised, or electronically generated, sound. In 1953 he helped found the electronic studio of the West German Radio in Cologne (with Herbert Eimert); he was permanent assistant to Eimert at this studio until 1962, since when he has been its sole artistic director.

In his own music electronics proved to be of seminal importance. Not only did he pioneer the use of electronics in live performed music (*Kontakte*, 1959, *Mikrophonie I and II*, 1964–5) but he also introduced related techniques into music for conventional instruments, notably in 'spatial' works such as *Gruppen* for three orchestras (1957) and *Carré* for four orchestras (1960). In all these works, sonority is of supreme importance. But in some other works of the 1950s, Stockhausen experimented with chance, or aleatoric, techniques (notably the Piano Piece No. 11, of 1956) which inevitably eroded the precision and fastidiousness which characterise most of his music before 1960. At first the free element was only the order of events, never their actual content. But in due course improvisation became a factor, culminating in a group of works called *Aus den sieben Tagen* (1968), where the 'composed' score consists only of short verbal texts in the light of which the performer invents the music himself.

None of these various devices has ever dominated Stockhausen's music to the exclusion of the others. However a certain consistent pattern can be detected in his work over the last twenty-five years. In the brief early phase the composer exercises a rigorous intellectual control over every detail of his music, and this leads him naturally to electronic music, from which even the vagaries of performance can be excluded. By far the best works here are *Gesang der Jünglinge* (1956) and the tape-only version of *Kontakte*. Thence the direction is outwards, towards what Stockhausen calls 'open' form and eventually towards a music of trance and telepathy, where the actual music is less important than the process of inducing a certain state of mental and spiritual empathy between the performers, and also between performers and audience. In this situation the composer is little more than a guru or, more cynically viewed, a master-conjuror. In a recent work like *Alphabet pour Liège* (1972) the 'score' even calls for elaborate equipment not unlike a conjuror's apparatus, the musical outcome being negligible, as it is also in *Indian Songs*

(1973). Such pieces have indeed a very nebulous existence as works of art. But Stockhausen has also many large recent works to his credit of a more substantial kind, mostly exemplifying his pop existentialist philosophy, and in some cases influenced by eastern religion. Notable among these are *Hymnen*, a live and electronic work based on national anthems (1966–7), *Stimmung* (1967) and *Mantra*, a large work for two pianos and ring modulators (1970).

S.W.

STRAUSS, Johann
(b. Vienna, 14 March 1804; d. Vienna, 25 Sept 1849)
STRAUSS, Johann Jr
(b. Vienna, 25 Oct 1825; d. Vienna, 3 June 1899)
STRAUSS, Josef
(b. Vienna, 22 Aug 1827; d. Vienna, 21 July 1870)
STRAUSS, Eduard
(b. Vienna, 15 March 1835; d. Vienna, 28 July 1916)

The story of the famous Strauss family is the story of Viennese dance music. Strangely there was no family musical heritage when the first Johann Strauss was born in Vienna on the 14th March 1804. His father was the innkeeper of the 'Zum guten Hirten' tavern in the Leopoldstadt not far from the banks of the Danube. It was a seedy place much used by the riverboat men and Franz Strauss, a morose and moody man, and his wife Barbara made only a modest living from it. Johann's mother died when he was seven and his father, shortly after remarrying, was found drowned in the Danube, a suspected suicide. The boy continued to live at the inn with his stepmother and at thirteen was apprenticed to a bookbinder. Long before this he had been attracted to the music made by the strolling musicians who earned their keep by playing such instruments as the violin, 'cello, harp and zither for the entertainment of the inn's customers. His new stepfather, named Golder, took a kindly interest and gave him a small violin which be-

Title-page of waltz, Souvenir de Vienne, *dedicated to the three Strauss brothers, by Albert Jungmann.*

AUX FRÈRES STRAUSS de VIENNE

SOUVENIR DE VIENNE

Valse-   Caprice

JOHANN STRAUSS

JOSEPH STRAUSS   EDOUARD STRAUSS

Op: 321.   Prix: 7.50

POUR **PIANO** PAR

ALBt. JUNGMANN

Du même Auteur:
des Elfes — Retraite Militaire.
du Guet — Chant du Printemps.

à quatre mains, 9f.

Du même Auteur:
Gavotte du bon vieux temps — Berger
Le départ du Matelot.

Piano et Violon, 9f.

Paris, AU MÉNESTREL. 2bis Rue Vivienne, HEUGEL et Cie. Éditeurs pour France et Belgique
Vienne: F. SCHREIBER.

came his preoccupation. It distracted him from his lessons at school and later from his work as an apprentice.

One day he ran away and headed for the famous inns of the Vienna Woods, the Heurigen, the haunts of Beethoven and Schubert where somewhat higher class musical groups, such as that led by the Schrammel brothers, provided entertainment. There he met a professional musician named Polischansky who heard his story and of his ambitions; then not only persuaded him to return home but also persuaded his step-parents to let him study music with him. Within a year Strauss had surpassed his teacher and had got his first professional job as a viola player in the orchestra led by Michael Pamer, then the leading dance orchestra in Vienna. In the same orchestra was Josef Lanner (1801–43) an attractive and accomplished young musician destined for a short but gay life. He and Strauss became close friends and when Lanner left to form his own band, Strauss joined him in 1819. Both, following in the steps of Pamer who was a talented composer, now began to write their own works. In 1824 when the Lanner orchestra had grown considerably in size and popularity, it split into two with Strauss conducting the second orchestra. Quarrels arose, mainly as to whose compositions should be played, and after a heated argument which led to blows one evening they parted company, and Strauss formed his own orchestra. They remained friends and followed their own fortunes and styles, Lanner continuing to write in a folk-song like vein, Strauss advancing his dance techniques toward the later glories of the Viennese waltz.

He made his orchestral début in 1826 and soon made a reputation with fine compositions like his *Kettenbrückenwalzer*. In 1830 he moved to the large and popular, but somewhat disreputable Sperl dance hall in the Leopoldstadt where his reputation was spread abroad by visitors who came to hear him, amongst them Chopin and Wagner. The main work was to provide dance music but there was an increasing tendency for the orchestra to display itself in interludes intended for listening which demanded more ambitious music to be written. With an orchestra of some 28 players Strauss now began to make tours abroad, visiting Germany, France, Belgium, Holland and England. In Paris he was lavishly praised by Berlioz and added the quadrille to his repertoire. He visited England in 1838 and 1849. In 1834 he was appointed

Johann Strauss Jnr by August Eisenmenger, 1888.

bandmaster of the 1st Wiener Burgerregiment; and in 1835 he was made director of the Imperial Court Balls.

Strauss had married, in 1824, and in keeping with family tradition, the daughter of an innkeeper who claimed some noble blood in her ancestry—Anna Streim. It was not a particularly happy marriage. In the first place Strauss had such a busy professional life that he was rarely at home; in the second place he carried 'on a curious, persistent affair with another woman. Why he chose to neglect the good-looking, intelligent and musical Anna for a rather plain, unintelligent and unmusical hatmaker named Emilie Trampusch who was mainly interested in his money seems inexplicable. However, he spent more and more time with Emilie in a rather drab flat in the Kumpfgasse. Meantime Anna maintained his opulent home in the Hirchenhaus and bore him six children, Johann, Josef, Nelli, Therese, Eduard and finally Ferdinand who only

Poster for a French production of Die Fledermaus.

lived a few months. Anna stood it for many years while Strauss increased his financial burdens by having five illegitimate children by Emilie. The final straw was said to be when he had the tactlessness to christen one of

THÉÂTRE DES VARIÉTÉS

LA CHAUVE-SoURiS

Opérette en 3 actes   (DIE FLEDERMAUS)

d'après H·MEILHAC et L·HALÉVY   Musique de

LIVRET de PAUL FERRIER   JOHANN STRAUSS

Imp. CH. WALL et Cie (Atelier DOLA)

these Johann. No longer seen with him in public, Anna made her ultimatum, upon which Strauss moved in permanently with Emilie and only kept contact with his legitimate family by sending them a meagre monthly allowance.

Strauss's musical life, in the meantime, was one of constant success and praise until he became over-ambitious. In the end, his orchestra, tired of endless travelling and afraid that he might, indeed, never settle in Vienna again, refused to accompany him to America and one night refused to play at all. In the end they agreed to one more trip to England provided that Strauss would take them back to Vienna for good after it was over. It was a chilly winter in the British Isles and, after a particularly wet and miserable trip to Edinburgh, Strauss and half his orchestra were taken ill. He managed to conduct further concerts at Newcastle, Leeds, Hull and Wakefield, but was so racked with coughs that a concert at Derby had to go on without him. They packed up and returned to Europe but in a hotel in Calais he collapsed and for days was in a coma. The orchestra returned to Vienna, Strauss eventually following on a cold and nightmarish journey via various hotels and hospitals. The sounds and sights of Vienna revived him, in spite of his coach crashing, and a forgiving Anna came to meet him and take him home. He recovered and was once more able to give concerts with his orchestra. Meanwhile the younger Johann, against the wishes of his father, was leading his own orchestra to rival success. In 1849, father Strauss, by now back with his mistress Emilie, contracted scarlet fever, caught from one of his illegitimate children, and within four days he was dead. Josef Strauss, called at the flat, found Emilie and her possessions gone and his father naked on the floor. Anna and her family were the mourners. Emilie and her brood sank into obscurity, her only claims to attention being some years later when 'she was caught attempting to steal a bronze lantern from her lover's grave.

On one unpleasant day, the elder Strauss had caught his oldest son playing the violin, gave him a severe whipping and forbade him to enter the music profession. No doubt, in his heart he felt justified in keeping his son from a profession which had led him to so much unhappiness, but Anna openly encouraged him. Johann Jr wrote his first waltz when he was only six. After finishing his schooling he was found a position as a bank clerk. With his

mother's help he had, however, taken violin lessons and, after the separation of his parents, he was given proper musical and instrumental training with a well-known choirmaster Joseph Drechsler. The family blood dictated his interest in dance music and at the age of nineteen he formed his own orchestra of fifteen players and made his début at Hietzing on the 15th October 1844. The concert, at which he played some of his own works and his father's *Loreley-Rheinklänge* waltz, was a tremendous success and his fame quickly rivalled that of the elder Johann, who was, perhaps, secretly pleased.

When Johann Sr died in 1849 the two orchestras merged and were taken over by the son. Soon he was forced into the same whirlwind tours as well as fulfilling several important posts at leading Viennese ballrooms. After touring the whole of Europe, including Russia, he paid his one and only visit to England in 1869, commemorating it with a set of quadrilles, based on popular English songs such as *Champagne Charlie*, and several other tactfully named works. The 1860s were the period of Strauss's most impressive compositions, like the controversial *Blue Danube* of 1867 which initially aroused some antagonism by being, in its original form, a setting of slightly controversial words with political overtones.

Strauss might have worked entirely within the dance-music field if he had not heard, as so many other composers over the world did, the sparkling strains of Parisian operetta often staged in Vienna in the 1860s and, in particular, if he had not met the arch-priest of French operetta, Jacques Offenbach, visiting Vienna in 1863 to produce some of these works, notably *Orpheus in the Underworld*. Offenbach and Strauss were involved in a contest to write a waltz for the annual ball of the Vienna Press Association and, remarkably, it was Offenbach who won with his *Abendblätter* pushing Strauss's *Morgenblätter* into second place. Perhaps when Offenbach suggested that Strauss should try his hand at operetta, the memory of that defeat encouraged Strauss to try to surpass the master in his own métier. Success in this area of endeavour did not come right away or every time as Strauss was inclined to be somewhat uncritical about the librettos offered to him. When two good ones came along he wrote two supreme operettas, two of the finest ever written—*Die Fledermaus* in 1874 and *Der Zigeunerbaron* in 1885.

In 1863 Strauss followed his father's foot-

Title page of the Demolition Polka *by Johann Strauss Jnr.*

steps by being appointed Director of the Imperial Court Balls. He had some of his father's matrimonial inclinations too. His first wife Jetty Treffz, a remarkable singer who was once rated as a rival to Jenny Lind, was an ideal companion who made his home a happy and comfortable place while her wealth made it easier for him to give up the orchestra and concentrate on composition. But the roving eye was a fatal inheritance and a taste for actresses disrupted the marriage bliss. Jetty herself was by no means innocent and Strauss was to find to his surprise that she had offspring other than those he knew of from her previous marriage. She died in 1877 thus resolving the unhappy situation. Strauss then married the actress Angelica Dietrich but she did not enjoy the solitary life of wife of an endlessly travelling musician and they were divorced. Finally he married Adele Deutsch, when he was fifty-eight, and she gave him the happiness he needed, keenly interested in his work and incidentally drawing Brahms into their circle of friends.

Strauss led a hard and industrious life, continually composing anywhere and anytime, but he was blessed with a youthful vigour that stayed with him until almost the end. In his last years he resorted to a quiet melancholy and was deeply depressed when his friend Brahms died in 1897. In 1899 he contracted double pneumonia and within a day or two had died.

When Johann Strauss decided to give up the family orchestra the mantle of leadership fell upon the next brother Josef who had always shown a strong gift for the arts but had started a career in architecture and engineering. Having deputised for Johann at one time, he took up a musical career, studied theory and learned the violin. He first conducted performances of his own compositions in 1853. Unlike Johann, he was of an introspective and nervous nature. He collapsed on the rostrum at a concert in Warsaw when the orchestra got out of hand, and died shortly after in Vienna.

Eduard, the younger brother, was persuaded by Johann to take up a musical career and for some time played in the family orchestra. He made his own début as conductor and composer in 1859, deputised as conductor of the family orchestra and finally took it over when Johann died. He toured the whole of Europe and appeared in England in 1885. His son Johann also continued in the family tradition. If Anna Strauss failed to cement the partnership with her husband, she certainly found fulfilment in the musical rewards that her talented sons gained for her.

Although it is the younger Johann Strauss whose music means most to Vienna and the world, each of the Strauss dynasty had much to offer. The elder Johann wrote mainly in a straightforward ländler idiom but much advanced the art of the waltz and other dances

during his short composing career. He rarely achieved the same melodic memorability of his son's works, but, well-schooled in the dance tradition, his pieces showed a great flair for rhythmic ingenuities and variations, while his harmonies were fairly conventional. Some of his more substantial waltzes have a refined elegance that gives them strength and many are still played. The one work that was to remain his memorial was the dashing *Radetzky* march, written in 1848, which became very much the symbol of the old Hapsburg dynasty. That will never be forgotten.

The sweep and splendour of the younger Johann's great waltzes need hardly be emphasised, nor the refreshing novelty of his polkas and mazurkas and other dances. *The Blue Danube* is probably the best known and most often played waltz ever written, but others challenge its supremacy with their ambitious, almost symphonic introductions and endlessly inspired themes: the gay *Voices of Spring* (*Frühlingsstimmen*), the haunting *Tales from the Vienna Woods* (*Geschichten aus dem Wienerwald*) and the noble *Emperor* waltz which has a truly majestic strength of purpose. Works like the *Annen* and *Pizzicato* polkas (the latter written with Josef) are models of simple ingenuity, while the two great operettas are simply the best of their kind and immortal.

The scope and magnitude of Josef's genius may not have matched Johann's but some of his waltzes are of equal rank, notably *Dorfschwalben aus Oesterreich, Sphärenklange* and *Mein Lebenslauf ist Lust und Lieb* with their gay themes strangely at odds with his moody nature. Perhaps one of the most touching dance pieces of all the family Strauss compositions is Josef's delicately beautiful *Die Libelle* polka-mazurka which the Vienna Philharmonic always play so affectingly. Eduard's 250 or so compositions are soundly wrought but never seem to match the inspiration of his brothers.

The Strausses between them took the spirit of the Schrammel quartets, the music of the lowly inns of Vienna, and transformed it into music that composers like Brahms and Wagner admired and which the great conductors and symphony orchestras of the world are eager to play. They took the captivating rhythms of the waltz to their heights and yet never lost sight of their dance origins or the world's great need for light music and strong melodies.

P.G.

STRAUSS, Richard
(b. Munich, 11 June 1864;
d. Garmisch, 8 Sept 1949)

Generally considered today last in the line of German romantic composers, Strauss was in his early years thought of as a revolutionary, shocking a musical world brought up on Brahms and Wagner. He lived long enough to see most of the major changes in 20th-century music, but chose to ignore them, remaining faithful to his own muse, but never quite matching the glorious works of his early years. He will remain a front-rank composer through the vigour and invention of his greatest tone poems and through his most original operatic scores.

He was born the son of Franz Strauss, a brilliant horn player. He had his first piano lessons when he was four, and wrote his first composition, a Christmas song, when he was six. He went through the normal schooling of a German boy entering the University of Munich in 1882, where he studied philosophy and aesthetics, while continuing his musical training, begun in 1875. He graduated in 1883, by which time he had already written a con-

Richard Strauss and his wife Pauline, 1914.

siderable body of works, among them the attractive songs of Op. 10.

During the winter of 1883–4 he visited Berlin, where he met Hans von Bülow, the famous conductor, who played the young composer's Wind Serenade, Op. 7, and asked him to write another piece for the Meiningen Court Orchestra. This was another work for wind, of which Strauss conducted the première with the orchestra at Munich, where it was then on tour, on the 18th November 1884. As a result, Strauss was appointed as assistant music director to that orchestra. This was the beginning of his secondary career as a conductor, which continued more or less to the end of his days. While at Meiningen he was also converted from a reasonably conservative composer in the Brahms mould into a follower of 'Music as Expression', as exemplified in the works of Berlioz, Liszt and Wagner. Strauss himself wrote that *Aus Italien*, the first of his symphonic poems (1886), 'is the connecting link between the old and new methods'. That work was the product of a visit to Italy, and it was first performed the following year at Munich, where Strauss was now established as third conductor at the Munich Opera, a post he held until 1889, when he moved to Weimar, as director of the Court Orchestra.

While at Munich he met the singer Pauline de Ahna, whom he soon married, and wrote his first major success, *Don Juan*, although it was not given its première until Strauss reached Weimar. *Tod und Verklärung* followed in 1890. Both provoked controversy, which was to become more fierce with succeeding works during the following years. While he was away convalescing from a serious illness in 1892, he was engaged in the writing of his first opera *Guntram*, not considered a success when it was first given at Weimar in 1894, after which Strauss returned with some relief to a more senior post than he had previously held at Munich. He commented on his departure from Weimar: 'I had recklessly squandered some of the goodwill borne towards me, by my youthful energy and love of exaggeration, so that they were not sorry to see me and Pauline go.' However, the Munich première of *Guntram* proved disastrous, and once again made Strauss angry with his home city.

Before he went to Berlin as first conductor of the Court Opera and Orchestra, he had already established himself as a leading conductor. He first appeared at Bayreuth in charge of *Tannhäuser* in 1891 and visited London for the first time in 1897. There was still time for composition. *Till Eulenspiegel* (1895), *Also Sprach Zarathustra* (1896), *Don Quixote* (1898) and *Ein Heldenleben* (1899) all had their first performances during this period. They are among the most brilliant and typical of his tone-poems. When *Till Eulenspiegel* was given in Britain in 1896, the first of Strauss's works to be presented here, it was considered so complex that it was played twice to justify the time spent on its preparation.

Strauss remained at his post in Berlin until 1908, when he was promoted to general music director (a job he held until 1924) and chief conductor of the Berlin Philharmonic until 1918. Meanwhile in 1900 he met Hugo von Hofmannsthal, who was to prove a seminal influence on Strauss's operatic development. Before their collaboration began Strauss had caused the biggest furore of his turbulent career with the production of *Salome* at Dresden in 1905, the second of his many operas written for that house (the first was *Feuersnot*, 1901). The story, based on an Oscar Wilde play, was fairly revolutionary as a subject for a libretto; the music, grand scale, sensual and sometimes ferocious, brought a new sound into the operatic theatre. Similarly the single-act structure, with its direct and powerful scenario, was novel. *Elektra*, fruit of his first cooperation with Hofmannsthal was, if anything, more violent, more imposing in its effect. To the passionate excitement of *Salome* was added an even more daring use of harmony and *leitmotif*, to express the unhinged psychology of Sophocles's heroine, but with a more noble characterisation than had been possible in the case of Salome.

Strauss could hardly go further in that direction, and for their next collaboration he and his librettist turned to the much more *gemütlich* world of 18th-century Vienna. *Der Rosenkavalier*, first given at Dresden in 1911, is in consequence a much softer-grained, more sentimental score, where the Viennese waltz finds its apotheosis and character is delineated as surely in a humorous vein as it had been in a dramatic one for the earlier operas. *Ariadne auf Naxos*, the following product of the partnership, was produced in its original form by Max Reinhardt at Stuttgart in 1912. This included a German translation of Molière's *Le Bourgeois gentilhomme*; in the 1916 revision made for Vienna, Strauss wrote an explanatory Prologue, thereby making the work self-sufficient and eliminating the need for a

wholly separate acting cast. As such it is a charming work, simply scored. Strauss successfully combined *commedia dell 'arte* episodes with the drama of Ariadne, and in the Prologue created the delightful character of the Composer. Its successor was a very different matter. *Die Frau ohne Schatten*, first given in 1919 at Vienna, where Strauss had become Director of the State Opera (remaining in the post until 1924), is a symbolic fantasy conceived on a large scale, in which much that is banal and pretentious marches with much that is striking and touching. *Die ägyptische Helena* (Dresden, 1928), a fanciful drama on the Helen and Menelaus theme, and the much more successful *Arabella* (Dresden, 1933) were the last products of the Strauss–Hofmannsthal partnership before the poet's death. *Arabella* comes closest to *Rosenkavalier* in mood and musical matter, but it is more intermittently inspired.

His direction of the Vienna Opera, together with the conductor Franz Schalk, was a controversial period, which ended in 1924 with Strauss's resignation. However, his sixtieth birthday was marked by that city and Munich giving him their freedoms. From then to the end of his life, he held no permanent post, but he continued to travel extensively, conducting opera and attending festivals. Most interest continued to lie in his works rather than his life, at least until 1935 when he was disgraced by the Nazi regime and resigned his position as President of the state music council, to which he had been appointed in 1933. Nevertheless his attitude to the regime remained ambivalent. He disliked interference of the government in artistic matters, and was uninterested in political developments, but not wishing to leave his home, acquiesced more or less passively in the doings of the Nazis, thus assuring that his works continued to be performed.

Meanwhile he had completed the domestic–autobiographical opera, *Intermezzo* to his own libretto, a comedy, containing much full-blooded music in the interludes and cultivating the conversational style, of which he was such a master, in the various scenes. After Hofmannsthal's death, Stefan Zweig adapted Ben Jonson's play *Epicoene* as a libretto for *Die schweigsame Frau* (Dresden, 1935). Josef Gregor (with help from Zweig, now as a Jew banned by the Nazis, and later Clemens Krauss) wrote the texts for his next three operas, *Friedenstag* (Munich, 1938), *Daphne* (Dresden, 1938) and *Die Liebe der Danae*

(Salzburg, 1952), none of which has held the stage in regular performance but each of which has points of interest and inspiration. *Capriccio* (Munich, 1942), to a libretto by the composer and Krauss, is a discussion on the relationship between words and music set at the time of Gluck, and related to the choice of a Countess between the love of a poet and a

composer. It is a fitting close to Strauss's operatic work, elegant and often autumnal in mood but in no way showing a decline in his powers. His last years also saw a late flowering of orchestral works. After the huge size of his last tone poems, such as the *Symphonia Domestica* (1904) and the *Alpine Symphony* (1915), these final pieces show a considerable refinement of his style, a mellowing of manner, but no lack of exuberance. Chief among them are the Second Horn Concerto (1943), two works for wind band (1945, 1946),

Poster for a Strauss week in Munich, 1910. The character depicted is Clytemnestra in Elektra.

RICHARD STRAUSS-WOCHE

MÜNCHEN 1910   23-28 JUNI

Metamorphosen for 23 solo strings (1946), an oboe concerto (1946) and the Duet Concertino for clarinet, bassoon and strings (1948).

In the early part of his life Strauss composed songs at a prolific rate. They are mostly lyrical in mood and free in form. Too few of these delightful pieces have found their way into regular performance. Strauss crowned his career with the valedictory *Four Last Songs*, first performed in 1950. At the time of his death, on the 8th September 1949, he had begun a fifth. They are written for the soaring soprano voice he so much loved, and for orchestra. They distil the essence of a style that changed little over the years and show to perfection the fusion of the romantic and neoclassical.

After World War II, Strauss was much fêted, particularly at a London festival of his music in 1947 and at his eighty-fifth birthday celebrations in 1949, during both of which he once more took up the baton, but he was old and tired by then and the end was obviously near for a composer whose world had already departed.

In his prime, Strauss was tall and elegant. He looked as much the practical man of business (which to an extent he was!) as the composer. He was a genial, sociable man who enjoyed nothing more than a game of *Skat*, of which he was a master (several hands are played during the course of one scene of *Intermezzo*). He was not above arranging his scores for any practical, but possibly musically dubious purpose and he would conduct almost anywhere for good money. His relations with his wife were frequently stormy.

The place of his most popular works is assured in the repertory. *Elektra, Salome* and *Rosenkavalier*, in that descending order of merit, are all works that add conspicuously and individually to the store of 20th-century music-drama, and the first two considerably advanced musical development and were influential on other composers. *Ariadne, Capriccio* and *Intermezzo*, in their more minor way, have also stood the test of fairly frequent performance. *Die Frau ohne Schatten* is perhaps more for the composer's total adherents.

Similarly in the orchestral field, *Till Eulenspiegel, Don Juan, Heldenleben* and *Zarathustra* remain in the mainstream of orchestral programmes while some of the later tone poems (and the very early ones) are of more specialised interest. The best show Strauss's big bravura writing and his flexible melodic gift at their most potent. These, and the operas

mentioned, make the kind of unique contribution to which any leading composer must aspire.

A.B.

STRAVINSKY, Igor
(b. Oranienbaum, 17 June 1882; d. New York, 6 April 1971)

Igor Fedorovich Stravinsky passed his youth in St Petersburg, where his father was a prominent bass-baritone at the Imperial Opera. Igor was one of four brothers. The family spent their winters in St Petersburg and their summers in the country. He was particularly fond of Ustilug in Volhynia where his mother's brother-in-law had a large estate. As a boy he was devoted to music. He learnt the piano and was given harmony and counterpoint lessons; but his parents refused to allow him to pursue a musical career and sent him to St Petersburg University to read criminal law and legal philosophy. By the time he was twenty, how-

Stravinsky, 1921.

Stravinsky by Picasso, 1917.

ever, he was determined to become a composer, and shortly before his father's death in 1902 he consulted Rimsky-Korsakov, who advised him to continue with private tuition, and himself acted as a kind of tutor and supervisor over the next six years.

Shortly after leaving the University, Stravinsky married his first cousin, Catherine Nossenko, in 1906, and in the course of the next eight years they had two sons and two daughters. Rimsky-Korsakov died in 1908; and the following year Serge Diaghilev, who was planning a mixed season of Russian opera and ballet in Paris that summer, heard *Fireworks*, a new orchestral work of Stravinsky's, at a concert; and this impressed

Rite of Spring *danced by The Royal Ballet.*

him so favourably that he decided he would like to enlist his services for the Russian Ballet. The first important commission he offered Stravinsky was *The Firebird*, a ballet based on a Russian fairy tale. *The Firebird* was the sensation of the Russian Ballet season at the Paris Operahouse in the summer of 1910 and helped to establish Stravinsky's status as a composer of international importance. Later that summer he started to compose a piece for piano and orchestra; but Diaghilev found ways of diverting it from the concert hall to the stage, where it became *Petrushka*, a ballet with its setting in the Shrovetide Fair that used to be held regularly in the Admiralty Square, St Petersburg. A kind of spring symphony based on the pagan rites of primitive Russian tribes was also produced in ballet form as *The Rite of Spring*, and its first performance (Paris, 29th May 1913) provoked one of the most lively theatrical scandals of all time. Stravinsky's next major work, an opera called *The Nightingale*, was a chinoiserie which he had started to compose as early as 1908 and which he now completed, ostensibly for the Free Theatre of Moscow. But when that enterprise collapsed, he allowed Diaghilev to produce it in Paris and London in the summer of 1914. The composition of another important Russian work was interrupted by the outbreak of war. This was *Les Noces* (*The Wedding*), a ballet cantata depicting Russian peasant wedding customs. Stravinsky made his own libretto from snatches of Russian folk songs and peasant dialogue and worked on the score when he and his family were living in Switzerland. Although the sung portion of this cantata, which is continuous, was ready by 1917, it took him another six years to find the right instrumental solution, and the first performance of *Les Noces* was not given by the Russian Ballet until 1923.

The year 1917 brought a complete change in Stravinsky's personal fortunes. It was only for health reasons that he and his family had been staying in Switzerland at the beginning of the war; and it had always been their intention to return to Russia – at least to their estate in Volhynia – when the war was over. The news of the February Revolution was received with acclamation; and Stravinsky telegraphed his mother, who was in St Petersburg, saying: 'Toutes nos pensées avec toi dans ces inoubliables jours de bonheur que traverse notre chère Russie libérée'. But the October Revolution brought a very different story. He then began to realise that his income from Russia would dry up and his property in St Petersburg and Ustilug would be confiscated. He decided not to return to his native country and opted for exile in Western Europe.

Something of the effect of this decision on his composing could be seen as early as 1918 when he wrote *The Soldier's Tale*, a piece to be read, played and danced. Its action was based on some popular tales from a Russian collection; but responsibility for the text was entrusted to C. F. Ramuz, a distinguished writer living in the Suisse Romande, who made the action of general, rather than national, application. Similarly, Stravinsky chose eclectic musical material for his score, which was written for a chamber ensemble of seven players. Any specifically Russian element was excluded.

After the war, when Diaghilev tried to persuade Stravinsky to resume his collaboration with the Russian Ballet, the project that won him over was the suggestion that he should adapt some music by Pergolesi for a *commedia dell'arte* ballet. *Pulcinella* (1920) was a landmark in his musical development. He himself said it represented his discovery of the past, the epiphany through which the whole of his late work became possible. This led to a marked change of musical style, away from Russian nationalist influences to procedures deriving from European classical traditions. How quickly this new idiom established itself can be seen from an early neo-classical masterpiece like the Octet for wind instruments (1923).

In 1920 Stravinsky and his family left Switzerland and settled in France. Obsessed by the need to earn enough money to meet mounting expenses, he decided to embark on subsidiary careers as a conductor and pianist. He reserved to himself for a few years the exclusive performing rights in his new Concerto for piano and wind (1924) and *Capriccio* for piano and orchestra (1929); and some years

later when his second son, Soulima, had become a professional pianist, he wrote a Concerto for two solo pianos (1935), which the two of them played on tour. He also formed a partnership with the violinist Samuel Dushkin, which led to the composition of a Violin Concerto in D (1931) and a *Duo Concertant* for violin and piano (1932). His touring activities took him all over Europe, and also to North America in 1925, 1935, 1937, and to South America in 1936.

During the 1920s and 1930s his neo-classical works did not always meet with approval; and many people lamented the fact that he seemed to have abandoned the 'exotic' Russian idiom of his earlier popular period. Yet it seems difficult now to understand how masterpieces like the opera/oratorio *Oedipus Rex* (1927), the *Symphony of Psalms* (1930) and the ballet *Persephone* (1933) could have been so underestimated at the time.

In 1934 he became a French citizen; and the following year, as if to commemorate his naturalisation, he published his autobiography in French. But the same year (1935) he was unsuccessful in his attempt to get elected to the Institut de France. Then ill-health started to take its toll of his family. His elder daughter, Ludmila, died from consumption in 1938. His wife died (also from consumption) in 1939; and his mother, who had

Stravinsky by Chagall.

been living with them since 1922, died a few months later. He himself spent five months in a sanatorium in 1939; and as war appeared inevitable, he decided to leave Europe and start a new life in the United States. He accepted an invitation to hold the Chair of Poetry at Harvard University for the academic year 1939/40 and delivered a series of six lectures there (in French) on the Poetics of Music.

Since 1922 he had been deeply in love with Vera de Bosset, formerly the wife of the artist Serge Soudeikine; and early in 1940 she joined him in the United States, and they were married in Bedford, Massachusetts. They settled in Hollywood; and shortly after the end of the war their naturalisation papers came through, and they became American citizens. His compositional activities continued unabated in America. A number of rather minor works appeared during the war; but these were flanked by two masterly symphonies – the Symphony in C (1940) and the Symphony in Three Movements (1945).

In the past his music had been published by a number of different firms; but in 1946 he entered into an exclusive agreement with Boosey & Hawkes for the publication of all his future works. Boosey & Hawkes also bought up the rights of those of his earlier works previously published by Edition Russe de Musique, from *Petrushka* to *Persephone*. For many years he had suffered from the fact that, as Russia had not subscribed to the Berne Copyright Convention, he had been unable adequately to protect the copyrights of his earlier music. Now that he was an American citizen, he was able to safeguard his current position; and this seemed a good moment to revise and correct some of his earlier scores and so establish new copyrights.

In 1948 he agreed with his new publishers to write a full-scale opera. The subject chosen was based on a series of paintings by Hogarth called *The Rake's Progress*. The English libretto was written by W. H. Auden and Chester Kallman; and the work of composition lasted three years. The first performance of *The Rake's Progress* was given at the Fenice, Venice (11th September 1951) with the composer conducting. This marked the first time he had been to Europe since the war.

The Rake's Progress was virtually the last major work of his to be written in the neoclassical idiom he had made peculiarly his own over the last thirty years. While working on the opera, he invited to his house in Holly-

wood a young American musician called Robert Craft, then in his early twenties. Craft made himself useful to Stravinsky in many ways and in course of time became a close and valued member of the household. He had always admired the music of the 20th-century Viennese School; and in 1953 he introduced Stravinsky to a wide range of recordings of Schönberg, Berg, and Webern. Stravinsky found that he was particularly attracted by the music of Webern; and henceforth his compositions began to show a cautious tendency to investigate the possibilities of serialism.

In Memoriam Dylan Thomas (1954) used a limited row of only five notes; but by the time he had reached *Agon* (1953–7), a ballet suite of twelve numbers, the music, though it opened and closed with a firm affirmation of C major tonality, explored a number of serial possibilities in some of the middle movements. *Threni* (1958), a large-scale work for soloists, chorus and orchestra, was his first completely serial work; and his mastery of this new medium was confirmed in *Movements* for piano and orchestra (1959). The concentrated power of his use of serialism can be seen from miniatures like the *Epitaphium* for flute, clarinet and harp (1959), *Double Canon* for string quartet (1959), and *Fanfare for a New Theatre* for two trumpets (1964), which, though lasting for scarcely more than a minute leave a full-scale projection behind them.

Craft's invaluable assistance enabled Stravinsky in his latter years to resume touring on virtually a world-wide scale; and in 1962, the year of his eightieth birthday, he made a triumphant visit to Moscow and Leningrad, forty-eight years after he had left his motherland in 1914. Craft also helped him to make gramophone recordings of his complete works; and together they devised a form of literary collaboration that enabled them to publish half a dozen books of personal reminiscences and discussions on musical topics written in English between 1959 and 1969.

His last major work was the *Requiem Canticles* (1966); but after that ill-health led to a slowing-down of all his activities. In 1969 the household moved from Hollywood to New York, where he died on the 6th April 1971. He was buried a few weeks later on the island of San Michele, Venice.

E.W.W.

SULLIVAN, Arthur
(b. London, 13 May 1842,
d. London, 22 Nov 1900)

The good fairies have rarely gathered at an infant's bedside in such numbers as they did in the case of Arthur (Seymour) Sullivan, lavishing on him the gifts of good looks, charm and musical talent. By the age of eight he had learned to play every instrument in the band of his father, then bandmaster at the Royal Military College of Sandhurst, and four years later he was admitted to the Chapel Royal as a chorister. In 1855, while still only thirteen,

Sullivan. Cartoon by Carlo Pellegrini.

two things happened which pointed towards the success he was later to achieve in both the musical and the social worlds: his anthem *O Israel* was accepted for publication, and the Duke of Wellington, paying a visit to the Chapel Royal choristers, patted him on the head and gave him a golden sovereign. A year later he became the first holder of the newly established Mendelssohn Scholarship at the Royal Academy of Music, under the terms of which he went to Leipzig in 1858 to continue his studies. During his three years there he studied diligently, appeared in public as both pianist and conductor, and had the satisfaction of hearing his incidental music for *The Tempest* played in a concert at the Conservatoire. He also developed an enthusiasm for the music of Schumann, whose music he championed on his return to England in 1861 with a generosity that was typical of him. By playing his own piano arrangement of Schumann's First Symphony to the principal of the Royal Academy of Music and the secretary of the concert society at the Crystal Palace, neither of which gentleman had previously heard a note of Schumann, he secured its first performance in England.

Once back at home, Sullivan set out to establish himself as a composer. Radically revised and improved, *The Tempest* was given at a Crystal Palace concert on the 12th April 1862, making him famous overnight. (The work was repeated the following week in response to overwhelming public demand.) Meanwhile he had to make a livelihood, so he took up various posts as organist, one of them at Covent Garden, where he also composed the music for a ballet, *L'Ile enchantée,* in 1864. The same year saw his cantata *Kenilworth* performed at the Birmingham Festival, and there were other compositions which made it appear as though he could not make up his mind whether to become a composer for the church or the concert hall. He did in fact continue to follow these paths, but in 1867 he was to be introduced to the form of musical entertainment which was to make him world-famous and wealthy, and for which his fluent but frankly limited talents were really best suited – operetta. His first collaboration, however, was not with W. S. Gilbert, with whom his name would finally become as irrevocably linked as those of Fortnum and Mason or Rolls and Royce, but with F. C. Burnand, who had made a libretto from Maddison Morton's farce, *Box and Cox*. With its title reversed to *Cox and Box* the one-act

Gilbert. Cartoon from Punch.

operetta was first given a private performance, then launched on the public stage. It did
not, however, set the Thames on fire, so Sullivan was soon back to the organ loft and
directing his creative energies once again to
hymns and other church music. It was not
until 1871 that he met Gilbert, and the first
fruit of their collaboration, *Thespis*, ran only a
month at the Gaiety Theatre in London
before vanishing without trace. Four years
later they came together again for the one-act
Trial by Jury, this time hitting the jackpot with
their skit on the legal system. It remains
unique among their operettas in that it contains no spoken dialogue. Then in 1877
Richard D'Oyly Carte formed a company for
the express purpose of presenting operettas by
Gilbert and Sullivan, beginning with *The Sor-
cerer*, which enjoyed a continuous run of 175
performances.

Gilbert and Sullivan were among the oddest
couples whom fate has ever brought together.
Gilbert, craggy and tousled in appearance,
was a cantankerous egoist who quarrelled
with everyone he met and was never happier
than when taking people to court, even Sullivan and D'Oyly Carte. Sullivan, handsome
and always smartly turned-out, combined
consistent charm with a gift for making
friends above his station, even among royalty.

The nature of their stormy collaboration has
been summed up perfectly by Caryl Brahms
in her two-tier biography:

> For a composer to have thought that his
> work was better in *The Lost Chord* than it
> was in *The Mikado*, and for a librettist to
> be convinced that a Bab Ballad – written,
> incidentally, in the train to Folkestone on
> his honeymoon – excelled the libretto of
> *HMS Pinafore*, may have been under-
> standable; but it did not make their work-
> ing relationship easier.

Yet this collaboration resulted in a series of
operettas which were not only wildly
acclaimed at the time but have retained
their popularity for a century. Gilbert's
contribution to this uniquely successful
partnership was his treatment of whimsical
situations in verse of considerable wit and
inventiveness. Sullivan met the demands of
these librettos with a quick melodic response
to their lilt and patter, and a keen sense of
parody which is never more hilarious than
when he guys the Verdian conspirators'
chorus. The operettas have attracted an
almost fanatical following, the majority of
D'Oyly Carte audiences consisting of aficion-
ados who attend every night of a Gilbert and
Sullivan season yet will never even sample one
operetta by Offenbach or Strauss, let alone
expose themselves to an opera. The term
'Savoy Operas' applied to the works of Gilbert and Sullivan is, incidentally, a complete
misnomer. Those who are not what might be
called practising Savoyards may find the
satire of Gilbert somewhat naïve on occasion,
the music of Sullivan too facile and repetitive,
and the operettas fatally lacking in moments
of genuine emotion. There is a so-called 'love
interest' in almost all their operettas, but
Sullivan's music never expresses even a hint of
sexual feeling. In spite of this, his operettas
continue to draw capacity houses every night
of the year. The run of successes, of which the
satirical targets range from the peerage and
the Aesthetic movement to women's rights
and the Victorian cult of *japonaiserie*, includes
The Pirates of Penzance (1880), *Patience*
(1881), *Iolanthe* (1882), *Princess Ida* (1884),
The Mikado (1885), *Ruddigore* (1887), *The
Yeomen of the Guard* (1888), *The Gondoliers*
(1889), *Utopia Limited* (1893) and *The Grand
Duke* (1896).

In his professional life apart from Gilbert,
Sullivan consistently received huge acclaim
for a variety of works ranging from innumer-

Sketch from The Mikado, *on its first production at the Savoy Theatre, London 1885.*

able drawing-room ballads and hymns to cantatas and sacred music dramas. He restricted himself to vocal works, however, failing to follow up the early Symphony in E, later called the 'Irish', and the 'Cello Concerto of 1866. He also attempted full-scale opera with *Ivanhoe*, produced at the now Palace Theatre in 1891, and wrote incidental music for various productions of Shakespeare. Today these works feature only as footnotes in volumes of musical history, and to attempt to revive them has ever proved of more than curiosity value. It should be remembered, however, that Sullivan lived at a time when the gibe that England was a 'land without music' had genuine validity. (Elgar, a late starter, did not make any strong impression on the musical world until he produced the *Enigma Variations* in 1899, a year before Sullivan's death.) To the British musical public, steeped in the choral tradition, Sullivan appeared as a major native composer, and he certainly had no serious rival. He brought to all his composition a craftsmanship that is not to be despised, and he was

never slow to provide a suitable piece to celebrate a national occasion. Since he was virtually the only English composer of the time, it was only natural that he should be held in high public esteem and given honours by the universities of Oxford *and* Cambridge. It was only fitting, too, that he should receive a knighthood in 1883. He devoted himself wholeheartedly, moreover, to the various conducting posts he held, showing complete dedication to every aspect of active musical life.

It was the tragedy of Sullivan's life that he succeeded almost extravagantly in a genre that he rather despised. His ambition was to compose on the level of Handel, whom he revered, and Schumann, whose music he selflessly championed in England. His friends must be blamed for making his dilemma all the more painful by complaining that he was wasting his talent on a kind of music that was beneath him. Just as Johann Strauss the Second has achieved immortality with his waltzes, and Offenbach with his French operettas, Sullivan is assured of permanent fame by virtue of operettas which embody an unmistakable English spirit. Like the comedian who spends his life regretting that he has never been asked to play Hamlet, Sullivan was disappointed that he never became the 19th-century Handel or the English Schumann, but the world is richer for its great comedians and richer too for the Sullivan operettas which sparkle as joyously today as they did a century ago.

F.G.B.

SUPPÉ, Franz von
(b. Spalato [Split], 18 April 1819;
d. Vienna, 21 May 1895)

One of the most important of Viennese theatre composers of the 19th century, Suppé began life surrounded by Italian influence, for he attended the University of Padua and studied music with Cigala and Ferrari. When his father died, he and his mother settled in Vienna and Suppé became conductor at the Josephstadt Theatre. He composed the incidental music and songs for a play so successfully that he went on to provide music for more than a hundred other plays not only at the Josephstadt but also for the Theater an der Wien and the theatre at Baden, near Vienna. He began also to compose his own operettas, one of which, *Das Mädchen vom Lande,* had a triumphant success at the Theater an der Wien in 1847. Among his other successful operettas are *Die schöne Galatea* (1865) and *Boccacio* (1879). Another, *Dichter und Bauer,* survives only in its overture, the popular *Poet and Peasant,* and the same might be said of *Leichte Kavallerie* or 'Light Cavalry'.

C.O.

SWEELINCK, Jan
(b. Deventer, *c.* May 1562;
d. Amsterdam, 16 Oct 1621)

Dutch organist, composer and teacher who lived at the end of the brilliant period in which the Netherlanders were the musical leaders of Europe, Sweelinck received his early musical education from his father who was organist of the Oude Kerk Amsterdam from 1564 until 1573; his only other teacher appears to have been Jan Willemszoon Lossy (*c.* 1545–1624) first town musician at Haarlem. Except for the period of study in Haarlem, it seems that Sweelinck rarely left Amsterdam; he is sometimes said to have visited Italy, but there is no evidence to support this. His journeys seem to have been restricted to the Low Countries (Rotterdam, Antwerp, Deventer) to advise on the construction or purchase of instruments.

Sweelinck probably succeeded his father as organist of the Oude Kerk in 1577 (the year of his father's death) and he retained the appointment with great distinction for the remainder of his own life. He was required to play the organ every day before and after the sermon, and also to entertain visitors to the church. In 1590 he married Claesgen Puyner, and of their six children Dirck, the eldest son, later proved himself a worthy successor at the Oude Kerk. Sweelinck dedicated the second volume of his *Psalms* to the musical society at Amsterdam, and he may well have been its leader. He died on the 16th October, 1621 and was buried in the Oude Kerk.

Sweelinck's importance and influence was wide-ranging, as a composer of vocal and instrumental music, and as a teacher of organ and composition. His pupils became established as musical leaders throughout Northern Europe; at Hamburg, for instance, they held the three most important organists' posts. Among his most celebrated pupils were Heinrich Scheidemann in Hamburg, and Samuel Scheidt in Halle, and through them Sweelinck influenced the development of the North German organ school which later included Bach.

Sweelinck's instrumental compositions are for organ or harpsichord, and include fantasias, echo fantasias, toccatas, and variations on chorale melodies (a form he is said to have instigated), secular songs and dances. His keyboard style shows certain affinity with the Elizabethan virginalists, and indeed four of his pieces are included in the Fitzwilliam Virginal Book. This influence may well have resulted from his personal friendship with two Englishmen who spent the last years of their lives on the continent: John Bull, who was Cathedral organist of Antwerp, and Peter Philips, sometime organist of the Royal Chapel in Brussels. John Bull wrote a fantasia on a '*fuga*' of '*M. Jan Pietersn*' and in 1593 Peter Philips visited Amsterdam 'to sie and heare an excellent man of his faculties'. It is possible that Sweelinck's variations on *Pavana Philippi* were composed on this occasion. Sweelinck, in company with many other Dutch composers, also produced a setting of John Dowland's famous 'Lachrymae'.

The fantasias display Sweelinck's great contrapuntal skill (eg. the *Fantasia Chromatica*) and are often cited as the earliest examples of worked-out fugues. The echo fantasias, particularly congenial to organ or harpsichord, delightfully exploit the form. Unlike the examples of some of his contemporaries, Sweelinck never allows the device to become mere pattern. The English virginalist influ-

Sweelinck.

ence is particularly clear in the toccatas and the brilliant figurations of some of the song variations – *Onder een linde groen*, for instance.

Apart from Sweelinck's contrapuntal ingenuity, his music is of great interest harmonically in that it occurs at a period of transition from modes to a major/minor tonal structure. The Onder een linde groen variations centre on G major whereas the 'Mein junges Leben had ein End' variations favour the Dorian mode. A similar duality is apparent in his vocal music – he uses 16th-century cantus firmus technique in several of the *Psalms*, parody technique in several of the '*Rimes françaises et italiennes*' (Leyden, 1612) alongside free composition in most of the *Chansons* and *Cantiones Sacrae* (Antwerp 1619). The range of expression is immense; from the lightest secular music – chansons – to the sublimest sacred music, the *Cantiones Sacrae* (for example the Christmas motet *Hodie Christus natus est*) Sweelinck's vocal works alone were published during his lifetime, but manuscript copies of his instrumental music achieved wide circulation throughout the greater part of Europe.

G.G.

SZYMANOWSKI, Karol
(b. Tymoszówka, 6 Oct 1882;
d. Lausanne, 29 March 1937)

The son of well-to-do landowning parents, Karol Szymanowski was born on their family estate in the Ukraine. Both his parents played the piano, so it was natural that he too should study this instrument from an early age. After three years study, aged ten, he went for further tuition to Gustav Neuhaus in nearby Elisavetgrad. Influenced by Beethoven, Wagner and his compatriot Chopin, he composed several piano pieces including two sonatas. His first published music was a set of nine piano preludes (1898–1900), which he dedicated to Artur Rubinstein: the pianist, whom he met after his entry to the Warsaw Conservatory in 1901, became a lifelong friend and champion of his music. A tall, slim and rather shy young man, the composer at this time must have been unhappily conscious of the slight lameness with which he had suffered from boyhood; his fastidiousness and reserve seem likely also to derive from a homosexual bias freely admitted by his biographers and which he later accepted and even turned to literary use in an unpublished novel (*c*. 1919).

In his early twenties, Szymanowski associated closely with other musicians and helped to form an organisation called 'Young Poland in Music'. In 1905 this in turn led to the foundation of a composers' publishing and concert-promoting association, and performance of a Concert Overture (1905) and piano pieces caused his fame to spread rapidly. However, he felt a need to seek wider experience, and following his father's death in 1906 he travelled extensively in 1907–14, visiting not only the great European cities of Berlin, Paris and Rome but also Algeria and Morocco. Musically, too, he moved away from the highly Chopinesque style of his earlier work (he composed at the piano) towards a more richly-textured idiom owing much to his new study of Richard Strauss. A First Symphony (1907) was performed in Warsaw, but the composer agreed with the critics who found it overelaborate and heavy, withdrawing it after the première. A Second Symphony (1910) showed that he had mastered large-scale forms and was well received both in Berlin and Vienna. A new and important influence, dating from about 1913, was that of Stravinsky and of the exotic elements found in his work (and in that of Debussy and Ravel also); the choral Third Symphony (1916) is a visionary piece with a pantheistic text by the 13th-century Persian

this period his music once again took on a nationalist flavour, for example in the ballet *Harnasie* (1932), a love story among wild mountain people. Despite his lameness, he liked to take long slow walks around Zakopane and, as he put it, 'listen to the mountains'. A religious work, perhaps his choral masterpiece, is the *Stabat Mater* (1926), in which he tried to avoid what he called 'archaic academicism'. Paradoxically, however, he accepted in 1926 the Directorship of the Warsaw Conservatory (he refused a similar, but better-paid, offer from Cairo); but he was unhappy during his two years in the post, composed nothing, and found his health declining. His lungs and throat were affected by tuberculosis (or perhaps cancer); he was ordered to rest and give up his heavy smoking, though he continued to drink a good deal of vodka. In 1930–1 he received an honorary degree from Cracow and other honours from abroad, and despite his declining health he travelled once again extensively, giving concerts and attending performances of his music until 1936. In that year a doctor predicted that the composer had only three months to live, though he was not told. Szymanowski died in a Lausanne clinic in 1937.

Szymanowski is the most important Polish composer between Chopin and the present-day musicians Lutoslawski and Penderecki, who indeed have acknowledged his influence. His sumptuous yet delicate style is wholly individual and intensely expressive, late-romantic in feeling yet technically adventurous; in the later works like *Harnasie* and the Second Violin Concerto (1932) there is perhaps an additional vigour and simplicity deriving from the folk-melodic flavour which the composer himself pointed out. He is to Polish music what his contemporary Bartók is to Hungarian.

C.H.

Szymanowski.

poet Jalal al-Din Rumi. The text praises the god Dionysus, whose worship, conflicting with orthodox Christianity, is also a central theme of the important opera *King Roger*, (1925) which took seven years to write: in this opera the composer gave full expression to his devotion to ancient culture.

World War I affected Szymanowski little at Tymoszówka, but the Revolution brought the destruction of his home (in his absence) and a financial hardship which was to affect him thenceforward. During the 1920s, however, he travelled once again in Western Europe (including London, where he had several friends) and also in the United States: little by little his music was becoming internationally known. Despite feeling unappreciated by his countrymen, he continued to live in Poland, often in the mountain resort of Zakopane; and during

TALLIS, Thomas
(b. London?, *c.* 1505;
d. Greenwich, 23 Nov 1585)

Thomas Tallis, who has been described as the 'Father of English Cathedral Music', was born during the first decade of the 16th century. The exact date of his birth is not known, but he was described as 'verie aged' in 1577, which infers that he was by then over 70. In 1532 he appears to have held an appointment at Dover Priory, and five years later is known to have sung in the choir of St Mary-at-Hill, London. He left the St Mary's choir in 1538, presumably to take up an appointment as organist or master of the choir at Waltham Abbey in Essex, where he remained until the Dissolution of the foundation in the spring of 1540. After a period of two or three years as a lay-clerk at Canterbury, Tallis, in 1543, was elected a Gentleman of the Chapel Royal, a position which he held with great distinction for the remainder of his life. In 1557 Queen Mary granted him a twenty-one-year lease on the Manor of Minster in the isle of Thanet; and further evidence of his continued favour is provided by the fact that during the first year of Queen Elizabeth's reign he received £40 from the Royal Household assets.

In 1572, William Byrd joined Tallis at the Chapel Royal, and three years later they were granted a royal licence which gave them the sole right for printing music and music paper in England. Initially, the venture was a failure. The two composers petitioned the Queen asking to be granted a lease of twenty-one years of the annual value of £30, and, commenting that the printing-licence had resulted in a loss of 200 Marks, pleaded that Tallis, 'is now verie aged and hath served yo mat tie and yo Royall ancestors these fortie yeres and hadd as yet never anie manner of preferment except onely one lease . . . which being now the best p te of his lyvinge is w th in one yere of expiration.' The lease was granted.

The title-page of the collection of *Cantiones Sacrae* which Tallis and Byrd published in

Tallis, from an engraving.

1575 and dedicated to Queen Elizabeth, informs us that they were acting as joint organists of the Chapel Royal at this time. In the preface of this volume there appears two Latin elegiacs, one, by Ferdinand Richardson, contains the celebrated line, 'Tallisius magno dignus honore senex.' Tallis spent the closing years of his life in Greenwich. He had married in 1552, but the marriage produced no children. He died in Greenwich in 1585 and was buried in the Parish Church of St Alphege.

Tallis's Latin music, which forms the major part of his output, demonstrates the wide range of forms and styles then in use. The extent of these Latin compositions may imply that he was reluctant to forgo his Roman Catholic beliefs and, of course, the return of Catholicism under Queen Mary must be regarded as another important contributory factor. His motet *Salvator mundi*, published in the *Cantiones Sacrae*, was very popular during the late 16th and early 17th centuries. The work is particularly characteristic of Tallis's skilful and dexterous handling of choral sonority, as is the motet *O Sacrum Convivium. O nata lux* is a simple homophonic compline hymn of great beauty; *In ieiunio et fletu*, on the other hand, is a polyphonic motet of strikingly original harmonic style. The gigantic motet *Gaude Gloriosa*, believed to have been composed at Waltham, is very much in the tradition of the early 16th-century votive antiphons; and his great assurance in handling rich multi-voiced textures is again demonstrated in the majestic 40-part motet *Spem in alium*, scored for eight 5-part choirs. The noble setting of the *Lamentations of Jeremiah* perfectly illustrates Tallis's supreme contrapuntal skills.

Tallis was among the first to write for the English Church according to Cranmer's requirement of a 'playn and distincte note for every sillable'. He produced 4- and 5-part settings of the English Preces, Responses and Litany shortly after the publication of *The Booke of Common Praier noted*, using Merbecke's standardised version of the plainsong. The Dorian Mode Service, which also conforms to Cranmer's request for brevity, is a simple homophonic setting dating probably from Edwardian times. John Day's *Certaine Notes*, published in 1565, contains a couple of anthems by Tallis which have become very popular: *Hear the voice and prayer* and *If ye love me*. The exquisite Whitsuntide anthem *O Lord give Thy Holy Spirit*, is believed to date from Tallis's later years – its varied textures and attractive style suggests the Elizabethan period. He also adapted several of the Latin motets to English words.

Tallis contributed a set of 'tunes' to Archbishop Parker's Psalter of 1567; one is now in general use as a hymn tune by the name of 'Tallis', and the so-called canon is an adaptation of the Eighth Tune. Vaughan Williams' *Fantasia on a Theme of Thomas Tallis* is also based on a melody from this set.

Tallis's instrumental music is of little importance. His outstanding ability was as an extremely versatile composer of vocal music. There are some delightful little keyboard pieces in the Mulliner Book (the setting of *Ex more docti mistico*, for example), but nothing to compare with the sublime *a capella* motets and anthems, which although written for use within the Roman Catholic or Reformed liturgies, transcends these denominational boundaries.

G.G.

TARTINI, Giuseppe
(b. Pirano, 8 April 1692;
d. Padua, 26 Feb 1770)

Tartini was an Italian violinist, composer and teacher. His father, Fanzango, a generous benefactor of the church, attempted to persuade Giuseppe to enter the University of Padua to study theology, but when the young Tartini eventually entered University it was to study law. He was able to nurture his great love of music, and also spent some time increasing his skills in fencing, at which he became extremely proficient. Tartini left university in 1713, by which time he had fallen deeply in love with Elisabetta Premazone, who is said to have been the niece of Cardinal Giorgio Cornario. Giuseppe and Elisabetta eloped and married. The Cardinal, who appears to have been Elisabetta's guardian, was incensed by this and ordered Tartini's arrest. Tradition has it that the young man fled the city disguised as a monk, and eventually entered the monastery of Assisi, where a relative was custodian. During his residence there, Tartini discovered the acoustic phenomenon known as *terzi tuoni* (or 'difference tones'), but was unable to offer any conclusive scientific explanation. The famous *Trillo del Diavolo* Sonata was written at Assisi. The composer related to Lalande, the astro-

nomer, that inspiration for the work's composition came from a dream:

I dreamt that I had made a bargain with the devil for my soul. Everything went at my command; my novel servant anticipated every one of my wishes. Then the idea suggested itself to hand him my violin to see what he would do with it. Great was my astonishment when I heard him play, with consummate skill, a sonata of such exquisite beauty as surpassed the boldest flights of my imagination. I felt enraptured, transported, enchanted; my breath failed me, and – I awoke. Seizing my violin I tried to reproduce the sounds I had heard. But in vain. The piece I then composed, 'The Devil's Sonata', although the best I ever wrote, how far it was below the one I had heard in my dream.

During his two years at Assisi he, in the words of Dr Burney: 'practised the violin to keep off melancholy reflections; but being discovered on a great festival in the orchestra of the church of the convent by the accident of a remarkable high wind, which forcing open the doors of the church blew aside the curtain of the orchestra and exposed all the performers to the sight of the congregation; when being recognised by a Paduan acquaintance, differences were accommodated, and he settled with his wife at Venice for some time.'

Tartini's fame as a violinist was now widespread and when the virtuoso Veracini visited Venice in 1716, a contest was arranged. Tartini, amazed at the skills of Veracini which far surpassed his own, resolved to undertake an exhaustive study until he had reached the perfection which he desired. Having achieved this, in 1721 he was appointed first violin at the famous Capella del Santo at Padua, the document recording the appointment describing him as 'an extraordinary violinist.' In 1723 he travelled to Prague where for the next two years he directed Count Kinsky's orchestra.

Tartini returned to Padua in 1726 and subsequently founded his school of violin playing which because of its excellence merited the title the 'School of Nations'; its founder was hailed as 'Master of Nations'. Tartini expounded his ideas on the theoretical aspects of music in a number of treatises, some of which were printed, whilst others have remained in manuscript. Tartini travelled extensively in Italy, but refused all offers from abroad, including the princely sum of 3,000 lire promised if he was to visit London. He spent his time playing, composing and teaching, and when old age prevented him from playing he still continued to compose. His last years were spent in suffering – he had a malignant growth of the foot. He died in 1770 and was buried in the church of St Catherine of Padua.

Frequently referred to as the successor of Corelli, Tartini imbued his own compositions with grace and elegance, and at times a passion which often summoned considerable virtuosity. These attributes, together with an innate sense of dynamic contrast, often manifest in the solo sonatas and concerti the taste of the *style galante*. It is interesting to note that several of Tartini's compositions have myserious literary quotations on them, often in cipher. Although a certain amount of church music by Tartini has survived, he was principally interested in instrumental composition remarking that 'the two types differ from each other in such a way that what is right for one cannot be so for the other. Everyone must limit himself to his talent. I have been asked to compose for the Venetian theatres, but have never wanted to do so, because I know that the throat is no fingerboard.'

As a teacher, Tartini was world famous. Among his pupils at the 'School of Nations' were Nardini, Pasqualino, Bini, Manfredi, Ferrari and Graun. In 1760, Tartini wrote a letter of instruction to Signora Maddalena Lambardini. The following extract, which is taken from Dr Burney's translation of 1771, affords a valuable clue in our understanding of Tartini's art: 'Your first study . . . should be the true manner of holding, balancing and pressing the bow lightly, but steadily upon the strings; in such a manner as that it shall seem to breathe the first tone it gives. . . .' Tartini's music is being restored to its rightful place thanks largely to the efforts of the Accademia Tartiniae di Padova, in reprinting his scores and theoretical works.

G.G.

TCHAIKOVSKY, Peter Ilych
(b. Kamsko-Votkinsk, 7 May 1840; d. St Petersburg, 6 Nov 1893)

Tchaikovsky was a sensitive and eager child, instinctively musical. His father was a successful mining engineer, feckless by nature but of distinguished stock. His mother was a sweet, sensitive woman: French by birth, musical, and a capable linguist. Peter Ilych, born on the 7th May 1840, was the second of her six children. He made rapid progress. At the age of four he was being taught alongside his elder brother; by the age of six his parents, tired no doubt of hearing the tunes from their handsome St Petersburg music box strummed on the piano, allowed him formal piano lessons. And though this 'child of glass' (his governess, Fanny Durbach's phrase) was prone to sudden fits of neurosis, often induced by the very music of which he was already so passionately fond, the first eight years of his life were comparatively settled.

But in 1848 his father resigned his safe government post at Votkinsk in the hope of a better position in Moscow. The position came to nothing (it was taken by a colleague to whom Ilya Petrovich had indiscreetly spoken) and the Tchaikovsky family began a difficult, migratory period in their lives. Peter and his elder brother were banished to boarding school; something which, like Dickens's blacking factory, Peter neither relished nor forgot. In 1850 he was transferred to the preparatory division of the St Petersburg School of Jurisprudence; but it was not until 1852 that the family itself settled in St Petersburg. Their new-found security was short-lived. In June 1854 Tchaikovsky's mother, of whom he was almost obsessively fond, died of cholera. It was a blow from which he never wholly recovered. Isolated now in an alien world of law and mathematics and the oppressive disciplines of an all-male institution, his life was already at odds with itself.

He made an indifferent lawyer. As a Clerk in the Ministry of Justice, which he entered in 1859, he was given to chewing official documents rather than delivering them. He travelled and continued his musical studies with the conservatively-minded Nicholas Zaremba. But it was the founding of the St Petersburg Conservatoire by Anton Rubinstein in 1862 that proved a decisive turning point. Tchaikovsky followed Zaremba to the Conservatoire and in 1863 resigned his post (and a secure salary) at the Ministry of Justice. It was a gamble – a characteristic gesture of faith in his own ability to survive as a musician. And it paid off. Within two years he had been invited by Anton's brother, Nicholas Rubinstein, to teach harmony at the Moscow Conservatoire.

Settled into Nicholas Rubinstein's house in Moscow, and brushing off embittered criticisms of his student pieces, Tchaikovsky bravely plunged into the composition of his First Symphony, *Winter Dreams*. It took a heavy toll of him. Throughout the early part of 1866

Tchaikovsky, 1892.

there were increasing signs of nervous disorders: colitis, hypochondria, numbness in hands and feet, even hallucinations. Yet the symphony is a quiet, almost elegiac offering, elegantly, economically scored, a staging post between Mendelssohn and the winter landscapes of Jean Sibelius. The symphony was poorly received in St Petersburg but Tchaikovsky (who was a good judge of his work) always retained a fondness for this 'sin of my sweet youth'.

In 1868 he was invited to meet the famous group, The Five, and their leader Balakirev in St Petersburg. If Tchaikovsky never fully espoused their cause it was because he was, for all his naturalness and sincerity of manner, essentially shy, independent and fearful of cliques. Of the group and its associates he despised only Cui. Rimsky-Korsakov he liked and admired, Borodin too, and when Nadezhda von Meck later compared Mussorgsky to Lalo, Tchaikovsky's retort was fiercely defensive. 'No Frenchman', he wrote 'has it in him to reach those pillars of Hercules which are accessible to the wide and turbulent Russian nature'. In 1869 Balakirev suggested,

and closely supervised, the writing of Tchaikovsky's memorable Fantasy Overture *Romeo and Juliet*. This work, written in the wake of Tchaikovsky's brief, abortive love affair with Désirée Artôt (a celebrated singer and courtesan, Verdi's Violetta to the life) is, like Strauss's *Don Juan*, the intoxicating first flowering of his genius: passionate, poised, brilliantly coloured, rich in melody.

The next few years of Tchaikovsky's career are, on the surface at least, comparatively untroubled. Working in Moscow in the winter, travelling and holidaying on country estates in the Summer (and, like Mahler, doing much of his composition during these Summer idylls), this is the period of the ebullient, folk-inspired Second Symphony, of the opera *Vakula the Smith* (later revised as *Oxana's Caprices* and full of delightful music) and the first two string quartets. But bigger things and bigger crises were in view. The first crisis – a crisis which involved the relationship between Tchaikovsky and Nicholas Rubinstein – came with the completion of the B flat minor Piano Concerto late in 1874. That the crisis was resolved, and that Rubinstein went on successfully to play the concerto he so derided, does not invalidate his criticisms of the work: that it is ill-proportioned, difficult to play and often vulgar in content. Interestingly, though, it is a work – full of deft, fantastic shapes and colours, beautiful melodies and ingenious formal devices – which has often drawn out the best in great, as opposed to second-rate, pianists.

The première of *Swan Lake* was also a fiasco for Tchaikovsky, poorly played and ill-conducted by a near-amateur, Ryabov. But in classical ballet he had found his *métier*, a world full of wonder and beauty; a sumptuous dreamscape of doomed and beautiful people. Put on the defensive by the failure of the production Tchaikovsky dismissed it: 'My own *Lake of Swans* is simply trash in comparison with *Sylvia*.' But for once Tchaikovsky had misjudged a masterpiece. In the richly scored dance episodes and in the plaintive oboe melody which is the swans' tragic *leitmotif* there is concentrated much of the essence of Tchaikovsky's genius and appeal.

But already Tchaikovsky was beginning to show renewed signs of depression. The Symphony he wrote at this time, the so-called *Polish* Symphony, is a fitful, desultory piece, saved only by its wonderful *Andante elegiaco*. Increasingly encircled in gloom, he was ordered to Vichy in the Summer of 1876 to take the waters. Whilst abroad he visited Bayreuth, where he heard *The Ring* (with displeasure) and met Liszt. The old Klingsor of Bayreuth appears to have worked his spell, though, for Tchaikovsky's next work, the tone poem *Francesca da Rimini*, is perceptibly Wagnerian. What is more, the poem's theme – the punishment of the lustful in Dante's Second Circle of Hell – and Tchaikovsky's conscious decision to marry are not unconnected. The guilt surrounding Tchaikovsky's long-endured homosexuality was preying deeply on him. 1876 also produced the elegant, beautifully crafted *Variations on a Rococo Theme* for 'Cello and Orchestra, but the stage was set for a period of overwhelming turbulence.

Depressed, and tired of his Conservatoire teaching, Tchaikovsky began work on his Fourth Symphony and on what was to be a masterly setting of Pushkin's tale of young love destroyed by ruthless charm, *Eugene Onegin*. Then, still nurturing his blind, misguided desire for marriage, and fearful that he too may be acting out the role of an Onegin, Tchaikovsky fell prey, in July 1877, to the combined charms, tantrums and blackmail (she threatened suicide if unrequited) of a blonde 28-year-old music student, Antonina Milyukova. Antonina was pretty and quick-witted, but she was also unintelligent, neurotic (her nails were bitten to the quick till they bled) and a nymphomaniac, a disastrous choice for a man of Tchaikovsky's idolising, idealising sensibility. Aware of her nature, his homosexuality and his desire, as he put it, 'for a full freedom', she was convinced that her charms would win him over. But within five days of their marriage Tchaikovsky was beside himself. 'Physically she is totally repulsive to me', he wrote in a letter to his brother. On the 7th August he fled to his sister's estate at Kamenka; later, in Moscow, he attempted to end his life by drowning; by October he had all but lost his reason. That Tchaikovsky was saved must be attributed to the speed with which he was removed to Switzerland and to the steadying influence of another, greater woman in his life, Nadezhda von Meck. For late in 1876 – such are life's strange symmetries – Mme von Meck, wealthy, widowed, the mother of eleven children and indiscriminately fond of music, had engaged Tchaikovsky on a trifling musical commission. Thus discreetly and unobserved had begun one of the strangest and most moving relationships in musical history. By mutual arrangement the two never consciously met, though in Florence and on the von Meck country estate they did more than once embarrassingly coincide. Instead they corresponded, lengthily, lavishly, frankly. In the wake of the traumas of 1877 (which Nadezhda followed through Tchaikovsky's own letters) she settled on him an annual allowance of 6,000 roubles. In fine, she conferred on him his freedom. Yield nothing, admit nothing, was her advice on the Antonina affair; but she need not have worried. Antonina was herself too compromised to be a permanent threat. (She died, tragically, in 1917 in the lunatic asylum to which she had been committed, sexually deranged, in 1896.) Thus in Nadezhda von Meck Tchaikovsky had all the affection, security and lack of personal, sexual involvement he yearned for; and in him Nadezhda, who at forty-five considered her life 'nearly over', had a wonderful stimulus for her declining years. People gossiped, but Tchaikovsky's stance was always characteristically simple and direct: 'She is kind, delicate, generous and infinitely tolerant. To me she is simply the eternally kind hand of Providence.' And so she remained until the disturbing break in the relationship – occasioned by a misunderstanding and, perhaps, Nadezhda's own declining health – in 1890.

The first fruits of Tchaikovsky's new-found security were the completion of two great masterpieces, the Fourth Symphony and *Eugene Onegin*, in Florence in the spring of 1878. 'I want human beings, not puppets', wrote Tchaikovsky of *Onegin*, and this intimate, profound work perfectly meets that ideal. The new respose also produced the Violin Concerto, a work of fine lyric virtuosity. But security has its own private pitfalls for the creative artist. Tchaikovsky's next opera, *The Maid of Orleans*, is full of puppets, kings and rebellions. Joan of Arc had haunted Tchaikovsky's imagination (at the age of seven he had written a poem about her in French) but the opera lacks individuality and imaginative insight. The Second Piano Concerto, in spite of a lovely slow movement, and the Piano Sonata, are also inclined to be dry and uneven. Roused by the death of Nicholas Rubinstein in 1881 Tchaikovsky wrote his long and beautiful Piano Trio; and to this period belong the *Capriccio italien,* the Roman Carnival dazzlingly set down, and the glorious *Serenade for Strings,* written on impulse ('I felt it deeply from start to finish'). But money, increasing fame and recognition,

Tchaikovsky's notebook, with sketches for his Fifth Symphony.

and long, tranquil summers on Nadezhda von Meck's country estate at Brailov calmed the mind, dried up the well-source.

With his father's death, and the sudden enforced sale of the Brailov estate (shades of *The Cherry Orchard*), Tchaikovsky, already prematurely greying, settled himself at Maidkovo near Moscow. Nervous of change, he turned routine into a fetish. (On visits to foreign hotels he had always insisted on his room being laid out exactly as on the previous occasion.) He would rise at seven, take tea, read the Bible and start work at 9.30 ('The Muse', he once observed 'has learned to be punctual.') The afternoon was for walking – like many composers he created on the move – the early evening for more composition or proof-reading, an obsession in later years. Apart from the occasional heavy drinking bout, it was an orderly life in familiar and not always elegant surroundings. Tchaikovsky was too much a nomad to care for possessions and his taste in furniture seems to have been bizarre.

Apart from the powerfully written *Manfred* Symphony, the mid-1880s produced little of note. But in 1888 a new creative upsurge is evident and with it, once again, a growing sense of crisis, exacerbated by what was to be five years of exhausting, almost obsessive travel. To this period belong the Fifth Symphony, the most Apollonian of the later symphonies, a work which movingly and imaginatively meets and characterises the melancholy mood; as well as the symphonic poem *Hamlet*, and *The Sleeping Beauty*, the richest and most consistently inspired of Tchaikovsky's great ballet scores. *The Queen of Spades*, a powerful

opera which still holds the stage most effectively, was also completed before the tragic break with Nadezhda von Meck. The *Nutcracker* Ballet, written in 1891, during a year of further severe nervous collapse and an exhausting tour of the United States, is perhaps more fitfully inspired, piquant and beautifully scored as much of it is.

The end of Tchaikovsky's strange, eventful life came in 1893. Early in the year the Sixth Symphony, the *Pathétique*, was written, quickly and at a pitch of great intensity 'The theme of it', he told his beloved nephew, Vladimir 'Bob' Davidov, to whom it is dedicated 'is full of subjective feeling. I frequently wept as I worked it out in my mind during that journey.' In June Tchaikovsky travelled to Cambridge to receive an Honorary Doctorate of Music. In October the new symphony was coolly received by a baffled St Petersburg public. (A reaction which is hardly surprising; even Mahler must have gazed into the score with awe and wonder.) On the 2nd November 1893, after dining agreeably and in good temper the previous evening on macaroni, white wine and soda water, Tchaikovsky ate little lunch. But at the end of the meal he drew a glass of tap water in the adjoining room. His brother, Modeste, was appalled. Did Peter not know that it was November, the cholera season in St Petersburg? Oh, yes – 'but one can't go tiptoeing about in fear of death for ever. Now what about that performance of my First Suite in Prague. . . .' It is immaterial whether or not it was the tap water which gave Tchaikovsky the cholera which killed him. The end was fearful and humiliating: the white aprons, the smell of carbolic soap and sulphuric acid, the terrible thirsts, the convulsions, and finally the hot bath to stimulate the all but inert kidneys. It was his mother's fate all over again. He died at three o'clock on the morning of Monday the 6th November 1893. His body was laid in state in his brother's bedroom before being taken to Kazan Cathedral and thence to the Alexander Nevsky Cemetry. There is a legend in St Petersburg that of all the mourners who passed by his body and touched it in respect not one contracted the fatal, and highly contagious, disease. It is a piece of hagiography which it would be cruel to dispute.

It would be easy to characterise Tchaikovsky and his music as being excessively gloomy and self-preoccupied. His life, as we have seen, gave him motive and cue for much despondency: a life, at odds with conventional morality and seemingly fated. In the Sixth Symphony we have the pattern of a distinctly modern consciousness, troubled, aware, rootless, self-alienated. The music of Mahler and Berg, the novels of Proust and Eliot's *Waste Land* are not far behind. Yet Tchaikovsky had a deep and abiding, if fearful, love of life which he expressed in music of great richness, vigour, and a characteristically elegiac beauty. His great ballet scores reveal his enormous melodic fertility. It is aristocratic, unerringly stylish music which conjures a bygone age without resort to empty *pasticcio*. Significantly, Tchaikovsky's god was Mozart. *Don Giovanni* was the formative, seminal influence; and though Tchaikovsky offered us Mozart, with his 'sane and wholesome temperament', as his own anti-type, is there not in both composers a comparable feeling for the heartache, the true *pathos* of living that can be carried in and beneath the most perfectly shaped melodic line? The ballets also reflect the wonder of a childhood vision of good and evil – a play of dramatic forces which links the ballets to the late symphonies, the Fourth and Fifth symphonies especially, with their uniquely imaginative re-appropriation of dance elements as part of the structure of symphonic drama. Tchaikovsky's operas suffer from a dearth of good libretti in a Russia which was yet to produce Chekhov and Stanislavsky. The Russian genius for the expressive use of arioso and an especially fluid kind of recitative is wonderfully used in some of the operas (in *Eugene Onegin* above all) and in many of his songs; and Bizet's *Carmen*, with its brilliant orchestration, eroticism and sombre beauty exerted a fascination for Tchaikovsky which finally bore fruit in *The Queen of Spades*, an opera which recreates Onegin's world whilst at the same time looking forward, in its gloomy third act, to a world which would one day give us Berg's *Wozzeck* and

Puccini's fine Seine-side melodrama *Il Tabarro*.

As for the vulgar, popular elements in Tchaikovsky – those elements which have made him paradoxically the most famous and, by a certain type of musical snob, the most derided and undervalued of great composers – all one can say is that no one was more aware than Tchaikovsky of music which is vulgar or insincere. His music for *The Tempest* was, he said, 'a motley *pot-pourri*'; *Francesca da Rimini* was too full of 'false pathos', of 'whipped up external effects that do not arise out of the given subject'; his Fifth Symphony he knew was formally weak. About his beloved Fourth Symphony and *Eugene Onegin*, though, he would hear no ill. And indeed these are sincere, truthful works, the two faces of Tchaikovsky wrought in the same critical period of his life: *Eugene Onegin*, passionate and pellucid, with its unbearably haunting Letter Scene and true life ending; a work of Turgenev-like charm and sensibility; and the Fourth Symphony born, like Beethoven's *Eroica*, out of personal despair, yet, Beethoven-like, forging new dramatic forms, new modes of expression, with which to formulate, express and defeat the crisis. As a symphony it is surpassed in range, colour and organic unity only by the Sixth Symphony, the *Pathétique*, which remains one of the most personal, original and musically satisfying of all great symphonies. 'I can tell you in all sincerity', wrote Tchaikovsky to his nephew, 'that I consider this symphony the best thing I have ever done.' And to another friend, 'On my word of honour, never in my life have I been so satisfied with myself, so proud, so happy to know that I have made, in truest fact, a good thing.' And the symphony remains to us, a moving and telling portrait of a great musician and a dedicated, troubled man.

R.O.

TELEMANN, Georg Philipp
(b. Magdeburg, 14 March 1681; d. Hamburg, 25 June 1767)

The most important of Bach's and Handel's contemporaries, Telemann was the son of a clergyman. He was largely self-taught in music, by studying the scores of such masters as Lully and Campra, but continued his musical studies while also studying languages and science at the University of Leipzig. As a

Telemann.

young man he composed operas for the theatres at Leipzig, and then became a church organist. Later, he became *Kapellmeister* at various small courts, but eventually returned to the church and was Music Director of the five principal churches in Hamburg from 1721 until his death forty-six years later. He was an extremely prolific composer, and in his own day a highly regarded one. Handel said of him that he could write an eight-part motet as easily as most people could write a letter.

Telemann composed forty operas, six hundred overtures, forty-four liturgical passions, several oratorios, innumerable cantatas and psalms, and a vast amount of miscellaneous music for church use. Of his operas, only the short *Pimpinone* (1725) is occasionally encountered today, though some of his instrumental and orchestral music finds its way into concert programmes.

C.O.

THOMAS, Ambroise
(b. Metz, 5 Aug 1811;
d. Paris, 12 Feb 1896)

The son of a composer, Ambroise Thomas learned music at a very early age, and revealed a quite precocious talent for both the piano

and the violin. At the Paris Conservatoire, which he entered at the age of seventeen, he won several important prizes, including, in 1832, the Grand Prix de Rome. His early works, mainly chamber music, including a quartet, a quintet and a trio for violin, 'cello and piano, were of such quality that much was expected of him. But it later became evident that his talent was essentially a dramatic one, and he began to produce compositions for the stage, beginning with three works which, at yearly intervals between 1837 and 1839, were produced at the Opéra-Comique. From there, Thomas progressed to the Paris Opéra where two operas and some ballets for which he provided the scores were staged. The majority of his later operas, however, were produced at the Opéra-Comique. The only one of them to have survived is *Mignon* (1866), its libretto based on Goethe's *Wilhelm Meister*. Thomas and his librettists are even further removed from Goethe than Gounod (and the same librettists, Barbier and Carré) was with *Faust*, but the music is light, tuneful and elegant, and it is not difficult to see why *Mignon* is still occasionally produced in France and Italy.

In collaboration with Barbier and Carré again, Thomas composed an opera on Shakespeare's *Hamlet*, which was produced at the Opéra in 1868. It was enthusiastically received, and an indirect consequence was that Thomas was appointed Director of the Paris Conservatoire, succeeding Auber. After this, Thomas produced very little new music for the stage, with the exception of *Françoise de Rimini* (1882), based on Dante.

C.O.

THOMSON, Virgil
(b. Kansas City, 25 Nov 1896)

The American composer Virgil Thomson first became known as a music critic. After serving in the United States Military Aviation Corps during World War I, he went to Harvard and also studied in Paris with Nadia Boulanger. After his graduation from Harvard, where for a time he was assistant conductor of the Glee Club, he took a position as organist and choirmaster of King's Chapel, Boston, and also began to write on music for *Vanity Fair* and other journals. At this time he took up the study of the piano, and on a return visit to Paris between 1925 and 1932 where he had a scholarship to the École Normale de

Musique, he became closely associated with the Parisian group of 'Les Six', with Erik Satie and with the American expatriates in Paris, such as Gertrude Stein. The librettos of his operas *Four Saints in Three Acts* (1928) and *The Mother of Us All* (1947) are by Gertrude Stein. In 1940 Thomson became chief music critic of *The New York Herald-Tribune*, and it is from this time that his reputation as an influential critic dates. In addition to the operas, Thomson has written prolifically in a variety of forms: songs, chamber music, orchestral works, music for films and incidental music for plays. If he lacks a strong personal voice, this is to a large extent compensated for by the excellence of his technique, and the confidence of his taste.

C.O.

TIPPETT, Michael
(b. London, 2 Jan 1905)

Born in London of Cornish stock, Michael Tippett passed most of his early childhood in Suffolk. From 1919 onwards his parents lived abroad; and many of his school holidays were spent visiting them in the South of France, Corsica, or in Florence. From an early age he realised his life would be dedicated to music; and in 1922 he entered the Royal College of Music, where he studied composition under Charles Wood, and conducting under Adrian Boult and Malcolm Sargent. Of crucial importance to his development as a musician was the chance of hearing performances of classical and contemporary music in London; and although his musical tastes were to range widely, Beethoven always seemed to remain his lodestar.

On leaving College, he supplemented his modest income by teaching French at a school in Surrey for a few terms and spent as much time as possible in composing; but in 1930 when he heard the results of his labours at a local concert devoted to his compositions, he was so dissatisfied that he decided to scrap everything he had written to date and go back to college for further instruction. A rigorous course of counterpoint under R. O. Morris braced him for a fresh start; but even so it was not until 1935, when he was thirty years old, that he felt sufficiently sure of himself to acknowledge one of his compositions as being sufficiently mature to deserve inclusion in the canon of his works. This was the first String Quartet, which he revised some eight years

later. There followed the first Sonata for Piano (1937), also lightly revised a few years later, and the Concerto for Double String Orchestra (1939). World War II broke out just as Schott's agreed to become his publisher: so there was a delay until nearly the end of the war before his music began to be available in printed form.

Tippett was always interested in contemporary social problems. Early in the 1930s, at the time of the depression, he became the conductor of the South London Orchestra of unemployed professional musicians, which rehearsed regularly at Morley College. He also wrote and arranged music for special performances given by school children under the auspices of the Royal Arsenal Co-operative Society, and by the Ironstone Miners of Cleveland, Yorkshire. Shortly after the outbreak of war he was appointed Director of Music at Morley College. He was a pacifist by conviction, and when he appeared before a Tribunal for Conscientious Objectors he was given conditional exemption from active service provided he undertook some approved form of war work such as agricultural labour or hospital portering. This he refused to do because he was convinced that music was the field in which he could best serve the community, and he was sentenced to three months imprisonment for failing to comply with the conditions of his exemption.

Just before the war he had decided that he wanted to write an important work as a protest against the horrors of the Nazi persecution of the Jews. At first he was doubtful whether this should take the form of an opera or an oratorio; but once he had decided on the latter, he looked round for a librettist. He had been fascinated by T. S. Eliot's contemporary verse play, *The Family Reunion*: so he decided to approach Eliot to see if he would help. Eliot suggested Tippett should sketch out the sort of thing he had in mind; and when this was done, he advised Tippett to look no further afield, but to complete the text himself. *A Child of Our Time* was written during the first two years of the war, but had to wait until the 19th March 1944 for its first performance. The oratorio makes its protest forcibly, and also expresses deep compassion, largely through the imaginative use of negro spirituals sung by the chorus.

After the war, life began to fall into a more regular pattern; and Tippett's works began to be published and performed. Outstanding compositions of this period were the second and third String Quartets (1942 and 1946) and the first Symphony (1945); but his main energies were being directed to his first opera. Remembering Eliot's advice about *A Child of Our Time*, he decided to write the libretto himself. A moment of intense personal vision convinced him that he had become 'the

Michael Tippett at the first performance of his King Priam *at Covent Garden.*

instrument of some collective imaginative experience', and in this mood he set about writing *The Midsummer Marriage*. The opera, which was in three acts, was planned and composed in an unusual way. First the libretto for Act I was drafted, then the music composed; and the same process was repeated for Acts II and III. *The Midsummer Marriage* took seven years to complete. It was produced at the Royal Opera House, Covent Garden on the 27th January 1955. The lengthy gestation of

the opera inevitably delayed the completion of a number of other works, particularly the Fantasia Concertante on a Theme of Corelli (1953), the Concerto for Piano and Orchestra (1955), and the Sonata for Four Horns (1955). Two commissions from the BBC deserve special mention: the Suite in D, celebrating the birth of Prince Charles (1948), and the second Symphony (1957).

For his next opera Tippett chose a public instead of a private myth and based the action on a number of scenes from the *Iliad* featuring Priam and his sons Hector and Paris. This time the libretto (written by the composer) was completed before the music had begun. *King Priam*, which was commissioned by the Koussevitzky Music Foundation, took only three years to write (1958–61); and its first performance was given by the Covent Garden Opera Company at the Coventry Cathedral Festival on the 29th May 1962. In this opera Tippett found a need to curb the lyricism of *The Midsummer Marriage* and to cultivate a harder-hitting, more abrasive style. Some of the *King Priam* musical material was used and further developed in subsequent works, particularly the second Sonata for Piano (1962) and the Concerto for Orchestra (1963). Achilles's song to the guitar was excerpted from Act II of the opera to become the first of a suite of three *Songs for Achilles* for tenor and guitar (1961).

At this point Tippett decided to compose an oratorio for baritone solo, chorus and orchestra based on passages from the Latin text of the Confessions of St Augustine. *The Vision of St Augustine* (1965) is a hermetic work presenting the idea of eternity and the difficulty of comprehending that idea in music of transcendental beauty and power.

For his third opera he reverted to the world of the private myth. *The Knot Garden* (1966–9) deals with the loves and hates of seven persons in modern England, who meet in a garden, which is sometimes literally an ornamental outdoor setting and sometimes a metaphorical maze. In contrast with *The Midsummer Marriage* which was lengthy and diffuse, *The Knot Garden* is taut and succinct almost to a fault. It is one of the few operas of the 20th century that has opened up new operatic potential. Once again the appearance of a new Tippett opera led to the completion of a number of related works. The blues ensemble at the end of Act I of *The Knot Garden* anticipated the important vocal movement in the third Symphony (1971); and Dov's song at the

end of Act II became the first of a cycle of three *Songs for Dov* for tenor and orchestra (1970). The third Piano Sonata, composed in 1973, is perhaps a forward- rather than a backward-looking work.

His fourth opera, *The Ice Break* (1973–6), is contemporary in setting and deals with the difficulties of communication as between different generations, different races, different ideologies, and the search for living tenderness behind so much violence. His fourth Symphony followed immediately on the completion of *The Ice Break*.

In early years Tippett suffered from the fact that his musical idiom was unfamiliar. Sometimes it was the sprung rhythm of his polyphony moving counter to regular barlines and metres that proved baffling, or the proliferation of decorative detail that tended to obscure the main issue. Like Mozart he was occasionally accused of writing too many notes: but such criticism was only valid so long as the clusters of swarming semi- and demi-semi-quavers were so clumsily executed that the music began to clot instead of resolving into a fine shimmering radiance. Until conductors and executants had caught up with his idiom and acquired the mastery necessary to render it with understanding, it was difficult for the public to appreciate his originality and the compelling strength of the images, whether intellectual or musical, that lie at the basis of his art.

E.W.W.

TOSTI, Francesco Paulo
(b. Ortona sul Mare, Abruzzi, 9 April 1846; d. Rome, 2 Dec 1916)

It has become the fashion in musical circles to look down the nose at Tosti, yet he composed a number of songs which have remained for more than a century in the repertoires of the world's most eminent singers. Perhaps he is regarded in this unkindly light because he threw off songs in an unashamedly sentimental style and became the pampered darling of royal families. He belongs to that small band of composers who could console themselves, after the critics had had their say, by crying all the way to the bank. He was sent to study the violin and composition in Naples, where he subsequently held a musical post that was as ill-paid as it was humble. At the age of twenty-three he returned home, disillusioned and in poor health, but in spite of illness he managed to compose two songs, *Non m'ama più* and *Lamento d'amore*, which were to become highly popular. He next tried his luck in Rome, where he won a considerable success at the Sala Dante singing several of his own ballads. Princess Margherita of Savoy, later the Queen of Italy, was so impressed that she appointed him her teacher of singing.

The most important step in Tosti's career, however, was his decision to visit London in 1875. His simple yet memorably tuneful ballads delighted the taste of the English, then frankly unsophisticated in musical matters, and his songs winged their way round all the fashionable drawing-rooms in London. He was not slow to realise his good fortune and began to set English rather than Italian lyrics, which paid off handsomely by his invitation to become teacher of singing to the royal family. Queen Victoria, it seems, *was* amused for once in her life. With this appointment in 1880 he decided to settle in London: he had already composed *Goodbye* and *Forever*, but it was the latter which summed up his affection for England. No doubt it was the sentimental song *Mother* which finally made England adopt him as her son. Curiously perhaps, it was not the Queen but her more earthy successor Edward VII who gave Tosti the ultimate accolade of a knighthood in 1908.

It may be easy to make fun of Tosti, but his enormous output of songs nevertheless reveals an enviable talent in the field he chose. The elegance of their vocal line, which has a genuine Italian flow and expressive warmth, is ample compensation for the sometimes cloying sentimentality of their lyrics, whether these be French, Italian or English. Sometimes, as in *L'alba separa dalla luce l'ombra*, his music approaches an almost operatic intensity. And always his songs proved rewarding to the singer. Tosti never pretended to be a profound composer, but the fact that artists of the calibre of Enrico Caruso, Beniamino Gigli, Jussi Björling, Eva Turner and, more recently, Luciano Pavarotti and José Carreras have chosen to include his songs in their recital programmes surely speaks for itself. There is always a place for enchanting melody in the world of music, and because he provided so many melodies of lasting appeal Paolo Tosti should never be despised.

F.G.B.

VARÈSE, Edgar
(b. Paris, 22 Dec 1885; d. New York, 6 Nov 1965)

Edgar (Edgard) Varèse studied mathematics and natural history at the École Polytechnique, but at the age of nineteen he decided to make music his career, against his father's wishes; he left the parental home and never returned. He studied at the Schola Cantorum from 1904 to 1906, learning composition with d'Indy and counterpoint and fugue with Roussel: in 1907 he entered Widor's master class at the Conservatoire. During the season of 1906–7 he founded the Choeur de l'Université Populaire and organised the concerts of the Château du Peuple: he was awarded the 'bourse artistique' of the City of Paris. He was already interested in 'radical music'; he once said: 'At twenty I began to feel sound as a living material, to be formed without wilful limitations – from this time on I thought of music as only existing in space.' He got impulses from African drum techniques which led him in a new direction; he was also influenced by the Futurists and their 'art of noises' (bruitisme) which broke with traditional methods of organising sound. The only work of Varèse to be preserved from this period is the Verlaine song *Un grand sommeil noir*, which shows the influence of Debussy and also a feeling for stark medievalism.

Varèse spent the years 1909–14 in Berlin, where he founded the Symphonischer Chor for the performance of old polyphonic music. He wrote an opera, now lost, on the subject of Oedipus and the Sphinx, to a text by Hofmannsthal; his symphonic poem *Bourgogne* was performed in 1910. He became friendly with Busoni, who made a great impression on him. He was a guest conductor with Prague Philharmonic Orchestra in 1914. In that year he returned to France and joined the army; a serious illness led to his discharge in 1915, and in 1916 he went to America, where he spent the rest of his life. In 1919 he founded and conducted the New Symphony Orchestra, and in 1921 he and Carlos Salzedo founded the International Composers' Guild; the object of both organisations was the propagation of new music. His earliest work which he recognised, *Offrandes* (1921), is a setting of surrealist poems by Huidobro and Tablada; this was followed in 1923 by *Hyperprism*, which Stokowski performed with the Philadelphia Orchestra in 1926. The audience were scandalised by the music, which was quite unlike anything they had heard before; it in-

Edgar Varèse.

cluded tone clusters, continuous percussion effects and seemingly endless repetitions of short, violent phrases. Other works followed, including *Amériques* (1926), *Arcana* (1927), *Ionisation* (1931) for 41 percussion instruments, including sirens, *Intégrales* for chamber orchestra (1931) and *Espace* for orchestra (1937). *Ecuatorial* of 1943 is a setting of a Mayan prayer for men's voices, brass, percussion, organ and two 'Thereminovox' – Varèse was already anticipating the development of electronic instruments, and, probably for that

reason, his output over the next few years was smaller until the new electronic inventions of the 1950s. He made full use of these in *Déserts* of 1949–54, in which a live ensemble has a dialogue with a pre-recorded stereophonic tape, and in the *Poème Electronique*, written for the Brussels Exhibition of 1958 and meant to be performed by a stereophonic battery of loudspeakers. His last work, *Nocturnal*, was left unfinished at his death and was completed by Chou Wen-Chung; it is a setting of a text from Anais Nin's *The House of Incest* in which the music explodes with alarming violence. Varèse belonged to no school, and his influence did not begin to be felt in Europe until after his visit to the Darmstadt Summer School in 1950; but his works anticipated by nearly forty years the present generation of electronic composers in their original use of sound, and are among the most remarkable creations in modern music. He said: 'Composers who are gifted with an inner ear have heard for years a new music of sounds which the old instruments cannot produce for them.'

H.S.

VAUGHAN WILLIAMS, Ralph
(b. Down Ampney, 12 Oct 1872;
d. London, 26 Aug 1958)

The son of a clergyman, Ralph Vaughan Williams was born in the Gloucestershire village of Down Ampney on the 12th October 1872. His father died less than three years later; he was taken to live in Surrey in the family house of his mother. His intellectual ancestry was strong: lawyers on his father's side, Josiah Wedgwood and Charles Darwin on his mother's. There were pictures and books as well as music-making at Leith Hill Place. His mother installed a small organ for him to play, while his aunt taught him the piano and even put him in for a correspondence course in the theory of music; all this, as well as violin lessons, took place before he reached the age of nine. At his preparatory school near Brighton he went on with both his instruments, while at Charterhouse, which he entered in 1887, he presented his Trio in G major to an audience of staff and fellow-pupils.

By this time he had already decided to become a composer. After leaving Charterhouse he visited Germany and was able to hear Wagner's *Die Walküre*; he was overwhelmingly impressed, and later said that after hearing *Tristan und Isolde* he was unable to sleep. Now he entered upon what was to be a long period of apprenticeship, going first to the Royal College of Music in London, where he studied with Hubert Parry, and then in 1892 to Trinity College, Cambridge, to read history and obtain his Bachelor of Music degree. He next returned to the Royal College, however, where he worked under Charles Stanford, made friends with his fellow-student Gustav Holst and played the organ in a South London church. In 1897 he married Adeline Fisher: his wife was both beautiful and intelligent, but they were to have no child-ren and she was cruelly afflicted by arthritis for some forty years until her death in 1951. However, this was all in the future; for the moment things went well, and the honeymoon in Berlin was accompanied by Wagner's music (the *Ring*) and lessons with Max Bruch. In 1908 he was to go abroad again for his last formal instruction: this time it was Ravel who (mainly with orchestration exercises) was chosen to provide 'a little French polish'.

Vaughan Williams was fortunate in having a private income. But he devoted himself to composition in a professional manner, working regular hours, setting himself high standards and revising extensively. He was also in demand as a scholar, contributing articles to *Grove's Dictionary*, giving lectures, and editing the *English Hymnal* (1906). One of its tunes (No. 402) is a folk song named after the place where Vaughan Williams first heard it, Monks Gate near Horsham in Sussex: the composer had by this time developed what was to be a lifelong interest in English folk melody. His music was profoundly affected by the melodic shape, rhythmic character and above all the atmosphere which he found in folk song; 'the art of music above all other arts is the expression of the soul of a nation', he declared. Not only rural music, but also popular songs of barrel-organ or music-hall type were included: the composer of the *Pastoral Symphony* (1922) had already written a *London Symphony* in 1914.

When war broke out in 1914, Vaughan Williams, although over forty, volunteered for military service, and spent most of the war in the ranks although he was commissioned in 1918. After demobilisation he was invited to join the teaching staff of the Royal College of Music; his 'method' seems to have been that of drawing out his pupils' musical personalities rather than imparting ready-made, anonymous technical expertise. He also took on the conductorship of the Bach Choir in 1921. His reputation as a composer had spread steadily, and in 1922 he accepted an invitation to conduct his new *Pastoral Symphony* in the United States.

The last thirty years or so of Vaughan Williams's life are mainly a record of creative work, growing fame and honours. Long before his death at the age of eighty-five he had been dubbed the 'grand old man of English music', a bulky yet not formidable figure with a thatch of snowy hair, often to be seen in London at concerts or the opera. He lived at a house called The White Gates, near

until his death to enjoy all kinds of music-making. On the day he died, it had been arranged for him to attend a recording session of his Ninth Symphony.

Vaughan Williams was in some senses a nationalist composer, like Bartók in Hungary or Falla in Spain. But he felt that a composer's having roots was not the same as narrow provincialism, and he used to cite J.S. Bach's long residence in Leipzig as an example of how universal genius emerged without deliberate cosmopolitanism. He wrote in 1942 that the love of one's country and customs was essential, adding that only on such bases could be built 'a united Europe and a world federation'. But folk song never shackled his individuality, and works such as the Fourth, Fifth and Sixth Symphonies are English-sounding only in the way in which (say) a Brahms symphony sounds German. He has sometimes been described as an agnostic, and was reticent about his religious views, but the numerous sacred works he composed, including the opera *The Pilgrim's Progress* (1949), are instinct with visionary spiritual force. In his songs his wide knowledge of English poetry, coupled with his insight, provide an extensive and important repertory. He stands between Elgar and Britten as the outstanding figure of his generation in English music.

C.H.

Vaughan Williams.

Dorking in Surrey, and involved himself with the local Leith Hill Festival as a conductor and adviser. He defended contemporaries who fell foul of conservative critics and, though not sharing Michael Tippett's pacifist convictions, threw the weight of his name behind the younger composer's conscientious objection in 1943. After his wife's death in 1951, he married the writer Ursula Wood in February 1953. He was now eighty; the Surrey house was sold and he and his new wife moved to Hanover Terrace, Regent's Park, an attractive London home where he was to spend the rest of his life. But he had by no means retired from active work and diversion: there were two more symphonies yet to come and a visit to the United States in 1954 lasting four months during which, after one wearing day's sight-seeing, he insisted on observing the sunset from the top of the Empire State Building. The Americans greatly took to him, describing him as a 'Miltonic figure' whose music had 'splendour without tinsel'. Though he now had to use a hearing aid, he continued

VERDI, Giuseppe
(b. Le Roncole, 10 Oct 1813;
d. Milan, 27 Jan 1901)

Italy's greatest composer was born, the son of an inn-keeper, in the village of Le Roncole, near Parma. He revealed a talent for music as a child, and was taught the rudiments of music by the organist of the village church, just opposite the inn. By the time he was ten he was sufficiently advanced for his father to send him to the small town of Busseto, three miles away, for further tuition. Antonio Barezzi, a Busseto merchant, took the lad into his house and gave him a job in his business, and soon the young Verdi was composing marches for the local Philharmonic Society as well as music for the church. In his nineteenth year, aided by Barezzi and by a charitable trust, he left Busseto for Milan, where he hoped to study at the Conservatorium.

The examiners for the Conservatorium refused to bend their rules to admit Verdi, who was four years over the maximum age for

Verdi and the cast of Falstaff *acknowledging applause at La Scala, Milan, 1893.*

entrance, so the young composer instead studied privately with Vincenzo Lavigna, a conductor at La Scala. He made good progress with Lavigna, and after two years returned to Busseto to apply for the post of cathedral organist which had fallen vacant on the death of his ex-teacher, Provesi. The ecclesiastical authorities, however, appointed a rival candidate, and Verdi instead became Director of the Philharmonic Society. He married Margherita Barezzi, the daughter of his Busseto benefactor, and began in his spare time to work on his first opera, *Oberto*, the libretto for which had been provided by a Milanese journalist, Antonio Piazza. When *Oberto* was accepted by the impresario Bartolomeo Merelli, for production at La Scala, Verdi, accompanied by his wife and two infant children, returned to Milan.

Oberto was warmly received at its first performance in November 1839, but by this time tragedy had already struck the Verdi family, both of the children having died. While Verdi was at work on his second opera, *Un giorno di regno*, Margherita died of encephalitis. In a condition bordering on nervous collapse, he completed his comic opera which failed miserably at La Scala (though modern revivals have revealed it to be a quite agreeable *opera buffa*). Verdi wanted now to give up his operatic career and return to Busseto, but the impresario Merelli had faith in him and persuaded him to undertake a third opera, based on the biblical story of Nebuchadnezzar. *Nabucco*, staged at La Scala, was an enormous success, critics and public alike realizing that the natural successor to Bellini and Donizetti had now arrived.

Though the line of progress from *Nabucco* to *Falstaff* more than fifty years later was to prove anything but a straight one, Verdi's future as a composer was never in doubt after *Nabucco*. For the next few years, until the masterpieces of his middle-period, he was to turn out operas at the rate, sometimes, of two a year. Most of them are uneven, some of them contain passages which look crude or awkward in score, though rarely in performance; but they are never dull, and they all possess a vivid creative energy which is entirely Verdi's own, owing nothing to his predecessors. Most of these early Verdi operas are now finding their way back onto the stage after years of neglect: *I Lombardi, Giovanna d'Arco, Attila, Il corsaro*, and *I masnadieri*, for example. And some, like *Ernani* and Verdi's first Shakespeare opera, *Macbeth*, are great operas by any standard. Verdi was later to refer to his 'years in the galleys' when he was condemned to compose operas in quick succession, but there is none of these early works that one would willingly be without. His early audiences, suffering under Austrian occupation, liked to identify many of the early operas as rallying-cries for a united Italy and Verdi himself was quite willing to be thought of as the composer of the Risorgimento, the liberal political movement for a free and united Italy.

During a visit to Paris in 1847, Verdi revived acquaintance with the soprano Giuseppina Strepponi, whom he had first met in his early days in Milan. They became lovers, and lived together for twelve years before marrying. In 1848 Verdi wrote his one overtly patriotic opera, *La battaglia di Legnano*, and the following year produced *Luisa Miller*, based on Schiller's play *Kabale und Liebe*, the opera which is a kind of transitional work between the youthful excitement of the earlier operas and the maturer voice which speaks from *Rigoletto* onwards.

The most popular of Verdi's middle-period operas are the three which he produced between 1851 and 1853: *Rigoletto, Il trovatore* and *La traviata*. All three are remarkable for their melodic richness, and the first and last are superbly constructed dramatically, as well. *Rigoletto*, a particularly resilient work, triumphantly survives poor productions and the vain foibles of musically illiterate singers. Conversely, it offers magnificent opportunities to the intelligent interpreter of its title-role, a role infused, as is the entire opera, with great humanity, despite its basis in romantic melodrama. *Il trovatore*'s effects are broad and immediate. The wealth of melody, the passionate melancholy of the soprano's music, the almost brutal vigour and pace of the opera, these are merely a few of the ingredients that have ensured its popularity since the day of its first performance. Too popular for its own good, perhaps, since it was for many years a non-favourite with critics who, unimpressed by Verdi's honest directness of purpose, could hear in his score only the death of *bel canto*. To enlightened ears, however, *Il trovatore* is the veritable apotheosis of the *bel canto* opera with its demands for vocal beauty, agility and range.

Only a few weeks separate the premières of *Il trovatore* in Rome and *La traviata* in Venice. The first performance of *La traviata* was a fiasco, and it was not until a new production was mounted the following year that the opera achieved success. It is a work so well-known today, its melodies so much a part of the experience of most musicians and opera-lovers, that it is difficult to stand sufficiently far away from it to appraise it afresh. It is an opera in which all of Verdi's finest qualities are to be perceived: his technical mastery, his humanity, his psychological penetration and his unerring taste.

Verdi divided the five years immediately following *La traviata* between his farm at Sant' Agata and visits to Paris, where the Opéra had commissioned a new work from him. *Les Vêpres Siciliennes* suffers from its poor libretto, though it contains some of Verdi's most individual music. More successful were *Simon Boccanegra*, produced in Venice in 1857, though it was not to assume its definitive form until Verdi and Boito revised it twenty-four years later, and *Un ballo in maschera* (1859), one of Verdi's most elegant scores. After *Un ballo in maschera*, he began to slow his pace somewhat, preferring to spend more time, either on his farm or in Genoa, with Giuseppina whom he had formally married in April 1859. When, in 1860, the first free Italian parliament was instituted, Verdi reluctantly agreed to stand for election. He was duly elected to the Italian legislative assembly, and served assiduously for five years, though he found political office irksome. He was not entirely lost to opera during this period, however, for he accepted an invitation from Russia to compose a new work for the Imperial Theatre at St Petersburg. He and Giuseppina travelled to St Petersburg for the production of *La forza del destino* (1862), a sprawling masterpiece which covers a vast canvas, from the personal to the social, in the manner of the 19th-century novel. In other words, it is the opera of a man who has read Manzoni's *I promessi sposi*. In it, Verdi continued his move away from strict aria form, a move he had begun at least as early as *Luisa Miller*, towards a greater fluidity and an apportioning of more orchestral and melodic interest to the recitative or arioso passages.

In 1865, Verdi revised his *Macbeth* of 1847 for performance in Paris, and then set to work on a new opera for Paris. This was *Don Carlos*, whose French libretto was based on Schiller's

Verdi.

German play. The opera was performed forty-three times during the season, so it was certainly no failure, but the Empress Eugénie found it offensive, and some critics professed to detect the influence of Meyerbeer and even of Wagner, much to Verdi's indignation. He had at this time yet to hear a Wagner opera, and, although the formal structure of *Don Carlos* is that of Meyerbeer's Paris operas, this was virtually a condition of composing for Paris. However, whether there are traces of Meyerbeer in one or two scenes or not, its dark orchestral colouring, its rich, complex musical characterisation and the quality of its melody combine to make *Don Carlos* one of the most rewarding of operas to encounter in the theatre. Above all, it glows with its composer's humanity, which he was able to breathe into characters who, on the printed page of the libretto, must have seemed to him at first acquaintance to be frigidly formal.

In 1869, one of Verdi's *Don Carlos* librettists, Camille du Locle, sent him the synopsis of an opera set in ancient Egypt. It had been written by a French Egyptologist, and the Khedive of Egypt was keen to commission Verdi to turn it into an opera to be performed in Cairo at the opening of the Suez Canal. There was, however, not time enough for this, and when the new Cairo Opera House was inaugurated in November 1869, two weeks before the opening of the Canal, the opera performed was *Rigoletto*. Verdi's Egyptian opera, *Aida*, had its premiere in Cairo in January 1871. Verdi himself did not travel to Egypt; he stayed in Italy to rehearse the singers for the Milan production which followed shortly after Cairo.

Aida is a remarkable work which has almost become the victim of its own popularity. In a sense, it falls between two Verdian stools, possessing neither the rough vigour of the early works nor the psychological penetration of *Otello* and *Falstaff*. In purely musical terms, however, it is nothing less than a miracle of melodic beauty and imaginative orchestration. Despite many public scenes, it is the most intimate of grand operas, and at its heart one senses Verdi's profound melancholy. The sounds he created are not picturesquely Egyptian: Verdi created his own Egypt just as surely as his beloved Shakespeare did in *Antony and Cleopatra*. His dramatic use of recurring musical motives is nicely judged, and his balancing of objective description and sub-

A page from the manuscript of Aida, *from the finale of Act II.*

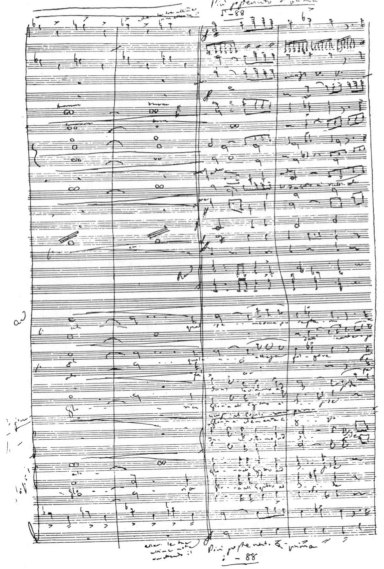

jective feeling is perfect. Both in its spectacular and its intimate aspects, *Aida* is a triumph of the creative imagination.

In 1873, the death of the great Italian novelist and patriot, Alessandro Manzoni, whom Verdi had venerated as a saint, led him to the composition of a Requiem Mass in Manzoni's memory. The Mass, first performed in a Milan church in 1874, conducted by the composer who subsequently took it on tour throughout Europe, is an unusual work in that it is written in a musical language closer to the dramatic than to the devotional. But the intention of the agnostic Verdi was to express the emotional meaning and implications of the liturgical text, just as in his operas he was concerned to express the meaning of the words and situations presented to him by his librettists. He is hardly to be blamed for writing with sincerity in his own style. Verdi brought his dramatist's art to the Requiem. Free to reveal something of his own attitude to death, he did not indulge in gentle resignation or joyful anticipation of an afterlife. Verdi's Requiem is a Mass not for the dead but for the living. The intensity and the compassion of his tragic view of the human condition are Shakesperian in stature.

By now Verdi considered himself to have retired from the world of opera. He devoted himself increasingly to his farm, and resisted the attempts of his publisher and others to lure him back to composition. In due course, however, he agreed to collaborate with the much younger Arrigo Boito, first on a revision of *Simon Boccanegra*, and then, most reluctantly, on an opera to be based on Shakespeare's *Othello*. He was, however, completely won over by Boito's libretto, and eventually began to work slowly but surely on the music. When *Otello* at last reached the stage in 1887, the world was able to acclaim another masterpiece by Verdi. In the opinion of many, it was his finest opera. It is certainly an incredibly fresh, youthfully inspired score for a man in his seventies to have created. Verdi's musical language and style are beyond praise. The melody is as glorious as in his more youthful days, but now freed from the harmonic constrictions of his earlier period, and able to range where it will.

After the success of *Otello*, Verdi and Boito were urged to begin another opera. But Verdi was not to be rushed. He busied himself with various philanthropic concerns, and five or six years were to elapse before he agreed to compose his next opera. In Verdi's eightieth year, 1893,

Falstaff had its première in Milan, and again the occasion was a triumphant success. There is so much to admire in *Falstaff*: scoring of chamber-music delicacy allied to a wide, Beethovenian range of orchestral expression, the magical evocation of forest and fancy in the last scene, and the fantastic energy and pace of the entire opera which seems to last no longer than one sudden flash of inspiration.

After the excitement and exhaustion of *Falstaff*, Verdi returned to his leisurely country life. He toyed with other operatic projects, and even travelled to Paris for the French première of *Otello*, for which he composed ballet music. In 1897, Giuseppina died of pneumonia. Verdi now felt completely desolate, but busied himself with setting up the Rest Home for Aged Musicians in Milan, which still bears his name and is supported by his royalties. He spent the Xmas of 1900 visiting his adopted daughter in Milan. It was there, at the Grand Hotel, that he succumbed to a sudden stroke in January. He was eighty-seven years of age.

C.O.

VILLA-LOBOS, Heitor
(b. Rio de Janeiro, 5 March 1887;
d. Rio de Janeiro, 17 June 1959)

The only internationally-known Brazilian composer of the 20th century, Heitor Villa-Lobos revealed his musical talent in early childhood, and was taught the viola, the clarinet and the piano. His father, who had encouraged his son's musical abilities, died when the child was ten, and his mother promptly forbade him to continue his studies, and insisted on his learning a respectable profession. Consequently, Heitor's musical studies went underground, and he would slip away from the house to play with street musicians. When he was sixteen, he ran away from home, and was helped by a sympathetic uncle to regularise his interest in music and his studies. Two years later, the young musician, who had already begun to compose small pieces, embarked upon a tour of the north of Brazil, listening to the folk music of the various regions, and composing his own songs as he travelled. After a period of study in Rio de Janeiro, he departed again, this time to the south of the country. Again he returned to conventional study in Rio, but was soon off again, this time into the interior.

Villa-Lobos.

During these years, Villa-Lobos amassed a great amount of knowledge of Afro-Brazilian music, and began to compose short operas, chamber music and songs, and to embark upon his first Symphony. It was when he was thirty-one that he met the pianist Artur Rubinstein, who introduced him to the music of Debussy which was to prove a beneficial influence. In 1923, Villa-Lobos travelled to Europe for the first time, staying mainly in Paris and coming now under the influence of Ravel. When he returned to Brazil in 1930, he began to compose his series of *Bachianas brasileiras*, pieces for various instrumental combinations, inspired by Bach. He became interested, too, in musical education and was instrumental in having many reforms made in the educational system, both before and after his appointment as Superintendent of Musical Education in Rio de Janeiro. Increasingly, he wrote for choirs, but also formed his own symphony orchestra with which he introduced a number of European classics to Brazil, including Beethoven's *Missa Solemnis* and Bach's B minor Mass. His *New York Skyline Melody* of 1939 came into being when an American journalist provided him with a photograph of the Manhattan skyline, and he worked out, on a system of his own devising, the melody which corresponded to it.

Villa-Lobos travelled abroad frequently as an unofficial musical ambassador for his country. The list of his compositions is voluminous, comprising operas and ballets, choral and orchestral works, chamber and piano music, songs, music for band, and arrangements of other composers, principally Bach.

C.O.

VIVALDI, Antonio Lucio
(b. Venice, 4 March 1678;
d. Vienna, 28 July 1741)

Antonio Lucio Vivaldi was one of the most important figures in the Baroque era. As a violin virtuoso and composer of instrumental music (particularly for the violin), he was to establish a reputation not only in Italy but throughout the whole of Western Europe.

We know little about Vivaldi's early musical training. His father, from 1685 employed as a violinist at San Marco, presumably gave him his first lessons; Giovanni Legrenzi (1626–90), director of music at San Marco, may also have coached him whilst he was still very young. At the age of fifteen, Vivaldi began his training for the priesthood. This extended over ten years, 1693 to 1703, during which time Vivaldi does not appear to have attended a seminary, at least not on a regular basis. Shortly after becoming a priest in 1703, he ceased saying Mass, complaining of a chest ailment which had caused him on several occasions to leave the altar in mid-celebration. His more fanciful biographers have imagined in these abrupt departures an impatient scramble to note down a musical idea whilst it was still fresh in the mind. They may not be so far from the mark. From all accounts, Vivaldi did not suffer from the same seizures when he was directing an orchestra or playing the violin. Nor, although in this respect he claimed the need of constant attention from his travelling companions, was he prevented from undertaking numerous journeys, some leading him far from Italy. In brief, it seems not unreasonable to suppose that he wished as a matter of preference to devote his life to music, and not to the Church. He did however remain indebted to the Cloth, and of course to his remarkably red hair, for the widely used nickname 'il prete rosso'.

From the same year as he was priested dates his association, which was to continue almost until his death, with the 'Ospedale della Pietà'. 'La Pietà' was one of four important charitable institutions in Venice which lodged and educated the numerous female foundlings with which city appeared to teem. The culti-

Vivaldi by Ghezzi, 1723.

vation of musical skills had become by the end of the 17th century the predominant activity in these orphanages. By Vivaldi's day, such was the attainment of the foundlings that their musical performances on Sundays and feast days drew large and appreciative crowds. Indeed, such were the resources, both musical and financial, of the Venetian Ospedali that they were able to attract into their service some of the most eminent musicians of the time, amongst others Antonio Lotti (1666–1740), Antonio Caldara (1670–1736), Johann Adolph Hasse (1699–1783), and, in 1703, Vivaldi. He began at La Pietà as *maestro di violino*, but there is no doubt that his activities were not confined to playing and teaching the violin, but extended also to composing. His Op. 1 trio sonatas were published in Venice in 1705, and his Op. 2 solo violin sonatas in 1709.

The second decade of the 18th century saw an enormous increase in the scope of Vivaldi's activities and his reputation, both as a violin virtuoso and as a composer. It was this decade in which he made his debut as an opera composer with the production in Vicenza in 1713 of *Ottone in villa*. This was the first of nearly 100 operas Vivaldi claimed to have written, and one of 46 which can now be traced. The composition and production of his stage works was an occupation which soon cut into

his duties at La Pietà. There was hardly a year between 1713 and 1738 which passed without the presentation of at least one, and more often three or four, new operas in some Italian city or other; and for many of these productions Vivaldi took upon himself the responsibility of rehearsing and - directing performances. This decade also saw the publication of his Op. 3–7, first in Amsterdam, and then throughout Europe. These publications, containing exclusively instrumental music (and including the famous Op. 3 set of concerti *L'Estro Armonico*), fully established Vivaldi's reputation, beside Corelli's, as the foremost Italian composer of instrumental music of his day. In 1716, the directors of La Pietà officially designated him *maestro dei concerti*, a title Vivaldi had sported since the appearance of his Op. 2.

The following years were accompanied by even more travelling and long periods of absence from La Pietà. Between *c.* 1718 and 1721, Vivaldi was in the service of Prince Philip of Hesse-Darmstadt, governor of Mantua from 1714 to 1735. It was during this Mantuan period that he met Anna Giraud (La Girò), who was to take so many of the leading soprano roles in Vivaldi's operas, and who, with her sister, became the composer's constant travelling companion. In 1723 and 1724, Vivaldi visited Rome, and on one occasion had the honour of playing before the Pope. In 1728 he equalled this signal recognition of his accomplishments with several audiences with the Emperor Charles VI. It is reported that the music-loving Charles spoke more with Vivaldi during two weeks than with his ministers in the course of two years. About this time Vivaldi dedicated two collections of his music to the Emperor, *La Cetra* (Op. 9), and a manuscript collection of twelve miscellaneous concerti. In 1729 he embarked upon a tour of Germany, including in his itinerary a visit to the Imperial Court at Vienna, and perhaps also to Prague.

If the 1720s marked the summit of Vivaldi's career (the Op. 8 concerti numbered amongst them the uniquely famous *Four Seasons*), the 1730s witnessed a slow decline. First the fickle Italian public began to show signs of tiring of his music; his powerful patron Philip of Hesse-Darmstadt died in 1736; the following year, 1737, the Church authorities, sensing perhaps their moment, banned Vivaldi from mounting his operas in Ferrara (a papal territory) on account of his lapsed priesthood and his association with Anna Giraud; and finally, the year after that, the directors of La Pietà refused to renew his contract. Towards the end of 1740, Vivaldi left Italy and travelled to Vienna. Was he seeking employment in the Imperial Court? We do not know; and in any case it was too late: Charles VI had died in October 1740, and the War of Austrian Succession was distracting Vienna from artistic pursuits. It was in Vienna that Vivaldi languished and died. He was buried on the 28th July 1741 in a pauper's grave attached to St Stephen's.

The number of known works by Vivaldi has risen dramatically this century with the discovery of two large manuscript collections now in the Turin State Library (the Foa and Giodarno collections). The figure now stands at 750 (total established by P. Ryom in 1971). Vivaldi belonged to an age of prolific composers, but there is still something extremely impressive about this achievement, not least because so much of his music is of such first-rate quality.

Today Vivaldi is known chiefly through his concerti; in his own day these works were no less responsible for his international reputation. The published concerti (Op. 3, 4, 7, 8, 9, 10, 11 and 12 – almost the complete range of his opus numbers) represent but a quarter of his total output in the concerto genre. This numbers over 400, including 220 solo concerti, some 60 concerti ripieni (or sinfonie), 48 bassoon concerti, 25 'cello concerti, plus divers works for flutes, oboes, clarinets (!), horns, trumpets and even mandolins. Pride of place must go to the solo violin concerti. In these works, including the famous Op. 3 set (*L'Estro Armonico*) and the *Four Seasons* from Op. 8, Vivaldi established and stabilised the 18th-century plan. These works contain no less the seeds of the 18th-century symphony: a strong sense of tonality, of harmonic thrust, and, most of all, drama. Many of the stylistic attributes associated with the early symphonists of the Mannheim school, and G. B. Sammartini, are also present: the rocketing scales and arpeggios, the graded dynamics, themes based on tonic triads and propelled by assertive, vigorously declamed rhythms, and a classically conceived use of wind, even to the inclusion of horns in some sinfonie. It should be noted that in his concerti Vivaldi was possibly the first composer to conceive of 'an essentially dramatic conflict between the virtuoso and the orchestra' and also the first 'to bring the pathos of the most impassioned Venetian opera arias into the slow movement' (Pincherle). It is not only works like Bach's Italian Concerto (BWV 971) which reveal the progeny of such pieces, but the piano concertos of Mozart. (Perhaps nothing speaks more eloquently for Vivaldi than the number of times J. S. Bach transcribed and arranged his concerti for organ and harpsichord, and indeed the evident debt he owed Vivaldi, particularly in the formal

Part of the autograph score of a concerto by Vivaldi.

organisation and the thematic construction of his ritornello movements.)

Vivaldi's vocal music includes various settings of items from the Ordinary of the Mass, numerous psalm settings (for Vespers) and Hymns, as well as three large-scale oratorios, *Moyses deus Pharaonis* (1714), *Juditha triumphans* (1716) and *L'Adorazione delli tre Re Magi* (1722). Of these works, his Gloria in D major has rightly become popular in recent years. The operas, which still remain largely buried in archives, and which contain much that was written hastily, and much that will remain locked in an irretrievable culture, reveal nevertheless that Vivaldi possessed considerable dramatic insight, and could write for the stage with the same degree of skill and fecundity as for the purely instrumental media.

E.H.

WAGNER, Richard
(b. Leipzig, 22 May 1813;
d. Venice, 13 Feb 1883)

It is now generally accepted that Wagner's father was not Karl Friedrich Wagner, his mother's husband, but the actor Ludwig Geyer whom his mother married the following year, after the death of her husband. Considering that Richard Wagner was to become so virulently anti-Semitic, it is one of life's ironies that his father was someone of Jewish ancestry. Geyer proved a benevolent stepfather to Richard, and supervised his education, but he died while Richard was still a child. The boy proved to be interested both in the theatre and in music. He had been taught to play the piano and, in his teens, having written a play, began to take lessons in composition in order to be able to provide incidental music for it. Soon, he was involving himself in music to the exclusion of all his other studies. His family were, one day, amazed to discover that he had not been to school for several months. He became passionately interested in opera, after attending a performance of Beethoven's *Fidelio* in which the title-role was sung by the famous Wilhelmine Schroeder-Devrient. Beethoven was his idol, and he remained a keen admirer of the great composer for the rest of his life. In 1831, at the age of eighteen, he entered Leipzig University, though his interest in academic studies was slight. He was attracted more by the appurtenances of student life: the societies, the drinking, the duelling.

In his eighteenth year, Wagner had an orchestral work, an overture, accepted and performed in Leipzig. The audience was, however, more amused than impressed by his overture, and Wagner returned to his musical studies before submitting any more works to public scrutiny. He next produced a piano sonata, which was published, and a symphony which was performed. But his main interest was in combining his literary and musical talents in an opera, and to this end he began work on *Die Hochzeit*, an opera which he left incomplete. Almost immediately, Wagner embarked upon the composition of another opera, *Die Feen*, again based on a libretto he had written himself. At no time in his life did he ever seriously contemplate using another librettist. Wagner, the composer of genius, was inspired by none but Wagner, the writer of clumsy and prolix libretti. At the age of twenty, thanks to the influence of his brother Albert who was on the musical staff of the theatre at Würzburg, Wagner obtained an engagement there as Chorus-master. During his season at Würzburg he managed to complete *Die Feen*, but did not succeed in getting the opera performed. For his next opera, *Das Liebesverbot*, he based his libretto loosely upon Shakespeare's *Measure for Measure*. His next professional engagement was as musical director of the Magdeburg company. Joining them in Lauchstadt where they were performing during the Summer, he soon fell in love with a young actress with the company, Minna Planer. Two years later, they married.

The marriage took place in Königsberg, for by this time the Magdeburg company had collapsed, and Minna had accepted an engagement in Königsberg. Wagner had run up debts in Magdeburg, which he avoided paying and he proceeded to do likewise in Königsberg. In despair, Minna fled to her parents in Dresden, but Wagner followed her and effected a reconciliation. When he was appointed musical director of the theatre at Riga, Minna followed him there. During his two years in Riga, Wagner planned and began to compose his next opera, *Rienzi*, based on a novel by Henry Bulwer-Lytton. In March, 1839, Wagner was dismissed from his post, and he and Minna were forced to surreptitious flight in order to escape their creditors. Their intention was to

Wagner by Franz von Lenbach.

The final scene of The Flying Dutchman, *from a Leipzig newspaper, 1843.*

reach Paris, but they were forced to do so by a most circuitous route. Smuggled on board a vessel bound for London, they found themselves blown off course by a fierce storm. The ship took refuge in a Norwegian fjord: Wagner was able to draw on the experience later, when composing *Der fliegende Holländer*. Eventually they reached London where they stayed for a week at an inn in Old Compton Street before proceeding to Paris. On the channel steamer Wagner got into conversation with two Jewish ladies who were friends of the famous composer Meyerbeer. Meyerbeer was staying in Boulogne, and Wagner secured a letter of introduction to him from the ladies. Meyerbeer greeted him amiably and agreed to examine what existed of the score of *Rienzi*. He also helped Wagner with introductions to people influential in musical circles in Paris, and over the years was to assist him on several occasions. His reward was to be referred to scurrilously in the anti-Semitic tract, *Jewishness in Music* which Wagner published anonymously.

Wagner had hoped to find immediate fame as a composer in Paris, but his hopes were not to be realised. He failed to interest the Director of the Opéra in his music, and succeeded only in selling him the libretto of *Der fliegende Holländer* for another composer to set. He made a little money out of journalism, but after a year or so he and Minna were penniless, and he was forced to borrow from friends. At one point, Wagner spent some weeks in a debtor's prison. But then the tide began to turn. Although Paris continued to display a lack of interest in his compositions, the Dresden Opera, to whom he had submitted *Rienzi*, accepted the opera for production. He completed the music of *Der fliegende Holländer* and sent the score to Berlin; on Meyerbeer's recommendation, it too was accepted. Borrowing the fare from his brother-in-law, Richard and Minna left Paris for Dresden. Though *Rienzi* was far too long, and musically uneven, the Dresden première was reasonably successful, thanks to the presence in the cast of two first-rate singers,

Joseph Tichatschek in the title-role and Wilhelmine Schroeder-Devrient as Adriano. There is much of Meyerbeer in the opera; in the processional rhythms, the huge choruses, even in the inordinate length. But, in *Der fliegende Holländer*, there is no trace of Meyerbeer. This, the first of Wagner's operas in which his genius shines forth unencumbered, was produced in Dresden in 1843, Berlin having relinquished its rights in the work. Although, according to Wagner, Schroeder-Devrient was magnificent as Senta, the opera was not a success. The composer blamed the 'distressingly corpulent' and apparently phlegmatic performer who sang the role of the Dutchman. Nevertheless, Wagner's stocks in Dresden were high. A month after the première of *The Flying Dutchman*, he was appointed Kapellmeister to the Saxon Court.

Wagner spent the next six years in Dresden, during which time *Tannhäuser* was completed and produced, with the composer's nineteen-year-old niece as Elisabeth and the loyal Schroeder-Devrient as Venus, and *Lohengrin* was composed. Despite all this activity, as well as his day-to-day work which involved the direction of the opera house, Wagner continued to amass debts, for he consistently and luxuriously lived beyond his means. In 1848 he attracted trouble of a different kind by allying himself with the revolutionary movement of intellectuals and students. When revolution broke out in the streets of Dresden, it was quickly suppressed. Wagner fled to Weimar, where Liszt was preparing a production of *Tannhäuser*. The Dresden authorities issued a warrant for his arrest, and the Royal Kapellmeister now found himself a political exile. He made his way to Switzerland, where Minna and her daughter joined him in Zurich.

Tannhäuser is a curiously slow and stately work, given that its subject is the relationship of sacred to profane love, but *Lohengrin*, first performed under Liszt in Weimar in 1850, marks a real advance for its composer. In fact, it stands at the crossroads of his interests. Romantic in its almost pre-Raphaelite purity, it also contrives to anticipate the direction Wagner was to take in his next completed work, *Tristan und Isolde*, by virtue of its delicate balance, though not yet complete fusion of music and drama.

In Zurich, Wagner at first concentrated on writing and publishing essays of musical polemics, though he found time also to have an affair, in Paris, with the twenty-year-old English wife of a Bordeaux wine-merchant. When the girl came to her senses and decided that she would not, after all, endow him with a yearly income, Wagner extricated himself from the situation, and returned to Minna. He now began to plan his tetralogy of operas based on the old Nibelungen legend. The libretti of the four operas were written in reverse chronological order, and all were completed before he began to compose the music, beginning with *Das Rheingold* in November 1853, and continuing with *Die Walküre* in 1854–6 and then *Siegfried*. By August 1857 he had completed two acts of *Siegfried*, at which point his composition of *Der Ring des Nibelungen*, as the cycle was to be called, was interrupted for twelve years when he began his romantic liaison with Mathilde Wesendonk.

Otto Wesendonk was a wealthy Zurich silk merchant, who became friendly with the Wagners and installed them in a villa close to his own. His wife Mathilde fell victim to the Wagner spell, and it was as an expression of his passion for her that Wagner turned aside from *The Ring* to write first the libretto and then the music of *Tristan und Isolde*. But the personal situation of the two families soon became intolerable. The two wives quarrelled openly, and Wesendonk tactfully took Mathilde on a visit to Italy. *Tristan und Isolde* did not reach the stage until 1865 in Munich. One of the great works of 19th-century romanticism, it is the masterpiece of Wagner's mature years. The score's heavily sensuous chromaticism and the ecstatic richness of its orchestration combine to give the opera a curious psychological strength. In *Tristan und Isolde* Wagner discovered how to reach simultaneously his audience's conscious and subconscious responses.

In 1859 the Wagners settled again in Paris. A production of *Tannhäuser* at the Paris Opéra in 1861, for which Wagner made changes to incorporate the necessary ballet, was interrupted by organised demonstrations. Soon, Minna returned to live permanently in Dresden, while Richard kept on the move in an attempt to promote his operas, and consoled himself with one or two new love affairs. He also became emotionally involved with Cosima von Bülow, illegitimate daughter of Liszt and wife of the conductor Hans von Bülow, a disciple of Wagner. Very soon, yet another person forced an entry into Wagner's emotional life: none other than the eighteen-year-old Ludwig II, King of Bavaria. The homosexual monarch, already advanced along the road to the insanity in which he was to end his days, fell in love with both Wagner and his music. Wagner immediately went to Munich, where he became the close friend of Ludwig. When Cosima bore Wagner a daughter, Bülow accepted the child as his own. But Wagner's relationship with the King was considered scandalous by Ludwig's Ministers, and he and Cosima removed themselves to a villa on Lake Lucerne, the rent of which was paid by Ludwig. Even after Cosima had borne a second child to the composer, Ludwig's adoration of Wagner remained constant. In the summer of 1868, Wagner's new opera, *Die Meistersinger von Nürnberg*, was performed in Munich. Intended as a light comedy, *Die Meistersinger* turned out to be a hymn to artistic compromise with, in its last scene, an irrelevant aside appealing to the baser aspects of nationalism. There can be no denying that the music of this passage is of extraordinary emotive force, of the kind which was peculiarly Wagner's own. The question it presents is whether the nasty taste of the words is redeemed by the beauty and power of the music, or whether these very qualities render more dangerously effective a message which, left in Wagner's raw words, would have less appeal. It is a question which has never been satisfactorily answered.

In 1869, Cosima and Wagner produced a third child. The following year, as soon as Bülow had divorced her, they married. Wagner had now come to the conclusion that his operas would never be staged properly except in a theatre of his own design. With the help of King Ludwig, he began to plan his own theatre, which eventually was built on a hill outside the small Bavarian town of Bayreuth. Though it was at first intended only as a temporary structure, the Festival Theatre, which opened in 1876 with the first complete performance of *The Ring*, is still in use. A splendid house, the Villa Wahnfried, was also built for the Wagners, and is still occupied by the Wagner family. *Der Ring des Nibelungen*, for all its unevenness and disproportionate length, is Wagner's most important work and also the one on which most critical estimates of the composer are based. Such is the scale and nature of the enterprise that it can be interpreted in terms of sociology, politics, history, psychology or moral philosophy. In the years following *The Ring*, Wagner composed his final opera, *Parsifal*. He himself conceived it as a sacred, Christian music-drama: others have described it as an attempt to give aesthetic validity to his own racial prejudice, or even as a celebration of high-minded, ascetic homosexuality. Whatever else it may be, *Parsifal* is a complex work of art.

After the Bayreuth première of *Parsifal* in 1882, the Wagners went to Venice for the winter. They occupied part of the Palazzo Vendramin, and it was here that Richard Wagner succumbed to a heart attack on the 13th February, 1883.

C.O.

WALLACE, William Vincent
(b. Waterford, 11 March 1812; d. Vieuzos, 12 Oct 1865)

Born in Waterford, Ireland, William Wallace showed an early aptitude for music; and his father, who was a regimental bandmaster, taught him the clarinet and piano. In his teens he also learnt to play the violin and organ, and by 1828 he was engaged as second violin in the band at the Theatre Royal, Dublin. Two years later he was appointed organist of Thurles (Catholic) Cathedral. He entered the Roman Catholic Church, adopting the additional name of Vincent, and in 1831 married Isabella Kelly, one of the young boarders in the neighbouring Ursuline Convent. The couple settled in Dublin; but, becoming increasingly disenchanted with Dublin musical life, Wallace decided to try his luck in Australia. In November 1835 he sailed to Hobart Town with his wife and infant son, his sister and his brother. After giving a single concert there, the family moved on to Sydney, where they opened the first Australian music school in Bridge Street. In January 1838 Wallace organised the first Australian music festival in St Mary's Cathedral; and the following month he sailed away secretly for Valparaiso, leaving behind him debts of approximately £2,000.

During the next five years he travelled extensively in South America, the East Indies, the West Indies, Mexico, and the United States. Returning to Europe in 1844, he carried out a concert tour of Germany and Holland and made his début as a concert pianist in London the following May. During that summer a chance meeting with Balfe's friend, Hayward St Leger, led to a suggestion that Wallace should write an opera for Alfred Bunn to produce at Drury Lane. Edward Fitzball provided the libretto; and *Maritana* was produced at Drury Lane on the 15th November 1845 with enormous popular success. But Wallace's next opera, *Matilda of Hungary* (1847), to a libretto by Bunn was not liked.

During Berlioz's visit to London in 1848, the two men met and got on well together. Berlioz described Wallace as 'an excellent, eccentric man, phlegmatic in appearance like many Englishmen, bold and impetuous by nature like an American' and was impressed by the tales of his adventures – 'carrying off women, fighting several duels, which proved unlucky for his adversaries, he lived a savage life. . . .'

The same year Wallace started to write his third opera, *Lurline*, to a libretto by Fitzball based on the legend of the Lorelei; but a financial crisis at Covent Garden meant production had to be postponed. Wallace stopped composing and spent the next three years touring South and North America, becoming a citizen of the United States in 1850. Returning to London, he settled down as a piano teacher. When asked by the Pyne/Harrison English Opera Company for a new opera for their Covent Garden season, he offered them *Lurline*, and on its production in 1860 this proved to be nearly as successful as *Maritana*. He wrote *The Amber Witch* (1861) for Mapleson at Her Majesty's, and two other operas – *Love's Triumph* (1862) and *The Desert Flower* (1863) – for the Pyne/Harrison Company. He died at the Château de Haget near Vieuzos in 1865.   E.W.W.

WALTON, William
(b. Oldham, 29 March 1902)

Walton was born in Lancashire and at the age of ten won a place as chorister at Christ Church, Oxford, where he was encouraged by the Dean of Christ Church (Thomas Banks Strong) and by Dr (later Sir) Hugh Allen through whom he was enabled to matriculate at the exceptionally early age of sixteen. He passed his Mus.Bac. but not his B.A. and left Oxford degree-less; that was the end of his formal training. But while in residence at Oxford he had made a number of influential friends, the most important among whom from the point of view of Walton's later career was Sacheverell Sitwell.

For the next ten years Walton lived with the Sitwells in Chelsea on and off as a kind of adopted or elected brother; this broadened his horizons incalculably both through exposure to the visual arts and through European travel. Musically, too, the Sitwells introduced him to Constant Lambert, possibly the greatest single influence on his career, and to other significant composers of the day, among them Bernard van Dieren and Philip Heseltine. It was through the Sitwells too that Walton's name first came before the public in 1922 in the form of *Façade*, an entertainment originally devised by them for performance in their own drawing-room. Some years before, a youthful piano quartet had won a Carnegie Award, but after *Façade* the overture *Portsmouth Point* (1925) was more indicative of the true bent of Walton's development than the string quartet 'full of undigested Bartók and Schoenberg' which achieved performance at the 1923 ISCM Festival but was later withdrawn. Much more substantial were the Sinfonia Concertante for piano and orchestra (1927) and the Viola Concerto (1929); with the latter Walton achieved maturity as a composer and with his large-scale choral work *Belshazzar's Feast* (1931) public renown to boot. His Symphony No. 1 (1935) and the Vaughan Williams' F minor (1934) are the two most important British symphonies of the inter-war period, but by the time the Violin Concerto appeared (1939) Walton had found another outlet for his lyrico-dramatic talent – film music. His activities in this field culminated in three momentous Shakespeare collaborations with Sir Laurence Olivier (*Henry V, Hamlet* and *Richard III*) but there were no major concert works during the war years apart from the comedy overture *Scapino* (1940).

Afterwards, between the composition of the A minor String Quartet (1947) and the Violin Sonata (1949) Walton married Señorita Susana Gil in Buenos Aires and shortly after settled in Ischia, off the coast of Naples – whence comes the tendency to Mediterraneanise which informs most of Walton's music from now on: the opera *Troilus and Cressida* (1954), the *Johannesburg Festival Overture* (1956), the *Partita for Orchestra* (1957), the Second Symphony (1960) and the one-act extravaganza *The Bear* (1967). For the past twenty years, his life has been uneventful, though until recently he was quite active in many parts of the world as conductor of his own compositions. He was knighted in 1951.

Walton's best work was done by the time of *Troilus and Cressida*. Thereafter whatever his music gained in tautness or astringency it lost in magnificence and *grande envergure*, and in the opinion of many the loss has outweighed the gain. The latter qualities were two predominating hallmarks of his style as it crystallised in *Belshazzar's Feast* and the Symphony No. 1, and they also inform other memorable scores of the pre-war period – the choral setting of Dunbar's *In Honour of the City of London* (1937), the Coronation March *Crown Imperial* (1937), the music for Louis MacNiece's radio play *Christopher Columbus* (1942) and the *Hamlet* music (1944). Other characteristics include a type of extrovert physical assertiveness encouraged by familiarity with the scores of Stravinsky and Prokofiev and with jazz, and a vein of bitter-sweet lyricism which is particularly prominent in the Viola and Violin Concertos and in the slow movement of the Symphony and later flowered into the full-blown romanticism of *Troilus and Cressida*; the music for the film *Escape me Never* (1935) is only one instance of how well this innate tendency to quasi-conventional romantic expressiveness could serve Walton in the cinema, and much of his film music, belonging as it does to his best period, is deserving of closer evaluation (e.g., the score for the 1942 film of Shaw's *Major Barbara*). His idiom, though braced by infiltration of Continental elements, has never been ashamed to affirm its links with tradition, often of a specifically English kind; he has aptly described himself as 'a classical composer with a strong feeling for lyricism' and his genius is for triumphant conformity within the rules rather than for iconoclasm. As such he is a major figure in English music and musically speaking occupies a position midway between Elgar and Britten.

C.P.

WEBER, Carl Maria von
(b. Eutin, nr. Lübeck, 18 Nov 1786;
d. London, 5 June 1826)

If the major impetus given to the establishing of the Romantic movement in music can be credited to one particular composer, that man was Carl Maria (Friedrich Ernst) von Weber. He brought his genius to the musical scene at the time most propitious for its fulfilment, and though his life was to be cut tragically short he was to influence the whole course of music: his operas paved the way for Wagner, while his piano music led just as surely to the subsequent stylistic developments of Chopin, Liszt and Schumann. It is necessary perhaps to

sketch in the background to the Romantic movement before looking at Weber's life or attempting an evaluation of his music. As opposed to the Classical ideals of order, balance and perfection within acknowledged limits of form and expression, Romantic art reaches out beyond the immediate time and occasion, giving a new emphasis to freedom, movement and passion. Romantic composers and writers sought to break the bounds of their actual experience of the world about them, to recapture the spirit of the past and anticipate the spirit of the future. In their work they tried to create a world of fantasy that was inevitably remote from the real one, achieving this, in the words of Walter Pater, by 'the addition of strangeness to beauty'. In this process the personality of the composer tended to become merged with his works, which often reflected his personal joys and sufferings, as in the symphonies of Berlioz and Tchaikovsky which bear the titles of the *Fantastique* and the *Pathétique*, sometimes even his longing for some unattainable ideal. This led in turn to the rise of 'programme music' which broke with the traditions of the past by linking itself to poetic, descriptive or even, as in the Richard Strauss tone poems *Don Juan* and *Ein Heldenleben*, narrative subject matter. On a more mundane level, the movement was a response to the changing relationship between the composer and his audience. In the 18th century the system of aristocratic patronage had restricted composers to writing for small, homogeneous, highly cultivated audiences, but with the rise of the middle classes in the early part of the 19th century there was a large, diversified and mainly uninformed new public. Reaching this mass of people who flocked for entertainment to public concerts and festivals was the challenge thrown down to the composer, a challenge made all the more difficult because composers also began at this time to look to posterity, to a time when some ideal audience would understand them as their contemporaries might fail to do. And here lay a paradox: at the very time that composers grew more inward-looking in their works they needed to attract the paying customer to the opera house and the concert hall. Composers therefore began to cultivate, sometimes consciously and sometimes subconsciously, colourful personalities, with such extreme cases as Liszt and Paganini carrying this to outrageous lengths which make the pop stars of today seem shy violets by comparison.

Weber, however, arriving at the dawn of the

Weber conducting a rehearsal of his opera, Der Freischütz, *at Covent Garden.*

new movement, restricted his romanticism to his music, apart from the fact that he was to die, like Verdi's Violetta and Puccini's Mimi, from consumption in almost operatic circumstances. His family was in fact of more humble background than the spurious 'von' Weber suggests, but they were certainly musical: his father was Kapellmeister to the Prince Bishop of Lübeck in the small town of Eutin, while his mother was a singer of talent and experience. Soon after the composer's birth his father became director of a travelling theatre company, so his childhood was spent on tour, which meant that his education, musical and otherwise, was more than somewhat hit-and-miss. His father was determined from the start that his son should be an infant prodigy like Mozart, and so Carl Maria, who was afflicted with a congenital disease of the hip, learnt to sing and play the piano at the age of four while he was still unable to walk properly. He was fortunately able to study with Michael Haydn, brother of the famous symphonist, in Salzburg for a time, and it was there that the eleven-year-old Weber's first compositions

were published. Soon afterwards he began his career as a concert pianist, while in 1800 he saw his first opera produced in Freiberg, a romantic–comic work called *Das Waldmädchen* which was subsequently given in Vienna but all copies of which finally disappeared apart from two fragments. (It is possible the young composer destroyed them himself, for he once declared that 'puppies and first operas should be drowned.') Between 1801, when he was still only fifteen, and 1816, he held posts as Kapellmeister at Breslau, an ambiguous musical secretaryship in Stuttgart and as director of the Prague Opera. During this period, however, he also made successful concert tours and found the time to compose the bulk of his orchestral work – the two symphonies, two concertos each for the piano and the clarinet, a bassoon concerto and a horn concertino – as well as a variety of songs and the operas *Silvana* and *Abu Hassan*. Then in 1817 he took up the position he was to hold for the remaining years of life, the directorship of the Dresden Court Opera. These were hectic years, during which he put in an incredible amount of work preparing and conducting operas, giving concerts, visiting many European capitals as a now celebrated composer and writing the operatic masterpieces for which, above all, his name endures – and all this despite gradually failing health.

A close look at Weber's symphonies and concertos makes it clear that traditional sonata form had no great appeal for him. He appreciated that other composers had found it provided an inner drama of its own in the development of contrasted themes and its exploration of key relationships. It was a form, however, which he neither mastered nor apparently wished to master. In his symphonies, and in the orchestral parts of his concertos, the use of instrumental colour to create mood and atmosphere was more his concern, while he sought to give the soloist an almost vocal expressiveness, both aims suggesting the born operatic composer. In the bassoon concerto he even presented the soloist as a dramatic character. The piano concertos. which reveal his love of virtuosity for its own sake, involve a high degree of ornamentation which was so strongly to influence Chopin. His desire to break with traditional form was made clear in 1821 when he decided to give the name *Konzertstück* to what was to have been his third piano concerto, even providing it with a 'programme' to emphasise its dramatic as opposed to purely formal nature. His four piano sonatas may similarly be regarded as dramatic statements of feeling. It is a pity that performers and public alike are hidebound in their attitude towards these works, for by neglecting them, the concertos above all, we are deprived of music which not only exerts an immediate appeal but gives deeper satisfaction the better we come to know it.

The earliest of Weber's stage works to have survived is *Abu Hassan*, composed when he was twenty-four, a one-act *Singspiel* in the tradition of Mozart's *Die Entführung aus dem Serail*. The music is delightfully light-hearted, as befits the comic *Arabian Nights* tale, yet it melts into moments of tenderness which indicate something of the direction the composer was later to take. He found himself finally with *Der Freischütz*, premièred in Berlin on the 18th June 1821 with the composer conducting. It was an immediate triumph, resulting in no less than thirty productions in other German cities by the end of the following year. For audiences everywhere it exemplified every characteristic of German romanticism, its humble human characters, presented against a vivid background of wild and mysterious nature, each an agent of supernatural forces of good or evil. Weber gave a distinctively national character to the melodies of the many memorable arias and choruses, while even more revolutionary was his use of harmony and orchestral colour to achieve dramatic expression. The scene of the Wolf's Glen brought something entirely new to opera with the eerie atmosphere Weber created in his music for the casting of the magic bullets. *Der Freischütz* represents a turning-point in German opera, but it also constitutes a masterpiece in its own right, setting a standard the composer was not to reach again in the five years remaining to him.

For his next opera, *Euryanthe* (1823), Weber unwisely chose a libretto so chaotic that his music, though both powerful and inventive, was unable to save the day. The influence it had on later composers, however, is immense, Weber's flexible handling of recitative, arioso and aria providing a model without which Wagner could not have reached the heights he did in *Lohengrin*, to mention only one example. The same fate overtook his last completed opera, *Oberon*, composed to an English libretto for Covent Garden, where it was first performed on the 12th April 1826 under Weber's direction. Again there is a profusion of very beautiful music, but the opera almost defies stage production. (Like *Euryanthe*, however, it can be enjoyed on gramophone records.) Less than two months after the première Weber died in his London lodgings. His coffin remained in a grave at Moorfields Chapel for eighteen years until matters were arranged for its return to Germany. When the ship carrying it docked at Hamburg other vessels from all parts of the world dipped their colours in tribute, and the Funeral March from Beethoven's *Eroica* Symphony was played as the coffin was transferred to a small boat for its journey to Dresden. The body of the father of German romantic opera was finally buried in the city he had made his home, the graveside speech appropriately delivered by his great successor, Richard Wagner.

F.G.B.

WEBERN, Anton von
(b. Vienna, 3 Dec 1883;
d. Mittersill, 15 Sept 1945)

Anton von Webern (he dropped the 'von' when Austria became a republic after World War I) was born in Vienna in 1883. His father, Karl von Webern, was a mining engineer who came from an old aristocratic family which

Heinrich Isaac. He found the teaching of Graedener and Navratil somewhat barren, and looked round for a better instructor; in 1904 he went to Berlin to see Pfitzner about taking lessons with him, but when Pfitzner made some slighting remarks about Mahler Webern turned round and went straight back to Vienna. Probably on Guido Adler's advice, he showed some of his songs to Schoenberg, who accepted him as a pupil in the autumn of 1904.

This was a decisive step in Webern's life. Schoenberg was an inspired teacher who really built up the musical characters of his pupils, and this was just what Webern needed at this stage. He has described Schoenberg's methods in 'Arnold Schoenberg as Teacher' (published in *Anton Webern* by Friedrich Wildgans, London 1966). During this period he wrote a sonata movement for piano, some songs and a piano quintet in one movement which had a private performance in Vienna at that time but was not published till after Webern's death. None of these works are characteristic of Webern's later style, and nor is his official Op. 1, the Passacaglia for orchestra, which he regarded as ending his apprenticeship with Schoenberg in 1908. In that summer he obtained a position as conductor at Bad Ischl, but he loathed the work there. He returned to Vienna in the winter, obtaining occasional work as a conductor and chorus repetiteur. Schoenberg had begun to write his first so-called 'atonal' pieces in 1908, and after writing the tonal, but highly chromatic chorus 'Entflieht auf leichten Kahnen' Webern followed his master's example in his songs Op. 3 and 4, the Five Movements for string quartet Op. 5, the Orchestral Pieces Op. 6, the Four Pieces for violin and piano Op. 7 and the Rilke songs Op. 8, all written between 1908 and 1910: these are Webern's first really mature works, and show the characteristic brevity of his style.

In the winter of 1910–11 Webern held the post of assistant conductor at the Stadttheater in Danzig; here again he was extremely unhappy, and he returned to Vienna in the spring of 1911. Meanwhile he had married his cousin Wilhelmine Mörtl, who bore him a daughter, Amalie, in April. He spent the summer in Carinthia, having given up his Danzig contract; meanwhile, Schoenberg had decided to move to Berlin. Berg and Webern tried to set up a foundation for him so that he could live without financial worries: Webern followed Schoenberg to Berlin in the autumn

Webern.

had settled in Carinthia for centuries. In 1890 he was transferred to Graz and in 1894 to Klagenfurt; Anton attended the Gymnasium at Klagenfurt and also had private lessons in violin and 'cello playing from the Klagenfurt musician Dr Edwin Komauer. He also came across Mahler's works in piano arrangements, but he had little theoretical instruction. From about 1901 onwards he began to write songs, and when he matriculated from his school in 1902 he was rewarded by being given a trip to the Bayreuth Festival. His father wanted him to look after the family estates, but eventually agreed to him studying music at the University of Vienna and completing his studies with a doctorate in philosophy: this decision was partly due to Karl von Webern being appointed to a post at the Ministry of Mines in Vienna, so that the whole family moved back there. In Vienna Webern studied musicology with the famous Guido Adler and harmony and counterpoint with Hermann Graedener and Karl Navratil, and for his doctorate he wrote a thesis on the *Choralis Constantinus* of

and spent the winter there, visiting the Mahler Festival in Munich in November together with Berg. Webern spent some time in preparing a brochure in honour of Schoenberg to which a number of musicians, principally Schoenberg's pupils, contributed; this was published in 1912. In February 1912 Webern went with Schoenberg to Prague, where he was hoping to obtain a post at the German Theatre, of which the musical director was Schoenberg's brother-in-law, the composer Alexander von Zemlinsky. This did not materialise at the time, and Webern returned to Vienna; shortly afterwards he received a contract to conduct at the theatre in Stettin, and went there in June. His contract was for a year, but he disliked Stettin as much as Danzig, and early in 1913 he returned to Vienna on sick leave; he ended his contract with Stettin in the summer. From 1913 to 1914 he lived in Vienna, writing his six Bagatelles for string quartet Op. 9, his Five Pieces for orchestra Op. 10 and the Three Small Pieces for 'cello and piano Op. 11. In 1915 he joined the army as a volunteer, but owing to his weak eyesight he was excused active service; meanwhile he was frantically trying to get Schoenberg out of the army. Webern was released early in 1917 and went with Schoenberg to Prague in March; he arranged to take a post at the theatre there for the summer season. Returning to Carinthia he began some of the songs with instruments which were eventually incorporated into Op. 13 and 14. He did not like his work in Prague any more than that in Stettin, and by August 1918 he was back in Vienna. He found an apartment in Mödling, a district where he was to live till almost the end of his life.

Webern's wife had borne him a son and two more daughters and his financial position was not easy. He taught some pupils, helped Schoenberg in the organisation of his Society for Private Musical Performances, and returned to Prague to conduct for a short time in 1920. He began to be offered conducting work in Vienna – the Schubertbund, the Mödling Male Voice Choir and, from 1922, the Workers' Symphony Orchestra and chorus. Universal Edition were now publishing his works, and he constantly had to appeal to them for money. In 1924 he was given the Music Prize of the City of Vienna, and he was beginning to be asked to conduct his works abroad. He adopted the twelve-note method of Schoenberg in his songs Op. 17 (1924) and used it in all his subsequent works. In 1927 he

was appointed conductor and then musical adviser for the Austrian Radio, and he undertook conducting tours in Germany and England in 1929, 1932, 1933 and 1935. In 1932 he moved into Vienna for a short time, but soon returned to the Mödling area. The advent of the Dollfuss government in 1934 meant the end of Webern's activities with the Workers' Symphony Orchestra, and he had to live almost entirely by teaching. The Anschluss of 1938 made his position even worse; he had to work as a proof reader for Universal Edition and make piano scores for them; he was regarded as a 'cultural Bolshevik' by the Nazis, and his music was banned in Germany and Austria. In 1943 Webern travelled abroad for the last time, to hear the first performance of his Variations for orchestra in Switzerland. Although he was nearly sixty he was called up for work as an air-raid warden and had to live in barracks for part of the time. In the spring of 1945 he heard that his son had been killed on the Yugoslav front. At Easter he left Mödling and managed to reach Mittersill near Salzburg, where two of his daughters were living; Webern's other daughter also reached Mittersill, and so did the sons-in-law eventually. After the end of the war Webern received various offers of important posts in Vienna, but he was tragically killed in 1945. He had gone to visit his son-in-law Mattl at another house in Mittersill: Mattl had been engaging in black market activities, and American soldiers had come to arrest him. Webern had been given a cigar by Mattl and went outside the house to smoke it, not wanting to inconvenience his sleeping grandchildren. An American soldier, who was returning to barracks carrying a gun, bumped into Webern in the dark, and being of nervous disposition, fired three shots at him. Webern died shortly afterwards.

Webern's music has influenced the younger generation of composers even more than that of Schoenberg and Berg. He adopted Schoenberg's methods in a radical way of his own; his works are very brief and concise, and every note in them is essential. There are strong contrasts of colour and a most sensitive use of sound; he has certainly taught composers to look at music in a new way. Unfortunately some of his successors ascribed to him the principle of 'total serialisation', in which not only the notes but also all the other so-called 'parameters' in music, such as duration, dynamics, tone-colour, method of playing, octave pitch of individual notes, etc., are subjected to serial organisation. This was not Webern's aim; he always felt that he was combining Schoenberg's twelve-note method with strict classical forms, as may be seen from many passages in his letters. At any rate he was the originator of a new kind of music which springs from the past but has anticipated the music of the future. And his idealism and strength of character have set an example to all his successors.

H.S.

WEILL, Kurt
(b. Dessau, 2 March 1900;
d. New York, 3 April 1950)

Weill's earliest musical studies were with Albert Bing. Later, he was for a short time a pupil of Humperdinck. His earliest practical experience was as a conductor and coach for the opera companies at Dessau and Lüdenscheid. In 1921 he settled in Berlin, where he studied with Busoni for three years. Although his earliest works were instrumental, Weill always thought of himself as a composer for the theatre. His first operas, one-act pieces written in a contemporary idiom, were nevertheless traditional in that they were scored for normal orchestra and intended for conventional singing. But Weill longed for an art that would decisively mirror his own time, and the life of his adopted city of Berlin (he came from a Jewish family in Dessau). It was in this mood that he exclaimed: 'I don't give a damn about posterity, I want to write for today!' It was in this mood that he collaborated with Bertolt Brecht, who wanted to achieve in poetry the same aims as Weill in music.

The first collaboration of Brecht and Weill, Der kleine Mahagonny, was a sketch with songs, about a mythical city whose excitements and whose attitudes were very like those of Berlin. It was an immediate success: at one stroke, Brecht and Weill had succeeded in bringing opera to the people. When Weill's wife, the Viennese actress and dancer Lotte Lenya, sang 'Denn wie man sich bettet, so liegt man' ('For as you make your bed, so you must lie in it'), her audience got the message, underlined in an almost sinister manner by the half-satirical use of popular melody, at once beautiful and banal.

The next work of the collaborators had an English title, Happy End, and was set in an America both mythical and real, like Kafka's novel, Amerika. These United States were states of mind rather than of geography, though the emotional truth of Kafka, and of Brecht–Weill, is unquestionable. The association of Brecht and Weill continued when Mahagonny was expanded into a full-length work, The Rise and Fall of the City of Mahagonny, which proved a triumph when it opened in Berlin. The collaborators then decided to carry the new and popular operatic style they had invented further away from the stage, and into schools and colleges. They wrote a work for schools to perform: Der Jasager (The yes-man), a two-act opera based on an old Japanese Noh play. In so doing, they again created a new genre, the educational opera, which was taken up by Hindemith, Fortner and other German composers including, much later, Carl Orff. (Even Benjamin Britten's Let's Make an Opera and Noye's Fludde are legitimate successors of Der Jasager.)

In 1933 Hitler came to power in Germany. Weill and Lotte Lenya got out of the country the day the Reichstag was destroyed by fire. They arrived in Paris penniless, and for some months lived on the hospitality of French admirers while Weill attempted to rebuild his career. Brecht was also in Paris, and the two men worked together on what was to prove their last collaboration, The Seven Deadly Sins, which combined ballet and opera. Years earlier, when he was a twenty-one-year-old student, Weill had written a symphony. Now, in Paris a second symphony was commissioned by the Princess Edmond de Polignac, whose generosity brought into being several other important musical works, including Stravinsky's Renard and Satie's Socrate. During the summer and autumn of 1933, in a village outside Paris Weill completed his symphony which was given its first performance the following year in Amsterdam under Bruno Walter. Unfortunately it was poorly received, and for Weill the problem of how to earn enough to survive on became acute. In Germany his music was banned; the Gestapo raided the offices of his publisher and destroyed all copies of his scores as well as the plates from which more copies might have been printed.

In Paris, Weill realised he must adapt himself to the requirements of French musical theatre. He found a French collaborator, the

Kurt Weill.

retained its European accent: this was the kind of political and social musical theatre he had helped to create, and it seemed for a time as though he would be able to continue in America along the path he had taken in Berlin. But, in the America of Franklin Roosevelt and the New Deal, Weil became more relaxed politically. In Berlin he would never have considered writing for the established bourgeois theatre. In New York, however, he began to understand the lure of Broadway, and for a time he succumbed to it. His second American piece of musical theatre was a Broadway musical. A superior musical, certainly, with book and lyrics by Maxwell Anderson, and production by Joshua Logan, but a Broadway show nevertheless. It was called *Knickerbocker Holiday*.

With Weill's next musical, it seemed as though his capitulation to Broadway was complete. *Lady in the Dark* had a book by Moss Hart and lyrics by Ira Gershwin. In Broadway terms it was a hit, and Weill soon became America's favourite composer of musicals. His tunes lost their mordant quality, and his orchestration was now for the normal American theatre-pit orchestra, larger and more conventional than that of *Mahagonny*. Throughout these 'show-biz' years, however, Weill never lost sight of the kind of work he wanted to write. He used his Broadway shows in order to learn about his new audience, and how best to approach it. In 1947, he adapted Elmer Rice's play *Street Scene* for music, hoping to make it into a real American opera. Much closer in form to opera than to the Broadway musical of the time, *Street Scene* was accepted gratefully by the mass audience to which it was addressed, and ran for several months. Weill, in his middle forties, had found his mature voice as a composer in his adopted land. He certainly thought so at the time, and said that all his earlier works for the stage were stepping stones towards *Street Scene*. But his next one proved to be a more conventional Broadway entertainment, *Love Life*, for which his librettist was Alan Jay Lerner who had already written the book and lyrics for *Brigadoon* and was later to write *Camelot* and *My Fair Lady*, all three with composer Frederick Loewe.

The wheel of Kurt Weill's career was turning full circle. Just as, nearly twenty years earlier in Berlin he had turned his attention to writing for amateurs and students, so now he determined to provide an American one-act opera for amateur or school groups. *Down in*

playwright Jacques Deval, and together they produced *Marie Galante*, a play with music. Weill proved his versatility by writing for it songs which, musically slight though they undoubtedly are, sound indisputably French in character. But writing pastiche French light music was no solution to his problem, for his roots as a musician were in the Austro-German tradition. After a brief sojourn in London, where he composed music for a show called *My Kingdom for a Cow*, Weill and Lenya made their way to the United States of America, where Weill had been invited to provide the music for a spectacular production by the great Austrian director Max Reinhardt. While working on this, Weill began to look around for an American librettist to take the place of Brecht. Through the Group Theatre of New York, a socialist organisation, he met the playwright Paul Green, and together they produced an anti-war satire, *Johnny Johnson*, which was staged in 1936. Weill's music

the Valley, an opera based on American folksong, was first performed in July 1948 by students at the University of Indiana. Weill followed it in 1949 with another Broadway musical, but a musical with a difference. From Alan Paton's novel about racial conflict in South Africa, *Cry, the Beloved Country*, Maxwell Anderson fashioned a libretto, and Weill, an old victim of German racial theories, responded to it with passion and enthusiasm. For *Lost in the Stars*, as the musical was called, he composed a score which was one of his finest. It made no concessions to Broadway taste, yet it reached its audience and affected it. Now Weill had really arrived back at the point where he had started. He had begun his career in the theatre by writing

operas in such a way that they could be appreciated by the mass audiences of the light theatre. He ended it by writing for that mass audience a work which moved back towards opera, and in doing so he helped pave the way for Leonard Bernstein and *West Side Story*. Several months later, while he and Maxwell Anderson were beginning to collaborate once again, this time on an opera based on Mark Twain's *Huckleberry Finn*, Weill suddenly died of a heart attack in New York, shortly after his fiftieth birthday.

Throughout his career, Weill's basic intentions never altered: to produce music that was both popular and good. This was comparatively easy to do in the 18th century, rather difficult in the 19th, and virtually impossible, it seems (*pace* the Beatles *et al*), in the 20th. Weill's unique achievement is that he came close to this, not just once but at many points during his life. He may not be one of the very few great composers of the century, one of the

A scene from the English Music Theatre production of The Threepenny Opera, *1976.*

Bergs, Brittens or Stravinskys, but he has an honoured place in the hierarchy and also a finer melodic gift than two of those three great names.

C.O.

WOLF, Hugo
(b. Windischgraz, 13 March 1860;
d. Vienna, 22 Feb 1903)

Hugo Wolf was born at Windischgraz, a small town in southern Styria, now in Yugoslavia and renamed Slovenjgradec. The area is basically Slovenian. But though Wolf's mother was partly Slav (also with Italian connections), his father was a German, Philipp Wolf, a leather maker and musician *manqué*. Among other accomplishments, Philipp was a versatile instrumentalist, and Hugo was taught to play the piano and violin at an early age. Initially his parents' circumstances were reasonably prosperous. But in 1867 a fire destroyed Philipp's house and workshops, and from that day until his death Hugo was never to enjoy comfortable independent means. The position was aggravated by his own wayward and difficult temperament. Once music had taken hold of him he tended to treat all other subjects with some measure of contempt. In 1871 he was expelled from the Graz Gymnasium for inadequate school-work. He next spent two years at a Benedictine seminary in Carinthia, after which he was again rusticated for poor academic effort. Finally he attended the Gymnasium at Marburg (now Maribor) for two years. But here too his absorption in music, including his own first attempts at composition, drove his teachers to despair. In 1875, not without parental opposition, he was sent to Vienna to study at the Conservatory, living with his father's sister, Katharina Vinzenzberg.

In Vienna Wolf was at last able legitimately to expand his musical horizons. Above all he discovered Wagner, whose music was to remain an obsession with him for the rest of his life. When Wagner himself came to Vienna in November 1875, Wolf spent most of his time hanging round the great composer's hotel and eventually managed to gain access to the presence. Wagner seems to have behaved kindly enough, without taking the fifteen-year-old boy very seriously. At the Conservatory, meanwhile, Wolf survived for the by now traditional two years before be-

coming involved in a contretemps with the director, Josef Hellmesberger, to whom he announced his intention of leaving the Conservatory, whereupon Hellmesberger expelled him in any case. Later on the director received a threatening letter ostensibly from Wolf, but actually written by a fellow student in his name. The whole episode is typical. All his life Wolf would wreck his own opportunities by impulsive, rude or malicious behaviour towards those whom he regarded paranoically as his musical enemies. Thus, finding himself more or less indigent in Vienna in 1877, he could still not bring himself to behave with consideration towards the more or less untalented children and aristocrats whom he undertook to teach music, as a result of which he soon found himself virtually without pupils. For many years thereafter he was only able to stay alive through the good offices of friends like the composer Adalbert von Goldschmidt and the conductor Felix Mottl, who seem to have recognised his talent on remarkably little evidence. In 1881, for instance, Goldschmidt got Wolf a job as assistant conductor in Salzburg. But within two months Wolf had rowed with the principal conductor and been forced to leave. Moreover, he had still hardly proved himself, even *to* himself, as a composer. Of his published works, only a handful of songs and the D minor String Quartet date from this period, though a larger number of songs survive in manuscript. In 1879 he called on Brahms with some of these, but Brahms advised him brusquely to get some lessons in counterpoint. Thereafter the previously admired master joined the ranks of Wolf's imagined enemies. During Wolf's three-year stint as music critic of the *Wiener Salonblatt* from 1884 to 1887 (another post secured for him through the influence of friends) it was Brahms who bore the brunt of his invective. A meeting with Liszt in 1883 was more promising. Liszt praised the songs Wolf showed him but suggested he should compose something on a larger scale. Wolf promptly embarked on his one and only completed orchestral work, the symphonic poem *Penthesilea* (1883–5).

By 1887 Wolf may well have felt that his career was a failure. In his only real job, as music critic, his main achievement had been to make enemies, and this had actually hindered him in getting even such music as he had written performed. He had, admittedly, also made many friends, including respected and influential musicians. But he had hardly

Hugo Wolf.

reality suggest that he felt as if he were watching *someone else* write this wonderful music. In three months at Perchtoldsdorf he produced forty-three Mörike settings 'of which each one', as he put it, 'surpasses the others'. After a break for the summer, he moved into Eckstein's house at Unterach am Attersee, and the flow continued: this time a further ten Mörike songs and thirteen tone poems by Eichendorff. Back in Vienna in late October he took up Goethe and within just over three months composed all but one of the fifty-one Goethe Lieder. Then, in October 1889 he went back to Perchtoldsdorf and began what was to become the *Spanisches Liederbuch*, settings of poems translated from the Spanish by Heyse and Geibel. Forty-four Spanish songs were composed by April 1890. Finally, on a rising gradient, he produced six Keller songs (*Alte Weisen*) and seven Italian songs in Heyse's translations, before breaking off in mid-November to visit Schott's of Mainz in order to conclude a new publishing agreement.

This is one of the great creative outbursts in history: 174 songs in two and three-quarter years. And such songs. Even Schubert in 1815 and Schumann in 1840 had not bettered it for sheer sustained intensity of inspiration. Wolf himself was never again to achieve anything comparable, though late in 1891 he completed the first *Italienisches Liederbuch* (twenty-two songs in all) and five years later, in the spring of 1896, added a second book (twenty-four songs), not at all inferior to the first. Thanks to his network of friends and admirers, whom he occasionally summoned for impromptu performances, his songs began to be known almost as soon as they were written, and this naturally led to commissions from outside. Moreover, Wolf himself was ambitious to prove himself on a larger scale, particularly as an operatic composer. But in that field he was not destined to succeed. After years of agonising over the problem of finding a suitable libretto, he finally settled on one by Rosa Mayreder called *The Three-cornered Hat*, a comedy set in Spain. As *Der Corregidor*, his opera on this libretto was staged in Mannheim in June 1896, but was coolly received and had only two performances. Before this, in 1891, there had been music for a production of Ibsen's play *The Feast at Solhaug*. But in between Wolf's inspiration almost completely dried up. 'I could just as soon begin suddenly to speak Chinese as compose anything at all', he wrote to a friend.

justified their faith. Of this period he himself supplied the epitaph in a letter to his sister Käthe written much later, in 1892. Speaking of his father, who died in May 1887, he wrote: 'Now he lies in the quiet churchyard and none of my songs can reach him . . . he, who lived and breathed only in music, and for whom *my* music never sounded, to whom my song never spoke!'

But the tide was already beginning to turn. In May 1887 Wolf had completed his best-known work outside the songs, the *Italian Serenade* for string quartet (the orchestral version dates from 1892), and late that year a friend of his, Friedrich Eckstein, persuaded a small publishing firm, Wetzler, to bring out a dozen of Wolf's songs, including the very early 'Morgentau', written in June 1877. The effect on Wolf himself was amazing. In February 1888 he borrowed a friend's house in the village of Perchtoldsdorf, on the edge of the Wiener Wald, and settled down to composing songs with texts by one of his favourite poets, Eduard Mörike. Suddenly music poured out of him at a rate, and of a quality, that even he seems to have been scarcely able to credit. This is borne out by his letters of the time, which, though superficially conceited, in

Nevertheless by late 1896 his existence bore an altogether brighter appearance. Friends had installed him in a flat of his own in the centre of Vienna. Working on the proofs of *Der Corregidor* and on sketches for a new opera, *Manuel Venegas*, he felt at last optimistic about the future. When he was least prepared, fate struck him down.

One day in September 1897 friends who met him in a restaurant found him obsessed with the idea that he had been appointed Director of the Vienna Opera. The new director in fact was Mahler. It seems that Mahler had promised to produce *Der Corregidor*, but then, after a row with Wolf over the merits of Rubinstein's *The Demon*, had withdrawn the promise. Wolf's mind, the victim for years of overwork and nervous stress, gave way completely under the disappointment and fury. He was taken to a private asylum in the city. For a time he recovered, and was able to spend much of 1898 at 'liberty', working again on *Manuel Venegas*. In October 1898, however, his mind went finally. He tried to drown himself in the Traunsee, where he had spent a long summer with friends. He was taken to the Lower Austrian Landesirrenanstalt, and there, after an agonisingly slow process of mental decline, accompanied in due course by general paralysis, he died, on the 22nd February 1903.

Wolf's final insanity sheds extraordinary light on the character of genius. Between 1888 and 1891 he wrote a large number of inspired songs in an exalted state of mind which had some of the symptoms of madness. Later, when officially mad, he tried to compose but could produce only music of surpassing banality. In the whole history of music, there is no other example of genius flaring up and dying down so rapidly, like a supernova appearing suddenly in the night sky then as suddenly vanishing, leaving what only scientists know to be a faint, feeble star dying away to a lifeless husk.

Though Wolf's other music has merit, his name lives on in his songs. The range of these is extraordinary, from the pithy sketches in the Italian songs to the grander and more expansive pieces in the Mörike and Goethe collections. Wolf is famous, above all, for the exact literary perception of his song-writing. The quality is Schumannesque (though Schumann lacked Wolf's literary taste). Where Brahms and Strauss concentrated on a vocal quality of line, Wolf followed Schumann in fusing voice and piano into a more subtle and flexible entity that endeavoured to penetrate directly to the psychological core of the poem. But Wolf was also a lyricist of genius, as well as possessing a surer command than Schumann of the bigger rhetorical style perfected by Schubert. In his own day he was dubbed 'the Wagner of song'. But though he idolised Wagner and certainly adopted harmonic ideas of his, and though the texture of his music has a Wagnerian fluidity, his world was really quite different. His great genius was for portraiture, for bringing the characters in a poem to life. In opera he consciously avoided the heroic mythological Wagnerian ethos. Yet his greatest songs certainly have an epic grandeur of their own, and he was perhaps the only German songwriter after Schumann (and possibly excepting Mahler) seriously to face up to and solve the problems of words-and-music, as opposed to the much simpler issue of music-to-words.

S.W.